# Vietnam's Second Front

# VIETNAM'S SECOND FRONT

## Domestic Politics, the Republican Party, and the War

Andrew L. Johns

The University Press of Kentucky

Scholarly publisher for the Commonwealth,
serving Bellarmine University, Berea College, Centre College of Kentucky, Eastern
Kentucky University, The Filson Historical Society, Georgetown College,
Kentucky Historical Society, Kentucky State University, Morehead State University,
Murray State University, Northern Kentucky University, Transylvania University,
University of Kentucky, University of Louisville, and Western Kentucky University.
All rights reserved.

*Editorial and Sales Offices:* The University Press of Kentucky
663 South Limestone Street, Lexington, Kentucky 40508-4008
www.kentuckypress.com

Library of Congress Cataloging-in-Publication Data

Johns, Andrew L., 1968-
    Vietnam's second front : domestic politics, the Republican Party, and the war /
Andrew L. Johns.
        p. cm.
    Includes bibliographical references and index.
    ISBN 978-0-8131-2572-5 (hardcover : alk. paper)
    1. Vietnam War, 1961-1975—United States. 2. Politics and war—United States—
History—20th century. 3. United States—Politics and government—1961-1963.
4. United States—Politics and government—1963-1969. 5. United States—Politics and
government—1969-1974. 6. Republican Party (U.S. : 1854- )—History—20th century.
7. Executive power—United States—History—20th century. 8. Legislative power—
United States—History—20th century. I. Title.
    DS558.J64 2010
    959.704'31—dc22                                        2009044739

This book is printed on acid-free recycled paper meeting
the requirements of the American National Standard
for Permanence in Paper for Printed Library Materials.

Manufactured in the United States of America.

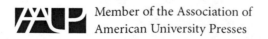
Member of the Association of
American University Presses

# Contents

# Acknowledgments

George Orwell believed that "writing a book is a long, exhausting struggle, like a long bout of some painful illness. One would never undertake such a thing if one were not driven by some demon whom one can neither resist nor understand." Most historians probably have similar feelings about their books at some point; I know I certainly did. But, overall, this has been a fascinating odyssey through one of the most intriguing and tragic periods in U.S. history.

It was not, however, a solitary journey. George Herring, David Anderson, David Schmitz, Walter Hixson, Jeff Livingston, David Kaiser, K. C. Johnson, Jeremi Suri, Laura Kalman, Jack Talbott, and Jim Matray all read various iterations and portions of the manuscript, provided excellent feedback and suggestions for improvement, and encouraged the project. Fred Logevall has been a tremendous adviser and friend. His scholarly expertise, constant support, and thoughtful advice on the book since its early stages have been invaluable. *Tack så mycket.* Valuable insights came from participating in the 2008 Society for Historians of American Foreign Relations Summer Institute program, directed by Peter Hahn and Bob McMahon; Jeff Engel, Matt Jacobs, Molly Wood, Chris Jespersen, Qiang Zhai, Tom Gaskin, Sandra Scanlon, Tom Zoumaris, Fabian Hillfrich, Michaela Hoenicke Moore, and Sayuri Shimizu all deserve credit for making me reconsider many of my arguments on the basis of their comments during the institute. Brian Etheridge, Terry Anderson, Kishore Gawande, Mark Stoler, Jessica Chapman, and Kyle Longley discussed the project with me when I visited their universities and gave me a great deal to think about, as did Tom Schwartz, Chester Pach, Andrew Preston, Tom Zeiler, Kurk Dorsey, Bill Miscamble, Andy Fry, Bob Schulzinger, Andrew Johnston, Hang Nguyen, Mitch Lerner, Jim Siekmeier, John Prados, and Bob Brigham in other venues.

A special thanks goes out to my three closest friends in the profession—Ken Osgood, Jason Parker, and Kathryn Statler. The past fifteen years of research trips to isolated archives, seminars, spilled coffee, barbeques, conferences, baseball and football games, and frequently making fools of ourselves would not have been the same without you. Ken and Jason read multiple drafts, gave cogent advice, justifiably ridiculed some of my more pathetic titles and ideas, inspired with their book prizes, entertained with their antics, and (maybe most important) threatened me if I didn't get finished. Kathryn read the entire manuscript at least twice, pushed me to get done, and provided indispensable advice and support—and administered a swift slap to the head when necessary.

Many others made helped make the book a reality. Chase Michaels, Lou Phillips, and the boys helped keep me marginally sane and solvent, and the WTFL and End Zone Maniacs gave me welcome diversions (and more cash). I couldn't ask for a more collegial environment than the one I enjoy at Brigham Young University. The institutional support for faculty research and writing is unsurpassed, and my colleagues have been fantastic. Particular thanks go out to Rebecca de Schweinitz, Chris Hodson, Matt Mason, Shawn Miller, Julie Radle, Aaron Skabelund, and Neil York for their support and lending an ear to my frequent ranting. My former colleague Brett Rushforth (now at William and Mary) furnished incentive to get the book finished during my leave—even if we didn't quite make our deadlines, I think I won. The Santa Barbara mafia—Jake Hamblin, Hubert Dubrulle, Rick Fogarty, Dennis Ventry, Justin Stephens, Kimber Quinney, Jennifer See, Jennifer Stevens, Lisa Larson, Traci Heitschmidt, and John Sbardellati—did its part as well. Curtis Solberg, Toshi Hasegawa, Tom Maddox, Matthew Jaffe, and Kevin Chambers helped keep me in touch with academe during the dark years. Finally, thanks to Julie Harris Adams, Michael Adamson, Jennifer Baker, Dan Combs, Sophie Hill, and Russell Stevenson for their research assistance.

Given the nature of my research, this book would not have been possible without generous financial support from multiple sources, including the Society for Historians of American Foreign Relations; the Organization of American Historians; the Historical Society of Southern California and the John Randolph Haynes and Dora Haynes Foundation; Sun West Endodontics; the American Foreign Policy Center; the Rockefeller Archive Center; the Carl Albert Congressional Research and Studies Center; the Herbert Hoover Presidential Library Association; the Dirksen Congressional Center and Caterpillar Foundation; the George Bush Presidential Library Foundation; the Bentley Historical Library; the Lyndon Baines Johnson Foundation; the Department of History and Graduate Division at the University of California, Santa Barbara; the Minnesota Historical Society; the Gerald R. Ford Foundation; the Regents of the University of California; the Interdisciplinary Humanities Center, the Graduate Division, and Department of History at the University of California, Santa Barbara; the David M. Kennedy Center for International Studies; and the Department of History, College of Family, Home and Social Sciences, and College of Undergraduate Education at Brigham Young University. I would also like to thank the Herb Block Foundation for its generosity.

Conducting research is a time-consuming process, particularly when dealing with material scattered in dozens of repositories across the United States.

While there are far too many people to thank individually (lest I neglect to mention someone at one of the nearly forty archives in which I worked), I am indebted to the archivists and staffs at the presidential libraries, congressional collections, historical societies, and university special collections and libraries cited in the book for providing invaluable guidance to the vast documentation and wildly divergent organizational systems. Their collective expertise made the research portion of this project much more efficient and productive. I would also like to thank the legal representatives of the family of Senator Wallace F. Bennett (R-UT) for granting access to his papers. I should also acknowledge the creators and maintainers of the Biographical Directory of the United States Congress (http://bioguide.congress.gov/biosearch/biosearch.asp), an invaluable resource for scholars working in congressional archives and collections.

Portions of this book have been developed from material published elsewhere and appear here with permission: "A Voice from the Wilderness: Richard Nixon and the Vietnam War, 1964–1966," *Presidential Studies Quarterly* 29, no. 2 (Spring 1999): 317–35; "Doves among Hawks: Republican Opposition to the War in Vietnam, 1964–68," *Peace and Change* 31, no. 4 (October 2006): 585–628; and "Achilles' Heel: The Vietnam War and George Romney's Bid for the Presidency, 1967 to 1968," *Michigan Historical Review* 26, no. 1 (Spring 2000): 1–29.

George Herring—an unparalleled historian of the Vietnam War and U.S. foreign relations and an even better person—prompted me to submit the manuscript to the University Press of Kentucky, and I could not be more thrilled with my association with the the Press. Steve Wrinn, the Press's director, exhibited an enthusiasm for this book from the beginning and demonstrated extraordinary patience and support over the past several years. Every author should be fortunate to work with someone of Steve's caliber and dedication. I am also grateful to Anne Dean Watkins, Candace Chaney, Joseph Brown, David Cobb, John Hussey, and the staff at the Press for their assistance and guidance in getting the book through the publication process and to the anonymous readers who went above and beyond in their detailed comments and provided excellent suggestions for improving the manuscript.

Finally, my deepest and most profound gratitude and love go out to my family, to whom "thank you" seems wholly inadequate. My wife, Kayli, tolerates me and has kept our lives steady and pointed in the right direction for the past two decades through the seemingly endless research trips, family challenges, long days at the office, the months I spent away at Gonzaga and the Department of State, and my (several) moments of doubt and uncertainty. Her unfailing support and willingness to run the show—and make it appear effortless— boggle my mind. She means more to me than she will ever know, and this book is dedicated to her. My children—Mitchell, Jenna, and Matthew—are now teenagers, which seems utterly impossible. They remind me daily of the importance of maintaining balance and perspective in my life and what my true priorities should be. I take pride in, and am in awe of, their respective commitments to basketball, volleyball, and Guitar Hero. My parents, Larry and Judy Johns, provided overwhelmingly generous support and encouragement and always try to "make things better." They are two of the most remarkable people I have ever known, and I am extremely proud and grateful to be their son. And last, but not least, Dobby and Witty help make our house a home, as did Rebel . . . I miss my dup.

# Introduction

## Ares, Virginia, and the Myth of the Water's Edge

We see, therefore, that War is not merely a political act, but also a real political instrument, a continuation of political commerce, a carrying out of the same by other means . . . for the political view is the object, War is the means, and the means must always include the object in our conception.
—Carl von Clausewitz, *On War*

The division between "domestic" and "foreign" policies no longer has meaning.
—Chester Bowles, writing in the *New York Times* in January 1960

In his sweeping history of the Peloponnesian Wars, the Greek historian Thucydides lamented the tendency for those in charge of the Greek city-states to allow domestic political considerations to affect questions of national security. In particular, he regretted how the Athenian leadership "adopted methods of demagogy which resulted in their losing control over the actual conduct of affairs. Such a policy . . . naturally led to a number of mistakes." Eventually, the Sicilian expedition ended badly owing to the various elites "quarrelling among themselves," which "began to bring confusion into the policy of the state. . . . And in the end it was only because they had destroyed themselves by their own internal strife that finally they were forced to surrender."[1] Had Thucydides lived two thousand years later, he could have written virtually the same words about the American experience in Vietnam. The nexus of domestic politics and foreign policy defined the U.S. commitment to South Vietnam, shaped American policies, and fundamentally influenced decisionmaking and choices in both the executive and the legislative branches.

Casual observers of the history of U.S. foreign relations might be surprised by this assertion. After all, there has been a long-standing and deeply ingrained

1

axiom that politics stops at the water's edge for American politicians. Essentially, this myth posits that there will be all manner of dissension and partisanship when debating domestic policies but that, when it comes to international affairs, the country will stand firmly together, placing the national interest above a political party's temporary advantage or a politician's personal gain. This assumption, however, is demonstrably false. Indeed, the myth of the water's edge, although prominent even in some scholarship, is thoroughly debunked when examining the historical record of U.S. foreign policy. Even during the Cold War, while a consensus on *strategy* prevailed among most Americans, debate always raged about the *tactics* that would be employed to implement containment. Tension and conflict inhere within the framework of the U.S. constitutional system, and foreign policy is no different than any other aspect of governance. Many of these debates derive their strength from the parochial—that is, domestic political—concerns of elected officials.

The problem, of course, is that decisionmakers have a strong aversion to admitting that domestic political calculations play any role in the policies they craft and the choices they make. In their study of the Vietnam conflict, Leslie Gelb and Richard Betts argue that *domestic politics* "is a dirty phrase in the inner sanctums of foreign policymaking." They contend that the water's edge myth "is unfounded but nevertheless potent. It creates great pressure to keep one's mouth shut, to think and speak of foreign affairs as if they are something above mere politics, something sacred."[2] Anthony Lake, who served on the National Security Council during the Nixon administration and later as Bill Clinton's national security adviser, once compared the discussion of domestic politics in foreign policy decisionmaking to the discussion of sex by the Victorians: "Nobody talks about it but it's on everybody's mind."[3]

If one relied solely on the documentary record, it would be easy to suppose that presidents, members of Congress, and the foreign policy bureaucracy paid little to no attention to public opinion, the electoral calendar, or how their decisions could affect them personally or politically. But even a cursory perusal of American history—not to mention a careful reading of the documents and an examination of the context in which they were created—demonstrates that the opposite is true, from the partisanship inherent in the Federalist and anti-Federalist debates during the 1790s, to the anticommunism of the Cold War, to the war on terrorism. To be sure, this nexus should not be construed to be monocausal; military and diplomatic considerations also contributed to the character and trajectory of U.S. policy. But, in the hierarchy of influence, domestic politics clearly played (and continues to play) a critical and, quite frequently, decisive part in the evolution of American engagement in the Vietnam conflict.

This book focuses on how domestic politics influenced the trajectory, scope, and character of U.S. Vietnam policy from 1961 to 1973. More specifically, it examines how the Republican Party played a central role in the process of policy formation and execution, the nature of the imperial presidency and its relationship with Congress, and the remarkably consistent behavior of three consecutive administrations in dealing with the conflict. A complete understanding of U.S. policy on Vietnam during this period cannot be obtained purely from analyzing decisionmaking in the White House or considering the views and influence of notable Democrats. Much of the early literature on the war did just that, ignoring Congress, public opinion, and the role of the GOP while focusing almost exclusive attention on Lyndon Johnson, Robert McNamara, McGeorge Bundy, and Walt Rostow. One of the primary goals of this study is to decouple the Vietnam experience from the myopic perspective of the executive branch and the Democratic Party and demonstrate not only the significant degree of Republican culpability for Vietnam but also the broader implications the war had for the presidency, executive-legislative relations, and the role of domestic politics in U.S. foreign relations. Theodore White wrote after the 1972 presidential election, "For eighteen years, in a way no historian can yet trace quite clearly, Vietnam had slowly grown to be the nightmare of American Presidents."[4] Nearly four decades later, with the benefit of perspective and a vast evidentiary record, this book analyzes the way in which Vietnam proved to be the nightmare of John Kennedy, Lyndon Johnson, and Richard Nixon as a result of their preoccupation with domestic political calculations.

The story of the second front of the Vietnam conflict—the domestic political battles fought at home simultaneously with the military conflict in Southeast Asia—and the Republican Party's influence on U.S. Vietnam policy has five primary and interrelated themes running through it. The fault lines in the Republican Party on the issue of the Vietnam conflict is the first theme. Most previous scholarship on the war identifies the GOP as the party of the hawks, supporting the escalation of the conflict in 1965, and advocating military victory well into the 1970s. The extensive research on which this book is based conclusively demonstrates that the Republican Party experienced the same divisions and upheavals as the rest of the country during the American experience in Vietnam. While the party was home to such überhawks as Barry Goldwater, John Tower, and Dwight Eisenhower, it also boasted some of the most devoted doves in the nation, John Sherman Cooper, Mark Hatfield, and George Aiken. Further, the intraparty squabbling over Vietnam, especially after the 1964 presidential election, would prove to be one of the major catalysts in bringing conservatives into an ascendant position in the GOP.

The second theme relates to the imperial presidency, which many scholars argue reached its apex during the Vietnam conflict.[5] The research presented herein simultaneously supports and calls into question that conclusion. On one hand, the evidence demonstrates that Congress's inability or unwillingness as an institution to directly confront the president underscores the expansive power of the presidency during the Cold War. Any success that members of Congress might have enjoyed was diminished by a myriad of executive actions. To be sure, individual congressmen did challenge the three administrations directly on the war, especially as the United States became more deeply engaged in Southeast Asia. Yet, even then, success was rare and would quickly be overwhelmed by the president, using the power and influence at his disposal. But perhaps the most striking fact is that, throughout the conflict, Congress proved that it lacked the will to stand together and challenge the White House even when public opinion was firmly on its side.

Conversely, however, the concept of the imperial presidency is undermined when one considers the extent to which the expansive powers posited under that model clash with the very real limitations of domestic political considerations. Although freed from many of the intended constitutional checks and balances vis-à-vis Congress, all three presidents faced constraints rooted in domestic political considerations. As a result, Kennedy, Johnson, and Nixon failed to exercise their vaunted authority to its fullest extent because they feared the even greater influence of public opinion, the ballot box, and the potential harm to their reputations and legacies. Thus, the parameters of the imperial presidency are not as broad as they might appear at first glance. While seemingly contradictory, these two facets of the presidency's relationship to its two publics—Congress and the American people—help us understand the dynamics at work in the decisionmaking processes in each administration. As Andrew Bacevich observes, "What is most striking about the most powerful man in the world is not the power that he wields. It is how constrained he and his lieutenants are by forces that lie beyond their grasp and perhaps their understanding."[6]

The third theme is congressional complicity in the war. One of the often-repeated refrains throughout the 1960s and early 1970s was that Vietnam was Lyndon Johnson's or Richard Nixon's war. There is no doubt that both presidents—along with John Kennedy and Dwight Eisenhower—deserve much of the responsibility for the conflict and its evolution.[7] But to deny any congressional culpability misreads history. Through their actions and—perhaps more important—inaction, members of Congress played an essential part in the escalation and duration of the Vietnam conflict. The deference shown to the three administrations, the collective failure to challenge the presidents, and the willingness to continue approving appropriations for a war that most opposed—

even as late as 1972—provide sufficient evidence to implicate Congress deeply in the entire tragedy. Lt. Col. Oliver North, the key figure in the Iran-Contra scandal of the 1980s, accused Congress of being "fickle, vacillating, unpredictable."[8] That description accurately summarizes how the legislative branch of the U.S. government approached the issue of Vietnam for two decades.

The fourth theme is the similarity between administrations regardless of party, experience, or timing. All three presidents discussed in this book—John Kennedy, Lyndon Johnson, and Richard Nixon—did everything they could to avoid public debate on the Vietnam issue, making decisions on the conflict that might jeopardize their political standing, and becoming "the first president to lose a war." Fear of a right-wing backlash drove their policymaking, and each had to rely on the Republican Party to a much greater extent than has been appreciated by scholars to this point. Moreover, each made a concerted effort to manipulate public opinion and domestic support to his advantage in an attempt to maintain his own personal credibility, demonstrate the dependability of America's commitments to its allies, and achieve electoral success. Of course, in this they were not alone; selling war and other controversial U.S. foreign policies has a long tradition among presidents.[9] The degree to which the Vietnam-era chief executives did so, however, was extraordinary.

The fifth and final major theme is, perhaps, the most crucial and pervades the entire book: the role played by domestic political considerations—public opinion, electoral calculations, personal credibility—in America's international affairs. The role and influence of domestic political considerations in making and implementing U.S. foreign policy—and the reciprocal relationship in which foreign relations influences political decisions at home—have long occupied scholars and observers. By its very nature, as Alexis de Tocqueville noted in the nineteenth century, the American political system consistently exerts a profound effect on the nation's international affairs. Democracies, he argues, tend to have "confused or erroneous ideas on external affairs, and decide questions of foreign policy on purely domestic considerations."[10] Although reductionist, Tocqueville's comment is instructive, particularly in the American context. Concern over public opinion and electoral success can lead U.S. policymakers to pursue foreign policies "excessively geared to short-term calculations," as William Quandt suggests.[11] More recently, Jussi Hanhimäki has argued, "One simply cannot understand foreign policy and international relations without relating it to domestic contingencies and vice versa."[12]

Yet, just as politicians demonstrate a disinclination to admit the influence of politics, partisanship, and elections on foreign policy, most scholars have underestimated the importance of these factors in analyzing and understanding the history of U.S. foreign relations generally and the Vietnam War specifically. Many diplomatic historians write their narratives as if "partisan wrangling and electoral strategizing have generally not been significant determinants of the nation's foreign policy."[13] Important interpretive histories such as Michael Hunt's explanation of the rise of the United States to global dominance, the global context into which Odd Arne Westad places the Cold War, the scholarship of the eminent Cold War historians John Lewis Gaddis and Melvyn Leffler, and even the paradigm-changing monographs of revisionists like William Appleman Williams focus primarily on the international aspects of America's foreign affairs.[14] To be sure, part of the emphasis in recent years derives from increased access to foreign archives, greater foreign language and area studies expertise among scholars, and prodding by historians and political scientists who urged diplomatic historians to decenter the United States and write truly international histories of American diplomacy.[15] But the lack of attention given to domestic political considerations stands as a stark reflection of the imbalance in the literature.

In an overview of the recent historiography of U.S. foreign relations in the *Journal of American History* in 2009, Thomas Zeiler underscored this problematic trend. In his article, written for a nonspecialist audience, Zeiler rightly celebrates the health and vibrancy of the field, focusing on the sophisticated scholarship addressing "traditional realism's engagement with ideology (*mentalités*), the embrace of international history, and the study of culture and identity." But politics? Barely even a passing reference. To his credit, Zeiler admits that "rooting the field in international history risks losing sight of the Americanness that is the very character of U.S. diplomatic history." Unfortunately, he then fails to explore the historiographic and interpretive implications of this statement. Even the broader disciplinary trends adopted by foreign relations scholars that examine the influence of race, gender, identity, and culture—all topics rooted in the "domestic" realm—have obscured the political aspects of policymaking.[16]

There are exceptions, of course. In his presidential address to the Society of Historians of American Foreign Relations in June 2008, Thomas Schwartz implored his fellow scholars to correct this glaring oversight by recognizing the importance of these considerations and incorporating the domestic political context of U.S. foreign relations into the historical conversation.[17] And a handful of scholars, like Fredrik Logevall and Campbell Craig, emphasize the existence and influence of the "intermestic"—the convergence of international and domestic—dimensions of policy in their work.[18] But, for the most part, the role of domestic political considerations remains conspicuously absent in the contemporary history of U.S. foreign relations, limiting our understanding of how and why the United States acts internationally. This study seeks to restore the proper balance of causality and influence. Throughout the book, the power, consequences, and centrality of these forces and the constraints—both real and perceived—they placed on America's presidents and politicians during America's longest war will be demonstrated conclusively.

The sheer tonnage of scholarship and documentation on the Vietnam War boggles the mind.[19] Newly available archival sources, recently declassified documents, examination of previously obscured aspects of the conflict, and reconsideration of long-held assumptions have created a vibrant and thriving debate. But, as Gary Hess noted in a historiographic article on the conflict, the "duration of the war and its antecedents . . . makes this a lengthy story and one being told more in fragments than in its entirety."[20] Like the expanding universe theorized by physicists, the canon of literature on Vietnam continues to proliferate almost exponentially with no end in sight. Yet, given the volume of literature on the conflict, it is surprising that the Republican Party has received so little attention in existing scholarship. Most accounts of the war relegate the GOP to obscurity, portraying it like a groundhog coming out of its hole every two or four years to make an appearance in an election campaign and then resume hibernating while the Kennedy and Johnson administrations unilaterally made and implemented U.S. policy. Even those who recognize the role of Congress tend to direct their attention to key Democrats like J. William Fulbright, Mike Mansfield, and Frank Church.[21]

Nothing could be further from the truth. Republicans played critical roles in the entire American experience in Southeast Asia. The GOP used the "loss" of China as a weapon to attack the Truman administration, which certainly contributed to the decision in NSC-64 to support the French in their colonial war in Indochina in March 1950. The Eisenhower administration continued to underwrite the French war effort until 1954, when it assumed responsibility for the fledgling regime of South Vietnamese premier Ngo Dinh Diem and began sending ever-increasing amounts of aid and military advisers to Saigon.[22] But most important—and obscured to the greatest degree in the scholarship—Republicans exerted significant influence on U.S. policy in Vietnam during the Kennedy, Johnson, and Nixon administrations.

Granted, Republicans remained the minority party in Congress throughout the 1960s and lacked direct access to decisionmaking positions until Richard Nixon assumed the presidency in January 1969. But the GOP acted as a pillar of support for all the presidents of the Vietnam era. Faced with opposition from opponents of the war, and preoccupied with the fear of a right-wing backlash if Vietnam "fell" to communism, each chief executive needed Republican backing for his foreign policies. Many notable figures within the GOP supported the

U.S. involvement in Southeast Asia from the beginning and would continue to urge increased military, political, and economic support for the various Saigon regimes throughout the conflict. Indeed, the most strident hawks in the party pushed Kennedy, Johnson, and Nixon to do more than the presidents themselves were ready or willing to do. This occurred, not from within the administrations, but from power bases outside the White House. As the political scientist James Lindsay has opined, "Even when members of Congress fail to dictate the substance of foreign policy, they frequently influence it indirectly."[23] This is exactly what happened during the Vietnam conflict.

It is important to note that the party was not a unitary actor as meaningful differences between liberal and conservative Republicans existed. The traditional division within the GOP between internationalists and isolationists/noninterventionists would undergo a watershed change in the 1960s as the right wing of the party emerged as the dominant force, leaving the liberals virtually powerless within their own party—and prompting many like New York City mayor John Lindsay to defect to the Democrats. The result of this split would be the formation of new and shifting coalitions that permanently altered the political calculus in both domestic and foreign policy in the party and in the country. Conservatives would play a major part in the war, through both the pressure they put on the administrations to win a military victory and the potential domestic political specter they represented to Kennedy, Johnson, and Nixon.

But, while the hawkish Republicans were numerically superior in the party, they represent only part of the story. Liberal members of the party figured prominently in providing a brake on the more vigorous options for prosecuting the war, working with key Democrats on the Senate Foreign Relations Committee to temper suggestions for additional escalation by making it politically unfeasible to do so. Opponents of the war in the GOP included some of the most influential members of the party and became a much larger and more vocal cohort as the conflict evolved.[24] Moreover, the strong sentiment within the Republican Party both for and against the war contributed to the divisiveness experienced by the country during the conflict and would merit consideration by scholars on that basis alone. Republicans played vital roles in the origins, escalation, and ultimate settlement in Southeast Asia; to tell the story of the Vietnam War without the GOP would be like watching "Seinfeld" without Kramer.

Perhaps the most important Republican during this entire period with regard to Vietnam was Richard Nixon. As president, Nixon obviously assumed direct responsibility for U.S. policy in Southeast Asia. But, while his role in the Vietnamization of the war and the negotiations that led to the fatally flawed Paris Peace Accords in 1973 has received wide attention, his function as an agent provocateur during the previous administrations has been seriously underestimated.[25] He pushed both Kennedy and Johnson to act more forcefully in Vietnam, urging expansion of the war, and looming as the personification of the fear of the Right that so heavily influenced both presidents (and, ironically, would affect Nixon himself as well during his administration). Moreover, his ability to effectively manage the Vietnam issue in 1968 allowed Nixon not only to capture the GOP nomination but also to defeat Hubert Humphrey in the general election. Along with Lyndon Johnson, Nixon stands as the central figure in the American experience in Vietnam.

While Nixon appears regularly in scholarship on the war, he is one of the few Republicans who has garnered significant attention. That is not to say that their story is entirely absent from the literature. Terry Dietz, Robert Mann, William Gibbons, and Gary Stone all ascribe some degree of influence to the GOP during the war.[26] Of course, biographies of key GOP figures—such as Nixon, Eisenhower, and Barry Goldwater—inform our understanding of the specific roles they played, but the common theme running through all those works is the presidency. Only a small body of scholarship exists on significant Republican congressional leaders, and even those works focus almost exclusively on the men who held senior leadership positions within the party—Everett Dirksen, Gerald Ford, and Melvin Laird. Virtually no literature exists on the breadth of congressional opinion among Republicans.[27] More generally, there has been an increasing focus on the evolution of the Republican Party and the broader rise of conservatism since the 1950s, but few of these studies explore the linkage between the conservative ascendancy and the war.[28] This book seeks to redress these historiographic lacunae.

It is fitting that this book began with a reference to Thucydides and Greek history. In looking back on the Vietnam conflict, Henry Kissinger later described the war as a "nightmare" and a "Greek tragedy" and suggested that the United States "should have never been there at all."[29] This frequently used analogy is appropriate, especially when considered from the perspective of the presidency. Tragedy depicts the downfall of the hero through some combination of hubris, fate, and the will of the gods. The tragic hero's desire to achieve some goal inevitably encounters limits (e.g., domestic politics). The hero need not die in the end, but he must undergo a change in fortune and may have an epiphany regarding or come to some understanding of his destiny. The experiences, actions, and decisions of Kennedy, Johnson, and Nixon during the Vietnam conflict could not be described more accurately.

In recognition of these parallels, each chapter title in the book references a character or concept from Greek mythology as a way of describing and framing a particular moment in the U.S. experience in Southeast Asia. The title of this introduction, for example, refers to the Greek god of war (Ares) and the goddess of politics (Virginia), a combination that would prove explosive during the twenty-five-year ordeal that the United States endured in Southeast Asia. If war is a continuation of politics by other means, then surely in the American context politics is war by other means.[30] Unfortunately, the saga of the Republican Party and domestic politics during the Vietnam conflict is not a myth but a tragedy. It is a story filled with protagonists with tragic flaws, imperfect institutions, and lessons suffused with consequences that continue to be felt to the present day.

# CHAPTER 1

# Trapped between Scylla and Charybdis

## JFK, the GOP, and Domestic Politics

The line dividing domestic and foreign affairs has become as indistinct as a line drawn in water. All that happens to us here at home has a direct and intimate bearing on what we can or must do abroad. All that happens to us abroad has a direct and intimate bearing on what we can or must do at home. If we err in one place, we err in both. If we succeed in one place, we have a chance to succeed in both.

—John F. Kennedy

One of the recurrent and dangerous influences on our foreign policy—fear of the political consequences of doing the sensible thing.

—John Kenneth Galbraith, *A Life in Our Times*

Shortly after his defeat by Franklin D. Roosevelt in the 1940 presidential election, Wendell Willkie advised his fellow Republicans, "Let us not, therefore, fall into the partisan error of opposing things just for the sake of opposition. Ours must not be an opposition against—it must be an opposition for."[1] Willkie's attitude reflected the prevailing sentiment in the party and the country at the time. Politics, argued leaders such as Senator Arthur Vandenberg (R-MI), had no place in making U.S. foreign policy. Vandenberg, who served as the chair of the Senate Foreign Relations Committee during the Truman administration and is widely credited as being the architect of postwar bipartisanship in foreign policy, opined, "To me, 'bipartisan foreign policy' means a mutual effort . . . to unite our official voice at the water's edge so that America speaks with maximum authority against those who would divide and conquer us and the free world. It does not involve the remotest surrender of free debate in determining our position." On the contrary, he continued, "Frank cooperation and free debate are indispensable to ultimate unity. In a word, it simply seeks national security ahead of partisan advantage. Every foreign policy must be *totally* debated . . . and the 'loyal opposition' is under special obligation to see that this occurs."[2]

Henry Cabot Lodge Jr., the GOP senator from Massachusetts who would serve as ambassador to South Vietnam on two occasions during the Vietnam War under Democratic presidents, agreed. The opposition party should function as "the voice of conscience though not of power" in foreign affairs, undertaking a "calm and deliberate reappraisal of the facts" while offering "constructive suggestions."[3] Such lofty ideals did not prevent Republicans and Democrats alike from consistently questioning the tactics employed by the United States in opposing the perceived Soviet threat or in getting political mileage out of the fall of China and other foreign policy failures. Additionally, as former secretary of state Dean Acheson wryly noted, one of the benefits of a bipartisan foreign policy was that the president could characterize any critic of that policy as "a son-of-a-bitch and not a true patriot."[4] During Dwight D. Eisenhower's administration, the president worked with Democrats such as Senate majority leader Lyndon Johnson to continue the tradition of cooperation. Although the consensus frayed occasionally, the Democrats worked fairly well with the White House during Eisenhower's two terms in office. With the election of John F. Kennedy in 1960, the Republicans found themselves thrust back into the role of the loyal opposition.

Should this rhetorical commitment to bipartisanship, an enduring hallmark of the Cold War, be considered posturing by politicians seeking electoral and policy advantages? Did a bipartisan consensus on foreign policy actually exist in the postwar period? The answers to those questions are not simple. To be sure, both political parties adhered to containment in its many iterations. But to translate the superficial agreement on the broad contours of strategy into any realistic, nonpartisan consensus on foreign policy—one in which politics stopped at the water's edge—misreads history. Republicans and Democrats fought vicious political battles during the 1940s and 1950s over questions of foreign policy, both in Congress and on the campaign trail. The presidential contest between Kennedy and Richard Nixon in 1960 demonstrated that fact vividly. Nevertheless, the rhetorical attachment to the ideal of bipartisanship remained a potent political force.

Such bipartisan rhetoric would not endure, however, as the burgeoning conflict in Indochina moved to center stage during Kennedy's thousand days.

Owing to the emerging problem of Vietnam—not to mention the perceived missile and bomber gaps, Fidel Castro's continued presence in Cuba, and the ongoing struggle with the Soviet Union—the Republican Party moved toward a more confrontational stance with the administration, consistently attacking the president for his foreign policy failures and inability to effectively engage and defeat the global Communist threat. Moreover, as the stakes in Southeast Asia increased, the Vietnam conflict emerged as a potent electoral issue in 1964. This chapter will examine Kennedy's preoccupation with domestic political considerations and the evolution of GOP criticism of his foreign policies. As will become clear, the new president would find himself trapped between the Scylla of the 1964 election and the Charybdis of Republican attacks, a position that strongly influenced the decisions he made and, more often, postponed as he maneuvered toward his reelection campaign.

In the aftermath of Kennedy's victory over Nixon, the Republican Party appeared to renew its support of rhetorical bipartisanship. Senator Wallace Bennett (R-UT), one of the leading voices on financial policy in the Senate, who believed in a stout foreign policy, sounded a conciliatory note as the GOP found itself out of the White House for the first time in eight years. Echoing Willkie and Vandenberg, Bennett told his constituents, "Opposition for the sake of opposition serves no real purpose." He hoped that "the new administration and the minority in Congress can get together on many basic problems. In the field of foreign affairs, particularly, the tasks we face are so monumental that we must avoid anything that will unnecessarily divide our people and dissipate our strength." Describing the GOP as "the party of constructive and responsible criticism," Bennett promised that the Republicans would "support the proposals made by the Kennedy Administration when we believe them to be right, but when we believe them to be wrong we will oppose them."[5]

As an example, Bennett spoke specifically about the situation in Laos, where the administration eventually decided on a policy of neutralization. Several columnists criticized Kennedy's policy for dealing with the Communist threat in the region, but the Utah senator noted that the Republican leadership in Congress had "openly and vigorously come to the President's side in support of a firm stand against the Communists in Laos." This, he insisted, represented the essence of the loyal opposition. While recognizing that the president played a "paramount role" in foreign affairs, he nonetheless asserted that the parameters must be shaped in public and that it would be "highly dangerous and unwise" for the president to exercise sole control over U.S. policy. To this end, Bennett called for full consultation with and complete information from the administration so that the Republicans would, as Vandenberg famously suggested, be in on the takeoffs as well as the crash landings.[6]

Building on this theme, Richard Nixon, perhaps his party's leading voice in foreign affairs, argued that criticism of the new president's foreign policy "for purely political purposes when his policy is right is irresponsible and unpatriotic. But, failure to criticize when his policy is wrong is just as irresponsible and unpatriotic."[7] Of course, Nixon in his own inimitable way simply meant that it was, in fact, OK to criticize Kennedy if it would help the Republican position. Nevertheless, on the surface it would be very easy for contemporary observers to believe that the two parties would present a united front to the world in terms of U.S. foreign relations. The media contributed to this notion as Republican rhetoric did not go unnoticed in the early days of the administration. A week after Kennedy's inauguration, a *Washington Post* editorial praised the GOP members of the Senate Foreign Relations Committee for demonstrating "their interest in fair appraisal rather than in mere partisan opposition. . . . Such a role for Republicans concerned with foreign affairs may not conform to some of the urgings of the Minority Policy Committee. But it conforms, we think, to the public interest."[8]

Yet *loyal* did not negate *opposition;* the honeymoon period between the Republicans and the administration would not last long. The GOP took advantage of every opportunity to attack Kennedy's foreign policies and began formulating its strategy for opposing the president even before the inauguration. Eisenhower summoned the party's congressional leadership to the White House just before he left office and reminded them of their responsibility to voice concerns over Democratic policy once the presidency no longer rested safely in GOP hands. Without a Republican president to oversee and formulate a unified party agenda, he argued, some other mechanism would be required to centralize and correlate Republican positions on the issues. Determined to chart, define, and maintain an integrated minority political strategy, the conferees created a joint Senate-House leadership group. In addition to their weekly press conferences, the leadership met regularly with prominent Republicans such as Nixon, Senator Barry Goldwater (R-AZ), and Governor Nelson Rockefeller (R-NY) in recognition of the need to unify the various wings of the party into a cohesive voice for national policy.[9]

Unity—and the lack thereof—would become an increasing concern for the GOP as the Kennedy years coincided with the acceleration of a tectonic shift in the Republican Party. Nixon's defeat in 1960 empowered the right wing of the party, a cohort that had never accepted the New Deal but had been "temporarily quiescent" during the Eisenhower administration. This faction gained strength as the Republicans increased their support in the South and the West, a demographic and electoral shift that would form the cornerstone of the party's support for the next five decades. This was a different brand of conservatism than that of Robert Taft, the Ohio senator who had lost the 1952 nomination to Eisenhower. Not only did it include Goldwaterites and economic conservatives, but it also counted on social and cultural conservatives, personified by William F. Buckley Jr., the editor of the conservative *National Review* and the host of television's "Firing Line." Buckley's support for conservative causes and groups like Young Americans for Freedom challenged the notion of consensus politics within the party and would form the nucleus of the insurgency that would, ultimately, control the party and dominate its agenda. Indeed, the next decade would witness a struggle for the soul of the GOP.[10]

In 1961, however, these intraparty tensions had not yet been fully manifested, and congressional Republicans remained under the stewardship of Charles Halleck (R-IN) and Everett Dirksen (R-IL). Halleck served as the leader of the party in the House from 1947 to 1955 and again from 1959 to 1965. A traditional conservative from Indiana, he was tough, pragmatic, and intelligent and felt at home both in the circles of power in Washington and in his home district.[11] Much the same could be said about Halleck's counterpart in the Senate. A conservative isolationist who evolved into a staunch cold warrior and presidential confidant, Dirksen became minority leader in 1959 and remained in that position until his death ten years later.[12] Although they faced increasingly sharp criticism from the "Young Fogies" on the right wing of the party, both men were formidable opponents and commanded Kennedy's respect. The president, according to Terry Dietz, would have been "foolish to discount their abilities to question, probe, and diminish policy decisions made by his administration."[13]

Halleck and Dirksen used those skills to publicly deride the administration's policies at the press conferences that followed the joint leadership's meetings in what became commonly referred to as "The Ev and Charlie Show." They devised these spectacles to identify for the public areas of difference between the parties and to demonstrate the Republican Party's superior position. Unfortunately, Barry Goldwater and other GOP hard-liners distrusted Halleck and Dirksen "for having prostituted themselves during the Eisenhower years" and regarded them as relics of a dark period in the party's history. As a result, disgruntled conservatives would undermine the facade of unity with criticisms of their own, a trend that increased during the 1960s. It did not help that the leadership's press conferences "proved a total disaster"—a "turn of the century vaudeville act," as *Commonweal* opined—in comparison to Kennedy's polished television presence; neither Halleck nor Dirksen would ever be considered a master of the medium.[14] As a result, the press conferences may have done as much to highlight the fissures within the party as they did to critique the administration.

The emerging intraparty schism did not stop the leadership from continuing to criticize Kennedy and his policies, however. On ABC's "Issues and Answers" nine days after Kennedy's inauguration, Dirksen summarized the GOP position on supporting the administration's foreign policy. "When it comes to bipartisan foreign policy in so far as that is possible obviously we would like to go along," Dirksen said, "but we have some firm notions about it." The senator stated that the Republicans wanted to avoid getting "our country in a position of appeasement which for all the world will look like weakness and that we are dealing from weakness rather than from strength."[15] Dirksen, like many of his colleagues, believed that the opposition party had greater responsibilities than mere opposition. As a result, he tried to view national affairs, especially those involving international issues, from a patriotic rather than a partisan stance, which led him to work closely with both Kennedy and Johnson.[16] Byron Hulsey suggests that the minority leader and the president had a "codependent relationship" during Kennedy's presidency, noting that the two men shared many similar philosophical and political beliefs. Yet overlapping political principles and rhetorical adherence to an ideal of bipartisanship did not mean that Dirksen considered his or his party's role as merely cooperating with the administration, as demonstrated by his enthusiastic support of the new Senate-House leadership group and his embrace of his role as a partisan fighter.[17] This would become evident as the Republican leadership challenged Kennedy on the emerging issue of Vietnam.

The new president had a long record of supporting America's commitment to South Vietnam.[18] As a senator, Kennedy had closely followed Eisenhower's post-Geneva Vietnam policy and never publicly indicated his opposition to the policies implemented by the administration, going so far as to call Vietnam the "finger in the dike" of communism.[19] While Vietnam did not become a pivotal issue during the 1960 presidential campaign, Kennedy's rhetoric foreshadowed an uncompromising global anticommunism that would eventually affect his policies in Southeast Asia and throughout the Third World.[20] Kennedy called for new and decisive leadership and in his inaugural address famously pledged that the United States would "pay any price, bear any burden, meet any hardship, support any friend, oppose any foe to assure the survival and the success of liberty."[21] After his election, he rejected any likelihood of a toned-down policy owing to his political insecurity, his lack of widespread popularity, and an abiding concern over a domestic political backlash if he softened his position vis-à-vis the Communist world—all of which stemmed from his narrow margin of victory in 1960. Fear of a right-wing counterattack would be a constant theme from 1961 to the end of the war; even Nixon dared not ignore the potential political threat from the Right.

Compared to the dramatic confrontations over Cuba, the showdown with

Soviet premier Nikita Khrushchev at Vienna, or the neutralization of Laos, the developments in Vietnam during most of Kennedy's presidency received relatively little public attention. But they would have a profound significance for his successors in the White House. JFK and his advisers saw Vietnam as a small and relatively manageable part of the global battle against communism whose significance derived from its role in that contest. They considered South Vietnam crucial because a Communist victory might demonstrate that the "national liberation" model the Soviets trumpeted early in 1961 could be applied successfully elsewhere in the Third World, thereby sparking a series of "brushfire wars" that would threaten world peace.[22] On 28 January 1961, Kennedy held a meeting with his top advisers to discuss Vietnam and concluded ominously, "This is the worst one we've got, isn't it?"[23] The president could not afford to ignore the problems in South Vietnam. As he told the columnist James Reston, "Now we have a problem in trying to make our power credible, and Vietnam looks like the place."[24] He knew that the Republicans would be waiting to exploit any stumbling by the administration in Southeast Asia. His confidence in the probable success of his strategy and fear of potential Republican criticism shaped the way he approached decisionmaking on Southeast Asia.[25]

Not everyone in the administration agreed about the importance of South Vietnam. The documentary record is replete with the contentious discussions that occurred among members of the president's cabinet and staff. As Kennedy's national security adviser, McGeorge Bundy, later said, Vietnam was "the most divisive issue in the Kennedy administration."[26] But the new president could not afford such dissension within his circle of advisers, or even in the Democratic Party generally, on Vietnam or other pressing foreign policy issues. Kennedy was highly cognizant of and concerned with domestic politics as they related to his foreign policy decisions, and that preoccupation led him to pursue bipartisan support—rather than empty rhetoric—for his initiatives. The president consistently sought GOP cooperation and support for political protection. Despite his efforts to reach out to Republicans, however, a coalition of Republicans and Southern Democrats emerged as an obstacle to his foreign policy and domestic agenda. As George Mayer has written, "In every Congress since 1939, this group exercised a life-and-death power over legislation; it killed much of the President's domestic program."[27]

Further, Republican charges of weakness or appeasement in the face of the Communist threat hit uncomfortably close to home and echoed JFK's criticism of Eisenhower and Nixon during the campaign. The widespread use of the "Munich analogy" in dealing with the threat of global communism had a significant influence on the way Cold War presidents formulated and implemented policy.[28] The fear of being branded as an appeaser—which had such negative connotations in the wake of Neville Chamberlain's failure to halt Nazi expansionism during the 1930s—shaped the Kennedy administration's response to the instability in Southeast Asia and foreclosed any realistic possibility of negotiations owing to the political peril that might result from failed diplomacy.

As a result, the upheaval in Indochina presented a constant concern for the president. Just prior to the April 1961 Bay of Pigs debacle—where CIA-trained Cuban exiles attempted and failed to overthrow the Castro regime—John Kenneth Galbraith sent the president a letter of warning about the situation in Vietnam. Galbraith, the new ambassador to India, called South Vietnam "a can of snakes" and warned that South Vietnamese premier Ngo Dinh Diem's efforts to cling to power could eventually draw the United States deeper into the conflict in Indochina. He also asked derisively, "Incidentally, who is the man in your administration who decides what countries are strategic? I would like to have his name and address and ask him what is so important about this real estate in the space age." Galbraith concluded that, in the case of Vietnam, "it is the political poison that is really at issue. The Korean war killed us in the early '50's; this involvement could kill us now."[29] The ambassador's astute advice was not lost on Kennedy.

In the wake of the disastrous invasion of Cuba, Kennedy made several moves intended to mute Republican criticism and mitigate the damage to his presidency. First, he met with Eisenhower at Camp David and solicited his predecessor's public support. Privately, the way Kennedy handled the crisis disturbed Eisenhower, but the former president reluctantly made the appropriate supportive comments in public. In addition, he exerted significant influence in restraining both Halleck and Dirksen; he convinced the two leaders to temper their remarks, cautioning that heated criticism could "sound like McCarthyism."[30] In doing so, Eisenhower acted as a firewall for the administration, as no Republican would directly challenge the party's elder statesman on a foreign policy issue. Kennedy also met with Nelson Rockefeller, a moderate Republican with significant foreign policy experience. Following that conversation, Rockefeller publicly announced that all Americans should "stand united behind the President in whatever action is necessary to defend freedom," providing the president with further political protection.[31]

In addition, Kennedy met with Richard Nixon. The former vice president urged bipartisan support for the president, stating that those with partial information and details about the invasion acted irresponsibly in criticizing the administration.[32] The following day, Nixon reiterated his support, saying that he told Kennedy that he would continue to back administration policies that were "consistent with our international obligations" and "designed to stop further Communist penetration in this hemisphere, or in Asia," including the commitment of American armed forces.[33] Yet Nixon would also obliquely attack the president's actions in the aftermath of the invasion. In early May, he stated that Republicans should not publicly criticize the president for "mistakes which have hurt our world position."[34] Such a statement in itself was implied criticism of Kennedy and typified the types of subtle verbal barbs Nixon—and, increasingly, other Republicans—would direct at both Kennedy and Johnson in the years to come. Nevertheless, the president's damage control efforts did bear fruit. Republican criticism, while significant, was tempered in the wake of the comments by the party leadership, giving the administration a chance to overcome a major policy failure. Of course, Kennedy expected to face attacks from his GOP rivals on the issue of communism. During their final transition meeting, Eisenhower told Kennedy that he and the Republicans would hold the new president responsible for any retreat in Southeast Asia.[35]

Eisenhower would remain true to his word. On leaving office, he retired to his Gettysburg farm. Yet *retirement* proved to be a misnomer as a description of his postpresidential years. Eisenhower remained a prominent public figure and had incredible demands on his time and for his influence. In addition to writing his memoirs, the former president was the patriarch of the Republican Party, "a burden at once honorary, inescapable, irksome, and gratifying."[36] Eisenhower kept abreast of domestic political issues and world events, often discussing administration policies with former subordinates. Kennedy and the congressional leadership arranged for Eisenhower to be reinstated to active duty status in the military by act of Congress, allowing him to receive the benefits of his five-star rank—most notably regular briefings on foreign affairs. As a result, Eisenhower could give informed advice to and exert influence on Kennedy when crisis situations arose.

While his successor struggled with and hesitated to make foreign policy decisions, Eisenhower became more openly opinionated on issues facing the country. Unfettered by presidential expectations and politics, his comments became more pointed and strident, particularly on the need to oppose communism in Southeast Asia. Although Eisenhower had misgivings about the way in which Kennedy conducted America's foreign policy, he made a conscious effort not to criticize his successor publicly, a policy he would continue in his relationship with Johnson. Having been in Kennedy's position, Eisenhower preferred to level his criticisms at domestic policies. He did, however, offer his counsel when asked.

For instance, Eisenhower joined Kennedy at Camp David on 22 April 1961 to discuss the situation in Laos. Kennedy "was quite sure that there was no possibility of saving Laos by unilateral military action" and remarked that he was less concerned about Laos than he was about Thailand. Eisenhower replied that, if that were the case, the best course of action would be the immediate strengthening of the Thai military and positions against Communist forces. But his public comments differed markedly from his private thoughts. In the wake of the Bay of Pigs fiasco, Eisenhower wrote confidentially that there would be a public outcry "if the whole story ever becomes known to the American people" and wryly noted that it "could be called a 'Profile in Timidity and Indecision.'"[37] Eisenhower's remarks in both public and private had to concern the president as they undoubtedly reflected the more acrimonious statements likely to emanate from the rest of the Republican Party.

Moreover, the former president remained committed to the Republican Party regaining the presidency and saw Kennedy's struggles as crucial weapons in the coming political struggle. At a meeting of the joint GOP congressional leadership on 1 May, Eisenhower "cautioned and urged the Republican leaders to keep an accurate record, for future reference, of any conversations they might have with the President in White House conferences on matters such as Laos and Cuba."[38] For Kennedy's part, while he disagreed with Eisenhower on many issues, he increasingly came to realize that his predecessor was one of only three other men in the nation—along with Herbert Hoover and Harry Truman—who fully understood the burdens of the White House. As a result, JFK's respect for Eisenhower grew throughout his presidency. Nevertheless, the president realized that Eisenhower's forbearance was not likely to be emulated by his Republican colleagues, particularly given the diplomatic and military problems that emerged during 1961.

In terms of anti-Communist foreign policy, Kennedy's first hundred days in office were less than auspicious. The failure of the Cuban invasion and the agreement to neutralize Laos provoked "Republican criticism which questioned his courage and competence."[39] Barry Goldwater claimed that the entire country should feel "apprehension and shame" at the failure of the invasion.[40] Senator Thruston Morton (R-KY), a respected moderate and former head of the Republican National Committee, declared that there was a lack of candor from the White House owing to the administration's refusal to admit its complicity in the invasion, foreshadowing the "credibility gap" critique the GOP would later use against Lyndon Johnson. The *New York Times* claimed that Morton's assertion "shattered the political calm" in Washington and upset the veneer of bipartisanship.[41] Similar comments followed the administration's decision to neutralize Laos.

As a result, Kennedy "sought a contrasting and compensating scenario of militancy in Vietnam," believing that, politically, he could not afford a third charge of retreat before the Communist advance so early in his presidency. His incentive to do so was bolstered by the perception that American credibility and leadership had suffered during his poor performance at the Vienna summit meeting with Khrushchev at the beginning of June.[42] He expressed his concerns to Walt W. Rostow, the deputy national security adviser, who would shortly move to State to chair the Policy Planning Staff. The president told Rostow that, unlike Eisenhower, who had been able to deflect political criticism for Communist success in Vietnam in 1954 by blaming the French, he did not have that luxury. He feared being portrayed as an appeaser—a charge that had crippled his father's political career after comments about Germany during the elder Kennedy's tenure as ambassador to Britain—and realized that Republicans like Representative Melvin Laird (R-WI) would assail him for failing "to act with sufficient vigor to frustrate the achievement of Communist objectives."[43] For Kennedy, then, the domestic political consequences were too steep to accept. Galbraith recalled that, during the Laotian crisis, the president told him, "There are just so many concessions one can make to the communists in one year and survive politically. . . . We just can't have another defeat this year in Vietnam." When the Laos agreement began to break down less than a year after its conclusion, "any possibility that Kennedy would even explore a negotiated compromise in Vietnam was foreclosed."[44]

Even without the possibility of a negotiated settlement, the Republican Party stood to gain regardless of what Kennedy did in Southeast Asia. The GOP could realistically criticize the president for being either too confrontational or too lenient with Communist demands, depending on the situation. In essence, it was a no-win situation for the president in domestic political terms. The nation's pundits recognized the dilemma Kennedy faced all too clearly. A Herblock cartoon portrayed Kennedy as a doctor operating on the Laotian crisis. Into the operating room came "The Ev and Charlie Show," Dirksen holding a paddle that said, "If you make concessions you're an appeaser," Halleck holding one labeled, "If you get tough you're a warmaker."[45] The commitment to the principle of the loyal opposition eroded as the president's options in Indochina narrowed and the Republican Party recognized the opportunity to damage his political prospects further.

Perhaps no Republican utilized rhetoric more effectively than Richard Nixon. In a speech in Chicago in early May, for example, he sounded a common refrain. "Our criticism of the Administration should be responsible, constructive, on issues of real substance," he said. "This is no time for nit-picking. . . . We certainly do not help America by running her down in the eyes of the world." Then Nixon said something that, in retrospect, defies explanation: "I believe that the current obsession about the level of America's prestige in the world obscures the principles that should guide us in developing foreign policy. Those who talk constantly about our prestige would seem to believe that we are in

7 April 1961: "The Slapstick Boys in the Emergency Room"

a popularity contest." During his own presidency, Nixon would become consumed with U.S. (and his own) prestige, and his decisions and policies reflected
that fixation. Further, he chastised the president for paying so much attention
to domestic political considerations, asserting, "Some political commentators
have suggested that President Kennedy cannot risk action which might involve
a commitment of American forces because of the fear of political criticism.
. . . I can think of nothing more detrimental to our national interest than for a
consideration of this type to have any effect in the high councils of the Administration."[46] In light of Nixon's obsessive concern with public opinion, electoral
politics, and political criticism during his own administration, these statements
seem extraordinarily contradictory.

Nixon was not alone. On 25 April, Representative John Rhodes (R-AZ)
charged that the administration's failure to "act in a resolute way in Laos, and
the recent fiasco in Cuba," reflected "incredibly bad intelligence, worse planning, but a complete lack of resolution to carry through to a desired goal."
Rhodes tied these foreign policy shortcomings explicitly to the loss of China,
exactly the type of rhetorical blast that the president feared.[47] The attacks by
Nixon, Rhodes, and other Republicans, combined with myriad foreign policy
challenges facing the administration, caused Kennedy and his advisers a great
deal of consternation. Not only did they worry about partisan criticism, but
they were also concerned about the effect of these problems on executive-
legislative relations. Walt Rostow mused that the administration would need a
"big new objective in the underdeveloped areas" of the world in order to keep
Congress "off our necks as we try to clean up the spots of bad trouble" in the
Congo, Cuba, Iran, Indonesia, Laos, and Vietnam.[48]

The combination of continuing problems in South Vietnam and the administration's struggles in foreign policy led the president to approve National
Security Action Memorandum (NSAM) 52 on 11 May 1961. The directive stated
clearly that the overriding American objective in Southeast Asia was to "prevent Communist domination of South Vietnam" and authorized various supporting actions in pursuit of that goal. NSAM 52 committed the United States to
South Vietnam, but not unequivocally. Kennedy approved only the actions required by present circumstances, postponing harder decisions until absolutely
necessary.[49] This approach to the situation in Vietnam would set a precedent
that the administration would follow over the next two years and that Lyndon
Johnson and Richard Nixon would replicate in their own deliberations about
the course of U.S. policy toward Southeast Asia. Rather than taking decisive action, the Vietnam-era presidents would deal with problems incrementally and
reactively.

While the administration studied its options for an expanded role in Vietnam, Kennedy sent Vice President Lyndon Johnson on a policy assessment trip through Asia, with a major stopover in Saigon. On completing the tour, Johnson testified before the Senate Foreign Relations Committee. He reported that the decision to negotiate with Laos had shaken Diem's confidence in the United States and warned that, if the United States intended to arrest the decline in South Vietnamese morale, "deeds must follow words—soon." Significantly, Johnson did not advocate the introduction of U.S. combat troops, a result of his meeting with Diem.[50] Representative Paul Findley (R-IL), who would later achieve notoriety as a major critic of U.S. policy toward Israel, called Johnson's statement that American combat troops were not needed in Vietnam at that time "an invitation to trouble." Findley advocated publicly offering combat troops to Vietnam because they would be the most effective deterrent against aggression. War might be avoided, he argued, if the administration committed combat troops before Communist action rather than committing them "midstream," which might trigger a larger war. Findley predicted that Vietnam could become another Laos and asserted, "We will be forced to send combat forces to a war already in progress, or once more be identified with failure."[51] As Findley's statement suggests, Republicans did not respect Kennedy's foreign policy decisions and expressed a distinct wariness of his reluctance to firmly oppose Communist aggression in Vietnam.

The president and his advisers took these comments very seriously. Domestic political considerations figured prominently in the calculations made by Kennedy and members of his administration during his first year in office. The National Security Council (NSC) aide Robert Komer, in a memo titled "Are We Pushing Hard Enough in South Vietnam?" concluded, "There are some strong political reasons for stepping up the momentum in South Vietnam. I believe it very important that this government have a major anti-Communist victory to its credit in the six months before the Berlin crisis is likely to get really hot." Recognizing the political and diplomatic realities that existed in mid-1961, he urged a more aggressive posture in Southeast Asia: "After Laos, and with Berlin on the horizon, we cannot afford to go less than all-out in cleaning up South Vietnam."[52] In fact, many administration officials pressed for escalation in Vietnam during the summer, but Kennedy, preoccupied with other foreign policy matters, approved only small increments of additional aid.

As the situation deteriorated without decisive action from the White House, Republican criticism continued throughout the summer and fall of 1961. In an opinion piece in the *Los Angeles Times* in late July, Richard Nixon slammed Kennedy for "unsure and indecisive leadership in the field of foreign policy," suggesting that the administration had been "plagued by a Hamlet-like psychosis which seems to paralyze it every time decisive action is required." Contrasting JFK's "bold talk" with the outcome of his decisions, Nixon derided the "confusion, indecision and weakness" of the administration's actions.[53] Kennedy grew increasingly concerned over the GOP's attacks, asking his close adviser and speechwriter Theodore Sorensen to speak with the columnists Walter Lippmann and Joseph Alsop and ask how the administration could counter Republican charges of appeasement. The president also urged Americans to display "national maturity" in the face of temporary gains and setbacks in the Cold War, an obvious effort to mute criticism before it occurred.[54]

Komer analyzed the domestic political situation for McGeorge Bundy in late October 1961. The man who became known as "Blowtorch Bob" and who would later head the Phoenix Program astutely observed, "I doubt if our position in [Southeast Asia] could survive 'loss' of S. Vietnam on top of that of Laos. Moreover, could Administration afford yet another defeat, domestically?"[55] Komer was certainly not alone in recognizing this relationship. Secretary of Defense Robert McNamara and Secretary of State Dean Rusk addressed Vietnam as a domestic issue on 3 November 1961 in a joint memorandum that assessed Gen. Maxwell Taylor's recommendations for further American action in Southeast Asia. "The loss of South Vietnam would stimulate bitter domestic controversies," they argued, "and would be seized upon by extreme elements to divide the country and harass the Administration."[56] Kennedy agreed. If the United States walked away from Southeast Asia, he opined, the Communist takeover would produce a debate in the country more acute than the loss of China.[57] Kennedy did not believe that he could weather such a storm on the heels of Cuba, Laos, Berlin, and Vienna. With his reelection hanging in the balance, he knew that he had to avoid making choices that would invite scrutiny and criticism.

The final weeks of 1961 marked a critical turning point in the American experience in Vietnam. Caught between those who wanted to extricate the United States from Vietnam and the aggressive proposals made by Taylor, Rostow, and others within (and outside) the administration who wanted to send troops to Vietnam, Kennedy put off the decision. He perceived the domestic political consequences of withdrawal to be too great a risk, and he realized what could happen if he gave the military permission to send combat troops at the end of 1961. Not only would the Republicans excoriate him for involving the United States in another war in Asia, but the conflict also had no foreseeable exit strategy, which would certainly endanger his reelection campaign in 1964. With a degree of prescience, the president told the State Department official Roger Hilsman, "They say it's necessary to restore confidence and maintain morale. But it will be just like Berlin. The troops will march in; the bands will play; the crowds will cheer." But even if that occurred, "we will be told we have to send in more troops. It's like taking a drink. The effect wears off, and you have to take another."[58] But Kennedy was already sipping; by the end of the year, there were over thirty-two hundred "advisers" in South Vietnam—a 400 percent increase since 1961—and, on 20 December, they were given the first official authorization to use their weapons in self-defense.

With an increasingly unstable Vietnam already posing difficulties and midterm elections looming in November, the administration demonstrated a keen sensitivity to political considerations as the new year began. The presidential adviser Chester Bowles, who had recently been relieved of his duties as undersecretary of state, expressed his concerns to JFK in early 1962. "One of the most critical problems facing this Administration in the field of foreign policy," he declared, "is the great and growing gap between the harsh, complex realities with which Washington policymakers must grapple and the generally limited understanding of these realities by most Americans, including the press and Congress. This gap is already dangerous."[59] Bowles's analysis proved to be perceptive. Senator Margaret Chase Smith (R-ME), a consistent and vocal critic of Kennedy's foreign policy, faulted the administration's limited escalation of more aid and advisers for Diem when Maxwell and Rostow called for American ground troops. As far back as 1953, Smith had lectured all over Maine on American responsibility in Indochina despite the fact that most Americans could not find it on a map, and the current situation concerned her greatly. In Smith's opinion, Kennedy was either "unrealistic" or "deliberately withholding or misrepresenting the facts." Whichever was the case, she feared that South Vietnam, and, indeed, all Southeast Asia, could be lost to communism.[60]

Smith and others within both parties were troubled by Kennedy's failure to follow Taylor and Rostow's hawkish recommendations the previous November. Nevertheless, during the first half of 1962, the decision to postpone a more robust prosecution of the war appeared to be succeeding. The incremental steps that Kennedy approved seemed to arrest the decline of the South Vietnamese regime. As a result, with other foreign policy crises consuming both the president's and the public's attention, Vietnam faded into the background to a certain extent. Moreover, many members of Congress hesitated, especially in an election year, to commit themselves on the conflict given the conflicting reports emerging from both Saigon and the administration. This reluctance to speak or act decisively on the issue of Vietnam would become the standard modus operandi for members of Congress throughout the entire conflict.

Yet, in their speeches and press conferences, Republicans highlighted their criticism of the administration's lack of candor regarding American involvement in Vietnam. When asked about statements to this effect by the Republican National Committee at a press conference in February 1962, Kennedy responded, "We have discussed this matter . . . with the Leadership of the Republicans and Democrats when we met in early January, and informed them of what we were doing in Viet Nam."[61] The president's comments did not stop Republican attacks. On "Washington Viewpoint" on 21 February 1962, Senator John Tower (R-TX) was asked whether he agreed with a statement by Richard Nixon that there should be "no partisan criticism of the Administration's policy in South Vietnam." Tower replied, "I certainly think that where we feel that the President is right and merits our support, we should . . . support him. . . . But where we feel the President is wrong on a foreign policy matter, assuming he's right in Laos and Vietnam . . . we should criticize him. If we fail to do that, then we have abdicated our responsibility as the opposition party."[62] Senator Jacob Javits (R-NY) and Representative Gerald Ford (R-MI) touched on the GOP policy differences with the administration on CBS on 1 April. Ford maintained that the Republicans would "be able to make a good position for the party in attacking the administration's vacillation, indecision, uncertainty in world affairs." He also indicated that he would have supported sending U.S. combat troops into Laos instead of neutralization. Javits followed this comment by stating that, given the lack of toughness in Laos, the GOP would support a stronger stance toward South Vietnam in order to prevail in "a terrific struggle."[63]

By mid-1962, Kennedy had become a prisoner of his decisions and failures in the realm of foreign affairs. His performance could not match the strident anti-Communist rhetoric of his 1960 presidential campaign, which led the GOP to collectively question his competence. Responding to the president's record during his first eighteen months in office, the Republican Congressional Committee released a "Declaration of Republican Principles and Policy" in June 1962 that harshly denounced the Kennedy administration's foreign policies. Although short on specific proposals, the statement decried the "bankruptcy" of American leadership during the Berlin and Cuba crises in 1961–1962 and in "the bluster followed by whimpering in respect to Laos."[64] Senator George D. Aiken (R-VT), one of the most respected voices in either party, who served on the Senate Foreign Relations Committee, complained that the relationship between Congress and the executive in matters of foreign policy had not been "quite as close and understanding as [he] would hope it would be" and questioned whether Kennedy was, in fact, the "key man" in formulating American policy abroad.[65]

The expansion of Republican criticism, combined with the ongoing problems in Southeast Asia, led the president to seek the counsel of Dwight Eisenhower again. Kennedy's advisers briefed Eisenhower on the situation in Laos in May 1962. The general agreed to support whatever decision the president made to resolve the situation, including neutralization. Eisenhower's endorsement, William Rust points out, "would not only help overcome objections to putting a limited force into Thailand but would also protect Kennedy's political flanks."[66] Indeed, administration officials constantly warned about the need "to be concerned about domestic reaction to our policies in South Vietnam" given the "considerable amount of bad publicity emanating from Saigon in recent months."[67] With Eisenhower's tacit blessing, the president felt less consternation about the resolution of the Laotian crisis, but he understood that little room to maneuver remained.

The margin for error shrunk further after Kennedy publicly referred to the aimless drift of foreign policy during Eisenhower's presidency. In response, the former president went on the attack. In a campaign speech for Massachusetts Republican candidates in Boston in October, he took the Kennedy administration to task for "an amazing burst of partisanship." Criticizing the president for using foreign policy "for purely political purposes," he declared (with tongue firmly planted in cheek), "I don't call attention to the dreary foreign record of the past twenty-one months. It is too sad to talk about." He went on to do just that, however, asserting, "I doubt that anyone can persuade you that in the past twenty-one months there has been anything constructive in the conduct of our foreign relations to equal any part of that eight-year record."[68] For Kennedy, Eisenhower's comments did more than simply influence the midterm elections; they served notice to the administration that the veneer of bipartisanship, already worn thin, could disappear completely at any time. What that meant for the president was that he would have to exercise extreme caution in dealing with the deteriorating situation in Southeast Asia.

Conservative political observers recognized Kennedy's precarious position on foreign policy. *Human Events* reported in early November, "The word is out that if the President is to keep a stiff spine in his posture on foreign policy, he needs a fistful of Republican helpers." Republicans around the country, the periodical continued, "were far ahead of Kennedy in calling for swift action against Cuba, and they sized up the situation in the Caribbean far better than members of the Democratic party."[69] Despite the accolades he earned with his firmness against Khrushchev during the Cuban Missile Crisis, the president's problems with the GOP and Vietnam remained. As Kennedy confided to Senate majority leader Mike Mansfield (D-MT) in mid-December 1962, "If I tried to pull out completely now from Vietnam, we would have another Joe McCarthy Red scare on our hands, but I can do it after I'm reelected. So we had better make damn sure that I am reelected."[70] JFK's decisions in 1963 reflected this strategy.

The Year of the Rabbit began ominously for the United States in Vietnam. By the end of 1962, while the Army of the Republic of Vietnam (ARVN) and its American advisers chased after the enemy's main unit forces, the National Liberation Front (NLF) had increased its hold on the countryside, gaining an estimated 300,000 members, and becoming increasingly bold militarily. The NLF demonstrated its superiority in the villages dramatically on 2 January 1963 when South Vietnamese troops using U.S. helicopters were ambushed by a battalion of Viet Cong forces at the village of Ap Bac. The subsequent fighting, marred by the reluctance to fight and disorganization exhibited by the ARVN forces, resulted in one of the bloodiest battles to that point in the conflict. Although the U.S. military leadership claimed victory because the enemy had abandoned the field, the Battle of Ap Bac represented the first major Communist victory over American technology, stiffened the Communists' resolve, and undermined confidence in Diem's armed forces. David Halberstam wrote that Ap Bac "epitomized all the deficiencies of the system: lack of aggressiveness, hesitancy about taking casualties, lack of battlefield leadership, a non-existent chain of command," and Roger Hilsman informed Kennedy that it had been a "stunning defeat."[71]

The battle drew an unprecedented level of media coverage. The *New York Times* columnist Arthur Krock suggested that the outcome of Ap Bac merited a "fundamental review" of U.S. policy to find an alternative to the administration's "starry-eyed diplomacy and . . . ingenuous commitments."[72] Despite extensive criticism of the situation in Vietnam in such mainstream periodicals as *Time* and *Newsweek,* however, Kennedy was not ready to undertake the reevaluation that Krock proposed. Vietnam remained an important symbol of the president's determination to oppose communism, but domestic political calculations foreclosed changing strategy to any significant extent at this juncture. Instead, the administration persisted in its public optimism with regard to Southeast Asia.

Kennedy missed an opportunity to divest himself and the country of the problematic situation in Vietnam early in 1963. Mike Mansfield, at the president's request, had taken three other Democratic senators to Vietnam in December 1962 to assess the circumstances and make recommendations. After disclosing his findings to Kennedy privately, Mansfield released his report to the public in late February. The senators warned that the struggle was quickly becoming an American war that could not be justified by existing U.S. security interests. Criticizing the Diem government as "less, not more, stable than it was at the outset" and "more removed from, rather than closer to, the achievement of popularly responsible and responsive government," the report warned that Vietnam could become "of greater concern and greater responsibility to the United States than it is to the Government and people of South Vietnam." Without a dedicated effort from the Saigon regime and the South Vietnamese people, the senators concluded, "the United States can reduce its commitment or abandon it entirely."[73] Mansfield's indictment of Diem was particularly telling given his vocal support of the South Vietnamese leader in the mid-1950s.

Had Kennedy chosen to change course in Vietnam, he could have used Mansfield's findings as both the justification for reconsidering American policy in Southeast Asia and domestic political cover. But, as the president told Kenneth O'Donnell, one of his closest confidants, he could not (or would not) take steps in the direction suggested by the majority leader "until 1965—after I'm reelected." O'Donnell later commented, "President Kennedy felt, and Mansfield agreed with him, that if he announced a total withdrawal of American military personnel from Vietnam before the 1964 election, there would be a wild conservative outcry against returning him to the Presidency for a second term."[74]

Perhaps Kennedy need not have worried so much about the Republican reaction. Admittedly, he had nearly quintupled the number of American advisers in Vietnam, devoted substantial economic resources to the maintenance of the Saigon government, and made South Vietnam a symbol of the determination of the United States to oppose communism. Yet the GOP position on Vietnam had been, as Terry Dietz has argued, "inadequate in relation to the issues at hand."[75] Prior to 1963, the Republican line generally consisted of repeated demands that the president stand firm against communism worldwide; Southeast Asia was simply another theater of operations and a minor one at that. Therefore, it is clear in retrospect that Kennedy likely had more room to maneuver politically than he perceived. As the situation worsened, however, key members of the GOP began to speak out more forcefully and directly on Vietnam. Senator Karl Mundt (R-SD), for example, considered the U.S. engagement in Vietnam a necessary bulwark against Communist encroachment in Asia and ignored suggestions that the administration abandon its South Vietnamese ally. A dedicated cold warrior, Mundt stridently criticized Kennedy for his failure to adequately support the Saigon regime, particularly after joining the Senate Foreign Relations Committee in 1963.[76] Many Republicans agreed with Mundt and suggested that the best way to salvage the situation in Indochina would be to increase the level of support.

Of course, the president was not oblivious to the potential for greater American involvement in South Vietnam. Many of his civilian advisers had recognized the problems confronting the United States in South Vietnam and pressed the president to take action before the situation got out of control. Chester Bowles sent the president a memo on 7 March 1963 recommending that the administration consider a new approach to the Vietnam problem. Bowles apologized for playing the role of Cassandra with regard to Southeast Asia but warned that Vietnam "may ultimately prove to be as troublesome as Cuba in its effects on the Administration's position at home and abroad." In addition to facing increased Communist opposition and growing American casualties, he feared rising public resentment at home followed "by politically inspired demands that we either 'admit our error' and withdraw, or go after 'the real enemy, which is China.'" Among the solutions he proposed was to "head off serious political pressures here at home well in advance of the 1964 open political season." This could be accomplished by "laying down a clear and realistic set of objectives" that would begin to "neutralize present and potential domestic critics of our position."[77] If Kennedy could get the Republicans on board, he would be able at once to take positive action in Southeast Asia and to protect himself domestically.

The shibboleth of bipartisanship, however, could be used by the Republicans as well as the president. As Barry Goldwater noted in his syndicated newspaper column on 26 March 1963, "Every time you turn around these days, some Democrat is urging the Republicans to stop criticizing the New Frontier in the name of foreign policy bipartisanship." Goldwater complained that many of those who showed "such touching concern for the Vandenberg tradition" felt "no restraint in belaboring a Republican administration for what they felt were policy mistakes."[78] With an eye on the White House, Goldwater made it clear that the GOP would not sit quietly and passively accept the administration's foreign policy. Dirksen underscored this attitude on 31 May 1963 when the joint leadership released a statement asserting, "We have always encouraged a bipartisan approach to foreign policy and want to continue to do so." Nevertheless, the statement continued, "one of the major problems in Washington today is discovering what the Kennedy Administration's foreign policy is." It concluded, "The concept of bipartisan support for foreign policy can only be effective when the supporters know what policy they are being asked to support."[79]

For JFK, the answer was quite simple. Despite heightened scrutiny from the Republicans and formidable obstacles to success, the president remained committed to the solvency of South Vietnam. On 24 April 1963, he told a friend, "We don't have a prayer of staying in Vietnam. Those people hate us. They are going to throw our asses out of there at almost any point. But I can't give up a piece of territory like that to the Communists and then get the American people to reelect me."[80] As a result, as Dean Rusk observed in late May, Vietnam had come to take up "more of the President's time than any other single subject."[81] While JFK wanted the war as a symbol of his administration's resolve to oppose communism, he also wanted it to return to its previously low priority among foreign policy concerns. He realized that, if the conflict continued to escalate, he would be faced with a potentially serious problem entering his reelection campaign the following year. The Republicans would be able to use Vietnam as a club with which to batter his candidacy, much as they had done to Adlai Stevenson in the 1952 presidential campaign with China. With these considerations in mind, he decided that the best course of action would be to appoint a strong ambassador to Saigon who could deal decisively with both the Diem regime and the press and deflect problems before they reached the Oval Office.

Kennedy's aides concurred. In a report on the situation in Vietnam prepared at the beginning of the year, Roger Hilsman and the NSC's Michael Forrestal argued, "What is needed, ideally, is to give authority to a single, strong executive, a man perhaps with a military background but who understands that this war is essentially a struggle to build a nation out of the chaos of revolution." Hilsman and Forrestal suggested that either "the right kind of general" or a civilian public figure "whose character and reputation would permit him to dominate the representatives of all the other departments and agencies" would make the ideal ambassador in Saigon.[82] Unfortunately, most observers considered the current ambassador, Frederick Nolting, unsuitable for the evolving situation. Kennedy needed a replacement who possessed an understanding of Vietnam's importance and who could act independently to support those interests. Although many pundits speculated that Edmund Gullion, the U.S. ambassador to the Congo, who already had experience in Vietnam, would be chosen to succeed Nolting in Saigon, Kennedy and Rusk had another candidate in mind.

The Kennedy administration always kept partisan considerations in the forefront when it came to foreign policy. For example, mindful of Woodrow Wilson's struggle with Congress over the Treaty of Versailles, the president invited Republican members of Congress to accompany the delegation traveling to Moscow to sign the Nuclear Test Ban Treaty in late July 1963.[83] Accordingly, rather than appoint a career diplomat like Gullion to the Saigon post, Dean Rusk argued that the ambassador should be a representative of even higher rank. He suggested that Henry Cabot Lodge Jr.—whom Kennedy had defeated in both the 1952 Massachusetts senatorial campaign and the 1960 presidential election—would be ideally suited for the ambassadorship. His national reputation and experience working with previous Democratic administrations, combined with his tenure at the United Nations and his familiarity in dealing with the media, gave him the credentials the administration sought.

Lodge's party affiliation provided an additional (and decisive) reason for his selection. The secretary of state believed that Lodge's status as a distinguished Republican would "reflect the bipartisan support which Kennedy had for his Vietnam policy" and would serve to blunt right-wing GOP demands for a more assertive posture in Vietnam. Rusk convinced Kennedy that Lodge was to the Republican Party in 1963 what John Foster Dulles had been in 1950—the personification of its liberal internationalist wing. Moreover, Rusk hoped that Lodge's appointment would serve to co-opt a major issue on the Republican agenda and erode support for Goldwater's candidacy in 1964. CBS's Eric Sevareid recognized the protection that Lodge would afford Kennedy given the growing instability in Southeast Asia. Sevareid believed that "a storm is coming, and it is permissible to think the President wanted a hostage to fortune in the form of a highly placed Republican against a day of political reckoning at home."[84]

Initially, some White House aides objected to Lodge's appointment to Saigon. Most glaringly, they cited the former senator's possible candidacy for the GOP presidential nomination the following year. Why, they wondered, should the administration give a potential rival a public platform from which to speak? But Kennedy did not worry about that eventuality. Arthur Schlesinger Jr. recalled, "The thought of implicating a leading Republican in the Vietnam mess appealed to [the president's] instinct for politics."[85] Indeed, JFK welcomed Rusk's choice, considering Lodge to be "Republican asbestos," insulation against the heat of possible future criticism of his foreign policy. As William Safire later wrote, Kennedy's appointment of Lodge was designed to "foreclose . . . Republican opposition to the way the war was conducted until 1967."[86] *Time* also noted that Lodge's selection would "make the Republicans think twice before attacking Administration policy in troublesome South Viet Nam."[87]

In addition, the president saw four advantages to appointing Lodge. First, it gave him an ambassador who was totally unsentimental toward Diem personally and could do the dirty work of discarding America's longtime ally, a course that increasingly seemed necessary. Second, Lodge's background and experience in acting decisively, if not always within bureaucratic restraints or protocol, would be invaluable in Saigon. Third, his appointment would give Kennedy a direct, personal line into the embassy and events in South Vietnam. Finally, Lodge was a politician with the ego required to straighten out the situation in Saigon.[88] In briefing Lodge about his new assignment on 17 June, Rusk explained part of the rationale for selecting the former senator. The administration needed "an ambassador out there who is tough; who can act as a catalyst; who will take responsibility and make decisions and not refer many detailed questions to Washington." Although he warned of a potential military escalation of the war if the Laotian situation continued to deteriorate, Rusk asserted that Kennedy wanted "to make the political side of things go as well as the military side has been going."[89] That, then, would be Lodge's charge as the representative of the United States in Saigon. Lodge appeared to be the perfect choice to deal with the uncomfortable and increasingly untenable situation in South Vietnam.

Yet, considering the recommendations made by Hilsman and Forrestal in January, Lodge's selection seems questionable in retrospect. Although skilled in public relations, the former senator possessed few of the qualities needed to negotiate the labyrinth of U.S.–South Vietnamese relations. Accustomed to working alone, he had no experience as an administrator or in coordinating the multiple fiefdoms that composed the American mission in Saigon. His vision of public service leaned more toward noblesse oblige than the bureaucrat's art traditionally associated with diplomacy. In his memoirs, Lodge wrote that he "believed that many mistakes had been made since 1945 and that if, in that period, the Indochina question had been wisely handled, the United States need never have gone there. In that sense the American presence there was a mistake." But, since American troops were involved in combat, he considered it his duty to accept the assignment from Kennedy.[90] Further, Lodge's own view of his role as ambassador—that he would be responsible only to the president, thereby circumventing the normal State Department channels and potentially even considering himself the ranking military authority for U.S. forces in South Vietnam—placed him in a unique position and inflated his sense of his importance and, perhaps, his responsibility.[91]

Ironically, however, in hoping to improve the situation in Saigon with Lodge's appointment, Kennedy almost certainly complicated it even further. The negative South Vietnamese reaction to Lodge's selection certainly supports that argument. On 27 June 1963, the administration officially announced the nomination of Lodge as Nolting's replacement. According to the CIA, a "considerably disturbed" Diem correctly interpreted Lodge's appointment to mean that "the United States [now] planned to wield a 'big stick.'"[92] Moreover, in the coming months, Lodge's actions in support of the administration's changing policy toward Saigon would exert tremendous pressure on the Diem regime, leading to increasingly strained relations and, ultimately, Diem's ouster—with the new ambassador leading the charge against the South Vietnamese leader.

The South Vietnamese were not alone in worrying about Lodge. The domestic political considerations attached to his appointment concerned his fellow Republicans as well. After his appointment, Lodge spoke with Dwight Eisenhower. The former president, who was somewhat troubled by the obvious political implications of the offer, conceded that Lodge had no choice but to accept the appointment. But he urged Lodge to make it "clear that you are a Republican and you are doing this as a matter of bi-partisanship" and not to let his service in Saigon dissuade him from returning to the political arena.[93] With less than eighteen months before the election, Eisenhower recognized that Lodge's presence in Saigon loomed as a wild card for both Kennedy and the GOP. Meanwhile, conservative Republicans considered Lodge to be their archenemy, responsible for a myriad of heresies, including contributing to Nixon's defeat in 1960 by being a lazy campaigner. In agreeing to represent the administration in Saigon, Lodge "had implicated the GOP in a potential foreign policy disaster," living up to the Republican Right's nickname for him: Henry Sabotage.[94] Their disdain for Lodge and concern for the implications of the appointment for the party led to severe criticism from the Right, divided the party, and contributed to the problems the Republicans faced during and after the 1964 presidential race.

As the election campaign got under way, bipartisan support for the administration's foreign policy broke down further. Conservatives attacked the 1963 foreign aid bill, the American wheat sale to Moscow, and the Nuclear Test Ban Treaty, which Kennedy had consummated that summer. Meanwhile, the leading Republican candidates for the presidential nomination—Nelson Rockefeller, Richard Nixon, and Barry Goldwater—waited eagerly for the president to make serious mistakes in South Vietnam, knowing that they could exploit those errors during the campaign. Even members of Kennedy's own party focused on the problem of Vietnam. Senator Richard Russell (D-GA) chided the administration for "trying to fight this problem as if it were a tournament of roses."[95] Kennedy knew that such criticisms could foreshadow political trouble in the months to come. Fortunately for the president, however, public opinion was not fully attuned to the Vietnam situation in 1963, and Southeast Asia still ranked behind Cuba as the leading foreign policy issue going into the 1964 race. Given that reality, he believed that he could continue to pursue a middle course on the conflict until the election. Unfortunately for him, events precluded that hope.

In late August, pressure for a change in leadership in Saigon peaked, with Lodge leading the way despite the fact that he had been in South Vietnam for less than a week. On 21 August, the American-trained South Vietnamese Special Forces carried out massive raids in Hue, Saigon, and other cities against discontented Buddhists, ransacking pagodas, and arresting over fourteen hundred. Diem's refusal to disavow the raids, which had been planned and implemented by his brother, Ngo Dinh Nhu, placed the onus of responsibility squarely on his shoulders and placed him in direct confrontation with the United States. As Hilsman later stated, "We could not sit still and be the puppets of Diem's anti-Buddhist policies."[96] Within days, ARVN generals opened secret contacts with U.S. officials about the possibility of a coup. Kennedy, still gun-shy after his early foreign policy failures, warned Lodge to be cautious in dealing with the disaffected generals and reserved the right to back away from supporting a coup against Diem. Nevertheless, ambiguously worded cables made JFK's intentions unmistakable—Lodge was to take whatever steps he deemed appropriate to either force concessions from Diem or prepare to abandon the regime.[97]

Fundamentally, Kennedy wanted to be seen taking action in South Vietnam. The president told Lodge, "I know from experience that failure is more destructive than an appearance of indecision." Yet, because of his reluctance to commit to a specific course of action that could conceivably backfire on him, he willingly gave his ambassador room to maneuver in this situation. As the CIA's William Colby observed, "Kennedy was quite content to give Lodge his head in deciding how far to go against Diem, because Lodge's involvement and Republican credentials would protect him [Kennedy] from recriminations whatever developed."[98] Lodge wasted no time implementing his instructions. According to George Herring, "From the day he set foot in Saigon, [Lodge] was deeply committed to a change of government."[99] With the broad discretionary powers at his disposal, Lodge informed the South Vietnamese generals that, while the United States would not assist them in carrying out a coup, it would support a new government that appeared to have a good chance of success. To the ambassador's dismay, however, the coup collapsed before it got started owing to a lack of will and organization among the military conspirators.

The stillborn overthrow of Diem marked a turning point in U.S. policy. The administration, through its actions in covertly supporting the generals' coup attempt, contributed to the instability of the regime by encouraging its opponents and making it virtually impossible for a return to the status quo ante. Clearly, as Lodge noted in a cable to Rusk, the United States had "launched on a course from which there is no respectable turning back."[100] In addition, the administration had become fiercely divided between those who supported Diem and those calling for his removal; the documentary record on the internal deliberations on whether to remove the South Vietnamese leader reflect the strong sentiments on both sides. But perhaps the most telling comments came from Attorney General Robert Kennedy, who would be elected to the Senate in 1964 and become one of the most vocal advocates of ending the war later in the decade. Bobby Kennedy presciently raised questions about the ability of any South Vietnamese government to win the war and wondered whether the United States should begin to extricate itself from the emerging quagmire.[101]

The administration had to figure out a workable solution to the Diem problem without exacerbating the situation either in Vietnam or at home. JFK and his advisers recognized the crucial importance of maintaining support for their foreign policy in Congress, in the press, and among the American people. Frederick Dutton, one of the administration's congressional liaisons, gave Theodore Sorensen a candid opinion of what needed to be done in this regard. He urged "a frank reappraisal of how, over-all our Administration is, and isn't, coping with the domestic side of foreign policy." Dutton cautioned: "Even while substantive policies are being examined, the political front needs to be shored up for domestic power purposes this year, for the credibility of this Administration abroad between now and the coming Presidential election, and for absolutely assuring success in '64." The Republicans, he continued, realized that "they must begin early this year to hack away at the Administration if they are to develop a plausible foundation for the campaign next year." What the administration needed in the next several months, Dutton concluded, was a better understanding "of the whole controversial field of foreign policy," particularly in Southeast Asia.[102] Unfortunately, finding that understanding in South Vietnam would prove to be difficult.

But the likelihood of the Diem regime possessing the ability to successfully defend itself against Communist encroachments and the domestic opposition Diem and Nhu had engendered continued to diminish. As the administration attempted to finesse a way out of the mess, it faced heightened criticism from the GOP. Despite the appointment of Lodge, the Republicans had continued to hammer away at JFK's foreign policy as lacking strength and direction. Representative Robert Wilson (R-CA), the chairman of the Republican Congressional Committee, attacked the "Kennedy Klan" in a speech on 2 October 1963, stating, "We have done nothing but back down, give in, retreat and lose ground before Communism." He called Kennedy's Southeast Asia policy "one of our most glaring failures," and he warned against losing Vietnam and the possible loss of "hundreds and perhaps thousands" of American lives.[103] Other congressional Republicans like Melvin Laird and Gerald Ford, pushing the administration to adopt a "more muscular approach" to defeating the Communist insurgency and save South Vietnam, also intensified their criticism of Kennedy's policy.[104]

The Republican attacks served only to fortify the administration's resolve to force the Saigon regime to change—one way or another. Ultimately, Kennedy approved recommendations to implement a policy of "selective pressures" on Diem; although not explicitly directed to foment regime change, "some of the things that [the administration] did encouraged the coup."[105] During the weeks leading up to Diem's ouster, Kennedy and his top advisers feared that premature negotiations would negatively affect American credibility. If the United States failed to make a stand in Vietnam, its allies and adversaries alike would question the country's dependability and determination in keeping its other commitments. But just as important were Kennedy's domestic concerns. Should South Vietnam fall, Kennedy believed, he would be open to charges of being soft on communism and would face the harsh GOP criticism that would come with withdrawal. Additionally, the loss of key Republican and conservative Democratic votes that would result from such a loss would certainly play an important role in the forthcoming election.[106]

In looking toward the balloting, Kennedy hoped that his opponent would be Barry Goldwater, who trailed the president 55 percent to 39 percent in opinion polls in October 1963. While Kennedy liked Goldwater personally—indeed, the two famously planned to hold joint appearances and travel on the same plane during the campaign—he and his advisers thought the senator to be unelectable and too conservative for most Americans. They displayed more concern about moderates like Nelson Rockefeller and Governor George Romney

(R-MI). Rockefeller had long aspired to the White House and had a sizable following in the center of the political spectrum. Fortunately for Kennedy, however, the governor's recent divorce, his quick remarriage, and the ensuing political problems it caused made a successful Rockefeller candidacy a long shot. On the other hand, Romney, recently elected as Michigan's governor, concerned Robert Kennedy greatly. Not only had he earned a fine business reputation as president of American Motors, but as a devout Mormon his personal life stood above reproach. "People love that God and country stuff," the president said. "Romney could be tough."[107]

Romney might be tough in 1964, but the situation in Vietnam posed immediate problems. Kennedy continued to vacillate between the pro- and the anti-Diem positions, but, as George Herring has observed, in this case "not to decide was to decide," especially since Lodge, who was effectively in control of American policy without explicit direction from Washington, so staunchly opposed Diem.[108] Machinations and intrigue pervaded Saigon in the last weeks of October; at one point, Nhu concocted a scheme for a fake coup as an excuse to eliminate suspected opponents. A last-ditch effort at conciliation by Diem on 1 November came too late; the coup had already begun. By the end of the day, the generals had seized key military installations, secured the surrender of Nhu's Special Forces, and demanded the brothers' resignation. When efforts to enlist Lodge's support for their position failed, Diem and Nhu attempted to escape the palace through a secret underground passage to a Catholic church. Shortly thereafter, they were captured and brutally murdered in the back of an armored personnel carrier (although the generals initially claimed that they both committed "accidental suicide" despite having been bound and mutilated).

The coup was extraordinarily popular in South Vietnam, and jubilant crowds smashed statues of Diem, danced in the streets, and covered ARVN soldiers with flower garlands. Washington responded with a combination of relief and misgivings. On hearing of the coup and the deaths of Diem and Nhu, Kennedy "leaped to his feet and rushed from the room with a look of shock and dismay on his face."[109] Arthur Schlesinger Jr. recalled that he "had not seen [Kennedy] so depressed since the Bay of Pigs. No doubt he realized that Vietnam was his great failure in foreign policy, and that he had never really given it his full attention."[110] Kennedy's immediate reaction did not change the fact that the United States now had a new ally in Southeast Asia for whose existence it was largely responsible (even more so than the Diem regime). On the surface, the change in government meant that the administration would have a more malleable regime in Saigon to work with toward American goals. But the implications of the coup for the United States were deeper and more profound. With its complicity in the demise of Diem and his government, the United States became inextricably linked to the Saigon regimes that followed. As a result of this perceived responsibility, the administrations of Kennedy, Johnson, and Nixon committed millions of American troops and billions of American dollars to support the synthetic entity known as South Vietnam lest the United States lose its international credibility. Domestically, Vietnam would become the leading partisan and electoral issue for the next ten years.

Indeed, the downfall of the Diem regime had important consequences for American domestic politics. The GOP had been split on U.S. support of Diem prior to his ouster. Some agreed with Senator Kenneth Keating (R-NY), who openly questioned whether Diem represented "the only alternative to communism in South Vietnam."[111] Others concurred with Richard Nixon, who argued that "'the choice is not between President Diem and somebody better, it is between Diem and somebody infinitely worse.'"[112] Following the coup, however, the party seized on the opportunity to criticize the administration's actions. The Republican Congressional Committee excoriated Kennedy's foreign policy in its newsletter, calling his diplomacy "jerry-built" and accommodationist. It also (rightly) accused the president of complicity in Diem's overthrow, noting ironically that the administration had restored military and economic aid that had been cut off in an effort to force Diem to make reforms.[113] Many Republicans considered the coup as a weakness of Kennedy's to exploit in the coming elections. Nixon in particular began to raise questions about Kennedy's moral responsibility for the administration's role in the events that led to Diem's death. The former vice president told *Time*—ironically in the issue dated 22 November 1963—that the coup might take on importance in 1964 should the war against the Viet Cong take a turn for the worse.[114]

Nelson Rockefeller also weighed in on the situation in Southeast Asia in a speech in St. Louis on 16 November. Rockefeller attacked the administration for its failures in both Laos and Vietnam, criticizing the "sacrifice" of Laos to an "illusory coalition" dominated by Communists, and arguing that the main result was to open another supply route for the Viet Cong. More generally, the presidential hopeful rhetorically asked how it was possible for "an administration composed of so many knowledgeable people to stumble from crisis to crisis, always the prisoner, never the master, of events?" Calling the neutralization of Laos and the increased military effort in South Vietnam "completely inconsistent with each other," he concluded by accusing Kennedy of pursuing a policy of "expedience which runs counter to our deepest traditions."[115]

The comments by Nixon and Rockefeller suggest that the GOP salivated at the prospect of an electoral campaign based on foreign policy issues. Not only could they assail the administration for its failures at the Bay of Pigs and in Laos, but now the situation in Vietnam gained new political stature and significance in the wake of the coup. Given Kennedy's strategy during the 1960 presidential campaign of attacking the Republicans as soft on communism, the GOP stood ready to return the favor in the 1964 race. Kennedy's biggest political fear, a right-wing backlash against his foreign policy, seemed to be materializing right before his eyes. How JFK would have dealt with Vietnam and foreign policy in the 1964 campaign remains a mystery, however. His assassination in Dallas on 22 November changed the nature and tenor of political discourse in the United States. For the time being, partisan considerations were put aside as the nation came together to mourn.

One of Kennedy's greatest faults was the tendency to approach Vietnam as a series of problems without fully considering the reasons for the commitment to South Vietnam or the ramifications of the steps being taken.[116] Furthermore, the politics of anticommunism played a critical role in shaping Kennedy's decisions on Vietnam. Having survived and prospered in Congress during the early years of the Cold War, Kennedy found the lesson of the aftermath of the loss of China looming large for him. Repeated attacks by Republicans for being soft on communism or submitting to a policy of appeasement hardened his resolve to stand firm in South Vietnam, and the potential resulting loss of swing votes in 1964 to the Republicans and conservative Southern Democrats provided additional motivation. Moreover, Kennedy "never questioned whether Vietnam was really a vital interest. Communism had to be contained; Vietnam was defined as a pivotal domino [perhaps *the* pivotal domino to Kennedy] in U.S. global policy. The text of the speech prepared for delivery in Dallas provides ample evidence."[117] Given the neutralization of Laos, the continuing specter of Cuban communism, and the isolation of East Berlin, Vietnam became a litmus test for his campaign promises.

As a result of the confluence of these forces, by late 1963 Kennedy had radically expanded the American commitment to Vietnam. He had ignored the possibility of negotiations (at least before the 1964 election), placed American advisers in harm's way and allowed them to participate in combat operations, disrupted South Vietnamese society through the strategic hamlet program, supported the removal of Ngo Dinh Diem from power, and placed American credibility in Southeast Asia on the line by committing the United States to the survival of a free and anti-Communist regime in Saigon. Yet he pursued this policy by doing just enough to satisfy the needs of the moment, fearing the domestic political consequences of either not doing enough to save South Vietnam or going too far in escalating the U.S. presence in Southeast Asia. Looming over all these decisions and evasions, the Republican opposition was an omnipresent reminder of the need for caution.

John Kennedy found himself trapped between the Scylla of the 1964 election and the Charybdis of Republican criticism of his foreign policy—both actual and anticipated—a position that limited his perceived options on Vietnam. Like Odysseus returning home from the Trojan War, he faced a multitude of obstacles as he attempted to navigate his way through Vietnam and GOP opposition to a second term. In doing so, he delayed critical decisions to avoid a heated political debate over fundamental questions about the U.S. commitment to South Vietnam, a debate that could have damaged him electorally. The GOP, for its part, adhered to the notion of the loyal opposition at the beginning of the Kennedy administration, but the party became increasingly strident in its attacks on the president as his foreign policy challenges mounted. Critical opposition from the emerging right wing and party leaders like Richard Nixon and Dwight Eisenhower meant that domestic politics were always a critical factor in Kennedy's foreign policy calculations. Yet like JFK, the Republicans were more than willing to wait and allow the situation in Vietnam to unfold in the months leading up to the election campaign, "waiting quietly for [Kennedy] to make mistakes and then use them against him in the 1964 election."[118] Indeed, the evidence is clear that, had Kennedy lived, the 1964 presidential campaign would have featured a debate over Vietnam prominently.

If the GOP seemed reactive during most of the Kennedy administration, that response reflected reality. There occurred very little internal debate within party circles about Vietnam at this juncture; more pressing issues like Cuba and Laos, along with the general trajectory of Kennedy's foreign policies, dominated the Republicans' attention. Republicans supported the military commitment to Vietnam overwhelmingly, but, since their constituents were relatively unconcerned with Vietnam, it never developed into a significant political issue for the party as a whole during the Kennedy years. Indeed, the unity displayed by the party on the Vietnam issue at this point in America's longest war stands in stark contrast to the fissures that would develop within the GOP and the country as a whole as the conflict evolved. The significance of the relationship between the Republican Party and the Kennedy administration on the issue of Vietnam is relatively simple. The two sides sowed the seeds of future conflict by boxing Kennedy in on Vietnam and limiting his perceived options, actions that would eventually (although not inevitably) lead to the escalation of the U.S. commitment by Lyndon Johnson.

# CHAPTER 2

# The Cassandra Conundrum

## GOP Opposition to LBJ's Vietnam Policy, 1963–1965

Political skill is the ability to foretell what is going to happen tomorrow,
next week, next month, and next year. And to have the ability afterwards to
explain why it didn't happen.
　　　　　　　　　　　　　　　—Sir Winston Churchill, *The Churchill Wit*

Vietnam is sort of going to hell . . . while all the center of political energy
of the Executive Branch is on the election . . . [LBJ's] living with his own
political survival every time he looks at those questions.
　　　　　　　　　　　　　　　　　　　—McGeorge Bundy
　　　　　　　　quoted in Gordon M. Goldstein, *Lessons in Disaster*

According to the *Iliad*, Cassandra, the daughter of King Priam of Troy, was so
beautiful that the sun god, Apollo, became infatuated with her. After agreeing
to become Apollo's consort, Cassandra received the gift of prophecy, but before the relationship was consummated, she rejected him. Enraged that a mere
mortal spurned his love, Apollo cursed Cassandra so that no one believed her
predictions. The gift became an endless source of frustration and pain for her.
During the war with the Greeks, her prophecies about the Trojan horse and
the destruction of Troy were either ignored or not fully understood; some ver-
sions of the myth suggest that people believed her words to be the product of
insanity, which caused them to dismiss her warnings out of hand. This chapter
will consider the Cassandras of the American experience in Vietnam: Barry
Goldwater, whose campaign statements foreshadowed U.S. policy in Southeast
Asia after the 1964 election; Richard Nixon, whose aggressive comments boded

ill for both the Johnson administration and his own; and John Sherman Cooper, whose dire warnings about the trajectory of the U.S. commitment to South Vietnam and its attendant perils would also be realized. It will also examine the role played by domestic political considerations in postponing decisions about the war owing to the 1964 presidential election.

Like most of his generation, Lyndon Johnson was a committed cold warrior who saw communism as an enemy that had to be defeated.[1] More specifically, he came into office as a strong believer in the necessity of standing firm in Vietnam as a bulwark against communism in Asia and of supporting the Saigon regime fully. This stance also reflected his belief that Kennedy's complicity in the coup that toppled Diem linked the fate of South Vietnam to the American commitment.[2] Yet Johnson was also driven by a notion he shared with his predecessor—should South Vietnam fall, he would face a domestic political backlash that would fracture the support he required to implement his nascent Great Society programs.[3] This sentiment would play a major role in every choice LBJ made leading up to the Americanization of the war. Not only would he base his decisions in significant measure on domestic political calculations, but he would also do everything he could to implicate the GOP in the process.

In the aftermath of Kennedy's death, Dwight Eisenhower called the White House and offered his advice and support. Johnson told Eisenhower, "I need you more than ever now." To this Eisenhower replied, "Anytime you need me Mr. President, I will be there."[4] The next day, the former president drove to Washington from Gettysburg to meet with Johnson. He made a number of recommendations, including those in a memorandum hastily composed at Johnson's request in which he left no doubts about where he believed the new administration should take the country in terms of both foreign and domestic policy. Although he did not follow many of Eisenhower's suggestions, particularly those dealing with domestic issues, Johnson recalled in his memoirs, "I had tremendous respect for the opinions of this wise and experienced man who knew so well the problems of the burdens of the Presidency."[5] Like Kennedy, Johnson would rely heavily on his predecessor on the issue of Vietnam in the years to come, both for his foreign policy expertise and for domestic political cover. For the time being, Johnson made it clear to the nation and the world that he would continue Kennedy's policies toward Vietnam.

One of Johnson's first acts as president was to reaffirm the American commitment to the Saigon regime. Drawing on the conclusions of the recently concluded policy conference in Honolulu, National Security Action Memorandum (NSAM) 273 essentially ratified the Kennedy administration's position on Vietnam. It announced U.S. support for the new government led by Gen. Duong Van Minh and stated that aid levels would be maintained consistent with American assistance to Diem. Further, NSAM 273 emphasized that the war would remain a primarily South Vietnamese effort; the United States would continue to provide support and training and serve in an advisory capacity. While not intended as a comprehensive statement of U.S. policy, NSAM 273 did clearly indicate the administration's intention to stand by its ally. As the president told a joint session of Congress on 27 November, "This nation will keep its commitments . . . [in] South Vietnam."[6]

The reason for Johnson's assertiveness on Vietnam so early in his presidency became clear when he sat down with Henry Cabot Lodge shortly after the assassination and effectively personalized the war. "I am not going to lose Vietnam," he told the ambassador. "I am not going to be the President who saw Southeast Asia go the way China went."[7] As David Halberstam explained, "If [LBJ] seemed weak as a President in dealing with Vietnam, he was sure it would undermine him politically. Hell, Truman and Acheson had lost China, and maybe it wasn't their fault, but they were blamed for it, and when it happened the Republicans in Congress were waiting and jumped on it. . . . Well, he did not want the blame for losing Vietnam."[8] Johnson later expressed his misgivings to Doris Kearns, asserting, "Everything I knew about history told me that if I got out of Vietnam and let Ho Chi Minh run through the streets of Saigon, then I'd be doing exactly what Chamberlain did in World War II. I'd be giving a big fat reward to aggression. And I knew there would follow in this country an endless national debate—a mean and destructive debate—that would shatter my Presidency, kill my administration, and damage our democracy." The "who lost China" debate and McCarthyism, Johnson believed, would be "chickenshit compared with what might happen if we lost Vietnam."[9] With that apocalyptic perspective, Johnson's options would be limited.

Shortly after the promulgation of NSAM 273, Johnson instructed Robert McNamara to fly to South Vietnam to assess the new government and the prospects for success. McNamara's report did not bode well for the future. He informed the president that the situation was "very disturbing. Current trends, unless reversed in the next 2–3 months, will lead to neutralization at best and more likely a Communist-controlled state."[10] Given the reality of the situation, Johnson broached the possibility of asking for a congressional resolution on Vietnam. Jack Valenti, one of LBJ's closest advisers, recalled, "Being sprung from the loins of the Congress, he was very, very disgruntled and discontented with the fact that we were messing around in Southeast Asia without congressional approval. This disturbed him greatly."[11] Of course, the domestic political considerations of a resolution were not lost on the president. When Johnson told Dean Rusk in December, "If we stay in South Vietnam much longer or have to take firmer action, we've got to go to Congress," he did so more for the sake of spreading the responsibility for escalating the war than for any perceived lack of legal standing for the American commitment.[12] Like Kennedy before him, Johnson wanted to avoid making any decision on Vietnam that would threaten his election in 1964.

Toward this end, Johnson sought advice from his former congressional colleagues. On the evening of 2 December, he spoke at length with Senator J. William Fulbright (D-AK) regarding a number of foreign policy issues, including Vietnam. Fulbright, the chairman of the Senate Foreign Relations Committee, called the situation "hopeless" and opined that "the whole general situation is against us, as far as real victory goes." He further suggested that Johnson allow the new government in South Vietnam time to prove itself rather than taking any drastic steps. Near the end of their conversation, Johnson asked Fulbright, "Why did you send *Lodge* out there, for God's sake?" Fulbright responded, "That was political." When the president broached the subject of relieving Lodge as ambassador in Saigon because he had "got things screwed up good," the Arkansas senator counseled him not to do anything immediately. "I think," he mused, "he was put there partly to conciliate the opposition."[13] Johnson heeded Fulbright's advice and left Lodge in place for the time being, partially to deflect Republican criticism, but also to prevent the presidential hopeful from gaining any traction heading into the upcoming campaign.

Whom Johnson would face in the race for the White House remained a mystery. If the 1964 Republican presidential nomination had a favorite at the end of 1963, it was Barry Goldwater.[14] An outspoken conservative, Goldwater came to the Senate in 1952 as an ardent opponent of Truman's foreign policy, which he labeled as little more than appeasement. He made opposition to communism the centerpiece of his political appeal, supporting McCarthy's crusade to purge the federal government of Communists, and regularly assailing Kennedy's foreign policy as weak and indecisive. His positions, while controversial, garnered him a great deal of support within the GOP, especially among the increasingly vocal and powerful right-wing. But his position as front-runner was tenuous to say the least. Running against Kennedy was one thing, but, as the *New York Times* noted, Goldwater's primary base of support was in the South, and he would be unlikely to match Johnson's strength in that region.[15]

The moderate-to-liberal wing of the party, which remained influential in the early 1960s, preferred both Lodge and Nelson Rockefeller to Goldwater's strident conservatism. Other viable candidates included Pennsylvania's moderate governor, William Scranton, and Richard Nixon, who, although he had lost the California gubernatorial election in 1962, remained a force within the party. On 8 December 1963, Eisenhower muddied the political waters even further. Newspaper reports suggested that the former president privately favored Lodge for the nomination. From Saigon, Lodge immediately discounted any interest in the campaign, citing the prohibitions of the Hatch Act, which barred federal employees from engaging in political campaigns. Further, he continued, even if he were not constrained by law, he would not run owing to his commitment to fulfilling his duties as ambassador. But his frequent public denials of interest in the nomination belied his true feelings. A man with lofty ambitions and a considerable ego, Lodge firmly believed that he could—and should—be the GOP candidate.

Arguably, Lodge probably posed the most serious Republican challenge to Lyndon Johnson in 1964. Unlike Goldwater's hawkish and divisive conservatism, Lodge's centrist views stood as a credible alternative to the president's given his solid record on civil rights, national security experience (which some believed Johnson lacked), and extensive contacts within the Eastern establishment. Nixon, whose credentials stacked up favorably against Lodge's, had experienced recent political misfortunes that undermined the appeal of his background and expertise. Rockefeller, whose connections and experience seemed equally attractive, never found sufficient traction with the GOP faithful on a national level. Thus, Lodge found himself well positioned to wrest the nomination from the other leading candidates. Even as he dismissed the idea of running to the media, he quietly began to coordinate his presidential bid through his son George Cabot Lodge, sent feelers out to prominent Republicans in an effort to determine the feasibility of his candidacy, and laid the foundation for a grassroots campaign to draft him for the nomination.[16] What neither Lodge nor his supporters realized, however, was the level of disdain that conservatives had for him, which would cripple his ambitions in 1964.

The president kept a close eye on the GOP infighting and was quite confident that he could defeat any of the potential Republican candidates. Johnson talked to the columnist James Reston on 8 January following his State of the Union address and boasted that he had successfully occupied the political center, leaving Goldwater, Lodge, and the others with no issues to exploit for the 1964 campaign. That statement belied reality. Vietnam loomed as the one issue that could explode in Johnson's face and on which the GOP would be able to pounce and use to their advantage. But that did not seem to worry the president. At one point in the conversation, he joked about what the young Republican said to the old Republican senator: "'Senator, he didn't leave much for us Republicans, did he?' And the old Senator said, 'Oh yes, he did. . . . We can always declare war.'"[17] Of course, contained in the joke were kernels of truth. While remaining rhetorically committed to the independence of South Vietnam, Johnson took only those actions that either evaded public notice or did not measurably increase the country's involvement. Knowing that, without provocation, he would do nothing to escalate the conflict before November, LBJ believed that he had painted his partisan opponents into a corner.

Nevertheless, Vietnam lingered in Johnson's mind as a potentially damaging problem. His growing concern over the issue was exemplified in a conversation he had with John S. Knight, the chairman of the board of the *Miami Herald,* on 3 February 1964. The president told Knight that the country had three choices. One was to "run and let the dominoes start falling over." Johnson refused even to consider that outcome because of the domestic political implications. "God Almighty, what they said about us leaving China would just be warming up, compared to what they'd say now. I see Nixon is raising hell about it today. Goldwater too." The other two options were neutralization of South Vietnam, which Johnson dismissed as "totally impractical," or "getting in" to the fighting with American troops.[18] Clearly, the president had given the final option a great deal of consideration, and the documentary record bears this out—contingency planning for the introduction of U.S. forces in significant numbers had already begun. Meanwhile, the administration would face increasing criticism from Republicans about its failure to stabilize the situation in Southeast Asia and defeat the Communist threat to Saigon. No member of the GOP would bang this drum more loudly than Richard Nixon.

When historians consider the most important and influential American political figures of the twentieth century, Richard Nixon will undoubtedly be near the top of the list.[19] Although reviled by many for his actions during the McCarthy era, the Vietnam War, and the Watergate scandal, he spent six years in the House and Senate, served in the executive branch longer than FDR (first as Eisenhower's vice president for eight years and later as the nation's chief executive), had an impressive and underappreciated domestic policy record as president, was involved in the decisions on the Vietnam conflict from the early years of the American commitment virtually until the end, and was one of the leading voices in U.S. foreign affairs for almost fifty years. Indeed, perhaps no American save Lyndon Johnson played as central and definitive a role during the country's experience in Vietnam as did Nixon.[20]

On 7 November 1962, Richard Nixon's political career appeared to be at an end. Having just been defeated by Edmund "Pat" Brown in the California gubernatorial election, the former vice president, sounding like a man who planned to fade into the footnotes of history, declared, "You won't have Nixon to kick around anymore." Indeed, as his aides led him out of the press conference, he exclaimed, "I finally told those bastards off, and every Goddamned thing I said was true."[21] ABC aired a thirty-minute show in 1963 entitled "The Political Obituary of Richard Nixon" in which Nixon told the reporter Roscoe Drummond, "Let's look at the facts. I have no staff. . . . I have no political base.

Anybody who thinks I could be a candidate for anything . . . is off his rocker."²²
Yet Nixon, who craved the limelight and whose ambitions had not diminished,
could not stand the slower pace of life as a private citizen in California. At one
point he told a friend, "If I have to play golf one more afternoon . . . I'll go out of
my mind."²³ Indeed, Nixon returned almost immediately to the public spotlight
and began his long journey back into contention for the presidency. First, on the
advice of the former GOP presidential candidate Thomas Dewey, he relocated
to New York in an effort to establish a base for his political ambitions. He then
became the senior partner in an old, conservative, and respected Wall Street law
firm, which enabled him to interact with domestic and international VIPs from
business and politics. He also began to travel extensively, making contacts with
foreign dignitaries, enhancing his knowledge of foreign affairs, and honing his
rhetorical and campaign skills.

Nixon had positioned himself for a political comeback. He could criticize
political insiders without being responsible for the consequences of his actions.
His nonincumbency gave him an important advantage over Johnson in particular. He was free to state his objections to policy without having to account
to Congress or the electorate. He had the luxury of being forthright, unencum-
bered by the restraints of office.²⁴ As a result, he could rehabilitate his public
image without running the risk of losing another election or being rebuked by
an official constituency. Demonstrating his astute grasp of geopolitics, Nixon
decided that the most politically sensitive region for the United States in the
coming decade would be Asia. He was particularly concerned with the Kennedy administration's commitment of sixteen thousand advisers in Vietnam and
believed that Kennedy's decisions regarding Vietnam would "turn sour." He began to educate himself on the military and political situation in Southeast Asia
so that he would be prepared for future campaign discourse. Vietnam became
the issue that would return Nixon to public life, most prominently as a critic of
Lyndon Johnson's policies and decisions.²⁵

In Lyndon Johnson Nixon had a convenient and stationary target. The president faced constraints from the demands of the presidency and was preoccupied with domestic political concerns. Logically, he could not afford to devote
all his personal and institutional resources to foreign policy and Vietnam—and,
indeed, did not want to do so—if he wanted to ensure the success of the Great
Society. Nixon, on the other hand, could hammer away at the administration's
indecisiveness and lack of initiative. Despite these handicaps, Johnson retained
the advantages of his office. The president of the United States has the ability to
set the national agenda and to focus attention away from problems—provided
those problems do not become too critical. He also has a massive bureaucracy to assist him in keeping abreast of potential difficulties, something Nixon

lacked. In addition, Nixon was still rehabilitating his image, while Johnson retained the aura of Camelot as Kennedy's legatee—a role he desperately wanted to shed but could use to his own benefit. The end result was like a political chess match between two grandmasters, each using his own strategy to project what his opponent would do, hoping to exploit an opening. In the turbulent political climate of the mid-1960s, Nixon and Johnson had ample opportunity to demonstrate their political skills.

Nixon understood that Johnson would pose a significant obstacle to recapturing the White House. Therefore, he determined that the best way to attack LBJ would be on an issue on which he himself possessed legitimate credentials and the president had a relative lack of experience. Of course, Nixon did not approach it so directly. As he told reporters in February, "I think it's very important that all Republicans who can get a national audience speak out, speak out critically and constructively [against Johnson's foreign policy]." He questioned the president's comments "in which he in effect implied that those who were criticizing him in the field of foreign policy were in the same group with enemies who were criticizing him abroad." He urged the administration to develop a "firmer, stronger, more consistent foreign policy than we have at the present time" because, in his opinion, "there is uncertainty into the world as to what America stands for."[26]

During a trip to Asia in March and April 1964, Nixon criticized America's policy on Vietnam for its "compromise and improvisations." In Saigon, a reporter asked him whether the administration's Vietnam policies would be a campaign issue in the fall. He responded, "I hope it doesn't; it will only become an issue if the policy has weaknesses worthy of criticism, if it is plagued with inconsistency, improvisation and uncertainty. That has been the case in the past."[27] Nixon later indicated that he intended to make South Vietnam an issue in the 1964 presidential election campaign, contending that Johnson's plans to defeat the Communists "may be inadequate." In reflecting on the situation he observed in Saigon, he stated that what he saw on the trip "convinced [him] that Johnson's Vietnam policy would not succeed."[28] For someone who claimed that his political career had come to an end, Nixon was making public statements that sounded suspiciously like campaign rhetoric. Consequently, Johnson instructed his aides to prepare campaign strategies and opposition research on Nixon's positions early in the year. The president was "worried enough about [Nixon's] potential candidacy that in January [1964] he considered making plans to hold a summit conference with Soviet leader Nikita Khrushchev as a way to blunt Nixon's greater experience in foreign affairs." Other administration officials, however, downplayed Nixon's chances at winning the GOP nomination.[29] They expressed more concern with Goldwater, Rockefeller, and Lodge, believing that it was far too soon for Nixon to realistically make a comeback on the national level.

While keeping an eye on Nixon, Johnson also instructed his advisers to establish a written record of accommodating the embassy in Saigon to prevent Lodge or other Republicans from using problems between Washington and the embassy against him in the fall. On 2 March, the president informed McNamara, "I think that politically—I'm not a military strategist—but I think that as long as we've got [Lodge] there, and he makes recommendations, and we act on them, particularly if we act favorably, then we're not in too bad a condition politically." If the administration did not do so, however, and "if something happens in between, I think we are caught with our britches down."[30] Later that day, LBJ spoke with Rusk and complained, "Lodge is a long ways from here, and he's thinking of New Hampshire, and he's thinking of defeats in the Republican Party, and he's feeling sorry for himself—and he's naturally a martyr." To avoid potential electoral complications, the president told Rusk to "watch what that fellow says, just be Johnny on the spot and have a runner the moment his cable hits coming right to you. And before it goes back, you write out a longhand one and check it, and let's get it right back to him so that he knows he's Mr. God, and we're giving him maximum attention." In the event Lodge won the GOP nomination, Johnson wanted proof of the administration's efforts to either approve Lodge's recommendations or "boost them up to do a little something extra."[31]

The paper trail would prove unnecessary as Lodge's support among Republican moderates did not extend to the emerging right-wing of the party. Although conservatives had not yet taken complete control of the GOP, the embryonic movement had already acquired a significant amount of influence within the party. The situation dripped with irony. Just as the Goldwater conservatives skewered Lodge for involving them in the problems in Southeast Asia, LBJ was cataloging Lodge's actions in Saigon to use against him in a potential electoral matchup—just as Kennedy intended when he originally offered Lodge the ambassadorship. Some observers argued that a Lodge candidacy would neutralize an important Republican issue in the fall and recognized the handicap the ambassador would face by being tied so closely to the administration's policies.[32] As a result of these factors, Vietnam became a major and, ultimately, fatal problem for his candidacy. Lodge would not, however, be the last Republican to see his presidential aspirations falter over the war.

Like John Kennedy, Lyndon Johnson had discovered that the platitudes about bipartisan foreign policy and politics stopping at the water's edge took on a different cast from the vantage point of the Oval Office. He had to tread cautiously during 1964, walking the fine line between propping up the revolving door governments and preventing military disaster, on the one hand, and doing too much in Southeast Asia and making it an issue in the fall campaign, on the other. One way to diffuse Vietnam in the fall would be to seek a congressional resolution in support of the administration. James Reston of the *New York Times,* who spoke with Johnson regularly, broached the issue in early March in his column, suggesting, "There is a good case to be made for seeking Congressional sanction on political and moral, if not on constitutional grounds." Reston did not believe that the president was contemplating expanding the war, "particularly in a Presidential election year," but pointed out that there was "plenty of time now to consider the question" so that U.S. policy did not "drift until the President has to act in an emergency."[33] In fact, LBJ had been thinking along those same lines for several weeks. He considered a congressional resolution as one way to deflect the attacks made by Goldwater, Nixon, and other opposition hawks. But he hesitated to take this crucial step, wanting to avoid the publicity that a debate over such a resolution would invite.

While Johnson worried about Republican criticism for not standing up to communism in South Vietnam, not every member of the GOP supported the war effort. Senator John Sherman Cooper (R-KY) stands as one of the least familiar but most influential dissenters on the Vietnam War. Cooper had a remarkable career, serving as ambassador to India and the German Democratic Republic, being elected to three separate stints in the Senate (the only person in U.S. history to achieve that feat), and being involved in some of the most defining issues and events of the Cold War. He was at once a stereotypical Southern gentleman and a thoughtful politician whose intelligence and persuasiveness made him extremely effective on Capitol Hill despite his low national profile and uninspiring rhetorical skills. Indeed, a 1960 *Newsweek* poll of Washington political correspondents ranked him as the ablest Republican in the Senate.[34]

Cooper had expressed doubts about the wisdom of American involvement in Southeast Asia since the mid-1950s and remained one of the leading voices for negotiation and settlement of the conflict throughout the American commitment to Saigon. Cooper had warned Kennedy against a large-scale U.S. military intervention and called on the administration to seek a negotiated settlement. As American involvement in South Vietnam expanded, Cooper became steadily more concerned about the prospects there, worrying about the chances of defeating the insurgency and the likelihood of getting a Saigon government possessing decent popular support. He supported the policy of providing assistance to the Saigon government but was convinced that anything beyond that superseded American interests. As tensions mounted following Diem's assassination, Cooper grew more concerned, especially after reports reached Washington that most South Vietnamese were tired of the fighting and wanted to reach a settlement. These efforts continued after Kennedy's assassination as Cooper lobbied Johnson to extricate the United States from the burgeoning quagmire.

In April 1964, Cooper urged the Johnson administration to make a serious attempt at negotiation. While he realized that the prospects for a satisfactory agreement were not very high, he understood that the military situation was poor and the outlook bleak and foresaw significant problems if the United States continued on its present course. In this, he was in complete agreement with the administration; their respective solutions to the problems, however, differed greatly. In May, Johnson asked Congress for $125 million in additional aid for Saigon. Cooper responded by saying, "I personally cannot see how we can hold our position in that country. Considering our obligations, we should give them a chance, but if they will not fight, I cannot see how we can bear this burden of men, money, and assistance in Southeast Asia." If the situation continued to deteriorate, he continued, the United States should pursue a reconvened Geneva conference.[35]

Cooper's pleas fell on deaf ears in the White House. Even as the Kentucky senator advocated negotiations, Johnson and his advisers secretly prepared for a significant increase in the American commitment to South Vietnam. The disintegration of the political and military situation, combined with the heightened resolve and determination of Saigon's enemies, challenged the administration to develop a more effective policy in Southeast Asia. Toward this end, Walt Rostow spoke about "the advisability of undertaking contingency planning, should Johnson decide to act more strongly against Hanoi." Shortly thereafter, the administration initiated a series of studies and planning exercises to determine the most effective—and politically acceptable—course of action in the event it became necessary to modify and/or escalate the American role in Vietnam.[36] Neither Johnson nor his advisers paid much attention to those in either party like Cooper (or U.S. allies, for that matter) who urged reducing the American commitment or pursuing some sort of mediated settlement.

Joining Cooper in dissenting on the war was George Aiken, who opposed both military escalation and precipitate withdrawal. Aiken said that the United States should maintain a "stalemate with the rebels for the time being if that is the best we can do." He favored efforts to achieve a political settlement but did express his willingness to station American troops in Thailand "for defensive purposes" if requested by the Thai government, only, however, if the move did not represent a prelude to an expanded war.[37] Throughout the decade, Aiken would occupy a familiar and increasingly stereotypical place in Congress on the war. Although he would consistently vote in favor of continuing funding for the war effort, he also urged negotiations at every opportunity. This seemingly inconsistent approach reflected the permissive context in which Kennedy,

Johnson, and Nixon worked with Congress during the war. Aiken also made a concerted effort not to make the conflict a partisan political issue and sought to work with the administration and his Democratic colleagues in the Senate to resolve the war as quickly as possible.

The specter of a partisan battle over Vietnam prompted Johnson to make it clear that nothing would or should be done to fundamentally change the American commitment prior to the November elections. The evidence clearly indicates that domestic priorities claimed the lion's share of the president's personal and institutional resources during the first half of 1964 as he sought to maximize his popularity, win his own mandate, achieve legislative success, and avoid or postpone potentially divisive decisions on Vietnam. Telephone transcripts from the Johnson White House clearly demonstrate the administration's domestic political focus, particularly Johnson's obsession with recapturing the presidency, and its influence on foreign policy decisionmaking.[38] For the president, Vietnam was the absolute last thing he wanted to deal with, and he "did everything to convey to his associates that their principal job in foreign affairs was to keep things on the back burner" in order to avoid "headlines about some accident." The impending election, McGeorge Bundy later recalled, "loomed over the political landscape, its shadow blotting out any sense of urgency, initiative, or imagination in the evaluation of America's strategic options in Vietnam." LBJ's "'preemptive concern'" was to "'win, win, win the election, not the war.'"[39] Johnson's priorities had a cascade effect on the administration's approach to policy in Southeast Asia. A note in the papers of Johnson's military aide, Maj. Gen. Chester V. Clifton, dated 5 March and written on White House letterhead, indicated that there should be "no joint resolution of Congress" regarding Vietnam and that no steps should be taken "that would lead us to a Korea situation before November."[40] Politics "became the enemy of strategy in 1964." The impending election constrained the president from either escalating the American presence or embarking on a strategic withdrawal.[41] The best way to avoid problems in the campaign and to deny the Republicans a gold-plated issue was to ignore or obfuscate Vietnam as long as possible.

While the administration continued to quietly plan for a potentially expanded American presence in Vietnam and the possibility of seeking a congressional resolution, the GOP—both doves and hawks—raised concerns about the country's involvement in Southeast Asia.[42] Nelson Rockefeller noted that "the situation appears increasingly critical" and blamed the deterioration of South Vietnam's position on the decision to neutralize Laos during the Kennedy administration—an astute and accurate observation to be sure. According to Rockefeller, "This has had a demoralizing psychological effect on the Vietnamese who must wonder if they will be the next U.S. ally to be sacrificed." He derided the current administration's policy for its "vacillation and confusion" and called on Johnson to "publicly define a firm, coherent, unwavering, precise, purposeful and determined policy for South Vietnam and Southeast Asia." Such a policy would halt troop withdrawals, allow "hot pursuit" of Viet Cong forces into Cambodia, Laos, or North Vietnam, and expand attacks on Communist supply lines and depots in Laos and North Vietnam. The only caution was a reminder that the war should remain a primarily South Vietnamese undertaking; Americanizing the war could, he concluded, provide the Communists with the "ability to rally public support on an anti-American or anti-colonialist propaganda campaign."[43]

Fellow GOP presidential hopeful Barry Goldwater used Vietnam as the foundation for his criticisms of the administration throughout the spring. In a speech at the Los Angeles Sports Arena in March, he expressed his astonishment at the administration's goal to bring the situation in Vietnam "under control." "Why in heaven's name," Goldwater asked, "*isn't* it under control? It isn't under control because it remains just what it has been for three years—an aimless, leaderless war."[44] The following month, he described American policies toward Vietnam as "inadequate" and predicted, "We'll be fighting in Vietnam for a decade [if nothing changes], and, at best, we'll end up with a draw or a slow defeat . . . there is no policy that sets a goal of victory for all of this!"[45] The Arizona senator also lampooned Johnson's overall approach to the Cold War, comparing it to his treatment of his dog: "Maybe Lyndon Johnson thinks that he can pick communism up by the ears and make it yell. . . . He seems to know as little about handling communism as he does about beagles." Goldwater slammed administration officials for mortgaging the future "in order to make political advantages for themselves today" and for their "near-sighted, political wheeling and dealing" over Vietnam policy. He implored his audience to "demand an accounting of our policy in Vietnam . . . demand the positive actions which can end the fighting there" and called on the president to meet with the Republican leadership immediately to listen to their advice on the situation in Southeast Asia.[46]

Other congressional Republicans followed Goldwater's example and became increasingly vocal in their criticism of the administration's policies on Vietnam, denouncing what they perceived to be a "no-win" strategy. To illustrate their displeasure, Representative William Broomfield (R-MI) introduced a resolution during the appropriations debate on 21 May to "put backbone" into U.S. policy in Vietnam. It called for the administration to explicitly declare its determination to defend South Vietnam—essentially a demand to win or get out. Broomfield, a key member of the House Foreign Affairs Committee, complained that the military situation was "visibly deteriorating" and that it was "apparent that our policy has not been purposeful and our determination has not been clear. . . . It is time we became the masters of events rather than the prisoners of our lack of policy." He hoped that his resolution would serve to "end the indecision" and commit the country to "an unwavering, precise policy for Vietnam."[47]

GOP congressmen like Broomfield agreed with the need to protect the Saigon regime but strongly disagreed with the tactics employed by the administration. Everett Dirksen derided the administration for its "indecision" on Vietnam and for "dribbling away both American lives and American prestige."[48] Senator Bourke Hickenlooper (R-IA) expanded on Dirksen's comments on ABC's "Issues and Answers." Arguing that fighting communism in Vietnam was "vital," the ranking Republican on the Senate Foreign Relations Committee stated, "We must be prepared to do whatever we have to do, and be prepared to meet the issues vigorously and let the world know that we are doing that." Hickenlooper also opined, "The November elections loom very greatly in President Johnson's mind, and I am quite sure he is not going to do anything that he can avoid doing that would cause any confusion in his election program for next November."[49] The majority of Republicans felt as did William Scranton, who stated, "We've either got to win the war in South Viet Nam in due time—or else forget it, lose it. It's that simple."[50]

But, in fact, it was not that simple. Lyndon Johnson had his own doubts about the war during 1964. He demonstrated no interest either in pursuing early negotiations that might lead to disengagement in Southeast Asia or in prematurely escalating the American role in the fighting, for a variety of domestic political reasons, as the vast documentary record clearly demonstrates.[51] Vietnam was a complex problem for Johnson that defied easy solutions. While the administration—and especially the Joint Chiefs of Staff—planned for the introduction of U.S. combat troops, Johnson's ambivalence about deeper involvement in the conflict manifested itself throughout the process. The president found himself facing a quandary: escalate the war to attempt to save South Vietnam from communism and risk criticism from significant national figures like Fulbright and Cooper, or allow some sort of negotiated solution that could result in a neutral or Communist regime, thereby exposing his presidency to exactly the kind of domestic maelstrom he desperately sought to avoid. Rather than making a decision, Johnson vacillated, took the "Goldilocks" option—not too hot, not too cold, but just right.

Speaking with his former Senate mentor and confidant Richard Russell about his dilemma on 27 May 1964, Johnson expressed his concern about the Republicans exploiting Vietnam as a political issue. Russell replied, "It's the only issue they got." Johnson also complained about Lodge's effectiveness as ambassador. When Russell suggested that Lodge be replaced with someone "more pliant," Johnson quickly responded, "He'd be back home campaigning against us on this issue, every day." Russell disagreed. He argued that Lodge would not be any more harmful to Johnson on Vietnam than MacArthur had been to Truman on the Korean War. In any event, he concluded that "this thing [was] so hopeless for the Republicans" that it would not matter what Lodge said or whether he even ran on the GOP ticket. But Johnson reiterated his apprehension about Nixon, Goldwater, and Rockefeller urging the administration to take the war into North Vietnam and the political repercussions of their public statements. Indeed, he suggested to Russell, "They'd impeach a President though that would run out . . . outside of Morse, everybody I talk to says you got to go in, including Hickenlooper, including all the Republicans."[52]

Johnson's generalization about the GOP reflected reality. In both their public comments and their private statements, Dirksen, Halleck, Ford, Eisenhower, Mundt, and Goldwater (to name a few) spoke to the need to win in Vietnam utilizing whatever resources were required. Indeed, a significant proportion of Republicans clearly would have supported any administration initiative to act more forcefully in opposing communism in Southeast Asia. While respected senators like Aiken and Cooper did advocate a negotiated end to the fighting and there were definitely rumblings of discontent on the back benches, the Republican leadership stood staunchly behind the overall objectives of America's policy in Vietnam and would continue to do so well into late 1967. If anything, they urged the administration to prosecute the war more vigorously. It is also accurate to state, however, that many members of the GOP preferred to give the administration enough rope to hang itself.

While his concerns regarding a Republican backlash were justified, Johnson overestimated Vietnam's importance to the American electorate. The deliberations over the war inside the Beltway notwithstanding, Vietnam did not resonate in the American consciousness in 1964 to the degree that it would later in the decade. Opinion polls indicated that two-thirds of those surveyed paid little or no attention to the war. To be sure, the initial stirring of dissent began to appear from Walter Lippmann and Hans Morgenthau, on college campuses, and among a handful in Congress.[53] In addition, a vocal minority of hawks urged the administration to demonstrate its backbone in fighting communism. But this elite opinion ran far ahead of the public, largely because the administration did everything it could to prevent the conflict from becoming more of an issue. Johnson had not yet reached the point where he needed to sell the war to the public.[54] More important, domestic politics remained his primary concern—not only the election but also his vision of the Great Society. Thus, Vietnam did matter to Lyndon Johnson, even if it did not to many Americans, but in a negative sense—he wanted to keep everything about Southeast Asia as quiet as possible until the voting in November. This would change radically in 1965. From that point on, and for the next decade, the Vietnam War would be America's primary foreign policy concern.

For the time being, public commentary on Vietnam remained the almost exclusive purview of the GOP presidential candidates, each of whom sought an issue that he could use to make headway against Johnson. This approach proved to be a double-edged sword for Barry Goldwater. His uncompromising anti-Communist rhetoric won him the support of conservatives, but it also served to undermine his appeal. The administration used his own statements against him, portraying him as a loose cannon who not only was out of touch with the majority of Americans but also posed a threat to global and national security. The lukewarm support from many of Goldwater's fellow Republicans did not help his candidacy, but then none of his rivals proved that they could capitalize on his liabilities. Nelson Rockefeller failed to take advantage of Goldwater's aggressive rhetoric in New Hampshire, but the controversy over the senator's hawkish foreign policy proclamations helped Lodge to an impressive win in the primary as a write-in candidate. Of course, given that Lodge hailed from Massachusetts, too much can be read into this victory. Rockefeller also generally chastised the administration's policies but displayed a curious reluctance to propose solutions or speak specifically about Vietnam.

Goldwater demonstrated no such reticence. In early April, he charged that Johnson's policies were devoid of "goal, course, or purpose," leaving "only sudden death in the jungles and the slow strangulation of freedom."[55] The following month, he intensified his attacks on the administration, blaming Johnson's inexperience in foreign affairs for the worsening conditions in Vietnam, and assuring voters, "We *can* and we should *end the fighting in Viet Nam* by taking . . . strong, affirmative action." A close political ally, Senator Milward Simpson (R-WY), echoed these sentiments: "We have been a de facto combatant in the inconclusive and bloody war in Vietnam for almost half a decade. Now the Administration maintains that we will win the war in Vietnam. 'Win,' however, means victory, and the Administration has been known to regard that word with derision and scorn." Simpson went on to suggest, "[There are] now two points on which we can be certain: The ground rules of Vietnam make total victory in the classic sense utterly unattainable, and just as surely, the lessons of history make anything less than victory totally unthinkable."[56]

Goldwater appeared on "Issues and Answers" on 24 May, just nine days prior to the California primary, which would make or break his presidential aspirations. The senator hoped to prop up his ailing campaign; in the weeks leading up to the voting, Rockefeller had gained ground on the front-runner, and there had been a great deal of speculation that Eisenhower was working behind the scenes to prevent Goldwater from capturing the nomination. Although Eisenhower would deny these allegations the day before the primary, Goldwater had to be concerned as he appeared on the air. During a discussion of the Vietnam conflict, the senator was asked how he would interdict Communist supply lines across the Laotian border. Sounding very much like the major general he was, Goldwater asserted, "There have been several suggestions made. I don't think we would use any of them. But defoliation of the forests by low yield atomic weapons could well be done. When you remove the foliage, you remove the cover."[57]

Both the AP and UPI released stories suggesting that Goldwater had called for the use of nuclear weapons in South Vietnam, an interpretation that at best can be considered a misrepresentation of the facts. Although UPI eventually retracted its story, Goldwater later commented that "the retraction never caught up" with the headlines and was "a near-fatal blow." Rockefeller used this second nuclear weapons statement to brand Goldwater as a nuclear extremist: "I do not believe that the answer to the failures of the present administration is to be found in a reckless belligerence typified by such proposals."[58] In the White House, Johnson realized that, even if Vietnam became an issue in the fall, he could now portray Goldwater as a fanatic who would use nuclear weapons if elected. Indeed, this strategy prompted one of the most effective political ads in history—the "daisy" commercial that so profoundly influenced voters.[59]

By the time the California primary took place in June, Vietnam had surpassed Cuba as the campaign's key foreign policy issue.[60] Goldwater described Vietnam as "soaked with American blood," a casualty of Johnson's secretive, indecisive, and dishonest policy.[61] While Rockefeller made an effort to counter Goldwater's appeal, he was unsuccessful, and Lodge had dropped almost completely out of the picture by this juncture owing to his inability to discuss his policies while serving as ambassador. Goldwater narrowly defeated Rockefeller in the California primary, thanks in large measure to the overwhelming support of conservative voters in Orange and Los Angeles counties. Despite the fact that Rockefeller carried northern California, the state's winner-take-all primary gave the Arizona senator eighty-six delegates, virtually ensuring his nomination. Rockefeller, whose presidential ambitions had been denied for a second time, stoically observed, "Sometimes with a defeat there's a gain—there are things you don't have to worry about any more, like do you have to take the country into war over Vietnam."[62] Rockefeller's relief at not having to deal with Vietnam would carry over the next four years; he would hardly address the issue publicly until late in the 1968 Republican primaries.

By June 1964, Vietnam had become, in the words of Robert Dallek, "a constant low-level irritant" to Johnson that threatened to evolve into much more.[63] The public and many in Congress seemed either indifferent to or confused about the war. A few senators cautioned against deeper involvement in the war at the same time as Richard Nixon and Barry Goldwater complained that the administration's actions were wholly insufficient to the task. In Vietnam, the prospects of a stable regime seemed more remote than ever, and the likelihood of continuing and escalating American military and economic support increased almost daily. The situation became so bad that Johnson finally decided that he would ask Congress for a joint resolution on Vietnam. Such a measure would accomplish several things. First, it would authorize stepped-up American aid to South Vietnam. Second, it would demonstrate to Saigon, Hanoi, Moscow, Beijing, and the rest of the world the resolve of the United States to stay the course in Southeast Asia. Finally, it would provide the president with domestic political protection by bringing Congress on board with the administration's policies. William Bundy, the former assistant secretary of defense, who had become the concept's primary advocate, believed a resolution to be, more than any other course, the "action that commends itself" to promoting the flexibility of "the Executive in the coming *political* months." He further argued that electoral considerations gave "such an affirmation of extra importance."[64]

Yet Johnson changed his mind and decided against seeking a resolution in June. A resolution, and the debate it would force, would place the political spotlight directly on Vietnam, the last thing he wanted to do. Moreover, several of his advisers informed him that any congressional debate on Vietnam could prove harmful to the administration. As Frederick Dutton, the head of the State Department's office of congressional relations, observed, "Even most of those supporting the Administration's present course are often wary about it." The actual level of interest in Southeast Asia, he continued, was "not at all high, which suggests to me not merely political caution in an election year but low understanding or care about the problem."[65] Knowing that they would have to explain themselves to their constituents in the fall, very few of the 468 members of Congress facing reelection campaigns wanted to take a controversial stand on the war. Better to allow the administration to take all the risks and sit back to gauge the public's response than jeopardize one's own reelection. Still, if Johnson had pressed the issue by asking for a resolution authorizing an expanded American commitment, he could not expect the GOP to refrain from an inquisition into his policies in Vietnam.

There is another potential explanation. The battle over the civil rights bill during the spring of 1964 evolved into one of the toughest of Johnson's political career. Its passage ranked as his highest priority, but the bill faced a potential filibuster in the Senate by a coalition of Republicans and Southern Democrats, and the president was determined to see the landmark legislation approved. On 10 June, coincidentally the same day as a key National Security Council meeting on the issue of a resolution, Johnson managed to convince Everett Dirksen—who had some reservations about the trajectory of U.S. policy in Vietnam—to support the legislation. Using his position as GOP minority leader, and cashing in a number of favors, Dirksen called for cloture on the bill, which led the way to its passage. Shortly thereafter, the administration decided not to pursue a resolution on Vietnam. One could be forgiven for reading too much into the meeting between Johnson and Dirksen (for which no documentary record exists), yet an intriguing question is worth considering: Is it possible that the two consummated a deal involving the civil rights bill and the resolution? Quite possible. Such a sub rosa agreement would have made sense on both sides given the ramifications of both measures in the fall campaign.

Without a resolution in hand, the administration had to tread cautiously when it came to Vietnam. Given the deterioration of the situation in South Vietnam, Johnson's advisers consistently reiterated, "It may be very difficult to postpone basic choices [on Vietnam] until November."[66] Such a scenario had to concern the president, who remained intent on maintaining the status quo as long as possible. Republicans eager to find a chink in the president's armor assailed such thinking. The same week that Johnson ultimately decided not to pursue a resolution, Charles Halleck held a press conference and stated, "We are seriously disturbed by repeated reports . . . that the Johnson Administration is postponing a decision on the war in Viet Nam until after election day." If this "indecision" was based on electoral considerations, Halleck warned, the administration "must be prepared to answer for it." The Republican leadership believed that "Americans will support a firm policy in Viet Nam, but they will never tolerate an election year gamble that could endanger the American position in the entire Far East."[67]

Halleck's comments were echoed by his GOP colleagues in the Senate. The "lack of definite, vigorous policy" left the country in limbo, according to Bourke Hickenlooper. Hickenlooper asserted that, if Vietnam was considered "vital" to U.S. interests, "then we had better do that which is necessary to obtain victory. . . . It is no time for equivocation and vacillation, we must stop groping and just fooling around."[68] In a public hearing on the 1964 foreign aid authorization bill, Hickenlooper told McNamara that he was concerned about American objectives in Vietnam and how serious the situation had become. He stated that he believed the time had come for a congressional resolution on Vietnam: "We have had lots of speeches on the vital necessity of some of these things. But in the past we have had resolutions concurred in by Congress establishing policy." In his mind, "the time had come when we had better have the administration and the Congress get together on some understood policy and some definite directional trends here so that we know what potentials we may have to face."[69]

A few days later, the House Republican Conference issued a statement criticizing the administration for "letting down our guard" against the Communists and not attempting to win the war in Vietnam. "A victory in South Vietnam over the military and subversive threats of communism is urgently required," the statement contended. Gerald Ford, who presented the report to the media, asserted that the United States should immediately "take command of the forces in Vietnam and not simply remain advisers." In addition, U.S. Special Forces should be sent to Vietnam in order to seal the borders against infiltration from North Vietnam. Expressing "bewilderment" with the administration's "flaccidity of determination," Ford called for a "victory in South Viet Nam over the military and subversive threats of communism." The Republican statement and Ford's remarks, while vilified by Mike Mansfield as a rhetorical prelude to the GOP convention the following month, demonstrated the Republican belief that Vietnam was the issue on which Johnson was most vulnerable.[70]

Johnson remained apprehensive about Vietnam and even considered making a nationally televised address on the war, something several of his advisers implored him to do. Such a speech, the presidential adviser and informal chief of staff Bill Moyers noted, could "de-fuse a Goldwater bomb before he ever gets the chance to throw it." Moyers believed that, if the president were to make such a statement, he should do so prior to the Republican convention. That would thwart a Goldwater strategy of "forcing [Johnson] to talk about Viet-Nam and also, in effect, actually admitting that Vietnam is a political issue."[71] Compounding Johnson's anxiety was a growing feeling of discontent in the country about Vietnam. Polls indicated that an increasing number of Americans believed that the situation was being poorly handled by the administration and that the United Nations should step in to help bring the conflict to a resolution.[72] Despite his concerns, however, as with so many other decisions related to Vietnam in 1964, Johnson eventually chose not to address Vietnam publicly before the GOP convention. Like Kennedy before him, he delayed making critical decisions on the basis of domestic political calculations. That inaction would come back to haunt him in the weeks after the November balloting.

On the eve of the convention, the presumptive Republican nominee remained steadfast in his support for the war effort. In an interview with Germany's *Der Spiegel* on 10 July, Goldwater was asked what he would do about Southeast Asia as president. He responded, "I would make it abundantly clear . . . that we aren't going to pull out of Southeast Asia, but that we are going to win in fact." Once that decision was made, he continued, he would turn the conduct of the war over to the Joint Chiefs of Staff and say, "Fellows, we made the decision to win, now it's your problem."[73] While potentially problematic—Goldwater never defined what "winning" would entail and essentially proposed giving the military a blank check in Vietnam—this statement presented a straightforward solution to the problem in South Vietnam, differentiating it from many of his more belligerent campaign pronouncements. Had the senator been somewhat more circumspect in his public speeches on the campaign trail, perhaps his fate in November would have been less assured. One aspect of politics that Goldwater never mastered was the importance of style as well as substance; his unyielding commitment to his ideals led to uncompromising and unvarnished language. As a result, he remained a flawed candidate who faced not only a serious image problem but also the expropriation by his opponent of his core issue, the one on which he attached his electoral hopes.

The GOP convention in San Francisco would prove to be less of a coronation for Goldwater than a stake through the heart of the party. Moderates opposed to Goldwater's agenda refused to support the nominee and jeered him and his acolytes as they spoke. The tensions became most apparent when the debate over the platform plank on Vietnam turned into a full-scale brawl between the two camps. Some delegates agreed with Margaret Chase Smith, who took a "pull out or fight" position, "continu[ing] to fear Americans did not have the facts on what was happening," and considering the situation in Vietnam to be a "quagmire" that the United States was losing.[74] The Goldwater forces prevailed in the internecine debate, although much to the detriment of Republican unity. In the final platform document, conservatives censured the administration for encouraging "an increase of aggression in South Vietnam by appearing to set limits on America's willingness to act." The plank pledged to "move decisively to assure victory in South Vietnam while confining the conflict as closely as possible."[75]

The setback for the moderates notwithstanding, opposition to the Vietnam conflict took center stage when Governor Mark Hatfield (R-OR) delivered the convention's keynote address. Given his dovish proclivities and serious policy differences with Goldwater, Hatfield was an odd choice to give the speech—indeed, he was heckled and booed mercilessly by Goldwater supporters as he attacked extremists like the John Birch Society and spoke in support of a progressive agenda and the United Nations, and someone even called in a bomb threat in an effort to disrupt his remarks. When it came to the subject of Vietnam, Hatfield did not pull any punches. He called the war "tragic" and "blatantly questioned the administration's Southeast Asian policy." While newspaper accounts downplayed his remarks, his open break with the party's platform on Southeast Asia and a host of other issues typified the dysfunctional nature of the GOP convention and highlighted the fissures that had developed in the party and that would be exacerbated in the wake of Goldwater's historic defeat.[76]

The contrast between Hatfield and Goldwater could not have been more pronounced. In his acceptance speech, Goldwater exhibited his typical inflexible conservatism and addressed Vietnam only briefly. He excoriated the administration for its timidity for "refusing to draw our lines against aggression . . . and *tragically* letting our finest men die on battlefields unmarked by purpose, pride or prospect of victory." Denying that the fighting in Vietnam was a "police action," the GOP candidate said, "Make no bones of this. Don't try to sweep this under the rug. We are at war in Vietnam. And yet the president . . . refuses to say, refuses to say, mind you, whether or not the objective over there is victory. And his secretary of defense continues to mislead and misinform the American people."[77] Yet Vietnam did not make much of an impression on the delegates assembled at the Cow Palace that evening. As Fredrik Logevall has pointed out, "Lost in the hubbub surrounding the convention and his nomination, Goldwater's pointed words about Johnson's Vietnam policy received little attention. But, of course, he had it exactly right." The United States was involved in a war, and the administration was withholding information from the public about the war and the contingency plans to expand the conflict to North Vietnam.[78] The outcome of the platform fight, the divisive convention, and the election would linger in the collective memory of the party and play a significant role in the construction of the 1968 plank on Vietnam, which would embody the GOP commitment to unity and a determination to avoid fratricide.

Less than two weeks after the convention, however, Johnson tacitly admitted the gravity of the dilemma in Southeast Asia by sending another five thousand American troops to Vietnam. The extra manpower did nothing to ameliorate the situation. The Saigon government remained unstable, and the National Liberation Front continued to make progress in the South, leaving LBJ to contemplate a politically unpalatable situation—taking affirmative and public action in support of America's ally. On 26 July, Johnson invited Fulbright to the White House for dinner and to discuss the situation in Vietnam. With the new Khanh regime in serious trouble, the president told Fulbright, the United States might have to deploy additional troops to Vietnam in order to save it. In order to do so, the administration would have to go to Congress and request a resolution. Johnson also told Fulbright that he was determined to take the "soft on communism" issue away from Goldwater in the fall campaign.[79] Vietnam specifically and foreign policy generally stood as the president's only true obstacles in the campaign against Goldwater. While he knew that he could easily marginalize his opponent as an extremist on domestic issues, Johnson understood the potential political difficulties that could be caused by a flare-up in Vietnam.

LBJ's concerns were personified by Richard Nixon. Despite his pessimism about Johnson's strategy, Nixon did not believe that Vietnam was a lost cause. In an article in *Reader's Digest* in August 1964, he claimed that the crisis in American policy toward Vietnam was one, not of competence, but rather of confidence. Nixon reproached the administration for "demonstrat[ing] that we have no real intention of winning this war. Instead, we are trying to achieve a precarious balance of not-quite-winning and not-quite-losing."[80] This was unacceptable to Nixon, who argued that the war could be won if the resources available to the military were backed by the political resolve of the administration. Indeed, in Saigon he stated that one key to victory was to "take a tougher line toward Communism in Asia" and to expand the war to "'the sources of the trouble whether in North Vietnam or Laos.'"[81] He cited a "strong body of opinion, particularly among the military," that held that a simple increase in American economic and military assistance would be insufficient to guarantee success "unless some countermeasures were taken against the North."[82] If Johnson did not exhibit a willingness to commit the resources and make the decisions necessary for success, Nixon believed, America's Vietnam policy was doomed to failure.

As a result of this crisis of confidence, American allies in Asia were losing faith in the United States. Nixon referred to his discussions with a number of Asian government and opposition leaders, including a Thai colonel who disparaged the United States for backing down in Laos and for having "talked two ways on Vietnam." The officer charged that it was "hard for us to believe that you mean to win in Vietnam." Nixon also quoted Pakistani president Ayub Khan as saying, "Diem's murder meant three things to many Asian leaders: That it is dangerous to be a friend of the United States; that it pays to be neutral; and that sometimes it helps to be an enemy! Trust is like a thin thread, and when it is broken it is very hard to put together again." As Nixon later wrote, "To our Asian friends and allies it looked as if a combination of political expediency, public apathy, distorted reporting in the media, and partisan politics was undermining America's will to fight against communism in Asia."[83]

The former vice president firmly believed that "victory is entirely within our grasp." Only one obstacle stood in the way: "the will to win—and the courage to use our power—*now.*" Nixon feared that a repetition of the errors Truman made in Korea—the "Yalu River complex"—would result in disaster for the United States. He contended that, short of nuclear weapons, Johnson should use every means at his disposal "to win this crucial war—and win it decisively." At stake was not just the fate of the Saigon regime but the freedom of all Asia and, even more important, American prestige. Nixon ridiculed suggestions made by Fulbright and others that the United States withdraw its forces or push for the neutralization of South Vietnam. Either contingency would be devastating. A withdrawal of forces would lead to the loss of not just South Vietnam but potentially all Asia, for it was "the dam in the river." Nixon believed that "neutralization [was] but another name for appeasement. It is surrender on the installment plan."[84]

Nixon's persistent criticisms worried Johnson and again raised the problematic prospect of needing to address the Vietnam issue more specifically prior to the election. But the incidents in the Gulf of Tonkin in early August 1964 solved LBJ's problems—at least for the time being. After receiving news of the attacks, Johnson called a secret meeting at the White House. In addition to his national security team, he invited several of his old Senate colleagues—including George Aiken, Bourke Hickenlooper, Leverett Saltonstall (R-MA), and Everett Dirksen—and members of the House leadership. After briefing the legislators, Johnson asked for their opinions on the crisis and whether they would support a joint resolution to give congressional sanction to reprisal raids. Saltonstall asserted that the United States had "no choice" but to retaliate, going so far as to oppose LBJ's limited response as insufficient, but expressed concern that the administration was proceeding without allies or any clear sense of the next step in Vietnam. Hickenlooper compared the situation to the Cuban Missile Crisis and told Johnson that asking for a resolution was "appropriate and proper." But perhaps the most prescient and astute comment came from Aiken, who told the president, "By the time you send it up there won't be anything for us to do but support you."[85]

Aiken's comments reflected the sentiment among GOP critics of the administration. Most notably, Nixon supported the retaliatory strikes ordered by Johnson. He argued that the Communists were testing the United States during an election campaign, which made it "doubly important to overcompensate with firm action." Nevertheless, Nixon made sure to qualify his support for Johnson's show of force, commenting that America "should have been strong all along." Still, the air strikes stole some of Nixon's (and Goldwater's) thunder and appropriated his main point of contention with Johnson for a time. Stephen Ambrose contends that the Tonkin Gulf incidents and the ensuing resolution represented "the decisive moment in the 1964 election," in that Johnson "made himself invulnerable to the criticism that he was shilly-shallying on Vietnam and was too soft on Communism. . . . Nixon [was] very lucky he was not the nominee, as Johnson had just stolen his issue."[86] Goldwater, obviously, was not as fortunate.

The Tonkin Gulf incidents enabled LBJ to go to Congress and ask for a joint resolution authorizing him to "take all necessary measures to repeal any armed attack" against U.S. forces and "to prevent further aggression." Because of the obvious pretext for the request, he could continue to portray himself as a moderate on the conflict and further marginalize Goldwater. Predictably, the attacks resulted in an outpouring of patriotism and expediency in an election year; members of Congress could now demonstrate their support for U.S. forces without the threat of an electoral backlash. This reality ensured the rapid passage of the measure, providing Johnson with bipartisan support and domestic political protection, albeit temporarily.[87] The possibility of a Goldwater administration "helps explain the Democratic congressional leadership's relative passivity" when Johnson asked for the resolution.[88] But even more important is the continuing theme of a permissive attitude in Congress in an election year, a trend that would be repeated in both 1966 and 1968.

The results of the congressional vote on the Tonkin Gulf resolution are as familiar to historians as the lineup of the Big Red Machine is to baseball fans. Yet it is more intriguing and significant to note that, aside from the dissenting votes of Wayne Morse (D-OR) and Ernest Gruening (D-AK), there were numerous other members of Congress with serious reservations about the proposed resolution. Representative Eugene Siler (R-KY) announced that he was "paired" against the resolution, which meant in effect that, if he had been present for the vote, he would have voted against the measure. In a statement released by his office, Siler stated that he opposed the resolution as unnecessary and contended that the United States had no business fighting in Vietnam.[89] This strong anti-war stance was not new for the soon-to-be-retiring congressman. Indeed, on 8 June 1964, Siler had announced his candidacy for presidency on the floor of the House. His unique (and unsuccessful) platform read simply: "I am running with the understanding that I will resign after 24 hours in the White House and let my Vice President take over the duties thereafter. . . . What I propose to do in my 1 day as President is to call home our 15,000 troops in South Vietnam and cancel our part of that ill fated, unnecessary, and un-American campaign in southeast Asia."[90] Siler may have been an obscure political figure, but his willingness to come out in open opposition to the war at this early stage should be recognized.

Moreover, concern over the scope and potential meaning of the resolution was far more substantial than the vote would indicate. Particularly in the Senate, there were significant reservations and pointed inquiries about the exact meaning of the proposed measure. John Sherman Cooper spoke for many of his colleagues when he argued on the Senate floor against a deeper American involvement in the war. President Johnson, Cooper said, "has with respect to our action in South Vietnam, a certain maneuverability, and avenues of negotiation which should be assiduously used, however they may be received." Cooper questioned the importance of Southeast Asia to American interests and the realistic limitations of American military power when deployed on a global scale: "We are committed in Europe and believe our chief interest is in the Western Hemisphere and Europe. In the Pacific, we are committed to the defense of Formosa, Korea, Japan, and the Philippines. I do not know how widely we can spread our resources and our men in the military forces."[91]

In an often-quoted exchange with Fulbright, who had accepted the responsibility from the White House to assure overwhelming passage of the resolution in the Senate, Cooper asked about the powers that the resolution granted the president:

COOPER: Are we now giving the President advance authority to take whatever action he may deem necessary respecting South Vietnam and its defense, or with respect to the defense of any other country included in the [Southeast Asian Treaty Organization] treaty?

FULBRIGHT: I think that is correct.

COOPER: Then, looking ahead, if the President decided that it was necessary to use such force as could lead into war, we will give that authority by this resolution?

FULBRIGHT: That is the way I would interpret it.[92]

Despite his perceptive interrogation of Fulbright, Cooper never seriously considered voting against the resolution. While he shared the concerns of the more vocal opponents of the war, he did not share their willingness to openly break with the administration when U.S. forces were in harm's way—yet. Cooper was neither a maverick nor a fringe political figure; he was an independent thinker with serious doubts about the situation in Southeast Asia who voted for the resolution despite considerable reservations.

In the short-lived discussions of the resolution on the Senate floor, hawkish Republican senators gave wholehearted support to the measure while subtly—and not so subtly—criticizing the administration. Goldwater voted for the resolution and supported the president, stating, "I believe that it is the only thing he can do under the circumstances. We cannot allow the American flag to be shot at anywhere on earth if we are to retain our respect and prestige."[93] Margaret Chase Smith credited Johnson with adopting a "firm policy" but believed that, had he done so earlier, the United States would not be in such a "deplorable mess." She advised the president to declare a national emergency, call up the reserves, invoke price and wage controls, and "go all-out for complete victory."[94] Strom Thurmond (R-SC) praised the resolution but went even further in expressing his hope that the administration would abandon its "purely defensive posture in favor of a 'win policy' in Vietnam," urging "victory, not stalemate." Milward Simpson delivered a biting attack on the administration for failing to take the initiative in Southeast Asia. He told the Senate that he hoped the resolution and bombing raids indicated "an end of our policies of indecision, vacillation, and compromise and herald[ed] the beginning of a measure of commitment that will forge victory" over communism in Vietnam.[95]

House Republicans unanimously supported the administration's retaliatory raids in the floor vote, but many expressed their own concerns about the resolution. Melvin Laird, one of the most influential voices in the GOP caucus, said that he agreed with the president's action and the resolution but pointedly stated, "We still have a policy to develop." He also stressed the importance of deciding whether the country had "the will, the capacity and the determination to win this war in southeast Asia." Lacking that, he argued, "the time has come for us to pull out."[96] This all-or-nothing attitude would become a common refrain for the many Republicans who disdained the incrementalism of the administration. Paul Findley questioned the resolution's broad language and asked for additional time to discuss the significance of the request on the House floor. He was told by Gerald Ford that he should not be worried because this was "a symbolic gesture of support to the President at a critical time . . . but it didn't have any far-reaching implications." Ross Adair (R-IN) agreed. He backed Ford's opinion, stating that the resolution did not "say in effect that we are approving all of the U.S. policies in southeast Asia in the past and are giving approval, in advance, for such actions as the President may see fit to take in the future." One of the most striking reservations came from Bruce Alger (R-TX). Although he subsequently voted for the resolution, Alger displayed his concern during the debate over what he saw as "congressional abdication of responsibility in declaring war." Fearing Johnson would use the resolution to further involve the country in the conflict, Alger voted for it "only assuming that Congress will not be bypassed later."[97]

The uneasiness displayed by Alger would soon be justified. Lyndon Johnson would unilaterally Americanize the war in Vietnam, relying almost exclusively on this ill-defined grant of authority. This left members of Congress scrambling to explain why they approved such an open-ended measure. In retrospect, many members of the GOP tried to justify their support as part of their commitment to anticommunism and freedom. Jacob Javits later stated that he voted for the resolution because he believed that America "must defend freedom in that area, or else see the balance of a large segment of the population of the world tipped against freedom."[98] In the years that followed, many Republican legislators (not to mention their Democratic counterparts) expressed their regret at having voted for the resolution. Some, including Cooper, made their feelings known at the time but voted in the affirmative anyway out of a sense of patriotism and support for the troops. Cooper recalled, "Well, I can say and, of course it's proved, that I knew exactly what it meant. So I was not in any way deceived because I knew that we were giving him the authority to send troops if he made up his mind to do so. There wasn't much thought at the time that it would happen." Others, like John Rhodes, considered their vote the one they would "like to take back" and made it clear they did not intend to give the president a "blank check." Rhodes lamented that he "did not read the Tonkin Gulf Resolution carefully" and, thus, did not realize the broad discretionary authority it granted the president.[99]

For the time being, Johnson enjoyed a windfall of public support for ordering the reprisal raids. A Harris poll found that 85 percent of the American people supported the air strikes, leading the *Los Angeles Times* to opine, "In a single stroke, Mr. Johnson has, at least temporarily, turned his greatest vulnerability in foreign policy into one of his strongest assets." The poll numbers supported that conclusion. In July, 58 percent of Americans criticized the administration for its handling of Vietnam policy. After the attacks, the president received a 72 percent vote of confidence in his approach to the war. More important for the election campaign, those who believed that Johnson could handle Vietnam better than Goldwater rose from 59 to 71 percent.[100] The numbers for Johnson are even more impressive when one considers that Vietnam was Goldwater's only wedge issue; the GOP challenger had better numbers against Johnson on Vietnam than overall.

Although they had voted en masse for the Tonkin Gulf resolution, Republicans almost immediately resumed their attacks on the president's Vietnam policies. In the 20 August edition of "The Ev and Charlie Show," Dirksen complained that the war "continues to go from bad to worse" and asserted, "The time has come to ask a blunt question: Why?" The administration, he said, needed to decide "what it does want to do in Southeast Asia and then do it. The American people will support . . . any necessary effort to thwart Communist aggression if a clear-cut objective is set and then vigorously pursued." Halleck picked up the attack in his statement. The House minority leader stated that the country's confused policy on Vietnam "can be contributed to a basic defect in the Johnson Administration. It has one eye on the Presidential election in November instead of both eyes on the affairs of this nation."[101]

But no amount of criticism about Johnson's Vietnam policies could salvage

Barry Goldwater's campaign, which seemed doomed almost from the start. He "groped futilely for a *winning issue*" and focused a great deal of attention on the Kennedy-Johnson record of being soft on communism.[102] One of the clearest expositions of his position came in his campaign book, *Where I Stand,* in which he argued, "There is no substitute for victory. We are at war in Vietnam, and we must have the will to win that war." He called for the interdiction of supply lines in neutral areas and the end to "privileged sanctuaries." He concluded, "The security of all Asia hinges on this crucial battle."[103] Could the campaign have turned out differently? Probably not.[104] The administration had already started planning for the escalation of the American presence in South Vietnam, and it is clear that, by late 1964, it had decided in principle to increase the U.S. commitment to Saigon. Moreover, the Tonkin Gulf resolution insulated Johnson against the need to directly debate Goldwater on U.S. policy. Thus, there is no realistic counterfactual scenario that could make Goldwater president.

While Vietnam took center stage as a staple of Goldwater's critique of Johnson's foreign policy, the Goldwater-Miller ticket never gained traction with the voters on its signature issue. Still, though it was not the pivotal issue that it would be in 1968, Vietnam did play a larger role in the 1964 presidential balloting than historians generally recognize. The question of an alleged agreement between Goldwater and LBJ to keep Vietnam (and civil rights) out of the campaign is also open to interpretation. On 24 July 1964, Johnson and Goldwater met at the White House and subsequently released a joint statement noting that they had agreed not to inflame racial tensions over civil rights during the election. There was no mention of Vietnam in the statement. While Johnson's memoirs do not discuss the meeting, Goldwater does in each of his autobiographies. According to Goldwater, Johnson accepted his proposals that they not challenge each other on civil rights or Vietnam policy, and the agreement was honored by both men during the rest of the campaign. Even a cursory glance at the documentary and public record reveals that the latter claim is, at best, an exaggeration and, at worst, completely incorrect.[105] If such an agreement did exist, it did not appear to have any effect on Goldwater's attacks on Johnson during the fall of 1964.

Notwithstanding the support given the president during the Tonkin crisis, Goldwater maintained that Americans should recognize the general failure of his Vietnam policy. Indeed, Goldwater increasingly referred to the conflict as "Lyndon Johnson's War," claiming that it resulted from the president's "weak and confusing leadership," and questioning whether there had ever been "a more mishandled conflict in American history." In a September 1964 speech in Pikesville, Maryland, Goldwater said that four years of drift in foreign policy had led the United States into "Lyndon Johnson's war in Vietnam. . . . American sons and grandsons are being killed by communist bullets and communist bombs. And we have yet to hear a word of truth about why they're dying." The GOP candidate also made a prescient observation on 29 September: "Why does [the president] put off facing the question of what to do about Vietnam? Does he hope that he can wait until after the election to confront the American public with the fact of total defeat or total war in Asia?" In fact, that was precisely LBJ's strategy. Johnson sought to "preempt the high ground, the moderate thorough-fare, the middle of the road from his Republican opponents."[106] The implications of that decision, of course, would soon become apparent.

Johnson's campaign strategy was indirectly aided by Everett Dirksen. From the beginning of the American commitment to South Vietnam, the Illinois senator backed whatever steps had been taken to bolster the regime in Saigon, although his partisan comments as part of "The Ev and Charlie Show" tended to temporize his support rhetorically. Early in Johnson's presidency, Dirksen had taken a very simplistic view of the war. "When you are at war," he asserted, "and the enemy refuses to talk except on terms that would mean your surrender, you turn the screws on him. You do everything that is necessary to bring him down."[107] Because of his stance on the war and his long-standing relationship with the president dating to their service together in the Senate, Dirksen enjoyed a unique rapport with LBJ. While his support helped shore up Johnson's political flank, it forced Dirksen into the sometimes uncomfortable position of opposing some of his party's most respected members—both those who sought a more aggressive prosecution of the war, like Richard Nixon, and the Coopers and Aikens who lobbied for intensified efforts at negotiation. Dirksen repeatedly acted to blunt and even silence criticisms by Republican leaders of Johnson's policies in Vietnam. He would prove to be the president's staunchest GOP ally until 1968.

Even though Johnson seemed well positioned to win the White House in November, he took no chances during the campaign and harshly attacked the Republicans for their militancy on the Vietnam issue. But, in doing so, he sacrificed long-term U.S. interests for a short-term domestic political advantage. Indeed, his comments on the war during his race against Goldwater would have far-reaching ramifications. In a speech in Manchester, New Hampshire, on 28 September, he stated, "Some of our people—Mr. Nixon, Mr. Rockefeller, Mr Scranton and Mr. Goldwater—have all, at some time or other, suggested the possible wisdom of going North in Vietnam." Taking such a precipitous action was beyond the parameters of the American commitment as the president defined it. "I want to be very cautious and careful," he asserted, "and use it only as a last resort, when I start dropping bombs around that are likely to involve American boys in a war in Asia." Tom Wicker wrote during the campaign that, "having shown his strength [with the Tonkin reprisals], having diminished Goldwater's ability to charge him with a 'no-win' policy and with soft-headedness toward Communism, having established his own 'restraint,'" Johnson seemed free to "do what came so naturally to so political a creature." As Wicker concluded, "With every rattle of the Goldwater sword, every reference to the use of nuclear weapons by the Air Force general on the Republican ticket, every provocative remark about bombing the North from the avid jet pilot who was his opponent, Johnson was lured by politics into the profitably contrasting position of deploring—even forbidding—war, escalation, and nuclear brinksmanship."[108]

LBJ spoke even more bluntly as election day approached. Campaigning at the University of Akron on 21 October, the president stated, "We are not about to send American boys nine or ten thousand miles to do what Asian boys ought to be doing for themselves."[109] Republican (and Democratic) critics would point to this statement as evidence that Johnson misled the American public in 1964, a crucial element of the "credibility gap" that would become a key component of GOP attacks on the administration for the remainder of the LBJ's presidency. Johnson's caution was mirrored by his advisers. Bill Moyers urged the president not to send either McNamara or Rusk to Vietnam before the elections because such a trip would "only tend to *increase* public attention and concern about the situation out there. We ought to be hoping that public discussion of Vietnam could be kept to a minimum." Since Goldwater did not seem to be making any progress in making Vietnam an issue, he continued, anything that went wrong while an administration official was in Saigon could "play into Goldwater's hands and Vietnam might well become a major issue."[110] Moyers, William Bundy, and other members of Johnson's administration understood that nothing mattered more than reaching the election without the albatross of a Vietnam-related disaster around the president's neck. In this regard, the administration was successful, though the postponement of critical decisions and deceiving the public about the true trajectory of U.S. policy can hardly be considered a "success."

The voting on 3 November 1964 was anticlimactic. Not only did Lyndon Johnson win the greatest popular vote landslide in American history, but Barry Goldwater managed to capture only six states. In addition, the GOP lost seats in both houses of Congress, leaving them with only 140 in the House and 32 in the Senate. In the House, this was the lowest number of Republicans since 1936; the Senate totals were the lowest since 1940. Writing in the *New York Times Magazine,* Jacob Javits suggested that the Republican Party was "in more serious trouble today than it was in 1936." Javits recommended that the GOP leadership be overhauled to breathe new life into the stale "Ev and Charlie Show" and allow new voices in the party to be heard.[111] That is precisely what happened.

As one of the strongest Republicans left standing, Melvin Laird became a major force within the party. He convinced the GOP leadership to create the National Leadership Council—a group of the best minds in the party charged with rejuvenating the GOP. He then set out to remake the Republican House leadership. The disastrous electoral results "created a climate for internal dissension and change," and, shortly after the election, with Laird's assistance and support, Gerald Ford began a campaign to capture the minority leader's post from Charles Halleck. Laird expressed interest in becoming minority leader— and would have been favored by conservatives as he was more aggressive than Ford—but, once Ford announced his candidacy, Laird stepped aside for his longtime friend. In voting by the Republican caucus on 4 January, Ford defeated Halleck and, in the contest for chair of the Republican Conference, Laird defeated Peter Frelinghuysen (R-NJ), marking a key shift in the party's leadership. LBJ called Ford shortly afterward, congratulating him on his victory, and attempting to co-opt the new minority leader by assuring him that he wanted the Republicans closely involved in discussions about Vietnam.[112]

While replacing Halleck was more about age and style, the balloting for the caucus chair became more of a philosophical battle. Laird had "aroused the enmity of the eastern moderates and liberals by his firm and unbending management of the Republican party platform" the previous fall. Frelinghuysen had been nominated by the "Wednesday Group," a coalition of moderate-to-liberal Republicans, in an attempt to keep the young Turks of the party who had vocally supported Goldwater out of power. But Laird's conservatism resonated with the GOP caucus and signaled a quantum shift in the ideological makeup of the party. While moderates within the party tried to regain control and move it away from Goldwater and toward the center, it would prove to be a lost cause in the long run.[113] Over the next decade, conservative Republicans would seize power in the party and have yet to relinquish it. At the same time, moderate and liberal members of the GOP became increasingly isolated and disenchanted with the direction of the party's platforms and agenda, and a number of them left the party altogether.

Even beyond the shake-up in the Republican leadership, Johnson's landslide victory had devastating consequences for the GOP. One commentator went so far as to speculate that the Democrats might retain control of the White House until at least 1988 owing to the fact that the party was "hopelessly divided" between its Left and Right wings.[114] This division, which would become a focal point of debate on the Vietnam issue later in the decade, doomed Goldwater's candidacy and left deep and lasting scars on the party. Virtually the only prominent Republican figures to emerge with their public images intact were George Romney and Richard Nixon—Romney because he never endorsed Goldwater and Nixon because he campaigned diligently for a ticket in which he had little confidence. The other major figures in the party, such as Rockefeller and Lodge, had given tepid backing to the ticket but had not thrown their full support behind it. Edward Brooke, the Republican attorney general of Massachusetts who would be a key player in Congress during the last stages of the conflict, recalled that his refusal to support the ticket was considered "an act of disloyalty" that actually cost him a number of his own campaign staff.[115] According to Nixon, Brooke and others who did not give their full backing to Goldwater saw "their influence . . . largely destroyed" within the party.[116] The chairman of the Republican Governors Association, Governor Robert E. Smylie (R-ID), stated in December, "We are a defeated party with a defeated leadership. We have suffered a defeat as severe in quality and quantity as any that the Republican party has ever sustained."[117]

George H. W. Bush, who lost a close senatorial race to Ralph Yarborough (D-TX) that fall, wrote to Nixon in the wake of the debacle in an effort to contextualize the crisis the party faced. The problem with the Goldwater campaign, he suggested, was that it "got taken over by a bunch of 'nuts' whose very presence at a rally would shake up a plain fellow coming in to make up his mind." The problem for the GOP was not a rejection of Goldwater's conservatism, Bush argued, but rather the "false image that people had about Goldwater." Bush recognized the paradigm change occurring within the party, asserting, "Rockefeller's brand of liberalism just won't hunt."[118] Bush proved to be prophetic; the 1964 election would produce tectonic shifts in the Republican Party's ideological composition and philosophical approach that would reverberate for decades to come.

Many pundits openly questioned whether the party of Abraham Lincoln, Teddy Roosevelt, and Dwight Eisenhower could survive as a viable political entity. According to Lewis Gould, the question was "whether Republicans had become a permanent minority party which could no longer mount a credible challenge."[119] Yet out of the ashes of this defeat came a party that knew it had to refocus itself and broaden its voter appeal in order to survive as a national political force. The first order of business was to select a new chairman for the Republican National Committee to replace Goldwater's appointment, Dean Burch. The position went to Ray Bliss. A veteran party leader who had helped Nixon carry Ohio in 1960, Bliss stressed the importance of organization and financial strength over ideology. He and other senior GOP officials realized the need for party unity after the 1964 disaster, both in terms of supporting its own candidates and in terms of having at least a semblance of centralized policy statements under the auspices of the Republican Coordinating Committee. The Republican Coordinating Committee was created as an effort to, in the words of Melvin Laird, "bring people together and to have a discussion so that we could speak more with one voice, and to use our national leadership in a more effective way."[120] Each of these factors would help define the party more clearly and avoid the divisiveness and extremism that characterized the Goldwater campaign. The goal was simple and twofold: first, to make a strong showing in the 1966 midterm elections and, second, to regain the White House in 1968.

Virtually all right-wing Republicans unequivocally supported the U.S. role in Vietnam. For them, the conflict was an integral part of the global fight against Communist aggression. South Vietnam could never be allowed to fall. GOP conservatives strongly disagreed with Johnson's restraint and the administration's failure to delineate its policy goals and objectives.[121] They pushed to bomb Hanoi, mine North Vietnamese harbors, and expand the war into the North and sought to use the threat of nuclear weapons to force the Communists to the negotiating table. Yet they also faced a dilemma, both ideologically and politically. While they backed the war against communism, they also perceived it as "Johnson's war" and took steps to distance themselves from what the *National Review* described as "Hard-Soft Schizophrenia."[122]

Goldwater had sounded the same themes in his campaign. Ironically, as he went down in ignominious defeat in the 1964 presidential contest, the administration adopted his policy prescription for the Vietnam conflict. With the election won, the focus could now be shifted to taking the appropriate and necessary steps to shore up the Saigon regime and stave off military disaster. The National Security Council Working Group met on the morning of the election to discuss how best to implement the expansion of the war that Goldwater had so forcefully advocated during the campaign and for which the administration had been planning for the past several months. Indeed, Goldwater's approach to Vietnam before 3 November would become LBJ's Vietnam policy thereafter. The *Tulsa Tribune* editorialized, "It's strange what a difference just a few weeks make. What was 'trigger-happy' in October is no longer 'dangerous' or 'irresponsible.' . . . For in their hearts high officials here have known for some time that the policy in Viet Nam could not be left to flounder indefinitely."[123] Herblock recognized the irony; several months later he drew a cartoon depicting Johnson looking into a mirror and seeing Goldwater's face staring back at him.[124]

The Republican Party's Cassandras—Barry Goldwater, Richard Nixon, and John Sherman Cooper—accurately predicted the evolution of the American commitment in Vietnam and anticipated the political obstacles that Johnson and Nixon would face in the White House. But, just like the prophetess of Greek legend, they were either ignored as extremists or dismissed as pessimists during Johnson's first year in office. The reason? Domestic political calculations. The president refused to consider any actions or decisions that might prove detrimental to his electoral hopes in November 1964. The war in Southeast Asia was a "holding action" intended to "silence right-wing critics" long enough to implement the Great Society and recapture the White House.[125] Over the next four years, LBJ would have numerous occasions to reflect back on the warnings from Goldwater, Cooper, and others who agreed with them and would undoubtedly wonder what might have been had he heeded their prognostications by either making an all-out effort to win the war or definitively pursuing a strategy of withdrawal. But, with the election behind him, he could now turn his attention to the deteriorating situation in South Vietnam without fear of an immediate and negative reaction about the conflict.

# CHAPTER 3

# Opening Pandora's Box

## Escalation and Domestic Politics, 1965–1966

Decide: To succumb to the preponderance of one set of influences over another set.

— Ambrose Bierce, *The Devil's Dictionary*

It is always thus, impelled by a state of mind which is destined not to last, that we make our irrevocable decisions.

— Marcel Proust, *Remembrance of Things Past*

For Lyndon Johnson, the operative mythological characters in 1965 were not Scylla and Charybdis or Cassandra, but rather Pandora. According to Greek myth, the gods gave Pandora a box with instructions not to open it. Before too long, however, curiosity overcame her, and she opened the box, unleashing havoc and all manner of evil on the world. It is unfortunate that Johnson did not heed the lessons of the ancient story. In choosing to escalate the Vietnam conflict into a full-scale Americanized (though undeclared) war, he took the United States from what some considered its golden age—the prosperity of the Cold War, the glamour of Camelot, and the preponderance of American power—into a much more uncertain era. This chapter will examine the decision the Johnson administration made to open the Pandora's box of escalation during 1965, consider how the implementation of that policy irrevocably altered the course of American history, and assess the role played by both hawks and doves in the GOP in the process.

From a domestic political standpoint, Lyndon Johnson had considerable room to maneuver after the 1964 election. In an unpublished book manuscript detailing his service in the administration, William Bundy argues that the president could have carried American public opinion with him "on whatever course he chose" with respect to Vietnam.[1] While he would have taken political heat from GOP hawks like Nixon and Goldwater for abandoning South Vietnam in late 1964, it would not have been debilitating and would certainly have caused less consternation for him in the years to come than what ensued. It is also important to remember that the war was not a deeply divisive issue at this point. Opposition to the conflict remained embryonic, and no real consensus existed either in Congress or in the country on what to do. For Johnson, however, the pathological fear of a "who lost Vietnam" debate dominated his thinking, and decoupling the United States from South Vietnam—or at the very least disengaging militarily from the conflict—did not register as a realistic option.

But, as H. W. Brands points out, the China analogy was not entirely accurate in this case. Truman's narrow victory over Thomas Dewey in 1948 rendered him much more susceptible to the "slightest rocking of the boat" than did Johnson's defeat of Goldwater. Given the magnitude of his landslide, LBJ "could have weathered a much larger storm without swamping."[2] Yet he had already decided in principle to escalate the war by the end of 1964, though some uncertainty lingered. Abandoning an American ally, particularly one facing an imminent Communist challenge, seemed inconceivable to him. In addition, while his mandate would allow him to pursue his comprehensive domestic legislative agenda, he did not want partisan sniping over the war to interfere with the Great Society. The best way, in his mind, to keep the Republicans at bay would be to strengthen the U.S. commitment to the survival of the Saigon regime and the defeat of communism in Southeast Asia.

But Johnson also had to face increasing pressure from Republican doves. Most notably, John Sherman Cooper remained steadfast in his opposition to increased involvement in Vietnam in the months leading up to Johnson's decision to Americanize the war. In January 1965, Cooper urged a reevaluation of U.S. policy based in part on the lack of fortitude demonstrated by the South Vietnamese government and military. As he told reporters, "If these people in South Vietnam will not stand and fight, I don't see how we can stay there."[3] The administration worried about Cooper's potential influence on Capitol Hill. One internal memo referred to him as a "bellwether" who could convince others to reconsider their support of the war and the administration.[4]

Another thorn in the administration's side was George Aiken. He considered Vietnam as an unwinnable war that threatened to have devastating domestic consequences for the United States—high casualties, a weakened economy, a divided populace, the end of bipartisanship, and a dangerous extension of executive power. Although Aiken consistently maintained that the United States did have a limited commitment to South Vietnam, a commitment based primarily on its responsibility for having transported hundreds of thousands of refugees from the North after the 1954 Geneva Accords, he remained pessimistic about the prospects for success in South Vietnam. He told one constituent, "There is no doubt about it—the situation in Vietnam is a mess and is getting worse. I have made it clear that I am opposed to the expansion of military operations in Vietnam." The senator went on to lament, "I wish the American people would be told the facts—or at least the Congress should be told the truth. We are not kept adequately informed."[5]

The skepticism exhibited by Cooper and Aiken began to be shared by others in Congress. The State Department official Jonathan Moore, a Republican who would later serve as George Romney's foreign policy adviser in the 1968 presidential campaign, addressed the issue of "congressional attitudes on South Vietnam" in a memorandum for McGeorge Bundy in early 1965. Moore wrote that, on Capitol Hill, there was "a generalized frustration with the situation in Vietnam and our involvement there." Many members of Congress to this point, he observed, had been "willing to go along with the people who have the direct responsibility, the experts, in the Executive Branch." But noticeable adjustments in congressional attitudes had begun to occur, a development that Moore believed should worry the administration. Among those with strong opinions, he suggested, Senator Henry "Scoop" Jackson (D-WA) and Cooper "should be watched as indicators" of shifting opinion. Looking to the future, he concluded that greater efforts to "present and persuade on the Hill" were needed in order to "develop and solidify support." Without taking such steps, "the passage of time and unhappy developments in [Southeast Asia] could erode our position and enhance the persuasiveness and numbers of the opposition."[6] Clearly, as the *New York Times* reported in early January 1965, Congress was "just as baffled and frustrated over what the U.S. should do in Vietnam as the Administration."[7]

The reason for the widespread uncertainty in January 1965 was that the situation in South Vietnam had become virtually untenable. The instability that had plagued the country's government since the Diem coup continued despite the efforts of American officials. To compound the problem, Buddhist leaders renewed their protests against the regime, and the demonstrations took on an increasingly anti-American character. Meanwhile, the National Liberation Front (NLF) enjoyed mounting success against the South Vietnamese army, and North Vietnamese forces infiltrated the South in preparation for what appeared to be a major offensive. As Gen. Maxwell Taylor, who had succeeded

Lodge as ambassador in Saigon, told Johnson late in the month, "To take no positive action now is to accept defeat in the fairly near future."[8]

Despite the problems facing the administration in Southeast Asia, Johnson virtually ignored Vietnam in his 1965 State of the Union address, devoting a mere 140 words to the conflict. When he did mention the conflict, he stuck to innocuous clichés about helping friendly nations, suggesting that to "ignore aggression now would only increase the danger of a much larger war." What was at stake, he asserted, was "the cause of freedom and in that cause America will never be found wanting."[9] Looking back at the speech, one thing becomes painfully obvious: LBJ's effort to keep the conflict off the national radar by obscuring the ongoing planning for an enhanced U.S. military presence in South Vietnam led him to gloss over what had become the most pressing foreign policy issue facing the administration.

Republicans launched a blistering counterattack almost immediately. Bourke Hickenlooper assailed the speech, saying that it "was not remotely in line with the reality in foreign affairs. . . . Things have been going from bad to worse in Viet Nam, and the administration does not know what to do about it." He also referenced the credibility problems Johnson faced, noting, "The situation as described privately [in a secret White House briefing] was not at all like this general peace and happiness picture we were receiving in the State of the Union address."[10] Richard Nixon warned of the danger of losing the war, forfeiting the military initiative to the Communist forces, and, especially, considering premature negotiations to end the fighting. In a speech to the Sales Executive Club of New York on 26 January 1965, Nixon cautioned, "We will be thrown out in a matter of months—certainly within the year [unless there is a change in strategy]." He argued forcefully for an escalation of naval and airpower in an attempt to cut off supply routes into South Vietnam and destroy Communist staging areas in Laos and North Vietnam. He also derided those who called for neutralization. "Neutrality where the Communists are concerned," he asserted, "means three things: we get out; they stay in; they take over." Nixon believed that the United States "must realize that there is no easy way out. We either get out, surrender on the installment plan through neutralization, or we find a way to win."[11]

The Republican attacks underscored the importance of dealing promptly and decisively with the situation in Vietnam. Most of Johnson's advisers agreed with Taylor's recommendation, arguing that the persistent instability in the South would require the United States to bomb the North as "a faint hope of really improving" the situation. William Bundy went so far as to suggest that the continuation of existing policies could "only lead to a disastrous defeat." Even if the United States could not hold South Vietnam against the Communist forces, Assistant Secretary of Defense John McNaughton argued, it would appear stronger to allies and adversaries alike if the administration kept "slugging away" rather than simply accepting defeat. The general consensus, therefore, was that the United States should take the first opportunity to launch an air campaign against North Vietnam.[12] Characteristically, Melvin Laird put it more bluntly: the United States needed either to "pull out completely or go all out and go in to win."[13]

The opportunity to make that choice would come in early February. NLF forces attacked American military installations at Pleiku, killing nine Americans, and destroying a number of aircraft. That evening, the administration decided to strike back. Johnson ordered the immediate implementation of Operation FLAMING DART, a series of reprisal strikes already drawn up by the Joint Chiefs of Staff (JCS), and later that day U.S. aircraft struck North Vietnamese military targets just across the seventeenth parallel. The attacks did not deter the NLF. Four days later, they hit the American base at Qui Nhon. LBJ subsequently ordered a series of even heavier air strikes that shortly evolved into Operation ROLLING THUNDER.

Following the Pleiku attack, Johnson announced, "We have no choice now but to clear the decks and make absolutely clear our continued determination to back South Vietnam in its fight to maintain its independence."[14] He did not elaborate as to what actions the American resolve entailed, however. Unconvinced by the president's comments, Nixon wrote to Goldwater and expressed his concern: "[The raids] may not be an adequate follow-through. I think we must continue to urge that the United States make a command decision to use whatever air and sea power is necessary to cut off the flow of arms and men from North Viet Nam into South Viet Nam." Nixon also met with Johnson at the White House and pressed the president for further action on Vietnam.[15] And, at a party fund-raiser in Philadelphia, Nixon demanded a "day by day and night by night" bombing campaign in the North. "Failing to do more than we are doing," he stated, "will mean loss of the war . . . to imperial communism . . . the choice today is not between this war and no war, but this war and another much bigger war." The next day, Nixon implicitly reproached the administration again, arguing as he had for weeks that the United States should stop reacting and begin attacking Communist supply lines into South Vietnam.[16]

Congressional response to the American air strikes was muted, but the general attitude was one of support for the president's firm action. Still, a growing uneasiness among some legislators began to emerge over the trend of increasing military involvement without a clear statement of policy from the White House. Representative John Lindsay (R-NY), a liberal internationalist who became one of the GOP's most outspoken doves by 1968 and defected to the Democratic

Party in 1971, summarized the apprehension: "The President must define our policy in Vietnam. It is still apparent that we have no clear policy except an aimless patchwork of scotch tape and bailing [sic] wire that becomes more confused every day." Lindsay ominously warned that, if the pattern of strikes and counterstrikes continued, the fighting would escalate until "the little remaining cover is totally stripped away and the involvement that is euphemistically known as military support becomes a naked U.S. war that has neither front lines nor back lines, nor beginning or ending."[17]

In a television interview following the NLF attacks, Aiken expressed his frustration over the catch-22 in Vietnam: "I am sorry to say that the situation in Vietnam is still deteriorating. . . . We cannot withdraw at this time. The situation is intolerable. It cannot go on. We have the choice of either negotiation or all-out war. Negotiation will be difficult. All-out war unthinkable."[18] Cooper and Javits echoed Aiken's call for negotiations without preconditions on either side. Cooper affirmed his support for Johnson's policy of backing South Vietnam but said that the administration had to show more flexibility on the diplomatic front: "I do not believe that we can reach negotiations by imposing as a prerequisite that the Communists cease their intervention, rightful as our position is. For then we stand in confrontation, with a position of unconditional surrender and with the possibility of war as the only arbiter." The same day, Cooper introduced a resolution in the Senate calling for a full briefing by Rusk and McNamara for the entire Senate.[19]

On the other end of the political spectrum, conservatives remained agitated by the administration's lack of fervor and resolve in stabilizing the Saigon regime and committing to victory. John Tower put it plainly: "Make no mistake about it—we are at war in South Vietnam, no matter what it is called." Moreover, he faulted the president for failing to "come to grips with the seriousness of the situation.[20] The *National Review* editorialized, "These air strikes . . . can most readily be understood not as military actions but as . . . a method of negotiating . . . they were in reality more political than military acts." The fundamental issue at stake, the editors continued, was whether American power stayed in Southeast Asia or got out. With remarkable foresight, they concluded, "If a decision is not made deliberately, it will come by default in any case, and that is much the worse way for us. Conceivably the drift could be into a full-scale war that no one intended. More likely it would be in the opposite direction: a further collapse, military and political, in South Vietnam."[21] Of course, the conservative preference was for immediate and decisive victory and a more vigorous application of U.S. military capabilities. Anthony Harrigan, writing in the *National Review,* advocated a blockade of North Vietnamese ports if "the United States seriously intends victory over the Viet Cong." Karl Mundt went even further, calling for massive bombing to create a "seared earth borderline of five to ten miles" to prevent the Communists from threatening South Vietnam.[22]

Conservatives pressed forcefully on Vietnam primarily because of their commitment to eradicating the scourge of international communism. Mundt believed that the United States had to demonstrate its "resolve and dedication to stop aggression when it starts, or appeasement that would lead to our eventually finding our backs to the wall again, as we were 25 years ago." Otherwise, the result could easily be "an all-out nuclear war to save our country."[23] Republicans on the Right linked the conflict in Southeast Asia to the global fight against Communist aggression and called on the administration to draw a line in Vietnam. Failure to do so, argued Representative John Byrnes (R-WI), would mean that a line "will have to be drawn later somewhere else, with the odds heavier against us."[24] Conservatives underscored these arguments with constant references to appeasement and the lessons of history. Senator Len Jordan (R-ID) instructed one of his constituents, "As history has proven, accommodation and appeasement only encourage a hostile nation to remain belligerent and aggressive." And Senator Norris Cotton (R-NH) warned that Vietnam could become another Korea if the United States did not use its strength to halt the advance of communism since "knuckling to the invaders in Vietnam is the surest path to ultimate war."[25]

Yet, while the hawks clamored for a stronger American effort in Vietnam, none of the leading opponents of the war in either party—including Mansfield, Aiken, and Cooper—were prepared to fully confront the administration in public over the war. To be sure, their criticisms of administration policy and support of negotiations were credible, but they weakened their cause by ultimately supporting the president's meager rhetorical efforts at peace and reaffirming their belief in a nominal American responsibility to provide assistance to Saigon. Very few members of Congress were willing to say what they really believed at this juncture: that South Vietnam was not worth the price of a major U.S. military effort and that a negotiated settlement would not harm American credibility and prestige in the long run. This reticence—and, to be truthful, complicity—on the part of leading congressional figures opposed to the expansion of the war had to be a relief to Johnson, who desperately wanted to avoid a probing, full-scale debate on the issue during the first half of 1965.

A discussion did ensue behind closed doors, however. With pressure from the Joint Chiefs and hawks like Walt Rostow to expand the U.S. military presence substantially, Johnson faced critical decisions regarding the direction of the American commitment.[26] Some historians have argued that this process was nothing more than window dressing, that Johnson had already made up his mind. But the documentary record clearly indicates that, while the administration recognized the need to escalate and had made a preliminary decision to do so, the president struggled when it came time to make the final call. A few of his advisers counseled caution. Undersecretary of State George Ball has received much attention for his dissent in the early months of 1965. Though Ball was dismissed by some as Johnson's in-house "devil's advocate," his opposition to escalation is well chronicled in a series of prescient memoranda to the president.[27]

Others weighed in against the Americanization of the war as well. In a memorandum to Johnson on 17 February 1965, Vice President Hubert Humphrey expressed serious reservations about escalating the U.S. military commitment in Vietnam. Humphrey reminded Johnson of the campaign statements in which he promised not to enlarge the war and urged him to consider the ramifications of escalation. In the wake of the landslide victory over Goldwater, Humphrey wrote, the Johnson administration was "in a stronger position to [cut losses in Vietnam] now than any Administration." The vice president argued that 1965 was "the first year when we can face the Vietnam problem without being preoccupied with the political repercussions from the Republican right." Moreover, Humphrey continued, a greater commitment to Saigon could lead to new political difficulties from liberal Democrats, independents, and labor. The best possible outcome would be "a Vietnam settlement which turns out to be better than was in the cards because LBJ's political talents for the first time came to grips with a fateful world crisis and did so successfully." The president would then reap the "subsequent political benefits from such an outcome."[28]

Johnson listened to and then ignored Ball and his vice president, accepting the verdict of his hawkish advisers. In retrospect, neither had much hope of having their position adopted by the administration. The decision had effectively been made already—Johnson's lingering doubts notwithstanding—and the weight of opinion within the national security hierarchy stood against them. In fact, Humphrey found himself banished from meetings dealing with Vietnam for an entire year; when invited back, he became one of the leading proponents of administration policy in Vietnam until after the 1968 Democratic convention. At this stage, all that remained for the president was to figure out when to implement the decision and how to sell the escalation to his "publics"—Congress, the American people, and the international community—without initiating a debate that could have devastating ramifications for the administration's goals.

In an effort to maneuver his way through the political minefield that his planning created, as Johnson made his crucial decisions on the conduct of the war in Vietnam, "he both sought and was influenced by Ike's advice."[29] The presidential aide Marvin Watson suggested that LBJ meet with Eisenhower on the Vietnam situation. Such a move, he argued, would "cause the Country to maintain this unanimous support" on the war issue.[30] Thus, during perhaps the most important week of the entire American involvement in the war, Johnson asked Eisenhower to attend a meeting at the White House on 17 February 1965. According to the record of their conversation, Johnson tried to play down the significance of the meeting: "I don't want to put it up like we're in deep trouble, because I don't think it's reached that point." "But," he continued ominously, "it's deep enough that I want to talk to you."[31] This pivotal meeting also included Robert McNamara, McGeorge Bundy, Gen. Earle Wheeler, the chairman of the JCS, and Gen. Andrew J. Goodpaster, Eisenhower's former aide.

The attendees listened for over two hours as Eisenhower explained his views on the U.S. military role in Vietnam. The American objective was "that of denying Southeast Asia to the Communists." In order to accomplish that goal, the former president argued, the administration needed to do several things. First, more support was needed from America's NATO allies. Second, the security of Vietnam could not be guaranteed through the use of American troops; rather, the Vietnamese had to stop supplies from reaching the Viet Cong. Third, American and South Vietnamese morale—"the key factor"—needed to remain high, while the confidence of the North Vietnamese needed to be undermined. This, he believed, should be achieved through an effective propaganda campaign in concert with the military actions under consideration.[32] Fourth, Eisenhower strongly advised decentralization of the military effort, arguing that it was essential "to back a commander and trust him. This requires that policies and missions be defined." This emphasis on a sense of mission also influenced Eisenhower's views on the importance of maintaining a credible and strong posture for international consumption. If the United States could not do so, it would appear weak in the eyes of Hanoi and the Soviet bloc, and the former president firmly believed that "negotiation from weakness is likely to lead only into deceit and vulnerability, which could be disastrous to us."[33]

Therefore, cessation and then renewal of air strikes would prove ineffective. Eisenhower argued for continuous pressure and further expansion of the attacks into North Vietnamese airspace. He also asserted that, if handled properly, such a course would not provoke a dangerous response from the Chinese or the Soviets. The United States simply needed to pass the word privately that it would take action against Beijing or Moscow if necessary, using "any weapons required" up to and including nuclear. "We should let it be known," he asserted, "that we are not bound by such restrictions." Never, he concluded, should the United States negotiate from a "position of weakness."[34] Eisenhower's recommendations should not surprise anyone familiar with his approach to foreign policy during his presidency. His comments to LBJ are completely consistent with his employment of the massive retaliation doctrine and use of strident rhetorical diplomacy in dealing with the Soviet threat.[35]

As a gesture of gratitude to his predecessor, Johnson arranged for General Goodpaster to provide regular briefings to Eisenhower on foreign policy in general and Vietnam specifically and to serve as the administration's liaison with the former president. Johnson did this for two reasons: first, to keep the former president informed and up-to-date so as to be able to call on his experience and insights on the war; and, second, to have the leading figure in the Republican Party publicly on the administration's side, an important consideration politically. These briefings continued through May 1968, and the record of these conversations provides us with the clearest statements of Eisenhower's views on the war as it evolved.

Shortly after their White House meeting, Johnson sent Eisenhower a letter discussing "the volume of vocal support for and unity behind our Southeast Asian effort." American purposes, he continued, would benefit from "the fact that neither friendly nor hostile governments doubt the unity or determination of our people or our governments." Johnson went on to praise the GOP for "standing up magnificently" and following Eisenhower's example of "putting the country first." He later wrote, "The cooperation of the Republican leadership in Congress continues to be a source of the most important strength for me—and, I am proud to say, support from many of the leaders is coming for our domestic policies as well as international policies."[36] These final comments demonstrate Johnson's concern for consensus and the importance he placed on domestic political considerations when making policy. The president was encouraged by comments like those from Senator Hugh Scott (R-PA), who believed that the United States could not withdraw from Vietnam. "If we do," Scott argued, "we will be forced to defend countries closer to our own soil and security . . . [and to] show the world the strength of our conviction and the resolution of our purpose." In an effort to support the administration's position and to clarify American policy, Scott introduced a resolution in March 1965 stating that Congress "approves and supports the President's actions" in South Vietnam. Later in the month, Jacob Javits proposed a similar resolution, this one emphasizing America's willingness to negotiate while helping establish a stronger public consensus behind America's policy toward Vietnam. The resolution warned against the danger "caused by an erosion of support" and urged Johnson to outline U.S. objectives to the public.[37]

Eisenhower made it clear that he would endorse the administration's policies in Vietnam. He supported Johnson's actions, as he had Kennedy's, because to do otherwise would be a disservice to the incumbent president and to the country. Moreover, he correctly assumed that Johnson had set his course and sought advice only on how to best carry out the administration's policies.[38] Privately, however, Eisenhower expressed concern about the expansion of U.S. military involvement in Vietnam, believing that it would be very difficult for American forces to be used successfully. Further, he doubted whether there would be the determination to apply the resources necessary to prevail if they were used.[39] Nevertheless, "Eisenhower held practically the same views as Johnson's key advisers: bombing the north was essential to the morale of South Vietnam and to the weakening of morale in North Vietnam."[40]

Behind the scenes, Eisenhower asserted an even more hawkish line and urged the use of overwhelming force to win the war. Given that the situation in South Vietnam had deteriorated so badly, many leading Republicans joined him as he pushed the administration to take firmer action. Despite having lost the presidential election the previous November, Barry Goldwater remained active in criticizing the administration's policies in Vietnam in his syndicated newspaper column.[41] As he later wrote in one of his autobiographies, "The war became one of the driving forces of my life." Goldwater met with Johnson in early 1965 and urged the president to remove the political restrictions from American forces in Vietnam, arguing, "When you go to war, the first decision you must make is to win it."[42] The quick destruction of North Vietnam through massive airpower remained his prescription for victory because he was certain that the guerrilla war could not continue in the South without logistic support. In April, he praised the president for initiating the bombing of supply routes, declaring, "Today, the United States is moving firmly and decisively on a foreign policy course charted straight out of the Republican campaign of 1964."[43] He went further, however, and advocated bombing industrial complexes and the port of Haiphong, measures that he and other Republican hawks would continue to stress in the years to come. But his involvement with the war was not limited to politics. He spoke regularly with American troops in Southeast Asia through the Military Affiliate Radio System network, toured military bases in South Vietnam on five different occasions, and continued to discuss the war with his fellow air force reservists during his time on active duty.

Pressure also came consistently from Richard Nixon, although as usual it appeared in the guise of full agreement with the president. At a press conference on 1 April, for example, Nixon endorsed Johnson's policy of retaliatory raids and urged his Republican colleagues to support the administration. Later that month, Richard Berlin of Hearst Publishing told one of Johnson's advisers that Nixon "did an outstanding job particularly in praising the President and defending the President's position in Viet Nam. When he got finished someone asked him: 'Dick, have you become a campaigner for Lyndon Johnson[?]'"[44] The key, according to Nixon, was to maintain pressure on Hanoi even if the situation in Vietnam seemed to be worsening. He predicted that the continued bombing campaign would eventually force Hanoi to submit to American demands and negotiate on the basis of South Vietnamese freedom. This was vitally important because America could not afford another defeat in Asia: "[The United States] must find a way to stop indirect aggression . . . [and] must be prepared to meet the issue squarely and to commit whatever forces are necessary. I would personally support whatever measures are made to achieve this objective."[45] Nixon never accused Johnson of doing too much; his politically motivated criticisms focused on Johnson's failure to fully commit whatever means necessary to ensure an American victory. Indeed, as Stephen Ambrose argues, "Whatever move Johnson made in the direction of escalation, Nixon was always one step ahead of him, demanding more."[46]

Eisenhower and Nixon corresponded frequently during this period and agreed on the approach to take against the administration. The former president continued to express his support for Johnson's policies during the spring of 1965, but he did so by highlighting ways in which U.S. policy could improve. In a briefing with Goodpaster in early May 1965, he focused on the importance of nation building in South Vietnam. He backed the movement of additional troops to support the American air bases, but stressed that "the military operations are only a part of the story. Our task is not merely to win a military victory, although this is an essential preliminary to pacification." What America needed to do was help the Saigon regime become strong enough to govern itself effectively. Eisenhower recalled that it was said of Hannibal that he knew how to win victories but did not know how to use them; he wanted to prevent the same problem from occurring in South Vietnam.[47] Several weeks later, he reiterated his concerns to Goodpaster: "A first question to consider is what the end of all this can be." Since the United States had "'appealed to force' in South Viet-Nam . . . 'we have got to win.'" Toward this end, Goodpaster reported to Johnson, Eisenhower "thought we should not only support Vietnamese forces in action, but should on occasion undertake offensive operations ourselves."[48] Indeed, as Robert Mann has written, many members of the GOP "doubted that the president was willing to go far enough. They goaded him to ratchet up the fighting."[49]

An important contingent of Republican doves like Cooper and Aiken did not want to see the conflict escalated. Perhaps more significant, however, a substantial cohort of party members sat on the fence, making the appropriate critical comments in response to key events without definitively committing to any specific course of action. At first glance, this seems a questionable strategy. But any notion of Republican equivocation on the war in 1965 can be considered "a calculated desire not to preclude options that might become attractive at a later date."[50] The Republican Policy Committee, the "semi-official sanhedrin of governors, congressmen, and GOP bigwigs," pledged to continue to support Johnson's "firm actions to halt communist aggression" but also called for "a full-scale debate on overall foreign policy."[51] As much as Johnson wanted to avoid such an eventuality, had the crisis in the Dominican Republic in April not resulted in him dispatching U.S. forces to restore order—temporarily diverting attention from Vietnam—it is entirely possible that there could have been a major public review of American Vietnam policy.[52]

Karl Mundt agreed about the necessity of reconsidering the trajectory of U.S. actions, questioning the basis for further expansion of the American commitment under the auspices of the Tonkin Gulf resolution. The senator called the resolution "a pretty ambiguous base on which to project reasons why we continue what we are doing in Southeast Asia." He argued that the administration needed to solicit an updated grant of authority from Congress given that the parameters of U.S. involvement had changed drastically since August 1964. Jacob Javits, an unlikely ally to be sure, joined Mundt in his advocacy. Javits complained, "I want to be consulted again. . . . We should not sneak in with the use of American troops for ground combat in South Vietnam." In June 1965, he introduced a new resolution and argued that the Tonkin Gulf resolution was "out of date. . . . It was passed under wholly different circumstances." While Johnson "may have the legal authority to make these decisions," as a matter of policy "they should not be made by him alone, without congressional approval and support." Javits hoped to spark a debate in Congress to "bring out the relevant facts and clarify the issues." He submitted his resolution to the Senate Foreign Relations Committee (SFRC), where it was shelved by Fulbright—who remained loyal to the president at this point—and no further action was taken.[53] The subject of an updated congressional authorization for U.S. military actions in Vietnam arose repeatedly during the years that followed, but no such resolution ever came to a vote during Johnson's presidency, owing primarily to the efforts of the administration and its congressional allies.

Nevertheless, these sentiments found another forum during a debate in the first week in May over an additional $700 million appropriation for the American effort in Vietnam. The lack of extended discussion on the bill—administration allies limited deliberations to a mere one hour—ensured both a lack of substantive exchange and overwhelming approval. The House passed the bill 408–7, while the margin in the Senate was 88–3. The funding enabled the administration to claim another legal precedent for the war. The State Department legal adviser Leonard Meeker took the position that, by voting for the appropriation, Congress sanctioned Johnson's actions and authorized the further use of U.S. forces in Vietnam. Johnson had managed to place Congress in a catch-22: vote for the funding, or face the political consequences of "abandoning" American forces in harm's way. Such tactics, however, contributed to the emergence of the credibility gap and would come back to haunt the president as the war progressed. In the House, Peter Frelinghuysen complained, "The size of the amount requested, the way in which this resolution is being rushed through the House, and the failure of anyone who has thus far spoken today to give any details regarding the way in which this money will be used, make it difficult to make an honest evaluation of a resolution of such tremendous significance." In response to such feelings, Senator Gordon Allott (R-CO) simply stated, "The fact is that we are there and that we must win."[54]

Republican supporters of the commitment to South Vietnam wanted to win the war, but they also wanted the administration to provide details regarding how U.S. policy would accomplish that goal. In an acerbic statement released on 14 June, Melvin Laird suggested that the GOP "may be dangerously close to ending any Republican support of our present Vietnam policy." Laird emphasized that such a move was possible because "the American people do not know how far the Administration is prepared to go with large-scale use of ground forces in order to save face in Vietnam." The GOP should base its future support for the administration on the president's response to this question, he argued. "If our objective is a negotiated settlement, it is time to use other means than the needless sacrifice of American lives to attain that objective." In the meantime, he continued, the administration needed to make better use of its bombing of North Vietnam, particularly in attacking Haiphong.[55] While he definitively fell into the hawk camp in 1965, Laird was "a very specific type of hawk—he thought the United States should quickly and massively pound the enemy into submission by air and sea power—not by the use of ground troops." He believed that there were several alternatives to the administration's policies, including trade restrictions and a naval blockade, that made more strategic sense than shipping tens of thousands of troops ten thousand miles away to fight a war in Asia.[56]

A few days later, Goldwater and Hickenlooper reiterated Laird's position in speeches to the Young Republican National Convention. Goldwater said that SEATO forces from Asian countries should be used in ground operations while the American role should be primarily one of air and sea support. "Our sea and air power should strike at all the means by which the enemy either supports or commits aggression," he asserted. Hickenlooper agreed, questioning the administration's emphasis on negotiations. Both Goldwater and Hickenlooper worried that a neutralized Vietnam—an outcome that they believed would result from negotiations from a position other than overwhelming strength—would lead to Communist control of South Vietnam "virtually overnight."[57]

Attacks on the administration by Republicans, both hawks and doves, would have a significant influence on policy decisions. In June 1965 the president and his advisers seriously considered a bombing pause, in part because, as

McGeorge Bundy noted, it would "meet one persistent demand of our domestic critics and waverers." But Bundy also predicted that any halt in the ROLLING THUNDER campaign would also "arouse strong criticism among domestic hardliners—particularly among Republicans who are looking for a way to make capital out of any signs of our softness in Vietnam."[58] Johnson found himself confronting a thicket of domestic political opinion that encompassed every possible point on the political spectrum. But his desire to preclude a national debate, combined with his domestic political agenda, forced him to chart a middle course on Vietnam—doing enough to prevent disaster in Southeast Asia and pacify the hawks but not enough to incur the wrath of the doves.

Despite his efforts, however, by the end of June the situation in Vietnam had deteriorated to the point that Johnson provisionally authorized sending a ninety-five-thousand-man American force to Vietnam. Everyone recognized, as Ball wrote to the president, that "the South Vietnamese are losing the war to the Viet Cong."[59] The only way to salvage the situation, in Johnson's mind, would be to Americanize the war. Eisenhower agreed with this assessment. At a luncheon with McNamara, McGeorge Bundy, Wheeler, and Dirksen, the former president suggested candidly that additional American forces were needed in Vietnam.[60] Two days later, Eisenhower made a strong statement regarding the American commitment to the security of and freedom in Vietnam. In a telephone conversation, Johnson told Eisenhower that his advisers recommended the expansion of U.S. military forces while the State Department recommended following a modified plan until later in the year—essentially a holding pattern. The president said he would "have to call up troops" and that he guessed that was Eisenhower's view, "conforming to the advice you gave me on Wednesday." Eisenhower replied that it was his view that "when you go into a place merely to hold sections or enclaves you are paying a price and not winning." As the former president firmly believed, "When you once appeal to force in an international situation involving military help for a nation, you have to go all out! This is a war, and as long as they are putting men down there, my advice is 'do what you have to do!'" He concluded by telling Johnson, "We are not going to be run out of a free country that we helped establish."[61]

With Eisenhower standing staunchly behind him, Johnson certainly felt more secure in Americanizing the war knowing that the leading Republican figure in the country would support any action he took in Vietnam. Eisenhower's support, however, did not insulate Johnson from criticism from other members of the GOP. Representative Howard Robison (R-NY) urged both the House and the Senate to hold full-scale hearings on Vietnam in order for Congress and the American people to "know exactly where the President's policies are taking us" and to have "an effective viable foreign policy . . . founded on . . . consent and approval" after the widest possible public discussion of the issues involved.[62] A debate was the last thing Johnson wanted at this juncture. He preferred to carry out his plans under the aegis of the Tonkin Gulf resolution and the support implicit in the various appropriations bills and to reiterate the principles of consensus and supporting the president in times of crisis.

Johnson received a welcome boost from the fifty-seventh annual National Governors' Conference in Minneapolis in late June. Vietnam dominated the conversations among the state executives, especially after the president went on national television on 28 June to explain his position on the war. Immediately thereafter, Governor Carl Sanders (D-GA) proposed a resolution to put the governors on record "in support of the President of the United States and the policy he has just announced." Mark Hatfield, who had criticized Johnson's buildup in Vietnam, made it clear that he did not want to sign a blank-check statement in support of the president's policies, telling his fellow governors, "Vietnam would become quicksand for a no-win foreign policy if the people weren't given a true sense of Johnson's goals."[63] Hatfield was joined in opposing the wording of the resolution by George Romney, who stated, "I have no way of knowing if the course of action the President has taken is right or wrong. . . . [But] the lack of information is disturbing." Romney counseled waiting to vote on any resolution until the governors could be briefed at the White House the following day, but the conference decided to vote immediately. Hatfield and Romney were the only governors who opposed the measure, and it passed overwhelmingly. Following a White House briefing the next day, however, Romney changed his position (something for which he would become infamous in the months to come) and voiced general support for the resolution.[64]

Hatfield had emerged as one of the loudest GOP voices opposing the administration's policies on Vietnam. Since his keynote address in San Francisco, he had "advanced from merely questioning America's involvement in Vietnam to sharply criticizing aspects of the war." He strongly disagreed with the policy of bombing nonmilitary targets and urged that the United Nations take a leading role in pursuing peace.[65] Following the vote, Hatfield faced heated criticism from his fellow governors, many of whom had been pressured by the president to approve the resolution. This was best exemplified by the comments of Governor Haydon Burns (D-FL), who confronted Hatfield in an accusatorial tone in a press conference after the vote: "You, Mark Hatfield, . . . have done a grave disservice to your country."[66]

Hatfield obviously saw things differently. An intensely religious man whose beliefs informed his policy outlook, he referred to Vietnam as one of the most significant crises in American history. His determination to find an end to the conflict was, perhaps, the defining cause of his political career. Toward this end, he told Johnson that to "give meaning to his noble appeal for negotiation in regard to Vietnam," the United States should "publicly welcome a United Nations resolution for a cease-fire" and that American efforts in Southeast Asia and other undeveloped areas should be focused on economic development and political cooperation to combat communism rather than military means.[67] After Johnson announced the Americanization of the war on 28 July, a reporter asked the president about Hatfield's statement that the United States had "no moral right to commit the world and especially our own people to World War III unilaterally or by the decision of a few experts." Johnson's response was typical: Hatfield would come around and accept that the administration was following the correct course once he discussed the matter with him the next day.[68] Johnson's famed persuasive techniques did nothing to move Hatfield; the governor would not budge from his principled position. His criticisms would become more frequent and pointed when he moved to the Senate in 1967.

From a completely different perspective, Melvin Laird continued to assail the administration for its lack of bipartisan discussion about American Vietnam policies. He charged Johnson and Mike Mansfield with deliberately attempting "to silence the dialogue, impose conformity, and obliterate efforts to arrive at an informed and broadly supported policy toward Vietnam." He went on to accuse Mansfield of undermining discussion through partisan attacks on Gerald Ford and of changing his position on the war for political expediency. Laird referred to the president's decision in February to take the fight to North Vietnam. While Mansfield had, he stated, opposed such a move—which had been supported by Republicans—in an appearance on "Meet the Press" just a few weeks before, he fell in line with Johnson once the decision had been made. Laird also cited numerous instances from a Senate speech on 30 June 1965 in which Mansfield made "blatant distortions" of Republican positions. He concluded with a plea for the administration to "recognize the value of debate and discussion of foreign policy problems."[69] Such a debate never materialized.

Culminating weeks of intensive White House deliberations, Johnson held a bipartisan meeting at the White House to brief the congressional leadership on the evening of 27 July. He explained to the assembled group the gravity of the situation in Vietnam and laid out five possible courses of action, ranging from the use of massive power (including the use of the Strategic Air Command) to complete withdrawal. Of course, the decision to Americanize the war had already been made; Johnson held the forum to inform the congressmen and build a united front for the imminent escalation. After listening to the presentation of the options, Dirksen publicly and predictably threw his support behind the president, agreeing "fully with [his] premise. . . . We must stay in South Vietnam." Bourke Hickenlooper asserted that anything short of a result that would make South Vietnam a buffer against communism was "out of the question. . . . We win victories in war and lose in negotiations." While most of the assembled legislators supported the his actions, Johnson did face criticism from his own party as some Democrats urged him to end the commitment before it got out of hand. But, by the end of the meeting, despite reservations on both ends of the political spectrum, Johnson achieved his goal—the lawmakers agreed to support his decision.[70]

When the decision to Americanize the war is examined closely, several important points become immediately apparent. While many Democrats vocally expressed their support of the president's decision publicly, the bulk of the Republican Party maintained a conspicuous silence. Many within the GOP skirted the Vietnam issue during the first eighteen months of Johnson's presidency. While they had definite ideas about how to fight the war, a discussion of the fundamental issues involved in the American commitment seemed like something to avoid politically. As William Gibbons writes, the Republican Party was "only too willing to let the Democrats take responsibility for greater U.S. involvement in the war and the use of large-scale ground forces."[71] That was the safest course politically and allowed the party room to maneuver in the future. In addition, it is obvious that the pro forma discussions undertaken by the administration with Congress did not represent an opportunity to influence policy; rather, they were designed to enhance support for the administration's decision. As John Rhodes noted in his memoirs, Congress "'angled into' the war and never confronted the issue head-on until *after* U.S. troops had already been deployed in Vietnam."[72]

LBJ's decision to Americanize the Vietnam conflict irrevocably changed the political calculus on the war. Now that the United States had assumed primary responsibility for both the survival of South Vietnam and the military action against the NLF and North Vietnamese, everything the president did would be colored by the situation in Southeast Asia. After spending most of 1964 making every effort to keep Vietnam out of the public consciousness and the political arena, Johnson now confronted the possibility of both a partisan and an electoral backlash should his policies fail to achieve the goals laid out in his speeches. Thus, not only had the nature of American involvement in South Vietnam changed, but the potential cost of Vietnam as a political issue to the president also increased immeasurably. During the eighteen months that followed, Lyndon Johnson would have his hands full fighting on two fronts: trying to prop up the South Vietnamese politically and militarily and maintaining his domestic legislative agenda while attempting to balance constantly shifting coalitions on domestic and foreign policy.

In the wake of Johnson's announcement, General Goodpaster briefed Eisenhower again. After hearing the update on the situation in Vietnam, Eisenhower told his former aide, "It is important to avoid acting by 'driblets.' If we want to win, we should not base our action on minimum needs, but should swamp the enemy with overwhelming force." This Clausewitzian dictum became Eisenhower's common refrain throughout the war, and he consistently "reiterated his view that we do better to avoid specific numbers which tend to suggest to our enemies that we are limited in our determination." Instead, the administration should make absolutely clear to the international community that it would "do whatever is needed to defeat Communism" in Southeast Asia. Eisenhower concluded that the United States needed "to recognize that we are at war in Viet-Nam, and not base our action on 'minimum needs' or a weak strike program against the North, but to 'swamp them.'"[73] Two weeks later, Eisenhower repeated his position, accentuating "the importance of acting quickly and with a preponderance of force in military operations, and making use of the power of our forces." He also emphasized that he supported Johnson's decisions strongly.[74]

House Republicans disagreed vehemently. The following week, they issued a policy white paper titled "Vietnam: Some Neglected Aspects of the Historical Record" asserting that Democrats bore responsibility for the crisis in Vietnam. The report concluded that, under the stewardship of Kennedy and Johnson, U.S. policy in Southeast Asia had been "uncertain, providing a basis for miscalculation by the Communists. Conflicting statements have been issued. Deeds have not matched words."[75] In assessing the GOP statement, an editorial in the *Chicago Sun-Times* suggested that the white paper should be read as a political document "looking toward the 1966 congressional elections and the 1968 presidential election." Yet the editors also recognized the accuracy of many of the charges against the administration and the disparity noted between Johnson's comments during the 1964 campaign and his subsequent decisions.[76]

Reaction came swiftly from Johnson's supporters, both Republican and Democrat. Administration officials told the president that the white paper was "a pretty feeble effort and that it does not deserve top level reply."[77] Dirksen disavowed it almost immediately, suggesting that it did not represent the position of the party as a whole. Another Republican who supported the president was Ross Adair. Adair, a staunch conservative who served on the Foreign Affairs Committee as the ranking minority member, supported the war and any additional steps necessary to effect an earlier end to the fighting. He told a constituent, "As long as the President follows a strong and forthright policy in Southeast Asia . . . I shall support him. . . . The way ahead of us in Viet Nam is not easy nor will the burden be light, but—in my opinion—it is one that must be borne."[78] And, even when Johnson responded to the GOP attacks by claiming that his Vietnam policies dated to commitments made during Eisenhower's presidency,

Eisenhower himself refused to criticize the president. Gerald Ford pleaded with Eisenhower not to "undercut" congressional Republicans, but the former president told Ford and other GOP congressmen on a conference call that he always made it his business to "keep still while we are in a condition of crisis."[79]

Unfortunately for Johnson, not everyone agreed with Eisenhower and Adair. In a letter to Gerald Ford on 30 August, Paul Findley urged the Republicans to hit the president "hard and continuously" on his Vietnam policy. Findley wanted to "pin the responsibility for it clearly on LBJ and make it plain that ground war in Asia was not Republican making." Once that was accomplished, he continued, "If LBJ should find a way to pull back on ground commitment we should be in a position to claim some credit. If LBJ settles for half-measures, as seems apparent today, again he opens himself to valid criticism." Findley saw "no profit and considerable danger in advocating policies more militant than the Administration's," observing that such a tactic would simply give the president a greater range of action without risk of GOP criticism.[80]

Meanwhile, former governor Harold Stassen (R-MN) attempted to bring the administration and the GOP together in the interest of national unity and an acceptable end to the conflict. Stassen had been elected as the youngest governor of Minnesota in 1938 but left office to enlist in the navy during World War II, serving as Adm. William Halsey's assistant chief of staff. FDR selected him as a delegate to the UN conference in 1945, and Stassen later ran for president three times. The liberal Stassen believed that the United States should stay in Vietnam to "follow through in assistance to the people of South Vietnam." But he stridently opposed bombing North Vietnam, arguing that it threatened U.S. policy throughout Asia. Only a victory by the South Vietnamese on the ground, he believed, could "lead to a *military* solution with favorable long range consequences in Asia and in the world." But he did not want to see it come to that. Instead, he preferred a solution that would seat both North and South Vietnam in the United Nations.[81] The following week, Stassen sent a letter to the leading members of the GOP. In it, the former governor asserted that he was convinced that Johnson was "making major mistakes" and that the party should pressure the president to "make some new decisions." At heart, Stassen believed that an "attempt at quick military solutions will be self defeating in a tragic matter."[82]

The response to Stassen's missive reflected the lack of consensus within the GOP on the war. Hugh Scott responded that he was "in accord with our present policy in Vietnam," although he did agree that "the solution of our problems in Vietnam requires more than strictly military measures." Hickenlooper considered any negotiations undertaken without "a position of superior strength" a recipe for disaster. Gordon Allott strongly disagreed with Stassen's emphasis on the United Nations, pointing to the "heavy membership of Communist Nations," but exhibited more concern about the lack of "real access as to basic problems." He asserted, "I am not aware of anyone other than these two [Johnson and McNamara] who are determining policy . . . our own Republican situation is [as a result] completely disheartening in having access to any real communication."[83]

These fault lines within the GOP should not be surprising; they reflected the growing schism within Congress and the general public over the conflict. The *National Review* noted that the party "has floundered badly, never quite knowing whether on the one hand we should back the action over there because it is clearly anti-Communist, or whether we should oppose it because it got to be as bad as it got because of Democratic maladministration."[84] The Republican Congressional Committee's newsletter typified the confusion, suggesting that the "only way to be safe at the conference table . . . is to deal from situations of strength that come only after reducing the enemy's military potential." But it also posted a stern warning: "'The way things are going in Vietnam, it's only a matter of time before we have an American army there with South Vietnamese advisers.'"[85]

Despite the influx of tens of thousands of American troops in the summer and fall of 1965, the military and political problems in South Vietnam persisted, and the administration's goals seemed as unreachable as ever. Senator Jack Miller (R-IA), a key member of the Armed Services Committee, framed the situation appropriately. He told the Senate that, while ending the war in Vietnam through negotiations represented a "great priority," the price of peace could not ignore U.S. objectives. Those included the preservation of South Vietnamese independence and the end of North Vietnamese support for the Viet Cong. Any cessation of hostilities, he argued, "must be premised on the achievement of these minimal objectives. . . . When they realize that aggression does not pay off . . . they will agree to the President's minimal objectives in a settlement—and not before."[86] While Republicans like Miller clamored for a more vigorous policy in support of the Saigon government, administration officials worried about the need for more troops on the ground. In a 23 October memorandum discussing the policy choices facing the country, William Bundy argued for the need to increase the ceiling for U.S. forces to 325,000. He also recognized the influence of the GOP and domestic politics, noting, "We are faced with the pressures from various quarters, symbolized by General [Curtis] LeMay and the Ford, Adair line, to hit the North substantially harder."[87]

But, even as the hawks circled around the administration, opposition to the war began to coalesce around several widely respected public figures. By the end of 1965, an increasing number of Americans—including such powerful and respected voices as Hans Morgenthau, Fulbright, Cooper, Walter Lippmann, and the Reverend Martin Luther King Jr.—called for a negotiated settlement to the war involving concessions on both sides.[88] On 15 October, the International Day of Protest against the War in Vietnam witnessed teach-ins and demonstrations against the war throughout the country. Both Democratic and Republican leaders in Congress roundly derided the protests as "misguided . . . subversive acts which almost amount to treason." Ford warned that such actions could result in Communist miscalculation based on a perceived lack of unity in the United States, and Dirksen called the demonstrators "craven souls."[89] James Reston pointed to the growing discontent with the administration's conduct of war in the aftermath of the election, suggesting that, if trends continued, the conflict was "bound to have political repercussions in the Congressional elections of 1966." The Republicans "could probably have embarrassed [Johnson] more by taking a moderate line, and holding him responsible for the stalemate that is taking lives, dividing the alliance, and diverting the nation from its domestic programs." Reston concluded, "The debate is likely to go with the Republicans the longer the war goes on and the longer the casualty lists grow."[90]

That certainly was Richard Nixon's fervent hope. Nixon appeared on "Face the Nation" on CBS in late November and reasserted that the administration's conduct of the war would be a central issue in the 1968 presidential election. He accused Johnson of getting the country bogged down in a long and costly ground war and argued that U.S. military commanders in Vietnam should be given the authority to bomb all military targets in and around Hanoi. In addition, he urged the mining of Haiphong harbor. When asked about his reaction to Gerald Ford's suggestion that the United States should declare war on North Vietnam, however, Nixon expressed his strong opposition to the idea. He believed that a declaration of war would cause diplomatic complications that might lead Hanoi to turn to Moscow or Peking for open intervention in the conflict.[91] Apparently, there were limits, politically imposed to be sure, to Nixon's hawkishness.

Another theme on which Nixon focused was his adamant belief in unity. He argued in a December 1965 article in *Reader's Digest* that resolute determination would be required to achieve a victory in Vietnam. He asserted that negotiating with Hanoi before achieving military victory "would be like negotiating with Hitler before the German armies had been driven from France." He maintained that a negotiated settlement would place "our country and indeed the entire free world . . . in peril." He suggested that negotiation would be perceived by the North Vietnamese as a sign of weakness. "The lesson of all history warns us," he wrote, "that we should negotiate only when our military superiority is so convincing that we can achieve our objective at the conference table—and deny the aggressors theirs." In other words, America should negotiate only when there was nothing to negotiate. Nixon concluded, "There can be no substitute for victory when the objective is the defeat of communist aggression."[92]

Nixon's candor belied the fact that many political figures hesitated to commit themselves to any controversial stance as they began to focus on the impending elections in 1966. Stephen Ambrose described it as "the Great Political Evasion of the 1960s, the refusal on the part of Democrats and Republicans alike to confront the Vietnam issue head-on, in an up-or-down vote for war."[93] But, as the American presence in South Vietnam continued to grow without concrete signs of improvement in the situation, observers began to recognize that the war could loom large as an issue in the 1966 midterm elections. Republicans also realized, as the *Christian Science Monitor* reported, that the war "stirs people deeply" and could be the "big issue" the following November.[94] If this occurred, the polling could become a referendum on Johnson's policies. The likelihood of this occurring increased as critics of the war derided the lack of progress, failed strategy, and uncertain goals and derisively referred to the conflict as "McNamara's war" or "Johnson's war."

Not everyone agreed with this characterization, however. In an editorial on 6 January 1966, the *St. Louis Globe-Democrat* attacked those in both parties who sought to label the Vietnam conflict as "Mr. Johnson's War." The editors called it "reprehensible" for "a few Republicans and a few ambitious and self-seeking Democrats like Bobby Kennedy, to try to make political capital of the war" at the expense of the country's best interests.[95] While the editorial apologized for Johnson's actions in Vietnam more than necessary, the underlying sentiment remains accurate. History clearly demonstrates that the conflict in Vietnam was America's war, regardless of the political ramifications for either party. Even Richard Nixon refused to place the full responsibility for the war at Johnson's feet.

John Sherman Cooper declined to pin the label on the president as well. Despite failing to convince the majority of his party or the president of the validity of his viewpoint, Cooper consistently urged a political solution to the conflict. He released a statement in late December regarding the bombing pause: "The reports of proposals to extend the truce in Vietnam mean that a test is ahead over the willingness of North Vietnam to negotiate. . . . This will be a decisive period, toward either broad negotiations or a larger extension of the war. The action of the President in suspending the bombing of North Vietnam confirms the willingness of our country to negotiate, and he should be supported."[96] The conviction that a military solution to the war could never succeed was buttressed when Cooper visited South Vietnam in December 1965 and January 1966. In January, as the Johnson administration made clear it planned to resume bombing North Vietnam, he expressed strong opposition and urged Johnson to seek a negotiated peace. During a meeting in the Oval Office on 26 January 1966, he approached the president with his views. When Johnson would give no assurances that he would fully pursue a negotiated settlement, Cooper spoke forcefully on the Senate floor that afternoon to publicly call for the immediate beginning of peace talks: "Negotiations, not escalation, should be the dominant theme of our activity now." The process, he argued, could start with a cease-fire—supervised and enforced by the United Nations—lasting up to five years, after which there would be national elections.[97]

Cooper added that the Viet Cong would have to be included in any negotiations because, "distasteful as it is, the Vietcong are the main fighters—they are doing the bulk of the fighting. They are supplied, without question, by North Vietnam, and by both men and supplies and with weapons from China." "But," he admitted, "they are the backbone of the fighting in Vietnam and if we ever reach negotiations they will have to be included."[98] Above all, he stated, Americanization of the war was a mistake that had to be stopped:

> This is essentially a political and not a military conflict. It is a battle in Vietnam for the hearts and minds of the Vietnamese. It must be limited to Vietnam, and be fought by the Vietnamese if we are to have any realistic hope of an acceptable settlement. . . . It is crucial that the war in Vietnam not be allowed to escalate further. Now is the time to make every conscientious effort to de-escalate the conflict. For the escalation there is no practical hope of achieving our aims in that unfortunate country and the very real possibility of an Asian wide war in which America would waste her resources and young men in a slaughter that could achieve nothing but these desperate conditions of chaos ideal for the spread of communism.[99]

Although a powerful appeal for an alternative to the present situation, Cooper's speech fell on deaf ears in the administration. The bombing resumed, and the buildup of American forces continued.

Cooper and his colleagues on the SFRC met in executive session on 11 January to hear a report from Mansfield and Aiken on their recent tour of Asia. The senators reported that, though "considerable ground" had been lost in Vietnam over the past three years, the United States had succeeded in "preventing a collapse" of the Saigon regime. In order to reverse the situation, however, additional U.S. forces would be required. The report posited, "It is not too early to begin to contemplate the need for a total of upwards of 700,000." Mansfield warned that the struggle would continue "as long as North Vietnam wants it to go on and has the means to pursue it." In summary, he asserted, "This is a conflict in which all the choices open to us are bad choices. We stand to lose in Viet Nam by restraint; but we stand to lose far more at home and throughout the world by the pursuit of an elusive and ephemeral objective in Vietnam."[100]

Response to the pessimistic assessment was mixed, reflecting the divisions extant among Republicans on the committee. Bourke Hickenlooper asserted, "A decision is going to have to be made. Do we either mark time and keep on this endless pushing and shoving and backing up and probing, or will a decision have to go on the other side, on an all-out give 'em hell and complete destruction philosophy?" Senator Clifford Case (R-NJ), the newest Republican on the committee, complained that private hearings were not the answer; what was needed was to find "some logical, clear, feasible objective" to end the war in a bipartisan and public way.[101]

The White House, predictably, worried about the report's conclusions and its implications for domestic support of the war. Johnson instructed George Ball to solicit proposals from the committee, telling him, "Stress the point of putting the solution up to them. We don't want to destroy the morale of our people." Both Fulbright and Hickenlooper expressed their belief that the administration needed to develop a better understanding and explanation of American objectives in Vietnam.[102] Case took issue with the Mansfield-Aiken report in a speech to the New Jersey Chamber of Commerce on 4 February 1966. He refused to accept the conclusion that the country must accept either indefinite expansion of the war or any terms offered by Hanoi. Defining himself as neither a hawk nor a dove, he pressed the administration to let the American people know what they faced and that it "makes sense." He concluded by reiterating a common theme among Republicans during the mid-1960s: "On these matters, one voice, and one voice only, can speak for our Government, and that is the voice of the President of the United States."[103] Case was correct; only Johnson spoke for the United States. But Republicans continued to speak for themselves in criticizing the administration. Jack Miller, recently returned from a visit to Vietnam himself, called for an end to bombing restrictions. He said that the "toe nibbling" strikes had failed and called for attacks on key bridges, power plants, petroleum distribution centers, and the port of Haiphong. "Unless the enemy's logistics system is much more severely impeded," he concluded, "we can expect a longer and more costly ground war in the south."[104]

The pessimism displayed by the report mirrored the rising dissent within Congress, particularly among Democrats. Consider the influential members of the president's party who opposed the war. Mansfield had urged neutralization and negotiations for two years. Fulbright would shortly break with the administration and begin hearings about American involvement in the war. These two were joined by a significant number of other Democratic senators in expressing their concerns about escalation and the dim prospects for U.S. objectives. As a result, support for the war shifted and transcended partisan lines. The old coalition of conservative Southern Democrats and Republicans, which had thwarted so many of Kennedy's domestic initiatives and had stood as an obstacle to the 1964 Civil Rights Act, now stood as LBJ's strongest bastion of support for the war. Complicating matters was the fact that many liberals and moderates in both parties who opposed the war remained supportive of the president's Great Society program, whereas the conservatives who backed Johnson in Vietnam argued against increasing domestic expenditures in order to prosecute the war more effectively. Thus, the president found himself in the unenviable position of having to court multiple competing constituencies simultaneously in order to retain support for the Vietnam conflict and his domestic agenda, a challenge that taxed the resources of the administration and its politically adept leader.

Johnson's State of the Union address, delivered the day after Mansfield and Aiken presented their report to Congress, featured the Vietnam situation prominently. LBJ devoted over half the speech to the war, a sharp contrast from the 1965 State of the Union address, in which he made only brief references to the conflict. He acknowledged that Vietnam "must be the center of our concerns" but refused to accept that the Communists could "win a victory over the desires and the intentions of all the American people." Of course, "all" the American people did not support the administration's war effort, which undercut the president's argument. Undeterred, Johnson explained that the United States fought for freedom and self-determination for South Vietnam—conveniently leaving aside the more pragmatic issues at stake such as U.S. credibility and the Cold War—and argued that America was "mighty enough, its society healthy enough, its people are strong enough, to pursue [its] goals in the rest of the world while still building a Great Society here at home."[105]

The official GOP response, delivered by Dirksen a few days later, underscored Johnson's position. The minority leader declared, "Let us be crystal clear. Viet Nam is not our war. But we pledged ourselves to help a small nation. Our word was given. We are there to keep our word." In order to do so, the country should pursue both military victory and efforts at peace, but Dirksen concluded, "There is, after all, no substitute for victory."[106] Early in 1966, prominent Republicans reasserted their aggressive posture on the war. Hugh Scott rejected the idea of considering a negotiated settlement that provided for anything less than total capitulation by the Viet Cong, deriding the "quitnik policy" within the Democratic Party. As the *New Republic* perceptively observed, Republican attacks served to narrow Johnson's options and make escalation of the conflict more likely. The GOP was "prepared to sympathize with all who" had become "tired of the war" while dispensing a "severe patriotic drubbing" to those who favored a negotiated settlement with the Viet Cong.[107] But, once again, the lack of party unity was striking. George Romney, who had begun to have more serious doubts about the U.S. commitment to Saigon, commented after the speech, "If we should face the alternative of further military commitment in South Vietnam to the point where it ceases to be a support of South Vietnam's defensive efforts to resist and drive the aggressors out, and it's going to become an American war." There should, he felt, be a full-scale debate in Congress and a formal consideration of a declaration of war.[108]

Some influential Republicans were content to leave the attacks on Johnson to opponents of the war within his own party. As William White reported in the *Washington Post,* this group of senior advisers, fund-raisers, and other behind-the-scenes figures wondered, "Why should we go after Johnson when fellows in his own party are doing a job on him?" Death by a thousand Democratic cuts seemed preferable to going on the record against the administration's policies and would leave the GOP flexible going into the midterm elections.[109] It is quite likely that one of these unnamed Republicans was Richard Nixon. In a speech in New York, Nixon argued that Republicans should support the president and, indeed, had been doing so more strongly than the Democrats. "From a political standpoint," he asserted, "it would be tempting to join the Democratic critics. By doing so we would win politically either way. After all, if the policy succeeds, the President is going to take the credit." "If it fails," he continued, "we then would have been among the critics. But the security of the United States and the cause of peace must come above partisan politics."[110]

At a meeting at the White House on 25 January 1966, Dirksen echoed Nixon and reiterated his support of the administration. He declared that to withdraw from Vietnam would be a "disaster" and told the president, "If we are not winning now, let's do what is necessary to win. I don't believe you have any other choice. I believe the country will support you."[111] Bourke Hickenlooper put Vietnam's place in the larger battle against communism into perspective. "If only Vietnam were concerned," he stated, "I'd get out. But we are confronting the Communist world. Either get out or lick them. I've been restless with our light bombing. If we win, we must take out their ability to make war."[112] John Sherman Cooper agreed with Hickenlooper to a certain extent. While he believed that "negotiations, not escalation, should be the dominant theme of our activity now," he admitted that the United States might have to escalate if efforts to negotiate an end to the war failed. Cooper also took his position a step further, arguing that the Viet Cong should be included in the talks "because it is obvious that neither negotiations nor a settlement are possible without their inclusion. . . . This is essentially a political and not a military conflict."[113] The truth of that statement, at least from a domestic political perspective, became glaringly apparent that week.

In early February, Fulbright initiated nationally televised hearings on the war under the authority of the SFRC, which he chaired. Fulbright and his allies on the committee, including Wayne Morse and Albert Gore Sr. (D-TN), hoped to "produce a true national debate and sufficient public pressure to contain the war within manageable limits and to induce a negotiated settlement."[114] There had been calls for congressional hearings on the war for months. Jacob Javits suggested in mid-1965 that the Senate needed to "reclaim its status as an 'independent voice' rather than limping along as a 'Presidential echo.'" Javits's resolution, along with lobbying from Frank Church (D-ID), SFRC chief of staff Carl Marcy, and others, was buried by Fulbright, who held out hopes of privately influencing Johnson. When Fulbright discovered that the president could not be persuaded, he began to discuss the need for hearings with his staff.[115]

Seth Tillman, a member of the SFRC staff, sent Fulbright a memorandum suggesting that "public hearings on Vietnam are not only *appropriate* . . . but can even be regarded as a Committee *responsibility*." Fulbright agreed, but, before committing to the hearings, he sounded out the two senior Republicans on the committee—Hickenlooper and Aiken—as well as Mansfield in his capacity as majority leader at the meeting at which the Mansfield-Aiken report was presented. Hickenlooper and Mansfield resisted the notion of public hearings, arguing that a closed session would allow the members of the SFRC to express themselves more freely. But pressure from other senators who hoped to force the administration into a comprehensive debate on U.S. policy convinced Fulbright that the public hearings should be held. Thus, on 3 February, the SFRC met in closed session and agreed to hold the public hearings, leaving the selection of the witness list to Fulbright and Hickenlooper.[116]

For the next three weeks, the committee questioned key members of the administration, including Dean Rusk and Maxwell Taylor as well as retired lieutenant general James Gavin and George Kennan, the venerable father of containment. Remarkably for the days before C-SPAN, the hearings received extensive, gavel-to-gavel television coverage on all three networks, allowing the American people to get their first true glimpse of the tensions between the administration and Congress. Most of the Democrats on the committee challenged the witnesses on virtually the entire spectrum of issues related to the war, pressing Rusk especially hard on the trajectory of U.S. policy, the prospects for success in Southeast Asia, and the question of the latitude granted the president to escalate the conflict under the Tonkin Gulf resolution. In contrast, the Republicans, with the possible exception of Aiken, generally backed the administration's position, although it was by no means a full vote of confidence.[117]

The Fulbright hearings put the administration at a distinct disadvantage. On the SFRC, critics of Johnson's Vietnam policy outnumbered its defenders and presented a much more coherent line of attack. Indeed, as Gary Stone argues in his study of the Senate and Vietnam during the Johnson presidency, "Whatever hope the administration's supporters might have had of equalizing the relationship of forces within the committee room rested with the Republicans." Yet Stone also points out that Republicans "did much more to hurt than help the administration," accusing Johnson of "lacking clear goals or a coherent strategy." The GOP showed a "capacity to move easily between hawkish and dovish positions, all the while attacking the administration for its lack of clarity."[118]

The immediate impact of the hearings was an intensification of public interest in the war and the increasing legitimacy of criticism. No longer was opposition to the conflict the purview of fringe political figures like Wayne Morse or Eugene Siler. Now some of the most recognizable names in American politics had appeared on national television asking pointed and skeptical questions about the U.S. commitment to Saigon. As David Halberstam noted, the hearings "ended more than a generation of assumed executive branch omniscience in foreign policy, and congressional acquiescence to that omniscience." Halberstam also observed that "dissent was steadily more respectable" in the wake of the hearings; indeed, polling data demonstrate that support for the war would begin a steady decline in the months that followed.[119] For the administration, the hearings created an atmosphere of uncertainty and questioning about its Vietnam policy that replaced the complacency and acceptance that had existed in the public and media up to this point. Lyndon Johnson now had to grapple not only with instability in South Vietnam but also with an increasingly cantankerous press, a reinvigorated Congress, and a public looking for answers.

Shortly after the hearings concluded, John Sherman Cooper argued that the conflict in Vietnam should be submitted to the United Nations for mediation. Although not completely sold on this idea, Eisenhower expressed a willingness to at least consider the proposal. In a letter to Arthur Goldberg, the U.S. ambassador to the United Nations, the former president stated, "I think that it was probably desirable to bring the Viet-Nam situation into the Security Council, if for no other reason than that of showing how seriously we are striving to reach a peaceful solution that is both honorable and workable." Yet he cautioned that any U.N.-brokered agreement "will have to assure complete justice to South Viet-Nam; it must comprise something more than a bundle of Communist promises—which are always violated," an article of faith he had adopted during his presidency.[120] Even if such an agreement could be concluded, however, many Republicans stood firmly against allowing the NLF any place in South Vietnam.

As John Tower facetiously observed, "Rewarding the Communists with a place in a South Vietnamese government would make about as much sense as giving the Mafia a seat on the President's Crime Commission."[121]

Seeking a way to counter the growing commitment to Vietnam, opponents questioned the legal basis for American involvement. While some focused on the Tonkin Gulf resolution, Clifford Case argued that to "repeal that resolution today would make no sense unless one feels, as some of my colleagues may feel, that it is time for a vote of *no* confidence in the President. That is not my view."[122] Others openly considered pursuing a declaration of war. Ross Adair told a constituent, "There are many things that are unclear about our policy there. One way to clarify the matter would be a declaration of war, but it appears to me that the President is not likely to ask for such a declaration at this time."[123] Yet declaring war against North Vietnam never received serious consideration either at the White House or on Capitol Hill. In addition to the pointed and probing debate that such a proposal would engender—something the administration still wanted to avoid at all costs—fears of Chinese and Soviet intervention precluded such a move. As a result, the war continued under the tenuous authority of the Tonkin Gulf resolution, the various appropriations bills, and the country's commitment under the SEATO agreement.

One of the common themes sounded by the Republican Party during the second half of the 1960s was the deep division over the Vietnam War that plagued the Democratic Party. The Republican Policy Committee addressed this problem in a statement on 2 March 1966. The lack of unity among Democrats had the effect of "prolonging the war, undermining the morale of our fighting men, and encouraging the Communist aggressor." Another result of the fractured party was that the administration's position on the war "continues to be marred by indecision, sudden change and frequent reinterpretation. Under the circumstances, it is little wonder that the enemy has been encouraged, our friends dismayed, and the national unity that can do more to bring about peace negotiations than almost any other thing delayed." The solution, the committee concluded, would be for the president to "disavow" the dissenters and "take command of his party."[124] But Johnson could not afford to publicly attack the disillusioned members of the Democratic Party, most of whom he needed to shore up support for his domestic priorities. Instead, he relied on his powers of persuasion in private conversations and the support of his Republican allies in Congress.

Credibility became a key focal point for the Republicans in their criticisms of the administration. Speaking to a gathering of GOP congressional staffers crafting strategy for the midterm elections, Nixon pointed out that the significance of Vietnam as a campaign issue would vary from race to race and that, as a result, "there need not be a detailed Republican position applicable to all and each district." When it became an issue, Nixon believed that Republicans should stress Democratic mismanagement of the war, the credibility gap, and "the failure to move strongly earlier when Republicans urged this."[125] In a speech in Chicago, John Byrnes commented on the "strange record [the administration] has compiled of misleading the American people on the problems involved and our intentions" in Vietnam. This pattern of deception, Byrnes continued, dated to the 1964 campaign, when Johnson gave the country "the impression that there would be no enlargement of our military activities there." Subsequently, Congress and the public had "been consistently misled by Administration officials. . . . It is no wonder that Washington is talking about, and Americans are feeling, a 'crisis of credibility.'" As Milward Simpson put it, "Utter candor is not a hallmark of this Administration."[126] This pattern of dissembling led Gerald Ford to pontificate, "There's no longer a 'Credibility GAP'—it's become a Credibility CANYON!—and it's widening between the Johnson-Humphrey Administration and the American people with every week that goes by."[127]

Conservatives wasted little time in exploiting Johnson's problems. In March 1966, the right-wing radio commentator Fulton Lewis received a call from a listener (quoting the comedian Mort Sahl) that summarized how the conservative wing of the party felt about Johnson and Vietnam: "In 1964 I was told that if I voted for Barry Goldwater it would mean massive escalation of the war in Vietnam and defoliation of the jungles. Well, I did vote for Goldwater, and sure enough it happened."[128] Indeed, GOP conservatives took great satisfaction in the increased American military commitment to South Vietnam. As the war progressed, they attacked Johnson for his restraint in conducting the war and for his failure to explicitly define the goals and objectives of his policy. Karl Mundt commented, "I am not just sure yet how you fight that kind of war successfully under Marquis of Queensbury rules which are applicable only to us. . . . I would like to win a war without killing, but I do not think you can play it like you play touch football." Success depended on "using our strength instead of applying our weakness."[129]

John Tower was one of these conservatives. An expert on military affairs who visited Vietnam frequently during the war, Tower consistently lobbied for a stronger and more focused military effort in South Vietnam. He contended, "[The United States] must use the very great power we possess . . . to destroy the will of the enemy to wage war against South Vietnam. . . . When we prove to him that war is a costly instrument of national policy, then ultimately we can negotiate a reasonable peace with honor and in the process discourage the precipitation of any further wars of 'national liberation.'" Joining Tower were Gerald Ford, who charged the administration with "shocking mismanagement"

13 May 1966: "The Agony and the Ecstasy"

of the war, and Strom Thurmond, who suggested, "We have stopped short of a determination to achieve a military victory over the communist aggressors as quickly as possible."[130] This was too much for Dirksen to swallow. He leaped to the administration's defense, asking, "What mismanagement? I don't know that there has been shocking mismanagement. I don't deliver a judgment like that unless I have some hard facts."[131] The split between the two Republican leaders led one newspaper to editorialize, "Never has the Republican party been so dangerously fragmented as it is today. Never has it been in greater need of unity."[132]

Not only were the hawks in the party divided, but Cooper's constant advocacy of negotiations began to gain greater national attention. In April 1966, after Cooper declared publicly that the United States had long since fulfilled any obligation to the Saigon regime that it might have had and that it would be foolish to fight on behalf of a people who would not fight for themselves, the *New York Times* called him a man "whose views command respect on both sides of the aisle." The paper spoke of the growing misgivings in the Senate and speculated that the moderate and sober Cooper could pull many fence-sitting lawmakers to his side.[133]

The *Christian Science Monitor* addressed the problem of unity in early April. Although prognosticators believed that the GOP would make strong gains in the midterm elections, concerns lingered about how or whether the party would incorporate the war into its campaign strategy. The plan to make Vietnam a partisan issue, the paper argued, "could dilute, even destroy the party's bright prospects. . . . If the Republicans commit the mistake of trying to make a partisan brew out of Vietnam, they will . . . throw away one of the best things they can possess. Their greatest asset is that they now stand united on Vietnam." If candidates took the advice of the Republican Congressional Campaign Committee, which advocated a more hawkish stance on the war, however, Republicans would "lose far more votes than they would gain, and would divide the GOP over Vietnam the way the Democratic party in Congress is already divided."[134]

Poll numbers indicated that, at least at the grassroots level, the Republican Party did not agree with the *Monitor*'s assessment. A Gallup survey of Republican county chairmen across the nation found that 44 percent believed that the best issue for the GOP in 1966 would be the Vietnam War. When asked to be more specific, 47 percent believed that the United States should be more aggressive, 30 percent considered that the war was being mismanaged, as Ford had suggested, and only 8 percent believed that the country should withdraw from South Vietnam.[135] The results of the poll would lead one to believe that Vietnam would play a major role in the 1966 midterm elections. Yet events and pragmatism relegated the war to relatively insignificant status during the campaign. The "buzzwords 'hawk' and 'dove' were too simplistic to describe Laird and most of his generation. They had fought and won a world war, and had paid a dear price for victory." While they were "not afraid to stand up against tyranny . . . experience had taught them that the end had to justify the sacrifice."[136]

Not everyone in the party was as outspoken as Laird. The uncertainty about the situation in Vietnam did not lend itself to expressions of principle for many Republicans facing reelection campaigns in the fall. Indeed, some observers believed that the failure of the GOP to take a decisive stand against the war represented an opportunity lost. *Newsweek*'s Emmet John Hughes wrote, "[Vietnam] could have been seized by spirited and conscientious Republicanism. . . . What would have been more politically rational than a Republican opposition sharply questioning from the outset a military commitment so carelessly calculated?"[137] Similarly, Fulbright told Harold Stassen, "The Republicans should be carrying more of the burden of debate regarding our foreign policy, rather than accepting it so quietly."[138] While it is true that GOP opposition to the conflict remained muted in 1966, political pragmatism took precedence given the lack of clear signals from the American public about the war and the firm desire to reconstruct the party nationally.

Meanwhile, the administration continued to rely heavily on support from Eisenhower for its policies. Johnson constantly tried to exploit Eisenhower's presidential and military experiences and willingness to publicly support the administration, and Eisenhower generally allowed him to do so. In June he told Goodpaster that he supported "hitting the enemy where it hurts once the decision is made to resort to force, giving the widest possible authority to the commander in the field." He also expressed his concern over the possibility that "the feeling may become widespread among our people that the war is simply dragging on inconclusively."[139] As the commander of allied forces in World War II, and later as president, Eisenhower enjoyed unquestioned obedience from his subordinates and, to a large degree, the support of the public. Thus, it should not be surprising that he believed that the United States could not retreat from its announced objectives in Vietnam. As he told Arthur Goldberg in September, "I have no patience whatsoever with the people that want to pull out of Vietnam at once, or are otherwise prepared to surrender principle." "Once we should admit that aggression pays off," he asserted, "we can expect an intensification of Communist efforts to dominate the world."[140] Yet he also realized that the war "is not something that can go on and on, but is something that should rather be brought to an end as soon as possible." He feared that the American public would "get tired" if the conflict continued "with no end in sight."[141]

Eisenhower's concerns were not unfounded. Roscoe Drummond warned that Republicans faced a "grave risk" of turning their "biggest campaign asset—Vietnam—into a political liability unless they do better in showing what they would do about it. Everyone can see that there is political hay to be harvested in the elections from the Vietnam issue." Unfortunately, he continued, the GOP position had two major weaknesses: a lack of a clear and coherent proposal of how the party would handle things differently and the armchair strategists. These problems "could end by convincing many voters that the party was being irresponsible and reckless." Vietnam would, if handled properly, be "an inevitable issue for the GOP in the elections this fall." But, he concluded, "The Republican leadership has got to begin now to prepare the party with a coherent stance . . . to persuade the voters that more Republicans in Congress would mean a better conduct of the war, not worse."[142]

Harold Stassen inserted himself into the debate again in late July to propose just such a strategy. In a letter to the editor published in the *Washington Post* and other newspapers (and referenced in *Time* and a *New York Times* editorial), Stassen proposed a "Fourth Alternative"—the first three were to continue present administration policy, to further expand and intensify the U.S. military effort, and to withdraw from Vietnam—for resolving the Vietnam conflict. The United States should "deliberately take all feasible measures to quiet down the war; to de-escalate it; to change the priority emphasis to the economic, educational, social, and political factors; and to contemplate a decade or more of competition of systems in Vietnam." In addition, both Vietnams would be admitted into the United Nations in order to facilitate "changing the struggle into one of competition rather than of military action." Under this proposal, bombing and other military action would be limited to defensive measures and amnesty extended to members of the NLF.[143] Unfortunately for Stassen, like so many other proposals during this period, his outline for ending the conflict failed to gain any traction and quickly faded into oblivion.

In July 1966, the White House arranged for fourteen members of the House of Representatives who supported the war to visit Vietnam and then report their findings directly to the president. According to Tim Lee Carter (R-KY), the senior Republican on the trip, the group was supposed to "say the war's going all right, when we got back." But things did not go quite as scripted. When asked by the president about his perception of the war effort at the White House after returning from Vietnam, Carter asserted, "No, Mr. President, you're not winning the war." Johnson was "shocked" at Carter's comments given the latter's conservative background and previous support of the war effort. But, by August 1967, Carter was calling for the withdrawal of American forces from Vietnam on the House floor in a speech that William Gibbons notes "was viewed as a sign of the trend of congressional and public opinion."[144] Carter's defection signified an ominous development for the administration. As support for his policies eroded, Johnson must have been tempted to shift his resources and political capital to a less politically dangerous issue. Unfortunately for LBJ, the Republicans would not allow him to do so.

On August 9, the Republican National Committee released another white paper, once again bringing the credibility issue to center stage. The lack of support for the administration's Vietnam policies, the report argued, resulted from "its failures to inspire confidence in its utterances. . . . From the beginning, official government pronouncements have frequently had little similarity to the grim realities of the Vietnam conflict." Instead, the public "was being treated to a steady diet of rosy predictions and misleading statements." The core problem, the committee concluded, was that the American people "never know what they don't know—they never know what they miss."[145] It sounded like the GOP intended to use the Vietnam issue against the Democrats in the midterm elections, focusing on the administration's credibility problems and the lack of noticeable progress on the ground. Making that assumption, however, proved to be premature to say the least.

Jeremy Campbell of the *London Evening Standard* reported that the "Brains of the Republican Party, or at least its shrewder strategists on Capitol Hill," suggested to GOP candidates that "it may be a serious tactical mistake to make the war in Vietnam a principal campaign issue" in November. Campbell opined that it was "a remarkable action for a minority party in need of votes to take. For it has but a virtual *cordon sanitaire* around the most vulnerable and tempting weakness of the Democrats." So why, then, did the GOP leadership make this suggestion? Campbell believed that they were "convinced that the President intends to neutralize the war as an election issue by making a major peace offer to North Viet Nam in the autumn." The "wariness which is almost palpable among informed Republican politicians and the frank assumption that the great conjuror in the White House will produce a bunny of some kind from the hat by November are worth noting."[146]

But the feared "October surprise" did not materialize, at least in the way Republicans anticipated. It would be Richard Nixon who startled the political world as the election drew closer. After spending two years zealously advocating escalation, Nixon suddenly reversed himself on one issue: negotiations. On 23 August 1966, following a meeting with a group of Republican senators arranged by Thruston Morton, the former vice president announced his support for an all-Asian peace conference. The proposed summit, which also had been supported publicly by Eisenhower and had been gaining currency during the summer, would include both China and North Vietnam. Yet Nixon and his Republican colleagues also maintained that the war should continue to be prosecuted energetically while the talks proceeded. He called for America's European allies to join in an economic embargo against North Vietnam. Surprisingly, he also questioned the effectiveness of bombing Hanoi and other important targets, contending that such actions could possibly widen the war.[147] Superficially, this about-face on the question of Hanoi's status as a legitimate target seems to be contradictory. But the Machiavellian Nixon shrewdly hedged his bets with one eye on the 1968 nomination.

Richard Nixon walked a tightrope during the late summer and early fall of 1966. On the one hand, his attacks on Johnson continued unabated. On the other, he was positioning himself as a voice of reason in the face of an increasingly unpopular and escalating war. His willingness to support the peace conference and the subtle foreshadowing of what would become his Vietnamization policy showed that he was leaving his options open; the election results would give him the signals he needed on what road to take after November. In addition, he recognized that there were political risks for him in the 1966 election. If the Republican Party went down in defeat or even failed to make a reasonable comeback, the press and his political competitors within the GOP would be able to say that Nixon, the perennial loser, had once again dragged the party down to defeat, effectively killing his presidential ambitions in 1968. Yet the potential dividends were too tempting to pass up. If a Nixon-led campaign managed to achieve a Republican resurgence in the congressional and local elections, he would receive the adulation and gratitude of the party faithful that could lead to a second presidential campaign two years later.[148] So he challenged Johnson at every opportunity, cognizant of the potential pitfalls in his path, and remained aware of the direction the political winds were blowing.

An interview with *U.S. News and World Report* on 3 October 1966 typified the nature of the verbal barbs that Nixon lobbed at Johnson. As previously noted, Nixon's attacks were formulaic; he would state his support for the president and then proceed to attack the administration for its policy shortcomings. William Bundy has aptly characterized Nixon's rhetorical tactics as "maximum innuendo and pious dissociation."[149] In this instance, he pointed out that the administration's response to North Vietnamese aggression was too little and too late. He pointed out that, a year and a half earlier, Republicans had urged the use of airpower against strategic military targets north of the seventeenth parallel. By the time Johnson decided to use airpower, Nixon contended, the North Vietnamese had been forewarned and had dispersed many of the key targets. He also rebuked the president for failing to unite the American people. In particular, he focused on Johnson's failure to maintain the Democratic Party's support for the war, the first time "a President has been unable to unite his own party behind the war effort." Nixon, with characteristic hyperbole, described this as "the greatest single foreign-policy failure of any American war President in history." He argued that, if the American people stood undivided behind the war effort, not only would the United States win the war, but the administration would also be enabled to obtain the support of its recalcitrant European allies.[150]

On all these points, Nixon agreed with Eisenhower, and, in many ways, they formed a tag team to keep the administration on its toes. Keeping the war as the foremost priority for the administration was one of Eisenhower's main concerns during this period. Eisenhower and Johnson spoke by telephone on 3 October 1966, and the former president suggested that winning the war in Vietnam should be the first priority above poverty programs, reaching the moon, or other things. In keeping with his established practice, he also stated that, although many people "want me to say publicly how to win the war—I won't do it—I won't divide the United States when it needs unity—I wish you to know how annoying all of this is to me."[151] Eisenhower did not feel that it was his place to subvert the administration publicly, but privately he did all he could to convince Johnson to remain focused and committed to the war effort.

In a letter to Nixon shortly after this conversation, Eisenhower condemned opponents of the war, specifically Mansfield and Javits, for their lack of understanding of the conflict and for not supporting the president: "Frankly, it seems that the Vietnam War is creating more whimperings and whinings from some frustrated partisans than it's inspiring a unification of all America in the solution of a national problem." These partisan problems were not the only concerns Eisenhower had. He began to see signs that the administration might be losing its determination to employ all its resources to win the war. He wrote to Nixon again just prior to the Manila conference and urged his former vice president to "keep hitting!" the administration for its "hesitation, indecision, and even timidity" in conducting the war.[152] Nixon and Eisenhower used almost identical hawkish rhetoric during the months following the escalation decision. The key difference between them, however, was that Nixon was less reluctant—indeed, was quite eager—to criticize Johnson and his policies publicly in his speeches and writings.

And, to be sure, Johnson deserved censure for his actions in 1965 and 1966. After delaying key decisions about the U.S. commitment in Southeast Asia for a year, he opened the Pandora's box of escalation and Americanization of the conflict. Unlike his mythological predecessor, however, LBJ let the options go incrementally rather than all at once. But the effect was similar—if anything, the slow and torturous deliberative process the administration undertook before making its final decision only made things worse. The United States now faced an open-ended war with a committed enemy in Hanoi and the NLF with no foreseeable resolution. Meanwhile, the president would face domestic political threats to his policy on multiple fronts that not only restricted his options in both foreign and domestic policy but also made it virtually impossible to make decisions based solely on the military and political situation in South Vietnam. Pandora, at least, had hope left in her box. LBJ must have been jealous as the midterm elections in 1966 approached.

# CHAPTER 4

# Confronting the Hydra

## LBJ on the Defensive, 1966–1967

Debate on public issues should be uninhibited, robust, and wide open, and that . . . may well include vehement, caustic, and sometimes unpleasantly sharp attacks on government and public officials.
—William J. Brennan Jr., *New York Times v. Sullivan* (1964)

The man who adapts his course of action to the nature of the times will succeed and, likewise, . . . the man who sets his course of action out of tune with the times will come to grief.
—Niccolò Machiavelli, *The Prince*

The reaction to the Americanization of the Vietnam conflict posed serious political problems for the president. Like Heracles confronting the Hydra—the mythical beast that would grow two heads when one was severed—Johnson found himself dealing with opposition to his policies from both conservatives and liberals. In what became a political juggling act of monumental proportions, the president battled a multiheaded opposition on Vietnam as the war evolved. As he fought the forces advocating negotiations or withdrawal, he had to simultaneously fend off those who pushed for a more aggressive approach in Vietnam. Every time he put out one brush fire, several more would flare up, leaving him constantly on the defensive. But, because Vietnam was not his only concern, he was forced to attempt to placate both sides of the debate to preserve as much support for his domestic agenda as possible. What resulted was a middle course that lacked the ability to resolve the conflict. This chapter will focus on LBJ's efforts to manage these countervailing forces from the 1966 midterm elections, which brought a number of influential GOP doves into office, to the eve of the 1968 presidential election.

The 1966 election campaign provided the Republicans with an opportunity to regain some of the ground they lost in 1964 and position the party for 1968. Although Vietnam would not play a decisive role in every instance, it did loom in the background and contributed significantly to several key congressional races. The GOP leadership, including Gerald Ford and Melvin Laird, generally advised candidates not to rely exclusively on Vietnam as a wedge issue in their campaigns and tended to shy away from taking advantage of the administration's difficulties. Ford and Laird agreed, however, that the war could play a pivotal role in some races. Ford went so far as to comment that he believed that "Vietnam [was] going to be a liability to any incumbent" in November.[1]

The Democrats also realized the potential the war had for causing electoral problems. Frederick Dutton told Bill Moyers that the party was unraveling in large part because of Vietnam, which he said was "a fierce symbol and ulcer eating away at the local level support for moderate Democrats like [California Governor Pat] Brown. . . . The strength of feeling over it . . . overrides any public issue or political tie in the state at present." Perhaps the soundest advice came from Representative Wayne Hays (D-OH): "Keep your head down, don't get tangled up in the row over Vietnam if you want to come through the '66 election."[2] Still, some candidates did make an effort to use the issue to their advantage. The GOP congressional hopeful George H. W. Bush of Texas emphasized his support of "a policy of firmness against Communist aggression and a utilization of tactics which will enable American fighting men to win the war" and called unilateral withdrawal "unthinkable" during his campaign.[3]

The contradictory advice given by Republicans and Democrats to their candidates reflected the uncertainty that prevailed about the war. And, despite the public opposition of a few and the private doubts of many on Capitol Hill, congressional opinion remained generally supportive of the administration on Vietnam in the fall of 1966. A *Congressional Quarterly* survey found that, out of 313 members of both houses, 58.5 percent favored existing policy, 26.4 percent favored stronger military action, and only 15.1 percent favored deescalation and negotiations.[4] Given the fact that the entire House and one-third of the Senate faced reelection campaigns, it should not be surprising that so many continued to follow the administration's lead in supporting the war. Moreover, given the growing opposition to the war, a significant number avoided the issue whenever possible. Successful candidates on the Republican side—incumbents and challengers alike—showed restraint and temperance in their comments on the war, rarely taking a stand that placed them in either the strong hawk or the avid dove camp.

In three races for seats in the Senate in which opposition to the war figured prominently, the impact of Vietnam on the campaigns differed substantially. Charles Percy, running against the incumbent Paul Douglas (D-IL), criticized Johnson's Vietnam policy frequently. He opposed escalation but did not suggest that the United States unilaterally withdraw until and unless a satisfactory settlement could be reached. Toward this end, he recommended that an all-Asian conference be held to settle the conflict. While this idea did not originate with Percy, he became the first national political figure to promote it publicly. Many members of the GOP who sought an alternative to Johnson's policies became enamored with the idea of a conference, but the president's supporters, including Percy's fellow Illinoisan Dirksen, did not think much of the plan. Despite Dirksen's skepticism, the Republican congressional leadership issued a press release on 25 August 1966 that gave its "encouragement and endorsement of the proposal of an all-Asian Peace Conference." The statement declared that the GOP support of the idea emphasized "our determination that the Republican Party shall continue strongly to maintain its historic and cherished position as the party of peace."[5] Nixon, who always understood the importance of helping fellow Republicans (particularly when it did not run against his own ambitions), also announced his support for Percy's plan.

As one GOP observer suggested, support of the conference was a means of "getting the word peace into the Republican vocabulary." Commenting on this development, the *Boston Globe* opined, "Emphasis on diplomatic solutions could lead to a completely new Republican line on Viet Nam. It could put the Republicans in the position of charging that the Democratic administration is incapable of making peace in Asia."[6] If and when the Republicans adopted such a policy, it would provide important leverage in future campaigns. For the time being, however, the party did not fully embrace negotiations and left its candidates to chart their own course on the war. In Illinois, Percy's strategy worked, and he won election easily. He later attributed his victory largely to "voter dissatisfaction with . . . the war in Vietnam."[7]

Percy did not stand alone among Republican senatorial candidates in 1966 in advocating a dovish approach to the war. Edward Brooke ran for the seat being vacated by Leverett Saltonstall against the Democratic challenger, Endicott Peabody, the former governor. Brooke predicted as early as February 1966 that peace would be an important issue in the campaign and believed that the party could make it a winning issue. He advocated a full congressional debate on the war, direct peace negotiations with the Viet Cong, and a reassessment of the air war in the North.[8] A Republican in Massachusetts must be a moderate to have hope of being elected. Peabody whimsically noted this salient fact when he said in October, "The longer we campaign, the fewer issues there seem to be

23 August 1966: "Hello—Anyface to Oldface—I Think We Have the Enemy Surrounded"

between my opponent and me." But, significantly, Vietnam was one of those issues. Brooke recalled that the war was "the most important issue in my campaign." Indeed, the *Boston Globe* urged its readers to make their decision on the basis of the candidates' positions on Vietnam.[9] Brooke believed that the United States was "justifiably in Viet Nam" but favored an Asian peace conference and opposed precipitate withdrawal and escalation.[10] In an interview on the eve of the balloting, he noted that many within the GOP were "becoming a little more disaffected" with administration policies and argued for limiting—although not ending—the bombing of North Vietnam in an effort to reach a negotiated settlement.[11] Brooke reached out to opponents of the war by recommending new peace initiatives, while Peabody supported Johnson's policies fully. Brooke swept to victory in the election with a plurality of over 400,000 votes, becoming the first African American senator to be elected to the Senate by popular vote. His success can be attributed in large part to his stand against the war.

Opposition to the war did not automatically guarantee electoral success, however. In Oregon, the popular governor, Mark Hatfield, seemed certain to defeat his Democratic opponent, Representative Robert B. Duncan, in the 1966 Senate election, yet his vehement antiwar stance almost cost him the seat. Vietnam, Hatfield later wrote, "was the issue that called me to the Senate."[12] Hatfield's opposition to the war, derived from his strong religious convictions and conscience, altered a race that had been perceived as an easy win. Duncan, a strident hawk, hoped to turn the campaign into a referendum on Hatfield's views on the war and succeeded in doing so. While the governor did his best to prevent the campaign from becoming a single-issue race, reporters consistently asked him about his stance on the war. When Hatfield became evasive, the normally supportive Portland newspaper the *Oregon Journal* published a harsh editorial titled "Hatfield: The Dove Who Ducks" and asserted that he was "acting as if his strategy is to win by being vaguely remembered by the voters as that nice young man who is so worried about Vietnam." Ultimately, Hatfield was elected to the Senate by a slim margin (a mere twenty-four thousand votes), but his outspoken antiwar views made the race closer than it should have been, isolated him from the majority of the Republican leadership, and dampened his prospects as a dark-horse presidential candidate in 1968.[13]

These three races demonstrate the varied impact that the war had in campaigns around the country. The residual support for U.S. policy in Vietnam played an important role in limiting the attractiveness of campaigns based on opposition to the conflict. Meanwhile, hawkish Republicans censured the administration for its slow response to the crisis in Vietnam over the past two years and for not fully prosecuting the war at present. John Rhodes sounded a common refrain in late August in a letter to a constituent. "I firmly believe many of the problems we now face . . . could have been avoided," he asserted. "The policy which [Johnson] is now beginning to implement is one which I advocated as much as two years ago. It is fatally irresponsible to fight a war without attempting to win it." Using America's full military power and capabilities, Rhodes concluded, "will bring the most rapid end to our struggle there." John Tower made similar comments in a speech to a high school audience in Lubbock in July: "It seems to me that our only acceptable alternative is to resolve to achieve military victory. . . . We have the military capability to win. We must apply it. I believe we must bomb targets of military significance wherever they are."[14] The sentiments expressed by Rhodes and Tower, shared by so many around the country, restricted Vietnam's role in the midterm elections.

But that did not prevent the war from posing serious problems for Johnson. Facing criticism from all sides, the president decided to be proactive in seeking a resolution to the conflict. In September, he announced that he would travel to Manila the following month in an effort to work out a basis for settlement. Percy and other doves lauded the administration for its efforts at peace, but the GOP hawks pounced. Gerald Ford considered Johnson's efforts in Manila to be a politically and electorally inspired "gimmick." He chastised the president for mixing "domestic politics and honest endeavors for peace in Vietnam," calling the meeting "some gesture aimed at taking the heat off the Democrats on the Vietnam issue just prior to the Nov. 8 election." In response, Dirksen sharply reproved his counterpart for criticizing Johnson's motives. The friction between the two Republican leaders caused great consternation among the GOP hierarchy, but as Ford noted, "We have had to learn to live with it."[15] Other Republicans expressed their skepticism about the true nature of the Manila conference as well. Barry Goldwater asserted, "No matter how piously the President may deny any domestic political considerations, the very fact that the meeting is scheduled so close to the congressional elections . . . makes it impossible to separate the trip from pure and simple Johnson politics."[16]

Clearly, the GOP struggled with the war issue. Even when, in mid-September, the party released another white paper that nominally represented its perspective on the conflict and criticized the administration, it engendered tremendous controversy from conservatives. The policy statement, according to the *National Review,* "self-righteously washes from Republican hands the stains of 'Johnson's war.' Everyone with an objection, doubt, query or sorrow over the fighting in Vietnam will find it smugly echoed in a demagogic sentence or two of this banal document." What the white paper lacked, however, was "the smallest hint of any specific alternative to the President's policy."[17] Two weeks later, the journal continued its assault on the document. "What is a poor Republican to do?" asked the *Review's* editors. "If he denounces the war, he is unpatriotic.

If he supports it, he is an LBJ stooge." Critical of Romney, Laird, and Ford for "tripletalking as an election draws near," the conservative journal praised only Richard Nixon and Dwight Eisenhower. Nixon "has understood the necessity for resisting the Communist advance into Southeast Asia, and has unequivocally backed the President's actions insofar as he judges they serve that aim." Eisenhower, in supporting "'as much force as we need to win,'" represented "the surest, quickest, most efficient and in the end the most humane way of going about the job."[18]

With the conference approaching rapidly, Johnson tried to ignore GOP attacks and accept whatever support he could for both the negotiations and the war. He did not, however, expect George Aiken's proposal on the eve of the Manila talks. Aiken had "come to the conclusion that the conflict in Viet Nam cannot be resolved under this administration." The real goal of Americanizing the war, he argued, had been to rescue U.S. troops that were in "clear and present danger of military defeat," not the unobtainable objective of stopping Hanoi's aggression. Johnson's escalation had achieved this goal; therefore, he could declare "victory" and begin a gradual redeployment of American forces while simultaneously substituting intensive reconnaissance for ROLLING THUNDER. The combination of redeployment with the cessation of bombing and a declaration of victory would remove credibility as a factor precluding negotiations, force the burden of further escalation onto the enemy, and open the door to a resumption of the "political warfare" of the Eisenhower and early Kennedy years.[19] Although praised by Mansfield and Fulbright, Aiken's grand scheme—which almost immediately became mythologized as a "declare victory and go home" proposal—failed to move Johnson from his agenda in Manila. Aiken recalled in an interview several years later that his idea made Johnson extremely upset and suggested that it was "the only time he ever really got mad at me."[20]

The Manila conference had three primary aims: to review military and nonmilitary developments, to review the progress being made toward pacification, and to consider peace proposals and new measures for ending the war.[21] After meeting with both the South Vietnamese and American officials from Saigon, the conferees issued a statement. The announcement centered on what would become known as the "Manila formula" and reflected Johnson's main goals for the conference. American forces would be withdrawn from South Vietnam no later than six months after "the other side withdraws its forces to the North, cease infiltration, and the level of violence thus subsides."[22] While some members of the U.S. delegation lobbied for a three- rather than six-month waiting period, opponents knew that the South Vietnamese, the Thais, and the South Koreans would object to the proposal. There is one other critical aspect to the Manila formula that needs to be recognized. With its stipulation that the United

States would remain in Vietnam until the violence subsided, the Manila communiqué effectively committed the administration to a virtually open-ended war in Southeast Asia.[23] The ramifications of that guarantee proved to be a political windfall for the GOP and political disaster for Lyndon Johnson.

The Manila conference sparked an election eve dispute between Johnson and Nixon and highlighted the Vietnam issue for the electorate. When the announcement of the agreement came, the Republican response was rapid and predictable. Nixon charged that the formula would spell disaster for South Vietnam because it would leave the Saigon regime unprotected against renewed Communist activity. Moreover, he asserted that the time had come to "renew the debate on the Johnson administration's policy in Vietnam, for this war is not only the global issue in this election, it is one of the central issues of our time." He warned that the United States "should never rely on communist promises—but should always insist on guaranteed deeds." The Manila communiqué, according to Nixon, "raised some grave policy questions which should be answered by President Johnson" prior to the upcoming elections in order to regain domestic support and reassure America's allies.[24]

The president responded immediately and harshly to Nixon's attack and charged that the GOP would cause the nation to "'falter and fall back and fail'" in Vietnam. Nixon replied that the most prominent opponents of the war had been Democrats.[25] At a press conference the day after Nixon's statement, Johnson went further, labeling Nixon a "chronic campaigner" who "find[s] fault with his country and his government during a period of October every two years." He insisted that his Vietnam policy would remain the same regardless of the outcome of the elections and accused Nixon of trying to "pick up a precinct or two, or a ward or two," with his comments.[26] LBJ's political aides went even further in denouncing Nixon. They accused the former vice president of "talking out of both sides of his mouth" and suggested that the Democratic National Committee "get about five Members of Congress to take in after Nixon . . . for 'playing politics with our boys in Viet-Nam.'"[27]

The candid and biting personal comments that Johnson made against Nixon backfired. Gerald Ford leapt to Nixon's defense, saying that he had raised "legitimate questions about our foreign policy" and that the "American people should have forthright answers to all these questions from the White House."[28] Goldwater also reproached the president in his syndicated column, asserting that the former vice president "has done a good deal more to gain support for the administration's over-all policy in Vietnam than have leaders in the Democratic Party. But when Nixon dared question . . . the policy, the President blew his top." Goldwater also suggested that, in attacking Nixon, Johnson had "declared open political war on Nixon and, through him, the entire Republican Party."[29]

For his part, Nixon accused LBJ of breaking "the bipartisan line of Vietnam policy"—a line that he had frequently fractured himself. He later asserted that Johnson had challenged "the principle of the right to disagree, the right to dissent." Nixon emerged from the fracas with an astonishing amount of support as even journalists came to his defense.[30] For example, on 4 November 1966, Murray Kempton of the *New York Post* wrote that, if Nixon "were really the reckless partisan we had thought him and not the honorable exponent of national unity he showed himself yesterday," then the administration might have an argument. And the *Yonkers Herald Statesman* editorialized, "If Mr. Nixon is a chronic campaigner, this is perhaps what the country needs most. A responsible voice of opposition, of questioning, of clarifying the big issues is essential in a democracy and Mr. Nixon is filling that role."[31] On the eve of the elections, Nixon suddenly found himself the beneficiary of an outburst by Johnson, precisely the opposite scenario political observers had expected.

Yet Vietnam figured only peripherally in the campaign. Moreover, when it was an explicit issue, more people favored escalation of the American war effort than sympathized with the antiwar movement's call to negotiate or withdraw.[32] But the meaning of the elections vis-à-vis Vietnam was ambiguous at best. Ronald Reagan, an outspoken hawk on the war, overwhelmed the antiwar Pat Brown to win the California governorship just as the dovish Percy and Brooke won seats in the Senate owing to their opposition to the war. Mark Hatfield's opposition to the war nearly cost him what should have been an easy victory. The outcome of the midterm elections "anticipated GOP foreign policy conflict" during the next two years as loosely defined groups of Republicans challenged each other and attacked the president over the war issue.[33] In addition to the gains in Congress, the GOP won numerous races in traditionally Democratic regions of the country. Further, the party's victories were not confined to one end of the political spectrum. While the liberal Nelson Rockefeller won reelection in New York, conservative governors won in Ohio, Nevada, Idaho, Arizona, and Arkansas, and the GOP won the Florida governor's chair for the first time since Reconstruction. Indeed, the election of so many conservative Republican governors helps explain the radical shift in the National Governors Association from a bastion of liberal Republicanism to the springboard for the conservative movement's takeover of the GOP in the late 1960s and early 1970s. For Republicans, 1966 was "pre-eminently a party victory" rather than a victory of individuals, and voters identifying themselves as members of the party increased for the first time in over two decades.[34]

But one individual could certainly claim victory. Richard Nixon and his advisers had been planning the 1966 campaign since the 1964 Goldwater debacle. Postulating that the political pendulum had swung too far toward the Demo-

7 August 1966: "Don't Worry, They Couldn't Be Doing It to Us Again"

cratic Party in 1964, they believed that large numbers of traditionally Republican districts lost in the Johnson landslide could return to the GOP column. They therefore concluded that Nixon should be at the vanguard of the campaign to recapture those seats in order to reap the benefits that would accrue to the leader of the Republican revival. The *Wall Street Journal* agreed, suggesting, "When the votes are counted a week from today the biggest winner—or loser—in the Republican Party may well be a candidate whose name won't be on any ballot."[35] Thus, as he had in 1954 and 1958, Nixon campaigned relentlessly for Republican candidates across the country and predicted that his party would make significant gains in both the House and the Senate.[36] The results could not have been scripted better. The Republicans managed to gain 47 seats in the House and 3 in the Senate, capture 8 governorships, and win 540 seats in various state legislatures.[37] What had been inconceivable in 1962 had become a real possibility in the wake of the elections: a Nixon presidency.

After the election, Nixon's optimism over his prospects in 1968 was obvious. As the *St. Louis Globe-Democrat* noted, the former vice president could now be identified as a political winner, having finally shed the image of the sulking, defeated gubernatorial candidate of four years earlier: "Whether by design or not, the Nixon performance over the last two years . . . has annihilated the argument that Nixon is a 'loser,' a candidate who cannot win. . . . There is no question that Richard Nixon is the Big Winner in 1966." The paper went on to interpret the GOP victory and its implication for 1968: "The Republican Party pros know today Richard Nixon is the only man in their party to date who has lured Lyndon Johnson in open combat and whipped him hands down. Lyndon Johnson knows who won the first round."[38]

Noting the precarious position the administration faced, the *New York Times* editorialized that the election indicated "widespread dissatisfaction and uneasiness about the course and the prospects of the Vietnam War."[39] Nixon could now begin to temper his rhetoric to maximize his support in the coming presidential race. He realized that "the peace party always wins. I know my own party. If the war is still going on in 'sixty-eight, there is no power on earth can keep them from trying to outbid the Democrats for the peace vote."[40] Indeed, as Senator Stuart Symington (D-MO) told Rostow, "We are getting in deeper and deeper [in Vietnam] with no end in sight. In 1968 Nixon will murder us. He will become the biggest dove of all times. There has never been a man in American public life who could turn so fast on a dime."[41] If the administration failed to resolve the conflict by 1968, Nixon would be perfectly positioned to move to the center and portray Johnson as an extremist on the war, just as Johnson had done to Goldwater in 1964. As Nixon stated over a decade later, the 1966 election results were "a prerequisite for my own comeback."[42] The campaign represented a personal victory for him, and his persistent badgering of Johnson paid off in spades. Nixon was back on the road to the White House. He already had the motive, his criticism of Johnson over the previous three years had provided him with the means, and now he had the opportunity to finally achieve his greatest ambition.

In an interesting postscript, in the wake of the 1968 Republican convention Tom Wicker revealed a conversation he had with Nixon just prior to the 1966 election. Nixon told reporters that Vietnam would be "a devastating political issue that would defeat President Johnson." Unless the president found a way to end the fighting, he argued, the Republican Party would be "grievously tempted to run on a peace platform in 1968." This analysis corresponded with that of most political observers at the time. Off the record, however, Nixon went on to say that, if the GOP did wage a peace campaign in 1968, he doubted that he could be the candidate since his "record of hawkishness was too clear."[43] Nixon, perhaps purposefully, underestimated his ability to adapt his position on the war over the next two years to ensure electoral success.

Yet to call the election results a devastating setback for the administration's Vietnam policies would be an overstatement. Despite the fact that a majority of Americans considered Vietnam the most important problem facing the nation, commentators generally agreed that the elections did not negate the administration's policy. The *Minneapolis Star* wrote, "Ho Chi Minh and others who are examining the election results for indications of support or opposition to American policies in Viet Nam, will look in vain." The pollster George Gallup observed, "Probably the prime reason why the GOP did so well was the public's distress and concern over Viet-Nam." But the results did not necessarily mean that people disagreed with Johnson's policies. Instead, he argued, "The public is looking desperately and eagerly for an honest way out."[44] Republicans carefully denied the existence of an element of war weariness in the GOP triumph. Nixon stated after the balloting that he hoped it would be "absolutely clear to Hanoi and Peking that the new House of Representatives will be much stronger than its predecessor as a bulwark of support for a United States policy of 'no reward for aggression.'"[45]

The results contributed to the decline of the liberal wing of the GOP. Despite the overwhelming rejection of Barry Goldwater's candidacy in 1964, the conservative insurgency would soon become the primary motive force within the Republican Party. To be sure, liberal Republicans did well in the 1966 elections. Several contested governorships were won by liberal members of the party like John Chaffee (R-RI) and John Volpe (R-MA), and the Senate added Hatfield, Percy, and Brooke to its ranks. In addition, George Romney won reelection handily and moved into the unenviable position as the Republican front-runner for the 1968 presidential nomination. Yet, as the historian Matthew Dallek argues, "Reagan could not possibly have beaten Brown prior to 1966; only civil rights, Berkeley, Watts, and Vietnam made it possible." Reagan "sense[d] early that citizens were frustrated with the stalemate in Southeast Asia and with the left-wing opponents of the war." Thus, in his campaign, Reagan "wrapped himself in the cause of American patriotism, and assailed antiwar radicals at every opportunity."[46] The same held true for conservatives around the country, and, for every Percy or Brooke elected to Congress, a hawkish George H. W. Bush, Howard Baker Jr. (R-TN), or Clifford Hansen (R-WY) joined the ranks of GOP legislators. Moreover, hawks still controlled the party's leadership, although the doves were well represented on key committees like the SFRC. By the time the primary season opened for the 1968 campaign, Reagan and Nixon would far outpace Romney and Rockefeller, and Vietnam would play a key role in the shifting of the GOP's power center.

For the time being, however, the Republican Party basked in its electoral gains and expressed confidence about the future. Daniel Jackson Evans (R-WA) commented at a meeting of Republican governors in Colorado in December 1966, "What 1966 has given us is the luxury of choice [for the 1968 presidential nomination]."[47] Unlike 1964, where the party emerged from the balloting bereft of leadership and lacking any pretense of unity, the 1966 elections vaulted several GOP politicians into contention for the party's nomination two years hence and reaffirmed the importance of sticking together against the Democrats. The future of the party looked as bright in 1966 as it had appeared moribund two years previously, as the GOP enjoyed an "embarrassment of riches." With such popular, experienced, and charismatic leaders such George Romney, Richard Nixon, Ronald Reagan, Nelson Rockefeller, and Charles Percy, the Republicans could look forward to the 1968 presidential campaign with a "widespread expectation of victory."[48]

On the other side of the aisle, the Democrats conducted their own post-mortem on the election and its implications for 1968. A group of Democratic operatives argued that the GOP had won through a combination of better organization, outspending the Democrats by better than four to one in most races, and intraparty strife. Vietnam and race relations, according to their report, stood as the two most important issues, although the latter seemed to have much more of an impact on the balloting than the war. Indeed, they concluded, "It is impossible to document the thesis that there was a national vote against President Johnson or the Administration, even against the Vietnam situation." In looking ahead to 1968, the report recommended that the president "should set up a new program of explanations about why we are in Vietnam" and "attempt to get the people to accept some measure of progress in the war other than lines on a map." In addition, he should initiate a public relations campaign that stressed Republican obstructionism and narrow partisanship, in terms of both domestic policy and the war.[49] For both parties, then, 1966 merely served as a prelude to the 1968 presidential campaign.

But the war held the key to the Oval Office, and Republican optimism and Democratic uncertainty hinged as much on the conflict in Vietnam as on any other issue. Over the next two years, debate over the course of American policy consumed the attention of the nation and helped determine the political futures of both parties. As divisive as the campaign rhetoric had been during 1966, the following year would see even more fractures in the Cold War consensus as the commitment to Vietnam increasingly came under scrutiny. Republicans previously disinclined to speak out on the war felt more confident in addressing the issues of escalation and negotiation after being returned to office for another term, with many of them publicly distancing themselves from the administration's policies. Meanwhile, Lyndon Johnson desperately attempted to preserve the waning support for his policies and would come to rely on hawkish GOP allies more heavily as dissent expanded in 1967.

The hydra of opinion on Vietnam forced the president to realign his political support while simultaneously putting out brush fires on multiple fronts both within his party and among the American public. Democrats had deserted the president in greater numbers in the wake of the Fulbright hearings, but, during the year that followed the midterm elections, a number of prominent Republicans would openly join the ranks of the opponents of the war. In addition, throughout 1967, George Romney, Richard Nixon, and the other leading contenders for the GOP nomination jockeyed for position within the party and grappled with the war issue. As a result, they forced Johnson to devote substantial energy and resources to holding his coalition of support together and balancing his domestic and foreign policy agendas. If those domestic political considerations were not enough, LBJ knew that his own reelection campaign was not too far over the horizon. If he hoped to win another term in the White House, he would have to drastically improve his approval ratings and his performance in the polls against the leading GOP challengers. As promising as the Republicans' prospects for regaining the White House were, however, the party leadership realized that the war (or its conclusion) could still become a winning issue for the administration. Momentum in politics, as in sports, is an elusive and transient quality. In order to build on their success in November, the Republicans would have to avoid being dragged down with the administration should the situation in Vietnam take a turn for the worse.

Given the status quo, some observers believed that the party needed to be proactive in its approach to the war. In December 1966, Radio Moscow predicted what the GOP strategy for the 1968 election would be. By "pressuring the administration for more energetic action in Vietnam . . . [Republicans] realize that the Democrats, not they, will get the full blast of the growing anger over the war." Therefore, the GOP would "demand a larger U.S. commitment, knowing full well that the Democrats will have to do the answering." In a nod to the infamous Goldwater daisy commercial in 1964, Radio Moscow concluded, "It looks as though the Republicans hope to kill their opponents' chances in 1968 by representing the Democratic candidate in the midst of napalm flares."[50] The editorial astutely recognized that, should Johnson run for reelection without a peace settlement already in place, the GOP would certainly make an effort to marginalize him and claim the moderate middle ground for themselves, in essence using his strategy from 1964 against him. This, in fact, would be exactly the strategy employed by Richard Nixon for the next two years, but the rest of the party would continue to struggle with what to do about Vietnam.

But would the war prove decisive in the 1968 campaign? American elections, conventional wisdom holds, turn on issues of economics and domestic policy, not foreign policy. Yet the evidence clearly demonstrates that, during the race for the GOP presidential nomination in 1968, the candidates' positions on the Vietnam War proved to be pivotal. Indeed, all other issues (race, law and order, the broader Cold War) aside, the overwhelming importance of Vietnam in the 1968 Republican primaries cannot be disputed. To be sure, Vietnam transcended normal foreign policy problems. The ramifications of the conflict affected American domestic politics deeply (and vice versa) and caused fissures within American politics and society not seen since perhaps the Civil War, and the GOP was not immune to these divisions. By way of comparison, on most of the other substantive issues in the Republican primary campaign, each of the major candidates took positions that, if not identical, were certainly comparable. Dwight Eisenhower wrote in 1968, "In domestic affairs, I have been able to make very little differences in the political differences in the philosophies of Rockefeller and Nixon."[51] As one account of the 1968 election argues, "Nothing is clearer than the imperative that an account of the politics of 1968 must start with Vietnam, the progress of which dominated the struggle for the Presidency from first to last." To consider the campaign for the GOP nomination without recognizing Vietnam's importance "would be like *Hamlet* without the murdered king."[52]

Given the Republican inability to craft a consistent and unified party line on the war—not to mention the wide-open field of candidates—Democrats had cause for hope. As John Bailey, the chair of the Democratic National Committee, said in January 1968, "We know who our nominees will be. . . . I'm happy to be able to say the Republicans have all their bloody infighting to look forward to."[53] Although political prognosticators identified any number of potential Republican presidential candidates for the 1968 election and dark-horse candidates could have emerged, only four stood any realistic chance of winning the nomination at the end of 1966: George Romney, Nelson Rockefeller, Ronald Reagan, and Richard Nixon. The national media, supported by opinion polls from around the country, anointed Romney as the front-runner after the 1966 midterm elections. On the strength of his landslide reelection victory in the Michigan gubernatorial race, the Harris poll showed him with a 54 to 46 percent advantage over Johnson, while a Gallup poll had the governor comfortably ahead of Nixon by a 39 to 31 percent margin.[54] Yet, when it came to Vietnam, Romney demonstrated no indication of expertise or even competence in detailing his views. If he hoped to win the nomination, he would have to grapple more successfully with the war in his public statements.

Vietnam notwithstanding, George Romney was an extremely attractive candidate. Although frequently considered a stalking horse for Rockefeller's presidential ambitions, the former lobbyist and automotive executive's success and popularity during his tenure as governor forced the Democratic Party to take him seriously. Campaign officials tried to take advantage of every controversy to deflate his public support and reduce the risk he posed to Johnson's reelection bid. His potential as an opponent for Johnson in 1968 is demonstrated in the number of polls conducted by Johnson's political aides that focused on hypothetical matchups between the president and Romney and on issues such as Vietnam. The biggest obstacle Romney faced as he considered the move from state to national politics was his tendency to not always be clear or consistent on the issues, particularly in the area of foreign affairs, where his inexperience represented a glaring problem.[55]

Romney's main challenger for moderate and liberal Republican support was Nelson Rockefeller, a scion of one of America's wealthiest families, former Eisenhower administration official, and perennial GOP presidential hopeful. The personification of the Eastern establishment, he enjoyed the support of a significant segment of the party. Although Rockefeller flatly stated that he had no presidential ambitions in 1968 and expressed his support for Romney, party leaders agreed with the national media that he would likely enter the race at some point during the campaign. Early in the 1960s, Rockefeller had been a vocal anti-Communist who derided the Kennedy and Johnson administrations for their failure to contain the spread of communism in Southeast Asia; however, he had adopted a deafening silence on the war since 1964.

Like Romney, Rockefeller faced a number of hurdles to win the nomination. First, his personal life was in disarray (at least for a politician in the 1960s), having been through a very public divorce and quick remarriage earlier in the decade.[56] Another liability was his actions during the 1964 campaign. Strongly opposed to Goldwater's candidacy, he refused to support the GOP nominee, which contributed to the fracturing of party support and angered Goldwater partisans. Former president Eisenhower said that, if Rockefeller managed to win the nomination, it "would resurrect all the hard feelings of 1964, at a time when it is imperative to get the party together."[57] Additionally, his failure to capture the Republican nomination in his previous attempts left questions in the minds of some party members regarding his electability. Ironically, many contemporaries and scholars suggested that Rockefeller may have fared better in a general election campaign—where his moderate-to-liberal views would have attracted a sizable number of independent and swing votes—than in the Republican primaries. Indeed, White House political aides in 1967 focused on Rockefeller as a likely and dangerous opponent for Johnson in 1968.

The third candidate was Rockefeller's opposite in virtually every way. Ronald Reagan had little experience in government, lived on the West Coast far removed from the GOP establishment, and epitomized the growing conservative wing of the Republican Party. His convincing victory in the 1966 California gubernatorial election not only gave the Republicans a solid base for the 1968 campaign but also vaulted him into the national spotlight as a politician rather than as an actor. His conservative views and hawkish stance on Vietnam gave Goldwater voters a candidate they felt comfortable with and provided a stark contrast with the views of Romney and Rockefeller. Throughout 1967 and 1968, Harris polls showed Reagan running ahead of all other Republican candidates in the South and West, whether in conservative rural areas or areas with Goldwater voters.[58] He possessed a number of assets, including his high "Q" ratings and nascent "Great Communicator" skills. Yet his lack of political experience, combined with his uncompromising rhetoric and the third-party candidacy of Governor George Wallace (D-AL), made him the least likely nominee of the four main Republican candidates.[59]

The final major contender for the Republican nomination was Richard Nixon. Despite trailing Romney in the early polls, Nixon had painstakingly revitalized his political career as a loyal party man since 1962. His actions gained him critical support within the party, and he did not hesitate to call in those favors when necessary. Nevertheless, he had to deal with his negative public image, particularly the lingering perception that he was a political loser. He did all he could during his "years in the wilderness" to change those assumptions and create, in the words of his critics, a "new Nixon"—one who could overcome his tragic flaws to finally win the presidency.

James J. Kilpatrick, in a *National Review* overview of the main contenders for the 1968 GOP nomination, wrote, "Nixon goes into this campaign with a balance sheet far more complicated than ledgers of his chief opponents. Ronald Reagan has a long list of attractive assets, offset by inexperience and by an actor's background. George Romney, businessman, successful governor, has chiefly to contend with memories of his defection in 1964 and with his own remarkable gifts for obfuscation. Nelson Rockefeller's net worth stands politically about where it stood three years ago." Ultimately, Nixon possessed assets that should make him the prohibitive favorite. "Of all the prospective Republican nominees," Kirkpatrick continued, "he alone enters the battle with a solid record of experience on the federal stage: Congressman, Senator, Vice President. . . . Nixon has traveled more, seen more, and thought more deeply on foreign policy than all his opponents combined. . . . His views on domestic affairs are vintage Eisenhower, decanted and rebottled. He is an excellent, if unexciting, public speaker." Nevertheless, Nixon's "liabilities are formidable. . . . The old label clings like an outworn bumper sticker: Tricky Dick. . . . The tag is plastered invisibly on his back: two-time loser [in 1960 and 1962]. In the hot light of a political campaign, it gives a phosphorescent glow."[60]

Nixon would have to fight to complete his public rehabilitation while grappling with the war, although the same would be true of the other prospective nominees. Although numerous issues would be discussed in various forums, the most important issue in the primary campaign would be the war in Vietnam. Nixon, Reagan, Romney, and Rockefeller each had to take into consideration the views of both the hawk and the dove wings of the party in order to become the GOP standard-bearer and craft a policy that would appeal to the widest possible audience. Ultimately, however, Vietnam proved to be the undoing of two of the candidates's campaigns and would propel the third to the Oval Office despite the fact that he had presented no concrete proposal for ending the divisive and stalemated conflict.

One of the reasons that Vietnam turned out to be so problematic for the candidates was that members of the GOP had very different ideas about what position the party should take on the issue for the 1968 election. A large contingent within the party remained supportive of the war, and many wanted to increase the level of American involvement. Reagan, for instance, argued that consideration "should be given to an outright declaration of war in the Vietnam conflict."[61] Strom Thurmond believed not only that the United States should bomb strategic military targets throughout North Vietnam, regardless of their proximity to the civilian population, but also that the U.S. military should blockade North Vietnamese ports. Adopting these steps, he argued, would allow the administration to "wind up the war within a reasonable time."[62] Ross Adair assured a constituent that he was doing everything he could to "push the Administration for more forceful action in Vietnam." Adair believed that the administration had "in some measure responded to Republican pressure in this regard."[63] These hawkish Republicans seemed willing to bide their time and allow LBJ to take the brunt of the criticism for the war while calling for him to remain firm and support South Vietnam.

Meanwhile, several notable Republicans had serious doubts about the war and urged the administration to seek a political settlement. Harold Stassen interpreted the election results as support for "a reanalysis and reconsideration" of current policy—based, predictably, on his "Fourth Alternative" concept—suggesting that the election of Republicans like Hatfield and Percy meant that voters rejected the "advocate[s] of escalation" and championed the moderate and constructive critics of the war. He further called for a bipartisan effort to bring the war to an end.[64] As the party and country looked ahead to the presidential campaign, Margaret Chase Smith called for the Republican nominee to run as a peace candidate in 1968. Some Democrats believed that even the hawkish Nixon would run as a dove against Johnson. Yet, at the beginning of 1967, it seemed clear to observers that the liberal wing of the party had very little chance of controlling the Vietnam issue at the 1968 convention despite the fact that the 1966 elections brought to Washington a new crop of Republican lawmakers, many of whom had run their campaigns against the war and Lyndon Johnson. Earlier in the year, Barry Goldwater refused to consider the possibility of a GOP dove winning the nomination: "Republican doves today, therefore, are in a position of specifically standing outside their party in foreign policy. . . . Republican doves would be far more representative of Bobby Kennedy's part of the Democrat Party than of anything recognizable as Republican."[65] With Nixon, Reagan, Eisenhower, and virtually the entire Republican congressional leadership supporting the war and pushing for victory, however, it was "almost inconceivable that a Republican dove could be nominated," according to William S. White of the *Washington Post*. If the Romney and Percy wing of the party had any hope of gaining the nomination, they had to "clear themselves up on Vietnam."[66]

Regardless of how members of the Republican Party felt about the war, they recognized the centrality of Vietnam in the upcoming 1968 campaign. David C. Roller, an assistant professor of history at Bowling Green State University in Ohio, wrote to Thruston Morton in mid-1967 and told him that the GOP "may be on the verge of recapturing the support of academics," which had been a traditional Republican constituency until 1933. The issue that could return the professorate to the party fold, Roller wrote, was Vietnam—owing to the "considerable distrust of Johnson, disgust with the administration's deepening involvement, and apprehension over our escalating objectives and expanding military involvement." Roller's letter indicated support of a Rockefeller, Percy, or Romney candidacy in 1968 and noted that there was not much support for unilateral or immediate withdrawal.[67] The last part of the letter is intriguing given that the nation's university professors proved to be among the most vocal critics of LBJ's Vietnam policies during the 1960s. Given the disparity of opinion within the party, it remained to be seen whether the Republicans could capitalize on the public's disenchantment with the war to craft a coherent and unifying policy on the war for the 1968 elections.

Initial impressions in the new year suggested that the task would be a daunting one. The divisions within the nation and the parties were exemplified in January 1967 when five freshmen GOP senators appeared on NBC's "Meet the Press" on 8 January 1967 and Vietnam was the topic du jour. The discussion reflected the growing fault lines within the party—and the country—on the conflict. On one side, Howard Baker, who was Everett Dirksen's son-in-law, and Clifford Hansen spoke out against a unilateral bombing halt. Hansen also criticized the administration for making decisions "for political reasons." On the other hand, as Mark Hatfield argued, since, in his mind, bombing had not proved successful, "Why continue it?" In the middle were Edward Brooke and Charles Percy, both of whom had campaigned against the war the previous fall, neither of whom were willing to end the bombing, but both of whom suggested a reassessment of current policy as well as seeking negotiations. Interestingly, Brooke stated that he thought that the Republican Party was "going to move towards the center" on the war issue in the wake of the fall elections.[68] The divide among the new senators prompted one observer to comment, "That makes the score 2½ to 2½."[69] Not surprisingly, the ratio reflected the increase in opposition to Vietnam in the GOP, an increase that paralleled both the stalemated military situation on the ground and the public frustration with the lack of progress against the Communist forces in Southeast Asia.

Polls confirmed that the country's attitude toward the war had become increasingly skeptical. By the end of January 1967, a national survey found that only 41 percent of Americans approved of the administration's Vietnam policy. A poll in Minnesota brought even darker news to Johnson: 72 percent of those surveyed were dissatisfied with the progress of the war. Johnson's job approval rating fell correspondingly, reaching 46 percent in early February. Just as the divisions in Congress grew more pronounced, the country at large had expressed its frustration with the war and simply wanted the fighting to end, although the surveys did demonstrate a lingering belief in the possibility of victory in Vietnam. The one bright spot in the polls for LBJ was that most Americans thought that the president's potential rivals in 1968—Robert Kennedy, Richard Nixon, and George Romney—would do no better or might even be worse in dealing with the Vietnam conflict.[70] A small comfort for Johnson to be sure.

The change in public opinion was mirrored in Congress. The war issue split both parties and resulted in the emergence of new coalitions, with Republicans such as Cooper and Aiken siding with antiwar Democrats. The doves had been increasingly in the spotlight ever since the Fulbright hearings on the war in the Senate Foreign Relations Committee the previous year and with the lack of tangible progress on the military and political fronts. As dissent within the Democratic Party proliferated, Lyndon Johnson relied more and more on the GOP for backing. Barry Goldwater asserted in a letter to the editor published in the *Louisville Courier-Journal,* "I have probably been more active in the support of Johnson's policies in Vietnam as he is now conducting them than have most Democrats."[71] As the partisan lines blurred and Americans began to show signs of exhaustion with the fighting, congressional sentiment against the war began to pick up steam. Opponents of the conflict were no longer looked on as political mavericks, and even previously staunch supporters of the war, such as Thruston Morton, began to question the wisdom of the American commitment to Vietnam and broke openly with the administration. In August 1967, Morton admitted, "I've come to the conclusion now that I was wrong. We're on a bad wicket and we've got to try something else."[72] Melvin Laird, who had pressed Johnson so vigorously on the war in 1965, also expressed serious reservations about the trajectory of U.S. policy in Vietnam. He told a Chamber of Commerce meeting in Wisconsin in March that he saw "no real chance for a U.S. military victory in Vietnam."[73] The evolution of Laird's stance on the war continued through his tenure as Nixon's secretary of defense, where he became the primary architect of Vietnamization.

Jacob Javits publicly changed his position on the war on 12 February 1967. Javits had been "an ardent supporter" of the administration through the initial escalation of American involvement in 1965. Yet, even then, he had doubts about the direction of the war. He proposed a new congressional resolution on Vietnam on several occasions during the mid-1960s, and, when George Aiken asked him about Vietnam, the New York senator replied that "he had had strong misgivings about it but the President's course had to be followed through and he was supporting LBJ right down the line."[74] In March 1965, Javits introduced a resolution in the Senate that at once asserted congressional support for the administration and called for "honorable negotiations" to end the conflict. Nevertheless, he remained convinced of the "morality and necessity of U.S. military aid," especially after he visited Vietnam in January 1966. In a memo to the president after his return, he stated, "I concluded my visit to Vietnam convinced that there is enough of a chance to realize freedom's objective there to justify our military commitment." He did express concerns about the long-term needs of South Vietnam and the ability of the United States to stay focused on the objective of the war. He also criticized American efforts in the political, social, and economic areas as "far from adequate." He concluded by saying that the administration needed to "prepare the American people, and Congress, for the difficult decisions and commitments we will have to make in the years to come in Asia." He later called the speech "my personal peak of support for the war."[75]

As the conflict dragged on, however, Javits grew increasingly disturbed by the lack of progress in spite of the escalated U.S. commitment. He began to emphasize the importance of political action to complement military force and the need for the South Vietnamese to shoulder more of the burden of the fighting, and he stressed that the United States "must come forward with realistic peace proposals." But the final straw came when he learned through British prime minister Harold Wilson that Johnson had turned down the Warsaw proposal that would have gotten America out of the war and allowed some self-determination for South Vietnam. Javits decided that he could no longer support what he now viewed as "President Johnson's own war"; he believed that the president "had decided that he would become the savior of the world and earn a place in history." In his speech on 12 February, Javits said that Johnson had "become locked into the mistakes, illusions and overoptimistic predictions of his own policies. He is so busy defending himself, making excuses, and changing facts and figures that he appears to many to have lost the initiative and credibility to make peace on his own." According to Javits, the United States had to find a negotiated way out of the war, and the Republican Party had to demonstrate that it had learned the lesson of Vietnam—that the American people "cannot afford and are not interested in being the policeman of the world."[76]

Javits's criticisms of the president's policies came at a time when the administration faced critical problems in South Vietnam. The military situation had not improved or changed significantly despite the fact that there were now over 400,000 American troops in Vietnam. Gen. William Westmoreland's "search-and-destroy" tactics, increased aerial bombardment of the countryside, and technological superiority failed to deter the National Liberation Front (NLF) and the North Vietnamese. In response, Hanoi had intensified its guerrilla campaign and main unit operations to put maximum pressure on South Vietnam and keep U.S. casualties high, thereby eroding the American will to fight. This strategy helped disrupt the search-and-destroy operations and prevented the likelihood of a clear military victory for the United States. The best that could be said about the Americanization of the war by 1967 is that it was clear that "the infusion of American forces had staved off what had appeared to be certain defeat in 1965."[77] But the failure to defeat Hanoi and the NLF and increasing disillusionment with the war did not serve to motivate a fundamental change in policy. When Congress voted on an additional $12.2 billion for the war in late March 1967, the sole Republican in either house to vote against the appropriation was Representative Charles Mosher (R-OH).[78] The permissive attitude among the nation's legislators, even those vehemently opposed to the conflict, continued.

Compounding the military problems was the chronic instability of the Saigon regime. Although the revolving-door governments that had characterized South Vietnamese politics had ended following Nguyen Cao Ky's coup in June 1965, Buddhist demonstrations had resumed against the Ky government in 1966 and soon spread both geographically and demographically as students, labor unions, Catholics, and even factions within the South Vietnamese army joined the protests. While loyal troops suppressed the protests, the uprising illustrated the severe internal problems in South Vietnam. In addition, pacification efforts had achieved little success in the countryside, and the corruption both within the government and throughout the country undermined the economy and the morale of the people. Even the drafting of a new constitution and the scheduling of national elections later in 1967 would fail to bring the domestic situation in South Vietnam under control. Such were the challenges that Johnson faced as he attempted to hold together a fracturing coalition of support and increased public disapproval on the war.

Many Republicans realized that, as the 1968 elections drew closer, the party would be driven by the force of public opinion to present an alternative to Johnson's policy on Vietnam.[79] But, while Javits joined with Hatfield, Percy, Cooper, Aiken, and others in urging negotiation, the majority of the party remained supportive of the war effort and critical of the doves. Dovish statements by Percy, for example, led Goldwater, who had previously backed Percy's political career, to openly rebuke the Illinois senator. Eisenhower also remained steadfast in his support of the American commitment in Vietnam. In a letter to George Humphrey, his former secretary of the Treasury, Eisenhower reiterated his opposition to anything short of a military victory in Vietnam, arguing that an "abject surrender might be welcomed by a few of the Fulbrights, Morses, and members of the leftish sectors" but would "outrage the vast majority of our citizens." He considered it ridiculous that Johnson could "successfully 'sneak out the back door' of Vietnam" and did not believe that the nation would be satisfied with any agreement that the "communists would soon, and with impunity, violate." The former president asserted that the United States needed to remain strong and dedicated to the cause of freedom and victory in South Vietnam.

He also suggested a strategy for the GOP in the 1968 presidential campaign if "the war goes on as at present." If a Republican won the election, Eisenhower asked, what would he do in Vietnam? With no answer readily available, the former president suggested that the party's leadership begin developing programs and contingency plans for the coming year that would allow the party and its nominee to present a united front on the war. Eisenhower also clarified his position on how the presidential candidates should treat the president: "I still believe that in crises we must support the Commander-in-Chief. However, we are not barred from criticizing the record of past events; and we can advocate different policies for future adoption." Yet the soldier in Eisenhower made it perfectly clear where he stood. "As long as America is losing men in conflict," he asserted, "I, personally, cannot fail to stand by the duly elected President in his effort to protect America's interests."[80] For Eisenhower, partisan politics took a back seat to the national interest, even as a presidential election year approached.

But some members of the party lacked Eisenhower's conviction about the importance of Vietnam to American interests. Paul N. "Pete" McCloskey (R-CA), who defeated the former child actress Shirley Temple Black in a special House election in 1967, would become one of the harshest critics of U.S. policy in Southeast Asia during both the Johnson and the Nixon administrations.[81] A committed anti-Communist and decorated marine colonel, McCloskey had actually applied (unsuccessfully) for active duty in Vietnam in the fall of 1965 and was later offered the opportunity to be an Agency for International Development provincial adviser in Vietnam, which he declined. Despite his belief that there were situations in which the United States should use its military might to combat communism, McCloskey came to fervently believe that Vietnam was "a classic question of the wrong war in the wrong place at the wrong time."[82]

McCloskey's antiwar sentiments were readily apparent during his congressional campaign, where he called the war the "most urgent issue of the present time." He admitted that he had initially supported the war despite his misgivings about the conflict—suggesting that "a loyal American had no option but to support the President" because he was the only one "fully cognizant of *all* of the facts involved"—but he came to question the American role in the fighting. According to him, even an escalation that produced a military victory "would determine nothing except that we would thereafter be committed to years of continuing guerilla warfare." Moreover, he argued that, if self-determination was a basic principle of U.S. foreign policy, then "we may have no business fighting in Viet Nam for the benefit of a government which has no chance of becoming the choice of a majority of the Vietnamese people." Successive administrations, he concluded, had "backed the wrong horse in our selection of the Saigon government as a means of withstanding the advancement of . . . Communism in Asia." He recommended that American military involvement be terminated as quickly as possible (although not with a precipitous withdrawal), that negotiations with Hanoi begin immediately on the basis that "we agree to the reunification of Viet Nam under a single government as soon as an orderly process for such re-unification can be determined," and that deescalation begin unilaterally to demonstrate U.S. sincerity. If the administration refused to follow his advice, McCloskey stated that he would bring the matter before Congress.[83]

McCloskey's opposition to the war played a key role in his electoral victory; indeed, the growing antiwar sentiment in the country that swept Mark Hatfield, Charles Percy, and other Republican opponents of the war into office in the midterm elections in 1966 helped him defeat the more conservative Black. Almost immediately on taking his seat in the House, he began a sustained and comprehensive critique of U.S. policy in Southeast Asia. In doing so, he not only attacked the Johnson (and, later, Nixon) administration for its failures but also correctly chastised Congress for abdicating its constitutional responsibilities. As he told his constituents in one of his first reports from Washington, Congress had, "by passively enacting supplemental appropriations for increased assistance to Vietnam," effectively ceded its policy influence to the president.[84]

Throughout his first term and the 1968 presidential campaign, McCloskey—like most Republicans, both hawk and dove—continued to hammer away at the Johnson administration for its policy shortcomings in Southeast Asia. He consistently urged an end to the bombing and a recognition of the realities of the situation. In a newsletter to his San Mateo constituents, he urged the administration to "go further than just stopping the bombing." The key to a successful negotiation to end the conflict, he asserted, "lies in an unequivocal declaration by the United States that we are agreeable to a peace based on the Geneva Accords. This in turn requires our agreement to the re-unification of Viet Nam." He believed that the United States was not "strong enough or powerful enough to win the kind of victory in Viet Nam that would permit us to pull out, leaving behind a government of South Viet Nam which will not one day fall to a nationalist coup." According to McCloskey, "It is time we admit failure and agree to a reunified country."[85] McCloskey's views on the war, although diametrically opposed to those of Eisenhower, provide some of the clearest examples of GOP opposition to LBJ's policies.

Others had difficulty defining their own perspectives on the war. George Romney had been a supporter of the president's policies since he visited Southeast Asia in late 1965. Romney said in Japan during the trip that "the American presence in Vietnam is necessary, if the world is to maintain liberty and freedom," and gave his full support to the American effort in Vietnam.[86] He told Eisenhower on his return that he saw the situation in South Vietnam as a "clearcut and fundamental" struggle in which the "issues are the same that brought our country into existence."[87] The next day, in a speech at the University of Detroit, the governor told students he was "now convinced the war in Vietnam involves circumstances much more complex and fateful than any war in which our country has been involved," calling the conflict "morally right and necessary."[88]

Unfortunately for Romney, his subsequent statements on the war were neither as clear nor as convincing. In July 1966, *Newsweek* criticized both Romney and the GOP for their positions on the war: "[Since Johnson escalated the conflict in March 1965] the Republicans have been groping for a viable way to capitalize on it. No one has groped more earnestly than Michigan's Gov. George Romney—but he has shifted his ground on the issue so many times that by now probably not even Mrs. Romney is sure where he stands." *Harper's* sounded similar concerns: "[Romney's] confusing remarks are not the guileful ambiguities of a Nixon but rather the product of ignorance and genuine uncertainty complicated by a terrible need to be right, both ethically and politically." Mike Mansfield complained that his position on the war was, at best, inscrutable: "I wish [Romney] would be a little more specific and explicit on where he stands. He's going all over the rainbow and nobody knows where the Governor of Michigan stands. If he's going to be a presidential candidate, he'll have to take a stand, sometime, some way." Romney even faced ridicule in his home state despite his widespread popularity. The *Detroit News,* in an editorial titled "He's Still Confused," skewered the governor and suggested that he "compose his thoughts, do his homework," and "hire some experts on national and international affairs."[89]

During a speaking trip in the Western United States in February 1967, Romney continued to have trouble defining his stance on the war. Prior to leaving, his foreign policy adviser, Jonathan Moore, suggested that he say no more about Vietnam because of the complicated issues that made oversimplification and misunderstanding so easy—and so politically dangerous. Moore recommended that he state only that the Republicans had the advantage of being able to take a fresh look at Vietnam without the impediment of having been involved in earlier mistakes. Initially, Romney followed the advice, but, as the trip wore on, he fell into his old habits of vagueness and apparent confusion. The *Detroit Free Press* opined that his floundering on the war had exposed his "lean heel," and opinion polls showed Nixon surging ahead of him among Republican voters. Other Republican leaders expressed their doubts about his position as well. Barry Goldwater told a friend, "My objections to Romney as a candidate are not based upon what he did or didn't do for me in 1964, but rather on his extreme hesitancy in taking any position on Vietnam." What really concerned the former senator was that "an adult man who has been President of a large corporation and Governor of a large state who has read and heard about our difficulties in Vietnam should be able by this time to make some kind of statement either for or against or in the middle on the subject."[90]

In retrospect, it would have been wise for Romney to "say flatly at once, and for many months thereafter, that he simply did not understand Vietnam, that he was not equipped to discuss Vietnam at that early moment" in the campaign. Unfortunately for his presidential aspirations, he could not stop himself from addressing the questions posed by an inquisitive and increasingly hostile press. Instead, he discussed the war "in the most plodding prose, in open innocent confession of his non-understanding, over and over and over again, to the despair of his staff." Romney's staff was not alone in questioning his problems with Vietnam. Eisenhower remarked to a friend, "I do not know what Governor Romney is doing to cause the bad impressions. He has proved himself to be a real vote-getter in Michigan and I do hope that he is not allowing ambition to change his personality or to create bad impressions. I am certain that he is a man of integrity and character and a great deal of ability." What Romney needed, Eisenhower opined, was "a truly skilful [sic] speech writer. It just does not make sense for a man to be so capable as he is in every other way and to have him create among his audiences doubt and bewilderment."[91] As a result of his struggles with the war, Vietnam plagued the governor almost as much as it did LBJ.

In an attempt to clarify for the public (and, perhaps, himself) where he stood on the war, Romney made a speech in Hartford, Connecticut, on 7 April 1967. During the days prior to his address, he sent draft copies of the speech to members of the GOP to solicit their opinions on his proposed remarks. One copy went to Jacob Javits, who had a "generally favorable reaction" but thought "the demand that the NLF negotiate itself out of existence . . . [to be] unreasonable, unrealistic, and naive—an impossible condition that . . . renders the whole approach unworkable." Nevertheless, Javits promised "he won't be critical publicly."[92] In his speech, Romney called withdrawal "unthinkable" and declared that the United States "must use military force as necessary to reduce or cut off the flow of men and supplies from North Vietnam, to knock out enemy main force units, and to provide a military shield for the South." But he also asserted that the United States "must avoid such future entrapments" and "should continue to seek meaningful negotiations. . . . America's major objective and contribution must be a just peace."[93] Intended to be a defining statement on the war that would increase his appeal as a presidential candidate, Romney's ambiguous speech instead clouded public perception of his position.

Still, the reaction to the Hartford speech was generally favorable. The *Washington Evening Star* declared, "The charge of 'fuzziness' in his thinking on the war in Vietnam can no longer fairly be brought against George Romney."[94] John Tower wrote Romney and told him that his remarks were "thoughtful, constructive and well done," and Wallace Bennett praised Romney for showing that he understood the nature of the American commitment to Vietnam by warning against the dangers of both indiscriminate escalation and withdrawal and for "placing the national interest above personal or partisan advantage."[95] But not everyone was satisfied with the speech, and many identified equivocations about Vietnam in it. The editors of *Detroit Free Press*, for example, wrote, "Romney has not yet removed Vietnam as the most troublesome issue among Republicans." Calling Vietnam "the most important issue, in his campaign for the presidency," they interpreted Romney's remarks as giving at least superficial support to Johnson's policies while not becoming "one of Lyndon Johnson's converts." "But," they concluded, "he has taken his pew in the LBJ church. It remains to be seen if he will be a believer or a backslider."[96]

The *Christian Science Monitor* characterized Romney's position as: "(1) Avoids an immediate row with President Johnson, (2) Is acceptable to both dove and hawk wings of the Republican party, and (3) Leaves Mr. Romney with freedom of action if the situation in Vietnam . . . should change." The paper recognized, "Romney had to have a position on the war. That was required of him as proof of the seriousness of his candidacy for the Republican nomination. . . . Had he taken up an extreme position, either way, he could have attracted to himself much criticism which now knows only the President as its target." But, as it doled out faint praise to Romney, the *Monitor* also took the GOP to task. The Republican Party, it argued, "is in the safe position of not pretending to know how to run the war from the opposition benches. . . . It merely watches critically and remains ready to take advantage of any serious blunder by the White House." An editorial cartoon in the *Detroit Free Press* showed Johnson and Romney sharing the same shirt standing between "Dovesville" and "Hawksville," with Johnson saying, "Why George! What a pleasant surprise, seeing you here!"[97] The following week, Romney's staff assessed the performance in much the same way. Jonathan Moore told the governor, "It got the press off your back on not having a Vietnam position [and made it clear that] you stood basically with the President." Yet the "speech was *too* close" to Johnson's position: "I don't think, in general, there's enough George Romney in the speech."[98] The problem, of course, was that it *was* George Romney in the speech, and that would prove to be his undoing as a presidential candidate.

Lyndon Johnson and his advisers saw the speech as an opportunity to mute Republican criticism of the administration's policies. John Roche sent a memo to Marvin Watson arguing that Romney's "peace with amnesty" plan was the same as the "National Reconciliation" program the administration had been pushing. Roche opined, "[Romney's] speech is going to land with a dull, mushy thud. Let's not do anything by way of publicizing it."[99] In analyzing an advance copy of Romney's remarks, Walt Rostow noted several points of agreement between the president and the governor. Yet he also noted that Romney "tries to have it both ways to a certain extent" and that the administration would have to deal with several issues in the speech. Rostow suggested that Johnson "welcome his support for [administration] policy and for his perhaps important message to Hanoi." He also urged the president and his surrogates to "take [Romney] to task hard" on points of disagreement and "deal firmly with his credibility gap and constitutional arguments."[100] Johnson took the advice. The president heartily thanked Romney for his support, choosing to interpret the statement as a vote of confidence in his approach to the war. Romney quickly responded that his statement should not be taken as "blank-check approval" of the administration's policies. The conflicting rhetoric in the speech, while effective in temporarily neutralizing Vietnam as an issue for the governor, would return to haunt him as the campaign for the GOP nomination continued. His rivals for the nomination, his Democratic opponents, and the media would point to his enigmatic position as a sign that Romney did not have the requisite leadership qualities and foreign policy experience to be president.

The harshest attacks came from conservatives who were already wary of the moderate Romney's political philosophy. The Right ridiculed him and his speech mercilessly in the weeks that followed. In response to his suggestions that the United States pursue "peace with honor," Ronald Reagan stated, "My idea of honorable disengagement is that you win the war. When you commit men to fight and die for a cause, it must be worth winning."[101] The *National Review* jibed, "George Romney's staff finally told him what his position is on Vietnam." It then suggested that the speech "appears to have opened up a noisy split in the GOP." This concerned the editors, who understood that "the GOP position on Vietnam will be a critical item at the '68 convention" and that the party "could founder on its disagreements over Vietnam."[102]

The Hartford speech did nothing to arrest Romney's slowly declining popularity. Jules Witcover later called it "a temporary tourniquet," and Barry Goldwater argued, "'The American people like it black and white. . . . They don't want to do too much thinking for themselves. Romney's too gray, that's his problem.'"[103] National polls, which had initially showed the governor leading both his GOP rivals and the president by a comfortable margin, now placed him in a dead heat with Johnson for the first time. His vagueness on the war was taking its toll. While Americans no longer automatically believed Johnson's statements about progress in Vietnam, it seemed equally as clear that they could not understand what Romney was saying about the war in his public appearances.[104] The governor's poll numbers would stagnate for most of the summer, stabilizing slightly following the Detroit race riots in July after the president sent in regular army troops to restore order. But the bounce was only temporary, and the war issue remained a source of trouble for George Romney.

Trouble resulting from the war did not fall exclusively within Romney's camp. Edward Brooke had ridden on the cusp of the antiwar wave, having been elected on the strength of his opposition to the conflict. But things would change when he embarked on a fact-finding tour of Asia on 4 March 1967, a trip that he originally hoped would end with a discussion with the North Vietnamese leader, Ho Chi Minh, in Hanoi. Peter Lucas, a Brooke confidant, thought that such a trip would be a great opportunity for Brooke; an African American U.S. senator intent on crossing into "enemy territory" was "one hell of an idea." Had Ho Chi Minh agreed to meet Brooke, "a picture of their meeting would have circulated throughout the world, and Brooke would have become an instant global hero."[105] Aside from his proposed meeting with Ho, to which the State Department (predictably) objected strenuously, Brooke wanted to learn about the political and military situation in Southeast Asia. When he arrived in Saigon on 11 March, he toured the countryside, visited troop installations, and sat through "innumerable briefings." He also had the opportunity to meet with South Vietnamese officials, including Prime Minister Ky and both the military and the civilian leaders of the American effort, William Westmoreland and Henry Cabot Lodge, the latter having returned to Saigon for a second tour as ambassador.[106]

Brooke was so struck by what he discovered in Vietnam that it led him to make a startling announcement. In his first speech as a senator, he surprisingly changed his position on the war. Brooke criticized the "incessant harping on whether or not we ought to have sent troops to Vietnam in the first place." Rather than relying on hindsight, he asserted that the "inescapable fact was that we were in Vietnam in a massive way" and that the "challenge was to find the best way to end it."[107] He warned allies and adversaries alike, "The American people will persevere in their fundamental support of the South Vietnamese . . . [and] are beginning to accept, reluctantly but definitely, that this struggle could conceivably last another decade." He also observed that, given Ho Chi Minh's unwavering demand that negotiations were impossible without the cessation of bombing and the unilateral withdrawal of American troops from South Vietnam, it seemed apparent that Hanoi "shows no intention . . . to negotiate for peace at this time." Therefore, he concluded, "The general direction of our present military efforts in Vietnam is necessary."[108]

While Brooke continued to advocate containing the war and pursuing negotiations, his position had definitely changed from a moderate dove to a moderate hawk, moving him closer to the center of the GOP. In assessing his speech, the *New York Times* asserted, "President Johnson won a prize convert today in the congressional debate on the Vietnam war." Brooke's legislative aide, Alton Frye, later said that the senator was "unhappy, intellectually, and emotionally discontented that he had reached a policy judgment on the evidence different from his preferences." But he could not ignore what he had seen and heard during his time in South Vietnam. Johnson called Brooke later that week from Camp David and praised the senator for performing a great service to the nation for saying that the best path to peace lay in continued military pressure on the Communists. John Tower, an ardent hawk, also lauded Brooke's change of heart, calling it "one of the most courageous acts on the part of one of my colleagues I have witnessed since being in this body." Brooke maintained that he "was never a hawk"—and his subsequent statements and actions support his claim—but his about-face on the war must have come as quite a shock to the voters who sent him to Washington as an opponent of the conflict.[109]

Hoping to reassure both his constituents and his congressional colleagues about where he stood on the war, Brooke clarified his position in an appearance on "Face the Nation" in late March. His "personal reassessment" of the bombings during his visit to Vietnam convinced him that "Ho Chi Minh is not ready to negotiate for peace solely upon cessation of bombings." Moreover, given the U.S. commitment to the Saigon regime, the administration could not withdraw. As Brooke explained the situation, "We would leave them in a very weak, vulnerable position. Our word would mean nothing at all. And there could be takeovers in all of those countries." He refuted the notion that Johnson had "brainwashed" him or tried to twist his arm. Rather, he argued, he had revised his view of the war on the basis of his experience.[110] Brooke should be credited for taking an increasingly unpopular stance at the same time as many of his fellow legislators abandoned their own convictions for the sake of political expediency. Indeed, his conversion in 1967 is unique in the narrative of the U.S. experience in Vietnam.

A number of other Republicans would make the trek to Southeast Asia in 1967 to assess the situation for themselves. Richard Nixon returned in mid-April to "evaluate the situation in Vietnam and the importance of the conflict to Vietnam's neighbors." What he saw convinced him that "continuation of the administration's policy of fighting a defensive war of attrition would inevitably lead to defeat."[111] Despite the fact that public opinion had clearly shifted against the war, Nixon remained steadfast in his belief that it could still be won and that the country should do everything it could to ensure that outcome. Toward this end, he again derided the opponents of the U.S. military effort. In Saigon, he urged Democratic opponents to declare "a moratorium on all the kind of criticism that gives aid and comfort to the enemy." While acknowledging that "some division" existed within the GOP, he pointed out that those differences paled in comparison to the Democratic rift.[112] While he was probably correct in his assessment of the relative severity of the fissures in both parties, the evidence makes clear that the Republicans were not as unified as the former vice president believed.

The divisions within the GOP became publicly apparent in the spring. First, Clifford Case accused Johnson of producing a "crisis of confidence" through the "misuse" and "perversion" of the Tonkin Gulf resolution. Dirksen fired back, asserting that Case's speech "essentially called the 97 other senators . . . a 'bunch of dummies.'"[113] Then, the Republican Policy Committee drafted a report entitled "The War in Vietnam." The report reviewed American policy toward Indochina since World War II but failed to include any substantive alternatives to the current policy. It had been prepared following a meeting of the Republican Policy Committee in late March at which Javits suggested that Senate Republicans should reach a consensus on Vietnam.[114] Although lacking specific policy prescriptions, the report did ask Republicans to consider two fundamental questions: what the American national interest in Southeast Asia was and how much further the party and the nation were prepared to go in support of that interest. The underlying tone was decidedly more dovish than the line that had previously been taken by the GOP leadership, much to the dismay of many in the party. *Congressional Quarterly* reported on the consequences of dissent and the proliferation of doves in the Democratic Party. In discussing the problems faced by the Democrats as a result of their intraparty differences on the war, it observed, "The Republicans are not a great deal better off. A deep split in the party became apparent after the release May 1 of a staff paper which questioned the wisdom of American military involvement in Viet Nam. Republican leadership in the House and Senate quickly shelved the document, but the debate within the party continues. Openly or not, the Republicans have their share of 'doves' as well."[115]

John Tower expressed outrage at the release of the study. He dismissed it as "neither party policy nor a Senate Republican party position. It was simply a 'think piece.'" The hawkish senator took great pains to "disassociate" himself from "a number of its inferences and suggested conclusions."[116] The next day, Tower wrote to Bourke Hickenlooper, who chaired the Republican Policy Committee. "I deeply regret that the 'War in Vietnam' report was made public to the press before the originally planned conference was held on it," he said. The Texan had hoped to make "a number of suggestions and comments . . . before any such release" since "we were dealing with the issue probably primary to the 1968 campaign." Tower feared that the report in its raw form might be misinterpreted by Hanoi as "evidence that one of the major parties is on the verge of withdrawing support to the President in the war." Given the fact that Tower had spent more time in Vietnam than any other member of Congress, he was surprised not to have been consulted about the report. Ultimately, he concluded,

"It is not only the absolute demand of national security but also the best politics for our party not to seem to withdraw support from the war effort at a crucial time."[117] Tower was not alone in his criticism of the report. Ronald Reagan made it perfectly clear where he stood at a press conference on 2 May: "I have insisted for a long time that our goal should be to win and I think you win as swiftly as possible, that attrition over the long period of time will cost us more in lives than a sudden strike for victory."[118]

Unable to let the matter drop, Tower held a press conference on 4 May to further attack the white paper. Admitting that there were "shades of opinion" within the party over Vietnam, he nevertheless felt that the paper should not be seen as exposing "*considerable* division between and among us on the issue of our position in Southeast Asia." He reiterated his commitment to continuing "*unrelenting* military pressure on the enemy" and opposition to accepting any settlement that did not guarantee South Vietnamese independence. In making his comments, he stressed the need for unity on the Vietnam issue, echoing the statements of Nixon and Eisenhower when he said, "There is no question but what Hanoi interprets vocal dissent in this country as a sign of lack of resolve."[119]

In the wake of Tower's acrimonious response to the report, the Republicans scrambled to play down the emerging policy rift in order to maintain some semblance of unity on the war. Mark Hatfield, who supported the study's conclusions, noted, "Republicans may not all share the same view concerning the war in Vietnam, but they will all respect and welcome the truth." The senator stated that he hoped the paper would "initiate a frank review within the Republican party of this nation's policies and objectives in Vietnam."[120] Barry Goldwater wrote to Dirksen and suggested that the GOP "seriously consider a discussion of the Coordinating Committee's position on Vietnam at the coming July meeting." The former presidential candidate believed that it was "imperative that the Party . . . clear up a position that has become a bit cloudy." The same day, however, his newspaper column suggested, "The cooing of these doves is a distinctly off-key note in party councils."[121]

The Republican infighting piqued the interest of the nation's columnists. Gould Lincoln, writing in the *Washington Star*, noted that the GOP position on the war—should the fighting continue into 1968—"is of major importance. If it should become known as a 'peace party,' many of the party's leaders and rank and file would be outraged." These hawks, he wrote, believed that discontent "is confined to a mere handful." He concluded that, if there was "any genuine attempt by the GOP to make itself an anti-war, peace party, the Republicans will be treading on dangerous ground" because, if the doves were successful in making the war a partisan political issue, "it will be without the support of top people in the Republican National Committee" as well as leading presidential candidates like Richard Nixon.[122]

Everett Dirksen, whose herculean efforts to keep the GOP firmly behind the president throughout the war had been amazingly effective, clearly had his work cut out for him. On learning of the report's release, Dirksen—who had been hospitalized with pneumonia—stayed up all night drafting a policy statement of his own. The next day, he left the hospital for the Senate to read his speech, which, unsurprisingly, represented a total endorsement of Johnson's policies in Vietnam. Asserting himself as the leader of the GOP in the Senate, Dirksen announced, "Preserving wholly the right of full and fair inquiry and criticism, we reiterate our wholehearted support of the commander in chief of our armed forces. We reaffirm our position of standing four-square behind him." Echoing Tower's criticisms, Dirksen's speech effectively neutralized the report's potential for expanded criticism of the president, a fact that he acknowledged later (with no little hyperbole): "When I put on the silencer, they are silent!" A relieved Johnson called Dirksen and simply said, "Thanks."[123]

But just because Dirksen reasserted his support for LBJ did not mean that the party meekly accepted his statement or his endorsement of the president. An increasing number of Republicans—irrespective of their position on the war—began to publicly suggest that the war could not be concluded with Johnson in the White House. While this move would be an obvious campaign tactic in any election year, it is clear that, politics aside, many truly believed this to be the case. George Aiken argued that, regardless of the administration's good intentions, it was a prisoner of its past, "too bound by its own vague criterion, its own predictions, its own predilections, its own conceptions and emotional commitments to see the interest of the Nation *except in terms of its own survival as the Government in power.*" Only a Republican president, "unfettered by the past," could end the war.[124] Edward Brooke mused that perhaps Ho Chi Minh would feel freer to bargain with a Republican president. And Representative Florence Dwyer (R-NJ) told a group of reporters from her home state, "The Administration has become so locked-in on its policy, so totally committed to the course it has set out to follow, that it greets all proposals for change with thinly veiled contempt."[125]

Moreover, Dirksen's effort to bring dissident Republicans back into the fold quickly devolved into a losing battle. By late summer 1967, most of the Republican leadership began to maneuver to disengage the party from Johnson's policies in anticipation of the upcoming campaign. In addition, the divide between hawks and doves within the party grew more pronounced, and it became apparent that the party was becoming nearly as divided as the Democrats on the question of the war. Although Dirksen managed to rein in some of the criticism

4 May 1967: "The Widening War"

of the president's policies among Senate Republicans, his reach did not extend to others within the party. Some Republicans had also grown weary of Dirksen's constant support of the administration. One complained, "Old Ev keeps saying, 'We stand for this' and 'we stand for that,' but the 'we' is more apt to be Ev and Lyndon Johnson than Ev and us Republicans."[126] In a sweeping attack on the administration's "confused foreign policy," the former GOP presidential nominee Alf Landon joined the fray. He declared that the president's "basic mistake" was to "underestimate what Americans had to do to win in South Vietnam." He also criticized both Johnson's tactical military decisions and the administration's failure to capitalize on opportunities for a negotiated settlement. He proposed that the president create a bipartisan "council of state" that would "consider not only Vietnam, but all other perilous options calling for immediate consideration and decision."[127]

The same day, the *Christian Science Monitor* ran an article that referred to Vietnam as "the Republican's [*sic*] big issue" that could lead the party to victory in 1968. The paper opined that the GOP stood "to be the beneficiaries of the growing frustrations of the American people" and of the growing feeling that the Democrats were not likely to "come up with any fresh, new approach to finding a satisfactory way out of the war." The article did not project that the GOP would be dovish out of necessity, however. The Republican position on Vietnam "may well be characterized more by a certain imprecision than by either dovishness or hawkishness" in order to accommodate the views of Aiken, Percy, Dirksen, and Nixon. The *Monitor* concluded, "It seems clear that this approach would have a great drawing power among voters. It might be enough of itself to cause a change in administrations."[128]

The increased public concern about the war paralleled efforts by some Republicans to deescalate American participation in the conflict. For example, on 19 May 1967, Paul Findley presented a joint resolution in the House "to refer the war issues in Vietnam to the International Court of Justice at the Hague for adjudication." The proposal, which was introduced as an amendment to the Tonkin Gulf resolution, "would demonstrate forcibly our desire to settle the issues by judicial process rather than force, clarify them in terms of international law, and accept as binding the judgment of the tribunal." In addition, Findley continued, it would test Hanoi's sincerity for a peaceful settlement to the conflict. If the enemy accepted, the war would end. If they refused, they "would be weakened in the important field of international opinion because [they] would have scorned the world's highest tribunal." Further, if the court found in favor of the American position, the United States would secure an international mandate for its military efforts and political position in Vietnam. It would no longer be isolated. Findley considered international law to be "the missing piece of the Vietnam jigsaw puzzle" that would "strengthen our position" if it failed.[129]

While congressional Republicans struggled with the war, nongovernmental groups affiliated with the GOP served notice that their views would not go unheard. In June 1967, the Ripon Society released a paper titled "The Myth of Bipartisanship."[130] Organized by a group of young academics, lawyers, and businessmen at Harvard in 1962, the Ripon Society "tried to provide the GOP with political ideas that contribute to the American dialogue. . . . Ripon members have seen as their most important contribution to American politics a bridging of the gulf that has separated much of the GOP from the intellectual and professional community for the past fifty years." The society focused particularly on young Americans and espoused a moderate-to-liberal view of Republican politics. Influenced by the British Conservative Party's Bow Group, it sought to establish itself as an organization of youthful Republican intellectuals oriented toward discussions of policy and the publication of position papers on a wide variety of issues, including civil rights, the decentralization of political power, and an end to the draft.

Criticizing the Johnson administration's foreign policy generally as a "muddled and meandering mess," the Ripon Society's report accused the president and his advisers of being "unguided by principle" and "prisoners of events." Significantly, however, the paper did not limit its attacks to the administration. It also censured the GOP leadership in Congress for offering "little edification and no alternative" to the status quo, calling them "the worst 'me-tooers' on issues of foreign policy." In particular, the Republicans were reprimanded for repudiating the Senate Republican Policy Committee's "penetrating and thoughtful" study of Vietnam earlier in the year and for declaring they stood squarely behind the president on Vietnam. The party "too rarely questions the policies behind which it is asked to unite," thus failing in its duties within the American political system.

The misuse of "bipartisanship" had led, the Ripons continued, to "a myth which identified bipartisanship with unity itself, rather than with the procedures used to attain such unity." In order to restore a truly bipartisan foreign policy, the paper suggested four basic rules for the GOP to follow. First, the party should diligently pursue opportunities for genuine bipartisan cooperation. Second, the opposition party must demand to be kept informed and not accept mere briefings about actions already decided on. Third, the opposition must offer constructive criticism of the administration's policies, a task in which the Republicans had failed. This failure resulted in a lack of awareness among the public regarding the facts, alternatives, and issues of foreign policy decisions. Finally, the GOP needed to "debate and resolve its own foreign policy views, that policy the GOP would employ were it in control of the White House." Such policy should necessarily be based on the broad foreign policy consensus in the United States. The clear duty of the Republican Party, the paper concluded, was "to employ all its available resources in the responsible study and debate of the pressing issues of foreign policy."[131]

Virtually everyone ignored the Ripon paper's recommendation for productive debate on the Vietnam War. Instead, partisan sniping became increasingly common as the year unfolded. In late June, a group of Republican congressmen attacked the administration for allowing the United States to become bogged down in a hit-and-run war. They argued that the way to peace in Vietnam was by winning the war. Representative George Hansen (R-ID) argued, "History has proven that the only thing the Communists respect is strength." Although such a policy was "long overdue, it is not too late. With resoluteness and courage . . . we can end this bitter struggle." He concluded, "[If] Ho Chi Minh won't cease his aggression and negotiate, let's do what must be done to put an end to this absurdity. Let's have peace in Vietnam—let's win!"[132] Representative Durward G. Hall (R-MO) concurred, stating, "The American people want us to cease this impasse . . . they are very anxious that we win."[133] Senator Paul Fannin (R-AZ), who won Goldwater's old Senate seat in the 1964 election, supported the war effort as strongly as his fellow Arizonan. Arguing that the "only peace that has so far interested the Communists is a piece of South Vietnam," he urged the administration to "apply the necessary force to bring the conflict to an early and honorable conclusion."[134] Ronald Reagan consistently attacked the administration for failing to maximize American power in Vietnam. In a speech to the National Young Republicans Convention in late June, he asserted, "We have the power to wind it up fast, and I think we should use it. I think Ho Chi Minh should be sitting on an apple crate, begging for help." But he did not believe that the GOP should count on the war as a major campaign issue in 1968, noting, "I'd hate to think anyone was hanging a political campaign on keeping the war alive just to make it an issue."[135]

These hawkish statements belied the trend of heightened public concern and growing antiwar sentiment resulting from the administration's lack of progress on the war. In a July Gallup poll, 52 percent of those surveyed said that they disapproved of the way Johnson was dealing with the situation in Vietnam, and only one-third expressed approval. This was "the highest level of criticism reached to date" and represented a sharp rise in disapproval since the month before.[136] Stewart Alsop, writing in the *Saturday Evening Post,* opined that both doves and hawks disliked Johnson's middle course on the war. But, he continued, "In next year's campaign the Republican candidate will have to take a position, and he, too, will thus risk alienating hawks, or doves, or both at once."

And, unfortunately for the party, no Republican had come up with a "magic solution" as yet.[137]

More consistent with the Gallup findings was a suggestion made by a group of GOP congressmen led by Bradford Morse (R-MA) and Robert Stafford (R-VT). They unveiled a proposal for a staged deescalation of the bombing of North Vietnam on 10 July 1967. Under the Graduated Reciprocal Identifiable De-Escalation (GRID) plan, the United States would halt all bombing of North Vietnam north of the twenty-first parallel—including Hanoi but excluding Haiphong—for sixty days. If the Hanoi regime responded with a similarly limited but verifiable deescalatory step, America would extend the bombing ban north of the twentieth parallel. Through a series of reciprocal steps, the bombing of the North would eventually be ended along with the North Vietnamese support to the South. While Morse and his colleagues admitted that Hanoi had not shown "a sincere interest in peace," they pointed to the deficiencies in previous bombing pauses undertaken by the Johnson administration and cited a number of reasons why the new plan would succeed. They argued that the proposal involved minimum military risk to both sides, gave Hanoi the chance to "save face," and did not deal in ultimatums or threats. They concluded, "We are not yet convinced that Hanoi has no interest in peace, but we are convinced that the possibility has not yet been tested by creative and sensitive U.S. diplomacy."[138]

The response to the proposal was mixed. The *Salt Lake Tribune* gave it tepid support. Calling it a "trial balloon that may never get off the ground" because its proponents were not nationally known and did not hold GOP leadership positions, the paper nevertheless suggested that, from a domestic perspective, it "could give the Vietnam debate another dimension by substituting a flexible approach for hard-line arguments of hawks and doves."[139] In assessing the plan for Walt Rostow, the prolific and seemingly omnipresent William Bundy called it "thoughtful and constructive" and "a not unreasonable specific suggestion along the lines of mutual deescalation." Bundy did criticize the GRID plan as weak because it gave Hanoi a military advantage during the sixty-day bombing pause and would not ensure that Hanoi would respond favorably. The reaction among House Democrats, however, indicates that Johnson and the Democratic leadership wanted to discredit the measure, if for no other reason than that it originated from a Republican source.[140] And, indeed, no action was taken on the Morse proposal.

One member of the Republican leadership took a different tack, however. Melvin Laird, in his characteristically direct style, spoke in the House on 17 July, stating, "I see only two realistic choices facing us today: reaffirm our original objective and proceed from there; or pull out of Vietnam before another drop of American blood is needlessly spilled. These are harsh words . . . but they are spoken out of a deep conviction." Calling himself a pessimist on the war, Laird said that he believed that the Manila agreement was a recipe for a Communist takeover in South Vietnam. Unless the administration clarified its position, disavowed Manila, and pledged itself to the existence of a free and independent South Vietnam, he would support "an immediate unilateral withdrawal."[141] Johnson must have felt dismay on hearing Laird's statement. Losing the support of one of the most influential members of the Republican Party was a blow to the administration that would have serious ramifications in the coming presidential campaign.

But, as disconcerting to LBJ as Laird's comments were, the wide spectrum of opposition to his policies in Vietnam caused even more consternation. The Hydra of opinion on the war forced the president to juggle multiple constituencies as he attempted vainly to safeguard his domestic priorities and prevent a crippling debate about the trajectory of the conflict. Unlike the Greek hero Heracles, he could not figure out a way to slay the monster—or at least was not willing to take the steps necessary to do so. Instead, he chose to fight a running and tactical battle on the political front against an array of opposition rather than making a definitive strategic decision on the military front to prosecute the war more vigorously or deescalate American involvement. As a result, he would find himself in a totally untenable situation as he faced the likelihood of running for reelection with no end in sight for the conflict in Southeast Asia and a Republican Party salivating at the prospect.

# CHAPTER 5

# Sisyphus and Tantalus

## The Political Impact of the War, 1967–1968

Human blunders, however, usually do more to shape history than human wickedness.
> —A. J. P. Taylor, *The Origins of the Second World War*

The commonest error in politics is sticking to the carcasses of dead policies.
> —Lord Salisbury quoted in E. D. Steele,
> *Lord Salisbury: A Political Biography*

Hell, according to the English author Henry Gardiner Adams, is "truth seen too late." For Lyndon Johnson and George Romney, no statement could more accurately summarize their experiences with Vietnam during 1967 and early 1968. Both had public epiphanies about the war that would cost them a chance to win the presidency, and they would spend the rest of their lives looking back with regret. Indeed, Johnson and Romney could be easily compared to Sisyphus and Tantalus, the characters from Greek mythology condemned by the gods to eternal torture for their misdeeds—Sisyphus rolling his stone up a hill but always having it roll back down, Tantalus burning with thirst but never able to reach the water. Like these tragic figures, Johnson and Romney would never reach their political goals, even though they appeared to be tantalizingly close, as a result of missteps in dealing with the conflict in Southeast Asia. This chapter analyzes how Vietnam affected their political fortunes and how the Republican Party attempted to appropriate the war as a campaign issue.

By the summer of 1967, the administration had been escalating the war in Vietnam steadily for two years with "dismal results."[1] The massive bombing campaign had failed to interdict supplies flowing south and had only minimal impact on the North Vietnamese infrastructure. Even as the search-and-destroy strategy accumulated massive body counts and the American troop level approached 500,000, there was no discernible progress on the ground; the success trumpeted by the military leadership in Saigon was merely a mirage. In an effort to break the stalemate, General Westmoreland and Walt Rostow began working on plans to bomb National Liberation Front (NLF) sanctuaries in Laos and Cambodia and invade those two countries to cut the Ho Chi Minh Trail. They both urged the president to permit American military actions north of the demilitarized zone and sought permission to initiate a massive bombing campaign against every military and industrial target in North Vietnam. Meanwhile, the antiwar movement spread beyond the nation's universities as support for the war dropped below 50 percent. Although not a unified "movement" per se, the protests attracted a broad range of participants frustrated with the conflict and eager to see it resolved.

Caught in the middle of these countervailing forces, Johnson tried to change the paradigm of the war in a speech in San Antonio that September. The proposal he presented there represented the first modification of American demands for resolving the war. Instead of insisting on an immediate withdrawal of all North Vietnamese troops, he offered to stop bombing North Vietnam if Ho Chi Minh agreed to serious negotiations and promised not to use the bombing halt to increase infiltration into South Vietnam. He even hinted at allowing the NLF to participate in the South Vietnamese government. Undeterred, North Vietnam made no response and stuck to its position that the United States should cease all bombing, withdraw all troops from Indochina, remove Nguyen Van Thieu and Nguyen Cao Ky from office, and permit a coalition government in Saigon that included the NLF. The San Antonio formula was a worthy effort on Johnson's part, but it failed to extricate him from the quagmire he faced with the war.

The Republicans experienced similar problems in reconciling the Vietnam issue. The divisions within the GOP were very real in mid-1967. Even as sentiment grew within the party to find a way out of Vietnam, Republican hawks held their ground. Eisenhower urged Congress to declare war on North Vietnam in order to give the American war effort priority over the domestic programs of the Great Society. While most Republicans refused to consider a declaration of war, fearing that the Soviets and/or the Chinese might intervene as a result, many agreed with the former president about making the war the highest priority for the country. Jack Miller derided the Johnson administration for trying to pursue a "guns and butter fiscal policy which has caused inflation and high interest rates," and the Republican Coordinating Committee stood solidly behind Eisenhower's statement regarding the hierarchy of budget priorities.[2]

In addition to their desire for the war to take precedence domestically, Republican hawks hammered the administration on the need to use U.S. military power more effectively in Vietnam. Gerald Ford asserted that he saw "no justification" for sending more troops to Vietnam while the administration prevented U.S. bombing missions from attacking Communist supply lines and industrial centers in the North. "Why are we pulling our best punches in Vietnam?" he wondered.[3] In an editorial lauding these sentiments, the *Indianapolis News* asked, "Why fight an enemy and then let his sources of supply, or a key airfield, or a strategic port, go unmolested?"[4] On NBC's "Today Show" on 16 August 1967, Tower argued that the United States had "to maintain unrelenting pressure on the enemy, that we cannot pull out with anything like reasonable terms until we show the enemy that we are determined to achieve military success, that we're determined to militarily secure South Vietnam." The only way to accomplish that, he continued, was "by maintaining unrelenting military pressure by bombing every target of major significance in the North. . . . [and] clos[ing] the port of Haiphong."[5]

The party's doves spoke just as adamantly against the war. Harold Stassen, in an interview in *Esquire,* said that he might seek the GOP nomination again in 1968 to ensure "a progressive Republican Party" committed to "peace in Vietnam."[6] He expanded on his position in a speech in Rochester, Minnesota, arguing, "[The] number one plank in the Republican platform of 1968 should be: 'We will bring the War in Vietnam to an early and honorable end.'" He believed that "the only effective way to end this terribly mistaken course of action is for our Republican Party to make it a clear-cut issue and carry it directly to the American people for their decision."[7] Jacob Javits concurred, arguing, "The time has come to mark the beginning of an end to our commitment there."[8] The *Los Angeles Times* noted the division of opinion within the party, reporting that, among Republican senators responding to its survey, seventeen backed administration policy on Vietnam and fourteen opposed it. Interestingly, the Democrats who responded reflected a similar split, with twenty-seven senators in support and twenty-six opposing.[9]

Facing eroding support from both parties, Johnson redoubled his efforts to reach out to the GOP hawks. He continued to consult frequently with Eisenhower through briefings with Goodpaster and sought advice from Republican members of the "Wise Men." The president also worked closely with Dirksen to clamp down on dissent among Republican senators, although Dirksen's effectiveness in this vein had begun to wane. Johnson enjoyed only limited success as more and more Republicans—whether because of conscience or political convenience—reconsidered their stance on the war. Criticism from both doves and hawks mounted, and opposition to the war and to the administration's conduct of the conflict was increasingly voiced. Tim Lee Carter, who had stunned Johnson with his comments the previous year, declared in August that the United States should, "while we are yet strong, bring our men home, every man jack of them."[10]

Political expediency obviously drove many politicians to change their public stance on the war. Nowhere was this more apparent than with Richard Nixon. Throughout the latter half of 1967, Nixon began to back away subtly from his aggressive rhetorical stance on the war and foreshadowed the purposefully ambiguous position he would adopt in 1968. In an interview with Carl Greenberg of the *Los Angeles Times,* he made a distinction between his views on the war and those of the "super-hawks" who supported measures such as a declaration of war, using nuclear weapons, or a "win-or-get-out" ultimatum. The former vice president also made an acute distinction about ending the war. He stated that the GOP position on Vietnam should focus, not on "how we lose in Vietnam" through an unsatisfactory peace settlement, but rather on "how we win."[11] He would raise such carefully crafted statements to an art form during his campaign for the presidency the following year.

Nixon had reason for optimism about his prospects for winning the 1968 Republican nomination. Given Ronald Reagan's inexperience and lack of a national political base and Rockefeller's lackluster attitude, the race seemed to be a clear-cut choice between Nixon and Romney, with Vietnam serving as the critical litmus test. William White addressed the differences between the candidates in the *Washington Post* on 23 August 1967. In assessing Romney's chances, White identified his "persistently cloudy attitude toward the war in Vietnam, an attitude which presently appears to be more dovish than hawkish" as one of his most significant weaknesses. "If the nomination were to be made today," White continued, Romney's views on Vietnam "would surely not be the views of the convention." Within the GOP, there seemed to be a sense that, in 1968, the party as a whole, and, thus, its presidential candidate, could "manage to run as the 'peace party' without at the same time quite repudiating the hard line against communism," that it could "claim the best of both worlds" by continuing to "speak for military resistance in Vietnam but also promise to end it."[12] The conservative *National Review* echoed White's assessment. The Michigan governor's "oscillation" on Vietnam, Cato wrote, "only reflects both sides of a widening division here between those Republicans who want the President to win the war and those who simply want to end it."[13]

The differences between Nixon and Romney did not alter the fact that the Republican candidate would undoubtedly attempt to use Vietnam against LBJ in the 1968 campaign. Given the precipitous decline in public support for the war and his policies, Johnson realized that, barring a settlement or significant military progress in Southeast Asia, he would be extremely vulnerable to GOP criticism. Democrats shared the president's concerns about the "political albatross" of Vietnam. Senator Joe Tydings (D-MD) told the Johnson aide Harry McPherson, "People are so frustrated and negative in Maryland that any reasonably good Republican could clobber me this year and probably next." Although Tydings hesitated to do so, his political advisers urged him to attack the president on the war issue. In recounting this conversation, McPherson informed Johnson that he had heard similar concerns expressed by Senators Edmund Muskie (D-ME) and Birch Bayh (D-IN). He called his discussion with Tydings "long [and] dispiriting" and lamented that, prior to this point, Tydings had been a "pretty good supporter" of the administration's policies.[14] With Vietnam occupying a pivotal position in the upcoming presidential campaign, it would be incumbent on all candidates for public office to delineate their position on the conflict clearly and forcefully—a stark contrast from 1966. Unfortunately, Romney failed to accomplish this basic political task.

The *Washington Evening Star* quoted an anonymous Republican as observing, "A lot of people would like to support Romney. He's got so many other constructive things to talk about, why does he always have to keep putting his foot in his mouth on Vietnam?"[15] One of Romney's biographers has asserted that the governor "seemed obsessed with the need for talking about Vietnam and winning national recognition as a man with deep understanding of international affairs."[16] This compulsion would ultimately cost Romney a chance at the White House. On 31 August 1967, he made a statement that, in hindsight, would prove to be the death knell of his presidential ambitions. In a taped interview with Lou Gordon on WKBD-TV in Detroit, he said, "When I came back from Viet Nam [in November 1965], I'd just had the greatest brainwashing that anybody can get." He proceeded to announce a quantum shift in his position on the war. "I no longer believe that it was necessary for us to get involved in South Vietnam to stop Communist aggression in Southeast Asia," he declared. Decrying the "tragic" conflict, he urged "a sound peace in South Vietnam at an early time."[17]

The connotation of *brainwashing* following the experiences of the American military in Korea and the popular perception of the term in the wake of the film *The Manchurian Candidate* made Romney's comments even more devastating. The *New York Times* called them an example of his "crippling lack of agility and verbal precision," and they appeared to reinforce Nixon's belief that Romney would not be able to "hit big-league pitching" in the campaign. Ironically, the *Detroit Free Press* had editorialized just a few days earlier that Romney had made "meaningful progress" in terms of clarifying his position on the war and said that the governor "appeared to be brain-washed by the military during his 1965 trip to the front." Given the importance of the *Free Press* in Michigan, it is quite possible that Romney read this editorial and, consciously or not, found that *brainwashing* aptly described his experience.[18]

Initially, some members of Romney's campaign staff seemed unconcerned about the remarks. His press secretary, Travis Cross, explained that being brainwashed at a White House briefing had become a standard joke among the governors, who used *brainwashing* interchangeably with *LBJ arm-twisting*. Yet, once the program aired on 4 September, trouble clearly loomed on the horizon. Dr. William B. Prendergast, in charge of research for the Romney for President Committee, immediately understood the dangers implicit in the use of the term. He realized that political critics, cartoonists, and pundits would find it irresistible to skewer Romney and his lack of coherence in matters of foreign policy.[19] One journalist wrote, "To admit he'd been wrong, over-sold on President Johnson's war strategy, was ungainly enough. Worse, that word 'brainwash' had a curiously chemical effect on the minds of Washington columnists. They flipped."[20]

Romney did attempt damage control by clarifying his remarks. A week later, he stated, "I believe that the full record clearly indicates that there has been a systematic continuation of inaccurate reports, predictions, and withholding information. This has kept the American people from knowing the facts about the Vietnam war and its full impact on our domestic and foreign affairs." Reagan believed that Romney's explanation was sound: "Perhaps he expressed at the same time the concern that a lot of Americans should have as to whether they are getting all of the facts that they are entitled to have about foreign and domestic policy."[21] Other Republicans came to Romney's defense as well. Eisenhower told the hotel magnate and Romney backer Willard Marriott, "I have personally felt that his 'brainwashing' statement was a mere explosive expression rather than an attack upon others." George Aiken, while admitting that the choice of words was poor, defended Romney, suggesting that it was highly likely that the governors "got things glossed over" on the trip and posited that it would not hurt Romney's candidacy. He did characterize Romney as "not a very astute politician."[22]

Despite his best efforts and the supportive comments from some of his colleagues, Romney's "brainwashing" statement crippled his status as the GOP front-runner and generated a maelstrom of controversy and derision from the media and within the Republican Party. *Human Events* suggested that Romney "was counting his intellectual pillow cases and found that two of his tea towels were missing. . . . If a prospective candidate for that high office has staged a clumsier, more witless performance . . . the embarrassment does not read-

8 September 1967: "George, How Did You Get into That?"

ily come to mind."²³ The *St. Louis Globe-Democrat* editorialized that Romney's statement "had all the psychological implication of a political death wish" and asserted, "We feel he is through. He certainly ought to be. This would be a good thing for the nation and for the GOP. Who could want a nominee or a President who, in effect, confesses he was a pushover for a 'brainwash?'"²⁴ The critics reacted as if Angela Lansbury flashed the queen of diamonds and Romney responded as programmed.

John Tower had praised Edward Brooke's about-face in favor of the war earlier in the year, but the hawkish senator blasted Romney's change of heart. "I have been to Vietnam three times and I haven't been brainwashed," he proclaimed. "I don't see how anybody could charge top American military and diplomatic personnel with brainwashing unless it is believed those personnel are incompetent or deliberately devious." Tower did give Romney a little benefit of the doubt: "I doubt if the Governor meant he was 'brainwashed.' It was an unfortunate choice of words."²⁵ Robert Stafford sounded a common concern among party members in a television interview in his native Vermont. "'If you're running for the presidency,'" he said, "'you are supposed to have too much on the ball to be brainwashed.'"²⁶ The implication was that, if Romney could be fooled by Americans, how could he possibly conduct a meaningful foreign policy in the face of the Soviet threat? Much less charitable was Governor James Rhodes (R-OH), who later said, "Watching George Romney run for the Presidency was like watching a duck try to make love to a football."²⁷

Richard Nixon was "fascinated"—and "pleased"—by the reaction to the statement. As he told his speechwriter Richard Whalen, "I've never seen anything like it in all my years of politics. One moment he's the front runner, the next he's down. Words are so very, very important."²⁸ Nixon would adhere to that principle religiously in the 1968 campaign. He understood that, as Alexander Pope wrote nearly three hundred years ago, "at every word a reputation dies." Indeed, the former vice president had ample evidence of the validity of this sentiment; one need look no farther than his infamous "Checkers" speech to realize that he fully understood the power (and peril) of political utterances. The incident also underscores the centrality of perception in politics. Fortunes can rise and fall simply on the basis of the way in which comments are received and interpreted.

Notwithstanding the controversy it precipitated, the brainwashing statement placed George Romney in a singular position among the major Republican presidential hopefuls. He had come out in direct opposition to the administration's policies in Vietnam. In denying the validity of the war, CBS's Eric Sevareid commented, "Romney has broken the pattern of all the potential presidential candidates. None of the others has gone anywhere near this far."

To his credit, Sevareid continued, Romney had "joined a distinct and growing pattern involving scores of other serious minded citizens, in Congress and
out."[29] Sevareid's praise had to be of little comfort to Romney. The recognition
of his "unique" status did not insulate him from further criticism, even from
those who had previously backed him. But even those willing to accept the
sentiment behind his remarks recognized the damage that had been done to
his presidential campaign. An editorial in the *Yakima Daily Republic* provides
a perfect example. While recognizing that the administration designed briefing sessions to present a convincing case in support of its policy, the editors
cautioned that, even if the term *brainwashing* was accurate, Romney should "be
expected to produce reasonable evidence that he was given false information."
Since he could not, "the brainwashing claim is certain to damage Romney's image as potential presidential timber."[30]

The *Detroit News,* which had supported Romney as governor and in his
early forays into the presidential arena, ridiculed his statements. "The Romney
policy," the editors opined, "is a pretty tired retread of a disproved strategy. . . .
While we think Romney is a splendid governor of Michigan, his latest position paper on Vietnam proves he's an appallingly unrealistic strategist amid the
complexities of a confused and confusing war."[31] Even the governor's political
allies chided him publicly for his comments. Wallace Bennett, who had been
vocal in his advocacy of Romney's bid for the nomination despite his admira-
tion for Richard Nixon, wrote to a constituent, "Unfortunately, Governor Romney has not been too wise in some of the statements he has made, particularly
about Viet Nam."[32] John Chafee, a staunch Romney supporter who had been on
the trip to Vietnam in 1965, denied that he himself had been brainwashed but
lamely added in Romney's defense, "I don't want to disagree with what someone else felt." The ultimate irony, however, is that Romney's chief foreign policy
adviser, Jonathan Moore, served as the State Department official assigned to
accompany the nine governors on the 1965 Vietnam tour—and was, therefore,
indirectly implicated as one of the brainwashers.[33]

The governor's comments demolished his year-long lead in the polls. In its
first poll following the snafu, the *Los Angeles Times* found that, among Republican voters, support for Romney's candidacy had fallen dramatically. According
to the survey, Nixon was chosen as the GOP candidate by 28 percent of those
polled, Romney by 13 percent, Rockefeller 13 percent, and Reagan 11 percent.[34]
A mid-September Harris poll showed Romney plunging to fourth place, and,
when he officially entered the race on 18 November, his standing had sunk so
low that many observers considered him as little more than a placeholder for
Rockefeller.[35] Although, in retrospect, the brainwashing statement could appear
to be simply a footnote to the story of the 1968 presidential election, Romney's

comments were "huge in public thinking at the time," mortally wounded his promising presidential campaign. Indeed, the statement stands with James G. Blaine's 1884 slogan "Rum, Romanism, and Rebellion" as one of the preeminent examples of a one-sentence political suicide in a presidential campaign. In a postmortem editorial on Romney's candidacy, the *Fort Worth Star Telegram* noted, "History some day will record, no doubt, that George Romney's chances for the Republican presidential nomination gurgled down the drain on Sept. 4, 1967 . . . after Sept. 4, Mr. Romney the frontrunner became an almost certain loser. He never recovered in the eyes of the public or the politicians."[36]

There are several reasons for the precipitous and rapid decline in Romney's political fortunes following the WKBD interview. First, his lamentations regarding the dim prospect of achieving American goals in Vietnam did not resonate with voters as much as they would have after the Tet Offensive. In addition, his political views placed him to the left of the core of the Republican Party; the Charles Percy/John Lindsay/Nelson Rockefeller wing was clearly losing its influence to the more conservative forces led by Barry Goldwater and Ronald Reagan.[37] Moreover, as recently as May 1960, Romney had categorically disavowed membership in the Republican Party, preferring to remain nonpartisan. And, given his liberal views on civil rights and his failure to support Goldwater in 1964, he had much greater support among independents and Democrats than among conservative Republicans. No wonder, then, that his support within the party was the proverbial "mile wide and inch deep," based almost wholly on the assumption of his electability, a critical consideration for the party in the wake of the 1964 Goldwater catastrophe. When his relative lack of support was combined with his relative lack of experience in politics, it is clear that Romney had no long-term loyalists on whom to rely once the aura of inevitability of his nomination and probable victory over Johnson evaporated. All that remained for him was to attempt to rebuild his fragile support and hope that his opponents for the nomination would stumble later in the race.

Moreover, Romney often referred to himself as a plainspoken man who said what he meant. Although many other candidates have attempted to portray themselves as such, in Romney's case it was accurate. The governor spoke off-the-cuff frequently, much to the chagrin of his political aides and supporters. He also lacked political sophistication and demonstrated a lack of understanding of the differences between a state race, where eccentricities can often be an advantage, and a national race, where perceptions and appearances play a far greater role. His laudable propensity to be candid and to speak extemporaneously without considering the consequences clearly cost him in this instance. His failure to be thoroughly briefed prior to his press conferences compounded these problems. His critics within the GOP regarded him as "essentially a reciter of lines," particularly on international issues. As James J. Kilpatrick of the *National Review* wrote, "So long as Romney carefully memorizes the foreign policy statements prepared for him by his staff, he is all right."[38] Thus, Romney's lack of preparation and understanding of the issues compromised his ability to elucidate his views. After the interview, *Time* noted that, while politicians often changed their minds, "the good ones do so with such grace that people hardly notice, or such logic that everyone understands." Romney did neither in this case; he had "offered so inept an explanation of his shifting views on Vietnam" that his presidential ambitions could be over.[39]

In his subsequent statements and his campaign's "clarifications," Romney asserted that he meant to illustrate the chronic lack of honesty from the administration on Vietnam rather than to suggest that he had been the victim of mind control. Referencing the "credibility gap" that allegedly plagued the Johnson administration was a tactic used by most Republicans at some point during the 1966 and 1968 electoral campaigns.[40] Hawks and doves alike criticized Johnson, McNamara, and other officials for distorting the truth and misleading the American public about the progress of the war. Romney's fatal mistake was that, during the interview, he failed to frame his statement within the parameters of the credibility gap, although he did so subsequently with much more success. Several days later, Romney told a news conference at the Washington Hilton that the real issue was "whether the American people have been told the truth about the war." In his opinion, they had been subjected to "a systematic continuation of inaccurate reports, predictions and withholding of information." He went on to say, "I was not talking about the Russian type of brainwash but about the LBJ type." This was a clear reference to the credibility gap issue.[41] Yet, by using the emotionally charged term *brainwashing* rather than the political catchphrase *credibility gap*, Romney fell into a rhetorical trap from which he could not escape.

The incident left Nixon in control of the race for the nomination. Indeed, Mary McGrory of the *Washington Post* wrote in the wake of Romney's blunder, "Nixon is sitting in the catbird seat. . . . Now Nixon can begin his courtship of the moderates in earnest." Nixon, she continued, was now "trying to recruit personnel, if not ideas, from the camp of the Michigan governor." This shift in position would be essential to his presidential ambitions because the former vice president would "make Lyndon Johnson something of a 'peace candidate.' More importantly, a meeting between Nixon and Johnson at Credibility Gap would undoubtedly result in a standoff." Theodore Draper made a similar observation about the relative lack of credibility of both men: "For every such unguarded statement by Johnson, there must be a dozen by Nixon. The latter could make the famous problem of Johnson's 'credibility' vanish as if by magic."[42] A week later, the journalists Rowland Evans and Robert Novak reported that Nixon's close advisers implored him to adopt a softer line on Vietnam quickly and to focus more on domestic issues.[43] That advice would prove to be the exact formula Nixon would employ during the 1968 campaign to win first the GOP nomination and then the general election.

Nixon's approach to the war did not sit well with many Republicans, and some within the party searched for an alternative. Romney's gaffe led to increased speculation among the party faithful that Nelson Rockefeller would enter the fray. John Sherman Cooper threw his support behind Rockefeller, telling the press in the fall of 1967 that the New York governor was the best man for the job, in terms of both domestic policy and foreign affairs.[44] George Aiken contended that Nixon had been "'altogether too hawkish in his views and pronouncements on the war'" and hoped that his party would find an alternate nominee.[45] And Mark Hatfield argued that the GOP could be the "peace party" in 1968 and vocally supported an effort to "de-Americanize the whole Vietnam War," although he did not mention any candidate in particular whom he would support.[46] The common thread between virtually all these efforts to derail Nixon's candidacy was that these Republicans sought an end to the war.

These opponents of the conflict formed a tacit alliance with antiwar Democrats and lobbied Johnson to find a way for the United States to extricate itself from the conflict. Perhaps the most intriguing of these contacts occurred daily between Aiken and Mike Mansfield. Longtime colleagues and friends, the two had breakfast together every morning and knew each other so well that they would be able to play off of each other when it came to their views on Vietnam without having to discuss the strategy overtly. This came in handy since, out of respect for the president, Mansfield would not say things publicly that he wrote to Johnson privately, whereas Aiken would. Conversely, Aiken—who by 1967 was referring to the war as a "debacle" that reminded him of the ancient Romans, "so concerned with their own world prestige that they forgot what was going on at home"—chose not to confront the GOP hawks directly. Mansfield had no such restraints. He could laud Aiken's stance as the Senate's "wise old owl" and attack the hawks with harsher language than Aiken, who usually would state that he was "somewhat disturbed" by hawkish statements. Mansfield's regard for Aiken was apparent when he commented, "Any position Sen. Aiken takes automatically becomes respectable, just because it's held by George Aiken."[47] The two composed a formidable team with which the administration had to contend when making decisions on the war; since their critiques predated even Fulbright's break with Johnson, this bipartisan coalition could not simply be written off as merely partisan politics.[48]

Preoccupied with domestic political considerations, many Republicans were content to criticize without proposing solutions of their own. The Ripon Society proposed a comprehensive alternative to the administration's policies in September 1967. In a report titled "The Realities of Vietnam: An Alternative for Republicans," the liberal Republican organization proposed a "thorough reorientation of American foreign policy in Vietnam." The report began with the following premise: "A bureaucratic coalition within the administration has reached a rigid consensus that repels knowledgeable advice. It has set its own terms of discussion, enshrined its own version of the facts and has for the most part succeeded in imposing its internal verities on public debate as a whole." As a result, the "larger questions of our involvement remain to be asked"—namely, how "a conflict which has repeatedly been defined as 'political' and 'essentially Vietnamese' became a largely military, largely American undertaking?"[49]

The Ripons argued that the Johnson administration was "incapable" of carrying out the kind of reappraisal required because of its "prideful commitment to continuing a misconceived policy." They recognized that the war "may well shape American thinking on foreign policy for a generation to come. . . . It is important, therefore, that the proper lessons be drawn." They concluded that the GOP had both "an opportunity and a duty" to present a viable alternative to the American people in the 1968 campaign. But it could not be any Republican alternative, they asserted; escalation along the lines suggested by hawks within the party could not be contemplated. Instead, the Republican Party "must be committed to reducing the costs of the American undertaking in Vietnam" and "extricate America" from the conflict.[50] At its core, the Ripon critique recognized the investment of personal credibility by Johnson and others in his administration in the war. The concern for national credibility, domestic political credibility, and personal credibility—credibility cubed, as Fredrik Logevall describes it—drove LBJ's decisionmaking process during his presidency.[51]

Johnson's allies did yeoman's work in attempting to blunt the criticism the administration faced from the GOP. On 11 September, Melvin Laird made a sweeping indictment of U.S. policy and suggested that he was ready to withdraw his support from the war. While this might seem odd given Laird's conservatism and early advocacy of the war, it was actually consistent with his core conservative principles. Laird wanted to win the conflict; if that proved impossible, he did not want to expend American lives, treasure, and political capital tilting at windmills. Dirksen, miffed at Laird's defection and concerned about other wavering Republicans, demanded a strong resolution of support for Johnson at the upcoming Republican Coordinating Committee meeting, hoping to fix the party squarely behind the president's conduct of the war. Laird and Gerald Ford fired back, arguing that, with the presidential election a year away, the GOP should be developing its own position on Vietnam rather than "blindly following Johnson." They warned Dirksen that, if he proposed such a resolution, they would not support it, and Dirksen eventually backed away from his demand.[52]

Ford also expressed concern about the intraparty squabbling over the war. He and Hatfield exchanged a series of letters in September 1967. Ford told Hatfield that it was time to end the "divisive and pointless debate" between doves and hawks in order to present a united front in the 1968 election. Hatfield, noting that the war would "inevitably be a major issue" in the campaign, suggested "de-Americanization" of the fighting and was convinced that "the Republican Party would be over-whelmingly supported by American voters" if it committed to that stance. He concluded, "Republicans should make every effort to develop a united position on Vietnam and to avoid fostering situations that can create irreconcilable splits in the Party before the Convention. Perhaps if the major Republican spokesmen could sponsor the general concept of de-Americanization of the war, divisive and pointless debate between 'hawks' and 'doves' and between the pro-bombing and anti-bombing factions could be largely avoided." Ford responded positively, stating that he agreed that "the war is presently far too American in character and seems to be getting more so every day."[53]

Laird's about-face did not pass unnoticed. Robert Novak reported that, in recent weeks, there had been a sharp turn against Vietnam even among conservative and publicly hawkish Republicans. Novak's report came on the heels of a *Chicago Sun-Times* article that noted "a wary but distinct shift by top Republicans toward a more 'dovish' position on the Vietnam war." The article pointed out that the "political advantages of bipartisan responsibility for the war seem to have lost their glamour for the GOP." Novak concluded that Nixon's chances against Johnson in 1968 would probably "depend on how well he gauged this growing mood within the party and the population."[54] Novak's insights are crucial in understanding the evolution of Nixon's stance on the war in late 1967 and 1968. Richard Nixon was an original anti-Communist. His involvement with the Alger Hiss case and the "Pumpkin Papers," his vicious attacks on Helen Gahagan Douglas in 1950, and his fierce rhetorical support of South Vietnam throughout the early 1960s clearly identified him as a hawk whose support of containment was unquestionable. Yet he was also as shrewd and calculating a politician as the United States has ever seen. His pragmatic approach to politics informed him that his aggressive posture on the war would not play well in Peoria or at the GOP's Miami convention during the 1968 presidential campaign. In order to win the nomination and the presidency, he would have to reinvent himself, back away from his strident advocacy of escalation, and convince both his party and the public that, of the presidential candidates, he was the one best suited to resolve the conflict.

Fortunately for Nixon, the transformation did not have to be complete.

Supporting a settlement in Vietnam did not preclude continued opposition to communism or a rejection of the American role in international affairs. His task, then, would be to devise a strategy that would address both aspects of foreign policy. Thus, in an effort to shore up support for his candidacy and earn the respect of the nation's elite, he addressed these issues and sought to burnish his already impressive foreign policy credentials in late 1967. In a remarkably prescient article published in *Foreign Affairs* entitled "Asia After Viet Nam," he examined the Vietnam conflict and its relationship to and potential impact on U.S. relations with China and the rest of Asia. The article established Nixon as the first prominent American politician to clearly understand and address the importance of the emergence of modern Asia—including the "Asian tigers" such as Taiwan and South Korea in addition to the economic power of Japan—in world affairs.

The United States, Nixon argued, was a Pacific power. Nevertheless, he recognized that there were distinct limits to the power that the country would be able to project into Asia in the wake of the Vietnam conflict. One of the legacies of the war, he warned, would be that the experience would encourage Americans to withdraw from world affairs and reject future unilateral intervention to counter Communist insurrections elsewhere. Other nations "must recognize that the role of the United States as world policeman is likely to be limited in the future." That being said, however, he asserted that the United States needed to be cognizant of the rising power of China and argued forcefully that the same sort of priority afforded Western Europe after World War II should be given to shoring up Asia against communism in the near future. To counter Chinese ambitions and adventurism, he proposed a sort of successor organization to SEATO, a regional alliance composed of South Korea, Japan, Taiwan, Thailand, Malaysia, South Vietnam, the Philippines, Australia, and New Zealand. Such an organization would have both economic and military ties but would not include the United States. Instead, America should stand ready to come to the assistance of any member of the alliance threatened by internal Communist uprisings or external aggression. A key component of this program for the former vice president was the removal of the restrictions imposed on the size of the Japanese military in order to allow (or, more appropriately, force) Tokyo to assume responsibility for its own defense.

But China was the true focus of the article. "Any American policy toward Asia," Nixon asserted, "must come urgently to grips with the reality of China." This did not mean "rushing to grant recognition to Peking," but it implied that the United States could not afford to leave China outside the family of nations where it could "nurture its fantasies, cherish its hates and threaten its neighbors." Nixon made it clear that he had no intention of dealing with the Chinese as they were. "The world cannot be safe until China changes," he argued, and America's aim should be "to induce change." The ultimate goal of U.S. policy should be to persuade the Chinese leadership to "turn their energies inward rather than outward. And that will be the time when the dialogue with mainland China can begin."[55] Nixon's interest in China, which played a critical role in his administration's strategy of "linkage" and triangular diplomacy, culminated in his epochal visit to Beijing in 1972.

Nixon believed that, while the challenges to a successful Asia policy were great, the time for implementing a proactive policy was short. He warned that two events were imminent in the 1970s that together "could create a crisis of the first order." The first was that the Soviets would reach military parity with the United States; the second was that China would develop a significant nuclear capability. In order to induce China to make the requisite changes prior to the outbreak of the coming crisis, Nixon relied on his proposed regional alliance backed by American military and economic power. Once it was in place and non-Communist Asia had strengthened its position in relation to Beijing, the members of the new organization would "no longer furnish tempting targets for Chinese aggression." The article concluded with a pragmatic assessment of the current situation in Asia: "Weary with war, disheartened with allies, disillusioned with aid, dismayed at domestic crises, many Americans are heeding the call of the new isolationists." Rather than capitulate to these forces, he called for a Pacific community that would match the Atlantic community, with the United States playing a full role in each relationship.[56]

"Asia After Viet Nam" was "Nixon at his most original and prophetic."[57] It demonstrated his maturity as a politician, his expertise in foreign affairs, and his recognition of the realities of the contemporary situation in both Asia and the United States. The clarity and thoughtfulness of his proposed policies toward Asia stood in stark contrast to his vitriolic assertions in the 1950s as a leading member of the China lobby and even some of his fiery rhetoric on the war during the previous three years. The formula presented in *Foreign Affairs* was statesmanlike and forward-looking and eschewed the contentiousness previously demonstrated by the former vice president. Further, the article served to further differentiate Nixon from his rivals for the Republican nomination; neither Romney nor Reagan could bring anywhere near the same level of experience or knowledge to bear on foreign affairs generally or Vietnam and Asia specifically as could Nixon. If either of them hoped to upset the former vice president, they would need to formulate a coherent and widely acceptable policy on the war in Vietnam.

Given Romney's brainwashing gaffe, Reagan's hawkishness and inexperience, and Rockefeller's noncandidacy, Nixon seemed poised to sweep to the

GOP nomination. But his road to Miami did not lack obstacles. The growing antiwar sentiment within the Republican Party concerned him and complicated his campaign strategy. For example, on 25 September, Paul Findley introduced a bipartisan resolution that called on Congress to undertake formal consideration of U.S. policy in Vietnam. Passing such a measure, Findley stated, would provide the means through which Congress could "discharge responsibilities in foreign policy clearly placed upon it by the Constitution." The resolution was cosponsored by fifty-five members of the House, fifty of whom were Republicans.[58] The last thing Nixon wanted at this juncture was a detailed public debate on the war that would force the party (and him) to commit to a specific course of action.

Moreover, Nixon realized the dangerous possibility that LBJ could be "baiting a trap" for the GOP that he would spring on them through a peace offensive or attacks on their weakness and confusion on the war issue. But, in keeping with the new public mood, he realized the need to say something that at least sounded new on Vietnam and had begun to temporize his position. As Evans and Novak reported, "Just how flexible or inflexible he is about Vietnam within the next few weeks could ordain the final outcome of his long political career." They need not have worried; Nixon would find a way to reformulate his political rhetoric to conform to the prevailing national mood in order to win the White House. He fundamentally understood the challenges facing the United States in Vietnam, telling Richard Whalen, "Our national interest requires ending the war." As Evans and Novak opined, "A Nixon shift on Vietnam would fit snugly into his new strategy of wooing the Republican left as the only viable alternative to Reagan. Only the question of Vietnam now separates Nixon from some Republican liberals."[59]

Indeed, by the end of 1967, criticism of the administration's handling of the war continued from all points of view within the GOP. Clifford Case made a speech in the Senate in which he assailed what he considered Johnson's irresponsible misuse and perversion of the Tonkin Gulf resolution to deepen American involvement in Vietnam. Case charged that a "crisis of confidence" existed about the president and his policies. Furious at the comments, Johnson implored Senate Democrats and Everett Dirksen to defend him and attack Case. So outraged was the president at Case's remarks that he told Joseph Califano, "Call Case and tell him if I want advice like that I'll get it from Wayne Morse and Ernest Gruening. Tell him the President doesn't need advice from someone who waits until the *New York Times* editorial board decides to change its mind."[60] On the other side of the party's ideological spectrum, Ronald Reagan continued to sound the most aggressively hawkish views, going so far as to say that consideration should be given to a declaration of war in Vietnam since it would help curb antiwar demonstrations.[61] Johnson faced a constricting locus of options and would continue to lose key supporters in Congress.

Domestic political problems continued to mount for LBJ as more public figures renounced their support for the administration in Vietnam. Thruston Morton called the war a mistake and admitted—remarkably for a politician— that he had been wrong. He accused the administration of Vietnam myopia that prevented it from "effectively coping with major problems elsewhere." By failing to emphasize the political nature of the war, he continued, the administration had contributed to political polarization at home and threatened important domestic and foreign initiatives. He concluded, "We must make it crystal clear to the American people that there is no military solution in Vietnam. We must put an immediate ceiling on further U.S. military action and open up every possible avenue toward negotiations." The senator called for an immediate bombing halt, increased pressure on both Saigon and Hanoi for a settlement, and an all-Asia peace conference to seek "honorable disengagement."[62]

After Morton's speech, the president called him to the White House. As Morton later described, "He really twisted my arm. . . . He gave me a long lecture on how wrong I was and how vital it was for our country and its position of leadership in the world that we see this thing through in Vietnam." Johnson was right to be concerned about Morton's defection. The *New York Times* wrote that Morton was "emerging as the most outspoken Republican critic of the Administration policy." Don Oberdorfer of the *Washington Post* called the Kentucky senator a "political weathervane" and noted that his reversal on Vietnam created an "instant sensation" despite the fact that it was not unique in late 1967. According to Oberdorfer, it reflected the fact that, by the summer and fall of 1967, "millions of American voters—along with many religious leaders, editorial writers and elected officials—appeared to be changing their views about the war."[63] Not surprisingly, LBJ was unable to sway Morton with his efforts.

The documentary record demonstrates the extent to which the administration worked to maintain congressional support for the war. Johnson's advisers constantly kept the president informed about the level of congressional support and would invite wavering politicians like Morton to the White House for pep talks and the "LBJ treatment." And the president needed all the support he could get. By late 1967, Johnson's consensus on Vietnam had eroded as the country became polarized; while opposition to the war increased, hawks were becoming more hawkish.[64] Of particular interest to the president was Everett Dirksen. Acting Secretary of State Nicholas Katzenbach, in a 29 September memorandum to the president responding to Morton's speech, showed an awareness of increasing criticism on Capitol Hill and took steps to shore up support for the president's policies: "We have supplied material to Senator

Dirksen to counteract Morton's speech."[65] Armed with these resources, Dirksen spoke on the Senate floor on 3 October to remonstrate Republican opponents of the war. Pounding on his desk, Dirksen declared, "I cannot in my position, and I cannot under any circumstances, denigrate him or demean him in the eyes of the world.... Have you heard the British demean their King and Queen? No, you do not demean the ruler. The President is not our ruler, but you do not demean him in the eyes of the people abroad."[66] Hugh Scott also stuck by LBJ. The senator told the Johnson aide Mike Manatos that he had received a number of invitations from the press, radio, and television to "express criticism" of the administration's handling of Vietnam. Scott stated that he refused the offers and reaffirmed his support of the president.[67] Dirksen's statement did not sit well with many of his fellow Republicans. One anonymous congressman complained, "Dirksen is polarizing the party on the war issue, leaving a gap so wide that Johnson can drive a truck down the middle by election time."[68]

In yet another manifestation of the divisions extant in the GOP, the Ripon Society released another study on 2 October 1967 dealing with "The Realities of Vietnam." Hailed as "one of the most thorough and scholarly proposals yet injected into the Vietnam debate" by the *Boston Globe* and "a brilliant analysis" by James Gavin, it argued the Republican responsibility to provide an alternative to the president's policy and claimed that a meaningful alternative would require the election of a Republican president in 1968.[69] The paper chastised the administration for vacillating between hawkish and dovish actions and urged a reappraisal of the structure of America's Vietnam policy and of U.S. foreign affairs as a whole. It correctly predicted that the "course of this war may well shape American thinking on foreign policy for a generation to come"; as a result, the Ripon Society called on the GOP to "bring the issues of foreign policy to the people in the 1968 elections." Significantly, the paper asserted that it was not necessary to "blame the entire structure of present policy on any one man or party, or any small group of officials," but it did note problems with the executive-legislative relationship, the Johnson style of leadership, and bureaucratic inertia. The Republican Party, therefore, would have to capture the White House in order to make the requisite changes in American foreign policy, changes based on multilateral aid and new thinking in foreign affairs.[70] Whether the GOP would pursue such a strategy remained to be seen. Certainly much would depend on who captured the party's presidential nomination.

It was increasingly obvious to political observers that George Romney would not be that person. Democrats in Congress smelled blood in the water in the weeks following his blunder and moved in for the kill. Wayne Hays, the chair of the House Foreign Affairs Subcommittee, recognized the damaging effect of Romney's statement on his candidacy and acted to keep the brainwashing incident alive. He invited Romney and Moore to testify before his sub-committee to explain how Romney had been misled by American military and diplomatic officials in Saigon. Hays, of course, did not expect Romney to appear; the invitation was designed to further embarrass the governor and cripple his already faltering campaign. But, in a move that surprised many observers, Romney announced his willingness to testify in an investigation "to determine the accuracy and nature" of the official briefings in Vietnam. Romney felt that this related to the "larger issue of the candor and honesty of the Government with the American people" and suggested that this would be a perfect opportunity for "a full congressional review" of American policy in Vietnam. Hays quickly backpedaled and rescinded the invitation to testify. Romney's campaign heralded the exchange as a victory for the governor, but it did little to prop up his sagging candidacy.[71]

By October 1967, the Republican Party felt the divisions brought on by the war. Everett Dirksen found his patience with GOP critics of the administration wearing thin. He felt that attacks on the president by moderates like Percy, Morton, and Case had "gone beyond 'due bounds.'" Not so, retorted Case. Not only was dissent within due bounds; it was vital to democracy. It was important, he argued, "'for all of us to meet our responsibility, when we disagree with the conduct of affairs by our government, to state that disagreement as clearly and distinctly as possible.'"[72] Dirksen's "foursquare support" of the administration's policies made it difficult for Republicans to "cleanly break with the President" or to "maximize politically their differences over how best to manage the war" throughout Johnson's presidency.[73]

While the columnist David Broder considered a Republican debate on Vietnam as "likely to be of great use to the country," he believed that the doves would not prevail and nominate one of their own in 1968. He gave three reasons for his assumption: first, the Republican tradition of staunch anticommunism would not allow it; second, the traditional power centers of the party and its leadership all favored continuing or expanding the war effort; and, third, the main contenders for the nomination (Nixon, Reagan, and Rockefeller) were all hard-liners on the war. (Broder discounted Romney and Percy as factors because of their declining or sluggish poll numbers.)[74] Senator Thomas Kuchel (R-CA), who had just returned from serving as an observer at the South Vietnamese elections, expressed similar sentiments. He lashed out at his fellow GOP senators for seeking to make a partisan political issue out of the war by creating a "peace party" image for the Republicans and reiterated his opposition to a bombing halt without reciprocal actions by the North Vietnamese. According to Kuchel, "Domestic American politics does not offer a satisfactory basis for a winning strategy in world affairs." America, he insisted, "must not sully her commitment to the security of free Asia by groping for a nameless settlement."[75] In his syndicated column, Barry Goldwater underscored Kuchel's remarks and harshly attacked those who characterized the GOP as a party in crisis. The "major impression of Republican dove-ishness," he claimed, came from only Hatfield, Percy, Morton, and Romney. In the House in particular, there existed "tough-minded and very nearly total adherence to a victory position." The doves, Goldwater concluded, represented "a distinct minority among Republican realists. Republicans, for all the clamor, still want peace, not surrender."[76] This was a subtle but important distinction, one that would be important in the coming political season.

For some in the GOP, Vietnam represented only one symptom of a broader problem with the administration's foreign policy. Paul Fannin, speaking at a fund-raiser in Kentucky, listed eight key issues for the 1968 campaign, the most important of which was foreign policy. "Vietnam is the open wound, the open sore," he remarked, "but it is also a symbol of the deep decay of our foreign policy." He chided the administration for failing to solve the problem in seven years in office and concluded, "If the problem is to be solved—and I believe it can be solved—then it's going to have to be a Republican who provides the solution."[77] But the solution to which Fannin referred could prove elusive. As the *Saturday Evening Post* noted, the president's opponents were divided: "What, then, can the Republicans offer as an alternative?" Moreover, knowing how to trap his opponents (as he had with Goldwater in 1964) and with a year before the election "in which to preempt their alternatives," Johnson was in a political position that looked good to the editors at the beginning of October, given the policy discord within the GOP.[78]

Not every member of the party believed (at least publicly) that the war should play a role in the campaign. Hugh Scott said on 9 October, "The war in Vietnam is not, and must not become, a political issue. . . . It would be wrong to misconceive [our] role as to become a 'peace at any price' party." He pledged that he "would not play parcheesi with the war."[79] Although Scott was not alone in this feeling, the fact remained that the war was, not just *an* issue, but *the* issue in the 1968 electoral contest, and, with the campaign growing closer, it was clear that the GOP needed to establish a position on the war. The peril, however, lay in becoming too closely identified with a specific policy, especially one solely dedicated to ending the war. As John Tower told the Senate later that day, "There is a great danger in allowing either majority or minority to be cast as a 'peace at any price party.' It would be the greatest folly for Hanoi to think that if it can just hold out another year it will reap from a victorious Republican party a thinly-veiled surrender."[80]

But what did *victory* mean in Vietnam? Certainly, the definition of *victory* (in strictly military terms) had changed since World War II and Korea. No longer could tangible progress be found on a map; *victory* did not mean taking a hill or winning a conventional military battle. What mattered most in Vietnam was the perception that the United States could not defeat the North Vietnamese and their NLF allies—a perception that was, in fact, a reality by 1967. Clifford Case addressed this question in a Senate speech on 11 October, stating, "I want to win the war in the South and by win I mean bring about the creation of a South Vietnamese nation whose citizens support their government and the society in which they live, a government which is capable of giving South Vietnam protection against outside aggression and leadership internally in those reforms which are essential to bring that nation into the modern world."[81] As for the GOP, it is not clear whether either the hawks or the doves had fully worked out their own conception of what *victory* meant for the party and the nation. Goldwater's statement that the party wanted peace but not surrender provides part of the answer. Republicans did not want to capitulate to Hanoi's demands and would not support unilateral withdrawal or concessions, but most did support negotiations from a position of strength. The GOP's central task would be to define the parameters of an acceptable settlement, one that "won" the war and contributed to electoral success.

With the 1968 campaign looming on the horizon, Lyndon Johnson accelerated his preparations to run for reelection. Realizing that Vietnam would be both the central issue and his most glaring weakness, he instructed his aides to begin gathering material on the war views and statements of potential Republican candidates.[82] His aides also prepared a white paper on the upcoming campaign. Noting that "our object and goal is your re-election," the presidential adviser Lawrence O'Brien asserted that the 1968 presidential election "is not an election that can easily be won. Our effort must be massive." The report focused considerable attention on Vietnam and addressed the possibility of a Republican peace candidate opposing Johnson in the campaign, the problem of Johnson's credibility gap, and the argument likely to be used by the GOP that Johnson could not win or end the war. O'Brien concluded, "The Republicans will run a purely emotional and anti-Johnson campaign which can be tailored to any candidate who happens to get nominated." To counteract such a strategy, the president and his staff would need to begin immediately implementing a comprehensive approach to the campaign and the Republican Party.[83]

But Johnson's efforts to blunt the utility of the war issue to the GOP got off to a rocky start. At a meeting of the nation's governors on the SS *Independence* in late October, the Democrats proposed a resolution of support for the administration's global commitments, including Vietnam. This was not an original idea; similar resolutions had been proposed and passed the past three years at the governors' meetings. Yet the biggest news of the conference was a telegram made public by Ronald Reagan. Sent from the White House aide Marvin Watson to Price Daniel, the former governor of Texas, who served as the White House liaison to the governors and director of the Office of Emergency Planning, the telegram suggested that pressure be applied to GOP governors to get them behind a resolution of support for the president.

The disclosure of the telegram helped defeat the resolution. The Republican governors refused to support the measure and voted almost unanimously against it (James Rhodes being the only exception). John Chafee argued that the president would "wave it around just like he did the Gulf of Tonkin resolution. He'll say that all the governors support him and use it to embarrass the Republicans politically."[84] Nils Boe (R-SD) agreed and asked, "Why should we pull Johnson's chestnuts out of the fire?" As Evans and Novak reported, the Republican governors believed that opposition to Johnson's handling of the war would be essential for the 1968 campaign, both for hawks and for doves. Sensing a public loss of confidence in the president's policy, the governors, "far more than their congressional counterparts," saw the GOP becoming the anti-Vietnam party. Jules Witcover called the reaction to the telegram's appearance "a scene right out of a Marx Brothers movie as Republicans displayed or feigned outrage and Democrats dove for cover."[85]

With a little over a year before the election, the *New York Times* opined that the American public "deserves to know much better than it does now what [LBJ's] Republican rivals have in mind." Reviewing the contradictory statements and silence of Romney ("following a 'ping-pong' course"), Nixon ("does not say what he would do to end a long, grinding war on the ground"), Reagan ("forthright if less reassuring"), and Rockefeller ("retreated into total silence") on the war, the paper warned that "the United States is approaching a critical turning point in Asia" and that "the public expects more from both parties than evasion, obfuscation or easy answers to the hardest question of 1968."[86] But that is exactly what the country would get over the next twelve months. Social security may be the third rail of American politics, but the Vietnam conflict threatened the political fortunes of everyone in the late 1960s, and everyone who held public office understood the potential pitfalls the war could cause for political aspirations.

One governor's opposition to the war had already cost him dearly in the presidential race. With their candidate severely damaged, Romney's campaign brain trust gave serious consideration to how the governor should address the Vietnam issue in the coming months leading to the all-important New Hampshire primary in February. They concluded that "it would be a very serious mistake" to discuss foreign policy in stump speeches or interviews in New Hampshire if Romney were not "prepared to articulate a detailed specific Vietnam policy." They recognized that "there is no issue, foreign or domestic, which even begins to approach the Vietnam War in terms of the level of concern of New Hampshire voters." For Romney to avoid Vietnam would "make him appear either irrelevant or evasive, or both." They firmly believed that "the outcome of the primary here hinges on the Vietnam issue and the ability of Governor Romney to enunciate a clear, specific position different from Nixon's (and Johnson's), thus in effect turning the primary into a plebiscite on Vietnam." Two days later, Moore told Romney, "There is no doubt that Vietnam is a big issue, perhaps the biggest of all, in New Hampshire as elsewhere." But he cautioned, "A full-scale treatment [of your position] would be advisable . . . we have not yet been willing to leave the generally middle ground and declare for a more clearly dovish position, an unwillingness I heartily agree with at this juncture." Moore worried about "blow[ing] the thunder of the neutralization proposal too early."[87]

Toward this end, Romney was presented with a series of six options for his Vietnam policy, most of which were much more dovish than his previous public statements on the war. Although he chose the most neutral of these suggestions, it is clear that both he and his advisers would have been more vocally opposed to the war if it had been politically viable. Romney unveiled the new approach in a speech at Dartmouth the following week. Identifying himself as a "dissenter," he appealed for the support of the largely student audience by arguing that he was "looking for an alternative, not merely a more popular or devastating criticism of the way things are going."[88] This would be a common theme for Romney for the remainder of his campaign and, indeed, throughout the rest of 1968. Yet this approach did not help his candidacy. Criticism of the war effort angered many in the GOP, particularly Nixon and former president Eisenhower.

Eisenhower sought national unity and attempted to energize support for the war effort. He had become increasingly skeptical of Johnson's policies in private, although he remained supportive in his public statements. In November, he invited his old comrade, Gen. Omar Bradley, to Gettysburg to appear on a CBS news special designed to swing public opinion in favor of the war. Bradley was the cochairman of the Citizens Committee for Peace with Freedom in Vietnam, an organization that focused on opposing any settlement of the war short of total military victory.[89] Neither general accepted the privileged sanctuary concept, which allowed Communist forces to escape into neighboring nations with no fear of retaliation.[90] Eisenhower, sounding more belligerent than ever, stated, "This respecting of boundary lines on the map, I think you can overdo it." He suggested a foray into North Vietnam "either from the sea or from the hills" and asserted that he would not be bothered in the least if U.S. troops crossed into Cambodia or Laos in "'hot pursuit'" of Communist forces.

He also dismissed the "'kooks' and 'hippies' and all the rest that are talking about surrendering."[91]

Campaigning in Oregon, Nixon said that Eisenhower was "absolutely right" from a "military standpoint" but that such a move would be both diplomatically and politically unsound "at this time," for it might "run a substantial risk of widening the ground conflict in Vietnam."[92] Other Republican leaders also understood the combination of opportunity and danger that the Vietnam crisis presented to the party in 1968. Republican National Committee chair Ray Bliss sounded a warning to GOP candidates on 6 November. Similar to the cautionary advice given by Ford and Laird leading up to the 1966 midterm elections was his warning that Republicans not rely on Vietnam as a central theme in the campaign: "We cannot build a successful campaign on an issue that may disappear in the morning." Bliss based his comments on his recognition of the power of the president to influence events and his concern that the party could be "torn apart" if it engaged in a great debate on Vietnam. Instead, he argued, the party should "put Vietnam on the backburner over a low fire where it can stew without boiling over and scalding the cook."[93] Bliss hoped that the GOP could avoid being forced into a debate over specifics if it gave the administration enough rope to hang itself on Vietnam.

As 1967 drew to a close, pundits began to focus more closely on the presidential campaign. Tom Wicker wrote that the most difficult chore facing the GOP in 1968, "a task inextricably entwined with its choice of a candidate," would be to find a position on Vietnam that would "enable it to take advantage of President Johnson's undeniable weakness." An outspoken hawk would give the president "the same opportunity he capitalized on in 1964"; an outspoken dove would "undoubtedly push Johnson into the stern role of protector of freedom, defender of the faith, scourge of Communism, and tough overseer of American interests." Wicker disagreed with Nixon's assumption that the GOP could defeat Johnson "no matter what stand" the Republican nominee took, pointing in particular to Romney's "impenetrable" position.[94] And Nixon, privately, believed the same thing. After Eisenhower remarked in a late November television interview that U.S. forces should be authorized to cross the demilitarized zone and enter Cambodia and Laos to stop infiltration into the South, Nixon began to "put some distance" between himself and Eisenhower. While he agreed with the former president's military assessment, he was "not prepared to enter a political year promising to make Johnson's war policy more effective by invading three more Indochinese countries."[95]

While Nixon pragmatically backed away from the militant position that characterized his statements on Vietnam between 1964 and 1966, other GOP hawks stood firm. John Tower, appearing on "Face the Nation," was asked whether he could conceive of a peace candidate like Percy or Romney winning the nomination in 1968. Tower responded obliquely: "It depends what you mean by a peace candidate. I think that Republicans all genuinely want peace." That being said, however, Tower asserted, "The Republicans must take a position which is calculated to convince the people that we are best competent to bring the war to the earliest possible successful conclusion, and maintain the strength and posture of the United States throughout the globe."[96] In a nutshell, that would be the Republican challenge in the year that followed.

The Vietnam War would play a crucial role in the 1968 presidential election campaign for the Republican Party. Would the party follow the admonitions of its leading elder statesman, Dwight Eisenhower, and push for victory? Would it hark to Everett Dirksen's pleas to support the administration's policies? Or would the moderates and doves be able to nominate one of their own and seek a negotiated settlement to the conflict? Roscoe Drummond of the *Washington Post* opined that the primaries would have the double value of not only deciding on the nominees but also constituting "a national plebiscite within both Parties on Vietnam. The issue will likely be very clear-cut: Whether to stay the course or get out as fast as possible. . . . The nomination itself may turn principally on this single issue."[97]

Hoping to reinvent himself on that issue, Romney clung to the thread of his candidacy, "fortified by his conviction that he is right, even when his strongest friends think otherwise." Indeed, the governor insisted that he did not regret using the term *brainwashing* in the August interview. "'I was referring to . . . the systematic manipulation of the news for the purpose of influencing attitudes and viewpoints,'" he told Jules Witcover. His obstinance received some support when Republican governors on a conference cruise to the Virgin Islands in November intercepted the wire from the White House instructing the Democrats to pressure James Rhodes to support a resolution on the war. Romney "jubilantly called it 'just another example of the kind of manipulation from Washington I've been talking about.'" Unfortunately, few accepted Romney's logic. One national reporter claimed to have "installed a time-saving special key on his typewriter that prints at a single stroke: 'Romney later explained. . . .'"[98]

Realistically, however, few Republicans could claim to be as eager as Romney to specify where they stood on the war. Only small minorities within the party could be easily characterized as deeply committed to either the hawk or the dove position. Most demonstrated their willingness to "engage in damaging low-intensity political warfare against Johnson, alternately criticizing him for not doing enough to win the war and for not doing enough to achieve peace." Not only would this strategy provide the political flexibility the party would need the following year to adapt to the evolving situation in Vietnam, but it also robbed the president of the "compensatory support" he needed from the GOP given the desertion of much of his own party.[99]

Of course, not everyone exhibited such reticence. The proponents of military victory remained steadfast in their certainty of an American triumph. Perhaps the most bellicose was Ronald Reagan. Speaking on Veterans Day in Oregon, he asserted that the country needed to admit that "we are in Vietnam because our national interest demands that we take a stand there now so we won't have to take a stand later on our own beaches." It was time, he continued, that "we either win this war or tell the American people why we can't. . . . The war in Vietnam must be fought through to victory, meaning first, an end to North Vietnam aggression, and second, an honorable and safe peace for our South Vietnam neighbors."[100] In early January 1968, George H. W. Bush sounded similar themes after he returned from a sixteen-day trip to Southeast Asia. On the basis of his observations and discussions with Ambassador Ellsworth Bunker and other military and civilian officials, Bush wholeheartedly believed, "We can succeed if we have the will." The only thing required to defeat the North Vietnamese and the Viet Cong was patience. In a speech in Houston on his return, he stated, "We are winning. This is no stalemate. This is no directionless, bogged down effort . . . it is an effort which requires a tremendous amount of patience. The communists have it—do the American people?"[101] Bush's confidence ran counter to the growing pessimism pervading his party and public opinion, but it did reflect the sentiments in his own district. Running unopposed for reelection to his congressional seat, Bush would spend 1968 campaigning extensively for Nixon and other GOP candidates.

Arguably no year in U.S. history produced more controversy, tragedy, or excitement than 1968. From the shock of the Tet Offensive to the assassinations of Martin Luther King Jr. and Bobby Kennedy, and from the riotous Democratic convention in Chicago to the election of Richard Nixon as president, the country became polarized and divided to a degree not seen since the Civil War. The upheaval experienced both at home and abroad during these twelve months would prompt Alf Landon to characterize 1968 as "a most fateful election year—certainly one of the most fateful in our nation's history."[102] Looming behind everything that occurred that year was the ongoing war in Vietnam. As the GOP attempted to regain the White House, Republicans like George Romney and Richard Nixon realized two very important realities. First, they had to define for themselves a position on the war that would appeal to the majority of the party and the electorate. Second, and perhaps even more important, they had to avoid repetition of the mistakes of 1964 that ended up in the disaster of the Goldwater campaign. Unity, rather than ideological dogmatism, would bring them the key to the Oval Office.

Still stinging from the negative backlash from the brainwashing remarks and the dissenter speech from the previous fall, George Romney's advisers hoped that their candidate could maintain a low profile on Vietnam as 1968 began and focus instead on issues more congenial to the governor's experience and knowledge. But the media and the public would not allow him that luxury. Vietnam remained at the center of the presidential contest. Even had he not been confronted with questions about the war at every turn, Romney could not afford to avoid the issue if he hoped to wrest the nomination away from Nixon. John Deardourff, an adviser to the campaign, noted that, unless the governor could clarify his position to the satisfaction of the voters of New Hampshire and the press, "he will lose . . . Vietnam will be the issue," and the voters "don't know what Governor Romney's position is on Vietnam."[103]

Not all Romney's advisers agreed with Deardourff. In preparation for an appearance on "Issues and Answers," they told the governor, "We all agree that you should *not* try to make any headlines on Vietnam during this show. We don't want to go an inch beyond where we already are . . . stop short of too much specifics . . . in your continuing position on Vietnam you want to maintain some potential for responsiveness and not get static."[104] Interestingly, this advice contradicted a speech Romney had made a few days earlier in which he stated, "Candor is also vital if the President is to be an effective Party leader," and challenged Nixon to a series of debates on the issues to "spell out differences" and "forge a comprehensive, constructive, and progressive set of policies" for the GOP.[105] But the governor's aides wanted to avoid any explicit and binding statements on the war. They had finally figured out what Nixon had known all along: no comment on Vietnam is better than a bad (and unretractable) one.

But, given his precipitous fall in the polls and the limited time remaining before the New Hampshire primary, Romney did not have that luxury. With nothing to lose and everything to gain, he had presented a substantive proposal for extricating the United States from South Vietnam, one based on a multilateral agreement on Southeast Asia, that he characterized as "guaranteed neutralization." If the Soviet Union, China, France, and the United States all had a vested interest in keeping the region neutral, he argued in a 16 January speech in Keene, New Hampshire, then the fiasco of the Laos neutralization compromise would not be repeated, and America could honorably settle the war. Although many saw the idea as "reasonable and realistic as far as it goes," critics asked for more "concrete suggestions on how to get the warring participants to the negotiating table." Romney, one newspaper lamented, "still teeters between the hawks and the doves. Fence-sitting will not help get us out of this mess."[106]

As Romney's struggles with the war continued, Dwight Eisenhower became increasingly frustrated with the war effort—which was now costing the nation

$82 million a day to fight—and the public and media reaction to the administration's policies. The general simply could not understand why the importance of South Vietnam and the correct strategy for victory were not as apparent to everyone else as they were to him. Moreover, he was dumbfounded that Americans could protest against their own soldiers in the field. He told Gen. Andrew Goodpaster on 22 January that the television coverage of U.S. military bases being hit by mortar fire was "damaging our people's understanding of the war." He urged LBJ to hit the North Vietnamese harder, including the use of American ground forces and B-52 attacks on enemy forces and bases in South Vietnam. And, although he recognized the potential political pitfalls facing Johnson in a presidential election year, Eisenhower strongly felt that "now may be the time to increase our combat effort" because, while "this will be a partisan and political year," domestic politics should not be a concern when the lives of U.S. troops were at stake. He wanted "to see the President win the war."[107]

Shortly after this briefing, Eisenhower said, "I don't regard myself as a missionary and I don't want to convert anybody. But if any Republican or Democrat suggests that we pull out of Vietnam and turn our backs on the more than thirteen thousand Americans who died in the cause of freedom there, they will have me to contend with. That's one of the few things that would start me off on a series of stump speeches across the nation."[108] This statement served as a daunting challenge to the presidential contenders in 1968: if they suggested that the United States abandon its commitment to South Vietnam, they would have to deal with the opposition of America's most respected and distinguished military leader. Eisenhower was—next to Johnson—the most zealous in exhorting the nation to martial unity. Of course, he was by no means alone in the GOP in continuing to support the war. Paul Fannin, for example, told the Phoenix Kiwanis in January 1968, "I remain convinced that an even greater application of force, and I don't mean manpower, would in the end create less suffering and hardship for all parties involved. We have nothing to gain—and everything to lose—by fighting a war we ourselves are not prepared to win." Allowing the stalemate to continue in Vietnam "can only lessen the free world's resolve to resist the march of communism and tyranny. If we do not honor our commitment to keep people free, we can expect more Vietnams in more areas of the world."[109]

The war loomed as the dominant electoral issue, completely polarizing public opinion in the country. Even as vocal opposition to the war in Congress, on college campuses, and on the nation's editorial pages increased, hawks in both parties sought to escalate the war further to achieve victory. Caught in the middle of these forces, Johnson and his advisers struggled to salvage the military situation on the ground in Southeast Asia and concurrently fight an increasingly challenging political battle back home. The president's annual State of the Union address to the nation would be a signal to both the hawks and the doves as to which way the administration's policy on both fronts would evolve during the months leading to the November election.

Johnson realized that his speech would set the tone for the campaign. He also knew that he did not have much in the way of progress to report. Indeed, although the North Vietnamese attack at Con Thien had been repelled, the overall military situation remained stagnant despite subtle signs that the American and South Vietnamese situation had improved. Recognizing this, the president began to consider reviewing the American approach in Vietnam in consultation with both his national security team and an array of former government officials. But, even as he privately contemplated a change in strategy, one that would take the United States in the direction of Vietnamization, he publicly vowed to see the war through to a successful conclusion.

Johnson's remarks to Congress and the American people reflected both his commitment to success in Vietnam and his defensiveness when it came to his record. The president made much of his accomplishments in foreign and domestic policy, and, while admitting that America was "challenged, at home and abroad," he reminded his countrymen that Americans had the wherewithal to meet the current trials. The most striking aspect of the speech was his sense of restraint, a characteristic that had not been present in his optimistic State of the Union speeches the previous four years. The implicit message was that Vietnam had placed limits on what the United States could do both at home and overseas.[110] Nevertheless, the president reiterated that success in Southeast Asia remained an attainable goal as long as the national will endured the present challenges.

The address drew a strong response from the Republican Party, a response that gave a clear indication of the direction in which most members of the GOP's leadership were leaning on the war. A month earlier, Evans and Novak had written, "House Republicans are convinced that if the official position of the party on Vietnam is more or less a carbon copy of the Johnson administration's, the Republican Party will have kicked away one of their strongest resources in the election—the deep discontent over the war in every part of the nation."[111] In an effort to distinguish their policy from that of the administration, the Republicans designed a made-for-television response to the speech in which they intended to rebuke the president's position and stake out their own stance on the key issues of the coming campaign.

John Tower was among the senators selected to present the Republican rebuttal on the Vietnam section of the speech. Tower asserted that the GOP stood for "military success in Vietnam that will enable the Vietnamese to rebuild a free nation," denounced the administration for "a self-defeating policy of 'grad-ualism,'" and charged that the "war could be over today if the Johnson administration had acted with determination instead of vacillation."[112] The *Christian Science Monitor* opined that the response was "a mobilization of dissatisfaction, with no specific alternative to the present policy. . . . The approach laid down by congressional Republicans on Vietnam appears to foreshadow a difference of degree rather than of ideology." The Republicans "accept President Johnson's basic postulates on the causes and goals of the war. . . . It is the manner of fighting rather than the cause of fighting that is at issue." The paper complained that, if this continued to be the main thrust of Republican policy on the war, "the voter in November might not have a clear-cut choice between hawks and doves in the rival parties," which would serve to subordinate Vietnam as an issue in the election.[113]

Clearly, the GOP wanted to distance itself from the administration's war for the electoral season ahead. But the party's congressional leadership did not want to paint itself into a corner with a specific policy prescription; flexibility was the watchword. Should Johnson manage to resolve the conflict before November, the party needed to be in a position to take advantage of developments, not constrained by previous declarations. But not everyone in the party agreed with the Tower strategy. After the speech, Cooper and Javits asserted that it did not represent mainstream Republican opinion and called yet again for a negotiated settlement to the conflict. Cooper stated that Tower's presentation "misrepresented the Republican position of foreign policy." Tower quickly responded by pointing out that the scripts were prepared, reviewed, and approved by the joint leadership of the party in a "graphic example of the cooperation and determination with which Republicans are pulling together toward a 1968 victory." In assessing the Republican response, a *Los Angeles Times* editorial opined, "If the statement [by Tower] truly represents the GOP position, the American voters and a watching world can expect no reasonable alternative to present Vietnam policy from the Republicans next fall. The rebuttal to the State of the Union message reflects the Grand Old Party at its worst."[114]

Shortly after the president's speech, however, a watershed event in the history of America's involvement in the war occurred. The Tet Offensive of 1968, which began on 30 January, served to usher in a new phase of the conflict. Although, in strictly military terms, Tet resulted in debilitating losses for the Viet Cong and Hanoi, the psychological and political impact of the surprise attacks devastated the administration. Images of the U.S. embassy under siege, the on-screen execution of a member of the Viet Cong by a South Vietnamese general, and the saga of American forces in Khe Sanh came directly into American living rooms and stunned the nation. Having been assured for years that success in Southeast Asia was just around the corner, the public reeled when it heard Walter Cronkite's disbelieving reaction on national television during the crisis ("What the hell is going on?" he cried, "I thought we were winning the war!") and his scathing remarks after his own visit to Vietnam in late February. Other commentators sounded similar skepticism. When General Westmoreland claimed victory in the wake of the offensive, the humorist Art Buchwald wrote that the statement was like Custer saying at Little Big Horn, "We have the Sioux on the run. . . . Of course, we still have some cleaning up to do, but the Redskins are hurting badly and it will only be a matter of time before they give in."[115]

Nearly three years of ineffective escalation against an enemy perceived to be inferior to the United States in virtually every way combined to destroy most of the public's remaining support for the war and caused a fundamental reexamination of it in the minds of millions across the country. Gallup polls found that, in the month following Tet, the number of self-described hawks had plummeted from 60 to 40 percent while the number of doves rose from 24 to 42 percent.[116] The new level of public consciousness spawned by the offensive raised basic questions about the war and threatened to further undermine the administration's fragile support. Johnson and his advisers acted quickly to reassure the nation that the attacks had been repulsed and that there had been no major setback. In response to the administration's efforts to minimize the impact of the Communist attacks, George Aiken commented, "If this is a failure, I hope the Viet Cong never have a major success."[117]

Facing increasing criticism in the aftermath of the offensive, Johnson realized that he would have to rely more than ever on the remaining Republican hawks to back his Vietnam policies. The relationship between the GOP and the White House was, of course, maintained for their mutual benefit, but it gave the Republican leadership a meaningful opportunity to influence the direction of American policy. On 31 January, for example, the president met with Dirksen and Ford for almost two hours—longer than he had spent with his Democratic colleagues earlier in the day—to discuss the situation in the wake of the Tet Offensive.[118] But their support of the administration's policies clashed with their desire to refrain from committing to a specific plan for resolving the conflict in order to maintain political flexibility in the fall. This conundrum left some Republicans in an awkward position.[119]

Back in New Hampshire, Nixon and Romney continued to vie for support in the first, and, arguably, most important, primary of 1968. A January Gallup poll showed that Republicans favored Nixon three to one over Romney and three to two over Rockefeller for the nomination.[120] As the *Grand Rapids Press* pointed out, "The Vietnam War issue, to the almost exclusion of all other issues, continue[d]" to separate the two candidates, despite the fact that Nixon had made virtually no public statement about the war during his visits to the state.[121] In an effort to exploit that difference, Romney challenged Nixon to a debate to "make their positions on key issues facing us crystal clear." When Nixon declined on the grounds that such a debate would only help the Democrats in the fall, Romney retorted, "To go through the many stages of a Presidential primary without a face-to-face engagement between the two principals would be like insisting on touch football all season, with no real contact until the super-bowl game."[122] Nixon brushed aside Romney's protestations, and no debate ever took place.

Nixon did address Vietnam in his campaign speeches, but only in the most general terms and without committing to any specific policy. He took great pains to avoid specifics on Vietnam, realizing that his hawkish background was not in sync with the prevailing mood of the country, and wanting to keep his options open for the campaign against Johnson in the fall. A good example is seen in a 15 February 1968 speech in Boston. The former vice president reconfirmed his belief that "there shall be no reward for armed aggression" but concurrently asserted, "We must be equally firm in our insistence that peaceful progress for the people of that beleaguered country be pressed with a sense of compelling urgency."[123] Such general statements were designed to appeal to the broad center of the Republican and national electorate while making no promises or specific proposals.

Romney responded with a preemptive strike on Nixon's Vietnam stance. On 16 February, he announced that "the Vietnam War would be his major campaign issue in the New Hampshire Presidential primary" and called Nixon "'a me-too candidate on Vietnam,'" charging that the former vice president had "'presented to New Hampshire voters no more than a blurred carbon copy of the discredited Johnson policies for ending the war . . . He has offered nothing in the way of a positive plan for peace.'" The Republican Party would not regain the White House, Romney asserted, without an alternative to the policy in Vietnam.[124] While Romney correctly chided Nixon for failing to provide such an alternative, he could not take advantage of his opponent's lack of specificity. Despite his critique of the front-runner, he failed to clarify his own position, choosing to reiterate his standard campaign rhetoric.

Romney's tendency to refer to the "Johnson-Nixon" policy of escalation in Vietnam represented a sharp departure from the gentlemanly manner in which Republicans had conducted themselves since 1964. He frequently made statements that emphasized the similarity between Nixon's policy and Johnson's. As Tom Wicker noted in his column in the *New York Times* on 18 February, Romney had broken the "Eleventh Commandment." Decreed by Dr. Gaylord Parkinson, the chairman of the California Republican Party, this dictum bound members of the GOP to "speak no evil" of other Republicans in order to "avoid any further ideological rending and wracking of the battered old elephant." Wicker also opined that "there is not yet any clear guide to a responsible and winning Republican policy" on Vietnam and that it would be "extremely difficult for any Republican candidate to take a position that will not give President Johnson the middle ground and the opportunity to paint his opponent as either a soft-headed dove or a dangerous hawk."[125] To avoid a repeat of the Goldwater debacle, the party leadership had determined that unity and civility would take precedence over internecine struggles. Better to focus attacks on the opposition than to succumb to intraparty strife and face another four years out of the White House. But Romney's flagging candidacy led him to resort to vicious attacks on Nixon's Vietnam policy in a last-ditch effort to swing the voters back to his side. The deeply religious Romney, who would never consider breaking the Ten Commandments, considered the GOP Eleventh Commandment expendable.

A *Boston Globe* editorial the following day observed, "[Romney and Nixon] have crossed swords on one of the vital issues, the war in Vietnam, and this is all to the good so far as it has gone. . . . What should be demanded of each of them, now, is the fullest possible elaboration of his thinking on this toughest of all campaign topics." The editors believed that, if the candidates took their advice, "one of them unquestionably would seal his doom. But each has the duty fully to argue his convictions."[126] The *Globe's* wishes were not enough to prompt either candidate to provide any substantive details, but its prediction was accurate in one sense: Romney's fate was sealed.

New Hampshire proved to be the final burial ground for George Romney's presidential ambitions. Neither his attack on Nixon nor his efforts to redefine himself could salvage his sinking candidacy, which one observer described as having moved "beyond farce into straight tragedy" by late February.[127] His campaign already on shaky ground coming into the primary, the governor's own polls showed him facing a six-to-one deficit against Nixon. Rather than waiting until after the balloting, Romney bowed to the inevitable and announced the end of his campaign in a statement to Republican governors on 28 February. He asserted that his withdrawal was due to the fact that he had "not won the wide acceptance with rank and file Republicans that [he] had hoped to achieve."[128] Yet his failure ran deeper than that. His inability to present his views concisely and consistently limited his effectiveness as a candidate, and his ambiguous and dovish position on Vietnam had a negative impact on his standing with GOP hawks.

Romney himself recognized that his candidacy faltered owing in large part to the Vietnam War:

I did rather dramatically reverse myself in 1967 from the position I had taken in 1965 on Vietnam. I used strong words. But I had to in order to make it abundantly clear I no longer believed the war had as its purposes and was being directed in the manner I was advised earlier. I do not regret making this declaration. More important than the Presidency is that enough voices speak to the subject of Vietnam in such a way that we will extricate ourselves from that conflict. . . . It has been some satisfaction to see the likes of Senator Morton, Senator [George] Aiken [of Vermont] and others taking much the same position in recent months, and I have hopes that Mr. Nixon and Governor Rockefeller will develop positions along the lines I have advocated.

Shortly after his withdrawal, Romney was asked on "Face the Nation" if he could support Nixon as the GOP nominee, a relevant question given his refusal to support Barry Goldwater's campaign in 1964. Romney responded, "There again I want to know more about his position on Vietnam." This was an extraordinarily disingenuous statement, but one that reflected the importance of the war in the coming political contest in which he no longer played a leading role.[129]

Johnson and Romney must have felt the frustration of the damned as 1968 began to unfold. Both had hoped to represent their parties in the presidential election that fall, but, like Sisyphus and Tantalus, they failed owing to their respective problems with the war. Indeed, LBJ's speech on 31 March would serve as the ultimate acknowledgment of his failure to resolve the conflict that had become America's longest war. Meanwhile, the Republicans struggled to define their relationship to Vietnam, increasingly reflecting the divisions within the country as a whole as the party became startlingly polarized. Even without a consensus on the conflict, however, the campaign would continue with different protagonists, and the war would continue to exert significant domestic political influence on the election and the candidates.

CHAPTER 6

# The Zalmoxis Effect

## Vietnam and the 1968 Presidential Election

The politician is an acrobat. He keeps his balance by saying the opposite of what he does.

—Maurice Barrès, *Mes cahiers*

Depend on it, sir, when a man knows he is to be hanged in a fortnight, it concentrates his mind wonderfully.

—Samuel Johnson quoted in Boswell's *Life of Johnson*

The pantheon of Greek gods ranges from the almighty Zeus—king of the gods, supreme ruler on Mount Olympus, god of thunder and the sky—to lesser-known but colorful deities like Adephagia (goddess of gluttony) and Priapus (god of fertility). One of the more obscure gods was Zalmoxis, who assumed human form and disappeared in the underworld for three years before returning in the fourth. Although a ruler and god of the underworld to the Thracians, he could easily have been the god of elections. In the American political system, every fourth year witnesses the spectacle of a presidential election, where candidates make sweeping, grandiose promises for change, peace, and prosperity—and then the rhetoric disappears for three years until it returns again for the next campaign. In 1968, the Zalmoxis effect reared its head as Republican presidential aspirants jockeyed for position, with Vietnam acting as a fulcrum for the primary contests. The war also figured prominently in the fall campaign between Richard Nixon and Hubert Humphrey, exerting broad influence despite the candidates' best efforts (and hopes), and nearly determining the outcome of the election. This chapter is devoted to examining how the GOP grappled with Vietnam on multiple fronts—internally, against the Johnson administration, and during the race for the White House—during 1968.

With his nomination virtually assured, Nixon began to craft a centrist position on Vietnam. The *Baltimore Sun* reported in March 1968 that House Republicans had become increasingly dovish with regard to the war, noting that over half the 187 GOP representatives had signed a resolution calling for "a congressional review of fundamental policy in Southeast Asia." The bulk of these, the article notes, "want a 'de-Americanization' of the war."[1] Yet Nixon could not embrace opposition to the war completely. Many Southern Republicans stood considerably to the right of the national political mainstream on a variety of economic, social, and especially racial issues. This cohort within the party had vigorously supported Goldwater in 1964 and had not relinquished its hard-core conservative views. If Nixon hoped to gain and hold the allegiance of both groups, he would have to use all his political skills to maneuver among the factions within the party.[2]

Speaking to a Republican gathering in Nashua, New Hampshire, in March, Nixon pledged to "end the war and win the peace."[3] In this and subsequent statements on the war made during 1968, he "walked a tightrope of meaning, using nuanced words and phrases to keep his balance." For doves and moderates, he emphasized nonmilitary steps toward peace; for hawks and conservatives, he talked about maintaining pressure on Hanoi and the Viet Cong and winning the peace. This, then, was his challenge: to woo the doves while holding on to the hawks and staying true to his own foreign policy convictions. Fortunately for him, the diverse opinions on the war that pervaded the country in early 1968 allowed him to propose politically appealing courses of action to disparate parts of the electorate without abandoning his own foreign policy goals and strategies.[4] This "middle-of-the-road" strategy, Nixon's speechwriter Richard Whalen noted in his memoirs, was intended, not to discover the most valid solution for Vietnam, but rather "to find the least assailable middle ground"—recently abandoned by Romney and not yet occupied by Rockefeller—that would secure the GOP nomination.[5]

Nevertheless, Nixon still faced challenges to his candidacy. George Wallace, the outspoken and controversial former governor of Alabama, decided to run as an independent. While his campaign focused heavily on the issues of race and states' rights, Wallace's position on the war was simple and direct: he would turn the problem over to the Joint Chiefs of Staff, ask them what needed to be done, and then "get on with doing it"—exactly what Goldwater had proposed in 1964. According to Wallace, the United States should call on "all the military ability we have," excluding nuclear weapons, to win the war. He rejected the concept of inviting the National Liberation Front (NLF) to the peace talks and suggested requiring that Asians themselves help stabilize the continent for the future peace and safety of the world. In keeping with his unbending mind-set, he asserted that any university professor or student who supported the North Vietnamese should be fired or expelled. The war was not very popular with Wallace's core supporters, however. They were more concerned with the anti-war protest movement, led by "silverspoon brats" who rejected core American values and patriotism. As a result, his Vietnam position did not have a significant influence on the campaign. Most Republicans concerned with the prosecution of the war tended to gravitate toward Nixon.[6]

Meanwhile, Nelson Rockefeller continued to attract attention as a potential candidate. Governor William Guy (D-ND) wrote to Marvin Watson and suggested that Nixon's position was tenuous because his view "as a hawk is quite well known; and if the mess in Vietnam were traced back far enough into the past decade, it is easy to find Vice President Nixon as part of the original problem." Guy expressed more concern with the possibility of a Rockefeller campaign. Lacking the same constraints that shackled Nixon, Rockefeller could "electrify the nation and swamp" Nixon's chances at the nomination by announcing "a concrete plan with deadlines for ending the United States participation in the Vietnam War." Guy contended that the war needed to be brought to an end by the administration before Nixon or Rockefeller developed a "dramatic plan" that would lead the public to question any subsequent proposal by the administration as Republican influenced. He also suggested that Rockefeller, who strategically left the October 1967 Governors' Conference prior to the vote on the resolution on the war, "did not want to be in a position of having to record his vote on any amendment that might be offered to an otherwise innocent resolution." Ultimately, he concluded, "The public will vote for those candidates or that party in which they have the most confidence that a plan will be followed to get us out of this costly Vietnam war."[7]

At this point, Guy's assessment was premature. Rockefeller's reluctance to speak out on Vietnam made his candidacy seem unlikely, and Nixon's rhetorical gymnastics appeared to be working. In March, however, Nixon nearly tripped over his own words. In an off-the-cuff remark to reporters, he said that, if elected, he would end the war in Vietnam but would not now tell the Hanoi regime what he would offer it as president. The media jumped on this statement and announced that Nixon had a "secret plan" to end the war. This led to rampant speculation about what such a proposal would entail and skepticism that this was anything more than a political ploy on Nixon's part. Critics referred to his long record of hawkishness on the war and prior dissembling as indications that he created the "plan" simply to get elected.[8]

Contrary to contemporary media accounts and an astonishing amount of subsequent scholarship, Nixon did not actually say that he had a secret plan, although, to be fair, he never officially denied having one. Not even Eisenhower, who wrote his former vice president to ask for details, could elicit an explanation. Nixon told Eisenhower that he could not be specific because he did not want to "undercut whatever diplomatic negotiations might be underway at present" and because he did not want to restrict his own negotiating flexibility when he became president.[9] A memorandum in the files of the Republican National Committee acknowledges that Nixon did indicate that he had definite ideas on how to end the war through what would become known as Vietnamization.[10] Yet he did not reveal his thoughts to even his closest confidants.

Critics of the alleged plan were numerous. A perceptive editorial in the *New York Times* suggested that the Nixon and Rockefeller campaigns both believed that "the Republicans can win the Presidency by censoring Administration policies in Vietnam but keeping vague, their own proposals for change."[11] The *Houston Chronicle* charged that Nixon's reticence in defining his plans to end the conflict "may be creating his own 'credibility gap'" and could give Rockefeller a wedge issue to use at the GOP convention in August.[12] And the *Anderson Independent* sarcastically editorialized that, if Nixon had such a plan, he should "reveal without delay the scope and details of [it] to bring the world into a great golden age after this coming November."[13] Rockefeller went so far as to wonder why Nixon would "keep a plan [to end the war] a secret when hundreds die each week?"[14] Rockefeller's comments dripped with irony. While complaining about Nixon's secret plan, Rockefeller had maintained a wary and almost anxious silence on Vietnam for several years. This, in part, explains why GOP conservatives like Representative John Ashbrook (R-OH) believed that Rockefeller was "the only Republican who could not unite the party."[15] If the governor hoped to overtake Nixon in the race for the nomination, he would need to reach out to conservatives and end his silence on the war.

Despite his criticism of Nixon's statements on Vietnam, which sounded very much like campaign rhetoric, Rockefeller stunned the political community by announcing his "withdrawal" from the race on 21 March. Although he had never actually declared himself a candidate, he stated, "I have decided today to reiterate unequivocally that I am not a candidate campaigning directly or indirectly for the presidency of the United States."[16] Rockefeller told friends that he was "really agonizing" over the political effect of making a commitment on the Vietnam issue because he believed that Johnson would begin peace negotiations before the November elections.[17] Suddenly, Nixon stood alone. With Romney's withdrawal, Rockefeller's disavowal of interest, and the lack of a realistic challenge from Ronald Reagan, his nomination seemed to be a foregone conclusion.[18] On 25 March, a *Wall Street Journal* editorial put it succinctly: "Nixon has the nomination 'all but in the bag.'"[19] But Nixon and his advisers recognized that, in order to pose a serious threat to Johnson in November, the former vice president would need to make a definitive statement on Vietnam soon to silence skeptics who questioned whether he truly had an idea of how to end the war or whether it was so much political smoke and mirrors.

The Nixon aide William Safire advised the candidate to elaborate his position for the nation and make a major policy speech on Vietnam. Safire argued—correctly—that Nixon's public statements on the war had consisted of "a grab bag of phrases, from which audiences could draw whatever general conclusions they pleased." Herbert Brownell, the attorney general under Eisenhower, also counseled Nixon to make a statement on the war. Brownell suggested that Nixon "had to say he would end the war, just as Ike had done back in 1952 with regard to Korea."[20] Nixon told Safire, "It would be better for me not to do anything controversial for the time being. I don't want to get into the crossfire between LBJ and Bobby [Kennedy]—let them hit each other, not me." But, after his initial reluctance, Safire and others convinced him to give a series of national radio addresses to develop his position for the public.[21] Ever the political realist, Nixon had "come to the conclusion that there's no way to win the war." As he told his speechwriters, however, "We can't say that, of course. In fact, we have to seem to say the opposite, just to keep some degree of bargaining leverage."[22]

Had Nixon followed through on Safire's and Brownell's advice, the ramifications for his candidacy could have been serious. He would have committed himself publicly to a course of action that would have limited his flexibility in the fall. Fortunately for Nixon's campaign, however, he never had to give his speech, which he had scheduled for 31 March. Richard Whalen recalls that, on being informed of Johnson's intention to speak to the nation the same day, Nixon "put his head down for a long moment. Then he flipped the pages of manuscript in the air in a gesture of resignation. 'Dammit. We've got to cancel. That's all we can do.'"[23] Nixon, who must have been relieved as well, posited that Johnson "had adopted the very plan Nixon was going to propose" in the aborted radio message, and the GOP front-runner wanted to be in a position to take advantage of anything the president said. As Stephen Ambrose has noted, "This was no accident—the two men had been together on Vietnam right along, except that Nixon had always been just ahead of Johnson."[24] The president's statement paralleled Nixon's proposed comments almost exactly, except for the shocking coda in which Johnson stated categorically that he would not seek reelection in November. Even Washington insiders were astonished at this decision. Just a few weeks earlier, an interviewer asked George Aiken whether he could envision any circumstances under which the president would not run for reelection.

Aiken replied, "Not now. I can't see those circumstances now. I think that would be the surprise of the year, I mean the generation if he didn't run."[25]

Republican reaction to the president's announcement was mixed. Representative Catherine May (R-WA) told her constituents that, by "removing himself from the political struggle, the President has acquired a credibility and a flexibility in negotiating that is far greater than could be expected if he intended to make himself a candidate for re-election." His decision freed him to "quickly engage in strenuous escalation of attacks on North Vietnam" without fear of political repercussions if the leadership in Hanoi refused to negotiate.[26] Eisenhower was not as charitable. The former president "was filled with anger, his remarks about Johnson's cutting and running unprintable."[27] Just a few weeks earlier, the president had paid Eisenhower a visit in Palm Desert, California, and promised that he would persevere in Vietnam. Eisenhower considered LBJ's decision not to maintain the current level of pressure on North Vietnam cowardly and detrimental to the national interest. The withdrawal from the political contest was the last straw for Eisenhower. The former president had become increasingly disenchanted with the administration's war strategy after 1966. He disdained gradualism—ironic, given the way he approached Vietnam during his presidency—and believed that the administration centralized too many decisions, thereby preventing field commanders from having the freedom they required to fight the war effectively. Eisenhower also expressed concern about the duration of the conflict and the disappearance of public support, which had already begun to wane. Eisenhower firmly believed that only a nation united behind a determined leader could prevail in the fight against communism.

Only days after Johnson's abrupt announcement, *Reader's Digest* published an article by Eisenhower aptly titled "Let's Close Ranks on the Home Front." Eisenhower condemned the "arrogant flouting of the law" by antiwar protesters, although he recognized the legitimacy of their opinions: "The current raucous confrontation, however, goes far beyond honorable dissent. . . . It is rebellion, and it verges on treason." He also argued that "the behavior of the dissenters themselves is making honorable negotiation impossible" because it signaled to the North Vietnamese leadership a lack of American resolve. If the Hanoi regime perceived the United States as divided, it had no incentive to make concessions in negotiations and would prolong both the fighting and the peace talks in the hope of forcing Washington to settle on its terms. Only if both sides came to the peace talks with "honest and reasonable intentions" could a satisfactory settlement be reached, and, in Eisenhower's mind, the lack of unity at home gave Hanoi no motivation to negotiate.[28]

The article also gave an explanation for America's continuing involvement in the war. Responding to critics who considered the war immoral, Eisenhower asserted, "It would be grossly immoral *not* to resist a tyranny whose openly avowed purpose is to subjugate the earth." He went on to argue that the main reason to support the American efforts was because "we are trying to save a brave little country, to which we have given our solemn promise of protection, from being swallowed by the communist tyranny." He also reemphasized his deep-seated conviction that the domino theory was "frighteningly correct." But perhaps the strongest statement came when he discussed the fact that 1968 was an election year. "It is improper, and I think unpatriotic," he said, "to voice dissent in such a way that it encourages our enemy to believe we have lost the capacity to make a national decision and act on it." In a direct challenge to presidential hopefuls such as Robert Kennedy and Eugene McCarthy, he asserted, *"I will not personally support any peace-at-any-price candidate who advocates capitulation and the abandonment of South Vietnam."* To Eisenhower, the Vietnam War was a necessity: "These things we must continue to do, even when we stand alone." He ended with a plea for unity: "It is unthinkable that the voices of defeat should triumph in our land."[29]

Those voices had, however, helped convince Lyndon Johnson to withdraw from the presidential campaign, a move that changed the entire dynamic of the race. The president's announcement made the fall campaign more unpredictable since the Republican presidential candidate would not be able to specifically attack him for the stalemated conflict and the domestic political debate would now revolve around the battle over disengagement and what that would mean.[30] While the president would contribute to that debate, it would be as a spectator rather than a direct participant. In a moment of historical irony, Johnson's defeat in Vietnam resulted from the escalated war that Goldwater had warned the American people about and for which he had been reviled; now, Johnson would go home to Texas as Goldwater returned to Washington (he would be elected to the Senate again in the fall).

Johnson's exit from the campaign eliminated Nixon's need to present a detailed strategy to end the fighting prior to the Republican convention in August. Indeed, Nixon took full advantage of LBJ's withdrawal. The following day, he issued a statement declaring a self-imposed "moratorium" on comments on Vietnam. He also alluded to his planned statement on the war in his speech, saying, "I shall not make the comprehensive statement on Vietnam which I had planned for this week."[31] (As Richard Whalen points out, the discarded speech "had been something less than 'comprehensive.'")[32] By doing so, he intended to insulate himself from criticism while retaining the flexibility to break the silence when he saw fit since Vietnam remained a critical issue in the campaign. In his mind, neither Robert Kennedy nor Hubert Humphrey, the front-runners for the Democratic nomination, were as vulnerable on Vietnam as Johnson would have been. Yet, despite renouncing his candidacy, the president could still be in a position to use the war to his and his party's advantage. A meaningful peace gesture could give the Democratic nominee a significant boost in the polls and could, potentially, lead Johnson to reenter the race. Thus, Nixon continued his strategy of taking the middle course, saying as little as possible about Vietnam while maintaining the public posture that he did not want to interfere with the president's efforts or undermine his own negotiating position should he become president. He did, however, publicly warn Johnson against the "temptations of a camouflaged surrender" and told reporters that he believed that there was room to negotiate an acceptable settlement in Vietnam.[33]

Nixon's politically astute, if ideologically fickle, actions brought criticism from the Right. "Richard Nixon has been pickled, like an insect in Baltic amber," the *National Review* pontificated. "His next move cannot be made until Johnson, in effect, has told him what there is to talk about." The president's decision "rendered his policies untouchable by clothing them in the mantles of justice, peace, and hope." By announcing the moratorium on Vietnam commentary, Nixon not only put himself in a straitjacket but also "immobilized . . . all other shades of Republican opinion. The only Republicans who remain free to say what they think are those [like Reagan] who take a harder line than Nixon." The *Review* concluded: "Johnson's 'withdrawal' is a political masterstroke."[34] Conservatives never fully accepted Nixon, either as a candidate or as president, and proved to be a source of constant political concern for him.

Johnson's announcement shocked Everett Dirksen. "I could hardly believe it," he said, although the two friends had discussed precisely this scenario on several occasions. It also had significant implications for Dirksen's position in the Senate. Not only would it lessen his "compulsion" to defend LBJ's Vietnam policies, but it would also require him to reshape his own political stance to "accommodate the new reality of another President-to-be."[35] Several Republicans also praised Johnson's efforts to bring about an honorable settlement while concurrently pointing out that his plan echoed previous GOP initiatives to bring the fighting to an end. Other members of the party lauded his selfless act but, like Nixon, managed to simultaneously criticize the administration's policies and warn against an ill-advised (read: preelection) settlement.

In an article that appeared the week after Johnson's announcement, Thruston Morton argued, "Only one possible alternative can provide the United States with effective and realizable policies abroad and unity and progress at home. That is the nomination by the Republican Party of a candidate who is not committed to wanton globalism or domestic retrenchment, and his election to the Presidency in 1968." Morton addressed his own break with the administration over Vietnam, which he claimed had resulted—at least in part—from his "increasing awareness" that "the failures of U.S. policy in Europe, the Middle East, and elsewhere were in large part due to our obsession with victory in Asia." He opined that, if the GOP could "resist the siren song of those who counsel stepped-up military involvement," and if it would nominate someone "dedicated to the proposition that gradual disengagement in Vietnam offers the best and only hope for an eventual solution," then it would be in a prime position to win the White House in the fall. And, he concluded, because the Johnson administration's options were "closed," a Republican president "would be much more capable of administering the painful medicine that will be required to overcome the sickness that is our Asian policy."[36] If Morton had his way, the GOP nominee would be Nelson Rockefeller.

Johnson's withdrawal resurrected the possibility of a Rockefeller candidacy. In fact, the president secretly urged the governor to reenter the race as an alternative to Nixon on 4 April and again at a dinner at the White House on 23 April. Johnson had long admired Rockefeller and considered him one of the country's ablest and most dedicated public servants. As Lady Bird Johnson later commented, "Lyndon thought Rockefeller was by far the best of the Republicans and wanted the best running for the American people to choose from."[37] Since many saw Nixon and Johnson as indistinguishable when it came to Vietnam policy, Rockefeller presented a plausible alternative to Nixon and any of the dovish Democratic presidential candidates. But he would have to confront the war directly if he hoped to be taken seriously as a legitimate candidate because "on the dominant issue of the moment, Vietnam, he had neither public nor private posture."[38]

Prior to 1968, Rockefeller had supported American aims in Vietnam and Southeast Asia and had criticized the administration for not doing enough to successfully prosecute the war. Yet he had maintained an almost complete public silence on the Vietnam issue since 1964. According to the *New Republic*, "As late as last March 22 [1967], Rockefeller was endorsing what is being done in Vietnam 'as a matter of both patriotism and practicality.' The *New York Times* reported that Mr. Rockefeller had told Senator Javits that he considered the Senator's slightly dovish views 'very impractical politics.'" Theodore Draper noted in March 1968, "Governor Nelson Rockefeller, who is waiting for his foes in the party to beg him to run . . . was last on record with a vigorous pro-war position, but he has managed to retain his potential as a candidate by not repeating it and, indeed, by not saying anything at all on the subject for about three years."[39] Despite the criticism he faced for failing to engage in a discussion of the campaign's key issue, Rockefeller remained hesitant to discuss the war throughout the spring, which left his potential return to the race stuck in neutral.

The debate over Vietnam continued within the Republican Party without

Rockefeller's input. John Rhodes told a constituent on 29 April that the United States "should continue to keep up our strength" in Vietnam and rely on military force to bring the North Vietnamese to the negotiating table.[40] Indeed, hawkish Republicans refused to allow the party to be conquered by the proponents of withdrawal. Speaking to the Western Governors' Conference in Hawaii, Ronald Reagan reiterated his support of winning a military victory in Vietnam. Criticizing Johnson for losing the war already in political and moral terms—although not on the battlefield, "where wars are really decided"—Reagan argued that the United States "must not give in. Whatever the cost, the United States must honor its pledge to uphold the sovereignty and independence of South Vietnam." If that could be accomplished by negotiating from a position of strength, so be it. But if not, "We must return to the fighting—but determined to use whatever power and technology we have at our command to end the war and make sure the aggression really stops."[41] Meanwhile, more members of Congress came out in favor of a negotiated withdrawal, not very surprising considering that most of them faced reelection in the fall and public sentiment ran strongly against the war. The polarization of the party raised questions among the GOP leadership regarding the convention platform. How would the party deal with Vietnam? Could the Republicans avoid a disastrous split over the war and present a united front against the Democrats? Would Vietnam cause them to break the Eleventh Commandment as Romney had done in New Hampshire?

As the Republicans moved closer to their convention in Miami, Johnson pursued a settlement. Formal peace talks opened in Paris on 13 May and immediately deadlocked. Hanoi had agreed to the meetings as part of its broader strategy of *danh va dam* (fighting while negotiating), "an integrated approach to warfare that blended military and diplomatic activities and sought to stimulate 'internal contradictions' in the enemy camp."[42] The North Vietnamese made it clear that they established contact with the United States to secure the unconditional end to American bombing raids so that productive talks could begin. While the administration displayed a willingness to stop the bombing, it would do so only provided that Hanoi deescalated on a reciprocal basis, something the Communist leadership continued to reject. Although Averill Harriman, the chief American negotiator, tried to persuade LBJ to end the bombing in order to jump-start the negotiations, the president refused to consider the proposal and threatened to undertake additional military measures to force the North Vietnamese to the table. Meanwhile, the political and military balance remained unchanged throughout the spring and early summer.

Despite Johnson's rejection of Harriman's suggestion, the president truly wanted to resolve the war before the election to potentially position himself to reenter the race. But, as he pursued peace, he had to fend off pressure from hawkish Republicans like Eisenhower. The former president continued to advocate a sustained and unyielding commitment to the war, but his commitment to the conflict was tempered by his belief in supporting the president. His final briefing with Goodpaster on 7 May 1968 reflected this dichotomy. Frustrated with LBJ's decision and with the increasing clamor for a negotiated settlement, he asserted that the United States "should not expect to attain more at the conference table than we could attain on the battlefield." Yet, even after all that had transpired, he remained a loyal soldier. As Goodpaster reported, "Eisenhower indicated support of the course the President is following with respect to the war in Vietnam and the peace negotiations."[43] Realizing that the military victory he pushed for would not come to pass, Eisenhower decided to endorse LBJ's negotiating strategy and hope that the GOP could regain the White House in November.

But, as the saying goes, two weeks is a long time in politics. Three months remained until the Republican convention, and six months were left before the general election. While the administration negotiated in Paris, the race for the GOP nomination intensified. At a luncheon with Republican senators in late April, Rockefeller finally spoke out on the war. Noting that the party was far from "monolithic" on the issue of Vietnam, he questioned Nixon's proposal that Republicans should observe a moratorium on commenting on the conflict while the administration arranged peace talks with the North Vietnamese. If preliminary negotiations with Hanoi lasted until November and such a moratorium were applied literally, the governor argued, Vietnam would be barred from political debate for the entire election—of course, that outcome would have pleased Nixon greatly. Rockefeller stated, "'I think there can be and should be discussion and criticism, and if it is handled properly it will not jeopardize the nation.'"[44] With the support of several influential Republican senators, Rockefeller posed a significant threat to Nixon's nomination if he decided to reverse himself and run. The former vice president also had to contend with his lingering reputation as a political loser. Nixon could not shake his past electoral failures, and many within the party considered him a flawed candidate who could not win a national election against any Democratic opponent. This perception gained credence when Rockefeller won the Massachusetts primary on 30 April as a write-in candidate with 30 percent of the vote; Nixon managed to finish only third with 25.8 percent of the vote (also as a write-in).[45] One could sympathize with the wariness of GOP voters. After the 1964 experience, they wanted to ensure they nominated an electable candidate, and Nixon had not yet proved his viability.

Democrats watched the Republican intramural contest with intense interest. How would the GOP deal with the thorny question of Vietnam, and what would the Democratic response be? Addressing the latter question, the speech-writer John Roche sent a detailed memo to Humphrey on campaign strategy. Roche advised the vice president to "start running against Nixon *now*" rather than waiting until after the convention in August. He considered Nixon an "extremely formidable opponent," which made Humphrey's job more difficult. He urged Humphrey not to attempt to "placate" the (Eugene) McCarthyite forces in the party because "any efforts to do so will play into Nixon's hand. . . . Don't put your energy into getting your old liberal 'friends' to love you. If you do, you will end up locked in on the war—which you must try to keep out of the campaign." Roche believed that, as far as Vietnam was concerned, Humphrey should stay in a "sealed room until *after* the election" and resist the temptation to build an independent position. But perhaps the most intriguing idea Roche forwarded was to suggest Rockefeller as Humphrey's running mate. Such a move would create a "national reconciliation" ticket that would be able to overcome the "noisy" environment in the country.[46]

Rockefeller's lingering presence in the race demonstrated his popularity across partisan lines. In addition to LBJ's backing and Roche's suggestion, Rockefeller enjoyed the support of a substantial segment of the Republican party. Thruston Morton considered him to be an "able and proven administrator" and "a winner"—clearly a swipe at Nixon—and supported his dovish position on the war.[47] Charles Percy, who had considered his own run for the GOP nomination, eventually announced his support for Rockefeller, calling him "the only Presidential candidate who has set forth a detailed program to end the war. His recent peace plan is a constructive contribution to the dialogue on this issue."[48] And John Sherman Cooper contended that the country would "only vote for a candidate who clearly states his views on Vietnam and forthrightly explains in what ways he intends to lead the United States from the mistake in Vietnam." Among Republicans, he argued, "only Governor Rockefeller has spoken out with clarity and firm direction."[49] That Rockefeller had not yet done so did not diminish Cooper's advocacy of the governor's presidential potential.

The day after his surprising victory in the Massachusetts primary, Rockefeller broke what the *Oregon Journal* called his "lengthy and conspicuous" silence on Vietnam in a speech at the World Affairs Council in Philadelphia.[50] In his first concrete statement on the war, he advocated reversing the Americanization of the war and turning more responsibility over to the South Vietnamese. But he also cautioned against permitting opposition to the war to result in a renewed isolationism. Peace negotiations, he argued, should include nonacceptance of any solution dictated by force and acceptance in South Vietnam's life of any group that sought its objectives through the political process—a statement clearly referring to the NLF. The *New York Times* editorialized the next day that the Johnson administration "should not find much to differ with in this analysis" and demonstrated its obvious preference for Rockefeller over Nixon.[51] The governor's speech came too late to have any substantive impact on the nomination, but it did serve notice to the party that its moderate wing would have to play a role in developing the GOP platform plank on Vietnam at the August convention.

Rockefeller's statement forced Nixon to take immediate steps to solidify his control over the party's platform plank on Vietnam. Intending to be the motive force behind the official GOP position on Vietnam, Nixon asked Richard Whalen to draft a comprehensive statement on the war for submission to the platform committee at the convention. The former vice president left his instructions intentionally vague; the only stipulation he provided was to "keep Hubert lashed to the mast."[52] Whalen spent most of July researching the war and interviewing experts on military and political matters related to the conflict. From these sources, it became clear that "it was time for the U.S. to begin extricating itself from Vietnam and time to declare the goal of eventual withdrawal to the American people."[53] That sentiment would become the central assumption of Whalen's draft plank and would provide Nixon with a centrist position on the war for the fall.

With Nixon dialing back his hawkish rhetoric and doves like Percy, Rockefeller, and Cooper becoming more vocal in opposition to the war, it seemed as though the GOP could become the "peace party." Yet a sizable contingent of Republicans remained hawkish and believed that the war could still be won on the ground. Appearing on "Meet the Press," Ronald Reagan endorsed an invasion of North Vietnam—carried out by the South Vietnamese and "supported logistically by the United States"—in the event that peace talks failed to produce a settlement. The conservative icon went on to assert that, even if Saigon and Washington never had to go that far, "the enemy must believe and must see that you are willing to." Whatever the cost, Reagan argued, the United States needed to honor its pledge to uphold the sovereignty and independence of South Vietnam. If that could not be accomplished through negotiations, then the administration should commit to employing all the power at its command to end the war through military means in order to put an end to North Vietnamese aggression. He did, however, rule out the use of nuclear weapons in Vietnam.[54] That caveat aside, Reagan's position sounded very much like the "madman theory" that Nixon would employ during his presidency.

Strom Thurmond also stuck to his guns, suggesting, "This appalling situation is the result of pulling our punches . . . the bitter fruit of the policy of 'gradual escalation.'" Thurmond put forward ten hawkish suggestions—including a blockade of North Vietnam and extensive bombing of military targets—that he believed would "threaten North Vietnam with certain military defeat." Only then, he concluded, would Hanoi be forced to "negotiate in earnest."[55] Despite continued aggressive rhetoric from Reagan, Thurmond, and other hawks and the ongoing support of Eisenhower, however, the party as a whole had clearly moved closer to adopting a position in support of deescalation in an effort to regain the presidency.

Meanwhile, Nixon cruised to victory in the Oregon primary, which virtually assured that he would be the GOP presidential candidate in the fall. The *New York Times,* which took him so seriously as a critic of the Johnson administration from 1964 to 1966, editorialized after the Oregon primary that the Republicans were on the verge of making "a familiar mistake."[56] What the *Times* and other media outlets did not admit was the fact that Nixon's success owed everything to the fact that he did not make any mistakes during the campaign, especially in his statements on the war. This was not the corrosive Nixon of the 1950s, or the imperfect candidate of 1960, or the hawkish firebrand of even a few years earlier. The Republican front-runner demonstrated a political maturity, restraint, experience, and understanding that allowed him to soften his hard edges, capitalize on his opponents' miscues, and ride the electoral currents to victory—all without having to commit to a specific position on the Vietnam conflict. Regardless of one's opinion of Nixon, his political brilliance in 1968 cannot be underestimated.

Although Nixon's nomination now appeared to be a near fait accompli, it did not stop Rockefeller from continuing to attack both Nixon and Johnson on the war. The administration, Rockefeller believed, wrongly used the assumptions of World War II to inform the American presence in Vietnam. In a speech to the Commonwealth Club of San Francisco on 13 June, he criticized the Democrats for an "out-dated political understanding. On the whole, we have acted as if we were trying to defend stable European political structures, as in the 1940s." This approach, he argued, failed to recognize the need to "create entirely new political structures for Southeast Asia."[57] Three days later, Reagan weighed in on who should participate in those structures. On "Face the Nation," he asserted, "I don't hope for the kind of peace that would result in, say, a concession that would allow the Viet Cong to be a part of the South Vietnamese government." That would be "about the same as the United States government taking the Cosa Nostra in as partners."[58] Reagan's comments represented the views of many in the GOP who refused to consider any settlement that included participation of members of the NLF in a postwar government in South Vietnam.

The following week, Rockefeller decided to confront Nixon's stance on the war directly. Discussing Nixon's moratorium proposal, he said, "Did a refuge in silence seem the safest haven for a prophet who had been proven so wrong? . . .

There must be an alternative to indefinite war." Rather than accepting Nixon's "belligerent prophecies" on Vietnam—"'We have to stop it with victory, or it will start all over again in a few years'"—the governor called the prospect of military victory "imagined" and made a plea to "avoid the deadly spiral of endless escalation."[59] Rockefeller's criticisms of Nixon demonstrated both the divisions extant in the GOP on Vietnam and the governor's continued interest in running for the presidency. But, while most of his comments to this point had been designed to attack the positions of his rivals, Rockefeller would soon end his reluctance to assert his own policy proposal for resolving the Vietnam conflict.

Rockefeller's staff worked overtime to create a strategy to wrest the nomination from Nixon based on the candidates' differences on Vietnam. In a memorandum to the campaign adviser Professor Henry Kissinger of Harvard, the author of the Vietnam sections of most of the governor's speeches in recent weeks, Rockefeller's political guru Graham Molitor noted Nixon's own proclivity for silence on the war.[60] By avoiding any comment on the war, Nixon retained "the political advantage of being able to go any way the political winds may blow." Molitor also pointed out that the president's strategy "avoid[ed] overexposure of the issue; avoid[ed] speaking on the issue too early in the campaign; reduce[d] the possibility of putting his foot in his mouth"—as Romney did with his brainwashing statement—"avoid[ed] alienating either hawks or doves; and maintain[ed] political expediency on the issue; Vietnam is *the* issue." Molitor suggested that this "lack of forthrightness" and political expediency on the war represented Nixon's greatest vulnerability and urged the governor to attack him on this basis.[61] Rockefeller would do just that.

On 14 July, Rockefeller held a news conference at the New York Hilton and announced a comprehensive four-stage plan to end the war. It would be the most important foreign policy declaration of his renewed presidential campaign. The plan, which he drafted in consultation with Kissinger and Gen. James Gavin, a vocal advocate of negotiations, staked out a middle position between Nixon and the ultradove Democratic senator Eugene McCarthy (D-MN). The proposal called for the pullback of North Vietnamese troops toward the demilitarized zone and the borders of Cambodia and Laos, the withdrawal from South Vietnam of North Vietnamese regulars and "fillers" in Viet Cong units and most allied forces, the holding of free elections under international supervision, and the eventual reunification of Saigon and Hanoi. The following week, the *New York Times* found Rockefeller's plan to be analogous to "the direction in which U.S. military policy already appears to be moving under General [Creighton] Abrams."[62] Rockefeller intended the plan, which alienated the remaining hawks in the party, to serve both as a campaign speech and as a model for the Republican plank on Vietnam. As the *Yakima Herald-Republic* observed, "If the GOP stand is to mean anything at all to the thoughtful American voter . . . then the Republican party should [in its platform] accompany its criticisms with specific alternatives [for resolving the war]."[63] Rockefeller's speech filled that void and, because of its specificity and detail, stood in stark contrast to Nixon's position.

Once again, conservative opinion savaged Rockefeller. The governor "might as well have said, in showing us the way to Republican unity, that Reagan and Nixon should begin a mutual pull-back," the *National Review* observed. "He knows that his is no solution, but that it has the ring of action . . . he does not know what to do in Vietnam."[64] In reality, he did know what he wanted to do; it just flew in the face of conservatives who saw his position as defeatist. The Republican Right remained steadfastly supportive of aggressive prosecution of the war as part of the global fight against communism, and any proposal for negotiations or deescalation in Vietnam that appeared to cede an inch to Hanoi, Beijing, or Moscow quickly found itself on the receiving end of conservative attacks. Using blistering rhetoric, the Republican Right refused to even consider anything short of outright victory.

This intransigence did not extend to the party as a whole, however. The Republican congressional leadership consciously avoided saying anything inflammatory or controversial about the war, the candidates' positions, or the GOP platform on Vietnam during the weeks preceding the convention. They sought to prevent an incident akin to Romney's brainwashing comment from ruining a show of unity in Miami. During a press conference on foreign relations just two weeks prior to the convention, Everett Dirksen purposefully neglected to mention the war. As Terry Dietz has argued, he likely wanted to "leave all this business alone until after the Republican National Convention."[65] But not everyone in the party agreed with this strategy. Jack Miller stated that he intended to make an issue out of the administration's "deception" and "miscalculation." He asserted that the convention would be "derelict" if it did not include criticism of the administration's policies in the platform.[66] It seemed that the Republicans would have their work cut out for them in Miami.

On the eve of the convention, Nixon found himself very strongly positioned to win the nomination. He had a string of primary victories under his belt and possessed a sizable lead in committed delegates. He had the support of Strom Thurmond in the South—secured in a meeting some consider "probably the single most important event in the election of 1968"—which connected him with former Goldwater voters he would desperately need in his corner.[67] Thurmond threw his support behind Nixon in part because he offered "the best hope of recovering from . . . a bloody, no-win war in Southeast Asia." Nixon also enjoyed the support of a wide coalition of groups, including the Athletes for Nixon Committee, which allowed him to reach out to nontraditional audiences using surrogates like the NBA legend Wilt Chamberlain (who opined that Nixon was "the man to bring the Vietnam war to an end, the right way") and the Green Bay Packer quarterback Bart Starr.[68] Yet, for all these advantages, his hold on the nomination remained tenuous. If, for some reason, he did not win on the first ballot, his support might conceivably disintegrate, and the Rockefeller and Reagan partisans might be able to rally enough votes to deny him the prize for which he had positioned himself during the past four years.[69] Indeed, the prospect of an alternate Rockefeller-Reagan ticket concerned Nixon and his advisers greatly as the convention approached. Representative Rogers Morton (R-MD) even suggested that the GOP's chance to regain the presidency was "being eroded . . . by the campaign of Governor Rockefeller, who on several occasions has distorted Richard Nixon's public position and pat record in a way which I believe can be very damaging to our party."[70]

Furthermore, questions persisted about the content of the party's platform plank on Vietnam, which lingered as a likely point of contention among leading Republicans. John Tower, who chaired the Key Issues Committee at the convention and remained solidly behind the war, wrote to Nixon on 20 July and informed him that the committee was divided on whether the candidate should make a preconvention statement on Vietnam. "We are concerned," Tower said, "about the Rockefeller publicity offensive on the issue even though we feel the specific Rockefeller proposals fall of their own weight." In Tower's opinion, if any comment on Vietnam should be made, "it must be in the context of a credible transitional phase of your thinking and strategy from 'no comment' to 'comment' status."[71] Tower's concerns reflected the uncertainty in the party about Vietnam in the days and weeks leading up to the convention. Republicans of all stripes had expressed their opinions on what the party should stand for (or against) when it came to the war. The Foreign Policy and National Security Subcommittee of the GOP's platform committee, headed by Representative Glenard P. Lipscomb (R-CA), brought a draft plank on Vietnam to Miami. Amazingly, the hawkish document was "somewhat more martial than the Goldwater position of 1964." It indicted the administration for failure in Vietnam and attributed the debacle to insufficient effort; it "all but sounded the call for the march on Hanoi."[72] Clearly, the such uncompromising and belligerent language would have to be changed to more accurately represent mainstream GOP opinion if the party hoped to avoid a repeat of the 1964 fiasco.

These concerns were reflected in a *New York Times* article in late July. Nixon, the paper asserted, did not "want to be saddled with a platform so hawkish that it would permit Vice President Humphrey to outflank him on the left. Without knowing how to achieve it, [Nixon] is said to want a formulation that would put some distance between the Administration's Vietnam policies and his without at the same time corrupting his own fundamental view that the war has been necessary to resist Communist expansion in Asia."[73] Concerned indeed. In fact, Nixon flew to California on 21 July, ostensibly to work on his acceptance speech. But his real reason for seeking solitude back home was to work on the Vietnam plank for the convention. Since the party—and, more important, Nixon as the candidate—would clearly have to say something specific in the platform, he needed to stake out his position on the Vietnam conflict. Would he end the war by winning it militarily or by withdrawing?[74]

Nixon's draft statement provided the answer. Realizing that he had to be dovish enough to make Humphrey look like a hard-liner and hawkish enough to fend off challenges from Reagan and the GOP right wing, Nixon submitted a typically middle-of-the-road plank based on Whalen's earlier draft. "The war must be ended," the presumptive nominee asserted, "honorably [and] consistent with America's limited aims and with the long term requirements of peace in Asia." But, until the war did end, and in order to "hasten a negotiated end," the war "must be waged more effectively." Yet Nixon did not propose further military escalation; rather, he promoted "a dramatic escalation of our efforts on the economic, political, diplomatic and psychological fronts." Beyond these general statements, he left the proposed plank purposefully vague. If elected, he did not want to be held hostage "to the mistakes of the past . . . neither defending old errors nor bound by the old record."[75]

Others weighed in on the nature of the platform as well. Although no longer a candidate for the nomination, George Romney remained an important figure on the platform committee, and he made every effort to influence the Vietnam plank. He told the committee that the platform "must contain three basic elements. First, it must clearly set forth our aim in Vietnam. Second, it must present a conflict strategy to achieve that aim. Third, it must include a positive program for peace." If the plank resorted to vague generalizations, he argued, or if the GOP were to "pussyfoot or mince words on the Vietnam War issue, the American people will not turn to us for leadership, nor will we deserve it." He again proposed Vietnamization and guaranteed neutralization of Southeast Asia in concert with cooperative multilateral action as a substitute for the unilateral U.S. military action in South Vietnam and the basis for a GOP pledge for an honorable peace in Vietnam.[76]

Governor Raymond Shafer (R-PA), in his first strong public statement on the war, asked the platform committee to write a pledge of deescalation into the Vietnam plank. "The tenor and time of our nation," he contended, "demands a total assessment of foreign commitments which should lead us to deescalation of this war and a de-Americanization of foreign involvement wherever our influence had become a way of life."[77] Mark Hatfield's proposed plank sounded similar themes. He called for a neutral mediator at the peace talks, advocated the inclusion of both the Saigon government and the NLF in the negotiating sessions as well as an end to the bombing of the North.[78] Dwight Eisenhower told the party not to recommend anything approaching a camouflaged surrender. Meanwhile, John Lindsay, long an opponent of the conflict, said the party "'should assume forthright leadership for the cause of ending this unwanted war.'"[79] Clearly, then, even as the convention began, the party remained divided on the direction of its policy. The cacophony of views on the war made a compromise on Vietnam difficult, but agreement was mandatory for the party's unity.

Fortunately, the extremism and ideological rigidity of 1964 gave way to concessions by all sides. The columnist James Reston noted before the convention that "nobody is putting party ideology above party unity," and this sentiment dominated the platform discussions.[80] The *Christian Science Monitor* reported the following day, "The Republican platform committee appears likely to hammer out a 'peace plank' most any GOP candidate could walk. . . . Despite some differences on the two major issues—Vietnam and the cities—there were indications the 1968 platform would produce no major battle on the convention floor."[81] The differences in the party over Vietnam were real and nearly insurmountable. But the desire for harmony and the GOP's institutional memory of 1964 provided powerful incentives to restrain the objections of even the most vocal hawks and the most committed doves. Nobody wanted to be held responsible for the party's defeat in November.

The platform that came out of the GOP convention was "a masterpiece of political carpentry," taking the middle course between conservatives and liberals in domestic policy and between hawks and doves on Vietnam. Mindful of the contentious 1964 platform debate that had seriously hobbled Goldwater, the disparate voices within the party compromised on the Vietnam plank, "seasoning it with words of wartime resolve and future peace." The last draft prior to printing literally had numbered sentences and paragraphs highlighted by word and phrase with indications of where each section originated.[82] While ideologically correct for either Nixon or Rockefeller, it tended to be left of the positions advocated by Reagan throughout the past year and right of Lindsay's extreme dovishness. Nevertheless, its language was flexible enough to avoid offending the broad center of political opinion in the country and left Nixon free to adopt and pursue any course of negotiations to achieve peace.

One account of the convention called the Vietnam plank "therapy rather than policy" because of its lack of specific detail as to how the GOP objectives would be achieved. The Vietnam plank advocated a progressive Vietnamization of the war but said nothing regarding a bombing pause or a coalition government that would include participation by the NLF.[83] Best of all, the party adopted the plank without a single dissenting vote—a testament to its inclusivity and the overwhelming desire for unanimity. One editorial noted that, while not as hawkish as Reaganites desired, "the Republican platform gives no ground on Vietnam. The Hanoi warlords should read it carefully. . . . If Hanoi's strategy is to continue the fighting until after the election in hopes of making a better deal with the new President, Ho Chi Minh is due for disappointment . . . there's no comfort in it for Hanoi."[84]

Observers discerned Nixon's influence on the platform and what it meant for his campaign. Reaction to the platform was universally positive within party ranks. Ross Adair spoke for his colleagues when he said, "The platform adopted was good and one upon which all Republican candidates can, in good conscience, stand for election. Its plank on Vietnam was reasonable—as strong, I think, as one could be having in mind the desire of our citizenry for a speedy and honorable peace. At the same time, it was not so weak as to give encouragement to the Communists."[85] Rockefeller, "delighted" that the platform pledged "de-Americanization of both military and civilian efforts" in Vietnam, expressed his strong support of the plank given that it contained a "positive program for a fair and just peace."[86]

Meanwhile, the media recognized the platform for what it was: a workable and uncontroversial statement in keeping with the tenor of the entire convention and the views of a majority of Americans seeking an honorable way out of Vietnam.[87] Tom Wicker noted that, while the Vietnam plank "hardly lines up Nixon or the Republicans with Dr. Spock or the New York Review of Books," it appeared that he had found a way to become the party's peace candidate. Wicker knew that it would be "political madness" for the GOP's platform to support "a war so unpopular that Johnson has been forced to withdraw from the race." Wicker praised Nixon for not having made a single major mistake, but, more important, for being "imaginative, forceful, and flexible."[88] Nixon's approach to the war also influenced the other speakers on the program. Washington governor Daniel Evans gave the convention's keynote address, "stak[ing] out an explicit peace position on Vietnam," but saying nothing overly upsetting to those convinced of the need for victory in Southeast Asia.[89]

It should be noted, however, that the GOP platform plank on Vietnam essentially removed most of the substantive differences between the Republicans and the administration on the war issue. Reducing the American role and increasing South Vietnamese responsibility for the conflict had already been embraced by LBJ. The political, economic, and diplomatic initiatives mentioned in the platform remained intentionally vague and undefined. A voter perusing the GOP platform was basically being asked to accept that Nixon had been wise about Vietnam in the past, knew a great deal about it, probably had some kind of plan for moving toward peace, and was being a statesman in not commenting on issues under discussion in Paris.[90] It was, at its core, an astute political document and the perfect complement to Nixon's established strategy on the war. Moreover, it placed the onus of Vietnam squarely on Humphrey's shoulders. If the presumptive Democratic nominee wanted to change his policy prescription for the war to distinguish himself from Nixon, he would have to move either toward escalation (highly unlikely) or toward a more dovish stance similar to the discredited McCarthy position. Either way, he would alienate a substantial portion of the electorate and cede the center completely to Nixon. Humphrey's dilemma is further testament to the political dexterity that Nixon exhibited throughout 1968.

The Vietnam portion of Nixon's 8 August acceptance speech was emblematic of his entire campaign for the nomination. He told the assembled delegates that he would make ending the war in Vietnam his first priority on entering the Oval Office. While commending the party for its stand on the war and criticizing the Johnson administration for the way it prosecuted the conflict, he pledged peace in Southeast Asia under his leadership as president. Of course, the speech included phrases designed to appeal to both the hawks and the doves in the party and said little about the specifics of Nixon administration policies. For the hawks, Nixon asserted, "And I say to you tonight that when respect for the United States of America falls so low that a fourth-rate military power, like North Korea, will seize an American naval vessel on the high seas [a reference to the *Pueblo* incident], it's time for new leadership to restore respect for the United States of America." For the doves, he stated, "We believe this should be an era of peaceful competition. . . . And we work toward the goal of an open world."[91] Classic Nixonian rhetoric. The result was an uninspiring conclusion to a convention that had achieved its goal: nominating an electable candidate on a politically safe platform that would appeal to the broad center of the American electorate. As for the war in Vietnam, the country would have to wait until Nixon assumed the presidency to discover his plan to end U.S. involvement; unfortunately, that process would be an issue in Nixon's next presidential campaign as well.

The selection of a vice presidential candidate posed the next challenge for the newly anointed nominee. Richard Whalen suggested to Nixon that the two main issues in the campaign, Vietnam and law and order, should determine the selection of his running mate. He could, for instance, move left on the war by "saying hard things now that would have to be said later anyway and by choosing for the ticket someone like" Mark Hatfield. By giving "dramatic evidence" of a new administration's commitment to ending the war, he could turn from

Vietnam and devote more time during the fall campaign to focusing on domestic issues from a center-right perspective.[92] Although Nixon ultimately did not choose this route, it demonstrated the thinking within the candidate's inner circle about the proper stance on the war.

Edward Brooke might have been a winning choice all around. An "owl" on the war who was also black, moderate, and from an Eastern industrial state, he could have given Nixon a strong vice president and served as a sign of national unity in the midst of chaos at home and abroad. Yet he had thrown his support behind Rockefeller and, thus, received little serious consideration from Nixon's inner circle.[93] John Lindsay firmly believed that he was "blackballed" for the vice presidency because of his dovish stand on the war.[94] In the end, however, Vietnam did not play a role in the choice of running mate. Nixon ultimately decided on Governor Spiro T. Agnew (R-MD), a virtual unknown on the national stage. The campaign selected Agnew primarily on the basis of what he brought to the ticket politically: he was a border state governor who could sway vital electoral votes; he was acceptable to Strom Thurmond, whose support was needed to help deliver the South to the GOP ticket; and he was an outspoken campaigner who could play the role of attack dog to contrast Nixon's conciliatory rhetoric, similar to the role that Nixon had played for Eisenhower in 1952 and 1956 and that Henry Cabot Lodge had failed to do for Nixon in 1960.

Richard Nixon emerged from the Miami convention primed to win the presidency. He had overcome all the obstacles in his path to capture the GOP nomination for a second time without having to explicitly commit himself to a specific course of action in Vietnam. Indeed, contrary to the prediction he made to Tom Wicker after the 1966 election, he was nominated on a platform that ostensibly aimed to end the Vietnam conflict. In selecting Agnew, he chose to deemphasize the war and concentrate on other issues—Agnew had a particularly strong reputation as a law-and-order governor—and the realities of American electoral politics. The Republican Party had united behind him, albeit reluctantly in several cases, in an effort to regain the White House. The years of campaigning, diligent party work, and maneuvering had paid off in spades. All that remained to achieve his lifelong ambition was to defeat Hubert Humphrey in the fall.

The summer of 1968 saw little progress on the military front in South Vietnam. Since his withdrawal announcement, Johnson had insisted that the South Vietnamese take more responsibility for the fighting, and the South Vietnamese Army was increased to 850,000 troops and began to conduct increasing numbers of joint military operations with American forces. In addition, the pacification programs were expanded, including the notorious Phoenix Program.[95] But these steps did nothing to change the underlying facts—despite the vicious losses inflicted on them during the Tet Offensive, the NLF and North Vietnam-ese refused to buckle to American pressure, either on the battlefield or at the negotiating table. So the stalemate continued. At home, John Wayne's *Green Berets* was released to a skeptical American audience that no longer believed in the conflict championed in the film. Protests increased exponentially, with serious clashes between students and law enforcement even at such bastions of higher education as Columbia University. With over 30,000 American soldiers dead, over 500,000 still on the ground in South Vietnam, and no end to the fighting in sight, a weary public hoped that a new administration would be able to bring the war to a conclusion.

Since Johnson's withdrawal at the end of March, the Democratic party had struggled to find the best candidate to oppose Nixon. Eugene McCarthy's stun-ning upset of the president in the New Hampshire primary had given the dov-ish senator an early lead, but his candidacy faded as mainstream Democrats refused to support his agenda. It appeared likely that Robert Kennedy would take up the mantle as the peace candidate for the party. His strong performance in the primaries vaulted him to second place in the delegate count with tan-gible momentum only three months after entering the race on 16 March. When Sirhan Sirhan assassinated RFK in the immediate aftermath of his victory in the California primary, however, the Democrats were left with no realistic alterna-tive but Hubert Humphrey, who had delayed announcing his official entry into the race and whose candidacy had not inspired the party or any of its factions to any appreciable extent. With a combination of disillusionment, mourning, and resignation, the party held its own quadrennial meeting in Chicago, hoping to nominate someone who could defeat Nixon.

When the Democratic convention opened in late August, the party found itself "involved in a civil war about the war."[96] Humphrey in particular was caught in the middle of the internecine struggle. The vice president realized that many of the Americans protesting the administration's policies in Vietnam were as anxious to escalate the war as others were to disengage. Further, since he relied so heavily on LBJ's core supporters for his own backing (Humphrey would never be confused for a dynamic vote getter), he dared not dissociate himself from the president despite the fact that the antiwar forces at the conven-tion were extremely critical of the absent Johnson. In an effort not to alienate his already fractured party, therefore, Humphrey took a middle course on the war rather than taking the path of least resistance and declaring himself a peace candidate to placate the most vocal delegates.

As if the fratricidal problems inside the International Amphitheater were not enough, the Democrats were not helped by the state of near anarchy that engulfed and overshadowed their convention on the streets of Chicago. The absurdity of the chaotic spectacle was almost unbelievable. Led by activists like Abie Hoffman, approximately ten thousand protestors came to the convention and called for an end to the war, the legalization of marijuana, and the abolition of money. They even nominated a live pig for president to mock the "pigs" who ruled America. In response, Chicago mayor Richard Daley called out the police, and several nights of skirmishes ensued. One Democratic senator called Daley's actions "Gestapo tactics," but Daley did not seem to care about national perceptions. At one point, the cameras panned to Daley as, clearly outraged, he was mouthing obscenities at intransigent delegates. With the city's police force attacking demonstrators with nightsticks and tear gas—claiming to be putting down a revolution—the nation watched transfixed as the Democrats, only four years removed from one of the largest landslides in American history, imploded. The televised riots cemented the impression of a party in disorder and helped fuel the law-and-order issue that Nixon would use effectively in the fall campaign.

After nominating Humphrey with barely disguised apathy, the convention turned to its Vietnam plank. Insurgents argued in vain that Humphrey could not win the election if he were shackled to a discredited policy of limited war as usual. Their effort to place a deescalation/negotiated settlement plank in the platform, however, was defeated handily. Protests broke out, and a few hundred antiwar delegates donned black armbands and sang "We Shall Overcome." Nevertheless, the final version of the Democratic platform on Vietnam called for an end to bombing as long as it did not endanger the lives of American troops, negotiations, and the inclusion of the NLF in a postwar government and asserted that the United States wanted no permanent role in Vietnamese affairs. The Democratic plank differed very little in substance from the one adopted by the GOP, but it saved the vice president from having to break with the administration. That was a small consolation for Humphrey. After the week of upheaval in Chicago, he would have been ecstatic not to discuss Vietnam at all during the campaign.

Humphrey emerged from the convention with a twenty-two-point deficit in the polls.[97] Had it been up to the two candidates, Nixon and Humphrey would have gladly agreed to a moratorium on discussing the war. But the American people felt otherwise. A Gallup poll in early September confirmed what most politicians and pundits already knew: Vietnam was—by an overwhelming margin (51 to 21 percent) over crime, the runner-up—the most important problem facing the United States.[98] Nevertheless, Nixon fervently clung to his public position that he would not specifically discuss his plan to end the war during the campaign to avoid undermining the negotiations in Paris. While this had been his posture for several months, it left a sour taste in the mouths of some of his

GOP colleagues. In September, Mark Hatfield made a little-noticed but telling comment about the forthcoming election and the war. "In the democratic process, voters should not be forced to go to the polls with their fingers crossed," he asserted; "they should not be forced to rely on blind faith that the men they vote for will share their views on the most important issue of the election."[99] Hatfield's skepticism, shared by many in both parties, did not change Nixon's strategy of silence.

From the beginning, the focus of Nixon's campaign was entirely defensive. He intended to run in place and protect his lead until election day. This strategy ceded the initiative to Humphrey, who would eventually have to detail his differences with the administration on Vietnam if he had any hope of overtaking the Republican candidate. Unfortunately for the vice president, such a move would at once allow Nixon to attack him for inconsistency when it finally came and obviate the need for specifics that could jeopardize Nixon's election. As the Nixon aide Patrick Buchanan noted in a memo to the candidate, "If HHH [Humphrey] shifts on Vietnam now, then he has spent four years deceiving the American people and he is unfit for any job in public life, let alone the Presidency."[100] Thus, Nixon could focus on his other campaign themes, most notably law and order, while waiting to counterattack when Humphrey finally disavowed the administration's policies.

With impressive discipline, Nixon stuck to his message, assuring the American Legion Convention in New Orleans that he would not "say anything to win votes that will cost us lives in Vietnam." He continued to assert that he would not comment on the conduct of the war or the progress of negotiations so that Hanoi would not get "the impression that a candidate for President who might be President might come into power and thereby give them an opportunity which they could not get from the present negotiations."[101] Ironically, that is exactly what he would do that fall in his sub rosa discussions with the South Vietnamese leadership.

Of course, Nixon was not alone in the campaign. Realizing that they had an excellent opportunity to regain the White House, GOP candidates focused on Vietnam and heaped criticism on Johnson and, by extension, Humphrey for the failed policies of the past five years. A representative speech by Dirksen, who was running for reelection for the final time, typifies the rhetoric used by Republicans in 1968. Dirksen admitted that the war had been "brutal and costly" but contended—somewhat hypocritically given his ardent support of Johnson since 1965—that the administration's policy of gradualism led to a failure of American conduct of the war. He also faulted the administration for failing to understand the nature of the war and stated, "When our political, economic and diplomatic efforts are given a priority equal to our military effort, we will get the kind of 'victory' we want . . . a durable peace." This recognized South Vietnam's right to self-determination and would be respected by North Vietnam and the international community. The speech closed with a line that could have been lifted directly from Nixon's stump speech: "This is the peace we must win."[102] The GOP did an admirable job staying on message throughout the 1968 campaign, rectifying another of the mistakes of the 1964 disaster.

One of the fascinating aspects of the 1968 campaign was the relationship between the president and the Republican candidate. Lyndon Johnson and Richard Nixon, for all their political differences, were fundamentally very similar. Historians and pundits have made comparisons between Nixon and Kennedy on several occasions, comparisons derived largely from the parallel courses their careers took and their showdown in the 1960 presidential election. But perhaps a more appropriate comparison can be made between Johnson and Nixon. Both came from humble backgrounds that not only instilled within them the ambition that carried them to the nation's highest office but also gave them an inherent distrust of the Eastern establishment, although both would ultimately rely on the advice of Eastern intellectuals like Bundy and Kissinger. Both were committed cold warriors and ardent foes of communism throughout their careers. And, at a very basic level, each was a pragmatist and a politician to the core and would do virtually anything to achieve his goals.

Indeed, despite their political differences, it appears that the two had a certain level of respect for one another. On 13 March 1966, for example, Johnson invited Nixon to the White House to discuss Vietnam. This was a typical Johnsonian tactic: bring an intransigent colleague or politician to the White House and attempt to overwhelm him with a combination of charm, arm-twisting, and LBJ's personal antics—such as inviting the guest to swim naked in the White House pool. Nixon, the crafty political veteran, was virtually immune to such tactics and used the opportunity to press Johnson to expand the war. Nixon told LBJ that he believed that the United States needed to take stronger actions to bring Hanoi to the conference table—an interesting position for one who had incessantly decried a negotiated settlement except under very specific conditions. He also assured LBJ that, although the election campaign was approaching and he would be campaigning for GOP candidates, "any criticism I make on issues [is not] directed personally at you." Johnson agreed: "We politicians are just like lawyers who get together for a drink after fighting each other like hell in the courtroom."[103]

Similar episodes took place during the 1968 campaign. Johnson spoke to Nixon on the telephone following the GOP convention to personally brief the Republican nominee on foreign policy developments. Nixon disingenuously told the president that he would avoid politicizing the war during the campaign against Hubert Humphrey and assured him, "I won't say a damn word that's going to embarrass you."[104] Shortly thereafter, the Reverend Billy Graham met with Nixon to discuss a variety of subjects. The former vice president asked Graham to convey a private message to the president. Nixon wanted to assure Johnson that he would not embarrass him after the election, wanted to continue a working relationship with him, would not reflect on him personally even while attacking his policy positions, and would give him "a major share of the credit" for settling the Vietnam war. A week later, Graham met with Johnson to pass along Nixon's remarks. Graham described the president as being "not only appreciative but . . . touched" by Nixon's gesture.[105]

Nevertheless, Johnson distrusted Nixon politically and did not hold him in the same regard as Rockefeller. Thus, despite not running for reelection, Johnson covertly kept tabs on Nixon's campaign throughout the summer and fall of 1968. The White House aide Fred Panzer, who served as LBJ's pollster and maintained detailed opposition research files, assessed Nixon's strategy on domestic issues in a 16 September memo for the president. Nixon's strategists, Panzer observed, "have set the major issues as Vietnam, Law and Order, and Inflation. So far, however, he is ducking the first, waffling on the second, and pushing the usual GOP line on the third."[106] That Nixon was "ducking" Vietnam should not have surprised Johnson and his advisers. The *Denver Post* charged that the GOP presidential candidate was "playing it cool. Perhaps a bit too cool." The paper also asked him to speak out "forcefully and candidly" on the significant issues of the campaign. The *New York Post* agreed, noting that it was strange that "Nixon the Silent," while "dodging the most authentic issue of the day [Vietnam], concentrates on building up what should really be a non-issue—law and order." And the *Baltimore Sun* asserted, "American voters need a clearer view than they now have of Mr. Nixon's position on the war in Vietnam. His repeated statement that he must keep his thoughts to himself in order not to interfere with the Paris talks does not relieve him of an obligation to explain his ideas to the American voters."[107] Whatever his differences with Nixon on policy and politics, Johnson did consider him to be capable and clearly preferred him to Humphrey as his successor in the Oval Office. Despite their mutual respect, however, Johnson would be infuriated when he discovered Nixon's involvement in efforts to undermine the peace process on the eve of the election.

One of the most fascinating and notorious episodes in American electoral history was the Anna Chennault affair.[108] Chennault—the widow of the air force hero Gen. Claire L. Chennault, who had commanded the famous Flying Tigers in Burma during World War II—had been an American citizen since 1950 and had become one of the country's most visible Asian Americans. Close to the China lobby, and active in Washington political circles, particularly among Republicans, she served as the cochair of the Women for Nixon-Agnew National Advisory Committee. But her real contribution to the 1968 campaign would come as an intermediary between the Nixon campaign and the South Vietnamese government.

In June 1968, Chennault had dinner with John Tower and the South Vietnamese ambassador to Washington, Bui Diem, and suggested that she and Diem meet with Nixon. The ambassador believed that establishing a better relationship with Nixon would be important; he feared that the Democrats were distancing themselves from the war and believed Nixon's election would bode well for South Vietnam's future. On 12 July, Chennault and Diem met with Nixon and John Mitchell, Nixon's law partner and later attorney general, at the Hotel Pierre in New York and gave the candidate an overview of the war and the problems facing the Saigon regime. After thirty minutes, Nixon, Mitchell, and Diem withdrew to talk privately for an hour and then returned to continue the conversation. The focus of the talks with Chennault was the election and the need for close and continuous communications between Nixon and Thieu. Near the end of the meeting, Diem raised the subject of the increasing unpopularity of the war in the United States and stated that he anticipated an eventual withdrawal of American troops. Diem went on to say that he wanted to see an intensive training program begun to facilitate the transition from U.S. to South Vietnamese responsibility for the fighting.

Nixon responded positively to the overtures and told Diem that his staff would contact him through Mitchell or Chennault. Nixon stressed that Chennault, whom he had known for many years, "would be the sole representative between the Vietnamese government and the Nixon campaign headquarters." The candidate explained their relationship succinctly: "Anna is a very dear friend. . . . We count on her for information on Asia. She brings me up to date." Thus, the Nixon campaign and the South Vietnamese government established a back channel using Chennault as the conduit. While it would be unusual in normal circumstances for the opposing party's presidential candidate to have private contacts with the leader of another nation, it was even more exceptional given the fact that the incumbent president was engaged in secret negotiations with that government.[109]

Throughout the campaign, Chennault maintained close contacts with a number of key Republicans, attended the convention in Miami, and traveled to Asia on several occasions to meet with various regional political figures. During one visit to Saigon, she met with Thieu in what she described as "an informal presentation of credentials." She asserted that she was "delivering a message from Nixon requesting that [she] be recognized as the conduit for any information that might flow between the two." She also discussed the Paris peace talks, later reporting to Nixon and Mitchell that the South Vietnamese "remained intransigent" in their "attitudes vis-à-vis the peace talks."[110] Diem also kept in close contact with Republicans such as Tower and George H. W. Bush in an effort to elicit support for a strong Vietnam policy. Diem understood that, as long as the United States faced domestic turmoil over the war, Hanoi and the NLF would simply wait patiently without budging from their demands.

While Nixon and his advisers worked behind the scenes to ensure his election, his public strategy remained constant, and he was able to maintain his lead over Humphrey. If the Democratic candidate hoped to catch his opponent, he would have to make a bold change in his position on the war. Humphrey's advisers believed that their candidate had to make one announcement on Vietnam and then stay away from the issue. The thinking was that "the war is irreparably viewed as a Democratic war; the less said about it the better."[111] Humphrey, like George Romney before him, could not afford to ignore the war if he hoped to win the election, but he remained torn on exactly what direction to take in the campaign. Humphrey's ambivalence about the war angered Johnson, who told Secretary of Defense Clark Clifford on 24 September that he doubted the vice president's ability to be president. According to LBJ, Humphrey "lacked the guts for the job."[112]

But the president's disapproval of Humphrey did not negate the fact that the Democratic ticket was in serious trouble. Humphrey may have preferred to focus on domestic issues, and, all things being equal, he may have attempted to make them the fulcrum of the race. But, in making his political calculations, he knew that he could not avoid Vietnam. Tipping the scales for the vice president was the fact that he was so far behind. Indeed, by mid-September, Humphrey's campaign was in disarray. He trailed Nixon by a substantial 43 to 28 percent margin (with Wallace right behind at 21 percent), and the polls indicated that his connection with the administration's Vietnam policy had crippled his candidacy. In an effort to revive his faltering campaign and to separate himself from Johnson's policies, Humphrey decided to change tactics. On the campaign trail on 21 September, he declared, "I'm going to seek peace in every way possible, but only the President can do it now. Come January, it's a new ball game. Then I will make peace." Humphrey promised that, as president, he would "stop the bombing of North Vietnam as an acceptable risk for peace," although he hedged his bets by saying that he expected Hanoi to restore the demilitarized zone prior to halting the bombing.[113]

Less than two weeks later, in a speech in Salt Lake City, Utah, he went even further and asserted that he would be prepared to risk a complete bombing halt, see what response might develop, and resume the bombing if there was no constructive response from Hanoi. Although deliberately vague and not explicitly more dovish than the Democratic platform, Humphrey's speech distanced him from Johnson's public statements and, for the first time, established an independent position on the war. In domestic political terms, the vice president's statement was a "resounding success."[114] It brought Democrats and independents who opposed the war back into Humphrey's column and provided him with a surge in the polls. It would not be overstating the case to state that it was the critical turning point in the campaign. For the next five weeks, Humphrey would inch closer to Nixon—passing him in the polls by the end of October—and would force Nixon to address issues that he would rather avoid. Victory, once considered a near impossibility by pundits, now seemed to be within Humphrey's grasp.

The GOP reaction to Humphrey's speech in Salt Lake City was predictable. In an attempt to shift the focus from his own position to that of his opponent, Nixon sent a telegram to all Republican members of Congress suggesting that they pressure Humphrey to say whether he was breaking with administration policy and urging an unconditional bombing halt. He also warned the American people that Humphrey's proposal would risk the lives of American troops in Vietnam. In response to Nixon's request, the Senate launched a debate on 3 October in which the Republicans attacked Humphrey's speech and the Democrats challenged Nixon to clarify his views on the war. Dirksen led the way for the GOP, raising a series of questions about Humphrey's remarks, and charging that the vice president's remarks had lost the war.[115] On the campaign trail, Spiro Agnew said that Humphrey's statements amounted to sending additional enemy divisions into the field.[116]

Despite the public criticism, the momentum generated by Humphrey's remarks concerned Republicans. Representative Burt Talcott (R-CA) sent a dire warning to his colleague Sherman Lloyd (R-UT): "Any of us who deludes himself into believing that Dick Nixon's election is a cinch ought to re-examine the political vicissitudes." While he liked Nixon's chances, he worried about "some real or feigned 'dramatic progress' to come out of the 'Paris talks' or Vietnam in October."[117] Wallace Bennett concurred, suggesting that any unilateral bombing halt by the administration should be considered "a desperate and dangerous attempt by the Johnson-Humphrey Administration to salvage Humphrey's sagging political hopes."[118]

In his memoirs, Lyndon Johnson made the dubious claim that the Salt Lake City speech effectively cost Humphrey the election because it made the Saigon government "extremely nervous and distrustful" of the administration and the entire Democratic Party. As a result, he argued, it encouraged Saigon to "thwart the negotiations in Paris in the decisive phase that was about to begin."[119] Whatever the effect the speech had on the race for the presidency, it certainly had a negative impact on the relationship between Humphrey and Johnson. The vice president's remarks angered LBJ and strengthened the president's reluctance to help Humphrey against Nixon.[120] Of course, to this point in the campaign, Johnson had done precious little in support of Humphrey's candidacy anyway, and, given Humphrey's rise in the polls following the address, it is probable that the vice president did not want any assistance from the Oval Office at this critical juncture.

As Humphrey drew closer to Nixon, the GOP nominee looked for any way to stem the tide of his opponent's momentum and found it through his behind-the-scenes maneuvering. After the Republican convention, the back channel had continued to convey information between the Nixon camp and Saigon. Adding to the intrigue of the campaign was the role played by Henry Kissinger. Kissinger, who had served as an adviser to Rockefeller and also as a member of the Johnson administration's negotiating effort in 1967, went to Paris during mid-September and talked with members of the U.S. delegation about the progress of the negotiations. Unbeknownst to the administration, Kissinger had secretly agreed to provide information on the talks to the Nixon team. On his return, he reported to Mitchell that, on the basis of his discussions in Paris, he believed that "something big was afoot." According to Nixon's memoirs, Kissinger was "completely circumspect" and did not reveal any details of the negotiations; he simply warned against launching any new proposals that might subvert developments in Paris.[121] Regardless of whether Kissinger violated security or confidences with his reports to Nixon and Mitchell, the information that he provided proved to be extremely useful to the campaign.

While the Nixon campaign pondered Kissinger's warnings, Bui Diem learned from Thieu that a deal might be imminent. He passed the information on to Chennault, who then contacted Mitchell and advised him that LBJ's "no breakthrough" statement in a conference call to the candidates on 16 October should not be taken literally. At the same time, she kept in close contact with Thieu, who, according to her account, consistently asserted that he opposed peace talks on the grounds that no one was ready, that he felt pressured by the Democrats to attend the Paris negotiations, and that he "would much prefer to have the peace talks after [the American] election." Chennault was asked to convey that message to "your candidate," a clear reference to Nixon.[122]

Nixon increasingly needed the indirect support provided by Thieu's covert information as his ace in the hole in the ever-tightening race. Indeed, by October, Nixon had begun to steadily lose ground to Humphrey, and it now appeared that the campaign would go down to the wire. Goldwater, who was running for a seat in the Senate, spoke with Nixon virtually every day and consistently urged the former vice president to "exploit the mismanagement of the Vietnam

War."[123] Nixon, however, did not express any pessimism about his chances, at least publicly, and refused to alter his approach. In an interview with Harrison Salisbury of the *New York Times* on 18 October, he seemed relaxed and outlined his foreign policy vision for his administration. He told Salisbury that he would "deal with [Vietnam] within six months" and described his intention to make an overture to China and to use triangular diplomacy in dealing with Moscow and Beijing.[124] His exterior confidence notwithstanding, Nixon secretly worried about the war in Vietnam and the possibility that Johnson would win the election for the Democrats with an "October surprise."

The surprise came in the form of a bombing halt negotiated by the administration in October. Once the agreement was reached, Rusk advised Johnson to officially inform the candidates. Nixon had repeatedly made clear his skepticism about any last-minute agreements, and the president was positive that Nixon would heap scorn and derision on the administration—and, by extension, Humphrey—for allowing electoral politics to interfere with the conduct of the war (and vice versa). But, in a White House meeting on 14 October, Rusk assured Johnson that the GOP candidate could be trusted. "Nixon has been honorable on Vietnam," he noted. "He has actually been more responsible on this than our own candidate." Clark Clifford agreed, telling the president, "I expect Nixon would play it fair with you."[125] Of course, at this juncture, neither Rusk nor Clifford realized the extent of Nixon's contacts with the Saigon regime through the Chennault back channel.

That concern appeared in sharp relief in a statement released by the campaign on 25 October. Nixon said that he had heard rumors of administration efforts to reach an agreement on a bombing halt and, potentially, a cease-fire in Vietnam. In typical Nixonian style, he stated, "I am also told that this spurt of activity is a cynical, last-minute attempt by President Johnson to salvage the candidacy of Mr. Humphrey. This I do not believe." The president "has made it clear that he will not play politics with this war." Yet it is clear that Nixon feared exactly that, and he wanted the voters to believe it as well. Jules Witcover noted, "It was an old standard Nixon ploy, giving wide publicity to a serious charge and then knocking it down himself. It was also standard Nixon to give testimony to his own purity in not taking political advantage of the rumor, which he proceeded to do." Nixon had no choice. Polls indicated that the race was essentially a toss-up at this point, and he needed every advantage he could muster if he was going to hold on and win.[126]

Meanwhile, observers remained skeptical about the so-called secret plan as the election approached. On "Issues and Answers," John Tower was asked to elaborate on Nixon's plan to end the war—if it existed. Tower responded in a similar fashion to the candidate. "Well, to begin with, you can't propose some pat solution and promise that you will put that pat solution into effect after you get into office," he said. That would "presuppose the cooperation of Hanoi which might not necessarily be forthcoming. In addition, it would be in the way of telegraphing your punch to the enemy."[127] The lingering skepticism about Nixon's plan, combined with Humphrey's post–Salt Lake City bounce, threatened to make the 1968 balloting a repeat of the photo finish of 1960. Only a major initiative or gaffe by one of the candidates, it seemed, could dramatically influence the race. Lyndon Johnson's startling announcement on 31 October provided just such an effect.

For several weeks, the administration had been negotiating with the North Vietnamese in Paris to institute a bombing halt that would allow peace talks to begin. Once informed by his military leaders that a halt would be militarily acceptable, Johnson threw his full support behind the effort. Although Thieu remained intransigent, LBJ decided to ignore the South Vietnamese leader and announce the halt on 31 October, the Thursday before the election. On the afternoon prior to the announcement, Johnson arranged a conference call with Nixon, Humphrey, and Wallace. He told the three candidates that he had decided to cease bombing North Vietnam as a prelude to peace talks and warned the presidential aspirants, "The fate of our country lies in your hands. . . . There would be serious trouble if anything anyone said were to interrupt or disrupt any progress we are trying to make to bring this war to a halt." Johnson directed this thinly veiled warning at Nixon and referred specifically to the Chennault affair.[128]

The administration's knowledge of the secret communications between Nixon and Saigon deserves a brief comment. On or about 29 October, as Johnson and his advisers realized that Thieu was being more resistant to American proposals, they received a report that startled them. Intercepted cables revealed that Bui Diem had reported to Thieu that he had "explained discreetly to our partisan friends our firm attitude" and "plan to adhere to that position." The ambassador concluded that, the longer the "situation continues, the more we are favored." Johnson subsequently ordered the FBI to tap Anna Chennault's phones, relying on national security concerns and possible legal violations as his justification. On 2 November, the tap picked up a call from Chennault to Saigon specifically urging that Thieu stand firm and saying that they would get a better deal from Nixon. When asked whether Nixon knew of her call, she responded that the candidate did not but that "our friend in New Mexico does." That day, Spiro Agnew was campaigning in Albuquerque.[129] Johnson suspected Nixon's machinations. He confided to Richard Russell, "Our California friend has been playing on the outskirts with our enemies and our friends both. . . . He has been saying . . . 'You better not give away your liberty just a few hours before I can preserve it for you.'"[130] As the evidence mounted of a conspiracy between the Republicans and the South Vietnamese, the administration privately debated what to do with the information. Publicly, however, LBJ focused on the bombing halt and the negotiations and began to speak out in support of Humphrey's candidacy—something he had been very reluctant to do until this point in the campaign.

The Nixon campaign scrambled to deal with the administration's eleventh-hour peace initiative. Immediately after LBJ announced the bombing halt, Mitchell spoke to Chennault on the telephone. He stated, "Anna, I'm speaking on behalf of Mr. Nixon. It's very important that our Vietnamese friends understand our Republican position and I hope you have made that very clear to them." Chennault responded that she was certain that Thieu would not go to Paris because he believed that it "would be walking into a smoke screen that has nothing to do with reality."[131] Mitchell's statement to Chennault underscored a cable Diem sent to Saigon the previous week in which he stated, "Many Republican friends have contacted me and encouraged us to stand firm. They were alarmed by press reports to the effect that you had already softened your position." He also reported that he was "regularly in touch with the Nixon entourage."[132] Thus, by the time LBJ spoke, Nixon knew that Thieu was adamant about his position and unlikely to consent to an early bombing halt or to participate in any talks. It is also clear that the Chennault channel had given Thieu an indication that South Vietnam would be better served by Nixon's election than by a Humphrey administration.

Further, Nixon had expected something like the bombing halt from Johnson: "Announcing the halt so close to the election was utterly callous if politically calculated, and utterly naïve if sincere." But, if Nixon had opposed the halt, it would have been political suicide. Thus, two days prior to the election, he announced that he would go to Saigon if it would help bring peace, much as Eisenhower, during the 1952 campaign, had asserted he would go to Korea.[133] Other Republicans displayed much less reluctance to call a spade a spade. Dirksen raged that the bombing halt was a blatant election stunt designed to swing the voters to Humphrey. Ronald Reagan asserted that the "political overtones of the bombing halt appeared rather obvious," and Bourke Hickenlooper added, "I think it's tragic that American lives are being played with this way." Other Republicans who criticized the timing of the announcement and its political motivations included Adair, Findley, Frelinghuysen, Laird, and Tower.[134] Republican skepticism was not entirely misplaced. Even if Johnson's motives for the bombing halt had been sincere, the timing was extremely questionable, and the public reacted negatively toward the perceived attempt to influence the outcome of the balloting. Humphrey's momentum slowed, leaving the race too close to call.

In Saigon, Thieu continued to indirectly aid the Nixon campaign. On 2 November, the South Vietnamese leader told the National Assembly that, despite Johnson's announcement, too many issues remained outstanding for him to attend the negotiations. The boycott by Saigon effectively suspended the opening of the substantive discussions until well after the U.S. election. In the wake of this diplomatic snafu, the GOP launched a counterattack on the administration, charging that it did not have "all its ducks lined up in a row."[135] Johnson became enraged. In a tense telephone conversation, he confronted Dirksen about an alleged Republican plot to sabotage peace, accused Nixon of "treason," and threatened to go public with the intercepts. Dirksen tried to placate the president, agreeing with LBJ's characterization of Nixon's actions.[136] Nixon must have learned of the president's anger. The following day, he appeared on "Meet the Press" and went out of his way to avoid criticizing the administration's Vietnam policy. Later that afternoon, Johnson spoke to Nixon directly and asked him point-blank whether he was involved. Nixon categorically denied any responsibility, asserting that he had no knowledge of or connection to either Thieu's decision or Chennault's activities. This blatant lie was his only possible defense. At this late stage of the campaign, any admission of guilt would more than likely cost him the election.[137]

Johnson faced both a moral and a political dilemma. As furious as he was with Nixon for the machinations with Chennault, Bui Diem, and Thieu, he did not want to be responsible for the chaos that would ensue if the contacts were made public. Thus, he left the decision to expose the scheme up to Humphrey. In a move that Theodore White has called one of the most decent and moral acts in American political history, Humphrey decided not to drop the bombshell that could have won him the election.[138] Most of his campaign staff and administration officials such as Clifford and Rusk advised him to keep the plot undisclosed because revelation of the secret deal could hurt the administration's attempts to get Saigon back to the negotiating table. Moreover, revelation could also backfire because, in such a close race, the legality of the methods used to obtain the information would have been called into question. Walt Rostow alluded to this in a memo to Johnson, stating, "The materials are so explosive that they could gravely damage the country whether Mr. Nixon is elected or not. If they get out in their present form, they could be the subject of one of the most acrimonious debates we have ever witnessed."[139] With the country already divided over so many issues, Humphrey concluded that discretion was the better part of valor. His decision "was either one of the noblest in American political history or one of the great tactical blunders. Possibly it was both."[140]

Scrambling for every advantage possible, Nixon made his final pitch to the public as the campaign reached its climax. On 3 November, he asserted that, if elected, he would "be willing to cooperate with the President and the Secretary of State and if they would consider it helpful for me to go to Paris or to Saigon [during the transition] in order to get the negotiations off dead center, I would be glad to do so." Nixon proclaimed, "This is not just a grandstand statement." But it is difficult not to view the offer in that light.[141] With only forty-eight hours left in the campaign, Nixon sought every advantage he could get in the race. While he tried to appear cooperative with the administration's peace initiatives, his GOP colleagues continued to denounce the eleventh-hour bombing pause. John Tower, who knew all the players but may or may not have been aware of the content of the Chennault discussions, claimed that the "reaction of President Thieu clearly suggests that the bomb-halt decision was hastily contrived, poorly planned, and undertaken without adequate coordination with or approval by South Vietnam." Tower went on to lambaste the administration for its action, stating that, since there was no "clear military advantages or concessions gained and since the chance for early, meaningful peace talks was botched by jerry-built diplomacy that was misunderstood by both ally and enemy, the whole thing smacks of politics."[142] But, this close to the election, everything the candidates, their supporters, or the administration did was political.

As the country went to the polls on 5 November, there was no consensus on who would win the presidency. As late as 21 October, a Gallup poll had given Nixon an eight-point lead over Humphrey; by 2 November, that lead had plummeted to two points in a Gallup poll, and Humphrey actually led by two points in a Harris survey. The day before the election, the final Harris poll showed Humphrey leading by a 43 to 40 percent margin—well within the margin of error. But, by that point, there was little that either Nixon or Humphrey could do. The race was so close that Nixon's advisers firmly believed in retrospect that, had the voting taken place three days earlier, Nixon would have lost the election; had it been held a week later, Nixon's margin of victory could have been doubled.[143] The election was now in the hands of the American people.

What are we to make of the Chennault affair and its influence on the 1968 election? Bui Diem asserts in his memoirs that "there was no secret deal" between the Nixon campaign and the Thieu government for Saigon to drag its feet on the Paris talks in order to sabotage the political momentum that Humphrey might have gained otherwise.[144] It is clear, however, that had Thieu participated in the announcement of the bombing halt—as originally intended and agreed to in mid-October—the initiative could have had a decisive impact on the race. Thieu's lack of support was crucial to Nixon's victory. Furthermore, Thieu emerged from the whole affair convinced that Nixon owed him a great political debt. Nixon, being the consummate politician that he was, also understood the importance of debts, especially those incurred during a campaign.

His intervention "may have been superfluous" since Thieu was already wary of negotiations and had already exhibited hostility toward Humphrey.[145] Thus, the effect of the debt—real or perceived—on future relations between the United States and South Vietnam was, perhaps, the most important legacy of the Chennault affair. Indeed, the single greatest problem for the United States in South Vietnam was how to bring influence to bear on Saigon so that the government would improve its performance and assume more of the burden of assuring its own survival. Nixon's debt to Thieu was, therefore, a "great handicap," but one that had been self-imposed for domestic political reasons.[146]

Contemporary observers recognized the pivotal nature of the secret talks as well. Clark Clifford opined in his memoirs that the Chennault affair "had been critical to [Nixon's] success."[147] William Safire, one of Nixon's aides during the campaign, agreed, arguing later that "Nixon would probably not [have become] president were it not for Thieu."[148] While the evidence is not incontrovertible, it is obvious that the communications between the Nixon campaign and the Saigon regime, facilitated by Anna Chennault, made each side's position perfectly clear to the other, and both the South Vietnamese leader and the Republican candidate were politically astute enough to realize the advantages of working together. Lacking the smoking gun—a document detailing a secret arrangement between Nixon and Thieu—perhaps the best way to describe what occurred during the campaign is through the political science game theory the "prisoner's dilemma," which essentially states that two actors are better off pursuing their joint interests than their individual self-interest—even if they do not directly coordinate their actions.[149] More disconcerting, the Chennault affair foreshadowed the type of covert operations and deniability that would later characterize the Watergate episode, an ominous portent for American politics.[150]

The story did not stay secret for long. Tom Ottenad, a reporter for the *St. Louis Post-Dispatch*, called Walt Rostow two weeks prior to Nixon's inauguration. He had uncovered evidence of the Nixon-Chennault-Thieu contacts and wanted to get confirmation from the administration that they had, indeed, taken place. Ottenad said to Rostow, "I've been told that during that period some Republican contacts were made with South Vietnamese officials urging them to go slow in the hope that . . . they might get a better shake under Nixon than they would otherwise." When asked whether the facts were accurate, Rostow replied, "I have not one word to say about that matter."[151] The story eventually did get out, but, given that the election results were a foregone conclusion, it did not have the explosive impact that it would have had in the days before the voting.

When Americans woke up on 6 November 1968, they discovered that Richard Nixon had defeated Hubert Humphrey by a razor-thin plurality in an election that was nearly as close as the 1960 election.[152] While Nixon received only

43.4 percent of the popular vote, the combination of Nixon and Wallace votes made it clear that a majority of Americans rejected the vice president's call for deescalation of the conflict. Contemporary observers disputed the significance of the war as a deciding factor in the election. *Time* reported, "Because so little light showed between Nixon and Humphrey on Vietnam, it is unlikely that the war played a large part in the presidential vote."[153] One unsuccessful senatorial candidate, John Gilligan (D-OH), perceptively noted that, if Humphrey "would have given the Salt Lake City speech earlier, the chances were he would have won."[154] Subsequently, scholars have differed on the influence of the war issue. The evidence demonstrates that, although it certainly was not as decisive a factor in the general election as it had been in the GOP primaries, Vietnam was an important aspect of the 1968 campaign and Nixon's reluctance to speak specifically about his plans for the war should he win the White House gave him a virtual tabula rasa with which to work after his inauguration.

During the transition period, Nixon remained as ambiguous about his intentions for his administration's policy on Vietnam as he had during the campaign. He did, however, make a public effort to work closely with LBJ during the two months remaining in his presidency. On 9 November, Bui Diem met with Everett Dirksen at the South Vietnamese embassy. Dirksen told Diem that he had a message of "utmost import" to deliver on behalf of both Johnson and Nixon: "South Vietnam has got to send a delegation to Paris before it's too late." Dirksen went on to state, "I can also give you firm and unequivocal assurances that under no circumstances will the United States recognize the National Liberation Front as a separate entity. I absolutely affirm that the United States does not contemplate a coalition government between the two sides in Vietnam."[155] In addition to the private lobbying, Nixon joined LBJ in pressing Thieu to participate in the negotiations. Ironically, this "drew [Nixon] into the framework of his [Johnson's] policy" and "imposed limits of a sort on his possible alternatives" once inaugurated.[156]

On 11 November, Nixon met with Johnson at the White House for a substantial briefing; naturally, Vietnam was the main topic of conversation. Nixon was totally supportive and cooperative, offering to do anything to help get substantive peace talks started, and stressing that the Johnson administration would speak for him in foreign affairs in the coming two months, suggesting that a one-voice policy might lead to "some very significant action and progress toward peace."[157] Republican senators expressed mixed feelings about the president-elect's decision to let Johnson speak for him on the subject of Vietnam. Both Clifford Case and Mark Hatfield questioned the wisdom of Nixon's statement that he would support the administration's decisions and carry them forward after 20 January. Dirksen backed Nixon's move as the best solution to a "sticky situation." Joining the minority leader in this sentiment were Senator Milton Young (R-ND) and Aiken, who said that Nixon "did the right thing—the only thing he could do for the welfare of the country as a whole at this time. If he had done otherwise, the whole Paris peace effort would have cracked up."[158]

Nixon did create a stir when he appointed Ambassador Robert D. Murphy, a State Department veteran who had advised both Kennedy and Johnson previously, as his foreign policy liaison with the administration. He intimated that Murphy should be consulted prior to any foreign policy decisions made by the president, a position that Johnson rejected out of hand. LBJ declared that all decisions would be made by him and his administration until 20 January and that, while Murphy would be consulted several times each week, the final authority and control over American foreign policy rested with the president.[159] Nixon's efforts to influence American policy during the transition were not unprecedented. Given the nature of the American political system, the period between the election and the inauguration inherently confuses the issue of responsibility, although, ultimately, the lame-duck president is the final arbiter of policy. In this instance, however, it is clear that the two-month delay prevented Nixon from initiating his vaguely defined strategy for peace and gave LBJ one final opportunity to settle the conflict. In the end, nothing significant occurred, as both Saigon and Hanoi awaited the new administration. Once again, domestic political considerations influenced the direction of U.S. policy on Vietnam.

Nguyen Cao Ky, the former South Vietnamese prime minister and general, said of the 1968 presidential campaign, "It is strange how a small country, so far away, could have such a profound effect on the destiny of a large nation."[160] The campaign for the 1968 Republican presidential nomination demonstrates clearly the importance of the nexus of foreign policy and domestic politics. Yet the preceding raises two important questions. First, why was Richard Nixon able to capture the party's nomination? Second, why was the war such a critical issue for the Republican party throughout the course of its selection process? Nixon used Vietnam effectively throughout the mid-1960s both to return to national political prominence and to position himself as the most attractive Republican presidential candidate. Prior to the 1966 elections, his rhetoric was hawkish and uncompromising, attacking Johnson at every opportunity for not doing more to win the war. But, once it was clear that he had a chance to win the GOP nomination in 1968, he retreated to a relatively more moderate position on the war in an effort to marginalize Johnson, just as Johnson had done to Goldwater in 1964.

For two years, Nixon managed to combine a call for an honorable peace with his traditionally tough anti-Communist rhetoric without stating precisely how he would bring about peace or where he would get tough. His approach paid off handsomely in 1968. As a result of his ambiguous stance on Vietnam during the primaries and the lack of a serious challenge by either Romney or Rockefeller, his progress toward the nomination in the late spring and early summer of 1968 "resembled a stately Spanish galleon coasting home under full sail from a fair wind."[161] This is consistent with the overall strategy that Nixon followed in 1967 and 1968 as he sought to capture the vital center and marginalize candidates on both extremes of the political spectrum.

More generally, the Republicans desperately wanted to avoid the mistakes of 1964 and nominate a centrist candidate who could at once unite the party and obtain national support in the general election. Nixon supported Goldwater (albeit reluctantly) in 1964, campaigned hard for GOP candidates in both local and national elections for years, proved to be a formidable fund-raiser, and consistently attacked the policies of the Johnson administration. Along the way, he collected countless political IOUs, enhanced his prestige among the party leaders and grassroots organizations, and, most important, kept himself in the national spotlight. Nevertheless, he still had to struggle to gain the nomination, and his victory was a testament to survival and luck as much as it was to his own appeal as a candidate. Indeed, critics of his nomination felt that the party had little choice but to settle for such an unattractive candidate. Garry Wills later wrote, "The Party had not undergone any great internal convulsion. It had simply caved, sifted and crumbled in upon its center, and the name of the resulting sandpile was Nixon."[162] Nixon benefited from inexperienced opponents, fortuitous events (such as LBJ's withdrawal), and his ability to avoid the misstatements and controversies that plagued his opponents. This combination contributed significantly to his electoral success.

Nixon's dominance of the nominating process also underscored the unarrested decline of liberal Republicanism. George Romney's stumbling over Vietnam and Nelson Rockefeller's uninspired and late-arriving campaign left GOP liberals without a viable candidate in 1968. Hatfield and Percy lacked the national visibility and organizational resources required to make a real bid for the GOP nomination, and virtually no one gave Edward Brooke or John Lindsay a second glance. In addition, the Goldwater supporters of 1964 united behind Nixon in opposition to the liberal wing of the party, especially when it became evident that Ronald Reagan was not yet ready to make the leap to the national spotlight. While 1964 marked the low point of the Republican Party, it also marked the beginning of the new conservative movement in America. The shift in power within the GOP was best exemplified in 1968 when the Republican Governors' Association, the only national bastion of power for liberal members of the party, unanimously elected Reagan as its chairman.[163]

The reasons for the decisive influence of the war are clear as well. Vietnam transcended traditional foreign policy concerns. It had, by 1968, become the overwhelming political, social, economic, and diplomatic consideration for the vast majority of Americans, cutting "across every vital sector of national life," as Romney stated in his Hartford speech in April 1967. As Theodore Draper noted at the time, the war should have been the "overshadowing issue of the election" because the country could "no longer deal with our domestic problems apart from the Vietnam war. The war is costing so much, it so devours the national energy, it is so divisive, that it is smothering everything else."[164] Given that the Republican Party's potential nominees had similar positions on other campaign issues, it was only natural that their differences over Vietnam, negotiations, and withdrawal would dominate the agenda during the primaries. In the fall, the Nixon-Humphrey race centered around Vietnam to a certain extent, but neither candidate wanted to focus on the war, preferring to discuss other, less politically inflammatory issues. But, even in spite of their reluctance, Vietnam did become a pivotal issue in the fall campaign with Humphrey's Salt Lake City speech and the eleventh-hour announcement of the bombing halt. The evidence clearly demonstrates that each event had a quantum influence on public opinion and figured prominently in determining who would succeed LBJ in the White House.

The Vietnam War has been blamed for the downfall of both Lyndon Johnson and Richard Nixon. To this list we should add George Romney and, to a lesser extent, Nelson Rockefeller. Their positions on the war acted as millstones around their necks—Romney because of his "garrulous and rambling" statements, vacillations, and brainwashing comment, Rockefeller because he failed to have a position and, when he finally did speak out, his peace proposal was too specific and failed to include anything for GOP hawks.[165] In contrast, Nixon deftly maneuvered around the Vietnam issue during the primaries and the convention, seeking to be all things to all members of the party. As David Broder predicted a year before the election, he was able to articulate the case for continuing the war more effectively than Romney was able to argue for limiting American involvement.[166] By subtly implying that he had a strategy to end the conflict—and thanks to unexpected help from the media, which publicized his purported secret plan—while maintaining his reputation as a staunch anti-Communist, Nixon walked the tightrope of opinion within the party without committing himself to a specific stance. As a result, he won the Republican nomination in Miami, maintained the requisite flexibility on Vietnam that served him so well in the campaign against Hubert Humphrey, and won the presidency. Vietnam definitely played a critical role in Nixon's victory in 1968. Yet, because Nixon and Humphrey both equivocated on the war, the election held no clear mandate for how the country wanted the war ended. The public's voice on the conflict "was muted and diffuse in November 1968." As a result, "Nixon had what he most wanted: maximum flexibility to end it on his own terms."[167]

At the end of the year, Zalmoxis would return to the underworld for another three years, leaving Richard Nixon to make good on his implied campaign promises. But the ambiguity with which he campaigned meant that the president-elect would have a free hand once he took office to resolve the war as he saw fit. The 1968 campaign was unusual in comparison to those of 1952 and 1960 in that the rhetoric of the campaign provided little indication of the direction in which the new administration would move once in office. For all the rhetoric, skepticism, and publicity about his secret plan, the president-elect gave no specific indication as to how he intended to resolve the Vietnam War. Even during the transition period, he and his advisers remained silent on the incoming administration's strategy, preferring to continue to support LBJ and his policy. The country, it appeared, would have to wait until after the inauguration to discover just what its new president had in mind. With the election behind him, would he revert to the old Nixon—the hawk who demanded a military victory in Vietnam—or would there be another new Nixon who would press for negotiations and reorient U.S. foreign policy for a new decade?

# CHAPTER 7

# The Icarus Agenda

## Vietnamization and Its Political Implications

Our researchers into Public Opinion are content
That he held the proper opinions for the time of year;
When there was peace, he was for peace;
when there was war, he went.
                    —W. H. Auden, "The Unknown Citizen"

Politicians, after all, are not over a year behind Public Opinion.
                    —Will Rogers, *The Autobiography of Will Rogers*

Richard Nixon had dreamed of being president for decades. With his defeat of Hubert Humphrey, that ambition was finally realized. Yet, on assuming the mantle of the presidency, he discovered that the freedom to say and do as he saw fit that he had enjoyed as a nonincumbent no longer existed. The new president attempted to free himself from these restrictions through secrecy and misdirection but came to realize that the vagaries of domestic politics limited him to a fairly restricted set of options. He faced constraints analogous to those of Icarus, the son of the skilled craftsman Daedalus. Imprisoned with Icarus on the island of Crete by King Minos, Daedalus crafted wings to allow him and his son to escape. Daedalus warned Icarus not to fly too close to the sun or to the sea—the heat could melt the wax on the wings, and the water could weigh the wings down. In either case, he would be doomed. That narrow corridor proved too restricting for Icarus. Overcome by the joy of flight, he got too near to the sun, the wax melted, and he plummeted to his death. Like Icarus, Nixon had to navigate between the military and the political fronts, forced to grapple with domestic opinion in his effort to win the peace. This chapter will focus on Nixon's first year in office, examining how his Vietnamization policy evolved from the perspectives of the Nixon White House and the Republican Party, which for the first time since the Americanization of the conflict had direct influence on U.S. policy decisions in Vietnam.

Nixon often complained that he inherited a war not of his making. Vietnam, he claimed, resulted from the "faulty strategies" of his predecessors, the "'architects' of the mess" he faced when he assumed the presidency.[1] No one can deny that Eisenhower, Kennedy, and Johnson made the decisions that created the morass in Southeast Asia. But the new president's protests should not obscure a critical fact: Nixon undoubtedly contributed to the situation he confronted. His hawkish criticisms of the policies implemented by the two previous administrations, not to mention his vague and ambiguous campaign statements on the conflict, convey a significant measure of responsibility for the situation he encountered on 20 January 1969 both on the ground in Vietnam and at home. Nevertheless, Nixon entered the Oval Office with supreme confidence in his foreign policy expertise. As he told an interviewer in 1967, "I've always thought this country could run itself domestically, without a President. All you need is a competent Cabinet to run the country at home. You need a President for foreign policy."[2] He firmly believed that he would be able to resolve the conflict in Vietnam quickly and produce a settlement that would win the peace, placate the Right at home, restore America's credibility and international prestige, and allow him to implement his grand design for U.S. foreign relations.

Nixon entered the White House with the freedom to follow virtually whatever path he thought best in Vietnam. Immediate withdrawal was not a realistic option; those who suggest that he could simply have declared the war a relic of Democratic administrations and disengaged from Vietnam ignore crucial structural and domestic political restraints. Unlike cardinals elevated to the papacy, presidential candidates are bound by the promises they made prior to their election. Nixon could not have realistically withdrawn precipitously from Vietnam without violating his ambiguous campaign promises. But the little that he had uttered during the campaign narrowed his freedom to maneuver as president.[3] That flexibility was underscored by the fact that, after Nixon's election in November 1968, several members of Congress joined in an informal moratorium on criticism of Nixon's Vietnam program. They hoped that, once Nixon took office, he would reveal the secret plan, and they wanted to give the president-elect an opportunity to implement his new strategy. Gerald Ford urged the country to "set no Vietnam deadlines for the Nixon Administration. To do so would be unrealistic. Impatience will not win the peace." George Aiken agreed and expressed his optimism that a settlement could be reached during

Nixon's first year in office: "There is a good chance the Viet Nam War will be de-escalated or ended in 1969, since both North Viet Nam and the U.S. genuinely want peace." Aiken's confidence was bolstered by his belief that Nixon's national security adviser, Henry Kissinger, would be an asset in the pursuit of peace because the former Harvard professor "helped Rockefeller to develop the policy of gradual disengagement from Viet Nam which Rocky proposed during the campaign."[4]

Cutting the umbilical cord of the Saigon regime proved to be problematic. The mythology that has come to surround Nixon's alleged secret plan has blinded many scholars to one undeniable fact. Nixon had no concrete strategic plan. He allowed the press and the public to believe that he did as a matter of political expediency during the campaign, but, in reality, he entered the White House with nothing more than a vague notion of how to bring the war to an end. On assuming the presidency, he likely "had no clear idea . . . of how to end the war quickly."[5] But such was Nixon's faith in his abilities that he remained confident that he could end the war with reasonable speed even without a definite blueprint. As he told Representative Donald Riegle (R-MI) prior to the inauguration, he believed that he could bring an end to the war within six months.

But self-assurance represented only part of the complicated equation. Resolving the war quickly mattered to Nixon for two additional reasons. First, he believed that he would be unable to conduct a cohesive and successful foreign policy toward the Soviets and the Chinese until after the Vietnam conflict ended. Second, and perhaps more important, he had already begun to think about his second term, not an uncommon occurrence for any president to be sure. Daniel Patrick Moynihan, who served on the White House staff as a counselor for urban affairs (and de facto domestic policy czar), wrote to Nixon two weeks prior to the inauguration and warned him that "his would be a one-term presidency unless the war in Vietnam ended soon."[6] Indeed, the domestic political implications of the war and its resolution dominated Nixon's early months as president. More than perhaps any politician in the country, he understood the consequences he would face if he could not demonstrate progress toward an honorable (victorious) peace by 1972. Could even as hawkish and committed an anti-Communist as Nixon survive a "who lost Vietnam" controversy initiated by the Democrats, a debate that Nixon feared just as much as Kennedy and Johnson had?

In fact, Nixon actually displayed more concern about conservative reactions to his policies than about antiwar forces throughout his presidency. Although privately preoccupied with domestic opinion, he publicly disdained the Left and the organized opposition to the war, dismissing them almost out of hand. But he did worry about challenges from the Right, and the pressure from conservatives was real. Strom Thurmond told his South Carolina constituents a week before the inauguration, "We have forgotten that the government of South Vietnam is not merely our ally, but our only hope for defending our interests in that part of the world." Thurmond advocated the resumption of bombing and other pressure on the North Vietnamese in order to achieve U.S. goals in the conflict. The only definition of *victory* he would accept included the evacuation of sanctuaries, the withdrawal of North Vietnamese troops from the South, and the independence of the Saigon regime.[7] The *National Review* would keep hounding Nixon on the war as well, consistently badgering the administration to employ U.S. military power more effectively and stay the course toward victory rather than capitulation to communism.

Although Vietnam would come to define his presidency in many ways, Nixon did not want to link his administration to the conflict explicitly. In his inaugural address, he did not directly mention Vietnam, but his remarks were replete with oblique references to ending the conflict. As Chief Justice Earl Warren administered the oath of office, Nixon's family Bibles were open to Isa. 2:4, which reads, "They shall beat their swords into plowshares, and their spears into pruninghooks: nation shall not lift up sword against nation, neither shall they learn war any more." Asserting that the "greatest honor history can bestow is the title of peacemaker," Nixon made a "sacred commitment" to "consecrate my office, my energies, and all the wisdom I can summon to the cause of peace among nations." He announced that the world had entered an "era of negotiation," although he cautioned (appropriately, it would turn out) that "peace does not come through wishing for it—that there is no substitute for days and even years of patient and prolonged diplomacy." Rather than victory, he concluded, America sought "peaceful competition" among nations.[8]

But Nixon's pledge to pursue peace in Vietnam did not appease some of the ceremony's spectators. For the first time in the nation's history, protesters disrupted the president's inauguration. Antiwar opponents chanted, "Four more years of death!" and "Ho, Ho, Ho Chi Minh, the NLF is going to win." Posters mocking one of Nixon's main campaign themes read, "Nixon's the One—the No. 1 War Criminal." All along the parade route on Pennsylvania Avenue demonstrators burned the American flags that had been distributed by the Boy Scouts and spat at police. Nixon's limousine was even pelted with rocks, bottles, and beer cans. Stephen Ambrose wrote that the spectacle was "a national disgrace."[9] The protests did, however, vividly demonstrate the challenges the new president would face in dealing with the war in Vietnam and accentuated the domestic political perils the administration would have to navigate.

How would the new president accomplish the monumental task at hand? In his book *No More Vietnams*, Nixon claims to have had a five-point strategy for ending the war: Vietnamization, pacification, diplomatic isolation, peace negotiations, and gradual withdrawal.[10] Hindsight may be twenty-twenty, but this retrospective claim does not correspond to the evidence. When Nixon and his advisers met in December 1968 to organize the transition, "it became clear that he had no plan, not even a general strategy, to end the war. Melvin Laird, who knew the president as well as anyone in the administration, later insisted, 'I don't care what anybody told you. He had no plan.'"[11] He instead relied on a collection of general guidelines that would inform his strategic and tactical policy improvisations. His policies toward the war when he took office were based on three premises. First, the public had to be prepared to settle for something less than a military victory. Many Americans were already willing to accept such an outcome if it meant that the country would disengage from the conflict. Second, the United States could not, Nixon adamantly believed, simply abandon the South Vietnamese to the mercy of the North. The long-standing American commitment to self-determination in South Vietnam and the omnipresent domestic political considerations militated against abdicating the U.S. role in Southeast Asia in that manner. The "decent interval" theory, although not yet part and parcel of American policy, would evolve from the tensions inherent in these contradictory requirements. Third, the war should be brought to an end "as quickly as was honorably possible"—not through precipitate withdrawal, but through a disengagement that would not negatively affect Nixon's political position at home.

In essence, there was nothing really new in Nixon's broad framework for ending the war. It resembled Dwight Eisenhower's approach of military and economic aid to the Diem regime coupled with a threat of direct American military action. It also paralleled the various means employed by Lyndon Johnson —back-channel diplomacy, overtures to Moscow, and bombing escalations to prod Hanoi into concessions—during his final year in office.[12] These imprecise criteria for resolving the conflict bore little resemblance to the sort of structured secret plan that Nixon intimated, and the public accepted, during the 1968 campaign. Instead, Nixon and Kissinger "constructed ad hoc and often contradictory strategies in reaction to military and political events."[13]

One of Nixon's central and most consistent strategies for dealing with the North Vietnamese was his "madman theory." Essentially a psychological warfare strategy, it was intended to coerce Hanoi into negotiations and concessions. As Nixon told his aide H. R. Haldeman, "I'm the one man in this country who can do it. . . . They'll believe any threat of force that Nixon makes because it's Nixon." The theory, he explained, was simple: "I want the North Vietnamese to believe I've reached the point where I might do anything to stop the war." He continued, "We'll just slip the word to them [through back channels] that, 'for

God's sake, you know Nixon is obsessed about Communists. We can't restrain him when he's angry—and he has his hand on the nuclear button,'—and Ho Chi Minh himself will be in Paris in two days begging for peace." But, as Lloyd Gardner observed, Nixon's other foreign policy actions as president—opening the door to China and negotiating with the Soviets over fundamental military and political questions—"belied the notion that a slathering madman with an itchy nuclear trigger finger sat in the White House."[14] Still, his fierce anti-Communist background and his reputation as a hawk gave the madman theory credibility.

But, just as Nixon hoped to keep Hanoi guessing about his true intentions, he wanted to be perceived by the American people as a strong leader who acted forcefully and who did not pander to popular sentiment. When a reporter suggested that, if he did not get out of Vietnam, he would be a victim of popular outrage just as Johnson had been, he instructed his domestic policy adviser John Ehrlichman to tell the reporter that, regardless of the polls, "RN will do what his long experience and conviction tells him is right." Despite this outward appearance, however, Nixon cared deeply about public opinion and understood the importance of molding that opinion in his favor. He realized that the American public possessed a limited amount of patience when it came to Vietnam and that only positive steps toward ending the conflict would allow him to retain popular support. To this end, he hired polling experts and commissioned private polls that gave the White House "a sophisticated capacity for public opinion analysis . . . of unprecedented scope."[15]

To assist him in implementing his as-yet-unfocused strategy for ending the war honorably, Nixon selected advisers who held a wide spectrum of views on the war. In terms of Vietnam policy, the two most important appointments he would make would be his national security adviser and his secretary of defense. Both men would exert a profound influence on the president, but for starkly different reasons and from frequently diametrically opposed positions. Together, they would push and prod him in such a way that U.S. Vietnam policy would come to resemble a patchwork quilt of contradictory and confusing decisions that simultaneously escalated the conflict and disengaged the country from its commitment to the Saigon regime.

As national security adviser, Nixon selected one of the most extraordinary and inscrutable figures in the annals of American diplomacy, Henry Kissinger.[16] A political scientist from Harvard University who had advised both the Johnson administration and the Rockefeller campaign, Kissinger considered Vietnam "the height of folly."[17] He believed that the United States should never have become bogged down in Southeast Asia. An acolyte of the Metternich/Castleraugh/Bismark realist tradition of balance of power diplomacy, he saw

Indochina as tangential to American national security interests and counseled disengagement. It is important to note, however, that Kissinger (and Nixon) believed that U.S. credibility and prestige were on the line in South Vietnam owing to the commitments made by previous administrations. This sentiment would complicate the negotiation process, as would Kissinger and Nixon's efforts to conduct the meaningful peace talks under a shroud of secrecy. Nixon's penchant for secrecy and control over foreign policy led him to keep members of the GOP—including most of his administration—out of the decisionmaking loop on the war. Whereas Johnson had consulted regularly with Dirksen, Nixon did not even keep his own minority leader, Hugh Scott of Pennsylvania, informed of administration thinking, a fact that Scott resented. In the aftermath of the invasion of Cambodia, for example, Scott was forced to belatedly shift his position from opposition to support for the president. He later complained to Kissinger that he needed to have "substantive evidence of support [from the administration] for my leadership," not simply "letters or statements," but "close consultation."[18] Nixon's approach to governing and negotiating resembled that of French president Charles DeGaulle (whom Nixon admired greatly), which was characterized by "secrecy, aloofness, an aura of mystery, limiting personal statements and achieving maximum surprise and effect with those he did make, frequent dissimulation of his true purposes in order to keep criticism at bay."[19]

In addition, although they shared many views on foreign policy, Nixon and Kissinger did not always see eye-to-eye on Vietnam policy. The president believed that it was necessary to turn the public's attention away from the war in order to bring it to a successful conclusion. Kissinger disagreed. The national security adviser cared little for public opinion (or so he claimed) and instead focused on ending the conflict in such a way that it would fortify America's standing with other nations, in particular the Soviet Union and China.[20] In addition, Kissinger believed that Vietnamization violated his cardinal rule of realism: military force and diplomacy must work together. As he had written eleven years earlier in *Nuclear Weapons and Foreign Policy,* "By stopping military operations we removed the only Chinese incentive for a settlement [to the Korean War]; we produced the frustration of two years of inconclusive negotiations." In short, he argued, "Our insistence on divorcing force from diplomacy caused our power to lack purpose and our negotiations to lack force."[21] Despite their differences, however, Nixon and Kissinger managed to work together to meet their mutual aims, preserve American credibility, and prevent a settlement that would have negative ramifications on U.S. policy elsewhere in the world.[22] As Kissinger later wrote in *Diplomacy,* "Nixon was eager to negotiate an honorable extrication, which he defined as almost anything except turning over to the North Vietnamese communists the millions of people who had been led by his predecessors to rely on America." Nixon, like Kissinger, "took credibility and honor seriously because they defined America's capacity to shape a peaceful international order."[23]

Kissinger and Nixon began working on Vietnam even prior to taking office. On 20 December 1968, Kissinger informed Nixon that he had used a back channel to assure Hanoi that the new administration was prepared to "undertake serious talks . . . based on the self-respect and sense of honor of all parties." He concluded on an ominous note, however. Nixon would accept an honorable settlement but would not settle for anything less.[24] Nixon and Kissinger wanted to extricate American forces from Vietnam as quickly and painlessly as possible as long as the withdrawal did not diminish U.S. credibility worldwide. Both were convinced that Johnson had overcommitted the United States in Southeast Asia; however, once there, the country could not afford to appear to have been pushed out by Hanoi. As Kissinger wrote in *Foreign Affairs* at the end of 1968, prior to his appointment as national security adviser, "The commitment of five hundred thousand Americans has settled the issue of the importance of Vietnam. For what is involved now is confidence in American promises. However fashionable it is to ridicule the terms 'credibility' or 'prestige,' they are not empty phrases; other nations can gear their actions to ours only if they can count on our steadiness."[25]

The other major force in the administration was Melvin Laird, the former Wisconsin congressman who had soured on the war during the last years of Johnson's presidency. Nixon's first choice to run the Pentagon had been "Scoop" Jackson, a Democrat and senior member of the Senate Armed Services Committee who was renowned for his support of a strong national defense policy. Not only were Jackson's credentials impeccable, but he would have given the administration a high-ranking Democrat in the cabinet as part of Nixon's "great coalition," which he hoped would at once unify the country and provide him with political protection in much the same way that Henry Cabot Lodge Jr. had for Kennedy and Johnson. But the nomination went beyond pragmatic considerations. Nixon "felt a kinship" with Jackson and wanted "at least credit for making the offer," which was legitimate (unlike the more pro forma invitations to join the cabinet given to Hubert Humphrey and other Democrats that Nixon knew would be rejected). Ironically, given the way events unfolded, it was Laird, who had advised Nixon and his transition staff to select Jackson, who ended up running the Pentagon in Nixon's first term.[26]

When Jackson declined the nomination, Nixon turned to Laird. The president alternately cajoled and threatened Laird on a cross-country flight from California to Washington, DC, to take the job. A political force within the GOP with impressive bureaucratic maneuvering skills, the congressman expressed a deep reluctance to accept the position and leave his powerful seat in Congress. Ever the crafty politician, he came up with a precondition to accept the offer that was "plausible yet so odious" that he believed Nixon would never accept it. He wanted a firm commitment that nobody in the administration—especially Nixon—would ever interfere with any appointment he made at the Pentagon while secretary of defense. Laird felt totally confident that no president would ever cede such power to a cabinet minister. Nixon thought it over for a moment and said, "Mel, you have my word on it." Laird was stunned. He had been tricked by Nixon. In a last, desperate hope to avoid accepting, he asked the president-elect to put the agreement in writing on a cocktail napkin. Nixon agreed. Although he had absolutely no desire to be secretary of defense, Laird succeeded in extracting an unprecedented promise from Nixon: control over the Defense Department's five million employees, especially the highly coveted political appointments that typically were doled out to repay political debts and surround the secretary with people loyal to the president. Given how well Laird knew Nixon, he kept the cocktail napkin and used it as the ultimate trump card in dealing with the new president.[27]

That leverage proved critical as Laird took over control of the U.S. military effort in Vietnam. He had come to the conclusion that the war could not be won. He realized that congressional opposition to the conflict was endemic on Capitol Hill. He felt that, if Nixon hesitated to bring the war to a conclusion, the president's small reservoir of political capital from his narrow margin of victory would disappear almost immediately. As a result, he became a leading voice of deescalation in the new administration and championed what would become known as Vietnamization. An outspoken advocate of military strength and a firm foreign policy during his tenure in the House, Laird became a passionate supporter of disengagement from South Vietnam during his four years at Defense. Indeed, Laird can accurately be characterized as the father of the Vietnamization program. As his military aide, Gen. Robert Pursley, recalled, the administration's policy was not formed during the campaign; it was "largely formulated on Laird's first trip to Southeast Asia."[28] Laird described the pressure he felt when he took over the Pentagon: "The primary role that I had was that I had a time bomb ticking—it was the public opinion in the country." He firmly believed that Nixon had been elected on the Vietnam issue and understood that a second term depended largely on the administration's progress in extricating the United States from Southeast Asia.[29]

Laird took steps to ensure that he did not fall victim to the same perceptions as his Democratic predecessors. In an effort to "insure that the SECDEF's [secretary of defense's] image is not successfully sold as the villian [sic] of the piece," it would "not be sufficient merely to coordinate domestic activities in the best PR tradition." Laird had to protect himself from becoming the "goat" of "misguided policy decisions or inept execution by others, lest he find himself the only man in the glass room who didn't fashion himself a cover before the lights came on." Given Vietnam's importance, "someone's image [was] going to fall or rise on this one," and Laird could be the victim "without ever realizing how the noose was fashioned." Political opportunists, he concluded, "will never permit a divorce of the Pentagon and the War. Right now, however, MRL is not the quarterback on the key plays."[30] Laird's actions demonstrated that, although the Republicans now controlled policy, the issue of personal credibility remained alive and well.

Aside from Kissinger and Laird, however, few members of the cabinet exerted any measurable influence on administration policy in Vietnam. In his senior appointments, Nixon drew a sharp distinction between those whom he included in his inner circle and those who, despite their nominal titles and positions, did not have his complete confidence. The president's modus operandi reflected his outlook on what would be required to resolve the situation he faced in 1969. The primary example of this hierarchy was his selection of William P. Rogers, Eisenhower's attorney general, with whom he had worked closely in the 1950s, to lead the State Department. Despite being the nation's leading diplomat, Rogers played virtually no role in the making of foreign policy. Owing to Nixon's deeply ingrained distrust of the Ivy League and the Nixon-Kissinger reorganization of the national security apparatus, Rogers became little more than a figurehead as secretary of state. Indeed, he often found himself explaining and defending policies before Congress and in the media that he had had little or no role in formulating. Nixon chose him primarily because of his loyalty and discretion.

Nixon also appointed Henry Cabot Lodge as his representative to the Paris peace talks. Lodge appeared to be a highly qualified choice on whom Nixon could rely for expert advice. During the transition, he advised Nixon to appoint someone of cabinet rank (preferably Lodge himself) to handle all matters relating to the war and to the negotiations.[31] Yet, despite assurances from Nixon to the contrary, he did not enjoy the authority to discuss substantive issues with the North Vietnamese delegation. The former ambassador and the negotiating team were little more than window dressing. The explanation for this is quite simple. Nixon and Lodge had nearly antithetical personalities and political beliefs, and the president would not entrust the resolution of the war—and, by extension, his political future—to the man who he justifiably believed had cost him the presidency in 1960. The real action in Paris would occur behind the scenes in the secret negotiations initiated and conducted by Kissinger.

Kissinger's private talks would supersede Lodge's public discussions, leaving the former ambassador hamstrung. Although he attempted to carve out a meaningful role for himself—going so far as to request permission to conduct his own confidential discussions, which Nixon granted—Lodge never played a central role in the negotiations or framing U.S. policy. By the end of the summer of 1969, he became extremely "disillusioned" and eventually requested to be relieved of his position. Nixon and Kissinger used Lodge's "credibility and reputation" and then "deliberately enfeebled his authority to carry out his assignment properly" because they believed that it was a necessary step to bolster the Saigon regime, even if it meant undermining progress in the Paris negotiations.[32] Thus, Nixon aggregated Vietnam decisionmaking and policy influence in the hands of a select few, essentially compartmentalizing his foreign policy and ignoring voices within the administration and the GOP that did not conform to his overall strategic vision. The only real exception to this rule was Laird, whom Nixon respected and whose power base at the Pentagon made him virtually untouchable.

In early January 1969, a special task force prepared a set of contingencies on Vietnam for Nixon to consider, ranging from an open-ended and gradual withdrawal of American forces to an indefinite American presence. After reviewing the alternatives, Nixon directed that the option for an immediate commitment to a complete withdrawal within a year or two be excised. Such a course of action "would have meant capitulation, a 'bug out,' something Nixon could not tolerate viscerally or intellectually," to say nothing of the domestic political implications.[33] Meanwhile, RAND's Daniel Ellsberg, who later played a central role in the Nixon administration by leaking the Pentagon Papers, prepared a list of questions for the Pentagon, the State Department, and the CIA on Vietnam. The resulting document, National Security Study Memorandum (NSSM) 1, made it clear that the kind of military pressure applied in Vietnam by the Johnson administration, especially the bombing campaign, had not worked in the past and likely would not work in the future.

Both Nixon and Kissinger challenged the conclusions of NSSM 1. They believed that they could win the war through a massive and unprecedented escalation of the intensity of bombing throughout Indochina. Previously, they argued, bombing had not been effective because it had not been employed to its maximum levels. Both supported the idea that American diplomacy would be more productive and Hanoi more willing to compromise if decisive military action were taken. Winning both the war and the peace while convincing the Communists that the United States was serious about the possible escalation of the war, they concluded, required intensive bombing in Southeast Asia. American policy toward Vietnam from 1969 to 1973 reflected that belief. Even Laird, who championed Vietnamization, believed that more effective use of U.S. airpower would shore up the Saigon regime and allow the administration to begin troop withdrawals at a much more rapid pace.

These preliminary discussions took place behind the scenes. Given the natural honeymoon period for any new president and the informal congressional moratorium on criticism of the administration on Vietnam, Nixon's first weeks in office saw little public discussion about the war. As the columnist Joseph Alsop wrote to the chief of U.S. intelligence in Saigon, Gen. Phillip Davidson, in February 1969, Nixon "has been extremely adroit in lowering the decibel count of the argument about Vietnam, and this will give him much more time than Humphrey would have had."[34] Nearly all Republican critics of the Johnson administration like George Aiken now counseled patience to give the new president a chance to work out a solution to the war.[35] In fact, Pete McCloskey stood virtually alone with the party in opposing Nixon's policy publicly during 1969. Nevertheless, Vietnam remained a central concern for the nation. At Nixon's first news conference, Helen Thomas of UPI bluntly asked the new commander-in-chief, "Now that you are President, what is your peace plan in Vietnam?" Nixon responded with a characteristic lack of specifics, citing a good start to negotiations, but warning that progress depended on the reaction of Hanoi. Answering a question later in the briefing, he also asserted that, while he wanted to bring the war to an end "as early as possible," the "hard, tough ground" of the negotiating process remained ahead and would take time to bring to a successful resolution.[36]

Kissinger later noted in his memoirs that Nixon did not believe that negotiations would amount to anything until the military situation changed fundamentally. The president thought that Hanoi would accept a compromise only if it had no other choice—hence the emphasis on increased bombing.[37] Moreover, he understood that he did not have unlimited reservoirs of goodwill and time. Recognizing this reality, he pushed Kissinger for results, telling his national security adviser, "It seems vitally important to me at this time that we increase as much as we possibly can the military pressure on the enemy in South Vietnam. . . . I believe it is absolutely urgent if we are to make any kind of headway in Vietnam that we find new ways to increase the pressure militarily without going to the point that we break off negotiations." He "[did] not like the suggestions . . . in virtually every news report that we anticipate a 'Communist initiative in South Vietnam.'" Kissinger concluded that he "believe[d] that if any initiative occurs it would be on our part and not theirs."[38] Rather than being reactive, as he believed Johnson to have been, Nixon wanted to force Hanoi to respond to U.S. initiatives in order to extract the maximum concessions from the North Vietnamese in any negotiated settlement.

The task facing Nixon was a daunting one, not only from an international perspective but also from a domestic political standpoint. Not only had he been elected by a slim margin, but he was the first president since Zachary Taylor in 1848 to work with a Congress in which both houses were controlled by the opposition party. Many Democrats who had only reluctantly supported Johnson's Vietnam policies could oppose Nixon more easily for partisan reasons. Indeed, given the nature of Johnson's lack of candor on the war, congressmen of both parties treated every statement from the Nixon White House with skepticism. Furthermore, after years of being in the position of supporting an unpopular war being directed by a Democratic president, Democrats in Congress moved quickly to hammer Nixon for his conduct of the war. John Rhodes later noted, "Gone was the cooperation of Congress with the White House on this and other foreign policy issues. After years of slavishly approving every Vietnam appropriation requested by Kennedy and Johnson, the Democrats in Congress shifted gears and began sounding a drumbeat to end the war immediately, at any cost."[39] While Rhodes overestimated the Democratic support enjoyed by LBJ and the willingness of Congress to push back against the administration, his point was valid. The tables had been turned, and the Democrats now took every opportunity to attack Nixon's Vietnam policies. Yet, despite the growing dissent in the Senate, there would "always be a crippling and pronounced lack of cohesion and organization among the Senate's doves." At this stage, they simply lacked the votes to reverse America's involvement in Southeast Asia in any meaningful way.[40]

On the other hand, Republicans who had pressured Johnson for over five years to act quickly and aggressively toward Hanoi now counseled patience. John Tower, the archetypical hawk during the Johnson administration, suggested that South Vietnam could win a political contest with the Viet Cong if the United States did not too hastily withdraw with too few safeguards: "Only if American patience falters can we fail to achieve our reasonable goals in Southeast Asia."[41] On the other end of the spectrum, George Aiken gave Nixon "a large plus sign for the manner in which he has handled affairs of the Nation to date." He also urged everyone to give the president time to implement his plan, arguing that the United States could not "pull out of South Vietnam tomorrow unless we have a pretty good idea of the situation we are leaving behind."[42] Even Mark Hatfield, perhaps the most outspoken Republican opponent of the war during Johnson's presidency, demonstrated a willingness to give Nixon time. After the election, he warned the president-elect not to ignore Vietnam, predicting that he would be doomed politically unless the war ended by 1970. But as he later recalled, "Shortly after Nixon was sworn in, Bill Rogers . . . came to see me suggesting, 'Let us get our act together, Mark. Lighten up on the secret plan, will you? Give us a legitimate amount of time to get our Vietnam peace policy established.' It seemed a reasonable request, and only fair. I acquiesced."43

The apparent calm on the issue of Vietnam that the administration enjoyed at the outset masked the turbulence beneath the surface. The obstacles that Nixon would face were readily apparent to contemporary observers. On 6 March, two editorials detailed these challenges. The *Christian Science Monitor* understood a critical point: "There is a combination of pressures impelling the new President from ever letting 'Johnson's war' become 'Nixon's war.' Hanoi will have read more calculatingly than most the reports that Mr. Nixon feels the domestic political need to be seen to be winding up the war before the end of this year. The Nixon administration is in fact in a tight corner on Vietnam and will need to keep its head."44 Meanwhile, the *New York Times* observed that Nixon was trying to "keep all his options open and to avoid any hint of what new approaches the Administration intends to pursue in its quest for a more stable world."45

Hanoi refused to grant Nixon the luxury of patience. The same day Tower made his comments, the North Vietnamese launched the 1969 Tet Offensive. Over the next three weeks, 1,140 U.S. soldiers were killed in the intense fighting, and antiwar criticism increased in intensity. Nixon responded by ordering the bombing of Communist sanctuaries in Cambodia, a step the Joint Chiefs had urged for several weeks. But, under pressure from Laird and Rogers, who felt that the bombing could not be kept secret and that the press and Congress would be furious at such an escalation, he rescinded the order.46 At a press conference on 4 March, Nixon was asked about the offensive's effect on public opinion. He told the reporters, "The American people will support a President if they are told . . . why we are there, what our objectives are, what the costs will be, and what the consequences would be if we took another course of action." He added that there were no plans to withdraw any American troops in the near future, although he admitted that such actions were under consideration.47

Nixon later wrote that the United States "should have dealt a swift blow that would have made Hanoi's leaders think twice before they launched another attack in the South." But, he lamented in retrospect, "I was stuck with Johnson's bombing halt." Even though he believed that the administration could prove unequivocally that the North had violated the agreement, he also believed that "bombing North Vietnam would produce a violent outburst of domestic protest. . . . This, in turn, would have destroyed our efforts to bring the country together in support of our plan for peace."48 Nevertheless, Nixon considered his failure to take decisive military action at this juncture his "biggest mistake as President" because he believed it would have ended the war in 1969.49 Kissinger agreed, telling William Safire, "We should have responded strongly [once the offensive began]. We should have taken on the doves right then—starting bombing and mining the harbors. The war would have been over in 1970."[50]

Taking on the doves, as Kissinger suggested, would have been totally in character for the president. Recall that, prior to his election, Nixon had consistently and vocally denounced critics of U.S. policy in Vietnam. Neither politicians nor the antiwar public at large escaped his wrath. From the Oval Office, his tenets did not change; indeed, if anything, his abhorrence of dissent, obsession with domestic enemies, and fear that the American people lacked the will and character required for the country to assert itself vigorously in the world intensified dramatically during his presidency and reinforced his penchant for secrecy.

Although Nixon rescinded the order to bomb Communist sanctuaries, he did so primarily because of the potential for a negative public response. He remained convinced that intensive aerial bombardment represented the only strategy that would force the enemy to make substantive concessions in the negotiations. In an effort to demonstrate to the North Vietnamese leadership in Hanoi that he could escalate the air war without sparking an outbreak of domestic protest, he began a covert bombing campaign of the Ho Chi Minh Trail in Cambodia in March 1969.[51] The attacks were a belated response to the February offensive, an action that he perceived as a direct challenge to his Vietnam policies. In his mind, Hanoi had thrown down the gauntlet to test the new American president, and Nixon wanted to demonstrate his resolve. This time, however, he did not give Laird or Rogers an opportunity to sway his decision.

While the president escalated the air war in an effort to force Hanoi into a settlement, he simultaneously pursued other avenues to rapidly resolve the conflict. As he recalled in his memoirs, he told the cabinet in March that he "expected the war to be over in a year."[52] Part of the reason for his optimism was his belief that the Soviet Union "would like to use what influence it could appropriately to help bring the war to a conclusion."[53] Foreshadowing the policies he pursued later in his administration, he attempted to leverage Soviet cooperation by linking a settlement to other issues of common interest. Unfortunately, Soviet influence was not pervasive enough in Hanoi to change the North Vietnamese bargaining position. Nixon underestimated the tensions between the two Communist nations, which dated to the 1954 Geneva conference, at which Hanoi believed that Moscow and Beijing had betrayed it to the West. That enmity undermined his plan to use the Soviet's leverage with North Vietnam to his advantage. This is a clear example of peripheral powers understanding and taking advantage of the Cold War for their own benefit, with the superpowers left at the mercy of their Third World allies and adversaries.[54]

The recalcitrance of Hanoi was only one of the challenges with which the president had to contend. As the war dragged on, he began to understand and appreciate more fully the problems that Johnson faced as the nation's commander-in-chief during an increasingly unpopular war. The skepticism about the war's progress and the lack of candor from the administration that had plagued LBJ also loomed as an issue for Nixon. John Ehrlichman told Kissinger on 20 March that Donald Riegle had just returned from Vietnam—a trip undertaken at his own expense—and reported to his colleagues that "the information being disseminated by the Department of State and the Department of Defense is not a fair representation of the trend of the conflict." Recognizing the difficulties that could arise from a Nixon administration version of the credibility gap, Ehrlichman recommended that Riegle be scheduled for a White House visit to avoid a public scene. The memo also noted that Pete McCloskey, who, like Riegle, was "essentially dovish and represent[ed] the young turks of the Republican party in Congress," planned to visit Vietnam the following week and should also be invited to meet with administration officials.[55] Nixon concurred and tried to exert influence on both. His efforts would prove to be spectacularly unsuccessful.

But, even though he opposed the administration's approach to the war, McCloskey wanted Nixon to succeed. While his critique of U.S. Vietnam policy did not abate, he was hopeful that Nixon might be able to end the war quickly. In late March 1969, he wrote the first in a series of letters to Nixon in which he urged the president to act on his ambiguous campaign promises to bring a swift end to the conflict. He realized that the only way that U.S. policy on Vietnam would change would be to convince Nixon that such change was in his best interest. In the letter, McCloskey flatly stated, "In Viet Nam, we are wrong. We were wrong to seek to contain communism through massive victory force. . . . We were wrong in thinking we could win, or that we can yet win." Essentially, he asked Nixon to admit that Americanization of the war had been a mistake and announce that troop withdrawals would begin shortly. Using subtle flattery, McCloskey argued that "both you and the United States are big enough to admit past mistakes" and that doing so would restore the credibility of the government in the eyes of the American people, a "far more valuable" commodity than "the credibility we will lose abroad and which Mr. Kissinger has urged as requiring our continued involvement in Viet Nam."[56]

Attached to the letter was a more detailed memorandum from the congressman explaining his rationale. He argued, "Our policy has been predicated upon the expectancy that with *enough* assistance, over a *reasonable* period of time, the Saigon government could achieve a sufficient degree of national cohesion to maintain its independence." For McCloskey, those assumptions were false, and no level of U.S. support for Vietnamization would change the fact that the conflict was "essentially a civil war." He urged Nixon to begin withdrawal of U.S. troops within ninety days, suggesting, "[The] success or failure of the Nixon administration will be determined by its ability to extricate the U.S. from its massive military commitment in Viet Nam . . . by the 1970 congressional elections."[57]

Much to McCloskey's dismay, Nixon did not reply directly to his letter—that was left to an aide—and McCloskey's hope for a quick settlement to the conflict faded rapidly. By the middle of 1969, he began questioning both the rate of withdrawals the administration had announced and the ultimate goal of Nixon's policy, taking the president and his advisers to task on the war at every conceivable opportunity. For the most part, the administration chose to ignore McCloskey's attacks, much as the Johnson administration had done to early Democratic critics like Ernest Gruening and Wayne Morse. Yet it did keep an eye on the congressman's remarks and the response they received in public and in Congress, and Nixon did make a token effort to placate McCloskey's dissent. For instance, the congressman visited the White House in September to meet with Henry Kissinger to discuss the conflict. This was McCloskey's second trip to the White House since Nixon's inauguration. In March, he (along with Riegle) pressed Kissinger to bring the war to a rapid conclusion. They were asked to "be patient" for sixty days as the president had a plan to end the war. In the second meeting, McCloskey confronted Kissinger about the lack of progress over the preceding six months. The national security adviser replied that the original plan had not worked and that the administration was "now working on another plan."[58]

Fortunately for the president, however, he—like LBJ—enjoyed the support of Everett Dirksen. The minority leader spoke on the Senate floor on 26 March and reiterated his support of the administration's approach to the conflict. Nixon, he asserted, "has repeatedly expressed his intention of settling the war in Vietnam. A plan is now being implemented, but slogans are not being shouted from the roof tops, rather action is underway." To those who criticized the administration for moving too slowly, Dirksen cautioned that ending the conflict "will require patience and perseverance, but a just and honorable peace will be achieved, something the previous Administration was unable to achieve." Nixon was "proceeding calmly, cooly, prudently, and responsibly—laying the foundation before it tries to put up the walls and roof."[59] Nixon would benefit from Dirksen's support until the senator's death in September.

It is easy to understand why Americans could be skeptical of Dirksen's defense of Nixon. By April, the number of American troops in South Vietnam reached its peak at 543,400, and the war looked no closer to being resolved. Meanwhile, Nixon and his advisers labored to redefine the U.S. role in Southeast Asia. Laird appeared on "The CBS Morning News" to defend the Vietnamization program, asserting that the American people needed to give the administration a few months to reach a negotiated settlement. He refused, however, to consider unilateral withdrawal and expressed some hopefulness about the progress of the private talks with the North Vietnamese.[60] In keeping with the strategy of deescalation, on 10 April 1969 Nixon and Kissinger issued National Security Action Memorandum 36, which directed Laird to prepare "a specific timetable for Vietnamizing the war."[61]

Laird pushed aggressively for the most rapid withdrawal possible throughout 1969. As Lewis Sorley suggests, he arguably "had the more perceptive view of the rapidly waning patience of the American public," and that understanding helped him have a great deal of influence on the administration regarding the pace and magnitude of the American troop withdrawals. Sorley cites William Colby's opinion that "Laird was the unsung hero of the whole war effort" who "saw the need to adjust American strategy to maintain the support of the American people in political terms—'the art of the possible.'"[62] Indeed, Laird's political acumen rivaled—some would argue surpassed—Nixon's, and he clearly recognized the nation's weariness with the war. Other Republicans echoed his advocacy of a phased withdrawal. Charles Percy, for instance, asserted that at least fifty thousand U.S. troops should be withdrawn from South Vietnam in 1969: "Anything else than that would not do the job of convincing the South Vietnamese that they should not place total reliance on our security forces." Despite his concerns, however, Percy did not go so far as to demand a definite withdrawal date, as some senators would do throughout Nixon's first term.[63]

Among the most outspoken Republicans in 1969 was Jacob Javits. He warned Nixon that the administration would have to make a "major shift" in its negotiating position if it were to "fulfill the mandate to end the war as well as to avoid 'very serious' domestic political problems." Javits's comments, the most blunt and critical by any GOP senator since Nixon took office, reflected growing congressional impatience with the administration's handling of the war. Both George Aiken and Hugh Scott had raised concerns about the pace of disengagement previously, but Javits's concern that Nixon was caught up in "the old myths, the old self-delusions, the old phraseology" of the Johnson administration resonated with the White House.[64]

Nixon also had to deal with a confrontational attitude from the other end of the GOP spectrum. As the administration moved closer to officially announcing its Vietnamization plan, conservatives expressed serious reservations about the direction of Nixon's policies. They believed that the war could still be won militarily and decried any political settlement that might make too many concessions to Hanoi. Their anxieties were encapsulated in an article in the *National Review* on 6 May that provided a long and detailed statement of the conservative position. The article, "What Now in Vietnam," supported the country's role in Southeast Asia, insisting that "American security and interest, understood in a given strategic and political context, required intervention." Arguing that a failure to maintain the current course of action would render the United States an untrustworthy and unreliable ally, it called for a "minimum intelligible objective . . . simply stated: to guarantee South Vietnam against communist takeover for the next period." In essence, the editors willingly accepted the prospect of a long-term military struggle—no surprise since conservatives maintained that the war was going well—and rejected the ongoing negotiations in Paris. American and North Vietnamese objectives were mutually exclusive, the conservatives argued, and any settlement would represent only an unacceptable political compromise.[65]

Administration officials and supporters expressed more optimism with the progress of Nixon's program. John Tower announced after arriving home from a ten-day visit to Vietnam that he felt the country's "current posture in Vietnam is the best it has been at any time since 1965." Tower, who visited Southeast Asia more than any other member of Congress during the war, returned convinced that Hanoi knew it could not win a military victory and continued to fight only in hopes of "prolonging the war in the apparent hope that the American people will weary of it and generate popular pressure on the President to accept a camouflaged surrender that would be advantageous" to the North Vietnamese.[66] At a press conference a few days later, Nixon suggested that progress had been made in Paris and that "the chances for peace in Southeast Asia have significantly improved since this administration came into office." He also asserted that the United States would not make unilateral troop withdrawals from Vietnam.[67]

Granting Nixon the benefit of the doubt, Donald Riegle urged Congress and the public to give the president "40 to 60 more days to turn the war around before he is pressed too hard for new actions." Riegle asserted that he believed that the administration was developing a blueprint for a de-Americanization of the war that would lead to significant troop withdrawals.[68] Jack Miller pleaded with his constituents to give the administration an opportunity "to give these talks every reasonable chance of succeeding." Nixon had inherited "an extremely bad situation," and it would be "most unrealistic to expect a dramatic change" so soon. The appropriate course of action according to Miller? Allow the president a chance to implement his Vietnamization program.[69] The nation would not have to wait that long for the administration to announce its plans.

On 14 May 1969, Nixon addressed the country on television to provide an update on the progress of the administration's efforts to resolve the war. H. R. "Bob" Haldeman, the White House chief of staff, noted in his diary the president's nervousness about the "Big Speech on Vietnam." Not only did Nixon work on the speech all day in the residence, but he worried about the smallest details, such as the light on the podium.[70] In his remarks, he publicly repudiated the "Manila formula"—offering to withdraw U.S. forces from South Vietnam six months after Hanoi withdrew—which had been worked out by LBJ. In its place, he offered the North Vietnamese simultaneous withdrawal to be followed by an exchange of prisoners-of-war and free elections in South Vietnam. He also intimated that the U.S. withdrawal would begin shortly, with or without an agreement. "The time is approaching," he stated, "when the South Vietnamese forces will be able to take over some of the fighting fronts now being manned by Americans." Yet the president was not entirely conciliatory, forcefully asserting, "Let me be quite blunt. Our fighting men are not going to be worn down; our mediators are not going to be talked down; and our allies are not going to be let down."[71]

Hanoi's response to the speech was entirely predictable. The North Vietnamese retorted that the administration's plan "is not to end the war but to replace the war of aggression fought by U.S. troops with a war of aggression fought by the puppet army of the United States." They rejected Nixon's proposal outright.[72] Their position was understandable. Why should they agree to reciprocal withdrawal when Nixon all but stated that the United States would be withdrawing its forces unilaterally in the near future regardless of any decisions made by the North Vietnamese? To accept the proposal would have represented an abandonment of the goals for which they had been fighting for three decades. Nixon, who believed that he had made a major concession, was furious with Hanoi's intractable position.

Domestic reaction to the speech was mixed. Wallace Bennett praised Nixon for seizing the initiative for peace and placing the burden to respond on Hanoi. The plan he presented was "creative," and Bennett strongly urged the American people to unite behind the president: "If we cannot get together on a mutual withdrawal and a negotiated settlement allowing a free choice in South Viet Nam, what hope do we have? . . . It is time to close ranks."[73] Representative John "Happy" Camp (R-OK) praised Nixon for his "wise course of action" and asserted that what the country needed was "the full support of the American people for the president's proposal." Camp "sincerely hope[d] that the time [had] come when we [could] show a little restraint—when the American people [could] withhold criticism. . . . We must provide [U.S. negotiators] with silence so essential to an honorable and peaceful conclusion of this war."[74] And the prevailing attitude within the party was summed up by Sherman Lloyd: "He has been in office less than five months. I believe we must unite behind him at this critical time. Give him a chance. Give him a little time."[75] Moreover, several

Republicans who had been consistently critical of American policy in Vietnam voiced their approval of Nixon's efforts to negotiate a settlement. The *Washington Evening Star* quoted Percy as expressing his "confidence that President Nixon is doing his utmost to bring the war to an end and to do it responsibly." In the same article, Barry Goldwater was quoted as deriding several Republicans and Democrats for undermining Nixon's position by advocating "peace at any cost."[76]

On NBC's "Today" the following morning, Tower and Frank Church appeared together to analyze Nixon's comments. Tower considered the president's offer to Hanoi to be "rational and generous . . . tempered with toughness." He reconfirmed the Republican willingness to stay in Vietnam until the country had achieved its minimum objectives. Church, predictably, expressed his disappointment in Nixon's lack of a fresh approach: "His statement last night was merely a restatement of the position that President Johnson had taken many times." Nixon, he observed, was "pouring the same old Johnson wine." Tower quickly retorted that he saw a striking difference between Nixon and Johnson. Under the Nixon plan, the United States would be willing to agree to a phased withdrawal of troops of both countries rather than forcing the North Vietnamese and NLF forces to leave South Vietnam prior to any American disengagement.[77] These would be the primary battle lines throughout much of Nixon's presidency—Republicans willing to give him the benefit of the doubt, Democrats seeking to make partisan gains at his expense.

Democrats like Church were not the only ones to find fault with Nixon's comments. When it became clear that there would be no immediate breakthrough in Paris and that Nixon's "comprehensive peace plan" fell on deaf ears in Hanoi, public approval of the administration's handling of the war dropped sharply, and the antiwar movement became more vocal. The breadth of the negative reaction to the speech demonstrated that Nixon's honeymoon on Vietnam had ended. According to his aides, the president sensed the "end of the easy going" and began gearing up to "deal with adversities, both internal and external, plus bad press coming up."[78] Media coverage of the speech ranged from neutral to negative, which depressed the president. If JFK had made the speech, he believed, "they would have been ecstatic." But perhaps the most pointed criticism came from Kissinger, who condescendingly complained that the speech had been "too complex with too many nuances that are totally unintelligible to the ordinary guy." In hindsight, he believed that Nixon should have presented the peace initiative as a diplomatic white paper and used the televised address to summarize the plan and give a brief, inspirational speech on the direction of the war.[79]

The president's sensitivity to the rising discontent over the war was illustrated in June. Ever the calculating politician, Nixon instructed Ehrlichman to invite Lyndon Johnson to the White House to celebrate his predecessor's birthday. The president carefully told his aide, however, not to make the occasion too big "because it will tie us too closely to [Johnson]." Even though he piously refused to label Vietnam as *LBJ's war* both prior to and during his presidency, Nixon carefully distanced himself from any perceived taint of the previous administration's failures despite the fact that his program for ending the war bore remarkable similarities to that implemented by Johnson in 1968. Ironically, the same memo asked Ehrlichman to invite Hubert Humphrey to the White House since he had expressed his support for Nixon's policies on Vietnam, a move that could have been taken directly out of LBJ's political playbook and reflected Nixon's efforts to maintain bipartisan support for his constantly evolving policies.[80]

Nixon would take the next step in formulating his deescalation strategy in June. Following a meeting with South Vietnamese president Nguyen Van Thieu on 8 June at Midway, Nixon announced that, with Thieu's assent, he had decided to "order the immediate redeployment from Vietnam of . . . 25,000 men," to be completed by the end of August. Nixon later admitted that Thieu, Gen. Creighton Abrams—the new U.S. commander in Vietnam—and the Joint Chiefs of Staff privately raised objections to the withdrawals prior to the announcement. In addition, Thieu later told a high-ranking American military official that "Nixon had told him that he had a mandate to withdraw the forces."[81] Although Abrams publicly supported Nixon's announcement, senior military officials privately expressed serious reservations about the withdrawals as it "became clear that the timing and pace were being decided in Washington on the basis of primarily domestic opinion requirements."[82] Yet Nixon had few real options. The contradictory tensions of American congressional and public opinion—"get out, but don't run out"—made the gradual disengagement from Vietnam virtually inevitable. Like Kennedy and Johnson before him, domestic political pressures forced Nixon to take the middle course between two unpalatable options, and, just like his predecessors, he fell victim to the Aesopian fallacy of trying to please everyone.

The president's decisions regarding the pace and structure of disengagement from the war did not sit well with Henry Kissinger. At a press conference on 19 June, Nixon gave what the national security adviser considered to be some "rather startling answers" to questions on the war. He announced that he hoped to beat Clark Clifford's goals on withdrawals of American troops from Vietnam, asserted that he was not "wedded" to the Thieu regime in Saigon, and said that he was not opposed to a cease-fire.[83] Kissinger reacted with great surprise. He believed that Nixon's comments meant the likely collapse of the Saigon government and that the president had decided to pull out of Vietnam. According to Haldeman, Kissinger had been "discouraged deeply" in mid-June because he felt that the administration's plans for Vietnam were not working out right. He complained that "Rogers and Laird are constantly pushing for faster and faster withdrawal," which he believed meant a "cop-out" in twelve months. If that were the policy, he argued, the administration might as well cop out now.[84] Other administration officials recognized the hazards of gradualism as well. U. Alexis Johnson, the undersecretary of state for political affairs, recalled that Rogers believed that a partial withdrawal of U.S. troops would check the rising domestic pressures for total withdrawal. Johnson disagreed, believing that "feeding the crocodiles" would "only whet their appetite."[85]

The news was not all bad for the president. Despite the consternation expressed by Democrats, conservatives, and the antiwar movement, Nixon's peace initiatives received substantial support from Republicans in Congress. Ross Adair, in a speech in the House, stated: "Although the Communists have either responded negatively or not at all . . . this is no reason to call for more concessions to Hanoi."[86] The Republican National Committee issued a report a few days later that echoed Adair's praise. Nixon, the report asserted, "has developed an effective strategy for peace. And the fruits of that strategy are already apparent. In Vietnam, the tide has finally been reversed." The question now, the statement claimed, was "no longer how fast our involvement in the war will escalate but rather how rapidly it will be contracted." The report noted that a Gallup poll from earlier in the month showed that 63 percent of those surveyed approved of Nixon's performance in office.[87]

Even the long-time critic of U.S. involvement in Vietnam John Sherman Cooper gave the administration credit for its efforts in early July. Rather than "default on the commitments of four Presidents" by taking the position that "we inherited the war," Nixon recognized his responsibility to bring it to a successful conclusion. In the six months he had been in office, Cooper continued, Nixon had made progress in putting forth "realistic, definitive proposals as a basis for negotiation" and beginning the Vietnamization of the conflict. The administration "wants to end this war. This means we must stay long enough to secure the self-determination for the people of South Vietnam." In 1969, the senator concluded, "Richard Nixon is fighting a battle to find an honorable solution to the war in Vietnam. I can assure you that Richard Nixon, like Eisenhower [in Korea], will win this battle."[88]

In his effort to win the peace in 1969, Nixon pursued contradictory policies of escalation and disengagement. A good example of this dual approach occurred in July. Following a high-level meeting on the presidential yacht *Sequoia* on 7 July, the administration changed the mission statement of the Military

1969: "You Can See Why We Had to Have Two White Houses"

Assistance Command in Vietnam from that of defeating the enemy and forcing the withdrawal of the North Vietnamese army from South Vietnam to one
of providing maximum assistance to Saigon, strengthening its armed forces,
bolstering pacification, and interdicting supplies to the enemy.[89] Meanwhile,
Nixon took the next step in his scheme to force the North Vietnamese to make
concessions at the bargaining table. In the wake of the bombing of Cambodia,
he issued a secret ultimatum to Ho Chi Minh: change your negotiating position
by 1 November, or face "measures of great consequence and force."[90]

Concurrently, White House aides began to sketch out the parameters of
Operation DUCK HOOK, a series of punishments directed at the North should
it fail to heed Nixon's ultimatum. Included among the proposed reprisals were
the mining of Haiphong harbor, the invasion of the North, and the bombing of
the network of dikes in North Vietnam to produce catastrophic flooding (all
measures long suggested by hawks). This carrot-and-stick strategy reflected
the faith that both Nixon and Kissinger had in the utility of combining force
and diplomacy. At the same time that Nixon made his overture to Ho Chi
Minh, he instructed Henry Kissinger to approach Nelson Rockefeller and ask
him to organize a group of prominent Americans to make a case against antiwar advocates. Nixon hoped that this group would blunt the desire to end,
rather than de-Americanize, the war. Nixon also asked the prominent conservatives William F. Buckley and Leo Cherne to organize an attack on the Student Mobilization Committee to End the War in Vietnam, using the specter of
a surrender to communism as red meat to gain the support of the conservative
movement.[91]

While the administration maneuvered behind the scenes, Republicans
continued to speak out publicly in support of Nixon's approach to settling the
war. Wallace Bennett chastised "advocates of a total unilateral withdrawal" for
doing a "disservice to the cause of peace by failing to support" the president's
efforts. He called on critics of the war to "rally behind the administration and
play a responsible role in convincing Hanoi that Washington and Saigon have
made significant peace efforts, and that the American people are united in their
determination to withhold any further concessions until there is a reciprocal
move by North Vietnam."[92] The following day, Gerald Ford spoke and asked
Americans "to rise in vocal and ardent support of President Nixon's strategy
for peace in Vietnam." Praising Nixon's accomplishments since (and prior to)
taking office, Ford assailed those critics of the administration who demanded
immediate, massive, and unilateral withdrawal of American forces from South
Vietnam. "It is time," he asserted, "to ask as with one voice: What is *Hanoi* doing
to bring about peace in Vietnam? What are *Hanoi's* initiatives for peace?"[93] As
Nixon had discovered, however, Hanoi remained committed to its long-stated

demands. It seemed that it would be up to the administration to take decisive action to break the stalemate.

By mid-July, Nixon confronted a situation in Vietnam not dissimilar from that faced by Lyndon Johnson during 1968. Most notable was the looming threat from the Right. The *National Review* stated unequivocally that Vietnam "is ineluctably Nixon's war." Had Nixon "bugged out fast" on taking office, its editors opined, "he could have avoided any identification with either the war or the defeat; he would have been seen merely as the liquidator of Lyndon Johnson's war. It is too late for that." Given that reality, if the war ended in "a defeat, a sellout," the president would be "politically kaput." He "would not have the slightest chance of re-election in 1972; little chance, probably of renomination . . . the broad Right—without the overwhelming support of which Nixon has no serious political base—would never forgive him." In essence, they concluded, "Nixon is lost unless South Vietnam is saved." This meant that Nixon "has got to make up his mind that this war can be won, and start winning it."[94] Incendiary statements to say the least. The strident rhetoric from conservatives dovetailed with the fear of a right-wing backlash that Nixon shared with Kennedy and Johnson and reinforced the potential domestic political threat he faced if he did not press for victory.

The political pressure that Nixon faced from both sides influenced the course of the negotiations. In his conversations with the chief North Vietnamese negotiator, Xuan Thuy, Kissinger made it clear that, if the North Vietnamese prolonged the conflict and "turned it into 'Mr. Nixon's War,'" it would work against them. If it became "Mr. Nixon's War," Kissinger asserted, then the president would have to win it. In essence, he put Hanoi on notice that "America's world position was at stake and the prospect of domestic instability resulting from two administrations in a row defeated by the war was impermissible."[95] Nixon could not afford to allow the war to interfere with either his broader foreign policy agenda or his political success at home, nor could he imperil his or America's credibility. Thus, any perception of ownership of the conflict had to be ruthlessly countered with actions that would reinforce his commitment to victory.

With Hanoi's intransigence, rumblings of congressional discontent, and fading approval ratings for his handling of the war, Nixon must have yearned for some good news. Thus, the third week in July must have seemed like Christmas. His reelection hopes were boosted in the wake of Teddy Kennedy's incident at Chappaquiddick.[96] Nixon had considered the young senator as a dangerous potential rival for 1972 but realized that the accident effectively eliminated another of the hated Kennedy clan as a political threat. The next day, Apollo 11 landed on the moon. The president, despite being criticized by the *New York Times* for engaging in "a publicity stunt of the type Khrushchev used to indulge in," appeared worldwide on television and spoke to the astronauts, Neil Armstrong and Edwin Aldrin.[97] Basking in the moment, he flew to the South Pacific to greet the astronauts as they splashed down. He then set off on a round-the-world trip, a "typical Nixon whirlwind extravaganza, complete with meetings with the various leaders, handshaking excursions into marketplaces, and state dinners."[98]

During the trip, Nixon stopped off at Guam. In an informal discussion with reporters, he announced a fundamental change in U.S. foreign policy. Expanding on his Vietnamization program, he unveiled what would become known as the Nixon Doctrine on 25 July 1969. To Kissinger's astonishment, he asserted that in Asia "as far as the problems of military defense, except for the threat of a major power involving nuclear weapons, . . . the United States is going to encourage and has a right to expect that this problem will be increasingly handled by . . . the Asian nations themselves." In essence, he asserted that the United States would expect client nations to handle more of the burden of internal security with their own troops, backed up with American military, political, advisory, and economic aid.[99] Although little more than a clarification of Vietnamization, this statement signaled the symbolic end to twenty-two years of interventionist foreign policy that dated to Truman's announcement that the United States would aid Greece and Turkey against Communist insurgents. The Nixon Doctrine served the president's purposes in relation to Vietnam admirably. It quickly became the fourth stated pillar of his policy in Indochina, alongside negotiations, Vietnamization, and troop withdrawals.[100]

While Nixon completed his international tour, Kissinger took a discrete trip to Paris, where the national security adviser began a series of secret meetings with the North Vietnamese. Nixon, employing a variant of the madman theory, wanted him to make very clear to Hanoi that North Vietnam faced a stark choice—make concessions at the negotiating table, or suffer the military consequences. Yet the North Vietnamese negotiators were no more susceptible to the American threats than Hanoi had been in May. Xuan Thuy pressed Kissinger to specify the timetable for American withdrawals and clarify the relative importance of the secret versus the official talks and presented a point-by-point critique of the American terms. The meeting ended with Kissinger's rejection of the North Vietnamese demands and an undefined proposal by Thuy to meet with Kissinger again.[101] In various formats, these back-channel talks would continue on and off for three years as Nixon and Kissinger indulged in their propensity for secrecy. Unfortunately, they also had the effect of "completely downgrading all the work being done in Paris" by the official negotiating team. Lodge, uninformed and uninstructed, served merely as a figurehead while the substantive discussions took place behind closed doors elsewhere. It was not surprising, then, that Lodge resigned in November, and his successors, although equally senior, were not more than tokens themselves.[102] Alexis Johnson was one of the many members of the State Department kept out of the loop about these negotiations, a fact that he did not resent because, as he later said, "I would have had little to contribute in any case, because decisions were being made on domestic political grounds rather than the actual situation in Vietnam."[103]

Although neither the official nor the secret negotiations made any substantive progress, Nixon pressed forward with Vietnamization. He realized the popularity of the idea of troop withdrawals and an honorable peace in Vietnam with a war-weary nation and Congress. Jacob Javits, who had criticized him earlier in the year, praised the administration for "effecting a number of constructive and realistic changes in the Vietnam policy it inherited from the previous Administration." Nevertheless, he gently chided the president for "playing down the sharpness of difference between the policy innovations in Vietnam policy it has introduced and those of its predecessor." Javits considered the contrast between LBJ and Nixon to be significant: "The Nixon Administration's Vietnam policy has been much better than the rhetoric it has used to express it."[104]

But the policy of gradual disengagement was not pursued in a vacuum. Not only did Nixon selectively escalate the war in an effort to force Hanoi into concessions, but the administration also used the Vietnamization process as a weapon in the U.S. negotiating arsenal. Unfortunately for Nixon and Kissinger, manipulating the withdrawals as a means of diplomatic leverage represented a potentially dangerous public relations problem. As Kissinger noted in a 10 September memo to the president, troop withdrawals "will become like salted peanuts to the American public; the more troops come home, the more will be demanded." Nixon had to walk a fine line between withdrawing too quickly to pacify domestic sentiment and too slowly to maintain pressure on the North Vietnamese. In his memoirs, Kissinger made this same point. In recalling conversations with administration officials in September 1969, he wrote that he discussed the fact that Nixon was not willing to "capitulate" but had "lost confidence" in the current strategy of walking a fine line "between withdrawing too fast to convince Hanoi of our determination and withdrawing too slowly to satisfy the American public." The president needed a "military plan designed for maximum impact on the enemy's military capability" in order to "force a rapid conclusion to the war."[105]

The beginning of September brought fundamental changes to the status quo. Ho Chi Minh died on 4 September, and, while doves urged Nixon to declare a cease-fire, he refused. Indeed, he was considering a major escalation of the conflict. With Ho Chi Minh off the stage, Nixon believed he had an opportunity to push the North Vietnamese harder and force a settlement on terms favorable to the United States. Less than a week later, the longtime GOP Senate minority leader Everett Dirksen also passed away. His replacement, Hugh Scott, was selected largely on the strength of support of the growing cohort of Republican liberals in the Senate. Yet Scott generally supported Nixon's foreign policy initiatives, backed the president's handling of the Vietnam issue, and, most important, shared Nixon's concern about the growing influence of the party's right wing. An original hawk on the war who had supported Johnson's escalation in 1965, he considered Vietnamization to be a "viable option" and demonstrated a keen loyalty to Nixon in the Senate throughout the conflict.[106] As important as Dirksen's support in the Senate had been, Scott's presence there provided the president with an important ally to help keep potentially wayward Republicans in line. This would be important given the decisions that would be made in the next two months.

On 12 September 1969, Nixon and his advisers met for a critical discussion on the war. The principals from the National Security Council (NSC) as well as U.S. Ambassador to South Vietnam Ellsworth Bunker and the military commanders met to consider the plan for the next phase of troop withdrawals. Kissinger argued that the administration needed "a plan to end the war, not only to withdraw troops." He urged that one more effort be made to appeal to the new leadership in Hanoi; if that failed, he recommended implementing the DUCK HOOK strikes on 1 November. Nixon was tempted by the suggestion, but the forces advocating deescalation were also powerful. While there had been a lull in the protests against the war in the summer, the signs of a resumption of major antiwar activity were widespread. Laird warned Nixon, "I believe this may be an illusory phenomenon. The actual and potential antipathy for the war is, in my judgment, significant and increasing."[107]

Meanwhile, domestic political problems continued to plague the administration. In addition to an effort to repeal the Tonkin Gulf resolution by Donald Riegle and Pete McCloskey, the White House picked up signals that critics were seeking to set a timetable for withdrawal of U.S. forces by 1970. Either move, according to Gen. Alexander Haig, an aide to Nixon and Kissinger, would be "counter-productive to the progress that the President is attempting to achieve on the battlefield, in Paris and in the orderly implementation of the 'Vietnamization' program" and would "exacerbate what have been surprisingly smooth Congressional attitudes on Vietnam since the May 14 speech." Haig urged Kissinger to meet with the disaffected GOP congressmen, emphasize the progress that had been achieved, and "make it clear that the President's program could be severely disrupted by the kind of emotional debate that the Tonkin or timetable proposal would surely generate."[108]

The president found himself in the midst of a dilemma. Although increasing the pace of deescalation ran counter to his preferences, he determined that escalation involved too many risks given the rising tide of opposition. As a result, four days after the NSC meeting, he announced an additional troop withdrawal of thirty-five thousand (bringing the total to sixty thousand) by December 15. The decision represented a move designed to appease the American public and to undercut the call from antiwar activists for a Vietnam War Moratorium on 15 October, which had prompted several congressional doves to start speaking out against the administration again. Nixon also gave an overview of what his administration had done to bring the war to a conclusion during his first eight months in office, asserting, "The time for meaningful negotiations has therefore arrived . . . the time has come to end this war."[109] Three days later, he stated that, because of the revised schedule of troop withdrawals, draft calls for November and December had been canceled and announced the first draft lottery for 1 December. Nixon later claimed that his withdrawal statement "was intended to let the new leaders of North Vietnam know that I was not assuming they were bound by Ho's reply to my letter" earlier in the month.[110] While that may have been part of the justification, domestic political considerations clearly dominated Nixon's decisionmaking process. In the wake of the announcement, the president addressed the UN General Assembly in New York. He told the delegates that his administration had taken "every reasonable step" to end the war in Vietnam. But he made it clear that the United States would not accept "a settlement that would arbitrarily dictate the political future of South Vietnam." Toward this end, he implored the members of the United Nations to "use [their] best diplomatic efforts to persuade Hanoi to move seriously into the negotiations which could end this war."[111]

But the president's public campaign for a resolution to the war remained at odds with his clandestine plan to escalate the war in the event of continued North Vietnamese intransigence. Nixon realized that, if he had to implement the military option, he would desperately need the full backing of his party to counter the outcry sure to erupt from the antiwar forces. Thus, on 30 September, he met with the joint GOP congressional leadership at Camp David. Using more bellicose rhetoric than he did in public, he made oblique references to the imminent DUCK HOOK operation, telling his fellow Republicans, "We are going to need unity more than we ever needed it before. I can't tell you everything that will be going on. . . . All I can tell you is this: I am doing my damnedest to end the war." Later during the meetings, Nixon let out the DUCK HOOK secret and told the legislators that he was considering blockading Haiphong and invading North Vietnam.[112] He also pointed out that Hanoi "misjudges two things": the time, since he still had three years and three months left in his term, and the man, since he had always maintained that he would not be the first president to lose a war. He concluded by saying that "our only hope for negotiation is to convince Hanoi we are ready to stay with it" and assured his Republican colleagues that the war would be over by the midterm elections.[113] Nixon's reassurances were not an insignificant factor given the electoral concerns many Republicans had in the face of the continuing conflict.

For the time being, the administration continued to vigorously prosecute the war. But, while Nixon and Kissinger were ready to "stay with it" in Vietnam, a large proportion of the rest of the country felt much differently. Protests against the war continued throughout 1969, and many Democrats intended to turn the tables on Nixon and the GOP and politicize Vietnam. Yet one of the leading Democratic critics of the war, Frank Church, categorically refused to "take part in any move designed to convert legitimate protest of the war in Vietnam into a partisan issue." Church noted with remarkable candor that it was "plainly too soon for Democrats to use Vietnam as a legitimate issue against the Republican Administration. After all, Democrats in the White House led this country into Vietnam." If Nixon did not extricate the country from the war, however, "it may become his war, but it isn't Nixon's war yet." The following day, Cooper commended Church for his remarks, noting, "You are, of course, in an unassailable position because your opposition to this conflict goes well back into the administration of a Democratic President."[114] Paul Fannin agreed with Church, complaining about critics "who will have given the President only eight months to undo what has been done in eight years."[115]

But, by the late fall of Nixon's first year in office, even some members of the GOP began to get restless at the slow pace of progress under his program. Clifford Case urged a more definitive timetable for American withdrawal from South Vietnam, arguing that, unless Saigon faced a specific deadline, "it will never make itself into a regime which commands the support of its own people or build a military force capable of its own defense, and we shall be locked into our present position indefinitely."[116] Nixon remained adamant about winning the peace. As he told Stewart Alsop in an interview at the White House on 2 October, "I can tell you we're not going to be defeated in Vietnam as long as I'm here." He also reiterated that he would not accept an American humiliation.[117] Nevertheless, the administration remained keenly aware of the need to reach out to its critics to blunt their effectiveness. Thus, Kissinger suggested to Nixon that they select critics of U.S. policy in Vietnam to visit the country "in the hope that their views would change and they would subsequently prove influential in helping sustain the support needed by the Administration." Of course, Kissinger wanted to ensure that the decision on whom to send to Vietnam would not backfire on the administration. "There is a danger," he warned, "that the critic, rather than opting for U.S. policy, would be confirmed in his opposition, and subsequently say so. . . . [This] should only make us more cautious in the selection process."[118] This was another tactic borrowed from the Johnson handbook, reflecting yet again the similarities of the dilemma both presidents faced in Vietnam.

By October, the president sensed that his options were limited. He believed that, without implementing DUCK HOOK, he could not end the war as quickly as he wanted, but he was also convinced that, if he authorized the strikes, he could not "hold the government and the people together" for the three to six months required for those strikes to work.[119] On 8 October, he told Haldeman that, although they had "bought" nine months, they could not expect to get any more time to deal with the war. Having kept the doves "at bay," the administration would now have to "take them on"—first with Agnew taking on the antiwar movement and the press and then with Nixon himself going on the attack. The problem, Haldeman and Nixon agreed, was that "this does make it [Nixon's] war."[120] After several more days of considering the alternatives, the president finally came to a conclusion. He rejected the "cop-out" option of precipitous withdrawal and abandoned the DUCK HOOK scheme, at least for the time being. Instead, he chose to ride out the Moratorium—Nixon felt that it "undercut the credibility of the ultimatum" he had sent Ho in July[121]—and then make a speech to the American people in which he explained his policies and asked for their support. Nixon and his advisers hoped that the anticipation generated by the announcement of the president's upcoming address would divert public attention from the protesters' message, keep the antiwar movement at bay, cause Hanoi to wonder what Nixon would do, and allow Nixon to withhold public comment until the night of the speech.[122] The strategy of postponement reared its head again as it had for Kennedy and Johnson during their presidencies and Nixon during the 1968 presidential race.

In a show of solidarity with the president's decisions, and to counter the appeal of the Moratorium, the House Republican Conference passed a resolution commending "Nixon's actions in reversing the course of the Vietnam War and expressing confidence in his efforts 'to end the war at the earliest practicable date. . . . Nixon has clearly demonstrated his desire for peace.'"[123] Republicans around the country concurred. Ronald Reagan spoke forcefully against the Moratorium, asserting that the administration, "entrusted with the awesome responsibility of the leadership of our nation" "deserve[d] not only our support, but our rejection of those in our midst who would arrogantly kibitz in a game where they haven't even seen the cards with which the game is played." He also derided those who tried to label Vietnam *Nixon's war* after eight years of Democratic control of policy, particularly since the president "has kept the door open in a hope for peace."[124] In fact, despite tepid support from GOP doves, in the end only two Republican senators formally endorsed the Moratorium—Mark Hatfield and Charles Goodell (R-NY).[125] Once again, the permissive attitude of Congress ceded the initiative to the administration.

Fortunately for Nixon, the strategy worked. When the Moratorium arrived in Washington and around the country, there were the typical suspensions of business as usual, teach-ins, memorial services, and other nonviolent actions. Yet the demonstration did not live up to the expectations of its organizers or meet the fears of the White House, in part because Agnew's attacks on the media helped reduce the coverage of the event. The demonstrations reminded the president of the need to "clearly state the case" in his November speech in order to "buy us another couple of months," but they did not change his underlying feelings about the antiwar movement.[126] His attitude is typified in a response to a letter from a Georgetown University student, Randy J. Dicks. Nixon made a distinction between listening to public opinion and being swayed by public demonstrations. "To abandon that policy merely because of a public demonstration," he told Dicks, "would therefore be an act of gross irresponsibility on my part." He then went on to remind him that "the road to peace . . . is not simple."[127]

Of course, Agnew's indictment of the leaders of the Moratorium as "hardcore dissidents and professional anarchists" rubbed many the wrong way. Hugh Scott called for an end to "name calling and accusations" in the Vietnam debate. Some saw this as a conscious administration strategy—"keeping the President on the high road, calmly, judiciously seeking public support for U.S. policy, while letting the Vice President travel the low road, dropping provocative epithets along the way as a sop to the more hot-headed crowd."[128] That did not stop Nixon from exerting influence to nip intraparty dissent in the bud. At one point in late October, for example, he ordered Bryce Harlow and Kissinger to "take [Hugh] Scott into the woodshed and make sure he stops his talk on [a unilateral] cease-fire."[129]

As he prepared to give the crucial speech in the face of significant public opposition to the war, Nixon retained the support of most Republicans in Congress. George Aiken backed the president, claiming that his withdrawal policy was "much like my suggestion of three years ago that we declare a victory and start bringing the troops home."[130] Yet some members of the GOP wavered in their willingness to grant the administration the benefit of the doubt owing to the slow progress of Vietnamization. Margaret Chase Smith, a longtime supporter of the war, complained that she had "no idea what Nixon's Vietnam plan is and that Nixon has asked the Republican leadership to take him on faith."[131] But the president maintained the support of the American people. A poll taken the day after the Moratorium showed that 68 percent of the respondents approved of Nixon's handling of the war.[132] Whether the president retained that support would depend largely on the response to his 3 November address. Moreover, conservative unrest lingered. While the *National Review* had backed away somewhat from the inflammatory comments made in July—admitting that the administration "appears to be pursuing a reasonable course"—its editors still pushed Nixon to present a plan on 3 November to "prevent the disaster of a Communist takeover." Failure to do so, they argued, would bring about "American defeat and international calamity."[133]

Nixon met with the GOP congressional leadership on 28 October to preview his remarks and enlist their support for the public relations offensive being prepared for the following week. The previous day, Bryce Harlow had suggested that the leadership needed to be positioned to "inform the public that a deliberate campaign is being conducted by peaceniks and doves to demand such extreme actions as a ceasefire and massive troop withdrawals in order to make your address appear inadequate." Harlow wanted the president to encourage the leadership, particularly Hugh Scott and Gerald Ford, to emphasize this theme when talking with the press after the White House meeting.[134] Nixon came away from the meeting reassured that Scott, Ford, and the rest of the Republican hierarchy would spin the speech in his favor.

The planning for the speech reflected the president's command of political maneuvering and sensitivity to the vagaries of American opinion. Nixon instructed Haldeman to assign a "strike force" to monitor the television networks, the *New York Times,* the *Washington Post, Time,* and *Newsweek,* directing it to counterattack if media coverage of the speech was negative. In addition, he told Haldeman to continue to solicit favorable statements from members of Congress. In this respect, he was sensitive to egos and protocol. "The calls to Reagan and Rockefeller should be made by Kissinger," while the other governors and congressmen "should be divided up among our best VIP types and calls made by those who have the greatest influence with them." He also suggested that a petition be circulated after the speech declaring congressional support for the administration. Again, domestic political considerations factored prominently. The president told Haldeman not to use a staunch supporter like John Tower to initiate the petition. Instead, he wanted to "bring in a fellow like Findley" in order for the administration to secure "the broadest possible support." Such a petition would "accomplish the objective of a resolution by the House and Senate supporting the President—an aim we do not want to take on frontally due to the fact that we would have to have extended hearings and we would lose our impact."[135] Lyndon Johnson had very little on Richard Nixon when it came to Machiavellian machinations.

Nixon claimed that his nationally televised address, originally scheduled to announce the initiation of DUCK HOOK but now titled "The Pursuit of Peace," was the most important of his presidency and, potentially, his political legacy. His preparations certainly reflected that sentiment; he worked through twelve drafts of the speech over a three-week period beginning the night of the Moratorium. William Safire offered to assist Nixon in drafting his remarks and "found that the President was treating this with the seriousness of an Inaugural or an acceptance address, doing it all himself."[136] But what would he actually say? Speculation ran rampant across the country. Most commentators agreed that the president would announce new troop withdrawals or propose a cease-fire. Given the nature of these predictions, it should not be surprising that criticism of the administration decreased dramatically in the days immediately preceding the speech. Haldeman noted in his diary that the "liberals have (very cleverly) shifted ground away from blasting P [Nixon] to saying they're with him." As a result, hopes for a major breakthrough percolated across the country despite the fact that administration officials knew that "there [wouldn't] be one" and that "the letdown [would] be tremendous." The White House tried to "squelch specific speculation" like Hugh Scott's call for a unilateral cease-fire, but these efforts were unsuccessful. Moreover, such conjecture "delighted Nixon, who loved to surprise and confound the experts."[137]

Melvin Laird believed that the speech should focus on Vietnamization, stressing, "We have a program; and we are moving." But the secretary of defense also urged the president to place the program within the larger context of the Nixon Doctrine. According to Laird, he told the president: "Properly understood . . . your policy in Vietnam is much more than an attempt to extricate America from more bloodshed on the battlefields of Vietnam. It is a major and essential foundation stone of your Asian doctrine for the 1970s and beyond." If Nixon made the connection, Laird continued, it could be "the most persuasive argument against precipitate withdrawal on a fixed timetable" that the administration could make and would help educate the public about the broader foreign policy goals Vietnamization served.[138]

Sitting behind his Oval Office desk on 3 November 1969, Richard Nixon spoke to the nation about the war in Vietnam. He began his comments by saying, "There were some who [when he took office] urged that I end the war at once by ordering the immediate withdrawal of all American forces." He stated that he did not choose that option, even though it would have allowed him to blame LBJ for the defeat and portray himself as the peacemaker. After reviewing the origins of the war, he stated the case for the continued importance of American involvement in South Vietnam. Losing in Vietnam, he argued, "would result in a collapse of confidence in American leadership, not only in

Asia but throughout the world." Precipitate withdrawal would be a "disaster of immense magnitude" that would not bring peace but rather would "bring more war."[139]

Nixon then turned to the steps the administration had taken to bring about a real peace, emphasizing U.S. flexibility: "Anything is negotiable except the right of the people of South Vietnam to determine their own future." He placed the blame for the failure to reach a settlement squarely at the feet of the Hanoi regime, which had refused to show even "the least willingness to join us in seeking a just peace." While he did not hold out much hope for negotiations, the president believed that his Vietnamization program could bring about peace. He did reserve the right, however, "to take strong and effective measures" in the event of increased American casualties:"This is not a threat. This is a statement of policy." The country did not understand the importance of this qualification immediately. While he pointedly told the protesters that he wanted peace as much as they did, Nixon called on the "great silent majority of my fellow Americans" to be "united for peace . . . united against defeat" and to understand that "North Vietnam cannot defeat or humiliate the United States. Only Americans can do that."[140]

In his memoirs, Nixon, with characteristic hyperbole, claimed that the televised address was one of the few speeches to "actually influence the course of history."[141] In reality, all the president's comments accomplished was to announce that he was going to continue his policies of the previous nine months; his "Checkers" speech two decades earlier had far more significance in the big picture. Robert Dallek contends that the speech "demonstrated that Nixon spoke like a hawk but was acting like a dove." As a result, the administration "gained no significant ground with either group. [The president's] tough language raised doubts among peace advocates that he would follow through on stated intentions to end the war, while Vietnamization convinced proponents of more aggressive military action that Nixon was pursuing a policy more attuned to a war-weary public than to a winning strategy."[142]

Nevertheless, the speech received widespread praise from the public. The White House received over eighty thousand telegrams and letters in favor of the address. In addition, over three hundred representatives and fifty-eight senators expressed their support for the president's remarks, and a Gallup poll recorded a 68 percent approval rating for Nixon. As the journalist Seymour Hersh noted, "The public seemed to believe that Vietnamization would end the war."[143] It helped that, after the first six months of bloody fighting in 1969, casualty figures had begun to decline, troops were being recalled to the United States, the peace talks showed some progress, and the public seemed confident in Nixon's plan to end the war.

The political and media reaction to the speech differed markedly, however. Joseph Alsop called the speech "one of the most successful technical feats of political leadership in many, many years," although he was much more charitable than his fellow journalists.[144] James Reston of the *New York Times,* whose comments were more typical of the media commentary, wrote that the speech would "merely divide and polarize the debaters in the United States, without bringing the enemy into serious negotiations."[145] Reston's column infuriated the president but did not reflect the sentiments of his readers. In response to what Nixon and his advisers perceived as negative media coverage of the speech, the administration's private pollster David Derge found that 63 percent of respondents agreed with the president's views on Vietnam while only 15 percent concurred with the commentators.[146] Another Gallup poll revealed an even stronger reaction; Nixon's approval ratings on Vietnam jumped from 58 to 77 percent, while his negative ratings plunged from 32 to a mere 6 percent. Three weeks later, Gallup found that 74 percent of Americans opposed an immediate total withdrawal from Vietnam.[147] Nixon was pleased at the feedback because "he succeeded in moving people to action without demagoging."[148] The survey results served to reinforce both Nixon's belief in the "great silent majority" of American citizens and his loathing of the media.

With his astute political mind and fervent need for popular approval, Nixon was not willing to let his remarks speak for themselves. The morning following the speech, he instructed Laird and Rogers to maintain "tight discipline throughout the Administration." Department spokesmen were instructed to "refrain from giving the impression that we are considering making any additional negotiating concessions in Paris or elsewhere" and ordered not to speculate on the issue of troop withdrawals. Nixon stressed to Laird the importance of standing firm on the point that "we have a plan but that we are not going to disclose it." Administration surrogates were told to focus on the fact that "progress under [the plan] has substantially exceeded our expectations" and that "flexibility in our withdrawal program is essential to its success." If these goals could be accomplished, Nixon concluded, "I feel that calm reasoned confidence following my speech can have a tremendous effect on building on what now appears to be a solid base of public support."[149]

The administration's spin machine worked tirelessly to underscore Nixon's speech. Bryce Harlow, appearing on "Issues and Answers" the following Sunday, stated, "I think that the country is largely behind what he said and I would hope that . . . this could help diminish the resistance to the President's effort for peace. . . . I do not believe that the 'silent majority' is going to leave their commander in chief on this issue."[150] Sherman Lloyd urged students at the University of Utah to give Nixon the chance to "unwind this war in a way that will allow him to withdraw American fighting men without leaving South Vietnam defense-less."[151] Daniel Evans pointed to the heartening tone of Nixon's remarks, noting that the withdrawal timetable was "more optimistic than it was in June."[152] One of the most interesting comments was made by Edward Brooke. With all the re-action to the speech, Brooke believed that the most important aspect had been overlooked, "the fundamental commitment which the President made . . . [to] the removal of all American combat troops from Vietnam as soon as possible. . . . President Nixon has turned the war around."[153] Other statements of support for Nixon's speech poured in from Republicans across the country, virtually all sounding these same themes. Response from the GOP was overwhelmingly positive. Idaho's Len Jordan wrote that Nixon had "given the American people new hope and a new direction."[154] House Republicans even sponsored a resolu-tion of support for Nixon's efforts to achieve "a just peace in Vietnam."[155]

John Tower also praised the address, stating that it "reflected confidence in our ability to control the situation in Vietnam." Tower saw Nixon's comments as "a sign to Hanoi that we are not going to bug out."[156] Meanwhile, Wallace Bennett cosponsored a resolution in support of the president's efforts. In dis-cussing the measure, Bennett asserted, "We seek to represent what we feel are the wishes of a great majority of Americans through supporting the President's efforts toward this goal." In contrast, he chastised those who sought to intimi-date the administration into drastic measures and concessions to Hanoi. What both groups had in common, he pointed out, was that each wanted to end the fighting in Vietnam War. The difference was the methods each side would ac-cept.[157] The bipartisan resolution demonstrated the support that Nixon enjoyed. Cosponsored by Mansfield, Scott, Hatfield, Tower, and Percy (among others), it read in part, "*Resolved,* That the Senate affirms its support for the President in his efforts to negotiate a just peace in Vietnam."[158] In essence, the president had succeeded in neutralizing the opposition and galvanizing a national major-ity behind his policy of slow, deliberate withdrawal. Even Nixon's critics had to admit that he scored a significant public relations victory with the address.

Indeed, Nixon's speech nullified the strength of the antiwar forces. Politi-cally sensitive dissenters backed off from criticizing the administration. Op-ponents of the war in Congress pressed Nixon on the pace of withdrawal but joined with the vast majority of their colleagues in endorsing his approach. Wil-liam Fulbright even postponed hearings on Charles Goodell's proposed "Viet-nam Disengagement Act" in order to avoid controversy. The fact that Nixon had turned popular opinion around so quickly and decisively stunned liberal critics. One antiwar organizer lamented that it was "inconceivable" that the president had "totally erased" the power and promise of the October Moratorium with a short television speech. Fundamentally, Nixon succeeded in giving a specific political focus to the national anxiety over Vietnam, a fact that helped him marginalize his opponents.[159] The great irony of these results, of course, was that his disdain for public opinion actually worked in his favor in this instance.

In the weeks that followed, Nixon acted to build on his successful address. Exactly one year after he had defeated Hubert Humphrey in the 1968 election, he told a television audience, "We have a plan now that will end the war, and end it in a way that we think will contribute to the cause of a just and lasting peace."[160] Laird told the Senate Foreign Relations Committee that Vietnamization offered "the best alternative to a negotiated settlement" and had "the best chance of minimizing U.S. casualties while resolving the war in the shortest possible time without abandoning our basic objective." Ultimately, Vietnamization provided "a practical middle course between isolationism and the role of world policeman."[161] On 24 November 1969, the president explained why the United States could not withdraw precipitously from Vietnam. "A nation cannot remain great if it betrays its allies and lets down its friends," he argued. "Our defeat and humiliation in South Viet-Nam without question would promote recklessness in the councils of those great powers who have not yet abandoned their goals of world conquest." Disengagement notwithstanding, Nixon concluded, the United States would keep its commitments and fulfill its international responsibilities.[162]

As well as events unfolded for Nixon in the aftermath of the speech, he continued to instruct his staff to keep a close watch on support. In the space of several hours on 24 November, for example, the president sent three separate memos to Bob Haldeman with detailed instructions and questions about the public and congressional reaction to the speech. He told Haldeman to "get the political group together (particularly Morton, Tower and Wilson) and see that they take a positive line on all scores." The goal was to "change the attitude of the Congress and also of the party leadership which has been too much one of telling us that we have to do things to please them and to win them rather than their coming to us asking how they can help us. Now is the time to strike on this issue while the iron is hot."[163] A few hours later, he focused on how to frame his own success, suggesting, "We should keep going back to the 'come-back theme.' No one has been written off more than RN. . . . Point out RN's resiliency." He also asked Haldeman (in the third person) to emphasize "Nixon's" effectiveness in using television in order to "keep our critics in the press and in TV off-balance."[164] Never satisfied, Nixon continuously sought to increase his approval ratings so that he could demonstrate a strong level of support for whatever actions he decided to take to resolve the conflict.

By the end of Nixon's first year in office, his efforts seemed to be working, in terms of both disengagement from the conflict and acceptance by the public and most of Congress. Perhaps the best indication of how successful his efforts at selling his Vietnamization program to the country was the reaction of the *National Review* at the end of December. It praised Nixon's "virtuoso performance on the homefront," noting the "remarkable fact that this President, a man with little discernable charisma, who was elected by only the narrowest of margins, has been able to mobilize public opinion behind his Vietnam strategy and almost completely quash the virulent 'peace movement.'" Clearly, Nixon's political acumen had trumped that of the Senate doves and the antiwar forces across the country, and that was enough for conservatives to temporarily forgive him for his other transgressions.[165]

After a year in office, Nixon had finally given the "secret plan" form and substance. Yet it would be another three years before the Paris peace agreement was finally concluded as implementing Vietnamization proved to be a much more formidable task than manipulating American opinion. In the interim, the United States would remain engaged in Vietnam, and Nixon would approve the devastating aerial bombardment of North Vietnam and sanction an illegal invasion of Cambodia. Additionally, nearly as many U.S. soldiers would be killed in Southeast Asia during the Vietnamization of the war as had died during the previous two decades of American involvement. While the nature of American commitment would change, the United States remained firmly dedicated to winning the peace under Nixon. But the strategy of gradual disengagement also meant that the war that had been widely considered to be "Lyndon Johnson's war" now, rightly or wrongly, became associated with the Nixon administration.

The commitment to Vietnamization led to additional troop withdrawals at the end of 1969. On 15 December, Nixon announced that 50,000 Americans would be out of Vietnam by the following April, bringing the total number of troops recalled to 115,000. He had considered a more substantial figure but decided to wait until spring in order to "make a dramatic public relations announcement of 150,000" between the fall of 1970 and the spring of 1971. The trick would be to strike a balance between pleasing the public and not making the withdrawals "so significant that they would undermine Vietnamization or deny the administration leverage in negotiations with Hanoi." This, as Kissinger observed, was the "basic dilemma" that the president faced as the war dragged on into 1970.[166]

Like Icarus, Richard Nixon dealt with crucial restraints in his efforts to resolve the Vietnam conflict. He could not move too quickly with Vietnamization or withdraw too many U.S. forces lest he lose leverage with Hanoi and face stinging criticism from the Right. But he also had to ensure that he did not proceed too slowly or take additional military measures that might escalate the conflict, or the antiwar forces in Congress and the country would pounce. When he flew too close to the sun—as in the case of the Cambodian incursion the following spring—the wax on his wings began to melt, forcing him to pull back to avoid crashing into the sea. This domestic political reality meant that, by the end of his first year in office, Nixon had taken only incremental steps toward an end to the war, a conflict that, at the beginning of his term, he had predicted would be over by the midterm elections. It remained to be seen whether he could tweak the Vietnamization strategy enough to allow that to occur.

# CHAPTER 8

# Whither Ariadne?

## Domestic Politics and Nixon's Search for Peace

And if we surrender, then all our hope is lost at once, whereas, so long as we remain in action, there is still a hope that we may yet stand upright.
— Thucydides, *History of the Peloponnesian War*

There are two things that will always be very difficult for a democratic nation: to start a war and to end it.
— Alexis de Tocqueville, *Democracy in America*

The pursuit of "peace with honor" proved frustrating for the Nixon administration. Why? Part of the answer is that, until the very end of the war, neither side had much incentive to negotiate. Both Washington and Hanoi believed that the other would fold under pressure if the right leverage was applied. But a more fundamental reason is that Nixon simply lacked a blueprint for departure. What he needed was his own Ariadne, a guide to assist his administration in extricating the United States from Vietnam. In the story of Theseus, the hero volunteered to slay the Minotaur in the labyrinth created by the master craftsman Daedalus. Ariadne, Daedalus's daughter, who had fallen in love with Theseus, taught him the way to reach the center of the maze, where the half-man, half-bull lived. She also gave him a ball of string that would help him escape after completing his task. Without the thread, Theseus would have been doomed to wander the labyrinth forever—or until he randomly stumbled on the right sequence of decisions that would lead him to the exit. This chapter will analyze how the Nixon administration did just that, taking multiple steps and missteps in an effort to end the war, all while facing keen domestic pressure from all sides and a new international system largely of Nixon's own making.

The new year did not get off to a very good start for the president. Hoping to keep the pace of withdrawals unpredictable in order to avoid undermining the U.S. negotiating position, Nixon and Kissinger were shocked when William Rogers announced in mid-January 1970 that the withdrawal plan was irrevocable. Of course, Rogers was absolutely correct; there would be no way for the administration to reverse the process of Vietnamization without incurring grave and unwanted domestic political damage. But Nixon recalled in his memoirs, "As 1970 began, I felt that we had to think about initiatives we could undertake to show the enemy that we were still serious about our commitment in Vietnam." He told Laird that "we must play a tough game" in order to achieve the kind of settlement that would allow Nixon to reach an "honorable peace"—not to mention "wage a successful presidential campaign in 1972."[1] That meant that Nixon did not want to have his options limited by Rogers or anyone else; if stopping or reversing the withdrawals (or even threatening to do so) was called for, he wanted the flexibility to carry out the threat lest the madman theory be completely discredited.

So Nixon did what he did best: he went on the offensive. The State of the Union address on 22 January 1970 provided him an opportunity to sell his Vietnamization policy and trumpet the success of his presidency thus far. He did so in broad terms. Stating unequivocally that the "major goal of our foreign policy is to bring an end to the war in Vietnam," he emphasized that the administration was "making progress toward that goal. The prospects for peace are far greater today than they were a year ago." He gave credit to Congress for allowing him time to implement his strategy "despite their differences on the conduct of the war." But he did not get into specifics and did not announce any additional troop withdrawals; instead, he promised a more detailed report on the trajectory of Vietnamization in a later speech. In fact, the bulk of the speech focused on domestic priorities such as inflation, crime, and pollution.[2]

Pete McCloskey challenged Nixon's claim about the success of Vietnamization shortly after the California congressman visited Vietnam again in February 1970. What he saw during his week there demolished any remaining hope he had for Nixon's policy. On his return, he told Lou Cannon, "I have real reservations that this policy is anything but a war crime. . . . To me what we are doing in Vietnam is an immoral thing." Whereas, before the trip, McCloskey focused on the failures of U.S. policy from a political, military, and diplomatic perspective, his critique of the commitment in Southeast Asia took on a decidedly moralistic tone after early 1970 (although he did not completely abandon these other avenues of attack). In this, his rhetoric paralleled that of Mark Hatfield, whose religious convictions informed his ongoing critique of U.S. involvement in the war. From this point forward, McCloskey recommitted himself to do "everything in his power to end" the conflict in Vietnam.[3]

Nixon had the same goal but was unwilling to compromise his desire for victory to achieve it. But comments like McCloskey's reminded him of the importance of suppressing dissent and maximizing support within the party. In early March, the president instructed Haldeman to convince the administration's supporters in Congress to fight an ongoing effort to repeal the Tonkin Gulf resolution vigorously, pointing out that "it is completely irrelevant" and that "we have not and will not commit American forces without going to the Congress." In addition, he continued, the passage of a resolution ending the grant of authority for the war might be "detrimental" to U.S. foreign policy beyond Vietnam. He made it clear that he did not want Senator Charles Mathias (R-MD), the motive force behind this iteration of the repeal proposal, "to get credit which he does not deserve."[4] Nixon had confidence in his strategy because the administration retained significant GOP support in Congress, the defection of Mathias, McCloskey, Hatfield, and others notwithstanding. Indeed, Haldeman succeeded, prevailing on a number of Republican congressmen to rally to the president's aid. A typical response came from Senator Henry Bellmon (R-OK), who scorned those who sought "to make Vietnam a political issue" and argued that they ignored "the effect of an American surrender in Vietnam on the peace of the rest of the world." Fortunately, he concluded, Nixon was not one of those.[5]

But, even with congressional support, Nixon chafed at the growing discontent within the GOP. Most problematic, unanimity did not prevail among the president and his senior advisers in the administration. The debate over whether to take action against the Cambodian sanctuaries demonstrated those tensions. William Rogers opposed the military action, as he had the previous March. Behind the scenes, Rogers tried to enlist Melvin Laird to oppose the president, writing to him privately to see if there were "steps we might take to influence Cambodia developments." Although he supported the incursion as both a means to neutralize a threat and a way to showcase the success of the administration's strategy, Laird expressed to Nixon serious concerns about the implications for Vietnamization. He feared that the president would seek to make this a primarily U.S. operation, which could set back the process of disengagement. Moreover, he worried that the American public would see the incursion as a "betrayal" of the president's promise to end the war. Hoping to convince the president to keep the troop withdrawals on track, Laird played the trump card that he knew would resonate with Nixon. If Nixon did not remove sixty thousand troops by the midterm elections in November, he argued, the GOP could suffer significantly at the polls.[6]

On the other side, among the most hawkish voices was Spiro Agnew, who urged "the strongest possible response." Agnew believed that the whole debate about the legitimacy of the incursion was "irrelevant. Either the sanctuaries were a danger or they were not. If it was worth cleaning them out, he did not understand all the pussyfooting about the American role or what we might accomplish by attacking only one."[7] The discussion brought out the worst in the president. As Henry Kissinger later wrote, "If Nixon hated anything . . . it was being shown up in a group as being less tough than his advisers." Given Agnew's comments and the reluctance of Rogers and Laird, Nixon "adroitly placed himself between the vice president and the cabinet." Kissinger firmly believed that Agnew's strident remarks during the meeting "accelerated" Nixon's ultimate decision to proceed with the incursion.[8] The president made it clear that the invasion would go forward and authorized the attack in National Security Decision Memorandum 58.

With the decision made, Nixon addressed the nation on 30 April to inform the public about the Cambodian incursion. He announced that U.S. troops were being dispatched into Cambodia to clean out enemy sanctuaries "completely occupied and controlled by North Vietnamese forces." Once the task was completed, American forces would withdraw from Cambodian territory. Nixon called the action "indispensable for the continuing success" of Vietnamization, reiterated that the United States would be "patient in working for peace" and "conciliatory," but warned Hanoi, "We will not be humiliated. We will not be defeated . . . our will and character . . . [are] being tested tonight." He also recognized the political risk that he (and, by extension, the GOP) was taking and claimed that he had "rejected all political consideration in making this decision." Whether the GOP "gains in November is nothing compared to the lives of 400,000 brave Americans," he asserted, claiming that he would rather be a "one-term President and do what I believe is right than to be a two-term President at the cost of seeing America become a second-rate power and to see this nation accept the first defeat in its proud 190-year history."[9] The level of Nixon's disingenuity—or, perhaps, self-deception—is remarkable. Nothing drove him more than the thought of a second term. That is exactly why he authorized the operation to clean out the sanctuaries—to attempt to win the war and assure his reelection.

Even though Nixon's press secretary, Ronald Ziegler, reported that calls were running six to one in the president's favor, critics condemned the speech. Tom Wicker, writing in the *New York Times,* argued that the invasion "makes it clear that he does not have and never has had a 'plan to end the war.'"[10] The *Chris-*

*tian Science Monitor's* George Ashworth called the decision "perilous, in both political and military terms."[11] The political reaction was equally negative, even within the Republican Party. Charles Goodell called Nixon's decision "pretty ghastly." Representative John Anderson (R-IL), the chairman of the House Republican Conference, said he was "deeply disturbed by the implications of the speech" and called the plan "a very real gamble with respect to expanding the war." John Sherman Cooper was willing to give the president a little bit of leeway and withhold judgment until the results of the incursion were known, but he still remarked, "I would have been happier if he had not chosen this."[13]

Opponents of the war on Capitol Hill responded immediately. On 1 May, Mark Hatfield and George McGovern proposed an amendment to the military appropriations bill currently under consideration in the Senate that would end all funding for the war after 31 December and require the withdrawal of all U.S. forces by 30 June 1971. The measure was obviously aimed at Nixon's conduct of the war, but there was also another point of concern for the sponsoring senators. According to McGovern, the time had come to stop deferring to the president and to begin taking responsibility. He asserted, "This amendment will place that burden on each Senator—a political risk that we should gladly bear rather than further risking the lives of our men in Southeast Asia."[13] McGovern recognized the problems caused by the permissive attitude of Congress. Hatfield hoped that Nixon's expansion of the conflict would provoke a backlash in Congress, stiffen the resolve of wavering senators, and force Nixon to accede to the demands of the doves. Nixon, understandably, resented the attempt to encroach on his prerogatives and pledged to resist any effort to do so.

Hatfield and McGovern realized that the only way their amendment would succeed was if public opinion forced the Senate to approve it. They determined that the best way to educate the American people and convince them to support the measure would be to present the amendment and an explanation for why it was necessary on a thirty-minute television spot. Both CBS and ABC declined to air the program, but NBC accepted it for the price of $60,000. Convinced of the necessity of the broadcast, McGovern took out a second mortgage on his home to finance most of the cost. As a result, on 12 May, NBC aired an edited, half-hour presentation of a four-hour antiwar panel discussion by Senators Hatfield, McGovern, Goodell (who cosponsored the amendment), Frank Church, and Harold Hughes (D-IA). In response to their plea for money to pay for the airtime and to continue the campaign to build support for the amendment, the group received well over $500,000, which helped establish the Committee to End the War. They also revised their proposal in an effort to win backing from a broader coalition, moving the cutoff date back to 31 December 1971. Unfortunately, these efforts bore little fruit. Hatfield and McGovern failed to attract support beyond the hardcore doves. The "very desirable group of moderate Republicans and Democrats who were tired of the war" were "not yet ready to force a dramatic showdown" with Nixon.[14]

The reason for the reluctance of this group to join forces with the doves was their concern about opposing the administration so blatantly in an election year. These senators worried about being portrayed as un-American by political groups sponsored by the White House like Americans for Winning the Peace and the Tell It to Hanoi Committee.[15] They had good reason for their concerns. Charles Colson, the Nixon aide in charge of coordinating the opposition to the amendment, described the cosponsors as "unilateral disarmers" and "salesmen of surrender" who wanted to undermine Nixon's conduct of foreign policy and sell out the U.S. forces remaining in Southeast Asia.[16]

But the battle over the Hatfield-McGovern amendment would have to wait until the senators completed their deliberations on a less drastic and more immediate proposal by John Sherman Cooper and Frank Church. On 11 May, the Senate Foreign Relations Committee (SFRC) adopted the Cooper-Church amendment, which called for the end to funds for U.S. ground troops and military advisers in Cambodia. Once the full Senate began to debate the legislation, the White House began to consider ways to mobilize public opinion against the measure. To counter the growing discontent in the Senate, especially among Republicans, Haldeman enlisted Barry Goldwater and Robert Dole (R-KS)—perhaps "the most ferocious Republican defender of Nixon's Vietnam policy"—to "really ram" Cooper and Church in the Senate debates and portray them as those who would stab U.S. forces in the back.[17] Henry Bellmon continued to support the administration, coming out strongly against the Cooper-Church amendment. Attacking the "obviously dangerous limitations put on Presidential action" that the amendment would have enacted, he also warned that the "encouragement that passage of this amendment will give to the enemy will probably mean that a final negotiated settlement will be substantially delayed." In effect, he argued, the Cooper-Church amendment was "an attempt by Congress to make short-range, tactical decisions as to how a military operation should be conducted . . . another example of good intentions leading to bad conclusions."[18]

Paul Fannin concurred, stating, "[The amendment] is perhaps not calculated to prolong the war, but in my view its enactment would inevitably prolong the conflict. . . . This is an attempt, in my view, to discredit the judgment of the President of the United States, to question his integrity and honor." Fannin reiterated his staunch support of the administration, suggesting that Cooper-Church would "hand the North Vietnamese a victory they have not won."[19] Despite this strong demonstration of support, Nixon worried that Goldwater, Dole, Thurmond, and other administration allies might not be able to sway the Senate to reject the amendment given the animosity generated by the revelations about the military action in Cambodia. In an effort to mitigate the political fallout, Nixon's staff organized a massive campaign in conjunction with the Veterans of Foreign Wars and the American Legion to attempt to move congressional opinion to the side of the administration.

Nixon's surrogates did their utmost to garner support for the administration's policies. Speaking to the Advertising Council, Bryce Harlow stated that the Cambodian incursion "gained invaluable time," time needed for Vietnamization to succeed, and had "added a major factor of security." Recent events had provided "the best opportunity that we have ever had since this terrible struggle began to achieve what most Americans want—to enable South Vietnam to make its own way in the face of a powerful aggressor."[20] Harlow also did what he could to retain support within the GOP. For example, he informed Len Jordan of private polls reflecting Nixon's strong approval ratings in the wake of his April 20 address on the war that preceded the announcement of the Cambodian operation.[21] Hugh Scott told the press in late May, "I believe there is definitely strong support for what the President is doing to wind down the war."[22] Gerald Ford told the House that the Cambodian operation did not represent an escalation of the war. "Nixon has kept his word to the American people," he argued. The public should "give peace a chance by giving the President a chance."[23]

Not everyone in the party was on board with the administration's strategy, however. Edward Brooke worried that Nixon's decision to invade Cambodia increased the prospect of a widened war. He expressed concern that "these developments may undermine the President's steady progress toward disengagement from the area."[24] Two days later, he criticized the administration, asserting that the incursion carried "obvious and enormous risks," and deploring the action. "It is particularly regrettable," he said, since Nixon acted "without consulting Congress." Brooke could not contemplate that the invasion was "indispensable to the success of the President's flexible withdrawal program." This "extremely hazardous policy" must not be allowed to prolong or expand the war.[25] Later, speaking to students at the Harvard Business and Law schools, he described a "three-phased strategy" for challenging Nixon's policies in Southeast Asia that had been devised by a group of Democratic and Republican senators. The strategy included using congressional appropriations power to prohibit further use of troops in Cambodia, repealing the Tonkin Gulf resolution, and seeking legislation requiring the withdrawal of U.S. forces by mid-1971.[26]

The incursion into Cambodia seriously disturbed McCloskey as well. He questioned its military value and regarded the whole operation "as a betrayal of the administration's commitment to withdraw from Vietnam." He wrote

Nixon to suggest that the president admit that the war was and continued to be a mistake. According to McCloskey, "[A] national war policy requires three things: military strength, the willingness of our people to pay the cost, and the willingness of our young men to fight. Is it not apparent to you that we have lost the latter two?" The antiwar movement had "a legitimate complaint" about U.S. policy, he opined, and "nothing you or the government can do is going to convince our young people that American purposes in this war are justified." The policy of "'no defeat, no humiliation' may have been justified in the 1950's and 1960's, but it is counterproductive today. . . . I plead with you to abandon your intransigent attitude on Viet Nam."[27] As with his earlier correspondence, McCloskey received no response from the president.

Even with such daunting opposition, Nixon felt assured that he would be able to overcome the doubters with the success of the Cambodian operation. But that confidence did not necessarily reflect reality, as antiwar Republicans continued to harp on him to hasten the process of disengagement. Charles Goodell, who was fighting for his political life, had become one of the loudest critics within the GOP. Not only had he been widely criticized by the party's leadership for his antiwar stance, but the administration had targeted him for defeat in the fall elections, especially after his televised appearance with Hatfield and McGovern. Nixon instructed his political operatives to throw the weight of the White House behind one of Goodell's opponents for his Senate seat, James Buckley, the brother of the *National Review*'s William F. Buckley. In an effort to distinguish himself from Buckley's conservatism, Goodell spoke out again in favor of the Hatfield-McGovern amendment in early June, arguing, "'The time has come for us to recognize that Congress must share the burden of responsibility' for ending the Vietnam conflict."[28] Goodell knew that, with the opposition of the administration, his only hope for reelection would be to appeal across party lines to Democrats and independents disaffected with the war.

Goodell and other disaffected Republicans made it difficult for Nixon to rally support behind the Cambodia incursion. Moreover, his efforts to sell the operation as critical to the country's success in Vietnam had little effect as the outrage that permeated the country and Congress over the invasion blunted the administration's public relations strategy. Nixon thus faced a dilemma—"suffer another humiliating defeat at the hands of the Senate's doves, or pragmatically embrace [the amendment's] language and acknowledge that it mandated a policy he had already endorsed." Ever the political realist, the president chose the latter option. But he did not submit meekly; instead, he acted to stack the deck in his favor to accommodate the new status quo. With the help of administration allies, he schemed to drag out debate on the amendment as long as possible so that it would essentially be a moot point. The Senate Republican leadership performed brilliantly, using a series of delaying tactics and legislative maneuvering that postponed the final vote on the bill for six weeks, until 30 June—the date that Nixon had set for withdrawing U.S. forces from Cambodia originally.[29]

The Foreign Military Sales Act, with the Cooper-Church amendment attached, passed the Senate by a vote of 58–37. The House subsequently rejected the version with the amendment by the fairly substantial margin of 237–153. David Schmitz has characterized the Cooper-Church amendment as "a landmark in the history of opposition to the war, congressional initiatives to bring the fighting to an end, and efforts to control executive power in foreign policy."[30] Indeed, Cooper-Church seemed to the administration more than an attack on Nixon's Vietnam policy; it was a challenge to the presidency itself. The doves did attempt to claim victory, arguing that the Senate had finally acted to limit the president's war powers. But the reality of the situation was that, given its failure in the House, the amendment did nothing more than underscore what Nixon had already done. Even with the advantage of public opinion in the wake of the Cambodian invasion, the Senate had again proved unsuccessful in fundamentally affecting the administration's policies in Vietnam. Although the seismic shift in public opinion made it easier for Congress to take on the administration, opposition had not yet reached the tipping point.

As the debate on Cooper-Church climaxed, Republican supporters of the president launched a preemptive attack on the still percolating Hatfield-McGovern amendment. They did so in the face of staunch opposition. Nixon's approval rating on the war had fallen to 31 percent, and a significant majority of 72 percent now supported a deadline for ending American involvement in Vietnam. Gordon Allott, the new chair of the Republican Policy Committee and a strong backer of the administration who had a reputation as "a master of legislative procedure," introduced the measure in the Senate "with the clear intent of sabotaging it." Indeed, the Colorado Republican urged the Senate to reject the amendment on the grounds that it represented an unconstitutional abridgement of Nixon's powers as commander-in-chief and would aid the enemy. McGovern savaged Allott for confusing the issue and preventing "the kind of discussion this most seriously deserves." Even opponents of the amendment like Barry Goldwater objected to Allott's strategy and joined with Hatfield, McGovern, and other antiwar senators to table the amendment on 29 June.[31] These two episodes demonstrate how far Nixon and his GOP supporters were willing to go to undermine the antiwar movement and opposition in Congress.

As if the two antiwar amendments were not enough, the administration had to deal with more legislative troubles as well. Efforts to repeal the Tonkin Gulf resolution continued as various members of Congress introduced revocation measures virtually every month. Henry Bellmon considered such efforts to be specious. "I don't see how we can 'undeclare war' while fighting is still going on," he said. "The repeal of this resolution . . . would not hasten the withdrawal of American troops from Vietnam. Instead it would make this nation appear to be vacillating and backing down on our national commitments." The resolution contained provisions for its expiration, he noted, and, if Nixon made the determination that those conditions had been met, then it would be appropriate to terminate the resolution. Otherwise, "As long as we have men in combat in Vietnam . . . I cannot in good conscience vote to repeal."[32] While some saw the situation differently, there were simply not enough members of Congress willing to support the repeal. As one Republican opined, "The Senate doesn't want to assume responsibility for the war and its aftermath. The senators want a time-table, but they don't want to set it themselves."[33]

With criticism assailing him from seemingly every direction, Nixon began to experience the same bunker mentality that plagued Johnson in the last years of his presidency. But, ever the canny politician, he identified ways to use the precarious situation he was in to his advantage. "They"—Democrats, dovish Republicans, the antiwar protesters—were the enemy, but "they" could also be useful. The administration's opponents could be "the villain, the object against which all of our supporters, as well as those who might become our supporters, could be rallied." Given the makeup of the "enemy," Nixon could claim to be a "superpartisan," acting in an "aggressively majoritarian" way in an effort to build a new coalition by "playing off the unpopularity of the minority."[34] Playing on the same themes that suffused his "silent majority" speech the year before, he made a concerted effort to denigrate and marginalize any and all opposition to his policies. While results varied, he did gain some room to maneuver.

In August, the complicated situation Nixon faced grew even murkier as domestic political pressure increased on members of Congress facing reelection. Gordon Allott suddenly shifted his position and urged Nixon to disengage from Vietnam quickly. Shortly thereafter, Hugh Scott joined a number of senators in signing a letter petitioning Nixon to consider a comprehensive cease-fire in Vietnam. The president, disturbed by these defections, complained to Kissinger, "We've got the Left where we want it now. All they've got to argue for is a bug out, and that's their problem. But when the Right starts wanting to get out, for whatever reason, that's *our* problem."[35] Much like Kennedy and Johnson, Nixon faced the prospect of a challenge from the Right on the Vietnam issue, and his fear of a right-wing backlash absolutely affected his decisionmaking on Vietnam.

And most conservatives continued to apply pressure on Nixon to prosecute the war more vigorously. Barry Goldwater, while applauding the president's decision to move into Cambodia as "the only decision he could make," believed that the decision to restrict the incursion to twelve miles inside the border failed to recognize reality. Limiting U.S. forces would simply mean that "the enemy will back up just as far as he has to to keep from being bothered."[36] The journalists Frank Mankiewicz and Tom Braden reported that Ronald Reagan's staff circulated a "secret internal memorandum" setting forth "a concerted Reagan plan to 'take the national leadership in opposing' Nixon." The goal of the plan, according to the report, was to "'keep pressure on President Nixon from the right in the hope disaster in Vietnam and increasing violence at home will cause the Republican National Convention in 1972 to dump the president and turn to Reagan.'" Reagan issued strong denials, calling the column "ridiculous," but the right-wing media criticism of the administration gave an indication of the discontent among conservatives within the GOP over the war.[37]

While conservatives ridiculed Nixon's lack of enthusiasm for the war, Edward Brooke wanted to hasten the process of disengagement. Although he supported Nixon's efforts, he believed that the time had come to "reinforce the President's commendable new directions by lending congressional sanction." He therefore supported the ideas behind the Hatfield-McGovern amendment, suggesting, "The conclusion that we have satisfied our commitment to the Vietnamese coupled with an extended timetable for troop withdrawal, could invigorate the efforts of the South Vietnamese to stand on their own. Hopefully it will heighten the willingness of all parties to negotiate an early political settlement."[38] Mark Hatfield made a similar argument. Using the president's logic from the Cooper-Church debate against him, Hatfield pointed out that the amendment only underscored Nixon's previously stated policy. By establishing a timetable for withdrawal, Congress would simply be supporting both the administration and the majority of Americans. If the president found it "necessary and advisable to maintain troops beyond that time," Hatfield suggested, "then he should simply obtain the authorization of the Congress." The amendment did not oppose Nixon's withdrawal plan; rather, it was "a means to share in the responsibility that is ours. Today, we shall choose to assume that responsibility, or to continue to abdicate it."[39]

Brooke's and Hatfield's concerns were not shared by the majority of their colleagues. The measure failed again by a vote of 55–39. Even had it passed the Senate, the Hatfield-McGovern amendment would have faced serious obstacles in the House, where the doves faced more hawkish supporters of the war. Moreover, in the unlikely event that it passed the House, Nixon could have easily vetoed it without fear of an override. Nevertheless, this stood as a watershed moment in the history of the war. Pressure against the conflict had been building for years, but, with congressional complicity in the form of appropriations and a lack of collective will to stand up to the administration in action as well as words, it did not translate into a change in policy. Yet, in looking back at the debate, *Time* observed that the "willingness of more than a third of the Senators to take the unprecedented step of handing the President a deadline for terminating" the war served as "a clear warning that senatorial patience was precariously thin."[40] Nixon's margin of error had decreased even further as a restless Congress inched closer to taking meaningful steps against the conflict.

Determined to keep the initiative with both congressional critics and the North Vietnamese leadership, Nixon announced another peace proposal on 7 October 1970. The new outline he presented called for a cease-fire to be put in place without preconditions and an Indochina peace conference to deal with the situation in the entire region, the rationale for the latter being that, since the war "has been proved to be of one piece[,] it cannot be cured by treating only one of its areas of outbreak." He stated that the United States stood ready to negotiate a timetable for complete withdrawal as part of an overall settlement, and he asserted that the United States was "prepared to be flexible on many matters" but that "we stand firm for the right of all the South Vietnamese people to determine for themselves the kind of government they want." He also proposed the "immediate and unconditional release" of all prisoners-of-war as a way to demonstrate "good faith, the intent to make progress, and thus improve the prospects for negotiation." These new terms were ostensibly designed to end the fighting and end the diplomatic impasse in Paris. He concluded by suggesting that an "unconventional war may require an unconventional truce; our side is ready to stand still and cease firing."[41]

Unlike the speech announcing the Cambodian incursion, this one was well received. The new plan garnered wide support, even from Nixon's domestic critics. The Senate unanimously approved a resolution endorsing the proposal, and Frank Church went so far as to opine, "The President has joined us. He is now on the same perch with the doves. So what is there to argue about? We've won this argument." Yet Church clearly misunderstood Nixon's thinking and the impetus behind the speech. The address "was primarily for domestic political consumption, not a genuine effort to restart the peace process." Nixon knew that Hanoi would reject the terms of the offer. He simply wanted to accrue the credit for making the proposal a month before the midterm elections. When reporters challenged his motives, characterizing this as an "October surprise" to aid the GOP in the upcoming voting, Nixon responded disingenuously, "If we had intended it for that, I am politically enough astute to have done it just about four days before the election. Then we would not have known what the results would have been and people would have voted their hopes rather than the realities."[42] But that is exactly what the president had done in an effort to affect the makeup of Congress positively for the administration. He banked on people not forgetting his willingness to negotiate with the North Vietnamese when they went to vote in November.

Eager to see some of his congressional opponents defeated, Nixon campaigned vigorously for GOP candidates in the weeks leading up to the voting. He emphasized two main issues: law and order and his plan to find a just peace in Vietnam. Both he and Spiro Agnew focused particular attention on the Senate races in an effort to defeat what Agnew described as the "radical-liberalism that controls the Senate."[43] Yet, as in 1966, the war did not turn out to be the definitive campaign issue that it could have been. The widely held view that Vietnamization was generally working limited the effectiveness of candidates who ran against the administration's policies. To be sure, in some races the war turned out to be decisive, but in many Vietnam factored in only peripherally as the economy, the cities, and other domestic problems dominated races across the country.

Nixon was not the only administration official to stump for Republican candidates. Melvin Laird loved campaigning, and he did so energetically in an effort to demonstrate the success of Vietnamization and the progress that he and Nixon had made toward peace. Speaking to the Chicago Council on Foreign Relations, Laird restated the administration's position on negotiations. If talks were to succeed, he asserted, "the willingness of one disputing party to negotiate must be matched by *equal* willingness on the part of other parties. It must be clearly understood that if this *mutual* willingness to negotiate existed . . . hostilities . . . could be speedily brought to an end." He also reminded the audience of one of Nixon's central talking points: "Neither peace nor freedom is secure if willingness to negotiate is not constantly complemented by military strength."[44]

The midterm elections dealt Nixon and the GOP a mixed hand, reflecting the divisions within the country. The Republicans lost nine seats in the House and gained two in the Senate but lost control of eleven state houses. The media in Washington portrayed the results as a defeat for the administration. Nixon immediately struck back in order to "put the whole thing in perspective" by denying that public disapproval of the way the administration was handling the war was a factor in the election.[45] Curiously, opponents of the war on both sides of the aisle won reelection—including Hubert Humphrey, who returned to the Senate after a six-year absence—although conservatives had banded together to defeat three notable Senate doves: Albert Gore Sr., Joseph Tydings, and, most satisfying for the president, Charles Goodell. Outspoken hawks faced challenges as well, and one of the president's strongest supporters on the war, George H. W. Bush, lost his senatorial bid to Lloyd Bentsen (D-TX). Still, the results left Nixon with concerns about his reelection campaign two years hence. He believed that the war "was sapping his domestic support and therefore had to be ended before 1972."[46] Without an honorable peace, his promises of 1968, vague and ambiguous as they had been, would come back to haunt him.

Unlike the president, Pete McCloskey felt much better about the election results. Having been returned to Washington by his district by a comfortable margin, he renewed his attacks on the administration. In a letter to Nixon at the end of November, he pleaded with the president to at least scale back the U.S. military actions in Vietnam. "If we cannot end the conflict," he wrote, "we can at least end American participation in a type of warfare which is inconsistent with our national goals, and our leadership in the cause of peace." "For this reason," he urged, "I would like to suggest your consideration . . . of the issuance of an order to stop the killing, or at least to order Americans to cease participation in the killing."[47] Once again, nothing concrete was forthcoming from the president. With no acceptable progress toward a resolution of the war, McCloskey concluded that it was "necessary to do something Nixon would understand" in order to force the administration to end the conflict.[48] That "something" would be a direct political challenge to the president the following year.

Despite the ambiguous election results and growing restlessness within the GOP, the situation in Vietnam seemed to be going as well as the administration could expect at the beginning of 1971. *Time* assessed the progress of the president's Vietnamization program positively, noting, "Things seem to be going according to Mr. Nixon's plan. The result, no doubt, is that not all that either the fluttery doves or the militant hawks might have wished, but Vietnam no longer seems like the morass Mr. Nixon inherited two years ago." Moreover, the upheaval brought about by the war had subsided, and, while "the President has not succeeded in bringing us together, at least things are no longer falling apart."[49] A rosy assessment to be sure, but one that certainly appealed to the administration. Others were less charitable. The *Philadelphia Inquirer* noted the schizophrenic nature of Nixon's policy, opining that the Nixon Doctrine had "fallen apart at the seams." Observing that administration officials frequently cited the doctrine as "the fundamental philosophy behind the U.S. troop withdrawal program from Vietnam," the paper contrasted that with Laird using the doctrine to justify increased U.S. military involvement in Cambodia, calling it the "perfect illustration" of the "Nixon Doctrine at work"—on the heels of another administration official denying the previous week that the doctrine was not an issue in the current situation in Cambodia.[50]

Nixon would have to deal with both the disparate opinion on the war and simultaneous crises that emerged at home and in Southeast Asia. In late January,

Hatfield and McGovern tried to establish a deadline for disengagement again, this time introducing a full-fledged bill—the Vietnam Disengagement Act of 1971—for consideration. The legislation would cut funds to any troop levels above 284,000 after May 1971 and would restrict the use of funds subsequently to supporting troop withdrawals, negotiations for the release of prisoners, and resettlement of Vietnamese. In presenting the measure, Hatfield declared, "A negotiated settlement is the means for ending the war. A timetable for withdrawal is the means to enable authentic negotiations. It is also the means for assuring the return of our prisoners of war."[51] The bill ran into a number of obstacles—including a vicious attack from Robert Dole—and, although a different version of the language would later be attached as a rider to a selective service bill, it fell short of adoption by a vote of 55–42. Even though Hatfield and McGovern picked up only three votes from the previous summer, the proposal definitely grabbed the attention of the administration.

Meanwhile, hoping to demonstrate that Vietnamization was, in fact, working, Nixon approved a major offensive aimed at the Ho Chi Minh Trail in Laos involving nearly twenty thousand Army of the Republic of Vietnam (ARVN) troops supported by U.S. airpower and artillery. Nixon had already authorized the heavy bombing of supply lines and staging areas in Laos and Cambodia on the basis of the rationale of "protective reaction"—that is, responding to attacks on U.S. reconnaissance planes. While neither the Laotian operation, code-named LAM SON 719, nor the bombing technically violated the letter of the Cooper-Church amendment, they did raise the ire of antiwar forces in Congress, who saw the development as yet another expansion of the war by an administration allegedly dedicated to ending the conflict in Southeast Asia. As the incursion unfolded, Nixon and his advisers played up the success of the operation, arguing that it was proof that Vietnamization was, in fact, progressing splendidly. But, in reality, the operation ended very badly as the ARVN disintegrated into chaos against a better-trained and larger North Vietnamese force, suffering a nearly 50 percent casualty rate and approximately two thousand dead. Even U.S. losses were substantial, as 712 helicopters were either damaged or shot down during the course of the operation.

Protests and demonstrations against the war continued as the details of LAM SON 719 filtered back home. The Vietnam Veterans against the War (VVAW) ceremoniously tossed their medals in the trash and gathered in front of the Capitol in faded uniforms with peace symbols. One of the members of the VVAW, former navy lieutenant John Kerry, testified in Congress and asked, "How do you ask a man to be the last man to die for a mistake?" Washington ground to a halt as the Mayday Tribe—a group of thirty thousand antiwar activists—disrupted traffic and caused one of the worst riots in the city's history. And the opposition in both parties in Congress continued to hammer away at the administration for escalating the war yet again.[52]

In response to the criticism of the Laotian incursion, the administration's defenders fired back. Robert Dole hammered his colleagues who were "unable to wait for the facts or results." Why, he wondered, attack the president for taking steps to win and end the war, especially since he was acting within his authority? The secretary of state, publicly supportive of the president despite his serious reservations, reassured the members of the SFRC that Nixon was honoring the spirit of the Cooper-Church amendment, although critics expressed deep skepticism about Rogers's testimony. But, in the end, the antiwar forces in Congress had no leg to stand on; the operation did not violate any legislation. As *Newsweek* opined, "Nixon appeared [for the time being] to have a free hand to test his theory that the war can be ended by expanding it."[53] Gerald Ford strongly supported the administration's action, asserting that it "promise[d] to destroy the enemy's ability to mount a major new offensive against South Vietnam" and helped ensure the continued success of Vietnamization.[54]

But LAM SON 719 also demonstrated the growing fissures within the GOP on the war. Nixon's aides informed him that a number of Republican congressmen, including staunch advocates such as Gerald Ford, Howard Baker, and Peter Frelinghuysen, were "badly shaken" by the results of the failed operation. Frelinghuysen commented that "Laos is one more straw—and a substantial one—on the camel's back" and asserted that "most Americans—myself included—have come to feel that this war has gone on too long."[55] These concerns would find a voice in the maverick campaign for the GOP nomination launched by Pete McCloskey. Although many members of the party opposed McCloskey's attacks on the administration—Ronald Reagan in particular was disgusted by McCloskey's statements—the disintegration of Nixon's base of support within the Republican Party was becoming increasingly evident.[56]

If the defection of GOP congressmen and declining poll numbers were not enough, Nixon began to see additional erosion of support from within his administration. The White House counselor Donald Rumsfeld—who would later serve twice as secretary of defense, most notoriously during the Second Iraq War, which resurrected so many memories of Vietnam—emerged as "a troublesome anti-war advocate." Along with other domestic policy officials like George Schultz, John Ehrlichman, and Clark MacGregor, Rumsfeld began asking why the Vietnamization process could not move more expeditiously. Nixon was predictably bitter, lashing out at Kissinger, "'They don't know a god-damn thing about foreign policy! . . . They're only concerned about, frankly, peace at any price really.'"[57] But this internal strife underscored the tenuous nature of Nixon's support in his own party.

Republican wavering on Vietnam was demonstrated clearly at a pivotal meeting that occurred on 5 April. Jacob Javits invited Melvin Laird to dinner at his Watergate apartment along with ten GOP Senate colleagues. Laird expected a cordial evening but soon realized that the senators had other ideas. According to one account, the Republican leadership was "sick of Laos, sick of Vietnam, and disenchanted with the president's exit plan, and they took it out on Laird." Hugh Scott warned Laird that the withdrawal increments Nixon would propose in his next announcement would not be enough. "He must make public some formula that clearly indicates the end of American participation of the war," Scott declared. Senator Marlow Cook (R-KY) asked how long it would take to completely withdraw if the order were given immediately. Laird responded that it would likely take nine months. The senators repeatedly told Laird that "they would not be able to hold their party together on war issues if Nixon did not announce an end date," something that Laird resisted as well, arguing that it would place the United States in an untenable negotiating position vis-à-vis the North Vietnamese. Senator Ted Stevens (R-AK) resignedly said, "I come from the most hawkish state in the union. I ran in '70 as a hawk. I couldn't do it in '72." But Hugh Scott summed things up the best: "You don't see any hawks around here. The hawks are all ex-hawks."[58]

The meeting served to underscore the problems Nixon faced both within his own party and with the country as a whole. Laird summarized the tone of the meeting for Nixon in a memorandum titled "Tempo of the War." He bluntly told the president, "The attention given to operations in Laos tends to obscure the fact that U.S. involvement in the war is declining rapidly." The following day, Laird wrote Nixon again and urged him to recognize that "congressional and popular U.S. support for our programs in Southeast Asia are now more tenuous than ever." He also pointed out that expenditures on the war were draining resources from the Cold War competition with the Soviets, a fact that could prove problematic in the 1972 election. The secretary of defense strongly urged the president to continue the rate of troop withdrawals, contrary to the advice of General Abrams and the Joint Chiefs. Laird's arguments proved persuasive.[59]

Taking Laird's advice, and furious with the disintegration of support, Nixon gave a speech on 7 April to blunt criticism and demonstrate that Vietnamization would be carried out on his own timetable. He announced that he would withdraw an additional 100,000 troops by 1 December, which would leave fewer than 200,000 in country. But Nixon, as usual, had ulterior motives for the address and announcements. He needed to divert attention from both the failed Laotian incursion and the recent conviction of Lt. William Calley on murder charges stemming from the My Lai incident. In evaluating the president's address, *Time* called it a "foxhole speech, digging in tenaciously in defense of his existing position." Mark Hatfield rejected the assumption that Nixon was moving quickly enough with disengagement, saying, "I expected an elephant and we got a mouse." But, even if Nixon had been inclined to heed Hatfield's advice, he still felt restrained by his fear of the political Right. One administration official anonymously told *Time*, "If we set a withdrawal date now, the domestic reaction would be worse than it was to the fall of China and the McCarthy period."[60]

Domestic political considerations drove administration decisionmaking throughout Nixon's presidency, his protestations to the contrary notwithstanding. Even more intriguing, the language used by the president and his advisers is stunningly similar to that of Kennedy and Johnson. But the evidence also clearly suggests that all three administrations exaggerated the potential threat posed by conservatives, and Nixon absolutely underestimated the burgeoning support—especially within the GOP—for hastening the disengagement process. Even after his latest proposal, Edward Brooke urged Nixon "in the name of humanity" to announce a timetable for withdrawal.[61] George Aiken suggested that the speech was not "'enough to put the lid back on,'" but he did believe that, "'come next December, he will accelerate the withdrawals still further so that he can meet or beat the Democratic goal' of withdrawing all troops by the end of 1972." Hatfield complained that Nixon "'failed to meet even the least of our expectations. The utter failure of the Paris peace talks demands that we set a specific date for our withdrawal in order to force action for the return of our prisoners of war. The casualty comparisons used to defend Vietnamization further reveals [*sic*] the moral insensitivity of this war policy.'"[62]

It was obvious that Republican opponents of the war were quickly losing patience with the administration's efforts to resolve the conflict. The *New York Times* reported that former senator Charles Goodell, who had been defeated with significant assistance from the administration the previous fall, was organizing a meeting of disaffected Republicans, including McCloskey and Donald Riegle, to "discuss their future 'insurgency' activities."[63] But the *National Review* observed that "the most significant defector from the House pro-Vietnam position is Georgia Democrat Phil Landrum." The reason for concern was that "much of the Administration's strongest support for the phased withdrawal policy . . . has come from Southern Democrats" and Landrum was seen as a "bellwether." While the GOP could "absorb and contain the carping of liberal Republicans," Nixon could not afford to lose Southern Democratic support, much like LBJ relied on the support of Republicans to compensate for defectors from his own party.[64]

By mid-April 1971, Nixon's presidency had reached a nadir. His conduct of foreign affairs, which had "always been his strongest appeal to the electorate," came under increasing scrutiny and criticism. With the Laotian offensive perceived as a failure, negotiations seemingly stalled, and the Calley trial laying bare atrocities by U.S. forces in Vietnam—not to mention the burgeoning problems of inflation and unemployment—Nixon dropped precipitously in the polls. Indeed, his popularity fell seven points from February to April in the Gallup Poll to 49 percent, a lower level than any president since Harry Truman at a comparable point in his administration.[65] Hoping to help shore up Nixon's support, a group of freshmen senators—including Robert Taft (R-OH), Lowell Weicker (R-CT), Glenn Beall (R-MD), and William Brock (R-TN)—counterattacked on the administration's behalf. Even William Saxbe (R-OH), a longtime critic of the administration's Vietnam policy, came to the president's defense, stating that what bothered him more than the war was "those who continually play politics with [it]."[66] As the weight of domestic opinion shifted against him, Nixon was forced to reevaluate his approach to ending the war or face the prospect of having to fight for his political life in 1972, not just against the Democratic nominee, but also in the Republican primaries.

For, as the *Washington Post* cogently noted in February 1971, Pete McCloskey knew that the "one thing Mr. Nixon understands is political pressure." That helps explain why McCloskey broached the idea of impeaching Nixon in a speech to a group of Stanford University students about ways to end the war. To McCloskey, it was clear that a national debate about the possibility of removing Nixon from office could "result in new policies to end the war quickly."[67] More realistic, however, was the notion that someone from the Republican Party needed to contest the 1972 presidential nomination on the grounds that Nixon had not fulfilled his pledge to bring the war in Vietnam to an end. After taking yet another trip to Southeast Asia in the spring of 1971, McCloskey all but decided that that someone would be him.[68]

This was no spur of the moment decision. It came after a protracted effort to convince the president to disengage from Vietnam dating back to January 1969. McCloskey did so, not because of any overarching presidential ambitions (in contrast to Nixon himself), but rather because he considered a primary challenge to be the only way to legitimately and fundamentally affect a change in U.S. policy. Of most concern to the congressman was the use of "unlimited air power" in Southeast Asia, which he suggested "violates the Hague Convention, let alone the Nuremburg principles." If Nixon refused to stop the bombing, McCloskey said, "no matter what his rate of withdrawal is, I think I would want to run against him."[69] McCloskey was realistic about his chances to upset Nixon in New Hampshire. He admitted that it might be political suicide to oppose the president but believed that it was worth doing if he could help bring an end to the war.

Yet, even as late as the summer of 1971, McCloskey held out hope that Nixon would see the light. He told his staff that he would seek the nomination only if Nixon continued the "unlimited use of bombing in Southeast Asia" and insisted on "keeping a residual force in South Viet Nam indefinitely." The primary reason for his candidacy would be "to create such a Republican base of voting strength against these policies that the President may have to consider changing his position in order to win renomination." McCloskey thought in strategic terms, hoping to attract traditionally non-Republican groups—housewives, students, union members, and minorities—to the GOP through his candidacy. He also recognized that he would not be able to count on much overt support, even from committed antiwar Republicans, who McCloskey asserted "understandably have to be (and should be) loyal to the party leadership, including the President."[70]

In a campaign book justifying his candidacy, McCloskey argued that he would not have challenged Nixon "had it not been for the gradual realization that [the president's] plan to *end* the war in Vietnam actually involved a drive to *win* the war." Using his own unanswered correspondence as evidence, he suggested (quite accurately) that the president had become isolated from the antiwar members of his own party.[71] By 1971, it was clear that the patience of GOP opponents of the war was waning, and antiwar politicians in the party like John Lindsay and Mark Hatfield pushed the administration to increase the pace of withdrawals and negotiations. Of course, Nixon and Kissinger pursued their own agenda and timetable in moving toward "peace with honor," irrespective of opposition from within the Republican Party, the media, or the public at large. They plunged forward relentlessly, firmly convinced that their strategy would prove effective and bring about, not just peace, but a victory in Vietnam that would enhance their overall foreign policy goals. Because of their confidence, they could ignore opinions that diverged or contradicted their worldview.

While McCloskey believed that Nixon was isolated from opponents of the war within the GOP, the congressman faced a different kind of isolation. For years, the party had committed itself to the so-called Eleventh Commandment. This doctrine derived from the experience of the 1964 presidential election, when many liberal Republicans (before that became an oxymoron) refused to campaign for or publicly support Barry Goldwater. In the ensuing elections in 1966 and 1968, Republicans made a concerted effort to restrict their criticisms to Democrats in an effort to build party unity and present a united front to the electorate, a strategy that helped the party make significant gains in the midterm elections and win the White House in 1968. McCloskey had already run afoul of the California Republican Party by violating the commandment in 1968, leading the Reagan wing of the party—which had assumed ascendancy both in the state and, to a growing degree, nationally—to distrust the congressman even more than it already did.[72] One member of California's congressional delegation, Representative Alphonzo Bell (R-CA), called McCloskey's presidential candidacy "needlessly divisive" and "hopeless."[73] That sentiment was shared by many in the party, who agreed with Attorney General John Mitchell's comment that, if "you can't get the GOP to listen to Nelson Rockefeller, you're not going to get it to listen to Pete McCloskey." The general feeling in the White House was that the ongoing troop withdrawals would sap the strength of an insurgency campaign, eliminating any threat it might pose to Nixon.[74]

McCloskey's friends in the GOP tried to reason with him and convince him not to run for the sake of party unity and his own political career. Representative Charles Wiggins (R-CA), who represented a district adjoining McCloskey's, told the congressman, "Neither the Republicans nor the Democrats are going to turn to McCloskey as their presidential candidate. . . . Although you personally may be excused for believing in the viability of your own candidacy, those around you are not so naive." Wiggins suggested that McCloskey was being "used," that his "enormous talents and potential for our party are being perverted and misdirected by those who are not pro-McCloskey, but are anti-Nixon." He admitted that McCloskey's differences with the administration were not unique but pointed out that other Republicans had "not permitted that opposition to be used as a vehicle for replacing the entire Republican Administration with a whole new team of Democrats." Wiggins suggested that McCloskey's political decisions led "in many directions apart from our policy in Vietnam" and urged his colleague to "reconsider the practical consequences of your efforts."[75]

Obviously, breaking the Eleventh Commandment did not sit well with many in the party, and as Robert S. Allen wrote in his syndicated column in May, "Local, state and congressional GOP leaders are angrily gunning for him, and admittedly canvassing the field for a potent candidate to run against him [for the Republican nomination for his House seat]."[76] Indeed, as Adam Clymer wrote in the *Baltimore Sun,* "The prevailing belief is that Republicans are less tolerant of insurgencies and dissent than are Democrats, and that there is little future for a Republican Eugene McCarthy. The thesis is probably right." But, Clymer continued, "Many Republicans who view his anti-war efforts with horror concede that they like him personally. . . . They see him as sincere, if wrong." If he made a strong showing in New Hampshire, McCloskey "might cause the President to speed up disengagement."[77] McCloskey, while a maverick within the GOP, was not alone in his opinions or in his campaign. Donald Riegle was outspoken in his support of McCloskey throughout his campaign, and Jacob Javits said that the congressman was "'acting constructively,'" suggesting that "ferment within the party was desirable." McCloskey likely had a number of "secret supporters" in the party as well, but even he recognized that the public support of any Republican would bring down the wrath of the White House on the perceived dissident.[78]

The national Republican leadership also tried to dissuade McCloskey from his harsh criticisms of the administration. In response to a letter from Gerald Ford pleading with him to blunt his attacks, McCloskey reiterated his case against Nixon. "I appreciate the concern many of my Republican colleagues have expressed about my intention to challenge President Nixon's Southeast Asia policies in next spring's primaries," he stated. Nevertheless, he reminded Ford that his opposition to the war dated to his 1967 campaign for Congress and that he was dismayed over the "transition of the Republican Party into its position of apparent support for winning the war in Viet Nam." Expressing a reluctance to challenge Nixon himself—"I would have preferred this program to have been presented by someone more experienced and knowledgeable than myself, but, as you know, no one has yet indicated a willingness to do this"— McCloskey asserted that he would do so unless Nixon ended the unlimited use of bombing and rejected the notion of leaving a residual U.S. force in Vietnam indefinitely.[79]

While the majority of the party dismissed McCloskey as either a self-aggrandizing publicity hound or a nuisance to the president, leading members of Nixon's staff refused to do so. This was partly due to the fact that the specter of Eugene McCarthy's showing in 1968 loomed as an object lesson for the administration, especially since it was the Vietnam War that led to McCarthy's success and Johnson's eventual withdrawal from the race. Moreover, Nixon took his politics very seriously, and, after the 1960 and 1962 election losses, he would never again leave anything to chance—which was, of course, what led to the Watergate scandal and the end of his presidency. John Ehrlichman, who was McCloskey's classmate at Stanford Law School, was tasked with trying to do something quietly about the maverick congressman to blunt any potential threat. Although holding "few illusions that he could talk McCloskey out of anything," Ehrlichman arranged for McCloskey to meet with Kissinger to discuss Vietnam and urged his friend to "soft-pedal personal criticisms of Nixon."[80] Ehrlichman's efforts were in vain; McCloskey steadfastly refused to reconsider his candidacy unless and until Nixon ended the war.

But Nixon was nothing if not an opportunist. Six days after McCloskey formally announced his candidacy in July 1971, Nixon announced his historic trip to China. Not only was he able to capture the public's imagination and set in motion his strategy of triangular diplomacy with the Chinese and the Soviets that would, he hoped, yield an honorable peace in Vietnam, but he "captured the political initiative" from McCloskey and his potential Democratic challenges leading up to the 1972 primaries.[81] In an interesting coincidence of timing, Nixon's trip to China in February 1972 also helped draw attention away from the looming New Hampshire primary, further burnishing his reputation at a key political moment and making it that much more difficult for McCloskey's message to gain traction. Richard Nixon knew how to use spectacle and distraction to his advantage, and he was a master of political timing.

As the progress of troop withdrawals proceeded, it appeared to some observers that Nixon would not need to concern himself with Vietnam in the presidential campaign the following year.[82] Over the next six months, McCloskey failed to attract voters to his campaign despite the fact that he moved beyond the single issue of Vietnam and challenged the president on a broader range of issues. A poll taken in November 1971 demonstrated several important facts about McCloskey's candidacy. Most notably, Republicans did not see him as a viable alternative to the current administration, favoring Nixon 73 to 13 percent. Even independents, on whom any chance of success rested, supported Nixon 54 to 23 percent, and the eighteen- to thirty-year-old demographic—the most likely antiwar voters—chose Nixon 46 to 33 percent. Yet McCloskey's significant minority support among non-Republican groups, according to a *New York Times* analysis of the poll results, "may be an indication that the President's troop withdrawals have not eliminated peace as an issue for 1972."[83] McCloskey almost certainly would not win, but he would force Nixon to confront the Vietnam issue during 1972.

This McCloskey did in a series of speeches and media engagements leading up to the New Hampshire balloting. Appearing on ABC's "Issues and Answers," he upbraided Nixon for using American military technology to protect his pride. According to the congressman, bombing villages in North Vietnam, Laos, and Cambodia was being carried out so that Nixon would not be the first president to lose a war: "You certainly can't say that it is preserving the liberty of the South Vietnamese anymore." The only thing worth fighting for at this juncture, he argued, was the return of U.S. prisoners-of-war; supporting the Thieu government "seems to me to be not a necessary part of our policy." He concluded by suggesting that even a Communist-dominated, reunified Vietnam would be less harmful to the Vietnamese people than continued American bombing.[84]

The antiwar wing of the party was not the only source of contention for the president. The GOP's right flank became increasingly problematic and worrisome. Nixon's presidency thus far had disappointed his conservative backers, particularly after the 1970 midterm elections. By the middle of 1971, conservatives had grown "quite restive" over the president's policies and decisions, notably his foreign policy decisions—such as his rapprochement with China and his pursuit of détente with the Soviets—and his declaration that the United States "sought no victory in Vietnam."[85] Criticism of his evolving liberal tendencies, as some conservatives described his policies, was encapsulated in an editorial in the South Carolina newspaper *The State*. The paper suggested a reason why McCloskey's candidacy for the 1972 GOP nomination failed to gain traction: "Nixon is giving him a steadily diminishing area in which to operate. More and more, the President is occupying the very ground whereon Rep. McCloskey seeks to build his ramparts." According to the editorial, Nixon's "liberal" Vietnamization program meant that any challenge to his candidacy "must come from the right. . . . Unfortunately, no formidable opponent within the party looms as a counterforce to what is beginning to appear as yet another 'new Nixon.'"[86] This stinging indictment came on the heels of William F. Buckley announcing that he and other conservatives were suspending support for the president and taking active steps to harass the administration during the 1972 campaign.

John Ashbrook became the focal point of conservative discontent. A former newspaper publisher who had been a member of Adm. Richard Byrd's final Antarctic expedition, Ashbrook was an ardent conservative and one of the most articulate anti-Communists in Congress. An energetic leader of the new Right, he helped found the American Conservative Union and was one of the leaders of the movement to draft Barry Goldwater to run for president. He represented the views of many on the Right when he gave a savage speech in the House in late 1971 in which he served up an indictment of Nixon's entire foreign policy agenda.[87] Two weeks later, he attacked Nixon for clinging to "the illusion of détente . . . in direct defiance of his statements across the years and many specific pledges made when running for the presidency." Although he generally supported Vietnamization—calling it "a commendable effort to fulfill our obligation to our allies"—Ashbrook hammered Nixon's "failure to exert the necessary presidential leadership," which "has endangered our national security." As a result of these shortcomings, he declared his candidacy for the presidency on 29 December 1971, asserting that he would challenge Nixon for the Republican nomination "to register conservative dissent from the increasingly liberal conduct of the Administration."[88]

Although Nixon's rapproachment with China loomed as a major issue for Ashbrook's campaign, the situation in Vietnam concerned him as well. Ashbrook had been a consistent opponent of timetables for withdrawal and unilateral U.S. action and strongly opposed what he saw as a "no-win" strategy. He "defined himself as a hawk who wants to 'get the blazes out'" of South Vietnam. But he held that withdrawal "should depend more on conditions than dates," and he derided limitations placed on U.S. military operations.[89] Most important, the Ohio congressman believed that U.S. national security was "in jeopardy" and that "our Republican Administration has simply retreated from the challenge and reneged on its promises to the electorate in 1968."[90] Conservative support for Ashbrook's candidacy irritated Nixon considerably. The administration denounced William F. Buckley for turning on the president. An angry Nixon aide called Buckley and reminded him, "Hadn't the Administration paid the proper attention to Buckley's patronage suggestions, the aide asked? Hadn't there been personal intervention on behalf of Buckley's brother in the 1970 New York Senate race?" Disloyalty was among the worst crimes in Nixon's book.[91]

Although conservatives had been "abysmally disappointed" with Nixon's policies since 1969, the support of the right-wing challenge was less a matter of power aggrandizement for conservative leaders than a reassertion of political principles.[92] But, for all the conservative angst about the direction of Nixon's policies, Ashbrook's candidacy never gained serious attention from Republicans. A *Boston Globe* poll in early February showed Nixon with 71 percent support among Republicans, with McCloskey garnering 14 percent and Ashbrook trailing with a mere 4 percent.[93] This demonstrates that, while conservative influence within the party had certainly expanded in recent years, it had not yet reached the level required to support a serious challenge to the sitting GOP president. By contrast, the effort to nominate Ronald Reagan in 1976 in place of President Ford very nearly succeeded.

Of course, not all conservatives united behind Ashbrook en masse. Two of the most notable, Ronald Reagan and Barry Goldwater, strongly opposed his candidacy. Reagan criticized Ashbrook on the grounds that "the party's got a big enough umbrella to keep all these people within it," a reflection of his faith in the Eleventh Commandment. Goldwater attacked with his characteristic bluntness. In a syndicated newspaper column in January 1972, he defended the Nixon administration on every charge leveled against it by Ashbrook and warned that divisiveness within the GOP could result in a Democratic president, an alternative "too horrible to contemplate."[94] Better Nixon, he believed, than to turn the White House over to the other party. Goldwater generally stuck by the administration and supported Nixon against attacks from both sides, although he did prod the president to be more forceful at times. Attacking congressional statements about an executive branch run amok, he told his Senate colleagues, "Congress is and has been involved up to its ears with the war in Southeast Asia. . . . No one can now claim innocence of what he was voting about."[95] Moreover, Goldwater argued that the recent bombing of Vietnam was not an escalation of the war but rather "a temporary move designed to speed the withdrawal of American troops, to save American and South Vietnamese lives, and to give the South Vietnamese some chance to decide their own destiny." Taking such action, he contended, would "speed the day when we will be rid of the Indo-China war with all its bloodshed and cost forever."[96] His overall support may have been evaporating, but Nixon could still count on a core group of GOP defenders to buttress the administration's policies.

Determined to reverse the tide, Nixon instructed his top aides to "sustain a massive counterattack" on his domestic critics for their lack of patriotism. "Keep nailing them," he ordered, and keep accusing them of "consciously giving aid and comfort to the enemy. They want the enemy to win and the United States to lose. They want the United States to surrender."[97] In yet another attempt to neutralize the administration's critics, Nixon made a major announcement on 25 January. He revealed to the public that Kissinger had been conducting secret talks with the North Vietnamese, which fact eliminated any suggestion that the president had not been trying to end the war peacefully. He also informed the country that he had proposed a deal that included a withdrawal of all U.S. forces within six months of a cease-fire agreement and the return of American prisoners-of-war and that South Vietnamese President Thieu had offered to resign one month before a new presidential election. Nixon's speech was a "political masterstroke that suddenly placed his congressional critics on the defensive." Although Mansfield, Church, and McGovern dismissed the plan, John Sherman Cooper called the proposal "fair and just," and most of the country was willing to give the president credit for the attempt.[98]

Some Republicans who wanted to give Nixon the benefit of the doubt, even those for whom the war had become anathema, had renewed hope. After the announcement, George Aiken wrote in his diary that he supported the proposal, fearing the "slaughter that would take place" if North Vietnam ever took control over the South. From a political perspective, Aiken noted, "The air is FULL of politics with the Democrats groping for issues. The progress in improvement of world relations made by President Nixon leaves them little hope for making any gains on the issue of the Indochina war."[99] But the president's steadfast critics were unswayed. In an appearance on "Face the Nation," McCloskey argued that his candidacy "may have played some part in causing [Nixon] to disclose the peace plans that he announced." Nevertheless, he refused to drop out of the race. "You can't believe the President anymore," he asserted. "I can't even begin to support the President in November if he's continuing this bombing policy in Laos and Cambodia." Fighting Nixon for the nomination "could end this bombing. It could force an American President to review and to change a policy that I can't live with."[100]

As the party prepared for another election year, one of the most influential political operatives in the GOP argued that Vietnam should be taken completely out of the election. Robert Hartmann, a legislative assistant to Gerald

Ford, told the minority leader, "It's my judgment that the less Republicans say about Vietnam the better." Hartmann's reasoning was simple: "I suspect that for most Americans the Vietnam War is as good as over." As for the rest, "Those who insist that President Nixon doesn't really want to get out of Vietnam, nothing we say is going to make any difference or get Republicans one vote."[101] If he decided to take Hartmann's advice, ignoring Vietnam would come naturally to the president—after all, he had done his best to follow that strategy in 1968. But the likelihood of that happening was slim, as the Democrats would certainly remind the country at every opportunity that Nixon's secret plan had not yielded a peace settlement in four years in the White House. Moreover, events would force the war back into the spotlight very quickly.

The Easter Offensive radically altered the political calculus on the war and forced the administration to make some difficult decisions in the face of substantial domestic political pressure. On 30 March 1972, North Vietnam launched a massive invasion of the South, hoping to take advantage of the fact that only six thousand U.S. combat troops remained in country. The North Vietnamese leadership believed that domestic pressures would prevent Nixon from reinforcing the ARVN with American soldiers, especially in an election year. They hoped not only to cripple Nixon, as they had Lyndon Johnson, but also to discredit Vietnamization, destroy the main units of the South Vietnamese military, disrupt pacification, and strengthen their position in the final peace negotiations.[102]

The aggressiveness displayed by Hanoi in attacking South Vietnam polarized an already divided country. Perceptions of the rationale behind the North Vietnamese invasion varied. George Aiken considered four reasons: to overrun the South if possible; to convince the world that Nixon's Vietnamization program had failed; to make it appear as if Nixon wanted the war to continue; and to strengthen Moscow's hand in the upcoming summit between Nixon and Soviet premier Leonid Brezhnev. Nevertheless, Aiken recorded in his diary that he believed the North Vietnamese attack would fail and "in the long run it may strengthen the hand of President Nixon in handling affairs in Indochina."[103] Paul Fannin said that the invasion "destroys any pretense that the war in Southeast Asia is anything more than a naked attempt by a Communist power to destroy a free nation." The issue at this point, he argued, was "how to end it—in honor or in shame . . . we are so close to leaving the people of South Vietnam with the chance to survive."[104] Barry Goldwater agreed but pressed the administration to go even further in its response. The president, he argued, "is going to have to make up his mind—and soon—whether we will continue to sort of dilly-dally in the bombing of supplies" or "whether we will go in after the source of the supplies," which would include bombing near Hanoi and Haiphong.[105] Conservatives pointed to the offensive as evidence that Nixon's Vietnamization program had failed and demanded that the president take immediate action to halt the invasion. Ronald Reagan typified the Right's response, arguing, "The bombing of military targets is the only recourse available to the President and the only way in which he can protect those Americans still remaining in South Vietnam."[106]

The congressional leadership met with Nixon on 12 April to discuss the offensive. In his notes from the meeting, Gerald Ford made some very telling observations. He wrote that the president wanted to emphasize that the conflict was "no longer a Civil War;" it was an "invasion," a distinction that would undercut a great deal of the criticism of U.S. policy in the antiwar movement. Ford recorded that the president argued that "Vietnamization [is] succeeding," which explained why Hanoi had launched such a desperate, perplexing attack. Nevertheless, Nixon strongly asserted: "*SVN [South Vietnam] must succeed.*" What the administration and the GOP leadership could not allow was for "turmoil in US [to] panic us. *We must stay strong.*" Ford also noted that Nixon was "taking sole responsibility" for success in Vietnam in order to maintain the "credibility of U.S. foreign policy." The president also criticized "those who got us in WAR [who] are sabotaging our efforts to get out. . . . If we dishonor our commitments the US will have no credibility." The minority leader characterized Nixon as "*calm & determined*" despite the upheaval surrounding the administration and marked his final conclusion: the United States would "prevent 'take-over' by communist forces, by an enemy invasion. Nuclear weapons—not necessary. . . . *We will do what is necessary. We will not lose.*"[107] If Nixon intended this to be a "come to Jesus meeting" with the leaders of the GOP, it worked. Ford and the rest of the leadership immediately began defending the president's reaction to the invasion.

To counter the negative publicity, Nixon's cabinet leaped into action. Spiro Agnew asserted, "If ever there was a time when an American President needed the support of all Americans, it is now. . . . If we hold firm, we may be able to complete our withdrawal and finally get our prisoners back—and we may be able to do so with the liberty and future of the South Vietnamese people intact."[108] William Rogers defended the administration's resumption of bombing in testimony before the SFRC, arguing that the decision was made to "protect American troops . . . while the President's withdrawal program continues." He deflected suggestions that the United States immediately withdraw from Vietnam, calling such ideas "ridiculous," and asserting, "It would destabilize the whole area. . . . It would be a mistake of major proportions." Vietnamization was working, he concluded. "What we need now is support. We don't need any immediate criticism."[109] But the invasion prompted a national outpouring of vitriol aimed at the administration. Editorials characterized the U.S. position as "tragically wrong." "To postpone stopping [the war effort] on some such spe-cious argument as loss of face is folly. America already has lost face." The only realistic option left was to get out of Vietnam completely "and leave Vietnam to its own solution."[110] The *Wall Street Journal* noted that the renewed bombing "is threatening to destroy the White House's shaky defenses against end-the-war legislation."[111]

Nixon was no doubt tempted to delay or cancel outright additional troop withdrawals in the face of the North Vietnamese invasion. But Melvin Laird would not allow that to happen. From years of working with Nixon, first in Congress and then as secretary of defense, he knew that there was always an avenue of appeal with the president: using domestic political considerations, especially in a presidential election year. That was precisely the tactic he used to convince Nixon to continue with the troop withdrawals in a memorandum on 24 April. Laird warned the president, "The denigration of Vietnamization is one of Hanoi's key goals in its current offensive." If Nixon were to suspend the "redeployment" of U.S. troops, he "would lend credibility to Hanoi's charge that Vietnamization is a defunct concept." "Of equal importance," although greater in Nixon's mind, "an announcement of redeployment suspension would have, in my judgment, a dramatic adverse political impact domestically."[112]

Looking back at the domestic reaction since the beginning of the Easter Of-fensive, John Roche wrote, "You might have thought that the question of who was doing what to whom would be conclusively settled. This was straight, na-ked aggression. Not even the most dedicated opponent of the war could argue that amphibious tanks were being constructed in peasant huts by the Vietcong." What surprised Roche, however, was the fact that "we have heard some of the strangest explanations of what allegedly occurred: Some commentators have virtually suggested that President Nixon personally sponsored the invasion. When the bombers went North, the howl went up that we had escalated the war." Roche concluded that "Johnson's War" had not become "Nixon's War. The war is now and always has been 'Hanoi's War.'"[113]

But, regardless of who claimed ownership of the conflict, it remained Nix-on's albatross for the time being. Compounding the problems he faced in the aftermath of the invasion, on 5 May seventeen House Republicans who had tended to support the administration's policies urged the president to propose a cease-fire in Indochina and appeal to the United Nations for a resolution. The motive force behind the plea was Howard Robison, who noted that the congressmen were "increasingly concerned over the pattern of events in Indo-china." Most disturbing were the bombing of strategic targets in North Vietnam and the apparently indefinite commitment of U.S. airpower to support ARVN ground forces. The open letter continued, "[We] do not see how even a near-total 'de-Americanization' of the ground war in Indochina can bring this conflict and its current carnage to an early end."[114] These additional defections made it imperative that Nixon regain the momentum that he had lost with the invasion and the subsequent chain of events, and that meant another television appearance to make another proposal to end the conflict.

Nixon did exactly that on 8 May. Explaining the administration's reaction to the North Vietnamese attacks, he asserted that there were only two issues remaining for the United States in the war. First, "Do we stand by, jeopardize the lives of 60,000 Americans, and leave the South Vietnamese to a long night of terror? This will not happen. We shall do whatever is required to safeguard American lives and American honor." The second was what the administration would do to counter the "complete intransigence" of the North Vietnamese in both the public and the private talks in Paris. Nixon made it clear that he would "not cross the line from generosity to treachery" in the negotiations. He laid out the three options open to the United States as he saw them: immediate withdrawal of all U.S. forces, continued negotiations, or "decisive military action to end the war." Recognizing that many Americans favored the first course, he admitted that, from a political standpoint, that would be the easiest choice since he had not been the one to "send over one-half a million Americans to Vietnam." But he refused to consider that option, suggesting that it would mean turning South Vietnam over to "communist tyranny and terror" and effectively sacrificing the remaining U.S. prisoners-of-war. Moreover, an "American defeat in Vietnam would encourage this kind of aggression all over the world. . . . World peace would be in grave jeopardy." While Nixon assured his audience that the administration wanted to negotiate, he claimed that the United States had "made every reasonable offer and tried every possible path for ending this war at the conference table."[115]

Thus, Nixon concluded, "What appears to be a choice among three courses of action . . . is really no choice at all." No longer would the United States exercise restraint "unprecedented in the annals of war." Instead, he announced, several measures would be implemented—all North Vietnamese ports would be mined, all supplies would be interdicted, rail and other communications would be cut off "to the maximum extent possible," and air and naval strikes against military targets in North Vietnam—code-named LINEBACKER—would continue. These steps would remain in place until Hanoi met his conditions: all U.S. prisoners-of-war must be returned, and an internationally supervised ceasefire throughout Indochina must be in place. Only then, he stated, would the United States proceed with "a complete withdrawal of all American forces from Vietnam within four months." Nixon closed by making a pointed statement to the Soviet Union. Noting that the two powers were near a major agreement on nuclear arms limitation, trade, and other key issues, he said, "Let us not slide back toward the dark shadows of a previous age." The country and the administration, he concluded, "must stand together in purpose and resolve."[116]

Following Nixon's speech, the GOP rose yet again to his defense. Paul Fannin lauded the president for not being "intimidated by either the military threat or the diplomatic risks abroad, nor by the political rhetorical here at home."[117] In Ford's eyes, Nixon's speech underscored the importance of U.S. credibility: "The President is proving to the world that the United States is not a pitiful giant. He is proving to the world that America's word is good, that it is clothed in integrity."[118] Senator Robert Griffin (R-MI) called the proposal "strong medicine but necessary," and James Buckley asserted that the president's decision was "both logical and inevitable given the political reality" and best designed to "compel Hanoi to go to the peace table in good faith and to preserve the credibility of American mutual security agreements around the world."[119] Ronald Reagan was effusive with his praise, stating, "For the first time in almost a decade of this war, a president . . . has given the people a clear-cut and completely truthful analysis of this war and has put it in perspective with regard to the all-important problem of world peace." In rejecting "the easy path of expediency and appeasement policies of the past," Nixon had embarked on "the only course which can bring peace and the return of our prisoners. He should have the support of every American."[120]

Barry Goldwater spoke vehemently against efforts to adopt an "end-the-war proposal." Referring specifically to an amendment proposed by Clifford Case and Frank Church, the Arizona senator said that it was "actually the kiss of death for almost everything we are trying to do. . . . It could easily result in the collapse of the South Vietnamese . . . [and] would spell the kiss of death for our peace negotiations in Paris." If the Senate wanted to bring the war to a resolution, he concluded, it should "exercise a courageous patience" and allow the administration's efforts to continue.[121] Strom Thurmond called Nixon's announcement "courageous and far-reaching" and said, "Hanoi will abandon her goal of military conquest in the South only if this Congress shows a solid unified wall of support behind our President." Nixon, he asserted, "has wisely refused to follow those who would surrender when the stakes are so high."[122] John Tower described Nixon's action as "eminently correct," and Milton Young argued that Nixon "had little choice but to make the decision he did to mine the harbors of North Vietnam and bomb their railroad and other supply lines."[123] But the protracted nature of the war made even committed hawks hesitant to support any additional military measures out of concern for domestic political considerations. With the election only six months away, members of Congress worried about what their districts would think if they backed an expansion of the bombing or mining North Vietnamese harbors. An example of this reluctance is seen with Representative Larry Coughlin (R-PA), a firm supporter of administration policy for years. Coughlin stated that, while he admired Nixon's "courage and resolve," he did not think "any possible threat against [U.S. interests] could justify the risks involved in the blockade."[124]

Opponents saw this as yet another opportunity to force Nixon to recognize the fatal flaws in U.S. policy and complete the disengagement process. McCloskey and Riegle, for instance, argued that the blockade violated international law and was unconstitutional without a declaration of war—a step they had no intention of ever supporting.[125] The longtime GOP critics Jacob Javits and George Aiken were not sold on Nixon's solution and did not hesitate to disdain the administration's strategy. Javits called the president's course of action "the inevitable result of a gravely mistaken course our country took in Vietnam." Aiken, discouraged with Nixon after having supported his efforts since the beginning of his presidency, argued that he did not believe that mining the harbors would have much effect on the status quo and that it simply represented the president practicing "brinksmanship."[126]

National media opinion differed widely on the administration's response to the offensive. "When predator nations are on the prowl," the *Phoenix Gazette* editorialized, "peace can be achieved only by fighting for it. Or by showing beyond even a fool's doubting the willingness to fight." The speech and the actions that Nixon proposed in it were "what President Kennedy and Johnson should have done."[127] The *Arizona Republic* commented that, while the speech "undoubtedly escalated American participation in the Vietnam war," it also "escalated the drive for peace." With significant hyperbole, its editors continued, "It was probably the bravest speech ever made by an American president, and it showed the only course that promises an honorable end to the war."[128] On the other side, Tom Wicker savaged Nixon in his column in the *New York Times*, calling his policy "a miserable failure." Wicker suggested that Vietnamization "is as grandiose a failure as Lyndon Johnson's land war," faulted Nixon and Kissinger's efforts at negotiating a peace settlement, and criticized the administration's decision to mine North Vietnamese harbors. He concluded by declaring that Nixon could not possibly achieve "withdrawal with honor" while maintaining a non-Communist government in Saigon.[129]

Despite the fact that Nixon was "catching hell about Vietnam," hawks like Barry Goldwater continued their dogged defense of the president, "supporting him to the hilt." In Goldwater's mind, Nixon's actions in mining Haiphong would not seriously jeopardize U.S.-Soviet relations. In fact, he argued, it "would be to the Russian's [*sic*] advantage to end this and it would certainly pull Nixon out of a hole and, frankly, I think the Russians are frightened that there might be a Democrat as President for they feel a Republican will reason with them in a sounder way."[130] Goldwater expressed his disgust with "the political roadblock which the Democrats in Congress are placing in the path of a Republican President who is trying to wind down and end their war." He questioned whether the Democrats wanted to end the war before the election and decried efforts to label Vietnam as "Nixon's War."[131]

The decision to mine Haiphong and expand the bombing of targets in North Vietnam had been a tremendous gamble—even Nixon characterized it as "go[ing] for broke."[132] The columnist James Reston suggested prior to Nixon's comments on 8 May that, because "nobody in Washington or Moscow or Peking, let alone in Hanoi, can calculate what Mr. Nixon will do if he is trapped," the decisions the president made and would still make in the wake of the Easter Offensive could "very well determine the outcome of the war and influence the Presidential election in November."[133] Yet, with the successful execution of the increased military tactics, with public opinion squarely behind the administration after his remarks—the American public had always been willing to accept bombing rather than the use of ground troops—and with a lackluster Democratic opponent, Nixon looked to be well on his way to a second term. Nixon's public approval ratings skyrocketed, and Congress did nothing substantive to impede his actions. As Theodore White commented, in the wake of the success of the president's speech and the shooting of Governor George Wallace one week later, Nixon's reelection "was finally, irrevocably, assured."[134]

That is not to say, however, that Nixon would not still face challenges. Pete McCloskey continued his quixotic campaign in an attempt to push Nixon closer to a settlement. But, despite his dogged determination and constant criticism, McCloskey's effort to upset the president ultimately fell far short of its goal. Nixon had won the Republican primary in New Hampshire easily over both McCloskey and Ashbrook. To be sure, the ongoing troop withdrawals and Nixon's announcement of Kissinger's secret talks with the North Vietnamese negotiator Le Duc Tho certainly undermined McCloskey's appeal. Yet, as the *New York Times* editorialized on 9 May 1972, McCloskey "achieved a highly creditable performance in obtaining one-fifth of the vote," demonstrating "courage and political leadership" in his principled crusade on issues on which Nixon was vulnerable—most notably, the Vietnam War and the administration's "mania for secrecy." The *Times* also recognized that, unlike other, more prominent Republicans, McCloskey refused to take "refuge in silence" or accommodate himself to a policy of which he disapproved.[135] The California congressman would continue to harass the administration for the remainder of the year, determined to press on until the last American came home.

But, even if they did not affect Nixon's renomination, McCloskey's constant attacks had their utility. As Don Oberdorfer had written in the *Washington Post* in September 1971, "The very existence of the McCloskey challenge is a warning to the President of the consequences of any sudden zigzag or crisis in the war zone."[136] Nixon had to be careful not to move too aggressively—at least in public—lest the antiwar forces pounce. Moreover, opponents of the war realized that their window of opportunity to influence the administration was quickly closing. As Leslie Gelb and Anthony Lake wrote in June, "If there is a chance of changing the President's policy, it is now when he faces an election campaign, not later, should he be re-elected."[137] Observers universally recognized that Nixon's vulnerability on the war issue was temporary and linked to domestic political constraints and electoral considerations. Once he no longer had to face the voters, there would be no restraints on what he might do to secure victory in Vietnam.

George McGovern was doing his best to ensure that Nixon did not get that opportunity. The outspoken dovish senator gained the Democratic nomination for president and continued to promote his strident message of immediate and unilateral withdrawal. Unfortunately for the Democrats, however, McGovern's strongest appeal—his commitment to an extreme antiwar position—also made him the easiest opponent for Nixon in the fall. McGovern's stance gave the president and his surrogates a great deal of room to maneuver and still hold on to the vital center of the electorate. For example, Ronald Reagan asserted that, if there had been an error in the conduct of the war from the U.S. perspective, it was "one of morality—the immorality over the long years of asking our young men to fight and die for a cause the administration at the time lacked the will to win." He criticized McGovern for suggesting that, as president, he would go to Hanoi "hat-in-hand" and give away "the last vestige of bargaining power"—not knowing whether it would affect the return of American prisoners-of-war. Nixon, he argued, deserved the assurance that he would have the support of the American people and would be able to "do whatever has to be done" to end the war honorably and bring the prisoners home.[138]

The country seemed to be willing to allow Nixon that latitude. That did not stop Congress from trying to hasten the process, however. Throughout the middle of 1972, more timetable and funding-termination proposals were forwarded, but none garnered much support. Hoping to diffuse the war issue for the fall campaign, the GOP leadership in the Senate made an effort to work out a compromise between Senate doves and the administration in late July. Nixon refused to consider any such legislation. "I recognize that there are differing views on how best to bring about the end to this war," the president stated in a letter to congressional leaders. "But I am also conscious that the responsibility for doing so is above all mine, and I intend to carry out this obligation in a responsible way." Congressional resolutions and amendments to appropriations bills that "deprive me of the flexibility to do so," he argued, "can not be the sound course. They will only serve to delay the end of the war by hampering the efforts for peace now being made."[139]

Nixon was not alone in his opinions. John Byrnes agreed with him and opposed efforts to end the war by congressional fiat. The Wisconsin congressman argued that it would give Nixon "no leeway in negotiating an end to the war, because it lays all of our cards on the table while the enemy's hand is still concealed, and because it lacks the safeguards which experience has shown us are necessary in any agreement we might make with the North Vietnamese."[140] With backing from Byrnes, Goldwater, Reagan, and other influential Republicans across the country, Nixon felt secure in his position. Indeed, by the late summer of 1972, he had essentially transcended the desire to cajole Congress into supporting his policies, including the intractable antiwar forces in his own party. In effect, he was basically ignoring everyone, counting on the boost in popularity he received from the LINEBACKER raids and other actions he implemented in May to carry him until Kissinger could make a breakthrough in the peace talks.

With this defiant attitude, Nixon looked forward to the adulation he would receive as the Republicans met to rally around him and celebrate the achievements of his first term. The party gathered in Miami again, the scene of Nixon's nomination four years earlier. Originally, the plan had been to meet in San Diego, but the threat of major protests by antiwar activists factored in to the decision to relocate the convention. In the days leading up to the president's acceptance speech, the party came together in keeping with the Eleventh Commandment and lauded the administration's successes, even on Vietnam, despite the earlier challenges from McCloskey and Ashbrook. Ronald Reagan contrasted McGovern's idealism, which he called a "flight of fancy," with Nixon's practical "idealism with integrity" and would be one of the administration's most vocal cheerleaders.[141] The two GOP senators from New York, James Buckley and Jacob Javits, could not have been more different ideologically. But the conservative Buckley and the liberal Javits put aside their problems with the president's policies—Buckley feared the administration might "fudge" on its commitment to Southeast Asia, while Javits "was not satisfied with the pace of diminishing the Vietnam war"—to show their support for Nixon at the convention.[142] And even Nixon's old rival Nelson Rockefeller appeared with Reagan both to demonstrate that the conservative and liberal wings of the party stood solidly behind the president and to deliver biting indictments of McGovern's handling of the war issue in the campaign.[143]

Of course, not everything went according to the carefully arranged script.

9 August 1972: "Now, as I Was Saying Four Years Ago—"

The administration was taken by surprise when William Rogers told the Knight newspaper chain at the beginning of the convention, "I think that either we will have a negotiated settlement before the elections, which I think is a possibility, or we will have one soon after." Nixon's staff quickly backpedaled from Rogers's remarks. Herbert Klein, the White House communication director, cautioned against reading too much into the secretary of state's comments and suggested that they be interpreted "as more a hope than any pinned-down date." Klein also made it clear that the situation remained stalemated despite Kissinger's ongoing negotiations and that reporters should not expect any "major developments" during the week of the convention.[144] What the president did not need at this juncture was an expectation of an imminent settlement that could blow up in his face if it did not materialize before the election.

Another problem occurred when Nixon's nemesis Pete McCloskey appeared with Daniel Ellsberg, the former RAND and Department of Defense official who had leaked the Pentagon Papers to the *New York Times,* the day before Nixon's speech. Ellsberg accused the president of planning the escalation of certain aspects of the war—especially the intensification of the bombing of North Vietnam—even before he was elected in 1968 as part of his alleged secret plan. The two men told reporters that they wanted to make Nixon's policies clear to the public before the GOP renominated him. McCloskey even tried to introduce some of Ellsberg's charges into the platform debate but failed to gain the access he needed to do so, largely because of the rules the party put in place to prevent dissension from disrupting the desired unanimity at the convention.[145]

The media also piled on, most vigorously when Anthony Lewis took Nixon to task in an article titled "The War President." Lewis described the "most remarkable achievement" of Nixon's first term as turning the Vietnam War from "a national mistake" into "an obsession." The president had squandered the "widespread goodwill" and "high public expectations" of those who believed that he would "liquidate" the war quickly once in office. Instead, he had "intensified the American commitment to an ignoble cause remote from the vital national interests." He remained, Lewis asserted, "determined to win the war, at whatever cost," which meant "getting the Communist side to accept an American-oriented anti-Communist Government in Saigon." He characterized the president's position as "imperviousness to changing realities," arguing that Nixon basically ignored the evolution of the conflict and its justifications and was prosecuting it for personal reasons. Ultimately, Lewis concluded, Nixon "has shown that it is possible for a determined President, with shrewd political advice, to carry on indefinitely a war unpopular in the country and in Congress. He has proved that there are no effective political mechanisms in the American system to restrain such a President between elections."[146] This fact of American political life recurs repeatedly during the Vietnam experience and helps explain why Kennedy, Johnson, and Nixon were able to take the actions they did with minimal congressional interference.

These minor irritants aside, the Republicans enjoyed another week of remarkable unity in Miami. The GOP platform once again muted the divisions within the party and spun the Vietnam War to the administration's advantage. In his four years in office, the platform proclaimed, Nixon had "marched toward peace and away from war," had "not abandoned an ally to aggression, not turned our back on their brave defense against brutal invasion, not consigned them to the bloodbath that would follow Communist conquest." His presidency had been a "saga of exhilarating progress." The Republicans pledged to continue to seek a settlement "which will permit the people of Southeast Asia to live in peace under political arrangements of their own choosing," although temporized by immediately declaring Nixon's "refusal to accept terms which would dishonor this country." The platform also recognized Nixon's "generous" peace proposal and attacked those who were "bemused with surrender"—those who would pursue peace at any cost.[147] In essence, the party's platform looked similar to the one it ran on in 1968 in that any Republican could run on the principles it championed. But in one respect the Vietnam plank in 1972 differed substantially: the ambiguous "win the peace" language of four years earlier had been replaced with a firm devotion to achieving an honorable peace—which still gave the president a great deal of latitude in interpreting exactly what such an agreement would look like.

In his acceptance speech, Nixon built on the language of the platform and asserted that his administration had "changed America and that America has changed the world" into "a safer place to live in than was the case 4 years ago." He claimed that "peace is too important for partisanship," suggesting (again, quite disingenuously) that he had not and would not play politics with Vietnam. After noting the progress made toward disengagement, he made three things absolutely clear: "We will never abandon our prisoners of war. . . . We will not join our enemies in imposing a Communist government on our allies . . . And we will never stain the honor of the United States of America." The last point was the wild card, and one could be forgiven for seeing it as portending ominous developments in Nixon's policies. He went on to declare that, while it might be "good politics" to accept Hanoi's demands and "just blame the whole catastrophe on [his] predecessors," the people who advocated this approach did not understand how "disastrous" it would be "to the cause of peace." But there was more to it than that. From Nixon's perspective, it would be a very poor political decision because of the potential backlash from the Right. He concluded by asserting that the country needed to ensure that the president "never has to negotiate from weakness" and that there was "no such thing as a retreat to peace."[148] This was a typical Nixonian speech, and it unequivocally demonstrated his willingness to stay the course in Vietnam until victory as he defined it was achieved.

The delegates, of course, loved every minute of the convention. But the accolades of his party notwithstanding, Nixon faced sharp criticism for his remarks and for the decisions made during his first term. Tom Wicker derided the Republicans for "having it both ways, turning black into white, and making something out of nothing" in Vietnam. Pointing to the GOP platform in which Nixon "ended the war in the prologue," he noted that "in the very same prologue the Republicans declare that the nation's choice this year is one between 'negotiating or begging with adversary nations.'"[149] McGovern also fired away at the president, desperately trying to overcome his sizable deficit in the polls and recover from the disastrous selection of Senator Thomas Eagleton (D-MO) as his running mate. But nothing McGovern did or said would make much of a difference. The public, weary of the war and anticipating news of a settlement from Kissinger's diplomatic efforts at any moment, focused on other pressing issues and relegated Vietnam to a relatively minor role in the campaign. As McGovern observed at one point, "When the corpses changed color, American interest diminished."[150]

That being said, Melvin Laird firmly believed that Nixon won a second term on the Vietnam War issue. Nixon realized, Laird recalled, that "the troop withdrawals and ending the draft were his biggest victories on which to campaign. He wound up with a huge majority in one of the greatest reelection victories any president has ever had." While certainly an overstatement, Laird's point is well-taken. Nixon agreed with Laird's assessment. In a letter to Laird that marked his valedictory as secretary of defense, he wrote, "To have bugged out the day after we got into office would have been easy—and some say—good politics. It would have won us a few good headlines and a great deal of public support in the short run." But, he concluded, it would have been "disastrous for America in the long run," and "historians will record we did the right thing."[151]

In the end, the race against McGovern was little more than a victory lap for Nixon. He made very few appearances and refused to debate the Democratic nominee, relying instead on surrogates and television advertising to make his case to the American public. Ford attacked McGovern's formula for peace in Vietnam, calling it "a formula for a Communist takeover in Saigon. George McGovern is unreal." Electing him would be tantamount to "an open invitation to Communist aggression throughout the world."[152] Paul Fannin, who admitted that not all was well in Vietnam, put the conflict into a broader context.

"The decision is being made," he said, "as to whether America will remain a force for good in the free world, or whether we will cower on our own shores." The primary obstacle to peace was that Nixon lacked the full support of Congress. With the support of Congress and the American public, he asserted, "this struggle to preserve a free nation can be won." Failure to do so would result in "a disaster." He concluded, "Peace is a wonderful goal, but peace lies in resolution and in strength—not in retreat or surrender."[153]

Although little doubt remained about the outcome of the election, the burgeoning story of Watergate loomed over the entire campaign. The break-in at the Democratic National Committee's headquarters in Washington, DC, was only the latest in a series of efforts by Nixon's "plumbers unit" dating back to the release of the Pentagon Papers to deal with the president's political adversaries. More important, the entire imbroglio derived directly from the Vietnam War. The scandal would consume an increasing amount of Nixon's time and attention even with the intensification of the peace talks with Hanoi as Kissinger inched closer to an agreement in Paris. The story of the break-in would not go away despite the administration's best efforts, and in September a grand jury indicted the "Watergate Seven." Revelations from the *Washington Post* reporters Bob Woodward and Carl Bernstein further complicated matters for Nixon and put him and his entire staff on the defensive. But the real importance of the entire Watergate situation was that its origins can be firmly located in Nixon's ongoing concern with the war and its relation to public opinion and his second term. Domestic politics caused his obsession with defending his policies, which led him to authorize the illegal cover-up by G. Gordon Liddy and the other key Watergate figures. Ultimately, his fixation on winning the peace in Vietnam and being reelected brought his presidency to a premature end with his resignation in August 1974.

For the present, however, Nixon went on to crush McGovern in the fall election in an unprecedented landslide. He carried forty-nine states and outpolled the Democratic candidate by over twenty million votes. McGovern's only support came from hard-core antiwar activists and the far left wing of his party; indeed, he even failed to win his home state of South Dakota (carrying only Massachusetts and Washington, DC). The GOP also picked up twelve seats in the House, a strong showing for Gerald Ford and his leadership team. But the Republicans lost more ground in the Senate, which meant that Nixon would have to do everything he could to wrap up the conflict in Vietnam before Congress could take definitive action. One of the war's strongest critics, John Sherman Cooper, retired, as did the hawkish Karl Mundt, and several other staunch supporters of the administration's policies lost their seats, including Jack Miller.

Still, reelection meant that Nixon could theoretically act with a greater degree of freedom in Vietnam given that he no longer had to worry about electoral calculations. He felt that the U.S. negotiating position would be stronger
after the election because the North Vietnamese would have to either "settle
or face the consequences of what we could do to them."[154] Kissinger informed
them as much, telling them that Nixon would not hesitate to "take whatever
action he considers necessary to protect United States interests" now that he
had defeated McGovern.[155] But, even with the election behind him, it is striking
that Nixon remained deeply concerned with domestic political considerations.
As George Aiken wrote in his diary three weeks after the president's historic
victory, "Assuming Kissinger is the conceited scamp that Thieu portrays him
to be, and that Thieu himself is an apostle of honor and integrity, Mr. Kissinger
will win the contest, for regardless of who is right and who is wrong neither the
American public nor the Congress will stand for our continued involvement in
Vietnam. Nor can President Nixon afford it at this stage of the game."[156] Even
though he would not face the voters again, Nixon needed a peace settlement for
three primary reasons: to allow him to pursue his broader foreign policy goals;
to achieve the long-promised "peace with honor" on which he had campaigned;
and to protect his legacy, something about which he always obsessed.

The prospects for a settlement did not look promising in December, however. Kissinger had come close to reaching an accord with the North Vietnamese
on the eve of the election and believed that it would be a boon for Republican
candidates. Unfortunately, he overlooked one minor detail—he did not inform
the North Vietnamese negotiators that Thieu could render any agreement inval-
id if he chose not to sign off on it. That is exactly what happened; the preelection
peace was thwarted by Thieu's intractable attitude and his fear that Kissinger
had sold South Vietnam out to Hanoi. Subsequently, negotiations stalled as the
South Vietnamese president insisted on sixty-nine "modifications" to the agreement; the North Vietnamese refused. Concerned that the newly elected Congress would cut off funding for the war when it convened after the beginning
of the year, the president faced a major dilemma: the prospect of negotiating
with a deadline with no additional leverage and an adversary in no mood to
make any further concessions. Kissinger summed things up for Nixon in mid-
December. The administration could either take "a massive, shocking step to
impose our will on events and end the war quickly" or allow matters to "drift
into another round of inconclusive negotiations, prolonged warfare, bitter national divisions, and mounting casualties." It was, for Nixon, an easy decision.
As Kissinger later wrote, Hanoi had "cornered him," and Richard Nixon "was
never more dangerous than when he seemed to have run out of options."[157]

On 14 December 1972, Nixon ordered the military to launch massive B-52 bombing raids against military targets in and around Hanoi and plant new mines in Haiphong harbor. The "Christmas bombings" targeted transportation, power, communications, and shipping facilities in the North on a scale not previously seen in the war. This was "jugular diplomacy," as Kissinger characterized it, a way to force the North Vietnamese into making sufficient concessions to allow Nixon to obtain his peace with honor.[158] Despite significant losses—twenty-six U.S. aircraft, including fifteen B-52s—and a major drop in the president's approval rating, the gamble paid off for Nixon. After two weeks of attacks, the North Vietnamese informed Kissinger that they were ready to talk again, setting a target date of 8 January. The two sides quickly reached an agreement, and two weeks later the Paris Peace Accords brought America's longest war to an end. But the overwhelming reaction to the bombings was decidedly negative. George Aiken, who had questioned the necessity and brutality of the attacks, calling them a "sorry Christmas present" for the American people, summarized the situation succinctly. The senior Republican believed that "both sides lost heavily, and the next meeting in Paris represents a 'mutual surrender party' which ought not to have ever been necessary in the first place."[159]

Accolades for the agreement poured in from across the political spectrum, but especially from Republicans. Barry Goldwater, in a widely published letter, praised Nixon: "This agreement is a tribute to the President's skill, perseverance and courage to make the right decisions in the face of overwhelming obstacles. But perhaps the greatest tribute must be paid to the patience and steadfastness of the President. He was able to attain the American goal of peace without surrender while under the most systemic, often hateful and nearly always intemperate attacks by his critics."[160] Aiken wrote that the agreement was "a masterpiece of diplomacy. Certainly it is a victory for us to be able to get out of our Vietnam predicament at all."[161] But some of the most fulsome praise came from the *Richmond News Leader,* which opined that Nixon had "accomplished what his people elected him, and re-elected him, to do. . . . The President's achievement cannot be overplayed. He did it when his domestic enemies were sedulous and singularly successful in their efforts to prevent the mobilization of national detestation for the Communist enemy. He did it as President of a people accustomed to speedy results. . . . He did it when many of the persons who should have supported him most enthusiastically had curled up in the corner like a sulky dog. He made up his mind and dug in his defenses and persisted. Now he has prevailed."[162] But not everyone showered Nixon with kudos. The *St. Louis Post-Dispatch* opined that peace was "marred" by "Mr. Nixon's shameful act" of bombing North Vietnam in December, while the *New York Times* congratulated Henry Kissinger but offered no words of support for Nixon.[163]

One of the ironies of the timing of the agreement was the death of Lyndon

Johnson on 22 January 1973. Is it possible that the North Vietnamese—or even the Nixon administration—postponed the announcement of the agreement in a last jab at Johnson? Certainly. Nevertheless, Nixon wrote to Lady Bird Johnson, "I only wish Lyndon could have lived to hear my announcement of the Viet Nam Peace Settlement tonight. I know what abuse he took—particularly from members of his own party—in standing firm for peace with honor."[164] Nixon could relate to his predecessor's plight. He had been subjected to similar abuse throughout his presidency, buffeted by the same domestic political pressures that had caused LBJ to withdraw from the 1968 presidential campaign. But, in the end, Nixon could at the very least point to the fact that he had fulfilled the promises of his inaugural address and brought peace, however flawed and transitory, to Vietnam.

During his presidency, Richard Nixon tried to find his way out of the maze created by his predecessors (and, truthfully, his own administration) without a guide and without a blueprint. The only direction he had, whether he would admit it in his private thoughts or not (and, judging by his memoirs, not), was the thread of domestic opinion. Nixon's decisions and choices from 1970 to the final peace treaty depended to a substantial extent on congressional pressure, American public opinion, and his concern for electoral success. Had Theseus attempted the same in his quest to kill the Minotaur, he would probably still be wandering Daedalus's maze.

And now, as the late Paul Harvey used to say, for the rest of the story. The domestic political considerations that had preoccupied Kennedy, Johnson, and Nixon prevented Gerald Ford and Kissinger from coming to South Vietnam's assistance in the last days of the regime in April 1975. The story of the "jabberwocky peace," as Larry Berman has characterized it, and its aftermath is a long and tortured one.[165] In the end, there was no peace, and there was no honor. The administration had every intention of abrogating the agreement that it had brokered—much as Theseus deserted Ariadne after escaping the labyrinth—an intention based on secret understandings that called for virtually indefinite U.S. involvement in Southeast Asia should the treaty be violated as Nixon and Kissinger expected. Indeed, "Thieu counted on the United States to be the final supervisor and enforcer of the peace."[166] But the agreed-on assistance never materialized. In his last eighteen months in office, Nixon faced an increasingly recalcitrant and assertive Congress, a public weary of war, and the Watergate crisis, which left the president politically impotent. In addition, Republicans abandoned the administration in droves. George Aiken called the ongoing bombing of Cambodia "ill-advised and unwarranted," and Norris Cotton spoke for many in the GOP when he said, "As far as I'm concerned, I want to get the hell out."[167] The political forces with which Nixon had successfully grappled during his first term now posed a mortal threat both to his presidency and to the residual U.S. commitment to Vietnam.

Nixon's entanglement in Watergate—a crisis with definitive links to Nixon's politically influenced Vietnam policy—consumed most of his attention and sapped his remaining political resources. By the time he resigned in August 1974, the Paris agreement was essentially in tatters, having been violated flagrantly by all parties. Nixon's successor, Gerald Ford, called for "strict observance of the cease-fire in Vietnam" and pushed Congress to continue to appropriate military aid for Saigon.[168] But Ford's primary concern was repairing the damage done to the country by Watergate; the war in Southeast Asia did not rank high on his list of priorities. That left Kissinger virtually alone and without the benefit of GOP support for the conflict in trying to convince "an increasingly defiant Congress" to expand military aid to South Vietnam.[169] But the logic that had maintained support for Saigon for three decades no longer resonated with Congress or the American public, and the new administration was forced to accept less than half the requested funding.

Domestic politics played a critical role during the denouement of the conflict. On the heels of Ford's pardon of Nixon, his offer of "earned amnesty" to draft resisters and the creation of the Presidential Clemency Board cost him substantially in terms of public opinion; his approval rating dropped from 72 to 49 percent by September. One Louisiana Republican called Ford's program "a direct insult to those servicemen who . . . did not shirk their duty."[170] Moreover, like Kennedy, Johnson, and Nixon before him, Ford had to deal with criticism from conservatives, not only for his amnesty program but also for his weak response to the North Vietnamese invasion. The administration's efforts came far too late for many on the GOP's increasingly powerful right wing, which expressed outrage at the "utter futility" of Ford's policies.[171] Moreover, observers like Vice President Nelson Rockefeller believed that the fall of Saigon would jeopardize Ford's chances of regaining the White House in 1976, placing the president's decisions into a political and electoral framework comparable to those of his three predecessors.

These domestic political factors limited Ford's room to maneuver and determined the nature of the U.S. response to Hanoi's final offensive. Congressional Republicans like Pete McCloskey and Edward Brooke believed that it was only a matter of time before South Vietnam fell, and the situation seemed desperate enough that Representative Robert Michel (R-IL) argued, "We can only provide humanitarian assistance."[172] As North Vietnamese troops closed in on Saigon in the spring of 1975, Ford and Kissinger pressed Congress for $722 million in emergency assistance to save South Vietnam, "setting off a final, bitterly emotional debate on the war."[173] With virtually no Republican support in

Congress to rely on, the administration lacked the leverage it needed to secure the aid package, which was summarily rejected. Kissinger finally had to admit that "the Vietnam debate has run its course," a reality Ford conceded when he told students at Tulane University on 23 April that the Vietnam conflict was "finished as far as the United States was concerned."[174] A week later, the North Vietnamese Army stormed into Saigon and toppled the regime whose survival had been at the center of the conflict on both fronts in America's longest war.

# Conclusion

## Sowing Dragon's Teeth

When you engage in actual fighting, if victory is long in coming, the men's weapons will grow dull and their ardor will be dampened. If you lay siege to a town, you will exhaust your strength, and if the campaign is protracted, the resources of the state will not be equal to the strain. Never forget: when your weapons are dulled, your ardor dampened, your strength exhausted, and your treasure spent, other chieftains will spring up to take advantage of your extremity. Then no man, however wise, will be able to avert the consequences that must ensue.

—Sun Tzu, *The Art of War*

In the White House, the future rapidly becomes the past; and delay is itself a decision.

—Theodore Sorensen in *Nation's Business* (1963)

From the tale of Cadmus in Greek mythology we get one of the first lessons about the dangers of *blowback,* a modern term for a timeless phenomenon—actions that provoke calamitous, although entirely unintended, consequences. Cadmus, a Phoenician prince, sent some of his men to draw water from the spring of Ares, the god of war. When they failed to return, he sent more men and then more men, until none remained. He then went to the spring himself, where he saw the dragon lying by the water, sluggish from his recent meal. Taking advantage of the situation, Cadmus slew the dragon by leaping directly into its mouth and killing it from within its jaws. The goddess Athena told him that, if he sowed half the dragon's teeth in the earth, his men would be replaced. Dutifully following her instructions, Cadmus planted the teeth. He did not expect the results. From the ground emerged ferocious warriors who attacked everything—and everyone—in sight. Athena advised Cadmus to strike one of them with a stone. He complied, and the warriors, assuming that they had been assaulted by one of the others, turned against each other. The band of *sparti,* as they were known, nearly destroyed themselves in the ensuing fratricidal blood-bath; the survivors became Cadmus's most loyal supporters when he founded the city of Thebes. In the end, Ares forced Cadmus to serve eight years of pen-ance for killing his dragon before being released to return home. Later, the re-mainder of the dragon's teeth fell into the possession of the hero Jason, whose experience paralleled that of Cadmus almost exactly.

Like Cadmus and Jason, three successive administrations and members of Congress reaped what they sowed in Vietnam. They sent increasing numbers of troops to Southeast Asia, fought among themselves politically, and served penance to the gods of war, although none of the presidents lasted eight years. In sowing the proverbial dragon's teeth, they precipitated an endless national debate that destroyed two presidencies, killed and maimed millions of Asians and Americans, wreaked incalculable harm on the fabric of culture and soci-ety in both nations, and fundamentally damaged and permanently altered the premises of politics and diplomacy in the United States. The war was fought on two fronts, with the actions in Southeast Asia invariably affecting the political battlefield at home, and vice versa. Hoping to save democracy on two fronts from the march of communism, they nearly destroyed it with their own "march of folly."[1] Such is the story of domestic politics and the Republican Party during the Vietnam conflict, a history marred by evasions, equivocations, delays, and postponements of critical decisions, actions and inactions that produced the most terrible of unintended consequences. The research in the preceding chap-ters suggests a number of conclusions about the centrality of domestic political considerations as they relate to the making and implementation of U.S. foreign policy, the significant contributions of members of the Republican Party to the policymaking process during the war, and the roles played by Congress and the three presidents of this period.

The historian David Skidmore argues, "Policy makers do not have the luxury of ignoring domestic political imperatives, even when these imperatives work against otherwise sound policies."[2] Presidents from George Washington to Barack Obama have pursued foreign policies based on domestic political calcu-lations. In doing so, they frequently subordinated the national interest to their own partisan or personal interests. Political expediency often trumped national security as presidents maneuvered to win reelection, boost their standings in opinion polls, or manipulate public and congressional opinion. The 1998 film *Wag the Dog* may have been a fictionalized account of a president staging a phony war to enhance his electoral prospects, but it revealed a deeper truth:

political leaders have often used foreign policy and international conflict as a way of bolstering their position at home.

Perhaps at no other time in the nation's history was this fact of American political life demonstrated more vividly than during the Vietnam era. Kennedy, Johnson, and Nixon all worried that the "loss" of Vietnam would open the floodgates of domestic criticism and that they would be attacked for being soft on communism by conservatives. Furthermore, they believed that these allegations would curtail their influence and expend their political capital, thus endangering their legislative agendas and weakening their presidencies. To borrow a poker metaphor, the "costs of raising the ante seemed clearly lower" than folding in South Vietnam.[3] Kennedy, Johnson, and Nixon all tried to bluff their way through the game; unfortunately, they were all playing with an unwinnable hand.

John Kennedy seemed particularly vulnerable on this issue. His early failures in Cuba, Berlin, and Laos contributed to his paranoia about a right-wing backlash against any signs of weakness in Southeast Asia. In his mind, the neutralization of South Vietnam, to say nothing of a Communist takeover, threatened a firestorm of conservative criticism that would doom his chances for reelection. Holding out for a more secure position in 1964, he and his administration remained in a holding pattern, delaying critical decisions in order to safeguard a second term. Whether Kennedy would have withdrawn from Vietnam is one of the intriguing, but ultimately unknowable, counterfactual questions in American political history.[4] But one thing is certain—domestic politics would have factored in to his deliberations even after winning a second term. As it was, the dragon's teeth Kennedy sowed had far-reaching ramifications for both his immediate successors.

Lyndon Johnson harbored similar fears. His experience in the Senate during the "who lost China" debate reinforced his concern over the potential problems he would face if he "lost" Vietnam. Constrained by the pervasive fear of the conservative reaction to losing the war or being branded an appeaser if he negotiated, he steadily Americanized the war as much for his own domestic political purposes as to save South Vietnam; indeed, the two causes had for him become intertwined. He wholeheartedly believed, as Jack Valenti later commented, that "the Democratic right and the Republicans . . . would have torn him to pieces" for losing Vietnam. Valenti believed, "If somebody had come forward with a specific plan, and was able to convince him [LBJ] that he wouldn't have the right wing, as he called them, the guys on the right, the Republicans, pillaging the political neighborhood, I think he would have considered it [i.e., a negotiated settlement]."[5] These fears influenced LBJ to the point that he ostracized or silenced anyone in his administration who dared speak of a negotiated settlement in Vietnam, as he did with his own vice president, Hubert Humphrey, in 1965.

Some historians suggest that Johnson misjudged the political environment, that the conservative threat was illusory and no right-wing monster lurked at his door.[6] Yet the evidence demonstrates two things quite clearly. First, whether the danger was real or imagined, LBJ's fear of the backlash was palpable. Former administration officials such as George Ball and Francis Bator recall that Johnson (like Kennedy and Nixon) feared the "Great Beast" of the Right more than any anxiety about pressure on the Left. They and others argue that LBJ was "traumatized" by what had happened to Truman and vowed not to let the same thing happen to him over Vietnam.[7] Second, Johnson's fear was grounded in a discernible political reality. Those who downplay criticism from the GOP and conservatives ignore the overwhelming documentary record to the contrary. As this book has conclusively shown, the anxiety about a right-wing backlash exhibited by Kennedy, Johnson, and Nixon reflected the extensive and serious criticism emanating from conservatives in the political environment in which all three made their decisions on the war.

Throughout his presidency, Johnson faced countervailing domestic political pressure from Republicans of every ideological bent. For each Barry Goldwater, Strom Thurmond, or Richard Nixon, there was a Mark Hatfield, John Sherman Cooper, or Pete McCloskey. Presidents must juggle multiple distinct and competing congressional constituencies in order to assure success in both foreign and domestic affairs, a task that became progressively more difficult for LBJ as the Vietnam War became increasingly unpopular. As the historian Melvin Small has commented, "The longer and larger the American commitment to Vietnam, the harder it became in domestic political terms to pull out of the war without, as Lyndon Johnson said, the 'coonskin nailed to the wall.'"[8] The fact of the matter is that Johnson's postponed decisions, politically motivated evasions, and intentional delaying tactics constricted the locus of realistic possibilities for his administration. The blowback from these decisions reflects a broader issue in the history of American foreign relations, the vast catalog of negative unintended consequences from U.S. policy decisions.[9] Ultimately, Johnson's Vietnam policies were designed less on the basis of whether they would achieve results in Southeast Asia than on whether they would sustain support for his administration's policies at home, especially in Congress. Domestic political pressures were instrumental in LBJ's decision to intervene, escalate, and remain in Vietnam.

Even Richard Nixon, the archetypical anti-Communist, worried about charges of being soft on Vietnam. He dreaded the repercussions he would face if he conceded too much to Hanoi or lost the war. Conservative forces within the

GOP—the *National Review* crowd especially—loudly criticized his Vietnamization strategy and forced him to disengage more slowly than perhaps he would have otherwise. In addition, the contradictory policies of disengagement and escalation that he employed simultaneously resulted directly from domestic political calculations. He did not want to be seen as giving up on the war or ceding too much ground to the North Vietnamese in negotiations. Thus, he escalated the bombing and expanded the war into Cambodia. On the other hand, domestic pressure required him to begin the process of withdrawal. But, even then, he faced constraints. Not only did the withdrawal need to occur methodically, lest he be accused of damaging American prestige, but, if it proceeded too slowly, he would also be accused of prolonging the conflict. These policies reflected a cognitive dissonance on Nixon's part. The president believed sincerely that the simultaneous yet contradictory policies of escalation and Vietnamization, both of which stemmed from his obsession with domestic political considerations, would lead to success in Southeast Asia.

The U.S. experience in Vietnam also makes clear that foreign policy exerts a tremendous influence on elections in the United States. It has long been an axiom of American politics that national security affairs and foreign policy do not play a significant role in deciding elections; scores of academic studies have argued that economic issues ("it's the economy, stupid!") far outweigh international ones in terms of voter interest and decisive influence on voting patterns.[10] Presidents know that this assumption is, at best, an exaggeration. In every election between 1952 and 1972, foreign policy clearly played a prominent role. Specific foreign policies might not affect a voter's decision, but they do speak to a president's job performance and the public's perception of his leadership skills. As a result, domestic political calculations exert a tremendous influence on the way in which presidents formulate foreign policy. The political scientist Miroslav Nincic argues that electoral logic "affects the timing of important decisions" and "creates discontinuities in the substance of foreign policy." As a result, "Politicians often adjust their stances according to expected political beliefs—a tendency implying that the conduct of U.S. international affairs is, in part at least, shaped by domestic political and electoral logic."[11] Melvin Small agrees. "During [an election] year," he writes, "because almost everything that presidents do or say in the international arena affects election prospects, they tread cautiously, or pander to popular nationalist sentiment in ways that are not always defensible in terms of the national interests." And Ralph Levering suggests, "Elections are significant because presidents and their advisers shape their policies and rhetoric partly out of fear of what the voters might do in the next election."[12] The argument made here reinforces and expands on these notions. Domestic politics and electoral calculations shaped decisionmaking on Vietnam from the beginning of the conflict to the fall of Saigon.

To an increasingly important degree, the Vietnam War played an integral role in the elections from 1964 to 1972. More significantly, electoral contingencies affected policy decisions in each year as candidates obfuscated the situation in Southeast Asia rather than acting to change public perceptions. Kennedy delayed making major decisions about the course of American policy in Southeast Asia in order to avoid alienating voters as he prepared for the 1964 election. After his assassination, Lyndon Johnson continued this approach. He made a concerted effort to avoid making any major decisions or commitments in Vietnam before facing Goldwater. He realized, as had Kennedy, that an escalation of the conflict without an overt attack on U.S. forces as the proximate cause would jeopardize his electoral success. Indeed, in a campaign that was in virtually every other way an unmitigated disaster for the GOP, Vietnam was Goldwater's best issue. LBJ's reluctance to engage him directly on the burgeoning conflict gave Goldwater a platform to criticize the president. The reality of these calculations is seen in the fact that, almost immediately after the balloting, Johnson decided to Americanize the war, knowing full well that he would not have to face the voters again for another four years.[13]

By the 1966 midterm elections, the murmurings of dissent and opposition began to grow louder. While neither party used Vietnam as a partisan issue to any significant extent—in fact, the Republican leadership advised its candidates *not* to use the war against their Democratic opponents—the conflict lingered in the background and decisively influenced several campaigns. Furthermore, Johnson's efforts at the Manila conference in October came under extreme criticism from the GOP as a political ploy to gain votes for the Democratic Party. Not only did the conduct of the war and the lack of progress become an issue during this campaign, but the administration's credibility did as well. Although it would be an exaggeration to assert that the GOP's electoral success represented a mandate for a change in Johnson's policies toward Vietnam, it did foreshadow the importance of Vietnam in the presidential campaign of 1968.

The pivotal 1968 election, and especially the Republican presidential nomination, clearly turned on the issue of Vietnam. George Romney's campaign failed primarily because he was unable to delineate his stand on the war. His waffling, not to mention the infamous brainwashing comment, proved a stark and decisive contrast to Nixon's adept handling of the war issue. Vietnam also tripped up Nelson Rockefeller. His reluctance to take a definitive stand on the war hampered his candidacy until it was too late. Ronald Reagan, a dark-horse candidate to begin with, was far too hawkish for the GOP, let alone the nation as a whole, to be seriously considered as a candidate. In the end, Richard Nixon's effective management of the Vietnam issue enabled him to secure the Republican nomination and craft an ambiguous platform for the fall campaign. On the Democratic side, Vietnam loomed just as large. Robert Kennedy's assassination prevented a potentially explosive convention at which the Vietnam positions of the two main candidates—Kennedy and Hubert Humphrey—could have been pivotal in determining the nominee. Yet, without RFK's presence at Chicago, and given Eugene McCarthy's dismal campaign efforts, Humphrey won the nomination almost by default. But, as the platform fight over the war demonstrated, the Democrats were deeply divided on Vietnam.

During the fall campaign, both Humphrey and Nixon would have preferred not to discuss the war at all. Humphrey finally broke with the administration because he believed that his best chance for winning the White House was to align himself with the doves; this tactical shift gave him a considerable boost in the polls and nearly won him the election. Nixon, while saying little of substance publicly, maneuvered behind the scenes for months with Anna Chennault, Bui Diem, and Nguyen Van Thieu in an effort to ensure his victory in November. The campaign took a dramatic turn at the end of October with the announcement of the bombing halt by Johnson; ironically, the evidence indicates that, despite the timing of the statement, the halt helped Nixon more than it did Humphrey. Clearly, Richard Nixon owed his presidency in large measure to his ability to present himself as the candidate best qualified to resolve the war through his secret plan to "win the peace" in Vietnam.

The role of the war in the 1970 midterm elections was definitely mixed; its impact varied from race to race, and both opponents and supporters lost their congressional seats. Yet Vietnam loomed large in the presidential election in 1972. The conservative and antiwar challenges from John Ashbrook and Pete McCloskey, respectively, meant that Nixon had to fend off criticism from both wings of his party. But McCloskey's failure to gain traction on the war issue foreshadowed George McGovern's inability to use Vietnam effectively in his campaign. As in 1968, Nixon handled the Vietnam issue deftly throughout the first half of 1972, as demonstrated by the solid support he received during the Easter Offensive despite his aggressive decision to mine Haiphong and radically expand the bombing of North Vietnam. In the fall campaign, the perception that Vietnamization was working—nurtured by Nixon, Laird, and their GOP surrogates—limited the appeal of McGovern's unyielding antiwar message and allowed Nixon to dominate the race on the basis of his appeal on other issues. The ultimate irony was best described by A. J. Langguth. One reason for Kennedy, Johnson, and Nixon to wage war in Vietnam "had been to ensure a second term, a term that none of the three was destined to complete."[14]

Just as domestic politics had a tremendous influence on the direction of

U.S. policy toward Vietnam, the war had a profound impact on the two major political parties. During the 1960s, the Republican Party began undergoing a total metamorphosis. The liberal wing lost most of its influence as conservatives like Goldwater and Reagan gained national prominence. As moderate and liberal Republicans faced derision for their weakness on Vietnam, the war transformed the GOP into a bastion of conservative ideals. On the Democratic side, the coalition that elected FDR and LBJ fractured as disillusionment with liberalism spread, forcing Johnson to cultivate support among Republicans on Vietnam. The war divided the Democratic party badly and contributed substantially to the Republican domination of the executive branch for the next twenty-four years. But Vietnam did more than disrupt the internal makeup of the Republicans and the Democrats. Without the war in Vietnam, it is unlikely that Richard Nixon and, perhaps, even Ronald Reagan would have been elected president. Moreover, the war fundamentally altered the basis of U.S. politics and foreign policy as the United States headed into the 1970s.[15]

The story of the Vietnam War also demonstrates the striking similarities and continuities between all three administrations and presidents. Kennedy and Nixon have frequently been compared by scholars given the parallels between their political careers and their presidential campaign in 1960. But it is intriguing how similar Johnson and Nixon were—and how little comment there has been about that fact. They both came from very humble backgrounds, both have accurately been described as "consummate politicians," both were committed cold warriors, and both saw their presidencies eviscerated by Vietnam. Kennedy and Johnson differed on a personal level, but they too saw the world through virtually the same lens and had analogous political beliefs.

But, more critically, all three acted in virtually the same manner when it came to Vietnam. Each avoided until it was absolutely necessary making crucial decisions that could have affected the course of the war significantly. Each declared that he would not be the first U.S. president to lose a war. Each did everything he could to manipulate congressional and public opinion in an effort to co-opt Congress into joint responsibility for the conflict and to maintain sufficient levels of support to ensure electoral success. For all the grandstanding and politicking, the three presidents approached Vietnam the same way. The policies, if not the tactics and troop levels, remained remarkably consistent during the entire conflict. All three presidents demonstrated a marked reluctance to negotiate from anywhere but a position of absolute strength (which none achieved), an unwillingness to compromise, and an inability to think outside the box that they had created for themselves. Delay, obfuscation, and political sensitivity characterized the Kennedy, Johnson, and Nixon approaches to Vietnam. In that sense, neither their party affiliation, nor their executive experience, nor the broader political context mattered a great deal.

Of course, all three presidents benefited from the ubiquitous congressional complicity that distinguished the Vietnam era. When responsibility for the war is apportioned, Congress should be held accountable for aiding and abetting the escalation and duration of the war. Despite the distinct divide between hawks and doves in both parties, the dominant attitude on Capitol Hill was permissive. Congress followed the same course as the executive: it chose the middle course on Vietnam, avoiding controversial and politically perilous positions. Most members of Congress were more than happy to allow the administration to take the lead in Vietnam and, thereby, assume the lion's share of the political and electoral risk.[16] Both parties consistently voted for appropriations for U.S. forces in South Vietnam on the grounds that to deprive troops in harm's ways of supplies would be unpatriotic. Yet, by supporting these spending bills, the Senate and the House implicitly ratified the policies pursued by Kennedy, Johnson, and Nixon in Vietnam and lengthened the country's involvement in the conflict. The same holds true for the failure of the Congress as an institution to support legislation like the Cooper-Church and Hatfield-McGovern amendments, which would have curtailed the executive's ability to wage war unchecked in Southeast Asia.

Yet to describe this context merely as permissive is to misjudge its influence and underestimate its affects. Perhaps *permissive* does not go far enough, implying as it does a passivity on the part of the House and Senate during the Vietnam era. Congress did not merely "permit" successive administrations to launch, escalate, and continue a ruinous war in Southeast Asia, although many of its choices can be interpreted that way. In many ways, and in several instances, Congress actively fostered the environment that led to these decisions: overwhelmingly approving the Tonkin Gulf resolution, continually authorizing massive military expenditures, and sanctioning a presidential war by failing to exercise its own prerogatives are only a few examples. Moreover, its conservative members cajoled, threatened, and encouraged Kennedy, Johnson, and Nixon to aggressively oppose communism in Southeast Asia, a political force that, as we have seen, could not be ignored by any of the presidents. *Complicity*, then, seems the appropriate description for the congressional context in this period.

Even for those who doubted the wisdom of the war, domestic political calculations softened their opposition. Because they wanted to be reelected, members of Congress had a strong incentive to be seen as addressing salient political issues, but they could not bring themselves to take the extra (and more politically dangerous) step of opposing funding for the war. This is the reason that the constitutional scholar Harold Koh suggests that the president almost always wins in foreign affairs. In the post–World War II period, the executive branch has taken the initiative in foreign affairs, and Congress has usually acquiesced because of legislative myopia or "sheer lack of political will."[17] In the long term, however, the conflict did have positive ramifications for the executive-legislative relationship. Vietnam made it "far less costly for members to challenge the president. The boundaries of acceptable political debate were widened."[18] One need only recall that, ten months after Kissinger signed the Paris accords, Congress passed the War Powers Act, overriding Nixon's veto. But, during the war, members of Congress failed in their constitutional, political, and moral obligations. In the final analysis, the demons of domestic politics shouted down the better angels of Congress's nature.

Congressional complicity resulted at least in part from the strength of the executive branch during the war. Kennedy, Johnson, and Nixon possessed an arsenal of weapons that could blunt, deflect, or undermine any initiative from the legislative branch; the preemptive strike by administration allies to kill the Hatfield-McGovern amendment is a perfect example. As Anthony Lewis concluded in an article critical of the GOP during the 1972 convention, Nixon had "shown that it is possible for a determined President, with shrewd political advice, to carry on indefinitely a war unpopular in the country and in Congress. He has proved that there are no effective political mechanisms in the American system to restrain such a President between elections."[19]

Yet the imperial presidency model goes only so far. For all the power and prerogatives that Kennedy, Johnson, and Nixon possessed, they all faced definite constraints—real and perceived—grounded in domestic politics. Concern over public opinion, electoral success, and their own credibility limited what each president could (or would) do. Furthermore, the war can accurately be described as the graveyard of presidential ambitions. The list of prominent U.S. politicians whose career trajectory fell short of the White House—or prematurely ended their tenure in the Oval Office—owing to Vietnam is lengthy: LBJ, Romney, Rockefeller, Nixon, Humphrey, McGovern, McCloskey, Ashbrook, and Ford.[20] As the former Johnson administration official James Thomson observed, the final domino of the Vietnam experience was "not some Asian country, it's the presidency itself."[21] This highlights an irony that future presidential aspirants should consider. Many political leaders have pursued a militaristic policy in the hope of maximizing political power, but all too often a misbegotten war serves as the undertaker of presidential power. America's wars abroad may have strengthened the imperial presidency, but they have also fatally damaged many an imperial president.

Given the pivotal importance of domestic political considerations during the Vietnam conflict, it follows that an understanding of the Republican Party's role during the war should be of central concern to historians of the conflict. The GOP had an important influence on U.S. policy during the war. Kennedy, Johnson, and Nixon all certainly understood the importance of their Republican colleagues in the domestic political process and catered to them to an appreciable extent. This was particularly true for Lyndon Johnson, who needed increasing levels of GOP support as Democrats deserted him in growing numbers. Republican governors, members of Congress, and national figures were in a unique position to exert pressure on the White House on both sides of the Vietnam issue, and they rarely passed up their opportunities to do so.

But the Republicans did not use their influence as effectively as they might have. In one sense, as Terry Dietz has asserted, the Republicans helped direct American policy toward Vietnam; in another, they were caught in the whirlwind of Vietnam and reacted to it.[22] The GOP reaped the benefits of criticizing or supporting American policy in Vietnam without having to shoulder the responsibilities of formulating that policy or answering for its outcome. Without being able to implement their own policies, the Republicans had to rely on the administration for briefings and action before they could respond either publicly or privately. The pussyfooting by Republican critics of presidential Vietnam policies (both hawks and doves) reflected their minority status. Even the most vocal hawks and the most outspoken opponents of the war studiously avoided the real issues at the heart of the administration's policies. A prime example was George Aiken, who consistently opposed the conflict throughout the 1960s but still voted for appropriations and accepted that the United States had made a commitment to South Vietnam that had to be upheld.[23] Of course, this was true for most members of Congress regardless of party affiliation. During the course of the war, Congress proved to be "a willing, if usually silent, accomplice in the formation of Vietnam policies. Dissent developed slowly and assumed significant proportions only at the very end of the war."[24]

As the preceding chapters have demonstrated, the Republican Party can be divided into three main categories when it came to position on the Vietnam War: hawks, doves, and those who shifted their positions during the course of the conflict. The hawks represented the largest faction within the GOP and included Richard Nixon, Dwight Eisenhower, Barry Goldwater, Gerald Ford, and John Tower. They supported LBJ longer and more vociferously than did the Democrats; ironically, the strongest support Johnson had for his Vietnam policies came from the GOP. Many of these Republicans advocated policies during the mid-1960s that were much more aggressive than those promulgated by the administration. Nixon, Eisenhower, and the others never accused Johnson of doing too little; their politically motivated criticism focused on his failure to commit whatever means necessary to ensure an American victory. The persistent hawkish rhetoric from this cohort within the party made it virtually impossible for Johnson, and, later, Nixon, to take any meaningful steps toward a negotiated settlement or even withdrawal from Vietnam.

By far the most important Republican figure during this period was Richard Nixon. The statements he made and the actions he endorsed during the first half of 1964, although hawkish even in the GOP, matched what Walt Rostow privately urged Johnson to do in Vietnam and were close to what Johnson actually did in 1965. Indeed, "Whatever move Johnson made in the direction of escalation, Nixon was always one step ahead of him, demanding more."[25] Nixon's vitriolic attacks on U.S. policy in Vietnam pressured the Johnson administration to act more aggressively in its conduct of the war or face the recriminations that Johnson most feared. Although Nixon moderated his rhetoric when it became clear that the war was unwinnable, he continued to point out flaws in LBJ's strategy while concurrently acting as the GOP's Delphic Oracle on the war. In the final analysis, Nixon himself and the other Republican hawks should be held accountable at least in part for the complex and exigent situation he faced as he took the oath of office in January 1969. By sowing their own dragon's teeth with their constant criticism of Johnson's Vietnam policies, they helped create it.

Yet, on assuming the presidency, Nixon confronted the same domestic pressures that had taunted his predecessors. While denying publicly that he allowed his policy decisions to be swayed by popular opinion or the antiwar protests, he was obsessed with the way the American people (especially the conservative wing of his party) and the media portrayed him. He constantly sought their validation—or tried to manipulate their perceptions. Nowhere was this more true than in the paradoxical and simultaneous escalation and disengagement policies pursued by the administration. Having been elected to "win the peace," Nixon now had to follow through on that promise. His rhetoric had placed him in an unwinnable situation in an unwinnable war. His contradictory policies were his only means of salvaging the support from all his disparate constituencies.

Nixon may have been the most important Republican on the issue of Vietnam, but the influence of Dwight Eisenhower cannot be discounted. During his postpresidential years, Eisenhower took a consistently hawkish stance on the Vietnam War and proved himself to be an unreconstructed cold warrior. The elder statesman and still revered general endorsed the escalation of the war, backed Johnson in supporting the Saigon regimes against the Communist threat, pushed for a decisive military victory, and lobbied for a comprehensive program of nation building in South Vietnam to secure that country's future survival. The only time he was critical of the administration was when he believed that Johnson was not doing enough to ensure success. Like Nixon's,

Eisenhower's uncharacteristically blunt rhetoric (at least for a politician) was due in large measure to his nonincumbency. Loosed from the constraints of office, he was able to be far more belligerent and suggest much more strident courses of action than he could have as president.

A second group of Republicans were those who either switched sides on the war or vacillated between support and opposition. The Republicans who changed their positions on Vietnam did so for a variety of reasons. Some, like Thruston Morton, had personal experiences that prompted them to renounce the conflict. Others switched their positions for purely domestic political reasons—that is, to appeal to the voters and ride the wave of public opinion. But, whatever the justification for abandoning the administration's policies, the fissures created by their actions closely reflected the divisions within American society. The most prominent examples of this cohort in the GOP are Melvin Laird, George Romney, Nelson Rockefeller, and Jacob Javits. Of course, Romney, Morton, and Javits had each expressed doubts and asked pointed questions about the conflict prior to their change of heart, but their defections seriously undermined the administration's support, particularly in the Senate. Laird's conversion occurred for different reasons, but he would become a central figure in the denouement of the conflict as the leading proponent of Vietnamization in the Nixon administration. The discomfort of this cohort, even if politically motivated, mirrored the struggles of millions of Americans who began to openly question the war and its architects.

If the Republican Party as a whole has been neglected in the historical literature, then the GOP doves have been almost completely ignored. This minority contingent opposed U.S. involvement in the war even prior to the beginning of Johnson's escalation of the conflict in July 1965. Given the way the conflict evolved, they could be forgiven for feeling like H. G. Wells, who once said, "I am not prophesying now; I am simply running along beside the facts and pointing at them." Yet the Republican doves—notably Mark Hatfield, John Sherman Cooper, George Aiken, and Clifford Case—were well represented on the Senate Foreign Relations Committee. They were extremely candid about the need for disengagement. They joined with Democratic dissenters on the war such as William Fulbright, Mike Mansfield, and Frank Church to move opposition to the Vietnam conflict from the left-wing fringe to the center of American political life and acted as a restraint on the Johnson and Nixon administrations' actions in Southeast Asia. Indeed, Aiken's "opposition gave early anti-war sentiment a degree of respectability and bipartisanship, helped to squelch calls for more escalation by Republican hawks, and may have led Johnson to reject even wider escalation of the conflict."[26]

Presidential fears also help explain the lack of recognition of the Republican opponents of the war. Kennedy, Johnson, and Nixon all calculated that the damage from appearing too soft on communism or failing to prosecute the war vigorously enough far outweighed the political trauma that might accrue from criticism by the opponents of the war. Nixon's dismissal of the antiwar movement exemplifies these calculations. In the final analysis, the arguments made by the doves simply did not have the political impact or leverage that those of their conservative and hawkish colleagues did. The implications for American democracy are both obvious and ominous.

In retrospect, it is indisputable that, like the rest of the country, the Republican Party experienced significant divisions over the conduct of the war. Thus, the lingering historical assumptions of "monolithic" Republican hawkishness on Vietnam are demonstrably false. The GOP never "spoke with one voice" on the war.[27] The hawks, while more visible and including the party's most recognizable names, should not overshadow the effective critique by the committed Republican opponents of the war. To be sure, there were elements of political opportunism among both the doves and those who switched their positions on the war; for every member of the GOP (and, truthfully, for any political figure in the country), the relation between sincerity and pragmatism is a tricky one to pin down. The doves were more idealistic at the beginning of the conflict, just as the hawks clung to their ideological principles at the end. Yet all the factions within the party acted on their convictions, reacted to domestic pressures, and exerted political influence on Kennedy, Johnson, and Nixon. But that just underscores the centrality of domestic political considerations in the Vietnam experience, the second front on which all three administrations fought from 1961 to 1973. Recognizing and understanding the influence of this "intermestic" dimension of politics and foreign policy should change the way historians interpret and assess the history of U.S. foreign relations, both during the Vietnam conflict and beyond.

More generally, the weight of historical evidence makes clear that Vietnam was not simply "Lyndon Johnson's war." Yes, the Johnson administration escalated the American commitment from 16,000 advisers to over 500,000 combat troops. Yes, Johnson's preoccupation with his own prestige, his national credibility, domestic politics, and his Great Society programs led him to escalate the war against his better judgment. And, yes, the war became identified in the public mind with Johnson and his administration. But the U.S. experience in Vietnam was long and complex; to hold LBJ accountable for all the errors in judgment and policy that occurred over three decades distorts the historical record. It neglects the realities of American politics, not to mention the responsibility that Truman, Eisenhower, Kennedy, and the GOP should bear for U.S. involvement in Southeast Asia. Nor should we forget Richard Nixon's undeniable culpability. He alone among American political figures contributed either directly or indirectly to every key decision on Vietnam from the 1950s to the Paris Peace Accords as a senator, as vice president, as a clarion voice for escalation, and as president. Furthermore, Vietnam can also be rightly considered to be a congressional war, a conflict supported by hawks and feebly enabled by the action and inaction of doves in both parties. All played a role in fostering the environment that led to and prosecuted war in Vietnam. Ultimately, as the *Washington Evening Star* editorialized in May 1967, "The fact remains that this is a war which involves, not one party or the other, but the United States."[28]

This should not be construed as an apology for Johnson. LBJ's decisions as president and commander-in-chief committed American combat troops to the conflict in Southeast Asia and escalated the fighting despite clear indications that U.S. efforts would be ineffective against a determined and patient enemy. Vietnam was not inevitable. Johnson *did* choose war, a choice based to a significant degree on his assessment of the likely political outcome. But he was neither alone nor unique in acting this way. Indeed, the decisions made by three consecutive administrations reflected the same sorts of political calculations. In attempting to fight the Vietnam conflict on two fronts—militarily in Southeast Asia and politically in the United States—Kennedy, Johnson, and Nixon ultimately failed to achieve victory on either. The consequences of their choices continue to resonate in contemporary American foreign and domestic policy decisions. One need only consider the 2003 vote for war in Iraq or John Kerry's equivocal campaign in 2004 to recognize the striking and parallel patterns of behavior that continue to demonstrably manifest the overwhelming influence of domestic political considerations on U.S. foreign policy.

# Appendix

## Republicans, 1961–1973

Members of the Republican Party mentioned in the book are listed alphabetically below with their state, congressional, national, or appointed offices; home state; and other pertinent identifying information.

| | |
|---|---|
| Ross Adair | Representative (IN) |
| Spiro Agnew | Governor (MD) |
| | Vice President |
| George Aiken | Senator (VT) |
| Bruce Alger | Representative (TX) |
| Gordon Allott | Senator (CO) |
| John Anderson | Representative (IL) |
| John Ashbrook | Representative (OH) |
| | Presidential candidate, 1972 |
| Howard Baker Jr. | Senator (TN) |
| Glenn Beall | Senator (MD) |
| Alphonzo Bell | Representative (CA) |
| Henry Bellmon | Governor (OK) |
| | Senator (OK) |
| Wallace Bennett | Senator (UT) |
| Nils Boe | Governor (SD) |
| William Brock | Senator (TN) |
| Edward Brooke | Senator (MA) |
| William Broomfield | Representative (MI) |
| George H. W. Bush | Representative (TX) |
| John Byrnes | Representative (WI) |
| John Camp | Representative (OK) |
| Frank Carlson | Senator (KS) |
| Tim Lee Carter | Representative (KY) |
| Clifford Case | Senator (NJ) |
| John Chaffee | Governor (NH) |
| Marlow Cook | Senator (KY) |

| | |
|---|---|
| John Sherman Cooper | Senator (KY) |
| Norris Cotton | Senator (NH) |
| Larry Coughlin | Representative (PA) |
| Everett Dirksen | Senator (IL) |
| | Senate minority leader |
| Robert Dole | Senator (KS) |
| Peter Dominick | Senator (CO) |
| Florence Dwyer | Representative (NJ) |
| Dwight Eisenhower | President |
| Daniel Evans | Governor (WA) |
| Paul Fannin | Senator (AZ) |
| Paul Findley | Representative (IL) |
| Hiram Fong | Senator (HI) |
| Gerald Ford | Representative (MI) |
| | House minority leader |
| Ed Foreman | Representative (TX) |
| Peter Frelinghuysen | Representative (NJ) |
| Barry Goldwater | Senator (AZ) |
| | Presidential nominee, 1964 |
| Charles Goodell | Representative (NY) |
| | Senator (NY) |
| Robert Griffin | Representative (MI) |
| | Senator (MI) |
| Durward Hall | Representative (MO) |
| Charles Halleck | Representative (IN) |
| | House minority leader |
| Clifford Hansen | Senator (WY) |
| George Hansen | Representative (ID) |
| Mark Hatfield | Governor (OR) |
| | Senator (OR) |
| Bourke Hickenlooper | Senator (IA) |
| Roman Hruska | Senator (NE) |
| Jacob Javits | Senator (NY) |
| Len Jordan | Senator (ID) |
| Kenneth Keating | Senator (NY) |
| Thomas Kuchel | Senator (CA) |
| Melvin Laird | Representative (WI) |
| | Secretary of Defense |
| John Lindsay | Representative (NY) |
| | Mayor (New York City) |
| Glenard Lipscomb | Representative (CA) |
| Sherman Lloyd | Representative (UT) |
| Henry Cabot Lodge Jr. | Ambassador to South Vietnam |

| | |
|---|---|
| Charles Mathias | Senator (MD) |
| Catherine May | Representative (WA) |
| Pete McCloskey | Representative (CA) |
| | Presidential candidate, 1972 |
| Robert Michel | Representative (IL) |
| Jack Miller | Senator (IA) |
| Bradford Morse | Representative (MA) |
| Rogers Morton | Representative (MD) |
| Thruston Morton | Senator (KY) |
| Charles Mosher | Representative (OH) |
| Karl Mundt | Senator (SD) |
| George Murphy | Senator (CA) |
| Richard Nixon | President |
| James Pearson | Senator (KS) |
| Charles Percy | Senator (IL) |
| Ronald Reagan | Governor (CA) |
| | Presidential candidate, 1968 |
| James Rhodes | Governor (OH) |
| John Rhodes | Representative (AZ) |
| Donald Riegle | Representative (MI) |
| Howard Robison | Representative (NY) |
| Nelson Rockefeller | Governor (NY) |
| | Presidential candidate, 1964 and 1968 |
| William Rogers | Secretary of State |
| George Romney | Governor (MI) |
| | Presidential candidate, 1968 |
| | Secretary of Housing and Urban Development |
| Donald Rumsfeld | Representative (IL) |
| | Counselor to Richard Nixon |
| Leverett Saltonstall | Senator (MA) |
| William Saxbe | Senator (OH) |
| Hugh Scott | Senator (PA) |
| | Senate minority leader |
| William Scranton | Governor (PA) |
| Raymond Shafer | Governor (PA) |
| Eugene Siler | Representative (KY) |
| Milward Simpson | Senator (WY) |
| Margaret Chase Smith | Senator (ME) |
| Robert Smylie | Governor (ID) |
| Robert Stafford | Representative (VT) |
| Harold Stassen | Presidential candidate, 1964 and 1968 |
| Ted Stevens | Senator (AK) |

| | |
|---|---|
| Robert Taft Jr. | Senator (OH) |
| Burt Talcott | Representative (CA) |
| Strom Thurmond | Senator (SC) |
| John Tower | Senator (TX) |
| John Volpe | Governor (MA) |
| Lowell Weicker | Senator (CT) |
| Charles Wiggins | Representative (CA) |
| Robert Wilson | Representative (CA) |
| Milton Young | Senator (ND) |

# Notes

Unless otherwise indicated, quotations are documented according to the order in which they appear in the text. Also, references to, e.g., "box 30/1" should be read as "box 30, folder 1."

## Introduction

1. Thucydides, *History of the Peloponnesian War,* 164. See also Small, *Democracy and Diplomacy,* xi.

2. Gelb and Betts, *The Irony of Vietnam,* 221.

3. Quoted in Miller, "The US-Israeli Relationship," 88. When the former State Department official Edward Djerejian moved to a position in the White House during the Reagan administration, he was shocked at "the interaction of domestic politics and foreign policy." According to Djerejian, "At the State Department you make the best judgments on the foreign policy interests of the U.S. Here you have to be abundantly aware, and put in the equation, domestic political considerations" (quoted in Farnham, "Impact of the Political Context," 445).

4. White, *The Making of the President, 1972,* 231.

5. The seminal work on this point is Schlesinger, *The Imperial Presidency.*

6. Bacevich, *The New American Militarism,* xii.

7. See, e.g., Berman, *Lyndon Johnson's War.* For a different perspective, see Cuddy, "Vietnam."

8. Lindsay, *The Politics of U.S. Foreign Policy,* 1. See also Olson, "The U.S. Congress."

9. For an in-depth look at this phenomenon, see Osgood and Frank, eds., *Selling War in a Media Age.*

10. Quoted in Kennan, *American Diplomacy,* 176.

11. Quandt, "The Conduct of American Foreign Policy," 88.

12. Hanhimäki, "Global Visions and Parochial Politics," 446.

13. Logevall, "Party Politics," 101. Levering contends that scholars who "seek to minimize the role of domestic politics in the making of U.S. foreign policy, and those who claim that the media and the public are easily manipulated by economic and political elites betray a gross misunderstanding of how the American political system actually works" ("Is Domestic Politics Being Slighted?" 35).

14. See Hunt, *The American Ascendancy;* Westad, *The Global Cold War;* Gaddis, *The Cold War;* Leffler, *For the Soul of Mankind;* and Williams, *The Tragedy of American Diplomacy.* While revisionists like Williams recognize that domestic forces did influence foreign policy, they generally pay scant attention to politics and electoral concerns.

15. See, e.g., Hunt, "Internationalizing U.S. Diplomatic History"; Leffler, "New Approaches, Old Interpretations"; and Hogan, "The 'Next Big Thing.'" It is instructive to note that, in the second edition of *Explaining the History of American Foreign Relations,* their important methodological overview of the field, Hogan and Paterson neglect the role of domestic considerations, inexplicably omitting Small's "Public Opinion."

16. Zeiler, "The Diplomatic History Bandwagon," 1053, 1060. Politics are similarly overlooked in Plummer, "The Changing Face of Diplomatic History."

17. Schwartz, "'Winning an election is terribly important, Henry.'"

18. Logevall and Craig, *America's Cold War.* See also Logevall, "Politics and Foreign Relations," a response to Zeiler's "The Diplomatic History Bandwagon."

19. On the historiography of the war, see Hess, "The Unending Debate"; the bibliographic essay at the end of Herring, *America's Longest War,* SR1–SR10; Catton, "Refighting Vietnam in the History Books"; and Johns, "The Vietnam War and the Expanding Universe Theory."

20. Hess, "The Unending Debate," 239.

21. See, e.g., Longley, "Congress and the Vietnam War"; and Schmitz and Fousekis, "The Emergence of Dissent."

22. On American intervention in Vietnam, see, e.g., Anderson, *Trapped by Success;* Lawrence, *Assuming the Burden;* and Statler, *Replacing France.*

23. Lindsay, *The Politics of U.S. Foreign Policy,* 3.

24. For an overview, see Johns, "Doves among Hawks."

25. Johns, "A Voice from the Wilderness."

26. See Dietz, *Republicans and Vietnam;* Gibbons, *The U.S. Government and the Vietnam War;* Mann, *A Grand Delusion;* and Stone, *Elites for Peace.*

27. On Congress and Vietnam, see, e.g., Herring, "The Executive, Congress, and the Vietnam War"; and Johnson, *Congress and the Cold War.*

28. Representative works include Brennan, *Turning Right in the Sixties;* Brinkley, "The Problem of American Conservatism"; Hijiya, "The Conservative 1960s"; Berman, *America's Right Turn;* Hodgson, *The World Turned Right Side Up;* and Reinhard, *The Republican Right.* On the effects of the rise of conservatism on the GOP, see Rae, *Decline and Fall.* On neoconservatives and U.S. foreign relations, see Ehrman, *The Rise of Neoconservatism.*

29. Small, *The Presidency of Richard Nixon,* 64.

30. The Prussian strategist Carl von Clausewitz wrote, "We see, therefore, that War is not merely a political act, but also a real political instrument, a continuation of political commerce, a carrying out of the same by other means . . . for the political view is the object, War is the means, and the means must always include the object in our conception" (*On War,* 119). Michael Foucault used this language in his writing, but I employ it in a different context here.

## 1. Trapped between Scylla and Charybdis

1. Quoted in Darilek, *A Loyal Opposition in Time of War,* xi.

2. Vandenberg, *Private Papers,* 342, 552–53. See also Hill, "Senator Arthur H. Vandenberg."

3. Quoted in Johnson, "Henry Cabot Lodge," 6.

4. Quoted in Paterson, "Presidential Foreign Policy," 17.

5. Newsletter, 27 December 1960, box 6B/2, Wallace F. Bennett Papers, L. Tom Perry Special Collections Library, Harold B. Lee Library, Brigham Young University, Provo, UT (hereafter Bennett Papers); Speech, 6 April 1961, box 6, Bennett Papers.

6. Speech, 6 April 1961, box 6, Bennett Papers.

7. Speech, Nixon in Sun Valley, ID, 30 September 1961, BBH, Personal Files, box 36, Bourke B. Hickenlooper Papers, Herbert Hoover Presidential Library, West Branch, IA (hereafter Hickenlooper Papers).

8. Editorial, *Washington Post,* 26 January 1961.

9. Dietz, *Republicans and Vietnam,* 36. The group began informal meetings on 24 January 1961, and it began keeping a record of formal statements on 23 March. Ritchie notes that, with Kennedy's election, the Republican Policy Committee in the Senate "switched from a defensive to an offensive stance" (*History,* 63).

10. Rae, *Decline and Fall,* 46–49. The literature on the evolution of the conservative movement has grown steadily. See, e.g., Critchlow, *The Conservative Ascendancy;* McGirr, *Suburban Warriors;* Edwards, *The Conservative Revolution;* and Regnery, *Upstream.* On the Young Americans for Freedom, see Schneider, *Cadres for Conservatism.*

11. On Halleck, see Scheele, *Charlie Halleck;* and Womack, "Charles A. Halleck and the New Frontier."

12. On Dirksen, see Hulsey, *Everett Dirksen,* and "Himself First"; Schapsmeier and Schapsmeier, *Dirksen of Illinois;* and MacNeil, *Dirksen.*

13. Dietz, *Republicans and Vietnam,* 35.

14. Reinhard, *The Republican Right,* 164–65. See also Scheele, "Response to the Kennedy Administration."

15. Transcript, "ABC's Issues and Answers," 29 January 1961, Remarks & Releases, Jan. 1961–Dec. 1961, Everett McKinley Dirksen Papers, Everett McKinley Dirksen Congressional Leadership Research Center, Pekin, IL (hereafter Dirksen Papers).

16. MacNeil, *Dirksen,* 186–87.

17. Hulsey, *Everett Dirksen,* 150–51.

18. For Kennedy's views on Vietnam during his years in Congress, see Bassett and Pelz, "The Failed Search for Victory," 224–28.

19. Paterson, "Introduction: Kennedy and Global Crisis," 12.

20. The Kennedy administration is analyzed in Giglio, *The Presidency of John F. Kennedy;* Parmet, *JFK;* and Schlesinger, *A Thousand Days.* Kennedy's foreign policy is examined by Beschloss, *The Crisis Years;* Hilsman, *To Move a Nation;* Kern, Levering, and Levering, *The Kennedy Crises;* Paterson, "Bearing the Burden"; Paterson, ed., *Kennedy's Quest for Victory;* and White, ed., *Kennedy.* The Kennedy administration's involvement in Vietnam is discussed in Jones, *Death of a Generation;* Hammer, *A Death in November;* Kaiser, *An American Tragedy;* Newman, *JFK and Vietnam;* Paterson, ed., *Kennedy's Quest for Victory;* Freedman, *Kennedy's Wars;* Rust, *Kennedy in Vietnam;* and Schwab, *Defending the Free World.*

21. Kennedy Inaugural Address, 20 January 1961, quoted in Belmonte, ed., *Speaking of America,* 2:725–27. Kennedy went on to say, "To those new states . . . we pledge our

word that one form of colonial control shall not have passed away merely to be replaced by a far more iron tyranny." As Gelb and Betts have noted, "Resolve to follow through in containment had palpable urgency in 1961" (*The Irony of Vietnam,* 79). Kennedy's inaugural address is representative of his entire approach to foreign policy rhetoric. On his use of rhetoric with regard to Vietnam, see Bostdorff and Goldzwig, "Idealism and Pragmatism."

22. VanDeMark, "A Way of Thinking," 26–27.

23. Quoted in Hammer, *A Death in November,* 34.

24. Quoted in Halberstam, *The Best and the Brightest,* 76. See also Brands, *The Wages of Globalism,* 220.

25. Pelz, "Kennedy's 1961 Vietnam War Decisions," 357.

26. Quoted in Hilsman, *To Move a Nation,* 413.

27. Mayer, *The Republican Party,* 515. See also Logevall, *Choosing War,* 31; and Brands, *The Wages of Globalism,* 220–21.

28. The Munich analogy and its relation to the Vietnam issue is discussed in Khong, *Analogies at War;* and Record, *Making War, Thinking History.* On the use and misuse of historical analogies, see Neustadt and May, *Thinking in Time.*

29. Quoted in Bassett and Pelz, "The Failed Search for Victory," 223.

30. Dietz, *Republicans and Vietnam,* 40–41.

31. *New York Times,* 26 April 1961.

32. *New York Times,* 21 April 1961.

33. *New York Times,* 22 April 1961.

34. *New York Times,* 3 May 1961.

35. Pelz, "Kennedy's 1961 Vietnam War Decisions," 363. On the transition meeting between Eisenhower and Kennedy, see Greenstein and Immerman, "What Did Eisenhower Tell Kennedy?"

36. Lyon, *Eisenhower,* 833.

37. Notes, 22 April 1961 (first quote), Dwight D. Eisenhower (DDE) Post-Presidential Papers, Augusta–Walter Reed Series, box 2, Dwight D. Eisenhower Presidential Library, Abilene, KS (hereafter DDEL); and Parmet, *JFK,* 177 (second quote).

38. Minutes, Joint Republican Congressional Leaders, 1 May 1961, RCL, folder 15, Dirksen Papers.

39. Kahin, *Intervention,* 132. For a brief look at the neutralization of Laos, see Wehrle, "'A Good, Bad Deal.'"

40. Quoted in Dietz, *Republicans and Vietnam,* 41.

41. *New York Times,* 28 April 1961. Morton had been involved in Vietnam policymaking in the 1950s as assistant secretary of state for congressional relations under John Foster Dulles and would become a vocal advocate of negotiations after 1967.

42. Kahin, *Intervention,* 132.

43. Small, *At the Water's Edge,* 13.

44. Kahin, *Intervention,* 129, 474 n. 16. See also Jacobs, "'No Place to Fight a War,'" 62.

45. Clipping, Cartoon, Herblock, 7 April 1961, Democratic National Committee Series I, box 47, Lyndon Baines Johnson Presidential Library, Austin, TX (hereafter LBJL).

46. Speech, Nixon in Chicago, 5 May 1961, BBH, Personal Files, box 36, Hickenlooper Papers.

47. Statement, 25 April 1961, 87th Congress, box 23/1, John Rhodes Papers, University Archives, Hayden Library, Arizona State University, Tempe, AZ (hereafter Rhodes Papers).

48. Memorandum, Walt Rostow to Kennedy, 2 March 1961, President's Office Files, Staff Memos, box 64a, John F. Kennedy Presidential Library, Boston, MA (hereafter JFKL).

49. *The Pentagon Papers*, 2:51; and Gelb and Betts, *The Irony of Vietnam*, 72–73.

50. Herring, *America's Longest War*, 95. Diem had displayed no interest in U.S. combat troops when the issue was raised by Johnson, but, in the wake of the meeting, the South Vietnamese leader requested additional American aid and advisers in order to expand his army by 100,000 troops.

51. Newman, *JFK and Vietnam*, 93.

52. Memorandum, Komer to Walt Rostow, 20 July 1961, National Security File (NSF), Countries, box 193, JFKL.

53. *Los Angeles Times*, 24 July 1961.

54. Bassett and Pelz, "The Failed Search for Victory," 237.

55. Memorandum, Komer to McGeorge Bundy, 31 October 1961, NSF, Regional Security, box 231, JFKL.

56. Reeves, *President Kennedy*, 257.

57. Rostow, *The Diffusion of Power*, 270. See also Patterson, *Grand Expectations*, 512.

58. Quoted in Reeves, *President Kennedy*, 261–62.

59. Memorandum, Bowles to Kennedy, 17 January 1962, President's Office Files, Staff Memos, box 62, JFKL.

60. Quoted in Wallace, *Politics of Conscience*, 177–78.

61. Press Conference Transcript, 14 February 1962, President's Office Files, Press Conferences, box 55, JFKL.

62. Transcript, "Washington Viewpoint," 21 February 1962, box 31/5, John Tower Papers, Special Collections, A. Frank Smith Jr. Library Center, Southwestern University, Georgetown, TX (hereafter Tower Papers).

63. Transcript, "Prospect for Republicans," 1 April 1962, box 31/6, Tower Papers.

64. Newsletter, Republican Congressional Committee, no. 21, 8 June 1962, box 41, E. Ross Adair Papers, Indiana State Library, Indianapolis, IN (hereafter Adair Papers).

65. *Burlington (VT) Free Press*, 11 June 1962.

66. Rust, *Kennedy in Vietnam*, 75.

67. Memorandum, Forrestal to Kennedy, 18 September 1962, NSF, Countries, box 196, JFKL.

68. Speech, 15 October 1962, DDE Post-Presidential Papers, Speeches Series, box 3, DDEL.

69. *Human Events* 19, no. 44 (3 November 1962): 832.

70. Reeves, *President Kennedy*, 444.

71. Quoted in Rust, *Kennedy in Vietnam*, 83 (Halberstam); and Herring, *America's*

*Longest War*, 106 (Hilsman). The American adviser to the South Vietnamese forces at Ap Bac, Lt. Col. John Paul Vann, called the battle a "miserable damn performance" and complained, "We sat there all day, did not close with the enemy, did not complete an encirclement of him, and that night, of course, he slipped away, as we knew he would." See Kaiser, *An American Tragedy*, 181–82 (Vann quotes); and Sheehan, *A Bright Shining Lie*, esp. 212–83. For a different perspective on the battle and its implications, see Moyar, *Triumph Forsaken*, 186–205.

72. Quoted in Kaiser, *An American Tragedy*, 183.

73. Kahin, *Intervention*, 146.

74. Ibid., 147.

75. Dietz, *Republicans and Vietnam*, 54.

76. For an examination of Mundt's contributions to the Vietnam debate, see Lauck, "Binding Assumptions."

77. Memorandum, Bowles to Kennedy, 7 March 1963, President's Office Files, Staff Memos, box 62, JFKL.

78. Goldberg, *Barry Goldwater*, 170.

79. Press Release, Joint Senate-House Republican Leadership, 31 May 1963, RCL, folder 37, Dirksen Papers.

80. Reeves, *President Kennedy*, 484.

81. Blair, *Lodge in Vietnam*, 11.

82. U.S. Department of State, *Foreign Relations of the United States, 1961–1963*, vol. 2, *Vietnam, 1962*, 60–62.

83. Parmet, *JFK*, 314. Although they were invited to accompany the president, the key GOP senators Dirksen and Hickenlooper declined, "pleading the desire to maintain their independence."

84. Article, Eric Sevareid, late August 1963, Roger Hilsman Papers, Countries, box 3, JFKL.

85. Schlesinger, *A Thousand Days*, 989.

86. Blair, *Lodge in Vietnam*, 12–13; and Cohen, *Dean Rusk*, 189.

87. *Time*, 5 July 1963, 22.

88. Matthews, *Kennedy and Nixon*, 228.

89. Blair, *Lodge in Vietnam*, 15.

90. Lodge, *The Storm Has Many Eyes*, 205.

91. Blair, *Lodge in Vietnam*, 18–19.

92. Quoted in Bassett and Pelz, "The Failed Search for Victory," 246.

93. Quoted in Johnson, "Henry Cabot Lodge," 13.

94. Reinhard, *The Republican Right*, 155, 184.

95. Bassett and Pelz, "The Failed Search for Victory," 244–45.

96. Quoted in Herring, *America's Longest War*, 116.

97. Telegram, Rusk to Lodge, 30 August 1963, and Telegram, Rusk to Lodge, 31 August 1963, in U.S. Department of State, *Foreign Relations of the United States, 1961–1963*, vol. 4, *Vietnam, Aug.–Dec. 1963*, 63, 76–78.

98. Blair, *Lodge in Vietnam*, 46–47.

99. Herring, *America's Longest War,* 117.

100. *The Pentagon Papers,* 2:738.

101. Herring, *America's Longest War,* 120.

102. Memorandum, Frederick G. Dutton to Theodore Sorensen, n.d. (ca. 1963), T. C. Sorensen Papers, box 34, JFKL.

103. Speech, 2 October 1963, 88th Congress, box 30/1, Rhodes Papers.

104. Small, *At the Water's Edge,* 19.

105. Herring, *America's Longest War,* 124.

106. Logevall, "First among Critics," 361. When asked in early October about the possibility of withdrawing troops from Vietnam, Lodge replied, "That's just politics" (Reeves, *President Kennedy,* 615).

107. Reeves, *President Kennedy,* 655–56 (quote); and Dallek, *Flawed Giant,* 32. Charles Bartlett, who conducted opposition research for the 1964 campaign for the president, noted that opinion polls indicated that Romney could "count on substantial switches by Kennedy voters who have been disenchanted by his handling of Cuba and the race problem. They found that Romney's connection with the Mormon church should prove advantageous, although most Southerners proved to know little about Mormonism. But there is a broad sense that the Mormons are anti-federal in philosophy and some feel a kinship between the past persecution of the Mormons and the present suffering of the South on the race question" (Summary, Charles Bartlett on Romney, n.d., T. C. Sorensen Papers, box 36, JFKL).

108. Herring, *America's Longest War,* 125.

109. Quoted in Herring, *America's Longest War,* 127.

110. Quoted in Patterson, *Grand Expectations,* 514.

111. *Congressional Record,* 23 September 1963.

112. Quoted in Dietz, *Republicans and Vietnam,* 55.

113. Newsletter, Republican Congressional Committee, no. 44, 8 November 1963, box 30/1, Rhodes Papers.

114. Matthews, *Kennedy and Nixon,* 233.

115. Speech, 16 November 1963, Graham T. T. Molitor Papers, box 30/26, Rockefeller Archive Center, North Tarrytown, NY (hereafter Molitor Papers).

116. Hess, "Commitment in the Age of Counterinsurgency," 83.

117. Berman, "NSAM 263 and NSAM 273," 200.

118. Kern, Levering, and Levering, *The Kennedy Crises,* 176.

## 2. The Cassandra Conundrum

1. The literature on Johnson's presidency is vast. See, e.g., Woods, *LBJ;* Bornet, *The Presidency of Lyndon B. Johnson;* Califano, *Triumph and Tragedy;* Goldman, *The Tragedy of Lyndon Johnson;* and McPherson, *A Political Education.* On Johnson's foreign policy, see Schwartz, *Lyndon Johnson and Europe;* Barrett, *Uncertain Warriors;* Berman, *Lyndon Johnson's War,* and *Planning a Tragedy;* Brands, *The Wages of Globalism;* Cohen and Tucker, eds., *Lyndon Johnson Confronts the World;* Gardner, *Pay Any Price;* Geyelin,

*Johnson and the World*; Herring, *LBJ and Vietnam*; Hoopes, *The Limits of Intervention*; Kunz, ed., *The Diplomacy of the Crucial Decade*; and VanDeMark, *Into the Quagmire*.

2. Matthews, *Kennedy and Nixon,* 246; and Gelb and Betts, *The Irony of Vietnam,* 156.

3. Woods, *Fulbright: A Biography,* 342; and Brands, *The Wages of Globalism,* 225.

4. Telephone Conversation Transcript, Lyndon Johnson to Dwight D. Eisenhower, 22 November 1963, LBJL.

5. Johnson, *The Vantage Point,* 31–32, 130.

6. NSAM 273, 26 November 1963, National Security Memoranda, NSF, box 2, and Speech, 27 November 1963, NSF, Speech File, box 1, LBJL. The Honolulu meeting took place on 20 November 1963. The *Pentagon Papers* characterize NSAM 273 as an interim, "don't rock-the-boat" measure whose central significance is that, despite the changes wrought by the dual assassinations in November 1963, American policy would remain substantially the same. See *The Pentagon Papers,* 3:17–20. Other scholars have dissented from this opinion. In *JFK and Vietnam,* Newman contends that Kennedy intended to completely withdraw America from Vietnam and that, through NSAM 273, Johnson reversed that plan and deepened the American involvement in the conflict. See also Dallek, "Lyndon Johnson and Vietnam."

7. Quoted in Patterson, *Grand Expectations,* 593.

8. Halberstam, *The Best and the Brightest,* 425.

9. Kearns, *Lyndon Johnson and the American Dream,* 252–53. Scholars recognize that decisionmakers are constrained by their past and their choices; clearly, the "who lost China" debate left an indelible imprint on Johnson's political psyche. See, e.g., Immerman, "Intelligence and Strategy."

10. Memorandum, McNamara to Johnson, 21 December 1963, NSF, VN, box 1, LBJL.

11. Quoted in Gittinger, ed., *The Johnson Years,* 18–19. In 1991, McNamara stated that Johnson left no doubt about his desire to include Congress. He quoted the president as saying, "By God, I'm going to be damn sure those guys are with me when we begin this thing" (see Woods, *Fulbright: A Biography,* 347).

12. Quoted in Johns, "Opening Pandora's Box," 179.

13. Telephone Conversation Transcript, Johnson to Fulbright, 2 December 1963, LBJL.

14. On Goldwater, see, e.g., Edwards, *Goldwater*; Goldwater, *The Conscience of a Conservative,* and *Goldwater*; and Goldberg, *Barry Goldwater.*

15. *New York Times,* 8 December 1963.

16. Johnson, "Henry Cabot Lodge," 18; and Blair, *Lodge in Vietnam,* 85–86, 94–100.

17. Quoted in Beschloss, ed., *Taking Charge,* 153–54.

18. Quoted in ibid., 213–14.

19. At Nixon's funeral in 1994, Senator Robert Dole (R-KS) predicted, "The second half of the twentieth century will be known as the age of Nixon" (quoted in Perlstein, *Nixonland,* 748).

20. On Nixon's early influence on U.S. Vietnam policy, see Johns, "A Voice from the Wilderness."

21. Quoted in Carter, *The Politics of Rage,* 325; and Press Conference Transcript, 12 November 1962, DDE Post-Presidential Papers, Speeches Series, box 5, DDEL.

22. Quoted in Wainstock, *The Turning Point,* 37.

23. Matthews, *Kennedy and Nixon,* 220–21.

24. Parmet, *Richard Nixon,* 455; Aitken, *Nixon,* 309.

25. Aitken, *Nixon,* 318–20.

26. Press Conference Statement, 12 February 1964, RG 15, Gubernatorial Papers, ser. 22, New York Office, subser. 2, box 27/826, Nelson A. Rockefeller Papers, Rockefeller Archive Center, North Tarrytown, NY (hereafter Rockefeller Papers).

27. *New York Times,* 2 April 1964 (quotes); and Logevall, *Choosing War,* 135.

28. *New York Times,* 4 April 1964; *Washington Post,* 14 April 1964; and Nixon, *RN,* 258.

29. Dallek, *Flawed Giant,* 128–29.

30. Telephone Conversation Transcript, Johnson to McNamara, 2 March 1964, LBJL.

31. Telephone Conversation Transcript, Johnson to Rusk, 2 March 1964, LBJL.

32. *Chicago Daily News,* 9 March 1964.

33. *New York Times,* 4 March 1964.

34. Schulman, *John Sherman Cooper,* 6. The extremely limited literature on Cooper includes Logevall, "A Delicate Balance."

35. Cooper Comments on WAVE-TV in Louisville, 24 May 1964, Senatorial Series II, box 570, John Sherman Cooper Collection, Modern Political Archives, University of Kentucky, Lexington, KY (hereafter Cooper Papers).

36. Karnow, *Vietnam,* 358 (quote); Rostow, *The Diffusion of Power,* 505; and *The Pentagon Papers,* 3:106.

37. Gibbons, *The U.S. Government and the Vietnam War,* 2:265.

38. The former Johnson adviser Eric Goldman wrote of the administration, "The main effort would go to domestic affairs. While taking every opportunity to dramatize his interest and his competence in foreign affairs, the new President hoped that he could hold world relations largely in their existing situation, and above all, that he could avoid crises" (*The Tragedy of Lyndon Johnson,* 25).

39. Goldstein, *Lessons in Disaster,* 97.

40. Note, 5 March 1964, NSF, Files of C. V. Clifton, box 1–3, LBJL. See also Transcript, Michael Forrestal Oral History Interview, 3 November 1969, by Paige E. Mulhollan, and Telephone Conversation Transcript, Johnson to Bundy, 2 March 1964 and 4 March 1964, LBJL; Kearns, *Lyndon Johnson and the American Dream,* 197–98; and Bornet, *The Presidency of Lyndon B. Johnson,* 71.

41. Goldstein, *Lessons in Disaster,* 132. Johnson "played the role of 'brakeman,' pulling the switch against both the advocates of 'decisive escalation' and the advocates of 'disengagement.' The key was to stake out the middle ground." In so doing, the administration would buy time. This strategy, however, resulted in "'disjointed incrementalism,' and deciding without choosing" (Farnham, "Impact of the Political Context," 452–53).

42. On the contingency planning for a congressional resolution on Vietnam during the first half of 1964, see Johns, "Opening Pandora's Box."

43. Speech, 27 April 1964, box 30/26, Molitor Papers.

44. Speech, 19 March 1964, 1964 Presidential Campaign (hereafter W), box 3/3, Barry

M. Goldwater Papers, Arizona Historical Foundation, Arizona State University, Tempe, AZ (hereafter Goldwater Papers).

45. Speech, 29 April 1964, W, box 1/10, Goldwater Papers.

46. Speech, 16 May 1964, W, box 1/8, Goldwater Papers; and *New York Herald Tribune*, 18 May 1964.

47. Press Release, 22 May 1964, Melvin Laird Papers, box A39, Gerald R. Ford Presidential Library, Ann Arbor, MI (hereafter GRFL).

48. Gibbons, *The U.S. Government and the Vietnam War*, 2:264–66.

49. Transcript, "Issues and Answers," 31 May 1964, BBH, Trips and Speeches, box 28, Hickenlooper Papers.

50. Quoted in Candidate Summary, *Detroit Free Press*, 5 June 1964, Gubernatorial Series, box 231, George W. Romney Papers, Bentley Historical Library, University of Michigan, Ann Arbor, MI (hereafter Romney Papers).

51. On Johnson's opposition to negotiations during this period, see Logevall, *Choosing War*.

52. Telephone Conversation Transcript, Johnson to Russell, 27 May 1964, LBJL.

53. On Lippmann's critique of the Vietnam conflict, see Logevall, "First among Critics." On Morgenthau's opposition and influence, see See, "A Prophet without Honor."

54. The nexus of foreign policy and domestic political considerations in the context of war and framing public perceptions of U.S. conflicts is the subject of Osgood and Frank, eds., *Selling War in a Media Age*.

55. Speech, 10 April 1964, W, box 3/4, Goldwater Papers.

56. Speech, 14 May 1964, 1964 Campaign Speeches, vol. 1, Goldwater Papers; Newsletter, 20 May 1964, box 6A/6, Bennett Papers.

57. Edwards, *Goldwater*, 223–24.

58. Ibid.

59. The "Peace, Little Girl" commercial—better known as the "daisy" ad—showed a little girl picking petals off a flower, her counting morphing into a missile launch countdown. The commercial ends with the detonation of a nuclear weapon. The ad aired only once, but the repeated media coverage of the controversy kept it in the public spotlight.

60. White, *The Making of the President, 1964*, 106.

61. Speech, 30 May 1964, 1964 Campaign Speeches, vol. 1, Goldwater Papers.

62. Quoted in Goldberg, *Barry Goldwater*, 194.

63. Dallek, *Flawed Giant*, 143.

64. Unpublished Manuscript, chap. 13, p. 25, William P. Bundy, Papers of William P. Bundy, box 1, LBJL (hereafter Bundy Manuscript).

65. Memorandum, Dutton to McGeorge Bundy, 2 June 1964, NSF, CF, VN, box 48, LBJL.

66. Memorandum, Robert H. Johnson to Walt Rostow, 27 July 1964, James C. Thomson Papers, box 24, JFKL.

67. Statement, Joint Senate and House Republican Leadership, 11 June 1964, James C. Thomson Papers, box 24, JFKL. Halleck cited recent stories in the *New York Times* (by

Arthur Krock), the *Washington Post,* and the *Washington Evening Star* to support his contention that Johnson based his Vietnam decisions on electoral strategy.

68. Letter, Hickenlooper to J. L. Ebeling, 11 June 1964, BBH, Foreign Relations Committee (FRC), Countries, box 158, Hickenlooper Papers.

69. Quoted in Gibbons, *The U.S. Government and the Vietnam War,* 2:278–79.

70. Senate Republican Memorandum, 2 July 1964, BBH, Political Files, box 71, Hickenlooper Papers; *New York Times,* 30 June 1964; Gibbons, *The U.S. Government and the Vietnam War,* 2:279.

71. Memorandum, Moyers to Johnson, 3 July 1964, WHCF, ND19/Co312, box 210, LBJL.

72. For poll citations, see Dallek, *Flawed Giant,* 147.

73. Interview Transcript, *Der Spiegel,* 10 July 1964, Office Files of Bill Moyers, box 30, LBJL.

74. Wallace, *Politics of Conscience,* 178.

75. Quoted in Goldberg, *Barry Goldwater,* 203.

76. Hatfield, *Against the Grain,* 94–95. The text of Hatfield's speech is reprinted in *Chicago Tribune,* 14 July 1964.

77. Middendorf, *A Glorious Disaster,* 131; Edwards, *Goldwater,* 272; Goldberg, *Barry Goldwater,* 205.

78. Logevall, *Choosing War,* 195.

79. Woods, *Fulbright: A Biography,* 348.

80. Nixon, "Needed in Vietnam," 37.

81. Telephone Conversation Transcript, Lyndon Johnson to McGeorge Bundy, 14 April 1964, LBJL.

82. *New York Times,* 10 April 1964.

83. Nixon, "Needed in Vietnam," 37, and *RN,* 256–57.

84. Nixon, "Needed in Vietnam," 38–43. Nixon referred to the "Yalu River complex" on several occasions. See, e.g., *New York Times,* 13 September 1965. For a general discussion of the issue of neutralization, see Logevall, "American Involvement in Vietnam."

85. Notes of the Leadership Meeting, 4 August 1964, in U.S. Department of State, *Foreign Relations of the United States, 1964–1968,* vol. 1, *Vietnam, 1964,* 615–21; Stoler, "The Tonkin Gulf Crisis," 84, 86–94; Hatcher, *The Suicide of an Elite,* 92.

86. Witcover, *The Resurrection of Richard Nixon,* 110 (Nixon quotes); Ambrose, *The Triumph of a Politician,* 55.

87. The argument that Johnson kept the congressional resolution in his coat pocket for use in the event of a crisis like the Tonkin Gulf incidents does not stand up to the evidence. The resolution presented to Congress in August 1964 owed more to prior joint resolutions than to the drafts that had been created during the first half of the year. See Johns, "Opening Pandora's Box." Edwin Moïse has convincingly argued that, while the first attack on American naval vessels in the Tonkin Gulf did occur, the second most likely did not; he also refutes charges of a conspiracy on the part of the administration. See Moïse, *Tonkin Gulf.*

88. Small, *At the Water's Edge,* 28.

89. *Burlington (VT) Free Press*, 7 August 1964.

90. Gibbons, *The U.S. Government and the Vietnam War*, 2:266.

91. *Congressional Record*, 7 August 1964.

92. Gibbons, *The U.S. Government and the Vietnam War*, 2:325–26.

93. *New York Times*, 5 August 1964.

94. Wallace, *Politics of Conscience*, 178–79.

95. Stone, *Elites for Peace*, 30–31.

96. *Milwaukee Journal*, 5 August 1964.

97. Gibbons, *The U.S. Government and the Vietnam War*, 2:309–10.

98. Javits, *Javits*, 393.

99. Oral History Interview, John Sherman Cooper, 11 March 1978, by Michael L. Gillette, LBJL, 45; Rhodes, *John Rhodes*, 99.

100. Harris Poll, 10 August 1964, WHCF, ND 19/CO 312, box 214, LBJL.

101. Statement, Joint Senate-House Republican Leadership, 20 August 1964, Republican Leadership File, folder 52, Dirksen Papers.

102. Reinhard, *The Republican Right*, 201.

103. Goldwater, *Where I Stand*, 28–29; Goldberg, *Barry Goldwater*, 391 n. 104.

104. Goldberg (*Barry Goldwater*, 216, 228) suggests that the Arizona senator could have forced Johnson to debate Vietnam policy, which could have prevented the Americanization of the war in 1965. (See also Edwards, *Goldwater*, 273, 317.) This is a questionable assertion. Thomas Powers and Jeffrey Matthews also disagree on this point; Powers argues specifically: "War and the fear of war dominated the presidential campaign of 1964 from its beginning" (Powers, *The War at Home*, 1; cf. Matthews, "To Defeat a Maverick").

105. Goldwater, *Goldwater*, 192–93, and *With No Apologies*, 192–95; Schneider, *Cadres for Conservatism*, 84. Powers (*The War at Home*, 19–20) suggests that Johnson engineered an agreement on race at the meeting but does not mention the war as part of the discussion.

106. Edwards, *Goldwater*, 332; Matthews, "To Defeat a Maverick," 671; Gould, *1968*, 9.

107. MacNeil, *Dirksen*, 271–72.

108. Quoted in Powers, *The War at Home*, 15–16; and in Gibbons, *The U.S. Government and the Vietnam War*, 2:357.

109. Quoted in Califano, *Triumph and Tragedy*, 172.

110. Memorandum, Moyers to Johnson, 3 October 1964, Office Files of Bill Moyers, box 10, LBJL. Moyers also pointed out that, the more McNamara went to Vietnam, the more likely the public would perceive a problem with the situation in Vietnam regardless of official administration statements.

111. Javits, "The Road Back."

112. Telephone Transcript, 19 January 1965, quoted in Beschloss, ed., *Reaching for Glory*, 164–65. See also Scheele, "Prelude to the Presidency" (quote).

113. Van Atta, *With Honor*, 68–69; Peabody, "Political Parties," 182–86; Critchlow, *The Conservative Ascendancy*, 76.

114. Donovan, *The Future of the Republican Party*, 10. Ironically, owing in large mea-

sure to Vietnam, the GOP would go on to win the White House in 1968 and retain control of the executive branch for twenty of the next twenty-four years.

115. Brooke, *Bridging the Divide*, 110. Brooke firmly believed that his opposition to Goldwater "haunted [him] for the rest of [his] political career." As he explained it, however, "I felt I was serving not only my conscience but the best interests of my country and the party" (110).

116. *Newsweek*, 9 November 1964, 31.

117. Quoted in Hess and Broder, *The Republican Establishment*, 1.

118. Letter, Bush to Nixon, 10 November 1964, Bush/Personal/Congressional/ General-Personal, box 1, George H. W. Bush Presidential Library, College Station, TX (hereafter GHWBL).

119. Gould, *1968*, 5.

120. Dietz, *Republicans and Vietnam*, 84. The membership of the new group included Eisenhower, all past presidential candidates, selected governors (including George Romney), and other party officials, but congressional representation was the dominating factor. Everett Dirksen and Gerald Ford announced the formation of the coordinating committee on 11 January 1965, saying that it would "guide Republican Party Policy at the national level, in the absence of a Republican President and Vice President, by the record they write in the Congress. It is their responsibility" (quoted in ibid., 84).

121. Reinhard, *The Republican Right*, 215.

122. Critchlow, *The Conservative Ascendancy*, 83.

123. *Tulsa Tribune*, 27 November 1964. Two days earlier, the *Chicago Tribune* noted, "When the administration spokesman, General Taylor, refers casually to the possibility of bombing the infiltration routes from Communist North Vietnam into adjoining Laos . . . no one cries that the administration is 'trigger-happy' and will wind up getting us in a nuclear war" (*Chicago Tribune*, 25 November 1964).

124. Logevall, *Choosing War*, 257–58.

125. Skowronek, *The Politics Presidents Make*, 343.

## 3. Opening Pandora's Box

1. Bundy Manuscript, chap. 18, p. 20. On this point, see also Logevall, *Choosing War*, chap. 9.

2. Brands, *The Wages of Globalism*, 231. Cuddy, however, argues, "After allowing the carnage to continue until he was safely re-elected . . . it would have taken an astonishing act of courage to cut the Gordian Knot at that late hour—the kind of moral heroism seldom seen in American politics" ("Vietnam," 372).

3. *New York Times*, 7 January 1965.

4. Logevall, *Choosing War*, 309.

5. Stoler, "The 'Wise Old Owl,'" 105; Letter, Aiken to John Wires, 26 December 1964, 39/3/8, George D. Aiken Papers, Special Collections, Bailey/Howe Library, University of Vermont, Burlington, VT (hereafter Aiken Papers). Unlike many congressmen, Aiken appears to have been more involved in responding specifically to the concerns of his

constituents in letters rather than simply sending out a form letter on a general subject. As a result, his correspondence is an excellent source of information on his views on a given subject at a given moment.

6. Memorandum, Moore to McGeorge Bundy, n.d. (January 1965), James C. Thomson Papers, box 25, JFKL.

7. *New York Times,* 11 January 1965.

8. Quoted in Johnson, *The Vantage Point,* 122.

9. State of the Union Address, 4 January 1965, BBH, Executive Office of the President, box 5, Hickenlooper Papers.

10. *Des Moines Register,* 6 January 1965.

11. Speech, 26 January 1965, Richard M. Nixon Pre-Presidential Papers, Speech File, box 83/2, National Archives and Records Administration—Pacific Region, Laguna Niguel, CA; Nixon, *RN,* 270; Witcover, *The Resurrection of Richard Nixon,* 109. See also Speech, 15 March 1965, GRF Congressional Papers, Legislative File, box B31-3, GRFL.

12. Herring, *America's Longest War,* 152.

13. *Shawano (WI) Leader,* 5 February 1965.

14. Quoted in Nixon, *RN,* 271.

15. Quoted in Parmet, *Richard Nixon,* 453; *New York Times,* 8 February 1965.

16. Gibbons, *The U.S. Government and the Vietnam War,* 3:82; AP Press Release, 11 February 1965, WHCF, Name File, box 120, LBJL. See also Ambrose, *The Triumph of a Politician,* 62; Witcover, *The Resurrection of Richard Nixon,* 110; and Donovan, "Over-Nominated," 92.

17. Gibbons, *The U.S. Government and the Vietnam War,* 3:71.

18. Transcript, Aiken Interview on WCAX-TV, 10 March 1965, 51/4/39, Aiken Papers.

19. *Washington Post,* 26 March 1965.

20. Press Release, 14 February 1965, box 973/2, Tower Papers.

21. *National Review,* 23 February 1965, 136–37.

22. Harrigan, "We Can Win in Southeast Asia," 187–88; Lauck, "Binding Assumptions," 287.

23. Newsletter, 9 March 1965, RG IX, box 1253, Karl E. Mundt Archives, Karl E. Mundt Library, Dakota State University, Madison, SD.

24. Newsletter (John W. Byrnes), 16 February 1965, Catherine May Papers, box 149, Special Collections, Washington State University, Pullman, WA (hereafter May Papers).

25. Letter, Len Jordan to Carolyn Cordwell, 26 February 1965, Len Jordan Papers, box 142/20, Special Collections, Albertsons Library, Boise State University, Boise, ID (hereafter Jordan Papers); Newsletter (Norris Cotton), 4 March 1965, box 149, May Papers. On the issues of appeasement and the lessons of history, see also News Release, 19 February 1965, box 149, May Papers.

26. For an in-depth look at the decisionmaking process in the first half of 1965, see Logevall, *Choosing War;* Berman, *Planning a Tragedy;* McMaster, *Dereliction of Duty;* and Ball, *The Past Has Another Pattern.*

27. Berman, *Planning a Tragedy,* 44–46. See also Ball, *The Past Has Another Pattern;* and DiLeo, *The Rethinking of Containment.*

28. Wainstock, *The Turning Point,* 6–7. The memorandum is reprinted in full in Humphrey, *The Education of a Public Man,* 320–24.

29. Ambrose, *Eisenhower,* 558. See also Brands, "Johnson and Eisenhower."

30. Memorandum, Marvin Watson to Johnson, 12 February 1965, WHCF, ND 19/CO 312, box 214, LBJL.

31. Telephone Conversation Transcript, 15 February 1965, quoted in Beschloss, ed., *Reaching for Glory,* 178.

32. For more on Eisenhower's belief in the importance of propaganda as a weapon, see Osgood, *Total Cold War.*

33. Memorandum of Conversation, 17 February 1965, DDE Post-Presidential Papers, Augusta–Walter Reed Series, box 1, DDEL.

34. Ibid.

35. On Eisenhower's use of rhetorical diplomacy, see Tudda, *The Truth Is Our Weapon;* and Osgood, *Total Cold War.*

36. Letter, Lyndon Johnson to Dwight Eisenhower, 5 March 1965, DDE Post-Presidential Papers, Augusta–Walter Reed Series, box 2, DDEL; Letter, Johnson to Eisenhower, 16 March 1965, White House Famous Names, box 2, LBJL.

37. Gibbons, *The U.S. Government and the Vietnam War,* 3:208–10.

38. Burke and Greenstein, *How Presidents Test Reality.*

39. Gibbons, *The U.S. Government and the Vietnam War,* 3:130n.

40. Gardner, *Pay Any Price,* 174.

41. The column, syndicated by the *Los Angeles Times,* resumed on 28 December 1964 after a hiatus during the campaign. Goldwater continued to write the column through 1968, when he returned to the Senate. The columns represent a great untapped source for historians largely owing to Goldwater's candid observations and frank statements—which, ironically, had been so devastating during his presidential campaign—on matters of both foreign and domestic policy. A significant percentage of his columns over these four years would address the war in Vietnam. In his first column, Goldwater described what his approach would be: "My column will now be devoted to commentary on current events. I shall be writing without the restrictions which as a United States Senator imposed limitations on what I could say in print. . . . *I am free to speak my mind* . . . a highly welcomed condition, particularly for a man used to speaking his mind with a large dose of candor" (Newspaper Column, 28 December 1964, box SP-8/13, Goldwater Papers [emphasis added]).

42. Goldwater, *Goldwater,* 221–22.

43. *New York Times,* 2 April 1965.

44. Memorandum, Jack Valenti to Lyndon Johnson, 28 April 1965, WHCF, Name File, box 120, LBJL.

45. Donovan, "Over-Nominated," 92; and *New York Times,* 2 April 1965 (quote).

46. Ambrose, *The Triumph of a Politician,* 64.

47. Memorandum for the Record, 4 May 1965, DDE Post-Presidential Papers, Augusta–Walter Reed Series, box 1, DDEL.

48. Memorandum for the Record, 16 June 1965, DDE Post-Presidential Papers, Augusta–Walter Reed Series, box 1, DDEL.

49. Mann, *A Grand Delusion*, 446.

50. Stone, *Elites for Peace*, 46.

51. *National Review*, 28 December 1965, 1180; Statement, Republican Policy Committee (Phil Brennan), 19 May 1965, 89th Congress, box 37/2, Rhodes Papers.

52. Bundy Manuscript, chap. 25, pp. 17–18.

53. Gibbons, *The U.S. Government and the Vietnam War*, 3:284–86.

54. Ibid., 3:237–50.

55. Press Release, 14 June 1965, GRF Congressional Papers, Press Secretary File, box D118, GRFL; *Waukesha (WI) Daily Freeman*, 14 June 1965.

56. Van Atta, *With Honor*, 105.

57. Gibbons, *The U.S. Government and the Vietnam War*, 3:306.

58. Memorandum, McGeorge Bundy to Johnson, 19 June 1965, NSC History, box 42, LBJL. Bundy also commented, "If U.S. forces were to get hurt during a pause, we would be giving a dangerous opening for Mel Laird; people just would not understand it."

59. Quoted in Berman, *Planning a Tragedy*, 89.

60. Although there are no notes from this meeting, a memo later that day from Marvin Watson to the president said that Johnson's military aide, Maj. Gen. C. V. Clifton—who had accompanied Eisenhower to the airport following the meeting—reported that Eisenhower had nothing but positive things to say about the manner in which Johnson was handling the conflict. See Gibbons, *The U.S. Government and the Vietnam War*, 3:344.

61. Memorandum of Telephone Conversation, Dwight D. Eisenhower to Lyndon Johnson, 2 July 1965, DDE Post-Presidential Papers, Augusta–Walter Reed Series, box 2, DDEL.

62. Press Release, Republican Congressional Committee, 17 June 1965, 89th Congress, box 38/7, Rhodes Papers.

63. Hatfield, *Against the Grain*, 97.

64. Mollenhoff, *George Romney*, 242–44.

65. Eells and Nyberg, *Lonely Walk*, 56–57.

66. Hatfield, *Against the Grain*, 98.

67. Statement, Mark Hatfield, July 1965, box 64, Adair Papers.

68. Califano, *Triumph and Tragedy*, 49.

69. Press Release, 16 July 1965, box 64, Adair Papers. On Mansfield, see Oberdorfer, *Senator Mansfield*.

70. Califano, *Triumph and Tragedy*, 41–46.

71. Gibbons, *The U.S. Government and the Vietnam War*, 3:447.

72. Rhodes, *John Rhodes*, 114.

73. Memorandum for the Record, 3 August 1965, DDE Post-Presidential Papers, Augusta–Walter Reed Series, box 1, DDEL.

74. Memorandum for the Record, 20 August 1965, DDE Post-Presidential Papers, Augusta–Walter Reed Series, box 1, DDEL.

75. Gibbons, *The U.S. Government and the Vietnam War,* 4:37.

76. Editorial, *Chicago Sun-Times,* 26 August 1965.

77. Gibbons, *The U.S. Government and the Vietnam War,* 4:37.

78. Letter, Adair to Rev. George B. Wood, 25 August 1965, box 64, Adair Papers.

79. Telephone Conversation Transcript, 24 August 1965, DDE Post-Presidential Papers, Appointment Book Series, box 2, DDEL.

80. Letter, Findley to Ford, 30 August 1965, GRF Congressional Papers, Press Secretary File, box D118, GRFL.

81. Letter, Stassen to Johnson, 16 August 1965, Harold Stassen Papers, box 108, Minnesota Historical Society, St. Paul, MN (hereafter MHS).

82. Letter, Stassen to Dirksen, Saltonstall, Hickenlooper, Scott, Javits, Kuchel, Ford, Laird, and Allott, 24 August 1965, Stassen Papers, box 108, MHS.

83. Letters, Scott to Stassen, 26 August 1965, Hickenlooper to Stassen, 27 August 1965, and Allott to Stassen, 2 September 1965, Stassen Papers, box 108, MHS.

84. *National Review Bulletin,* 14 September 1965, 1.

85. *National Review Bulletin,* 31 August 1965, 4–5.

86. Speech, 7 September 1965, box 3, Senator Jack Miller Collection, Iowa Historical Society, Iowa City, IA (hereafter Miller Papers).

87. Gibbons, *The U.S. Government and the Vietnam War,* 4:81.

88. For a discussion of Lippmann's views, see Steel, *Walter Lippmann and the American Century;* and Logevall, "First among Critics." On Fulbright and the war, see Woods, *The Search for a Cold War Foreign Policy.* On the antiwar movement in general, see Wells, *The War Within;* Small, *Antiwarriors;* and DeBenedetti, *An American Ordeal.*

89. Gibbons, *The U.S. Government and the Vietnam War,* 4:89–90.

90. *New York Times,* 19 November 1965.

91. *New York Times,* 22 November 1965.

92. Nixon, "Why Not Negotiate in Vietnam?" 50–54.

93. Ambrose, *The Triumph of a Politician,* 76–77.

94. *Christian Science Monitor,* 29 November 1965.

95. Editorial, *St. Louis Globe-Democrat,* 6 January 1966.

96. Statement, n.d. (December 1965), Press Release Series, box 879, Cooper Papers.

97. *Washington Post,* 27 January 1966. See also Statement, Cooper, 10 January 1966, Speech Series, box 905, Cooper Papers.

98. Transcript, 30 January 1966, Speech Series, box 905, Cooper Papers.

99. Gibbons, *The U.S. Government and the Vietnam War,* 4:139.

100. Ibid., 4:136. The public version of the senators' account of their findings can be found in Report, 6 January 1966, 28/4/4, Aiken Papers. Accompanying Mansfield and Aiken on the trip were Edmund Muskie (D-ME), Daniel Inouye (D-HI), and Caleb Boggs (R-DE).

101. Remarks, 11 January 1966, in *Executive Sessions,* 35, 37.

102. Gibbons, *The U.S. Government and the Vietnam War,* 4:137.

103. Speech, 4 February 1966, box 34/97-L, Clifford Case Papers, Special Collections and Archives, Rutgers University, New Brunswick, NJ (hereafter Case Papers).

104. Clipping, AP News Report, 5 February 1966, 33/3/21, Aiken Papers.

105. For the text of the State of the Union address, see Speech, 12 January 1966, Office Files of Henry H. Wilson, box 15, LBJL.

106. *New York Times*, 18 January 1966. The practice of an opposition response to the State of the Union address, accepted as commonplace today, was an innovation of the Republican minority in the 1960s. See Dietz, *Republicans and Vietnam*, 97–98.

107. Fry, *Debating Vietnam*, 20–21 (Scott quote); *New Republic*, 8 January 1966, 7.

108. Mollenhoff, *George Romney*, 244.

109. *Washington Post*, 26 January 1966.

110. Speech, 29 January 1966, Melvin Laird Papers, box A39, GRFL.

111. Quoted in Brands, *The Wages of Globalism*, 245.

112. Gardner, *Pay Any Price*, 282. Leslie Arends, the ranking Republican member of the House Armed Services Committee, also supported the resumption of bombing to bolster the American military position, as did Frances Bolton of the House Foreign Affairs Committee, who thought that bombing would send a signal that the United States planned to see its commitment in Vietnam through to the end. "Don't let them think we won't fight," she argued. See Brands, *The Wages of Globalism*, 245–46.

113. Gibbons, *The U.S. Government and the Vietnam War*, 4:139.

114. Fry, *Debating Vietnam*, 11. See also Longley, *Senator Albert Gore, Sr.*

115. Fry, *Debating Vietnam*, 27.

116. Gibbons, *The U.S. Government and the Vietnam War*, 4:222–23.

117. The hearings are excerpted in *The Vietnam Hearings*.

118. Stone, *Elites for Peace*, 91, 98.

119. Halberstam, *The Powers That Be*, 504–5, 706.

120. Letter, Dwight Eisenhower to Arthur Goldberg, 21 February 1966, DDE Post-Presidential Papers, Augusta–Walter Reed Series, box 1, DDEL.

121. Statement, 21 February 1966, box 25/14, Tower Papers.

122. Speech, 1 March 1966, box 34/103-L, Case Papers.

123. Letter, Adair to Flava Ploughe Halberstadt, 22 February 1966, box 78B, Adair Papers.

124. Statement, Republican Policy Committee, 2 March 1966, 89th Congress, box 37/6, Rhodes Papers.

125. Memorandum, Pavlik to Hickenlooper, 3 March 1966, BBH, Political Files, box 49, Hickenlooper Papers.

126. Speech, 2 June 1966, BBH, FRC, Countries, box 165, Hickenlooper Papers.

127. Press Release, 31 March 1966, Laird Papers, box A14, GRFL.

128. Reinhard, *The Republican Right*, 215.

129. Remarks, 12 May 1966, in *Executive Sessions*, 745, 748.

130. Press Release, 2 March 1966, box 973/7, Tower Papers; Newsletter, 16 May 1966, BBH, FRC, Countries, box 159, Hickenlooper Papers.

131. Quoted in *U.S. News and World Report*, 2 May 1966, 15.

132. Newspaper Clipping, Editorial, *Columbus (GA) Ledger*, 24 April 1966, Robert T. Hartmann Papers, box 72, GRFL.

133. Press Release, 18–22 April 1966, Senatorial Series II, box 597, Cooper Papers.

134. *Christian Science Monitor,* 4 April 1966.

135. Cited in Memorandum, Tom Johnson to Moyers, 20 June 1966, WHCF, ND 19/ CO 312, box 221, LBJL. Of the 1,597 respondents, 41 percent considered inflation to be second to the war as the best issue for the party.

136. Van Atta, *With Honor,* 118. Van Atta's point is compelling. The tendency of scholars to employ the overgeneralized binary categories of hawks and doves in analyzing the Vietnam era is reductionist and overlooks the fluidity of the political landscape.

137. *Newsweek,* 27 June 1966, 17.

138. Quoted in Johnson, *Congress and the Cold War,* 138.

139. Memorandum for the Record, 22 June 1966, DDE Post-Presidential Papers, Augusta–Walter Reed Series, box 1, DDEL.

140. Letter, Dwight Eisenhower to Arthur Goldberg, 1 September 1966, DDE Post-Presidential Papers, Augusta–Walter Reed Series, box 1, DDEL.

141. Memorandum for the Record, 19 September 1966, DDE Post-Presidential Papers, Augusta–Walter Reed Series, box 1, DDEL.

142. *Cedar Rapids Gazette,* 23 June 1966.

143. Letter to the Editor, *Washington Post,* 31 July 1966. Stassen sent a version of the letter to a number of politicians in both parties. See, e.g., Letter, Stassen to Percy, 2 August 1966, Stassen Papers, box 108, MHS.

144. Gibbons, *The U.S. Government and the Vietnam War,* 4:351–52. Accompanying Carter on the trip were ten Democrats and three Republicans, all of whom had served in either World War II or Korea.

145. Report, Republican National Committee, 9 August 1966, box 198, May Papers.

146. *Miami Herald,* 11 August 1966.

147. Gibbons, *The U.S. Government and the Vietnam War,* 4:392–93.

148. Nixon, *RN,* 271–72.

149. Bundy, *A Tangled Web,* 33.

150. "Outlook for Republicans Now," 60.

151. Notes, Telephone Conversation, Lyndon Johnson to Dwight Eisenhower, DDE Post-Presidential Papers, 3 October 1966, Augusta–Walter Reed Series, box 1 DDEL.

152. Letters, Dwight Eisenhower to Richard Nixon, 7 October 1966, and 21 October 1966, DDE Post-Presidential Papers, Special Names Series, box 14, DDEL.

## 4. Confronting the Hydra

1. *Christian Science Monitor,* 28 July 1966; *National Review Bulletin,* 5 July 1966, 3 (quote).

2. Quoted in Dallek, *The Right Moment,* 220; and *Washington Post,* 21 February 1966.

3. Campaign Pamphlet, n.d. (1966), Bush/Personal/Congressional/General, box 1, GHWBL.

4. Gibbons, *The U.S. Government and the Vietnam War,* 4:413.

5. Hartley, *Charles H. Percy,* 81; and Press Release, 25 August 1966, Republican Congressional Leadership File, folder 69, Dirksen Papers.

6. *Boston Globe,* 27 August 1966.

7. *New York Times,* 10 November 1966.

8. Cutler, *Ed Brooke,* 178.

9. Brooke, *Bridging the Divide,* 139, 154.

10. Transcript, "Issues and Answers," 4 September 1966, box 562, Edward William Brooke Papers, Manuscript Division, Library of Congress, Washington, DC (hereafter Brooke Papers).

11. Transcript, WBZ Radio Interview, 30 October 1966, box 562, Brooke Papers.

12. Hatfield, *Against the Grain,* 103.

13. Hess and Broder, *The Republican Establishment,* 387–88; and *National Review,* 23 August 1966, 856.

14. Letter, Rhodes to H. R. Andersen, 23 August 1966, 89th Congress, box 43/4, Rhodes Papers; Speech, 22 July 1966, box 718/3, Tower Papers.

15. Quoted in MacNeil, *Dirksen,* 292; News Release, 28 September 1966, GRF Congressional Papers, Press Secretary File, box D4, GRFL.

16. Newspaper Column, 5 October 1966, box SP-8/24, Goldwater Papers.

17. *National Review,* 4 October 1966, 966.

18. *National Review,* 18 October 1966, 1028.

19. Letter, Aiken to Irving H. Reynolds, 8 August 1966, 39/4/12, and Speech, 19 October 1966, 39/5/18, Aiken Papers; Stoler, "What Did He *Really* Say?" and "The 'Wise Old Owl,'" 110.

20. Quoted in Gibbons, *The U.S. Government and the Vietnam War,* 4:449. According to Stoler, "It is ironic that he appeared to have won fame and notoriety for something he never said and for a position he never held, over an issue he tried unsuccessfully to keep unimportant" ("The 'Wise Old Owl,'" 114). A few days after Aiken's proposal, Leonard Marks of the U.S. Intelligence Agency mentioned it to the president. According to Marks, "He looked at me—he had a way of staring at you—and finally I blinked. I said, 'What do you think?' He said, 'Get out of here.' I picked up my papers and left. . . . Several years after he left the White House I was invited to spend a weekend at the ranch. We were by ourselves. It was on my conscience and I said, 'Mr. President, I have to ask you something. In all the years we've been together, only once did you act in a way that I could really complain' and recalled this experience. 'Why did you do it?' He looked at me and he said, 'Because in my gut I knew that you and George Aiken were right, and I couldn't do anything about it'" (quoted in Berman, *Lyndon Johnson's War,* 203; see also Gibbons, *The U.S. Government and the Vietnam War,* 4:449–50).

21. Gibbons, *The U.S. Government and the Vietnam War,* 4:440–41.

22. Ibid., 4:442.

23. Gardner, *Pay Any Price,* 314–18.

24. Letter, Nixon to Eisenhower, 4 October 1966, and Newspaper Column, 16 October 1966, DDE Post-Presidential Papers, Special Names Series, box 14, DDEL; and Press Release, 4 November 1966, GRF Congressional Papers, Press Secretary File, box D55, GRFL.

25. *National Review,* 1 November 1966, 1126.

26. *New York Times,* 5 November 1966.

27. Memorandum, George Christian to Jake Jacobsen, 4 November 1966, White House Famous Names, box 6, and Memorandum, James R. Jones to W. Marvin Watson, 5 November 1966, WHCF, ND 19/CO 312, box 223, LBJL. Statements from Carl Albert, Mike Mansfield, and others criticizing Nixon can be found attached to the Jones memo to Watson.

28. Statement, 4 November 1966, GRF Congressional Papers, Press Secretary File, box D4, GRFL. See also Statement, 14 October 1966, Post-Eisenhower Administration Series, box 10, Fred A. Seaton Papers, DDEL.

29. Newspaper Column, 9 November 1966, box SP-8/26, Goldwater Papers.

30. *New York Times,* 5 November 1966; Nixon, *RN,* 276.

31. News Summaries, Fred A. Seaton Papers, Post-Eisenhower Administration Series, box 10, DDEL.

32. Schulzinger, *A Time for War,* 235.

33. Hulsey, "Himself First," 172.

34. Hess and Broder, *The Republican Establishment,* 5–6.

35. *Wall Street Journal,* 1 November 1966. See also Aitken, *Nixon,* 322–23; and Nixon, *RN,* 267.

36. A sample of Nixon's tireless campaign schedule for his fellow Republicans over a three-day period in late September 1966 is described in Kilpatrick, "Crisis Seven": "[Nixon] lived on hamburgers, canned soup, milkshakes, box lunches, banquet cardboard, soggy pie. *He was the party man.* This was the Nixon who fought for Goldwater, all the way, in 1964, while George Achilles [Romney] sulked in his tent and Nelson the Rock was otherwise engaged. This was Nixon in 1966, sweating it out for the GOP, the hard way, the exhausting way, giving party candidates everything he had" (1267–69).

37. Nixon, *RN,* 277. Of the sixty-six House candidates whom Nixon campaigned for, forty-four won; of the eighty-six Republican candidates for all offices whom he helped, fifty-nine were elected—a success rate of 68.6 percent. See Wicker, *One of Us,* 287.

38. *St. Louis Globe-Democrat,* 3–4 December 1966.

39. *New York Times,* 13 November 1966. Nixon considered the election as a repudiation of Johnson: "This election means: (1) more support, rather than less, for the principle of no reward for aggression. (2) A growing desire to increase our military, diplomatic and economic pressure on the Communists so as to end the war in Vietnam soon" (*RN,* 278).

40. Quoted in Schandler, *Lyndon Johnson and Vietnam,* 346.

41. Memorandum, Rostow to Johnson, 28 November 1966, WHCF, CF, box 72, LBJL.

42. Nixon, *RN,* 277.

43. *New York Times,* 6 August 1968. Wicker explained that he revealed the off-the-record comments because Nixon's statements were "too interesting a footnote" to keep secret.

44. American Opinion Summary, Department of State, 10–16 November 1966, Office Files of Harry McPherson, box 28, LBJL.

45. *New York Times,* 10 November 1966.

46. Dallek, *The Right Moment*, x, 186.

47. Quoted in Hess and Broder, *The Republican Establishment*, 1.

48. Hess and Broder, *The Republican Establishment*, 6–9.

49. Memorandum, Dick Scanlon and James Rowe to Johnson, 6 January 1967, Office Files of Marvin Watson, box 23, LBJL. The report was not written by Rowe; it was complied by Scanlon and a group of Democratic political operatives.

50. Transcript, Radio Moscow, 17 December 1966, WHCF, ND 19/CO 312, box 223, LBJL.

51. Letter, Eisenhower to Robert Cutler, 26 March 1968, DDE Post-Presidential Papers, Special Names Series, box 3, DDEL.

52. Chester, Hodgson, and Page, *An American Melodrama*, 21.

53. Ibid., 183.

54. Wainstock, *The Turning Point*, 34; Mollenhoff, *George Romney*, 253. The Gallup poll also showed Reagan with 8 percent, Rockefeller and Percy with 5 percent each, and Lindsay with a mere 2 percent.

55. The role played by Vietnam in Romney's candidacy is discussed in Johns, "Achilles' Heel." For an opposing view, see Lythgoe, "The Decline of George Romney."

56. On the impact of Rockefeller's divorce on his viability as a candidate, see, e.g., Califano, *Triumph and Tragedy*, 289; and Edwards, *Goldwater*, 176.

57. Quoted in Wainstock, *The Turning Point*, 40.

58. Wainstock, *The Turning Point*, 42.

59. Wallace and Reagan would have competed for similar constituencies during the campaign. On Wallace, see Carter, *The Politics of Rage*. On Reagan's political career in the mid-1960s, especially his successful gubernatorial campaign, see Dallek, *The Right Moment*.

60. Kilpatrick, "Crisis Seven," 1263. See also Riccards, "Richard Nixon and the American Political Tradition," esp. 743.

61. *New York Times*, 26 October 1967.

62. *U.S. News and World Report*, 23 January 1967, 41.

63. Letter, Adair to Mr. Kelble, 8 March 1967, box 81B, Adair Papers.

64. Statement, November 1966 (postelection), Stassen Papers, box 108, MHS.

65. *New York Times*, 9 September 1967; Newspaper Column, 10 May 1967, box SP-8/11, Goldwater Papers.

66. *Washington Post*, 18 March 1967.

67. Letter, Roller to Morton, 2 May 1967, National Republican Committee Series, Political File—National Campaigns, 1963–1968, box 19, Thruston B. Morton Papers, Modern Political Archives, University of Kentucky, Lexington, KY (hereafter Morton Papers).

68. Transcript, "Meet the Press," 8 January 1967, box 562, Brooke Papers.

69. Hess and Broder, *The Republican Establishment*, 236.

70. Dallek, *Flawed Giant*, 450.

71. Letter to the Editor, *Louisville Courier-Journal*, 31 March 1967.

72. *Louisville Courier-Journal*, 18 August 1967. Morton defends his decision to break

with the administration in Letter, Morton to Weathers Jr., 30 August 1967, box 22, Morton Papers.

73. Van Atta, *With Honor*, 119.

74. Memorandum to Aiken, October 1966, 39/5/18, Aiken Papers.

75. Memorandum, Javits to Johnson, 20 January 1966, WHCF, ND 19/CO 312, box 219, LBJL.

76. Javits, *Javits*, 393–99.

77. Herring, *America's Longest War*, 186. Robert Shaplen observed that a "state of irresolution" existed in 1967 (quoted in ibid., 190).

78. *National Review*, 4 April 1967, 378.

79. Hess and Broder, *The Republican Establishment*, 236.

80. Letter, Dwight Eisenhower to George Humphrey, 14 February 1967, DDE Post-Presidential Papers, Special Names Series, box 14, DDEL.

81. Aside from a biography (Cannon's *The McCloskey Challenge*) and a campaign autobiography (McCloskey's *Truth and Untruth*), virtually no scholarship exists on McCloskey's political career. For example, in White's *The Making of the President, 1972*, McCloskey rates only two very brief mentions; in Small's *At the Water's Edge*, his name appears once; and, in Kimball's *Nixon's Vietnam War*, McCloskey is conspicuously absent. Even in Nixon's memoirs, he is mentioned only in passing, as one of the Republican challengers for the 1972 nomination.

82. Cannon, *The McCloskey Challenge*, 127. Interestingly, despite his criticism of U.S. Vietnam policy, McCloskey declined an offer from Daniel Ellsberg to participate in making the Pentagon Papers public in early 1971. See Mann, *A Grand Delusion*, 686.

83. Statement, 12 September 1967, Robert T. Hartmann Files, Ford Congressional Papers, box R25, GRFL.

84. Newsletter, 13 March 1968, box 652, Paul Norton "Pete" McCloskey Jr. Papers, Hoover Institution Archives, Stanford University, Palo Alto, CA (hereafter McCloskey Papers). McCloskey's first speech in the House on the same day focused on the same theme, insisting that Congress shared responsibility with the president in approving further expansion of the commitment in Vietnam. See Cannon, *The McCloskey Challenge*, 128.

85. Newsletter, 20 September 1968, box 652, McCloskey Papers. The previous day, McCloskey told the *Hillsborough Boutique*, "The primary bar to a negotiated peace in Vietnam appears to be our insistence that South Vietnam be treated as a separate country on a permanent basis" (Statement, 19 September 1968, box 652, McCloskey Papers).

86. Newspaper clipping, *Japan Times*, 4 November 1965, Gubernatorial Series, box 129, Romney Papers.

87. Letter, Romney to Eisenhower, 15 November 1965, Gubernatorial Series, box 363, Romney Papers.

88. Speech, 16 November 1965, Gubernatorial Series, box 246, Romney Papers.

89. *Newsweek*, 18 July 1966, 21; Shannon, "George Romney," 61 (quotes); Editorial, *Detroit News*, 17 January 1967; and Transcript, "Face the Nation," 5 March 1967, Guber-

natorial Series, box 242, Romney Papers. A sampling of newspaper headlines during 1965 and 1966 demonstrates Romney's struggles with the Vietnam issue: "Romney Backs Viet Policy" (29 July 1965); "Governor Criticizes U.S. Policy" (30 July 1965); "Governor Opposes Escalation" (30 January 1966); "Romney Favors Widening Bombing of North Vietnam" (13 June 1966). See Hess and Broder, *The Republican Establishment*, 126.

90. Mollenhoff, *George Romney*, 263–64; Letter, Goldwater to Rt. Reverend Walter Mitchell, 27 January 1967, 90th Congress, box 9/2, Goldwater Papers.

91. White, *The Making of the President, 1968*, 56; Letter, Eisenhower to Barry Leithead, 24 March 1967, DDE Post-Presidential Papers, Special Names Series, box 18, DDEL.

92. Memorandum, Al Applegate to Romney, 7 April 1967, Gubernatorial Series, box 263, Romney Papers. On the memo, Romney's handwritten comments dismiss Javits's point: "I may be wrong, but I'm not unduly concerned about this criticism." Romney also solicited advice from Hugh Scott, Edward Brooke, and Nelson Rockefeller. See Powers, *The War at Home*, 254.

93. Speech, 7 April 1967, Gubernatorial Series, box 263, Romney Papers.

94. *Washington Evening Star*, 10 April 1967.

95. Letter, Tower to Romney, 10 April 1967, box 817/21, Tower Papers; Press Release, 11 April 1967, box 22, Bennett Papers.

96. *Detroit Free Press*, 9 April 1967.

97. *Christian Science Monitor*, 12 April 1967; Newspaper Clipping, *Detroit Free Press*, 16 April 1967, 90th Congress, box 18/4, Goldwater Papers.

98. Memorandum, Moore to Romney, 14 April 1967, Gubernatorial Series, box 263, Romney Papers.

99. Quoted in Mollenhoff, *George Romney*, 268; Memorandum, Roche to Watson, 7 April 1967, Office Files of Harry McPherson, box 28, LBJL.

100. Memorandum, Walt Rostow to Johnson, 7 April 1967, Office Files of Marvin Watson, box 30, LBJL.

101. *New York Times*, 19 August 1967.

102. *National Review*, 2 May 1967, 453.

103. Witcover, "George Romney," 39.

104. White, *The Making of the President, 1968*, 57.

105. Cutler, *Ed Brooke*, 222.

106. Ibid., 226–29.

107. Brooke, *Bridging the Divide*, 162.

108. Cutler, *Ed Brooke*, 234–35.

109. Ibid., 235–37; Gibbons, *The U.S. Government and the Vietnam War*, 4:595 n. 109; and Brooke, *Bridging the Divide*, 162.

110. Transcript, "Face the Nation," 26 March 1967, box 562, Brooke Papers.

111. Nixon, *RN*, 282.

112. *New York Times*, 15 April 1967.

113. Johnson, *Congress and the Cold War*, 138.

114. Gibbons, *The U.S. Government and the Vietnam War*, 4:674.

115. *Congressional Quarterly Fact Sheet,* 31 May 1967, Democratic National Committee Series I, box 131, LBJL. See also *Wall Street Journal,* 11 May 1967.

116. Statement, 2 May 1967, box 25/12, Tower Papers.

117. Letter, Tower to Hickenlooper, 3 May 1967, box 25/12, Tower Papers.

118. Quoted in Hess and Broder, *The Republican Establishment,* 279–80.

119. Press Conference Transcript, 4 May 1967, box 25/12, Tower Papers.

120. Newspaper Clipping, *Washington Evening Star,* n.d. (May 1967), Dirksen Working Papers, folder 2873, Dirksen Papers.

121. Letter, Goldwater to Dirksen, 19 May 1967, 90th Congress, box 11/2, and Newspaper Column, 19 May 1967, box SP-8/11, Goldwater Papers. Goldwater's columns from 1965 to 1967 are a wonderful resource for historians because he states clearly and distinctly what he means; reading between the lines is completely unnecessary. Such candor was, in part, a by-product of his nonincumbency. Indeed, the same qualities that helped derail his presidential campaign make him an excellent editorialist. As a result, charting his views on the Vietnam War and other issues during this period is very easy.

122. *Washington Star,* 6 May 1967. The *Wall Street Journal* published a similarly themed editorial two days previously.

123. MacNeil, *Dirksen,* 298–99.

124. Speech, 2 May 1967, 48/10/1967 book, Aiken Papers.

125. *Wall Street Journal,* 11 May 1967.

126. Hulsey, *Everett Dirksen,* 237.

127. Speech, 5 May 1967, 39/5/17, Aiken Papers.

128. *Christian Science Monitor,* 5 May 1967.

129. Statement, Findley in the House, 18 May 1967; Letter, Findley to Adair, 31 May 1967. Attached to the speech is a copy of the proposed joint resolution. See Memos and Statements 7/67, box 81B, Adair Papers.

130. See Ripon Society, *The Lessons of Victory,* ii–iv; and Rae, *Decline and Fall,* 81–86.

131. Huebner and Petri, eds., *The Ripon Papers,* 167–75.

132. Speech (George Hansen), 21 June 1967, box 234, May Papers.

133. Newsletter, Republican Congressional Committee, no. 25, 3 July 1967, box 84A, Adair Papers.

134. Press Release, 2 June 1967, 90th Congress, box 79/1, Paul J. Fannin Papers, Arizona Historical Foundation, Arizona State University, Tempe, AZ (hereafter Fannin Papers).

135. *Congressional Quarterly,* 28 July 1967, 1313.

136. *Ogden (UT) Star Examiner,* 30 July 1967.

137. Alsop, "Can Anyone Beat LBJ?" 31.

138. Press Release, 17 July 1967, box 81B, Adair Papers. Morse and Stafford were joined by John Dellenback (R-OR), Marvin Esch (R-MI), Frank Horton (R-NY), Charles Mathias Jr. (R-MD), Charles Mosher (R-OH), and Richard Schweiker (R-PA). The plan was originally conceived by Dr. Douglas Bailey, who worked for the Wednesday Group, an organization of Republicans that had been formed by Morse. Morse had been critical of the administration for being "unyielding and inflexible" in its approach

to negotiations and deescalation of the war. See Gibbons, *The U.S. Government and the Vietnam War*, 4:801. A full copy of the plan, including some initial press reaction, can be found in Pamphlet, GRID Proposal, Dirksen Working Papers, folder 2874, Dirksen Papers.

139. *Salt Lake Tribune*, 12 July 1967.

140. Gibbons, *The U.S. Government and the Vietnam War*, 4:802.

141. *Congressional Record*, 17 July 1967.

## 5. Sisyphus and Tantalus

1. Karnow, *Vietnam*, 503; and Herring, *America's Longest War*, 218.

2. *Brattleboro (VT) Reformer*, 24 July 1967.

3. *Congressional Record*, 8 August 1967.

4. Editorial, *Indianapolis News*, 14 August 1967.

5. Transcript, "Today," 16 August 1967, box 31/24, Tower Papers.

6. Clipping, *Esquire*, n.d. (August 1967), Stassen Papers, box 109, MHS.

7. Speech, 9 August 1967, BBH, FRC, Countries, box 161, Hickenlooper Papers.

8. Speech, 11 August 1967, BBH, FRC, Countries, box 161, Hickenlooper Papers.

9. *Los Angeles Times*, 20 August 1967.

10. Gibbons, *The U.S. Government and the Vietnam War*, 4:800–801.

11. *Los Angeles Times*, 31 July 1967. Gerald Ford made similar distinctions between "winning" the war and "succeed[ing]" in Vietnam in an address to the American Legion convention. See Speech, 30 August 1967, Robert T. Hartmann Papers, box 57, GRFL.

12. *Washington Post*, 23 August 1967.

13. *National Review*, 5 September 1967, 943. In a conversation with Hubert Humphrey, Barry Goldwater opined that Romney would "fall on his face" during the campaign and that that would lead to a Rockefeller candidacy, which Goldwater was "unalterably opposed to." See Memorandum in the Vice President's Files, 23 August 1967, Office Files of Harry McPherson, box 27, LBJL.

14. Memorandum, McPherson to Johnson, 25 August 1967, Office Files of Harry McPherson, box 29, LBJL.

15. *Washington Evening Star*, 21 August 1967.

16. Mollenhoff, *George Romney*, 288.

17. Interview, Romney on WKBD (Detroit), 31 August 1967, Gubernatorial Series, box 245, Romney Papers; and Mollenhoff, *George Romney*, 291.

18. *New York Times* quoted in Wainstock, *The Turning Point*, 35; Editorial, *Detroit Free Press*, 28 August 1967. See also Ambrose, *The Triumph of a Politician*, 105.

19. Mollenhoff, *George Romney*, 294–95. For example, an editorial cartoon showed "the Romney bird"—a three-headed bird with a dove on one side, a hawk on the other, and Romney in the middle. See *New York Daily News*, 8 September 1967.

20. Magazine Clipping, T. George Harris, *Look*, 12 December 1967, Lloyd Papers, 27/25, Sherman P. Lloyd Papers, Special Collections, Marriott Library, University of Utah, Salt Lake City, UT (hereafter Lloyd Papers).

21. Statement, 9 September 1967, Gubernatorial Series, box 245, Romney Papers; *Detroit Free Press,* 13 September 1967.

22. Letter, Eisenhower to Marriott, 3 January 1968, Gubernatorial Series, box 363, Romney Papers; Clipping, *Bennington (VT) Banner,* 16 September 1967, 38/6/13, Aiken Papers.

23. Kilpatrick, "Brainwashing George Romney," 5.

24. Editorial, *St. Louis Globe-Democrat,* 12 September 1967.

25. Statement, Tower on WTTG-TV, 7 September 1967, box 25/15, Tower Papers.

26. *St. Albans (VT) Messenger,* 2 October 1967. See also Newspaper clipping, *Philadelphia Bulletin,* 7 September 1967, Democratic National Committee Series I, box 131, LBJL.

27. Quoted in White, *The Making of the President, 1968,* 54.

28. Whalen, *Catch the Falling Flag,* 24.

29. Commentary, Eric Sevareid on "Face the Nation," 5 September 1967, Gubernatorial Series, box 266, Romney Papers.

30. *Yakima (WA) Daily Republic,* 9 September 1967.

31. Editorial, *Detroit News,* 13 July 1967.

32. Letter, Bennett to Durant C. Black, 10 October 1967, ser. 5, box 10, Bennett Papers.

33. *Newsweek,* 1 September 1967, 30–31. At the time he joined Romney's campaign, Moore was a foreign policy expert who was a fellow at the Institute of Politics of the John F. Kennedy School of Government at Harvard. He was serving as a special assistant to the secretary of state for Far Eastern affairs at the time of Romney's October 1965 trip to Vietnam.

34. *Los Angeles Times,* 17 September 1967.

35. Wainstock, *The Turning Point,* 35.

36. White, *The Making of the President, 1968,* 57–58 ("huge in public thinking"); Mollenhoff, *George Romney,* 289; Editorial, *Fort Worth Star Telegram,* 1 March 1968.

37. See, e.g., Rae, *Decline and Fall.*

38. Kilpatrick, "Brainwashing George Romney," 1382.

39. *Time,* 15 September 1967, 22.

40. On the credibility gap, see, e.g., *New York Times,* 23 April 1965; *Wall Street Journal,* 1 December 1965; *Washington Evening Star,* 26 January 1966; Report, "The Credibility Gap," May–June 1966, Republican National Committee, Robert T. Hartmann Papers, box 46, GRFL; Press Release, Sen. Milward Simpson, 2 June 1966, box 2B/43, Bennett Papers; and Speech, Alf M. Landon, 15 January 1968, 11/3/4, Aiken Papers.

41. *Newsweek,* 1 September 1967, 31.

42. *Washington Post,* 16 September 1967, 45; Draper, "Vietnam and American Politics," 28.

43. *Washington Post,* 22 September 1967, 49.

44. *Louisville Courier-Journal,* 15 November 1967.

45. *Burlington (VT) Free Press,* 3 December 1966.

46. *New York Times,* 11 August 1967.

47. Quoted in Stoler, "The 'Wise Old Owl,'" 105; *Wall Street Journal,* 3 March 1966 ("Any position"). It should be noted, however, that, by 1969, Mansfield's and Aiken's views on the war would diverge significantly.

48. Stoler, "The 'Wise Old Owl,'" 108–9; Letter, Aiken to Laina Gerrish, 4 May 1967, 39/4/35, and Statement, 22 August 1965, 48/9/1965 book, Aiken Papers.

49. Ripon FORUM Research Paper, September 1967, Bush Papers, Personal/Congressional/General—Vietnam, box 1, GHWBL.

50. Ibid.

51. Logevall, "'There Ain't No Daylight,'" 103.

52. Van Atta, *With Honor,* 124–25.

53. Letters, Hatfield to Ford, 8 September 1967, and Ford to Hatfield, 29 September 1967, Robert T. Hartmann Papers, box 103, GRFL.

54. *Chicago Sun-Times,* 10 August 1967; Whalen, *Catch the Falling Flag,* 17. David Broder made similar observations in his *Washington Post* column on 7 September 1967.

55. Nixon, "Asia After Viet Nam."

56. Ibid.

57. Aitken, *Nixon,* 329.

58. Press Release, 25 September 1967, Robert T. Hartmann Papers, box 103, GRFL.

59. Whalen, *Catch the Falling Flag,* 26; *Washington Post,* 22 September 1967.

60. Califano, *Triumph and Tragedy,* 248–49.

61. *New York Times,* 26 October 1967.

62. Gibbons, *The U.S. Government and the Vietnam War,* 4:827–28.

63. *National Review Bulletin,* 29 August 1967, 3; Gibbons, *The U.S. Government and the Vietnam War,* 4:829.

64. *Christian Science Monitor,* 26 September 1967.

65. Memorandum, Katzenbach to Johnson, 29 September 1967, Files of Marvin Watson, box 32, LBJL.

66. *New York Times,* 4 October 1967.

67. Memorandum, Manatos to Johnson, 19 September 1967, WHCF, ND 19/CO 312, box 228, LBJL.

68. *U.S. News and World Report,* 11 December 1967, 74.

69. Huebner and Petri, eds., *The Ripon Papers,* 182.

70. Ibid., 182–203.

71. Mollenhoff, *George Romney,* 310–11.

72. Maraniss, *They Marched into Sunlight,* 196–97.

73. Friedman, "The Battle of Ideas," 7.

74. *Washington Post,* 3 October 1967.

75. *Washington Evening Star,* 8 October 1967; *Tulsa Tribune,* 3 October 1967; and Speech, 3 October 1967, BBH, FRC, Countries, box 161, Hickenlooper Papers.

76. Newspaper Column, 11 October 1967, box SP-8/10, Goldwater Papers.

77. Senate Republican Memorandum, 12 October 1967, BBH, Political Files, box 72, Hickenlooper Papers.

78. "Vietnam: No Exit," 90.

79. Speech, 9 October 1967, Legislative File, 1957–1968, box 22, Morton Papers.

80. Speech, 9 October 1967, box 25/15, Tower Papers.

81. Speech, 11 October 1967, box 34/107-M, Case Papers.

82. Walt Rostow compiled a fourteen-page sample of representative statements by Nixon, Percy, Rockefeller, Reagan, and Romney. See Memorandum, Walt Rostow to Johnson, 19 October 1967, Office Files of Harry McPherson, box 27, LJBL. See also Memorandum, James R. Jones to Watson, 31 October 1967, WHCF, Name File, box 256, LBJL.

83. White Paper on the 1968 Presidential Election, 29 September 1967, Office Files of Marvin Watson, box 20, LBJL.

84. Quoted in Clipping, *National Observer,* 23 October 1967, Records of the Democratic National Committee, ser. I, box 23, LBJL.

85. *Washington Post,* 20 October 1967; Witcover, *The Year the Dream Died,* 30–31.

86. *New York Times,* 17 October 1967.

87. Memorandum, John Deardourff to Richard van Dusen, Leonard Hall, and Jonathan Moore, 19 October 1967, and Memorandum, Moore to Romney, 21 October 1967, Gubernatorial Series, box 263, Romney Papers.

88. Speech, 30 October 1967, Gubernatorial Series, box 263, Romney Papers.

89. The committee was, in fact, a front group for the White House, not a spontaneous outpouring of support for LBJ's Vietnam policy. It was the brainchild of the Johnson aide John Roche, who promised the president that he would "leave no tracks" of the connection to the administration. See Perlstein, *Nixonland,* 207–8. The Nixon administration would employ similar tactics in an effort to manufacture support for its policies.

90. Dietz, *Republicans and Vietnam,* 128.

91. Lyon, *Eisenhower,* 847; Memorandum for the Record, 21 November 1966, "Goodpaster and Wheeler Briefings (1967)," DDE Post-Presidential Papers, Augusta–Walter Reed Series, box 1, DDEL.

92. Bundy, *A Tangled Web,* 19; *New York Times,* 22 November 1965.

93. *Washington Evening Star,* 6 November 1967.

94. *New York Times,* 14 November 1967.

95. Black, *A Life in Full,* 504.

96. Transcript, "Face the Nation," 17 December 1967, box 31/25, Tower Papers.

97. *Washington Post,* 22 November 1967.

98. Witcover, "George Romney," 38–40.

99. Stone, *Elites for Peace,* 154, 187.

100. Speech, 11 November 1967, Ronald Reagan Gubernatorial Papers, 1966–1975, Press Unit, box P17, Ronald Reagan Presidential Library, Simi Valley, CA (hereafter RRPL). Reagan usually spoke from note cards based on a written speech but frequently spoke extemporaneously. Throughout his tenure as governor, his office consistently maintained that he would stand by quotations taken from the printed version.

101. Press Release, 11 January 1968, and Speech, 11 January 1968, Bush Papers, Personal/Congressional/General, box 1, GHWBL.

102. Speech, 15 January 1968, 11/3/4, Aiken Papers.

103. *New York Times,* 19 December 1967.

104. Briefing Memo for 21 January 1968 "Issues and Answers" Appearance, 19 January 1968, Gubernatorial Series, box 242, Romney Papers.

105. Speech, 17 January 1968, box 817/21, Tower Papers.

106. *Grand Rapids (MI) Press,* 17 January 1968.

107. Memorandum for the Record, 22 January 1968, DDE Post-Presidential Papers, Augusta–Walter Reed Series, box 1, DDEL.

108. Lyon, *Eisenhower,* 847–48. Eisenhower made similar comments in a pre-Christmas interview discussing the upcoming presidential campaign. See *New York Times,* 25 December 1967.

109. Speech, 2 January 1968, 90th Congress, box 79/2, Fannin Papers.

110. Dallek, *Flawed Giant,* 513–19.

111. *Grand Rapids (MI) Press,* 22 December 1967.

112. Transcript, Response to State of the Union, Republican National Committee, 17 January 1968, BBH, Executive Office of the President, box 5, Hickenlooper Papers. Among the others responding to the speech were Peter Dominick (R-CO), George Murphy (R-CA), and Howard Baker.

113. *Christian Science Monitor,* 27 January 1968.

114. UPI Report 149, 24 January 1968, box 25/15, Tower Papers; Editorial, *Los Angeles Times,* 25 January 1968.

115. Herring, *America's Longest War,* 233; and Small, *Johnson, Nixon, and the Doves,* 138.

116. Carter, *The Politics of Rage,* 326.

117. Quoted in Gould, *1968,* 36.

118. Barrett, *Uncertain Warriors,* 113.

119. Dietz, *Republicans and Vietnam,* 131.

120. Wainstock, *The Turning Point,* 35.

121. *Grand Rapids (MI) Press,* 12 February 1968. See also White, *The Making of the President, 1968,* 61.

122. Telegram, Romney to Nixon, 5 February 1968, Gubernatorial Series, box 240, Romney Papers.

123. Speech, 15 February 1968, Fred A. Seaton Papers, Post-Eisenhower Administration Series, box 11, DDEL.

124. *New York Times,* 17 February 1968.

125. *New York Times,* 18 February 1968.

126. Editorial, *Boston Globe,* 19 February 1968.

127. English, *Divided They Stand,* 80.

128. Statement, 28 February 1968, Gubernatorial Series, box 240, Romney Papers.

129. Letter, Romney to Joseph S. Karp, 13 March 1968, Gubernatorial Series, box 240, and Transcript, "Face the Nation," 10 March 1968, Gubernatorial Series, box 242, Romney Papers.

## 6. The Zalmoxis Effect

1. *Baltimore Sun*, 18 March 1968. Republican leaders had attempted to persuade Nixon that a "Republican hawk" could not win the presidency. See *National Review*, 14 November 1967.

2. Carter, *The Politics of Rage*, 327.

3. *New York Times*, 6 March 1968. See also Transcript, Radio Address, 7 March 1968, Fred A. Seaton Papers, Post-Eisenhower Administration Series, box 11, DDEL.

4. Kimball, *Nixon's Vietnam War*, 41–43.

5. Whalen, *Catch the Falling Flag*, 135. See also *Washington Post*, 8 March 1968.

6. *Christian Science Monitor*, 19 February 1968. Wallace and his followers tended to have a bifurcated view on the war issue. While he urged more aggressive prosecution of the war, Wallace voters as a group were much more likely than Humphrey or Nixon voters to agree with the proposition that the United States should never have become involved in Vietnam in the first place. See Carter, *The Politics of Rage*, 345, 506–80.

7. Letter, Guy to Watson, 9 March 1968, Office Files of Harry McPherson, box 27, LBJL.

8. For an example of media skepticism, see *Capital Times* (Madison, WI), 7 March 1968, Clipping in Office Files of Fred Panzer, box 119, LBJL.

9. Letter, Nixon to Eisenhower, 17 March 1968, DDE Post Presidential Papers, Special Names Series, box 14, DDEL.

10. Parmet, *Richard Nixon*, 506. The memo was designed as a guide for handling the "secret plan" controversy in March.

11. *New York Times*, 16 March 1968.

12. Clipping, *Houston Chronicle*, 16 March 1968, Office Files of Fred Panzer, box 119, LBJL.

13. Clipping, Editorial, *Anderson (SC) Independent*, 15 March 1968, Office Files of Fred Panzer, box 119, LBJL. See also *New York Times*, 21 March 1968.

14. *New York Times*, 16 March 1968.

15. *Business Week*, 9 March 1968, 27.

16. *New York Times*, 22 March 1968.

17. Wainstock, *The Turning Point*, 41.

18. In the New Hampshire primary on 12 March, Nixon received 84,005 votes, Rockefeller 11,691, Romney (despite having withdrawn) 1,743, Stassen 429, and Reagan (who was not an official candidate) 326. See Wainstock, *The Turning Point*, 45.

19. Editorial, *Wall Street Journal*, 25 March 1968.

20. Whalen, *Catch the Falling Flag*, 128; Ambrose, *The Triumph of a Politician*, 142.

21. Safire, *Before the Fall*, 47–48.

22. Quoted in Whalen, *Catch the Falling Flag*, 137.

23. Whalen, *Catch the Falling Flag*, 141. An entire draft of the penultimate version of the speech is found in ibid., 283–94.

24. Ambrose, *The Triumph of a Politician*, 147.

25. Interview, 21 January 1968, 48/10/1968 book, Aiken Papers.

26. Newsletter, 11 April 1968, box 283, May Papers.

27. Ambrose, *The Triumph of a Politician,* 563.

28. Eisenhower, "Let's Close Ranks," 50–52.

29. Ibid., 50, 52–53.

30. Berman, "Coming to Grips," 537. Tomes agreed, writing, "Johnson's withdrawal initiated one of the most unpredictable, uncharacteristic, and, at times, unimaginable political campaigns in the history of the American presidency" (*Apocalypse Then,* 167).

31. *New York Times,* 2 April 1968.

32. Whalen, *Catch the Falling Flag,* 143.

33. Quoted in Whalen, *Catch the Falling Flag,* 144. See also *New York Times,* 30 June 1968.

34. *National Review,* 23 April 1968, 382.

35. MacNeil, *Dirksen,* 329.

36. Morton, "Only the GOP Can Get Us Out of Vietnam," 10–12.

37. Califano, *Triumph and Tragedy,* 290. Johnson's regard for Rockefeller is discussed in Dallek, *Flawed Giant,* 544–45.

38. White, *The Making of the President, 1968,* 230.

39. *New Republic,* 10 June 1967, 3; Draper, "Vietnam and American Politics," 26.

40. Letter, Rhodes to Norbert J. Shubeck, 29 April 1968, 90th Congress, box 48/5, Rhodes Papers.

41. Speech, 11 May 1968, Reagan Gubernatorial Papers, box G0177, RRPL.

42. Herring, *America's Longest War,* 254.

43. Memorandum for the Record, 7 May 1968, DDE Post-Presidential Papers, Augusta–Walter Reed Series, box 1, DDEL.

44. *Baltimore Sun,* 25 April 1968.

45. Wainstock, *The Turning Point,* 89. Massachusetts governor John Volpe finished second as a favorite-son candidate.

46. Memorandum, Roche to Humphrey, 14 June 1968, Office Files of Harry McPherson, box 30, LBJL.

47. Letter, Morton to John Yarty, 17 July 1968, KY Misc. File, Morton Papers.

48. Statement, Charles Percy, 25 July 1968, National Republican Committee Series, box 20, Political File—National Campaigns: Rockefeller, Morton Papers.

49. Press Release, Senatorial Series II, 1956–1972, box 567, Legislative File—Reference, Cooper Papers. Cooper made his comments at a press conference in support of Rockefeller at which Percy, Morton, Javits, Brooke, Scott, and Senator James Pearson (R-KS) also appeared.

50. Quoted in Wainstock, *The Turning Point,* 90.

51. Editorial, *New York Times,* 2 May 1968. See also *Christian Science Monitor,* 2 May 1968.

52. Whalen, *Catch the Falling Flag,* 180–81.

53. Ibid., 184. For details on the draft and the convention, see ibid., 185–94.

54. Transcript, "Meet the Press," 26 May 1968, Reagan Gubernatorial Papers, box G0193, RRPL. See also *Los Angeles Times,* 12 May 1968.

55. Newsletter, 3 June 1968, BBH, FRC, Countries, box 162, Hickenlooper Papers.

56. Editorial, *New York Times,* 31 May 1969.

57. Speech, 13 June 1968, National Republican Committee Series, Political File—National Campaigns: Rockefeller, box 20, Morton Papers.

58. Transcript, "Face the Nation," 16 June 1968, box 28/13, Molitor Papers.

59. Speech, 20 June 1968, Senatorial Series II, 1956–1972, Legislative File—Reference, box 567, Cooper Papers.

60. Kissinger's Machiavellian machinations during the prelude to the 1968 election were truly extraordinary. At various times he provided advice and counsel to the Rockefeller, Romney, Humphrey, and Nixon campaigns, and he also served for a time as a special emissary for the Johnson administration in negotiations with the North Vietnamese. See, e.g., Black, *A Life in Full,* 547.

61. Memorandum, Molitor to Kissinger, 1 July 1968, box 23/22, Molitor Papers.

62. Editorial, *New York Times,* 23 July 1968.

63. *Yakima (WA) Herald-Republic,* 31 July 1968.

64. *National Review,* 30 July 1968, 733–34.

65. Dietz, *Republicans and Vietnam,* 136.

66. *New York Times,* 29 July 1968.

67. Perlstein, *Nixonland,* 283.

68. Statement, 22 June 1968, BBH, Political Files, box 50, Hickenlooper Papers (Thurmond quote); Statement, Wilt Chamberlain, 28 June 1968 (Chamberlain quote). The Athletes for Nixon Committee included over a hundred famous sports stars. See Press Release, Nixon for President Committee, 12 July 1968, BBH, Political Files, box 50, Hickenlooper Papers.

69. Wainstock, *The Turning Point,* 97.

70. Letter, Morton to Sherman Lloyd, 22 July 1968, box 54/24, Lloyd Papers.

71. Memorandum, Tower to Nixon, 20 July 1968, box 817/17, Tower Papers.

72. White, *The Making of the President, 1968,* 245.

73. *New York Times,* 21 July 1968. See also Nixon, *RN,* 308.

74. Ambrose, *The Triumph of a Politician,* 166.

75. Draft Platform Statement, 1 August 1968, Fred A. Seaton Papers, Post-Eisenhower Administration Series, box 11, DDEL.

76. Speech, 1 August 1968, Gubernatorial Series, box 362, Romney Papers.

77. *Philadelphia Bulletin,* 30 July 1968.

78. Draft Platform Plank on Vietnam, 28 July 1968, Dirksen Politics, folder 685, Dirksen Papers.

79. *Christian Science Monitor,* 2 August 1968. Lindsay also suggested a more comprehensive approach to peace in Vietnam in an open letter to GOP convention delegates published in *Look,* 20 August 1968, 61. See also Cannato, *The Ungovernable City,* 225–26.

80. Quoted in Wainstock, *The Turning Point,* 99.

81. *Christian Science Monitor,* 3 August 1968.

82. Van Atta, *With Honor,* 128; White, *The Making of the President, 1968,* 246. For example, "P" stood for "platform draft," "R" for "Romney's suggestions," and "N" for "Nix-

on's contributions." Charles Goodell (R-NY), who served in both the House and the Senate during the war and as the chief negotiator for Rockefeller's team in the platform deliberations, has stated that Nixon's advisers accepted most of Rockefeller's proposals, "sensing the need for a common ground among the GOP." See Dietz, *Republicans and Vietnam*, 139.

83. Republican Platform, 1968, BBH, Political Files, box 66, Hickenlooper Papers; Wainstock, *The Turning Point*, 101–2; Chester, Hodgson, and Page, *An American Melodrama*, 453 (quote).

84. *Tri-Cities (WA) Herald*, 11 August 1968.

85. Newsletter, 19 August 1968, box 89B, Adair Papers.

86. Statement, 4 August 1968, RG 15, Gubernatorial Papers, ser. 25, Press Office, subser. IV, box 76, Rockefeller Papers.

87. For media reaction to the GOP plank on Vietnam, see, e.g., Editorial, *Houston Chronicle*, 6 August 1968; and Editorial, *Christian Science Monitor*, 6 August 1968.

88. *New York Times*, 6 August 1968.

89. Chester, Hodgson, and Page, *An American Melodrama*, 454.

90. Bundy, *A Tangled Web*, 25.

91. Wainstock, *The Turning Point*, 113. The USS *Pueblo* was an American spy ship captured by North Korea in 1968. For a comprehensive look at the crisis and its implications for U.S. diplomacy, see Lerner, *The Pueblo Incident*.

92. Whalen, *Catch the Falling Flag*, 180.

93. Cutler, *Ed Brooke*, 301–9.

94. Hentoff, *A Political Life*, 218.

95. Created by William E. Colby—an OSS officer during World War II who had been the CIA station chief in Saigon, head of the CIA's Far East Division, and later deputy Military Assistance Command, Vietnam, commander in charge of pacification—the Phoenix Program was designed to destroy the infrastructure of the Viet Cong. With the assistance of the CIA and Civil Operations and Revolutionary Development Support, Colby charged South Vietnam with eliminating the Viet Cong's leadership through arrest, conversion, or assassination. By 1972, as many as twenty thousand people had been killed.

96. McQuaid, *The Anxious Years*, 33.

97. Langguth, *Our Vietnam*, 520.

98. *New York Times*, 8 September 1968.

99. Quoted in Whalen, *Catch the Falling Flag*, 220.

100. Whalen, *Catch the Falling Flag*, 217.

101. Speech, 12 September 1968, BBH, Political Files, box 50, Hickenlooper Papers.

102. Speech (sample Dirksen campaign statement), Politics, folder 627, Dirksen Papers.

103. Nixon, *RN*, 272–73.

104. Telephone Conversation Transcript, Johnson to Nixon, 28 August 1968, LBJL.

105. Memorandum of Conversation, Billy Graham, n.d. (September 1968), White House Famous Names, box 6, LBJL.

106. Memorandum, Panzer to Johnson, 16 September 1968, WHCF, CF, box 76, LBJL.

107. Editorial, *Denver Post,* 17 September 1968; *New York Post,* 18 September 1968; Editorial, *Baltimore Sun,* 3 October 1968.

108. On Chennault, see Chennault, *The Education of Anna;* and Forslund, *Anna Chennault.*

109. Diem, *In the Jaws of History,* 235–37. For Diem's account of the entire Chennault affair, see ibid., chap. 28. See also Bundy, *A Tangled Web,* 37–38.

110. Bundy, *A Tangled Web,* 39.

111. Memorandum, John Havelock to Humphrey, 13 September 1968, quoted in Sieg, "The 1968 Presidential Election," 1066.

112. Dallek, *Flawed Giant,* 577.

113. Ibid., 579.

114. Bundy, *A Tangled Web,* 29.

115. *New York Times,* 4 October 1968.

116. Sieg, "The 1968 Presidential Election," 1067. See also *Washington Post,* 2 October 1968.

117. Letter, Talcott to Lloyd, 2 October 1968, box 54/24, Lloyd Papers.

118. Senate Republican Memorandum, 24 October 1968, BBH, Political Files, box 72, Hickenlooper Papers.

119. Johnson, *The Vantage Point,* 548. LBJ's assessment is disputed in Clifford, *Counsel to the President,* 573.

120. Dallek, *Flawed Giant,* 579.

121. Nixon, *RN,* 323.

122. Bundy, *A Tangled Web,* 40; Telephone Conversation Transcript, Johnson to Nixon, Humphrey, and Wallace, 16 October 1968, LBJL.

123. Goldwater, *With No Apologies,* 208.

124. Aitken, *Nixon,* 362.

125. Meeting Notes, 14 October 1968, Thomas Johnson Meeting Notes, box 4, LBJL.

126. Statement, 25 October 1968, Laird Papers, box A39, GRFL; Mann, *A Grand Delusion,* 620–21; Witcover, *The Year the Dream Died,* 404.

127. Transcript, "Issues and Answers," 27 October 1968, box 31/27, Tower Papers.

128. Quoted in Matthews, *Kennedy and Nixon,* 269. In a memorandum on 31 October, Walt Rostow advised the president that, if Thieu did not agree to the talks, LBJ should talk to Nixon privately and "give him the evidence . . . that the South Vietnamese are thinking that they can turn down this deal and get a better deal after the election": "While sharing the information with Nixon, tell him flatly that you are confident that he has nothing whatsoever to do with this." Rostow also suggested that Johnson stress the domestic political advantages of Thieu's participation and that he invite Nixon and the other candidates to sign a letter to Thieu encouraging him to accept the negotiations. See Memorandum, Rostow to Johnson, 31 October 1968, NSF, Files of Walt W. Rostow, box 5, LBJL.

129. Bundy, *A Tangled Web,* 41–42.

130. Telephone Conversation Transcript, Johnson to Russell, 31 October 1968, LBJL.

131. Bundy, *A Tangled Web*, 41.

132. Diem, *In the Jaws of History*, 239–41.

133. Bornet, *The Presidency of Lyndon B. Johnson*, 320.

134. *Washington Post*, 1 November 1968. Johnson, ever concerned with domestic politics, had instructed his congressional aides to canvass the members of both the Senate Foreign Relations Committee and the House Foreign Affairs Committee regarding their stance on the bombing halt. See Memorandum, Benjamin H. Read to Walt Rostow, 3 November 1968, NSF, CF, VN, box 103, LBJL.

135. Ambrose, *The Triumph of a Politician*, 212–13.

136. Telephone Conversation Transcript, Johnson to Dirksen, 2 November 1968, LBJL.

137. Telephone Conversation Transcript, Johnson to Nixon, 3 November 1968, LBJL; White, *The Making of the President, 1968*, 381; Bundy, *A Tangled Web*, 43.

138. White, *The Making of the President, 1968*, 381.

139. Memorandum, 29 October 1968, NSF, Files of Walt W. Rostow, box 5, LBJL. See also Sieg, "The 1968 Presidential Election," 1072.

140. Witcover, *The Resurrection of Richard Nixon*, 441.

141. Transcript, 3 November 1968, NSF, Files of Walt W. Rostow, box 5, LBJL.

142. Press Conference Transcript, 4 November 1968, box 25/15, Tower Papers.

143. White, *The Making of the President, 1968*, 382–83.

144. Diem, *In the Jaws of History*, 243.

145. Mann, *A Grand Delusion*, 622.

146. Bundy, *A Tangled Web*, 48.

147. Clifford, *Counsel to the President*, 596.

148. Quoted in Diem, *In the Jaws of History*, 244.

149. The prisoner's dilemma scenario is a staple of social science game theory. Two people have been arrested separately and are held in separate cells. They are not allowed to communicate. Each is told the following: (*a*) We have arrested you and another person for committing this crime together. (*b*) If you confess and the other person confesses, we will reward your assistance to us, and your sparing us the expense of a trial, by sentencing you both fairly lightly (to two years in prison). (*c*) If you do not confess and the other person also does not confess, we will not be able to convict you, but we will be able to hold you here and make you as uncomfortable as we can for thirty days. (*d*) If you confess and the other person does not, we will show our appreciation to you by letting you go free. We will then take your testimony, in which you will implicate the other person as your accomplice and put that person in prison for forty years. (*e*) If you do not confess and the other person does, that person's testimony will be used to put you in prison for forty years, and your accomplice will go free. (*f*) Each of you is being given the same deal.

150. Bundy, *A Tangled Web*, 44–45.

151. Telephone Conversation Transcript, Ottenad and Rostow, 3 January 1969, NSC, HAK Office Files, box 3/9, Richard M. Nixon Presidential Materials Project, National Archives and Records Administration II, College Park, MD (hereafter NPMP).

152. Nixon received 31,770,237 of the 73,186,819 votes cast in the election. Humphrey and Wallace garnered 31,270,533 votes (42.7 percent) and 9,906,141 votes (13.5 percent), respectively.

153. *Time*, 15 November 1968, 19.

154. Wainstock, *The Turning Point*, 175. Carl Marcy, the longtime chief of staff for the Senate Foreign Relations Committee, agrees: "If Humphrey had come out much earlier and stated flatly that he was going to get us out of Vietnam, he might have won—because I think that was the crucial issue during that campaign." See Transcript, Oral History Interview, Carl M. Marcy, 2 November 1983, by Donald A. Ritchie, 213, Oral History Project, United States Senate Historical Office, Washington, DC.

155. Diem, *In the Jaws of History*, 245.

156. Gardner, *Pay Any Price*, 523.

157. *New York Times*, 12 November 1968.

158. *New York Times*, 14 November 1968.

159. UPI Press Release, 15 November 1968, NSF, Files of Walt W. Rostow, box 14, LBJL.

160. Ky, *How We Lost the Vietnam War*, 169.

161. Aitken, *Nixon*, 355; and Sieg, "The 1968 Presidential Election," 1063.

162. Quoted in Parmet, *Richard Nixon*, 516.

163. Rae, *Decline and Fall*, 84–85.

164. Draper, "Vietnam and American Politics," 24–25.

165. Mollenhoff, *George Romney*, 291, 324. Mollenhoff asserted, "Essentially all of Romney's political problems in 1967 and early 1968 can be traced to his comments on the Vietnam war" (ibid., 324). Senator Jacob Javits of New York asserted, "That one word [*brainwashed*] . . . destroyed his chance for the presidency—as if someone had pushed him off a cliff. Almost any other word would have been all right" (Javits, *Javits*, 356).

166. *Washington Post*, 3 October 1967.

167. Mann, *A Grand Delusion*, 623–24.

## 7. The Icarus Agenda

1. Nixon, *RN*, 269; Kimball, *Nixon's Vietnam War*, 28. Nixon's presidency has been the focus of a sizable and growing literature. See, e.g., Dallek, *Nixon and Kissinger*; Ehrlichman, *Witness to Power*; Hoff, *Nixon Reconsidered*; and Small, *The Presidency of Richard Nixon*. On Nixon and Vietnam, see Berman, *No Peace, No Honor*; Kimball, ed., *The Vietnam Files*; Kimball, *Nixon's Vietnam War*; and Hoff, "The American Home Front."

2. White, *The Making of the President, 1968*, 147.

3. LaFeber, *The Deadly Bet*, 173.

4. Hartley, *Charles H. Percy*, 190; Speech, 15 January 1969, GRF Congressional Papers, Press Secretary File, box D25, GRFL; Transcript, Interview with *Vermont Catholic Tribune*, 8 January 1969, 38/8/1, and Memorandum, Staff to Aiken, 18 December 1968, 39/6/19, Aiken Papers. The Senate Republican Policy Committee urged its members to "be in every possible accord" with Nixon's policies. See Ritchie, *History*, 79.

5. Small, "Containing Domestic Enemies," 130; Hoff, *Nixon Reconsidered*, 210 (quote).

6. Quoted in Small, *The Presidency of Richard Nixon*, 67.

7. Newsletter, 13 January 1969, box 343, May Papers.

8. Inaugural Address, 20 January 1969, in *Public Papers: Nixon*, 1–4.

9. Ambrose, *The Triumph of a Politician*, 245.

10. Nixon, *Real Peace*, 214–16. See also Nixon, *RN*, 349.

11. Small, *The Presidency of Richard Nixon*, 65.

12. Kimball, "'Peace with Honor,'" 157.

13. Small, *The Presidency of Richard Nixon*, 66. There have been sharp differences among both scholars and participants regarding Nixon's Vietnam policy and whether it produced tangible progress (the "better war" argument) or unnecessarily prolonged the war in exchange for marginal diplomatic gains. For examples of the two positions, see Sorley's *A Better War* and Kimball's *Nixon's Vietnam War*, respectively.

14. Gardner, *Pay Any Price*, 539; Kimball, *Nixon's Vietnam War*, 76–86. For an alternate explanation of the madman theory, see Johns, "The Rhetorical Diplomacy of the Vietnam War." One of the main proponents of psychological warfare as a component of U.S. foreign policy was Eisenhower. During his administration, the United States employed numerous methods of psychological warfare as part of its overall "total Cold War" campaign against the Soviets. See, e.g., Hixson, *Parting the Curtain*; and Osgood, "Form Before Substance," and *Total Cold War*.

15. Katz, "Public Opinion," 497. See also Jacobs and Shapiro, "The Rise of Presidential Polling."

16. The literature on Henry Kissinger is extensive. In addition to Kissinger's self-serving memoirs, *The White House Years*, see, e.g., Hanhimäki, *The Flawed Architect*; Suri, *Henry Kissinger*; Hersh, *The Price of Power*; and Schulzinger, *Henry Kissinger*.

17. Olson and Roberts, *Where the Domino Fell*, 216.

18. Herring, "The Executive, Congress, and the Vietnam War," 181.

19. Bundy, *A Tangled Web*, 55.

20. As Garthoff argues, Vietnam "played a singularly important role" in both the pursuit of détente with Moscow and the Nixon-Kissinger strategy of triangular diplomacy with China and the Soviet Union. See *Détente and Confrontation*, 10 (quote), 248–61. Nelson also argues that, by "making progress in Vietnam a *sine qua non* for future cooperation with the U.S.S.R. (and, hopefully, China), Nixon hoped to create leverage . . . that could be used to force Hanoi to stop fighting" ("The Domestic Side of Détente," 130). See also Schulzinger, *Henry Kissinger*, 30.

21. Quoted in Isaacson, *Kissinger*, 237.

22. Schulzinger, *A Time for War*, 276.

23. Kissinger, *Diplomacy*, 675.

24. Memorandum, Kissinger to Nixon, 20 December 1968, NSC, HAK Office Files, box 2/3, NPMP.

25. Kissinger, "The Viet Nam Negotiations," 218–19.

26. Letter, Laird to Bryce Harlow, n.d. (during transition), Laird Papers, box A98, GRFL.

27. On Jackson declining the post and Nixon's efforts to convince Laird to accept, see Laird Oral History Interview by Maurice Matloff and Roger Trask, 18 August 1986, Laird Papers, box D8, GRFL; Van Atta, *With Honor,* 3–6, 135–36; and Bundy, *A Tangled Web,* 53.

28. Sorley, *A Better War,* 115.

29. Laird Oral History Interview by Maurice Matloff and Alfred Goldberg, 2 September 1986, Laird Papers, box D8, GRFL.

30. Memorandum, n.d. (first half of 1969), Laird Papers, box A100, GRFL.

31. Sieg, "The Lodge Peace Mission," 176.

32. Sieg, "The Quest for Peace," 246, and "The Lodge Peace Mission," 192.

33. Steinberg, *Shame and Humiliation,* 172.

34. Merry, *Taking on the World,* 473.

35. See, e.g., Letter, Aiken to Hilda Daigel, 3 February 1969, 39/9/29, Aiken Papers.

36. Press Conference Transcript, 27 January 1969, in *Public Papers: Nixon,* 15–23.

37. Kissinger, *The White House Years,* 261.

38. Memorandum, Nixon to Kissinger, 1 February 1969, Laird Papers, box D11, GRFL.

39. Rhodes, *John Rhodes,* 106. See also Small, *The Presidency of Richard Nixon,* 67.

40. Mann, *A Grand Delusion,* 646; Ashby and Gramer, *Fighting the Odds,* 292.

41. Press Release, 22 February 1969, box 974/6, Tower Papers.

42. Speech, 1 May 1969, 48/10/1969 book, Aiken Papers.

43. Hatfield, *Against the Grain,* 134; Eells and Nyberg, *Lonely Walk,* 65.

44. Editorial, *Christian Science Monitor,* 6 March 1969.

45. Editorial, *New York Times,* 6 March 1969.

46. Ambrose, *The Triumph of a Politician,* 256–57.

47. Press Conference Transcript, 4 March 1969, in *Public Papers: Nixon,* 179–94.

48. Nixon, *Real Peace,* 107.

49. Quoted in Sorley, *A Better War,* 107.

50. Quoted in Safire, *Before the Fall,* 368.

51. Shawcross, *Sideshow.*

52. Nixon, *RN,* 390.

53. Garthoff, *Détente and Confrontation,* 249.

54. On this point, see Smith, "New Bottles for New Wine."

55. Memorandum, Ehrlichman to Kissinger, 20 March 1969, WHCF, Subject File, CO, box 84, NPMP.

56. Letter, McCloskey to Nixon, 20 March 1969, box 652, McCloskey Papers.

57. Memorandum, McCloskey to Nixon, 20 March 1969, Robert T. Hartmann Files, Ford Congressional Papers, box R25, GRFL.

58. McCloskey, *Truth and Untruth,* 14.

59. Speech, 26 March 1969, Remarks & Releases, August 1968—CR Index, "March 1969, 2," Dirksen Papers.

60. Transcript, "CBS Morning News," 3 April 1969, Laird Papers, box A78, GRFL.

61. Levite, Jentleson, and Berman, eds., *Foreign Military Intervention,* 51.

62. Sorley, *A Better War,* 116.

63. Hartley, *Charles H. Percy,* 190.

64. *New York Times,* 10 May 1969.

65. *National Review,* 6 May 1969, 418–21. The editorial garnered a great deal of support from conservative Republicans such as Strom Thurmond, Ronald Reagan, and John Ashbrook, who each wrote laudatory letters to the editors. See *National Review,* 20 May 1969, 475, and 3 June 1969, 526.

66. Press Release, 14 April 1969, box 974/6, Tower Papers.

67. Press Conference Transcript, 18 April 1969, in *Public Papers: Nixon,* 298–307.

68. *Washington Post,* 2 May 1969.

69. Press Release, 13 May 1969, box 1, Miller Papers.

70. Haldeman, *Diaries,* 56.

71. Speech, 14 May 1969, President's Personal File, President's Speech File, 1969–1974, box 48, NPMP.

72. *New York Times,* 16 May 1969.

73. Speech, 15 May 1969, box 6C/26, Bennett Papers.

74. Statement, 15 May 1969, Camp Papers, box 6/15, Carl Albert Congressional Research and Studies Center Congressional Archives, University of Oklahoma, Norman, OK (hereafter CACRSC).

75. Newsletter, 1 June 1969, box 100/26, Lloyd Papers.

76. *Washington Evening Star,* 17 May 1969.

77. Transcript, "Today," 15 May 1969, box 974/6, Tower Papers. See also Ashby and Gramer, *Fighting the Odds,* 292.

78. Herring, *America's Longest War,* 278–80; and Haldeman, *Diaries,* 59.

79. Kimball, *Nixon's Vietnam War,* 147–48.

80. Memorandum, Nixon to Ehrlichman, 16 June 1969, President's Personal File, Memoranda for the President, box 1, NPMP. See also Ambrose, *The Triumph of a Politician,* 283.

81. Statement, 8 June 1969, in *Public Papers: Nixon,* 443–44; Nixon, *RN,* 392; Sorley, *A Better War,* 423–37.

82. Bundy, *A Tangled Web,* 66.

83. Press Conference Transcript, 19 June 1969, in *Public Papers: Nixon,* 470–80.

84. Haldeman, *Diaries,* 65, 69.

85. Johnson, *The Right Hand of Power,* 528.

86. Press Release, 15 July 1969, box 89B, "News Releases 1968," Adair Papers.

87. Report, Republican National Committee, "The Nixon Administration's First Six Months," 20 July 1969, Working Papers, folder 1895, Dirksen Papers. In fact, aside from the Vietnam issue, Nixon's approval ratings remained strong throughout his first term.

88. Speech, 1 July 1969, Senatorial Series II, 1956–1972, Legislative File, Foreign Relations Committee, box 483, Cooper Papers.

89. Kissinger, *The White House Years,* 276.

90. Nixon, *RN,* 394.

91. Dallek, *Nixon and Kissinger,* 149.

92. *Congressional Record*, 14 July 1969. Other GOP senators who participated in the discussion included Scott, Percy, Tower, Mundt, and Dirksen.

93. Statement, 15 July 1969, Robert T. Hartmann Papers, box 61, GRFL.

94. *National Review*, 29 July 1969, 735–37.

95. Dallek, *Nixon and Kissinger*, 152.

96. The Chappaquiddick incident saw the death of Mary Jo Kopechne, a former aide to Kennedy's brother Robert who was a passenger in Teddy Kennedy's car. Kennedy drove off the Dike Bridge and was able to swim to safety, but Kopechne died. Kennedy left before talking to authorities and later pleaded guilty to leaving the scene of an accident.

97. *New York Times*, 19 July 1969.

98. Ambrose, *The Triumph of a Politician*, 285.

99. *Public Papers: Nixon*, 549.

100. Bundy, *A Tangled Web*, 68.

101. Kimball, *Nixon's Vietnam War*, 157.

102. Bundy, *A Tangled Web*, 61.

103. Johnson, *The Right Hand of Power*, 528.

104. Speech, 28 July 1969, 39/8/23, Aiken Papers.

105. Kissinger, *The White House Years*, 284, 1481. It is interesting to note the similarity in language between Kissinger's characterization of troop withdrawals and Kennedy's depiction of troop increases. Both suggested that, once started, the process would be extremely difficult to stop.

106. Kotlowski, "Unhappily Yoked?" 235–38, 254.

107. Ambrose, *The Triumph of a Politician*, 299.

108. Memorandum, Haig to Kissinger, 17 September 1969, NSC, Subject File, box 314/5, NPMP.

109. Speech, 16 September 1969, President's Personal File, President's Speech File, 1969–1974, box 51, NPMP.

110. Nixon, *RN*, 398. Ho had accused the United States of undertaking a "war of aggression" and violating Vietnam's "fundamental national rights." He demanded that the United States cease the war immediately, withdraw its troops, and allow self-determination for the Vietnamese people.

111. Speech, 18 September 1969, in *Public Papers: Nixon*, 724–31.

112. Nixon, *RN*, 400.

113. Haldeman, *Diaries*, 90; and Mann, *A Grand Delusion*, 639.

114. Statement, 29 September 1969, and Letter, Cooper to Church, 30 September 1969, Senatorial Series II, 1956–1972, Legislative File, Foreign Relations Committee, box 482, Cooper Papers.

115. Statement, 3 October 1969, 91st Congress, box 78, Fannin Papers.

116. Statement, 12 October 1969, box 35/79-P, Case Papers.

117. Merry, *Taking on the World*, 483–84.

118. Memorandum, Kissinger to Nixon, 6 October 1969, WHCF, Subject File, CO, box 84, NPMP.

119. Quoted in Kimball, *Nixon's Vietnam War,* 169.

120. Haldeman, *Diaries,* 96.

121. Nixon, *RN,* 405.

122. Kimball, *Nixon's Vietnam War,* 170.

123. Press Release, 14 October 1969, box 116/29, Lloyd Papers.

124. Speech, 14 October 1969, and Speech, 24 October 1969, Reagan Gubernatorial Papers, Press Unit, box P18, RRPL.

125. *National Review,* 4 November 1969, 1090. Other Republicans supported the Moratorium as well. John Lindsay called it "the highest form of patriotism." See Cannato, *The Ungovernable City,* 423.

126. Haldeman, *Diaries,* 102.

127. Letter, Nixon to Randy J. Dicks, 13 October 1969, in *Public Papers: Nixon,* 798–99. See also Letter, Dicks to Nixon, 28 September 1969, in ibid., 799–800.

128. *Yakima (WA) Herald-Republic,* 22 October 1969.

129. Memorandum, Haldeman to Harlow and Kissinger, 22 October 1969, Haldeman Files, box 4, NPMP.

130. Letters, Aiken to Stanton Bean, 2 October 1969, and Aiken to Mr. and Mrs. Joseph Patten, 16 October 1969, 39/9/28, Aiken Papers. It appears that Aiken used the mythology that had been created about his proposal much like Nixon had appropriated the secret plan myth for his own purposes during the 1968 campaign.

131. Quoted in Schulzinger, *A Time for War,* 280.

132. Small, *The Presidency of Richard Nixon,* 74.

133. *National Review,* 4 November 1969, 1101.

134. Memorandum, Harlow to Nixon, 27 October 1969, NSC, Subject file, box 339/8, NPMP.

135. Memorandum, Nixon to Haldeman, 26 October 1969, President's Personal File, Memoranda from the President, box 1, NPMP.

136. Safire, *Before the Fall,* 172.

137. Haldeman, *Diaries,* 102; Ambrose, *The Triumph of a Politician,* 308.

138. Memorandum, Laird to Nixon, 30 October 1969, Laird Papers, box A100, GRFL.

139. Speech, 3 November 1969, President's Personal File, President's Speech File, 1969–1974, box 52, NPMP.

140. Ibid.

141. Nixon, *RN,* 409.

142. Dallek, *Nixon and Kissinger,* 165.

143. Hersh, *The Price of Power,* 133.

144. Merry, *Taking on the World,* 485.

145. *New York Times,* 4 November 1969.

146. Katz, "Public Opinion," 499. Derge had been instructed to include the following leading statement before the question in the poll: "There has been considerable discussion surrounding President Nixon's speech on Vietnam Monday night. Criticisms have been made by some commentators who disagree with the President in his views"

(Memorandum, Higby to Magruder, 11 November 1969, Gallup Poll, box 134, H. R. Haldeman, Staff Members' Office Files, White House Special Files, NPMP).

147. Cited in Sorley, *A Better War,* 169.

148. Haldeman, *Diaries,* 105.

149. Memorandum, Nixon to Laird and Rogers, 4 November 1969, Laird Papers, box D11, GRFL.

150. Transcript, "Issues and Answers," 9 November 1969, Bryce Harlow Papers, box 1/51, CACRSC.

151. Speech, 6 November 1969, box 116/29, Lloyd Papers.

152. Statement, 3 November 1969, box 343, May Papers.

153. Speech, 9 November 1969, box 497, Brooke Papers.

154. Letter, Jordan to G. A. Trobrough, 17 November 1967, box 68/16, Jordan Papers.

155. House Resolution 614, 4 November 1969, Edward Hutchinson Papers, box 111, GRFL.

156. Statement, 4 November 1969, box 974/6, Tower Papers.

157. Press Release, 10 November 1969, box 26, Bennett Papers.

158. Senate Resolution 280, 7 November 1969, box 2A/35, Bennett Papers.

159. DeBenedetti, *An American Ordeal,* 259–60.

160. Statement, 5 November 1969, in *Public Papers: Nixon,* 913–16.

161. Statement, Laird to Senate Foreign Relations Committee (executive session), 19 November 1969, Laird Papers, box A95, GRFL.

162. Quoted in McMahon, "Credibility and World Power," 467.

163. Memorandum, Nixon to Haldeman, 24 November 1969, Memoranda from the President, 1969–1974, fiche 5/document 0090, Papers of the Nixon White House, American Foreign Policy Center, Louisiana Tech University, Ruston, LA (hereafter AFPC).

164. Memorandum, Nixon to Haldeman, 24 November 1969, Memoranda from the President, 1969–1974, fiche 5/document 0093–0094, AFPC.

165. *National Review,* 30 December 1969, 1302.

166. Kimball, *Nixon's Vietnam War,* 182–83; Kissinger, *The White House Years,* 436.

## 8. Whither Ariadne?

1. Nixon, *RN,* 445; Kissinger, *The White House Years,* 481; and Kimball, *Nixon's Vietnam War,* 183.

2. *Chicago Tribune,* 23 January 1970.

3. Cannon, *The McCloskey Challenge,* 138, 143, 141.

4. Memorandum, Nixon to Haldeman, 2 March 1970, Memoranda from the President, 1969–1974, fiche 7/document 0034, AFPC.

5. Speech, 10 March 1970, Allan Cromley Papers, box 3/8, CACRSC.

6. Van Atta, *With Honor,* 260–61.

7. Witcover, *Very Strange Bedfellows,* 93–94.

8. Kissinger, *The White House Years,* 491–92.

9. Speech, 30 April 1970, Laird Papers, box A58, GRFL.

10. *New York Times,* 3 May 1970.

11. *Christian Science Monitor,* 1 May 1970.

12. *Chicago Tribune,* 1 May 1970.

13. Quoted in Mann, *A Grand Delusion,* 659.

14. Mann, *A Grand Delusion,* 666–67.

15. On these groups, see Scanlon, "The Conservative Lobby"; and Thelen, "'Will you help our nation win the peace?'"

16. Ashby and Gramer, *Fighting the Odds,* 331–32.

17. Mann, *A Grand Delusion,* 660–61, 677.

18. Speech, 15 May 1970, Cromley Papers, box 3/8, CACRSC.

19. Speech, June 1970, 91st Congress, box 78/15, Fannin Papers.

20. Speech, 18 June 1970, Harlow Papers, box 1/81, CACRSC.

21. Memorandum, Harlow to Jordan, 27 April 1970, box 68/16, Jordan Papers.

22. Press Conference Transcript, 19 May 1970, Robert T. Hartmann Papers, box 106, GRFL.

23. Speech, 4 June 1970, Robert T. Hartmann Papers, box 61, GRFL.

24. Press Release, 29 April 1970, box 497, Brooke Papers.

25. Statement, 1 May 1970, box 497, Brooke Papers.

26. *New York Times,* 9 May 1970.

27. Letter, McCloskey to Nixon, 7 May 1970, box 652, McCloskey Papers.

28. *New York Times,* 7 June 1970.

29. Mann, *A Grand Delusion,* 662–63.

30. Schmitz, *The United States and Right-Wing Dictatorships,* 121.

31. Ritchie, *History,* 78; Mann, *A Grand Delusion,* 665–66.

32. Statement, 24 June 1970, Cromley Papers, box 3/8, CACRSC.

33. *Newsweek,* 28 June 1971.

34. Safire, *Before the Fall,* 308–9.

35. Kissinger, *The White House Years,* 969.

36. Letter, Goldwater to Jack B. Lubin, 22 May 1970, 91st Congress, box 11/8, Goldwater Papers.

37. UPI report, 19 May 1970, Reagan Gubernatorial Papers, box G0153, RRPL.

38. Speech, 27 August 1970, box 497, Brooke Papers.

39. *Congressional Record,* 1 September 1970.

40. *Time,* 14 September 1970.

41. Speech, 7 October 1970, Bush Papers, Personal/Congressional/General—Personal, box 1, GHWBL.

42. Mann, *A Grand Delusion,* 673.

43. *Time,* 26 October 1970.

44. Speech, 22 October 1970, Laird Papers, box A93, GRFL.

45. Kimball, *Nixon's Vietnam War,* 229.

46. Kissinger, *The White House Years,* 969.

47. Letter, McCloskey to Nixon, 30 November 1970, box 652, McCloskey Papers.

48. Cannon, *The McCloskey Challenge,* 158, 164.

49. *Time,* 25 January 1971.

50. *Philadelphia Inquirer,* 28 January 1971. In a meeting the following week, Laird observed, "We have to be able to answer those who will charge us for having abandoned negotiations for Vietnamization." To this Ellsworth Bunker replied, "I agree completely. You can see it coming; you can see the critics lining up on this." See Memorandum of Conversation, 4 February 1971, box D11, Laird Papers.

51. Longley, "Congress and the Vietnam War," 303.

52. Herring, *America's Longest War,* 298–99.

53. *Newsweek,* 8 February 1971.

54. Statement, 8 February 1971, Robert T. Hartmann Papers, box 61, GRFL.

55. Mann, *A Grand Delusion,* 678.

56. Memorandum, Buchanan to Nixon, 3 April 1971, President's Speech File, 1969–1974, fiche 297/document 0043–0044, AFPC.

57. Mann, "Young Rumsfeld," 90.

58. Van Atta, *With Honor,* 365–67.

59. Ibid.

60. *Time,* 19 April 1971.

61. Statement, 14 April 1971, box 497, Brooke Papers.

62. *New York Times,* 8 April 1971.

63. *New York Times,* 14 April 1971.

64. *National Review,* 20 April 1971, 410.

65. White, *The Making of the President, 1972,* 59.

66. *National Review,* 20 April 1971, 420.

67. *Washington Post,* 22 February 1971. See also Cannon, *The McCloskey Challenge,* 161–72. McCloskey gave a speech in the House four days previously in which he sounded similar themes, arguing, "The President's recent decision to employ American airpower in support of South Vietnamese and Cambodian forces in the neutral countries of Laos and Cambodia exceeds his constitutional powers, and is, at best, a deliberate flouting of the will of Congress" (*Congressional Record,* 18 February 1971).

68. On McCloskey's spring trip to Vietnam, see Cannon, *The McCloskey Challenge,* 176–208.

69. Transcript, "Face the Nation," 18 April 1971, box 652, McCloskey Papers.

70. Memorandum, McCloskey to Staff, 10 May 1971, box 652, McCloskey Papers.

71. McCloskey, *Truth and Untruth,* 13.

72. McCloskey suggested in mid-1968 that he would not support the conservative Max Rafferty—who had defeated the incumbent, Thomas Kuchel, in the GOP primary—in the fall election against the eventual winner, Alan Cranston. Reagan proceeded to excoriate McCloskey for violating the Eleventh Commandment. See Cannon, *The McCloskey Challenge,* 209.

73. *Washington Post,* 10 July 1971.

74. Quoted in Cannon, *The McCloskey Challenge,* 220.

75. Letter, Charles E. Wiggins to McCloskey, 13 May 1971, Robert T. Hartmann Files, Ford Congressional Papers, box R25, GRFL. Wiggins copied the letter to Ford and other GOP members of Congress.

76. Syndicated Column, 15 May 1971, Robert T. Hartmann Files, Ford Congressional Papers, box R25, GRFL.

77. *Baltimore Sun*, 2 May 1971.

78. Cannon, *The McCloskey Challenge*, 223.

79. Letter, McCloskey to Ford, 11 June 1971, Robert T. Hartmann Files, Ford Congressional Papers, box R25, GRFL.

80. Cannon, *The McCloskey Challenge*, 220–21. Ehrlichman's advice was reciprocated by Robert Dole, the chairman of the Republican National Committee, who for months went out of his way to avoid mentioning McCloskey since he believed "it improper for the Republican chairman to attack another Republican." See Cannon, *The McCloskey Challenge*, 222.

81. Cannon, *The McCloskey Challenge*, 234.

82. Memorandum, Hugh Scott to Clark MacGregor, 14 September 1971, Hugh D. Scott Jr. Papers, box 65, Special Collections, Alderman Library, University of Virginia, Charlottesville, VA.

83. *New York Times*, 21 November 1971.

84. Transcript, "Issues and Answers," 9 January 1972, box 652, McCloskey Papers.

85. Moser, *Promise and Hope*, 1, 3.

86. *The State* (Columbia, SC), 14 October 1971.

87. *Congressional Record*, 15 December 1971.

88. Speech, 29 December 1971, John M. Ashbrook Papers, 1972 Campaign Files, box 1, John M. Ashbrook Center for Public Affairs, Ashland College, Ashland, OH (hereafter Ashbrook Papers); *National Review Bulletin*, 28 January 1972, B14.

89. Newspaper Clipping, n.d. (March 1971), box 92/1, Ashbrook Papers. On Ashbrook's position on the war, see, e.g., Letter, Ashbrook to H. B. Kriebel, 10 March 1971, and Letter, Ashbrook to Frank E. Bailey, 1 June 1971, box 92/1, Ashbrook Papers.

90. Letter, Ashbrook to W. D. Workman Jr., 10 January 1972, 1972 Campaign Files, box 1, Ashbrook Papers.

91. *New York Times*, 4 March 1972.

92. Ibid.

93. Moser, *Promise and Hope*, 25, 27.

94. Ibid., 18.

95. Quoted in *National Review*, 24 September 1971, 1045.

96. Letter, Goldwater to Laura J. Kreis, 25 January 1972, 92nd Congress, box 33/11, Goldwater Papers.

97. Ashby and Gramer, *Fighting the Odds*, 380.

98. *New York Times*, 26 January 1972; Mann, *A Grand Delusion*, 693.

99. Aiken, *Senate Diary*, 10–11, 27.

100. Transcript, "Face the Nation," 5 March 1972, box 652, McCloskey Papers.

101. Memorandum, Hartmann to Ford, February 1972, Robert T. Hartmann Papers, box 104, GRFL.

102. Herring, *America's Longest War*, 304. See also Randolph, *Powerful and Brutal Weapons*.

103. Aiken, *Senate Diary*, 40.

104. *Congressional Record*, 7 April 1972.

105. Quoted in Editorial, *New York Daily News*, 6 April 1972.

106. Press Release, 17 April 1972, Reagan Gubernatorial Papers, Press Unit, box P13, RRPL.

107. Notes (Gerald R. Ford, handwritten), 12 April 1972, GRF Scrapbooks, box 14, GRFL.

108. Speech, 21 April 1972, Laird Papers, box A50, GRFL.

109. Transcript, Rogers Testimony to SFRC, 17 April 1972, Dewey F. Bartlett Papers, box 56/9, CACRSC.

110. *Arizona Daily Star*, 14 April 1972.

111. *Wall Street Journal*, 21 April 1972.

112. Van Atta, *With Honor*, 405.

113. *Baltimore News-American*, 24 April 1972.

114. *New York Times*, 6 May 1972.

115. Speech, 8 May 1972, William T. Kendall Files, box 6, GRFL.

116. Ibid.

117. *Congressional Record*, 1 May 1972.

118. Speech, 9 May 1972, Robert T. Hartmann Papers, box 61, GRFL.

119. *New York Times*, 9 May 1972.

120. Press Release, 9 May 1972, Reagan Gubernatorial Papers, Press Unit, box P13, RRPL. The same day, Reagan sent a telegram to each member of the California congressional delegation urging support of Nixon's actions. See Telegram, 9 May 1972, Reagan Gubernatorial Papers, Press Unit, box P13, RRPL.

121. Speech, 5 May 1972, 92nd Congress, box 33/11, Fannin Papers.

122. Speech, 9 May 1972, William T. Kendall Files, box 6, GRFL.

123. Speeches, 8 May 1972 (Tower), and 9 May 1972 (Young), William T. Kendall Files, box 6, GRFL. Similar speeches were given by Republican senators Lowell Weicker, Robert Taft Jr., Peter Dominick, William Brock, Paul Fannin, Hiram Fong, Jack Miller, Norris Cotton, Gordon Allott, Henry Bellmon, Wallace Bennett, and Roman Hruska (R-NE).

124. Summary of Reaction to Nixon Speech, 8 May 1972, William T. Kendall Files, box 6, GRFL.

125. Ibid.

126. *New York Times*, 9 May 1972.

127. *Phoenix Gazette*, 9 May 1972.

128. *Arizona Republic*, 10 May 1972.

129. *New York Times*, 11 May 1972.

130. Letter, Goldwater to Gen. Robert C. Richardson III, 11 May 1972, 92nd Congress, box 33/11, Goldwater Papers.

131. Speech, 11 May 1972, 92nd Congress, box 33/11, Fannin Papers.

132. Herring, *America's Longest War*, 307.

133. *New York Times*, 3 May 1972.

134. White, *The Making of the President, 1972*, 237.

135. Editorial, *New York Times*, 9 May 1972.

136. *Washington Post*, 19 September 1971.

137. *New York Times*, 14 June 1972.

138. Speech, 22 June 1972, Reagan Gubernatorial Papers, Press Unit, box P18, RRPL.

139. *New York Times*, 29 July 1972.

140. Letter, Byrnes to Rev. Harvey L. Kandler, 11 September 1972, John W. Byrnes Papers, box 63/3, Area Research Center, Special Collections, David A. Cofrin Library, University of Wisconsin, Green Bay, Green Bay, WI.

141. Speech, 21 August 1972, Governor's Office Files (Research Files), box G0153, RRPL.

142. *New York Times*, 24 August 1972.

143. *New York Times*, 21 August 1972.

144. *New York Times*, 21 August 1972.

145. *New York Times*, 23 August 1972.

146. *New York Times*, 22 August 1972.

147. *New York Times*, 21 August 1972; 1972 Republican Platform, Governor's Office Files (Research Files), box G0153, RRPL.

148. *New York Times*, 24 August 1972.

149. *New York Times*, 24 August 1972.

150. Boyer, *Promises to Keep*, 305.

151. Van Atta, *With Honor*, 422, 425.

152. Statement, 11 October 1972, Robert T. Hartmann Papers, box 61, GRFL.

153. Speech, 17 October 1972, 92nd Congress, box 81/1–19, Fannin Papers.

154. Mann, *A Grand Delusion*, 706.

155. Nixon, *RN*, 721.

156. Aiken, *Senate Diary*, 127.

157. Kissinger, *The White House Years*, 1447–48.

158. Mann, *A Grand Delusion*, 712.

159. Herring, *America's Longest War*, 317; Aiken, *Senate Diary*, 139.

160. Letter to the Editor, 4 February 1973, *Staunton (VA) News-Leader*. Goldwater's letter appeared in scores of newspapers around the country.

161. Aiken, *Senate Diary*, 153.

162. *Richmond News Leader*, 24 January 1973.

163. *Wall Street Journal*, 31 January 1973 (including *St. Louis Post-Dispatch* quote).

164. Letter, Nixon to Lady Bird Johnson, 23 January 1973, Name/Subject File, 1969–1974, fiche 73/document 0041, AFPC.

165. See Berman, *No Peace, No Honor*; and Asselin, *A Bitter Peace*. On the implementation of the accords during the period from 1973 to 1975 and the fall of South Vietnam, see, e.g., Haley, *The Fall of South Vietnam and Cambodia*; Jespersen, "Kissinger, Ford, and Congress"; Lee and Haynsworth, *The Abandonment of South Vietnam*; and Willbanks, *Abandoning Vietnam*.

166. Jespersen, "Kissinger, Ford, and Congress," 445.

167. Aiken, *Senate Diary*, 198; Herring, *America's Longest War*, 328 (Cotton).
168. *New York Times*, 14 August 1974.
169. Herring, *America's Longest War*, 331.
170. Quoted in Schulzinger, *A Time for War*, 318.
171. Reinhard, *The Republican Right*, 228.
172. Quoted in Schulzinger, *A Time for War*, 323.
173. Herring, *America's Longest War*, 334.
174. *New York Times*, 18 April 1975; Herring, *America's Longest War*, 336.

## Conclusion

1. Tuchman, *The March of Folly*.
2. Skidmore, *Reversing Course*, 149–50.
3. Gelb and Betts, *The Irony of Vietnam*, 79.
4. On the question of whether Kennedy would have escalated the Vietnam War had he lived, see, e.g., Dallek, "Lyndon Johnson and Vietnam"; Kunz, "Camelot Continued"; Logevall, "The Question of What Might Have Been"; Newman, *JFK and Vietnam*; Blight, Lang, and Welch, *Vietnam If Kennedy Had Lived*; and Paterson, "Introduction: Kennedy and Global Crisis."
5. Quoted in Gittinger, ed., *The Johnson Years*, 101.
6. Logevall questions the "right-wing beast" in 1964 and 1965, suggesting instead that there was "a remarkable *absence* of hawkish sentiment in public opinion [and] in Congress . . . in the key months of decision" ("Comment," 356).
7. Small, *Democracy and Diplomacy*, 117; Bator, "No Good Choices," 326.
8. Small, *Democracy and Diplomacy*, 117.
9. The litany of examples of blowback is extensive. See, e.g., Hixson, *The Myth of American Diplomacy*, 279–80.
10. For an alternate perspective, see Aldrich, Sullivan, and Borgida, "Foreign Affairs and Issue Voting."
11. Nincic, "Elections and U.S. Foreign Policy," 122–23, 127.
12. Small, *Democracy and Diplomacy*, xii; Levering, "Is Domestic Politics Being Slighted?" 20.
13. Gaubatz argues that "there is a discernable relationship between election cycles and the behavior of democratic states in international conflicts" and demonstrates that democracies tend to become involved in "more wars early in the election cycle and fewer wars late in the cycle" ("Election Cycles and War," 212).
14. Langguth, *Our Vietnam*, 637.
15. Mann, *A Grand Delusion*, 2. Kennedy (*The Rise and Fall of the Great Powers*, 404–5) compares the Vietnam War's impact on virtually every aspect of American civilization to the consequences of World War I on Europe.
16. In a speech on 19 June 1969 titled "Of Presidents and Caesars," Frank Church compared the growth of executive power and the creation of the imperial presidency to the caesars' grab for power in ancient Rome. He criticized the Senate specifically for its

acquiescence "while Presidents have steadily drawn to themselves much of the power delegated to Congress by the Constitution." The concentration of power in the hands of the executive, he warned, "has grown ever more rapidly, while the Congress has been reduced to virtual impotence in the making of foreign policy." See Schmitz, *The United States and Right-Wing Dictatorships,* 115.

17. Koh, "Why the President (Almost) Always Wins," 1291. See also Schlesinger, *The Imperial Presidency,* 181.

18. Lindsay, *The Politics of U.S. Foreign Policy,* 25; Johnson, *Congress and the Cold War,* 143.

19. *New York Times,* 22 August 1972.

20. Conceivably, this list could also include Lodge, Goldwater, John Kennedy (if one believes the conspiracy theorists who argue that his Vietnam policies led to his assassination), Carter (who could not defeat Reagan without the Vietnam issue, which had helped him defeat Ford), and John Kerry (whose Vietnam record came under attack).

21. Interview, James Thomson, "Vietnam: A Television History," pt. 3, "LBJ Goes to War, 1964–1965," 1983, transcript available at http://www.pbs.org/wgbh/amex/vietnam/series/pt_03.html (accessed 29 April 2007).

22. Dietz, *Republicans and Vietnam,* 2.

23. See O'Brien, "Aiken and Vietnam."

24. Herring, "The Executive, Congress, and the Vietnam War," 176.

25. Ambrose, *The Triumph of a Politician,* 64.

26. Stoler, "What Did He *Really* Say?" 107.

27. Johnson, *Congress and the Cold War,* 109, 138.

28. *Washington Evening Star,* 3 May 1967.

# Bibliography

Conducting research in congressional collections is a little like committing a crime: you need to have motive, means, and opportunity. The staggering volume of material on the American experience in Vietnam (archival documents, memoirs, and academic literature) makes the task even more daunting and requires not only significant resources but also difficult decisions on which materials to consult. Being comprehensive is simply not a realistic option.

In selecting the collections in which to conduct research for this book, I employed a number of criteria: importance of the individual within the Republican Party from 1961 to 1973 (not limited to members of Congress); membership on key congressional committees in the House and Senate; party leadership position, both official and unofficial; geographic and ideological diversity; the availability of funding to visit the archive (a major consideration for this kind of research); and pragmatic considerations like proximity to other relevant archives. A few collections that I would have liked to include—most notably the papers of Senator Mark Hatfield (R-OR) at Willamette University in Oregon—remain restricted or closed to researchers.

## Archival Collections

**American Foreign Policy Center, Louisiana Tech University, Ruston, LA**
Papers of the Nixon White House (Microfiche edition)

**Area Research Center, Special Collections, David A. Cofrin Library, University Wisconsin, Green Bay, Green Bay, WI**
John W. Byrnes Papers

**Arizona Historical Foundation, Arizona State University, Tempe, AZ**
Paul J. Fannin Papers
Barry M. Goldwater Papers

**Bentley Historical Library, University of Michigan, Ann Arbor, MI**
George W. Romney Papers

**Carl Albert Congressional Research and Studies Center Congressional Archives, University of Oklahoma, Norman, OK**
Dewey F. Bartlett Papers
Page Belcher Papers
John N. "Happy" Camp Papers

Allan Cromley Papers
Bryce Harlow Papers

**Dwight D. Eisenhower Presidential Library, Abilene, KS**
Dwight D. Eisenhower Post-Presidential Papers
Oral History Collection
Fred A. Seaton Papers
White House Central File
White House Office
Ann Whitman File

**Everett McKinley Dirksen Congressional Leadership Research Center, Pekin, IL**
Everett McKinley Dirksen Papers

**Gerald R. Ford Presidential Library, Ann Arbor, MI**
William J. Baroody Jr. Papers
Richard B. Cheney Files
Gerald R. Ford Congressional Papers
Robert T. Hartmann Files
Robert T. Hartmann Papers
Edward Hutchinson Papers
William T. Kendall Files
Henry Kissinger and Brent Scowcroft Parallel File
Melvin Laird Papers
Oral History Collection

**George H. W. Bush Presidential Library, College Station, TX**
George H. W. Bush Collection

**Herbert Hoover Presidential Library, West Branch, IA**
Bourke B. Hickenlooper Papers
Herbert Hoover Post-Presidential Papers

**Hoover Institution Archives, Stanford University, Palo Alto, CA**
Paul Norton "Pete" McCloskey Jr. Papers

**Indiana State Library, Indianapolis, IN**
E. Ross Adair Papers

**Iowa Historical Society, Iowa City, IA**
Senator Jack Miller Collection

**John F. Kennedy Presidential Library, Boston, MA**
Roger Hilsman Papers
Robert F. Kennedy Papers
National Security File
Oral History Collection
President's Office Files

T. C. Sorensen Papers
James C. Thomson Papers

**John M. Ashbrook Center for Public Affairs, Ashland College, Ashland, OH**
John M. Ashbrook Papers

**Karl E. Mundt Library, Dakota State University, Madison, SD**
Karl E. Mundt Archives

**L. Tom Perry Special Collections Library, Harold B. Lee Library, Brigham Young University, Provo, UT**
Wallace F. Bennett Papers

**Lyndon Baines Johnson Presidential Library, Austin, TX**
William Bundy manuscript
Democratic National Committee series
National Security File
NSC History
Office Files of Harry McPherson
Office Files of Bill Moyers
Office Files of Fred Panzer
Office Files of Marvin Watson
Office Files of Henry H. Wilson
Oral History Collection
Papers of William C. Westmorland
Telephone Conversations
Vietnam Country File
White House Central Files
White House Famous Names

**Manuscript Division, Library of Congress, Washington, DC**
Edward William Brooke Papers

**Miller Center of Public Affairs, University of Virginia, Charlottesville, VA**
Presidential Recordings Program

**Minnesota Historical Society, St. Paul, MN**
Hubert H. Humphrey Papers
Clark MacGregor Papers
Harold Stassen Papers

**Modern Political Archives, University of Kentucky, Lexington, KY**
John Sherman Cooper Collection
Thruston Morton Papers

**National Archives and Records Administration, College Park, MD**
Richard M. Nixon Presidential Materials Project

**National Archives and Records Administration—Pacific Region, Laguna Niguel, CA**
Richard M. Nixon Pre-Presidential Papers

**Ronald Reagan Presidential Library, Simi Valley, CA**
Ronald Reagan Gubernatorial Papers, 1966–1975

**Rockefeller Archive Center, North Tarrytown, NY**
Graham T. T. Molitor Papers
Nelson A. Rockefeller Papers

**Special Collections, A. Frank Smith Jr. Library Center, Southwestern University, Georgetown, TX**
John Tower Papers

**Special Collections, Albertsons Library, Boise State University, Boise, ID**
Len Jordan Papers

**Special Collections, Alderman Library, University of Virginia, Charlottesville, VA**
Hugh D. Scott Jr. Papers

**Special Collections and Archives, Rutgers University, New Brunswick, NJ**
Clifford Case Papers

**Special Collections, Bailey/Howe Library, University of Vermont, Burlington, VT**
George D. Aiken Papers
Robert T. Stafford Papers

**Special Collections, Marriott Library, University of Utah, Salt Lake City, UT**
Sherman P. Lloyd Papers

**Special Collections, San Diego State University, San Diego, CA**
Robert C. Wilson Papers

**Special Collections, Washington State University, Pullman, WA**
Catherine May Papers

**United States Senate Historical Office, Washington, DC**
Oral History Project

**University Archives, Hayden Library, Arizona State University, Tempe, AZ**
John Rhodes Papers

## Newspapers and Periodicals

*Anderson (SC) Independent*
*Arizona Daily Star*
*Arizona Republic*
*Armed Forces Journal*

*Atlantic Monthly*
*Baltimore News-American*
*Baltimore Sun*
*Bennington (VT) Banner*
*Boston Globe*
*Boston Herald*
*Brattleboro (VT) Reformer*
*Burlington (VT) Free Press*
*Business Week*
*Cedar Rapids Gazette*
*Chicago Daily News*
*Chicago Sun-Times*
*Chicago Tribune*
*Christian Science Monitor*
*Columbus (GA) Ledger*
*Commentary*
*Congressional Quarterly*
*Current History*
*Daily Oklahoman*
*Dallas Morning News*
*Denver Post*
*Des Moines Register*
*Detroit Free Press*
*Detroit News*
*Duluth (MN) News-Tribune*
*Economist*
*Esquire*
*Evansville (IN) Courier*
*Foreign Affairs*
*Fort Worth Star Telegram*
*Good Housekeeping*
*Grand Rapids (MI) Press*
*Harper's*
*Hemet (CA) News*
*Hillsborough (CA) Boutique*
*Houston Chronicle*
*Human Events*
*Indianapolis News*
*Indianapolis Star*
*Indianapolis Times*
*Look*
*Los Angeles Times*
*Louisville Courier-Journal*

*Madison (WI) Capital Times*
*Miami Herald*
*Milwaukee Journal*
*Minneapolis Star*
*Nashua (NH) Telegram*
*National Observer*
*National Review*
*National Review Bulletin*
*New Haven (CT) Register*
*New Republic*
*New York Daily News*
*New York Herald Tribune*
*New York Post*
*New York Times*
*New York Times Magazine*
*Newsweek*
*Ogden (UT) Star Examiner*
*Oregon Journal*
*Ottawa (IL) Daily Times*
*Philadelphia Bulletin*
*Philadelphia Inquirer*
*Phoenix Gazette*
*Reader's Digest*
*Richmond News Leader*
*Richmond Times-Dispatch*
*Rutland (VT) Herald*
*Salt Lake Tribune*
*San Diego Union*
*San Francisco Chronicle*
*Saturday Evening Post*
*Saturday Review*
*Shawano (WI) Leader*
*St. Albans (VT) Messenger*
*St. Louis Globe-Democrat*
*St. Louis Post-Dispatch*
*The State (Columbia, SC)*
*Staunton (VA) News-Leader*
*Swanton (VT) Courier*
*Tacoma News-Tribune*
*Time*
*Tri-Cities (WA) Herald*
*Tulsa Tribune*
*U.S. News and World Report*

*Vermont Catholic Tribune*
*Wall Street Journal*
*Washington Evening Star*
*Washington Post*
*Waukesha (WI) Daily Freeman*
*Wichita (KS) Eagle*
*Yakima (WA) Daily Republic*
*Yakima (WA) Herald-Republic*
*Yonkers Herald Statesman*

## Books and Articles

Aiken, George D. *Aiken: Senate Diary, January 1972–January 1975.* Brattleboro, VT: Stephen Greene, 1976.

Aitken, Jonathan. *Nixon: A Life.* Washington, DC: Regnery, 1993.

Aldrich, John H., John L. Sullivan, and Eugene Borgida. "Foreign Affairs and Issue Voting: Do Presidential Candidates 'Waltz Before a Blind Audience?'" *American Political Science Review* 83, no. 1 (March 1989): 123–41.

Allison, Graham T. "Making War: The President and Congress." *Law and Contemporary Problems* 40, no. 3 (Summer 1976): 86–105.

Alsop, Stewart. "Can Anyone Beat LBJ?" *Saturday Evening Post,* 3 June 1967, 27–31.

Ambrose, Stephen E. *Eisenhower: Soldier and President.* New York: Simon & Schuster, 1990.

———. *Nixon: Ruin and Recovery, 1973–1990.* New York: Simon & Schuster, 1991.

———. *Nixon: The Education of a Politician, 1913–1962.* New York: Simon & Schuster, 1987.

———. *Nixon: The Triumph of a Politician, 1962–1972.* New York: Simon & Schuster, 1989.

———. "Nixon and Vietnam: Vietnam and Electoral Politics." In *A Vietnam Reader,* ed. George Donelson Moss, 203–16. Englewood Cliffs, NJ: Prentice-Hall, 1991.

Anderson, David L., ed. *Shadow on the White House: Presidents and the Vietnam War, 1945–1975.* Lawrence: University Press of Kansas, 1993.

———. *Trapped by Success: The Eisenhower Administration and Vietnam, 1953–1961.* New York: Columbia University Press, 1991.

Anderson, David L., and John Ernst, eds. *The War That Never Ends: New Perspectives on the Vietnam War.* Lexington: University Press of Kentucky, 2007.

Angel, D. Duane. *Romney: A Political Biography.* New York: Exposition, 1967.

Appy, Christian G. *Patriots: The Vietnam War Remembered from All Sides.* New York: Penguin, 2003.

Ashby, LeRoy, and Rod Gramer. *Fighting the Odds: The Life of Senator Frank Church.* Pullman: Washington State University Press, 1994.

Asselin, Pierre. *A Bitter Peace: Washington, Hanoi, and the Making of the Paris Agreement.* Chapel Hill: University of North Carolina Press, 2002.

Austin, Anthony. *The President's War: The Story of the Tonkin Gulf Resolution and How the Nation Was Trapped in Vietnam.* New York: Lippincott, 1971.

Bacevich, Andrew J. *The New American Militarism: How Americans Are Seduced by War.* New York: Oxford University Press, 2005.

Ball, George W. *The Past Has Another Pattern: Memoirs.* New York: Norton, 1982.

Baritz, Loren. *Backfire: A History of How American Culture Led Us into Vietnam and Made Us Fight the Way We Did.* New York: William Morrow, 1985.

Barnhart, Michael, ed. *Congress and United States Foreign Policy: Controlling the Use of Force in the Nuclear Age.* Albany: State University of New York Press, 1987.

Barrett, David M. *Uncertain Warriors: Lyndon Johnson and His Vietnam Advisers.* Lawrence: University Press of Kansas, 1993.

Baskir, Lawrence A., and William A. Strauss. *Chance and Circumstance: The Draft, the War, and the Vietnam Generation.* New York: Simon & Schuster, 1978.

Bass, Jack, and Marilyn Thompson. *Ol' Strom: An Unauthorized Biography of Strom Thurmond.* Atlanta: Longstreet, 1998.

Bassett, Lawrence J., and Stephen E. Pelz. "The Failed Search for Victory: Vietnam and the Politics of War." In *Kennedy's Quest for Victory: American Foreign Policy, 1961–1963,* ed. Thomas G. Paterson, 223–52. New York: Oxford University Press, 1989.

Bator, Francis M. "No Good Choices: LBJ and the Vietnam/Great Society Connection." *Diplomatic History* 32, no. 3 (June 2008): 309–40.

Baumgartner, Jody C., and Peter L. Francia. *Conventional Wisdom and American Elections: Exploding Myths, Exploring Misconceptions.* Lanham, MD: Rowman & Littlefield, 2007.

Bell, Jack. *Mr. Conservative: Barry Goldwater.* New York: MacFadden, 1964.

Belmonte, Laura A., ed. *Speaking of America.* 2nd ed. 2 vols. Belmont, CA: Wadsworth, 2007.

Berman, Larry. "Coming to Grips with Lyndon Johnson's War." *Diplomatic History* 17, no. 4 (Fall 1993): 519–37.

——. *Lyndon Johnson's War: The Road to Stalemate in Vietnam.* New York: Norton, 1989.

——. *No Peace, No Honor: Nixon, Kissinger, and Betrayal in Vietnam.* New York: Free Press, 2001.

——. "NSAM 263 and NSAM 273: Manipulating History." In *Vietnam: The Early Decisions,* ed. Lloyd C. Gardner and Ted Gittinger, 177–206. Austin: University of Texas Press, 1997.

——. *Planning a Tragedy: The Americanization of the War in Vietnam.* New York: Norton, 1982.

Berman, William C. *America's Right Turn: From Nixon to Bush.* Baltimore: Johns Hopkins University Press, 1994.

——. *William Fulbright and the Vietnam War: The Dissent of a Political Realist.* Kent, OH: Kent State University Press, 1988.

Beschloss, Michael R. *The Crisis Years: Kennedy and Khrushchev, 1960–1963.* New York: HarperCollins, 1991.

———, ed. *Reaching for Glory: Lyndon Johnson's Secret White House Tapes, 1964–1965.* New York: Touchstone, 2001.

———, ed. *Taking Charge: The Johnson White House Tapes, 1963–1964.* New York: Simon & Schuster, 1998.

Bird, Kai. *The Color of Truth: McGeorge Bundy and William Bundy, Brothers in Arms.* New York: Simon & Schuster, 1998.

Black, Conrad. *A Life in Full: Richard M. Nixon.* New York: PublicAffairs, 2007.

Blair, Anne. *Lodge in Vietnam: A Patriot Abroad.* New Haven, CT: Yale University Press, 1995.

Blight, James G., Janet M. Lang, and David A. Welch. *Vietnam If Kennedy Had Lived.* Lanham, MD: Rowman & Littlefield, 2009.

Blum, John Morton. *Years of Discord: American Politics and Society, 1961–1974.* New York: Norton, 1991.

Bornet, Vaughn Davis. *The Presidency of Lyndon B. Johnson.* Lawrence: University Press of Kansas, 1983.

Bostdorff, Denise M., and Steven R. Goldzwig. "Idealism and Pragmatism in American Foreign Policy Rhetoric: The Case of John F. Kennedy and Vietnam." *Presidential Studies Quarterly* 24, no. 3 (Summer 1994): 515–30.

Boyer, Paul S. *Promises to Keep: The United States since World War II.* 3rd ed. Boston: Houghton Mifflin, 2005.

Bradley, Mark Philip, and Marilyn B. Young, eds. *Making Sense of the Vietnam Wars: Local, National, and Transnational Perspectives.* New York: Oxford University Press, 2008.

Brands, H. W. "Johnson and Eisenhower: The President, the Former President, and the War in Vietnam." *Presidential Studies Quarterly* 15, no. 3 (Summer 1985): 589–601.

———. *The Wages of Globalism: Lyndon Johnson and the Limits of American Power.* New York: Oxford University Press, 1995.

———. *What America Owes the World: The Struggle for the Soul of American Foreign Policy.* New York: Cambridge University Press, 1998.

Brennan, Mary C. *Turning Right in the Sixties: The Conservative Captures of the GOP.* Chapel Hill: University of North Carolina Press, 1995.

Bresler, Robert J. *Us vs. Them: American Political and Cultural Conflict from World War II to Watergate.* Wilmington, DE: SR, 2000.

Brigham, Robert K. *Guerrilla Diplomacy: The NLF's Foreign Relations and the Viet Nam War.* Ithaca, NY: Cornell University Press, 1999.

———. *Iraq, Vietnam, and the Limits of American Power.* New York: PublicAffairs, 2008.

Brinkley, Alan. "The Problem of American Conservatism." *American Historical Review* 99, no. 2 (April 1994): 409–29.

Brooke, Edward W. *Bridging the Divide: My Life.* New Brunswick, NJ: Rutgers University Press, 2007.

———. *The Challenge of Change: Crisis in Our Two-Party System.* Boston: Little, Brown, 1966.

Bueno de Mesquita, Bruce. "Domestic Politics and International Relations." *International Studies Quarterly* 46, no. 1 (March 2002): 1–9.

Bundy, William. *A Tangled Web: The Making of Foreign Policy in the Nixon Presidency.* New York: Hill & Wang, 1998.

Burke, John P., and Fred I. Greenstein. *How Presidents Test Reality: Decisions on Vietnam, 1954 and 1965.* New York: Russell Sage, 1989.

Burr, William, and Jeffrey Kimball. "Nixon's Secret Nuclear Alert: Vietnam War Diplomacy and the Joint Chiefs of Staff Readiness Test, October 1969." *Cold War History* 3, no. 2 (January 2003): 113–56.

Bush, George H. W. *All the Best, George Bush: My Life in Letters and Other Writings.* New York: Scribner, 2000.

Califano, Joseph A., Jr. *The Triumph and Tragedy of Lyndon Johnson: The White House Years.* New York: Simon & Schuster, 1991.

Cannato, Vincent J. *The Ungovernable City: John Lindsay and His Struggle to Save New York.* New York: Basic, 2001.

Cannon, Lou. *The McCloskey Challenge.* New York: Dutton, 1972.

Carter, Dan T. *The Politics of Rage: George Wallace, the Origins of the New Conservatism, and the Transformation of American Politics.* Baton Rouge: Louisiana State University Press, 1995.

Castle, Timothy N. *At War in the Shadow of Vietnam: U.S. Military Aid to the Royal Lao Government, 1955–1975.* New York: Columbia University Press, 1993.

Catton, Phillip E. "Refighting Vietnam in the History Books: The Historiography of the War." *Organization of American Historians Magazine of History*, October 2004, 7–11.

Cerny, P. G. "The Fall of Two Presidents and Extraparliamentary Opposition: France and the United States in 1968." *Government and Opposition* 5, no. 3 (1970): 287–306.

Chafe, William H. *The Unfinished Journey: America since World War II.* 3rd ed. New York: Oxford University Press, 1991.

Chanoff, David, and Doan Van Toai. *Vietnam: A Portrait of Its People at War.* New York: St. Martin's, 1996.

Chennault, Anna. *The Education of Anna.* New York: Times Books, 1980.

Chester, Lewis, Godfrey Hodgson, and Bruce Page. *An American Melodrama: The Presidential Campaign of 1968.* New York: Viking, 1969.

Clausewitz, Carl von. *On War.* Edited by Anatol Rapoport. New York: Penguin, 1968.

Clifford, Clark. *Counsel to the President: A Memoir.* New York: Random House, 1991.

Cohen, Warren I. *Dean Rusk.* Totowa, NJ: Cooper Square, 1980.

Cohen, Warren I., and Nancy Bernkopf Tucker, eds. *Lyndon Johnson Confronts the World: American Foreign Policy, 1963–1968.* New York: Cambridge University Press, 1994.

Colby, William. *Lost Victory: A Firsthand Account of America's Sixteen-Year Involvement in Vietnam.* Chicago: Contemporary, 1989.

Conley, Brian Matthew. "Party People: Bliss, Brock and the Rise of the Modern Republican Party." Ph.D. diss., New School University, 2008.

Converse, Philip E., Warren E. Miller, Jerrold G. Rusk, and Arthur C. Wolfe. "Continuity and Change in American Politics: Parties and Issues in the 1968 Election." *American Political Science Review* 63, no. 4 (December 1969): 1083–1105.

Cooper, Chester. *The Lost Crusade*. New York: Dodd, Mead, 1970.

Cosman, Bernard, and Robert J. Huckshorn, eds. *Republican Politics: The 1964 Campaign and the Aftermath for the Party*. New York: Praeger, 1968.

Crabb, Cecil V., Jr., and Pat M. Holt. *Invitation to Struggle: Congress, the President, and Foreign Policy*. 3rd ed. Washington, DC: CQ, 1989.

Craig, Gordon A., and Alexander L. George. *Force and Statecraft: Diplomatic Problems of Our Time*. 3rd ed. New York: Oxford University Press, 1995.

Critchlow, Donald T. *The Conservative Ascendancy: How the GOP Right Made Political History*. Cambridge, MA: Harvard University Press, 2007.

Crockett, David A. "The President as Opposition Leader." *Presidential Studies Quarterly* 30, no. 2 (June 2000): 245–74.

Crouse, Eric R. *Dear Senator Smith: Small-Town Maine Writes to Senator Margaret Chase Smith about the Vietnam War*. Lanham, MD: Lexington, 2008.

Cuddy, Edward. "Vietnam: Mr. Johnson's War—or Mr. Eisenhower's?" *Review of Politics* 65, no. 4 (Autumn 2003): 351–74.

Cutler, John Henry. *Ed Brooke: Biography of a Senator*. Indianapolis: Bobbs-Merrill, 1972.

Dallek, Matthew. *The Right Moment: Ronald Reagan's First Victory and the Decisive Turning Point in American Politics*. New York: Free Press, 2000.

Dallek, Robert. *The American Style of Foreign Policy: Cultural Politics and Foreign Affairs*. Oxford: Oxford University Press, 1990.

———. *Flawed Giant: Lyndon Johnson and His Times, 1961–1973*. New York: Oxford University Press, 1998.

———. "Lyndon Johnson and Vietnam: The Making of a Tragedy." *Diplomatic History* 20, no. 2 (Spring 1996): 147–62.

———. *Nixon and Kissinger: Partners in Power*. New York: HarperCollins, 2007.

Darilek, Richard E. *A Loyal Opposition in Time of War: The Republican Party and the Politics of Foreign Policy from Pearl Harbor to Yalta*. Westport, CT: Greenwood, 1976.

DeBenedetti, Charles. *An American Ordeal: The Antiwar Movement of the Vietnam Era*. With Charles Chatfield. Syracuse, NY: Syracuse University Press, 1990.

DeConde, Alexander. *Presidential Machismo: Executive Authority, Military Intervention, and Foreign Relations*. Boston: Northeastern University Press, 2000.

DeConde, Alexander, Fredrik Logevall, and Richard Dean Burns, eds. *Encyclopedia of American Foreign Policy*. 2nd ed. 3 vols. New York: Scribner, 2002.

Destler, I. M., Leslie H. Gelb, and Anthony Lake. *Our Own Worst Enemy: The Unmaking of American Foreign Policy*. New York: Simon & Schuster, 1984.

Diem, Bui. *In the Jaws of History*. With David Chanoff. Bloomington: Indiana University Press, 1987.

Dietz, Terry. *Republicans and Vietnam, 1961–1968*. New York: Greenwood, 1986.

DiLeo, David L. *George Ball, Vietnam, and the Rethinking of Containment.* Chapel Hill: University of North Carolina Press, 1991.

Divine, Robert A. *Foreign Policy and U.S. Presidential Elections, 1940–1960.* 2 vols. New York: Franklin Watts, 1974.

Donovan, Robert J. *The Future of the Republican Party.* New York: New American Library, 1964.

———. "Over-Nominated, Under-Elected, Still a Promising Candidate." *New York Times Magazine,* 25 April 1965, 14–15, 90–91.

Draper, Theodore. "Vietnam and American Politics." *Commentary,* March 1968, 15–28.

Duiker, William J. *The Communist Road to Power in Vietnam.* 2nd ed. Boulder, CO: Westview, 1996.

———. *U.S. Containment Policy and the Conflict in Indochina.* Stanford, CA: Stanford University Press, 1994.

Edwards, George C., III, and Stephen J. Wayne. *Presidential Leadership: Politics and Policy Making.* 3rd ed. New York: St. Martin's, 1994.

Edwards, Lee. *The Conservative Revolution: The Movement That Remade America.* New York: Free Press, 1999.

———. *Goldwater: The Man Who Made a Revolution.* Washington, DC: Regnery, 1995.

Eells, Robert, and Bartell Nyberg. *Lonely Walk: The Life of Senator Mark Hatfield.* Chappaqua, NY: Christian Herald, 1979.

Ehrlichman, John. *Witness to Power: The Nixon Years.* New York: Simon & Schuster, 1982.

Ehrman, John. *The Rise of Neoconservatism: Intellectuals and Foreign Affairs, 1945–1994.* New Haven, CT: Yale University Press, 1995.

Eisenhower, Dwight D. "Let's Close Ranks on the Home Front." *Reader's Digest,* April 1968, 49–53.

———. *The White House Years: Mandate for Change, 1953–1956.* Garden City, NY: Doubleday, 1963.

———. *The White House Years: Waging Peace, 1956–1961.* Garden City, NY: Doubleday, 1965.

Ellsberg, Daniel. *Secrets: A Memoir of Vietnam and the Pentagon Papers.* New York: Viking, 2002.

Ely, John Hart. *War and Responsibility: Constitutional Lessons of Vietnam and Its Aftermath.* Princeton, NJ: Princeton University Press, 1993.

English, David. *Divided They Stand.* Englewood Cliffs, NJ: Prentice-Hall, 1969.

Evans, Peter B., Harold K. Jacobson, and Robert D. Putnam, eds. *Double-Edged Diplomacy: International Bargaining and Domestic Politics.* Berkeley and Los Angeles: University of California Press, 1993.

Evans, Rowland, Jr., and Robert D. Novak. *Nixon in the White House: The Frustration of Power.* New York: Vintage, 1972.

*Executive Sessions of the Senate Foreign Relations Committee.* Vol. 18. 89th Cong., 2nd sess. Washington, DC: U.S. Government Printing Office, 1993.

Farnham, Barbara. "Impact of the Political Context on Foreign Policy Decision-Making." *Political Psychology* 25, no. 3 (June 2004): 441–63.

Ferguson, Niall, ed. *Virtual History: Alternatives and Counterfactuals.* New York: Macmillan, 1997.

Foley, Michael. *The New Senate: Liberal Influence on a Conservative Institution, 1959–1972.* New Haven, CT: Yale University Press, 1980.

Ford, Gerald R. *A Time to Heal: The Autobiography of Gerald Ford.* New York: Harper & Row, 1979.

U.S. Department of State. *Foreign Relations of the United States, 1961–1963.* Vol. 2, *Vietnam, 1962.* Washington, DC: U.S. Government Printing Office, 1990.

———. *Foreign Relations of the United States, 1961–1963.* Vol. 4, *Vietnam, Aug.–Dec. 1963.* Washington, DC: U.S. Government Printing Office, 1991.

———. *Foreign Relations of the United States, 1964–1968.* Vol. 1, *Vietnam, 1964.* Washington, DC: U.S. Government Printing Office, 1992.

Forslund, Catherine. *Anna Chennault: Informal Diplomacy and Asian Relations.* Wilmington, DE: Scholarly Resources, 2002.

Foyle, Douglas C. *Counting the Public In: Presidents, Public Opinion, and Foreign Policy.* New York: Columbia University Press, 1999.

Freedman, Lawrence. *Kennedy's Wars: Berlin, Cuba, Laos, and Vietnam.* New York: Oxford University Press, 2000.

Friedman, Michael Jay. "Congress, the President, and the Battle of Ideas: Vietnam Policy, 1965–1969." *Essays in History* 41 (1999). Available online at http://etext.lib.virginia.edu/journals/EH/EH41/Friedman41.html (accessed 29 March 2007).

Fry, Joseph A. *Debating Vietnam: Fulbright, Stennis, and Their Senate Hearings.* Lanham, MD: Rowman & Littlefield, 2006.

Fulbright, J. William. *The Arrogance of Power.* New York: Vintage, 1966.

Gaddis, John Lewis. *The Cold War: A New History.* New York: Penguin, 2005.

———. *Strategies of Containment: A Critical Appraisal of Postwar American National Security Policy.* Rev. and expanded ed. New York: Oxford University Press, 2005.

Gaiduk, Ilia V. *The Soviet Union and the Vietnam War.* Chicago: Ivan R. Dee, 1996.

Gallucci, Robert L. *Neither Peace nor Honor: The Politics of American Military Policy in Viet-Nam.* Baltimore: Johns Hopkins University Press, 1975.

Gardner, Lloyd C. *Pay Any Price: Lyndon Johnson and the Wars for Vietnam.* Chicago: Ivan R. Dee, 1996.

Gardner, Lloyd C., and Ted Gittinger, eds. *International Perspectives on Vietnam.* College Station: Texas A&M University Press, 2000.

———, eds. *Vietnam: The Early Decisions.* Austin: University of Texas Press, 1997.

Garthoff, Raymond L. *Détente and Confrontation: American-Soviet Relations from Nixon to Reagan.* Washington, DC: Brookings Institution Press, 1985.

Gartner, Scott Sigmund, Gary M. Segura, and Bethany A. Barratt. "War Casualties, Policy Positions, and the Fate of Legislators." *Political Research Quarterly* 57, no. 3 (September 2004): 467–77.

Gaubatz, Kurt Taylor. "Election Cycles and War." *Journal of Conflict Resolution* 35, no. 2 (June 1991): 212–44.

Gelb, Leslie H., and Richard K. Betts. *The Irony of Vietnam: The System Worked.* Washington, DC: Brookings Institution Press, 1979.

Geyelin, Philip. *Lyndon B. Johnson and the World.* New York: Praeger, 1966.

Gibbons, William Conrad. *The U.S. Government and the Vietnam War: Executive and Legislative Roles and Relationships.* 4 vols. Princeton, NJ: Princeton University Press, 1986–1995.

Giglio, James N. *The Presidency of John F. Kennedy.* Lawrence: University Press of Kansas, 1991.

Gittenger, Ted, ed. *The Johnson Years: A Vietnam Roundtable.* Austin, TX: Lyndon B. Johnson School of Public Affairs, 1993.

Goldberg, Robert Alan. *Barry Goldwater.* New Haven, CT: Yale University Press, 1995.

Goldman, Eric. *The Tragedy of Lyndon Johnson.* New York: Knopf, 1969.

Goldstein, Gordon M. *Lessons in Disaster: McGeorge Bundy and the Path to War in Vietnam.* New York: Times Books, 2008.

Goldwater, Barry M. *The Conscience of a Conservative.* New York: Macfadden, 1964.

———. *Goldwater.* With Jack Casserly. New York: Doubleday, 1988.

———. *Where I Stand.* New York: McGraw-Hill, 1964.

———. *Why Not Victory? A Fresh Look at American Foreign Policy.* New York: McGraw-Hill, 1962.

———. *With No Apologies: The Personal and Political Memoirs of Barry M. Goldwater.* New York: William Morrow, 1979.

Gould, Lewis L. *1968: The Election That Changed America.* Chicago: Ivan R. Dee, 1993.

Gourevitch, Peter. "The Second Image Reversed: The International Sources of Domestic Politics." *International Organization* 32, no. 4 (Autumn 1978): 881–912.

Granberg, Donald, and Edward E. Brent Jr. "Dove-Hawk Placements in the 1968 Election: Application of Social Judgment and Balance Theories." *Journal of Personality and Social Psychology* 29, no. 5 (1974): 687–95.

Greenstein, Fred I. *The Hidden-Hand Presidency: Eisenhower as Leader.* New York: Basic, 1982.

Greenstein, Fred I., and Richard H. Immerman. "What Did Eisenhower Tell Kennedy about Indochina? The Politics of Misperception." *Journal of American History* 79, no. 2 (September 1992): 568–87.

Haig, Alexander M., Jr. *Inner Circles: How America Changed the World, a Memoir.* With Charles McCarry. New York: Warner, 1992.

Halberstam, David. *The Best and the Brightest.* New York: Random House, 1972.

———. *The Making of a Quagmire.* New York: Random House, 1990.

———. *The Powers That Be.* New York: Knopf, 1979.

Haldeman, H. R. *The Haldeman Diaries: Inside the Nixon White House.* New York: Putnam's, 1994.

Haley, P. Edward. *Congress and the Fall of South Vietnam and Cambodia.* Rutherford, NJ: Dickinson University Press, 1982.

Hammer, Ellen J. *A Death in November: America in Vietnam, 1963.* New York: Dutton, 1987.

Hanhimäki, Jussi M. *The Flawed Architect: Henry Kissinger and American Foreign Policy*. New York: Oxford University Press, 2004.

———. "Global Visions and Parochial Politics: The Persistent Dilemma of the 'American Century.'" *Diplomatic History* 27, no. 4 (September 2003): 423–48.

Harrigan, Anthony. "We Can Win in Southeast Asia." *National Review*, 9 March 1965, 187–88.

Harris, T. George. *Romney's Way: A Man and an Idea*. Englewood Cliffs, NJ: Prentice-Hall, 1967.

Hartley, Robert E. *Charles H. Percy: A Political Perspective*. Chicago: Rand McNally, 1975.

Hatcher, Patrick Lloyd. *The Suicide of an Elite: American Internationalists and Vietnam*. Stanford, CA: Stanford University Press, 1990.

Hatfield, Mark O. *Against the Grain: Reflections of a Rebel Republican*. As told to Diane N. Solomon. Ashland, OR: White Cloud, 2001.

———. *Not Quite So Simple*. New York: Harper & Row, 1968.

Hayward, Steven F. *The Age of Reagan: The Fall of the Old Liberal Order, 1964–1980*. Roseville, CA: Forum/Prima, 2001.

Hentoff, Nat. *A Political Life: The Education of John V. Lindsay*. New York: Knopf, 1969.

Herring, George C. *America's Longest War: The United States and Vietnam, 1950–1975*. 4th ed. New York: McGraw-Hill, 2002.

———. "The Executive, Congress, and the Vietnam War, 1965–1975." In *Congress and United States Foreign Policy: Controlling the Use of Force in the Nuclear Age*, ed. Michael Barnhart, 176–86. Albany: State University of New York Press, 1987.

———. *LBJ and Vietnam: A Different Kind of War*. Austin: University of Texas Press, 1994.

Hersh, Seymour M. *The Price of Power: Kissinger in the Nixon White House*. New York: Summit, 1983.

Hess, Gary R. "Commitment in the Age of Counterinsurgency: Kennedy's Vietnam Options and Decisions." In David L. Anderson, ed., *Shadow on the White House: Presidents and the Vietnam War, 1945–1975*, ed. David L. Anderson, 63–86. Lawrence: University Press of Kansas, 1993.

———. "The Unending Debate: Historians and the Vietnam War." *Diplomatic History* 18, no. 2 (Spring 1994): 239–64.

———. *Vietnam and the United States: Origins and Legacy of War*. Boston: G. K. Hale, 1990.

Hess, Stephen, and David S. Broder. *The Republican Establishment: The Present and Future of the G.O.P.* New York: Harper & Row, 1967.

Hijiya, James A. "The Conservative 1960s." *Journal of American Studies* 37, no. 2 (August 2003): 201–27.

Hill, Thomas Michael. "Senator Arthur H. Vandenberg, the Politics of Bipartisanship, and the Origins of Anti-Soviet Consensus, 1941–1946." *World Affairs* 138, no. 3 (1975–1976): 219–41.

Hilsman, Roger. *To Move a Nation: The Politics of Foreign Policy in the Administration of John F. Kennedy*. Garden City, NY: Doubleday, 1967.

Hinckley, Ronald H. *People, Polls, and Policymakers: American Public Opinion and National Security.* New York: Lexington, 1992.

Hixson, Walter L. *The Myth of American Diplomacy: National Identity and U.S. Foreign Policy.* New Haven, CT: Yale University Press, 2008.

———. *Parting the Curtain: Propaganda, Culture, and the Cold War, 1945–1961.* New York: St. Martin's, 1997.

Hodgson, Godfrey. *The World Turned Right Side Up: A History of the Conservative Ascendancy in America.* Boston: Houghton Mifflin, 1996.

Hoff, Joan. *Nixon Reconsidered.* New York: Basic, 1994.

———. "A Revisionist View of Nixon's Foreign Policy." *Presidential Studies Quarterly* 26, no. 1 (Winter 1996): 107–30.

———. "Richard Nixon, Vietnam, and the American Home Front." In *An American Dilemma: Vietnam, 1964–1973,* ed. Dennis E. Showalter and John G. Albert, 187–97. Chicago: Imprint Publications, 1993.

Hogan, Michael J. "The 'Next Big Thing': The Future of Diplomatic History in a Global Age." *Diplomatic History* 28, no. 1 (January 2004): 1–22.

Hogan, Michael J., and Thomas G. Paterson, eds. *Explaining the History of American Foreign Relations.* 2nd ed. New York: Cambridge University Press, 2004.

Holsti, Ole R. *Public Opinion and American Foreign Policy.* Rev. ed. Ann Arbor: University of Michigan Press, 2004.

Hoopes, Townsend. *The Limits of Intervention: An Inside Account of How the Johnson Policy of Escalation in Vietnam Was Reversed.* New York: Norton, 1987.

Huebner, Lee W., and Thomas E. Petri, eds. *The Ripon Papers, 1963–1968.* Washington, DC: National Press, 1968.

Hughes, Barry B. *The Domestic Context of American Foreign Policy.* San Francisco: W. H. Freeman, 1978.

Hulsey, Byron C. *Everett Dirksen and His Presidents: How a Senate Giant Shaped American Politics.* Lawrence: University Press of Kansas, 2000.

———. "Himself First, His Party Second, Lyndon Johnson Third: Everett Dirksen and the Vietnam War, 1967." *Congress and the Presidency* 22, no. 2 (Fall 1995): 167–81.

Humphrey, Hubert H. *The Education of a Public Man: My Life and Politics.* Garden City, NY: Doubleday, 1976.

Hunt, Michael H. *The American Ascendancy: How the United States Gained and Wielded Global Dominance.* Chapel Hill: University of North Carolina Press, 2007.

———. *Ideology and American Foreign Policy.* New Haven, CT: Yale University Press, 1987.

———. "Internationalizing U.S. Diplomatic History: A Practical Agenda." *Diplomatic History* 15, no. 1 (Winter 1991): 1–11.

———. *Lyndon Johnson's War: America's Cold War Crusade in Vietnam, 1945–1968.* New York: Hill & Wang, 1996.

Immerman, Richard H. "Intelligence and Strategy: Historicizing Psychology, Policy, and Politics." *Diplomatic History* 32, no. 1 (January 2008): 1–23.

Isaacs, Arnold R. *Without Honor: Defeat in Vietnam and Cambodia.* Baltimore: Johns Hopkins University Press, 1983.

Isaacson, Walter. *Kissinger: A Biography*. New York: Simon & Schuster, 1992.

Isaacson, Walter, and Evan Thomas. *The Wise Men: Six Friends and the World They Made*. New York: Simon & Schuster, 1986.

Jacobs, Lawrence R., and Robert Y. Shapiro. "The Rise of Presidential Polling: The Nixon White House in Historical Perspective." *Public Opinion Quarterly* 59, no. 2 (Summer 1995): 163–95.

Jacobs, Seth. "'No Place to Fight a War': Laos and the Evolution of U.S. Policy toward Vietnam, 1954–1963." In *Making Sense of the Vietnam Wars: Local, National, and Transnational Perspectives*, ed. Mark Philip Bradley and Marilyn B. Young, 45–66. New York: Oxford University Press, 2008.

Javits, Jacob K. *Javits: An Autobiography of a Public Man*. With Rafael Steinberg. Boston: Houghton Mifflin, 1981.

———. *Order of Battle: A Republican's Call to Reason*. New York: Atheneum, 1964.

———. "The Road Back for the G.O.P." *New York Times Magazine*, 15 November 1964, 1–2, 129–30.

Jespersen, T. Christopher. "Kissinger, Ford, and Congress: The Very Bitter End in Vietnam." *Pacific Historical Review* 71, no. 3 (August 2002): 439–73.

Johns, Andrew L. "Achilles' Heel: The Vietnam War and George Romney's Bid for the Presidency, 1967 to 1968." *Michigan Historical Review* 26, no. 1 (Spring 2000): 1–29.

———. "Doves among Hawks: Republican Opposition to the Vietnam War, 1964–1968." *Peace and Change* 31, no. 4 (October 2006): 585–628.

———. "Opening Pandora's Box: The Genesis and Evolution of the 1964 Congressional Resolution on Vietnam." *Journal of American–East Asian Relations* 6, nos. 2–3 (Summer–Fall 1997): 175–206.

———. "Poker and the Rhetorical Diplomacy of the Vietnam War: A Reconsideration of Richard Nixon's Madman Theory." Paper presented at the conference of the Society for Military History, Ogden, UT, April 2008.

———. "The Vietnam War and the Expanding Universe Theory." *Diplomatic History* (forthcoming).

———. "A Voice from the Wilderness: Richard Nixon and the Vietnam War, 1964–1966." *Presidential Studies Quarterly* 29, no. 2 (Spring 1999): 317–35.

Johnson, Lyndon Baines. *The Vantage Point: Perspectives on the Presidency, 1963–1968*. New York: Holt, Reinhart & Winston, 1971.

Johnson, Robert David. *All the Way with LBJ: The 1964 Presidential Election*. New York: Cambridge University Press, 2009.

———. "Congress and the Cold War." *Journal of Cold War Studies* 3, no. 2 (Spring 2001): 76–100.

———. *Congress and the Cold War*. New York: Cambridge University Press, 2006.

———. *Ernest Gruening and the American Dissenting Tradition*. Cambridge, MA: Harvard University Press, 1998.

———. "Henry Cabot Lodge and Democratic Foreign Policy." Paper presented at the conference of the Society for Historians of American Foreign Relations, Toronto, June 2000. Copy in author's possession.

——. "The Origins of Dissent: Senate Liberals and Vietnam, 1959–1964." *Pacific Historical Review* 65, no. 2 (May 1996): 249–75.

——. *The Peace Progressives and American Foreign Policy.* Cambridge, MA: Harvard University Press 1995.

Johnson, U. Alexis. *The Right Hand of Power: The Memoirs of an American Diplomat.* With Jef Olivarius McAllister. Englewood Cliffs, NJ: Prentice-Hall, 1984.

Jones, Howard. *Death of a Generation: How the Assassinations of Diem and JFK Prolonged the Vietnam War.* New York: Oxford University Press, 2003.

Kahin, George McT. *Intervention: How America Became Involved in Vietnam.* New York: Knopf, 1986.

Kaiser, David. *An American Tragedy: Kennedy, Johnson, and the Origins of the Vietnam War.* Cambridge, MA: Harvard University Press, 2000.

Karnow, Stanley. *Vietnam: A History.* New York: Viking, 1991.

Kattenburg, Paul. *The Vietnam Trauma in American Foreign Policy.* New Brunswick, NJ: Transaction, 1980.

Katz, Andrew Z. "Public Opinion and Foreign Policy: The Nixon Administration and the Pursuit of Peace with Honor in Vietnam." *Presidential Studies Quarterly* 27, no. 3 (Summer 1997): 496–513.

Kearns, Doris. *Lyndon Johnson and the American Dream.* New York: Harper & Row, 1976.

Kegley, Charles W., Jr., and Eugene R. Wittkopf. *American Foreign Policy: Pattern and Process.* 4th ed. New York: St. Martin's, 1991.

——, eds. *The Domestic Sources of American Foreign Policy: Insights and Evidence.* New York: St. Martin's, 1988.

Kennan, George. *American Diplomacy.* Expanded ed. Chicago: University of Chicago Press, 1984.

Kennedy, Paul. *The Rise and Fall of the Great Powers: Economic Change and Military Conflict from 1500 to 2000.* New York: Vintage, 1989.

Kern, Montague, Patricia Levering, and Ralph Levering. *The Kennedy Crises.* Chapel Hill: University of North Carolina Press, 1983.

Khong, Yuen Foong. *Analogies at War: Korea, Munich, Dien Bien Phu, and the Vietnam Decisions of 1965.* Princeton, NJ: Princeton University Press, 1992.

Kilpatrick, James Jackson. "Brainwashing George Romney." *Human Events* 27, no. 38 (23 September 1967): 5.

——. "Crisis Seven." *National Review* 14 (November 1967): 1267–69.

Kimball, Jeffrey. *Nixon's Vietnam War.* Lawrence: University Press of Kansas, 1998.

——. "'Peace with Honor': Richard Nixon and the Diplomacy of Threat and Symbolism." In *Shadow on the White House: Presidents and the Vietnam War, 1945–1975,* ed. David L. Anderson, 152–83. Lawrence: University Press of Kansas, 1993.

——. *The Vietnam War Files: Uncovering the Secret History of Nixon-Era Strategy.* Lawrence: University Press of Kansas, 2004.

Kinzer, Stephen. *Overthrow: America's Century of Regime Change from Hawaii to Iraq.* New York: Times Books, 2006.

Kissinger, Henry. *Diplomacy.* New York: Simon & Schuster, 1994.

———. *Ending the Vietnam War: A History of America's Involvement in and Extraction from the Vietnam War.* New York: Simon & Schuster, 2003.

———. "The Viet Nam Negotiations." *Foreign Affairs* 47 (January 1969): 211–34.

———. *The White House Years.* Boston: Little, Brown, 1979.

Koh, Harold Hongju. "Why the President (Almost) Always Wins in Foreign Affairs: Lessons of the Iran-Contra Affair." *Yale Law Journal* 97, no. 7 (June 1988): 1255–1342.

Kolko, Gabriel. *Anatomy of a War: Vietnam, the United States, and the Modern Historical Experience.* New York: Pantheon, 1985.

Komer, Robert W. *Bureaucracy at War: U.S. Performance in the Vietnam Conflict.* Boulder, CO: Westview, 1986.

Kotlowski, Dean J. "Unhappily Yoked? Hugh Scott and Richard Nixon." *Pennsylvania Magazine of History and Biography* 125, no. 3 (July 2001): 233–66.

Kovenock, David M., and James Warren Prothro. *Explaining the Vote: Presidential Choices in the Nation and the States, 1968.* 3 vols. Chapel Hill, NC: Institute for Research in Social Science, 1973.

Kuklick, Bruce. *Blind Oracles: Intellectuals and War from Kennan to Kissinger.* Princeton, NJ: Princeton University Press, 2006.

Kunz, Diane. "Camelot Continued: What If JFK Had Lived?" In Niall Ferguson, ed., *Virtual History: Alternatives and Counterfactuals,* 368–91. New York: Macmillan, 1997.

———, ed. *The Diplomacy of the Crucial Decade: American Foreign Relations during the 1960s.* New York: Columbia University Press, 1994.

Kutler, Stanley I. *The Encyclopedia of the Vietnam War.* New York: Simon & Schuster, 1995.

———. *The Wars of Watergate: The Last Crisis of Richard Nixon.* New York: Knopf, 1990.

Ky, Nguyen Cao. *How We Lost the Vietnam War.* New York: Stein & Day, 1976.

LaFeber, Walter. *The Deadly Bet: LBJ, Vietnam, and the 1968 Election.* Lanham, MD: Rowman & Littlefield, 2005.

Langguth, A. J. *Our Vietnam/Nuớc Viêt Ta: The War, 1954–1975.* New York: Simon & Schuster, 2000.

Lauck, Jon K. "Binding Assumptions: Karl E. Mundt and the Vietnam War, 1963–1969." *Mid-America* 76, no. 3 (Fall 1994): 279–309.

Lawrence, Mark Atwood. *Assuming the Burden: Europe and the American Commitment to War in Vietnam.* Berkeley and Los Angeles: University of California Press, 2005.

Lee, J. Edward, and H. C. "Toby" Haynsworth. *Nixon, Ford and the Abandonment of South Vietnam.* Jefferson, NC: McFarland, 2002.

Lee, Steven H. *Outposts of Empire: Korea, Vietnam, and the Origins of the Cold War in Asia, 1949–1954.* Montreal: McGill-Queen's University Press, 1995.

Leffler, Melvyn P. *For the Soul of Mankind: The United States, the Soviet Union, and the Cold War.* New York: Hill & Wang, 2007.

————. "New Approaches, Old Interpretations, and Prospective Reconfigurations." *Diplomatic History* 19, no. 2 (Spring 1995): 173–96.

Lerner, Mitchell B. *The Pueblo Incident: A Spy Ship and the Failure of American Foreign Policy.* Lawrence: University Press of Kansas, 2002.

————. "Vietnam and the 1964 Election: A Defense of Lyndon Johnson." *Presidential Studies Quarterly* 25, no. 4 (Fall 1995): 751–66.

Levering, Ralph B. *The Cold War: A Post–Cold War History.* Arlington Heights, IL: Harlan Davidson, 1994.

————. "Is Domestic Politics Being Slighted as an Interpretive Framework?" *Society for Historians of American Foreign Relations Newsletter,* March 1994, 17–35.

————. *The Public and American Foreign Policy, 1918–1978.* New York: William Morrow, 1978.

Levite, Ariel E., Bruce W. Jentleson, and Larry Berman, eds. *Foreign Military Intervention: The Dynamics of Protracted Conflict.* New York: Columbia University Press, 1992.

Levy, David W. *The Debate over Vietnam.* 2nd ed. Baltimore: Johns Hopkins University Press, 1995.

Levy, Jack S. "Domestic Politics and War." *Journal of Interdisciplinary Studies* 18, no. 4 (Spring 1988): 653–73.

Lind, Michael. *Vietnam, the Necessary War: A Reinterpretation of America's Most Disastrous Military Conflict.* New York: Touchstone, 1999.

Lindsay, James M. *Congress and the Politics of U.S. Foreign Policy.* Baltimore: Johns Hopkins University Press, 1994.

————. "Deference and Defiance: The Shifting Rhythms of Executive-Legislative Relations in Foreign Policy." *Presidential Studies Quarterly* 33, no. 3 (September 2003): 530–46.

Lodge, Henry Cabot, Jr. *As It Was: An Inside View of Politics and Power in the 50's and 60's.* New York: Norton, 1976.

————. *The Storm Has Many Eyes.* New York: Norton, 1973.

Logevall, Fredrik. *Choosing War: The Lost Chance for Peace and the Escalation of War in Vietnam.* Berkeley and Los Angeles: University of California Press, 1999.

————. "Comment on Francis M. Bator's 'No Good Choices: LBJ and the Vietnam/Great Society Connection,'" *Diplomatic History* 32, no. 3 (June 2008): 355–60.

————. "DeGaulle, Neutralization, and American Involvement in Vietnam, 1963–1964." *Pacific Historical Review* 61, no. 1 (February 1992): 69–102.

————. "A Delicate Balance: John Sherman Cooper and the Republican Opposition to the Vietnam War." In *Vietnam and the American Political Tradition: The Politics of Dissent,* ed. Randall B. Woods, 237–58. New York: Cambridge University Press, 2003.

————. "First among Critics: Walter Lippmann and the Vietnam War." *Journal of American–East Asian Relations* 4, no. 4 (Winter 1995): 351–76.

————. "Party Politics." In *Encyclopedia of American Foreign Policy* (2nd ed., 3 vols.), ed. Alexander DeConde, Fredrik Logevall, and Richard Dean Burns, 3:99–111. New York: Scribner, 2002.

———. "Politics and Foreign Relations." *Journal of American History* 95, no. 4 (March 2009): 1074–78.

———. "'There ain't no daylight': Lyndon Johnson and the Politics of Escalation." In *Making Sense of the Vietnam Wars: Local, National, and Transnational Perspectives,* ed. Mark Philip Bradley and Marilyn B. Young, 91–110. New York: Oxford University Press, 2008.

———. "Vietnam and the Question of What Might Have Been." In *Kennedy: The New Frontier Revisited,* ed. Mark J. White, 19–62. New York: New York University Press, 1998.

Logevall, Fredrik, and Campbell Craig. *America's Cold War.* Cambridge, MA: Belknap, 2009.

Logevall, Fredrik, and Andrew Preston, eds. *Nixon in the World: American Foreign Relations, 1969–1977.* New York: Oxford University Press, 2008.

Longley, Kyle. "Congress and the Vietnam War: Senate Doves and Their Impact on the War." In *The War That Never Ends: New Perspectives on the Vietnam War,* ed. David L. Anderson and John Ernst, 289–310. Lexington: University Press of Kentucky, 2007.

———. *Senator Albert Gore, Sr.: Tennessee Maverick.* Baton Rouge: Louisiana State University Press, 2004.

Lunch, William L., and Peter W. Sperlich. "American Public Opinion and the War in Vietnam." *Western Political Quarterly* 32, no. 1 (March 1979): 21–44.

Lyon, Peter. *Eisenhower: Portrait of a Hero.* Boston: Little, Brown, 1974.

Lythgoe, Dennis L. "The 1968 Presidential Decline of George Romney: Mormonism or Politics?" *Brigham Young University Studies* 11, no. 3 (Spring 1971): 219–40.

Lytle, Mark Hamilton. *America's Uncivil Wars: The Sixties Era from Elvis to the Fall of Richard Nixon.* New York: Oxford University Press, 2006.

MacNeil, Neil. *Dirksen: Portrait of a Public Man.* New York: World, 1970.

Mann, James. "Young Rumsfeld." *Atlantic Monthly,* November 2003, 89–101.

Mann, Robert. *A Grand Delusion: America's Descent into Vietnam.* New York: Basic, 2001.

Manza, Jeff, and Clem Brooks. "The Religious Factor in American Presidential Elections, 1960–1992." *American Journal of Sociology* 103, no. 1 (July 1997): 38–82.

Maraniss, David. *They Marched into Sunlight: War and Peace, Vietnam and America, October 1967.* New York: Simon & Schuster, 2003.

Matthews, Christopher. *Kennedy and Nixon: The Rivalry That Shaped Postwar America.* New York: Touchstone, 1996.

Matthews, Jeffrey J. "To Defeat a Maverick: The Goldwater Candidacy Revisited, 1963–1964." *Presidential Studies Quarterly* 27, no. 4 (Fall 1997): 662–78.

Mayer, George H. *The Republican Party, 1854–1966.* 2nd ed. New York: Oxford University Press, 1967.

Mayhew, David R. "Wars and American Politics." *Perspectives on Politics* 3, no. 3 (September 2005): 473–93.

McCloskey, Paul N. *Truth and Untruth: Political Deceit in America.* New York: Simon & Schuster, 1972.

McCormick, James M., and Eugene R. Wittkopf. "At the Water's Edge: The Effects of Party, Ideology, and Issues on Congressional Foreign Policy Voting, 1947–1988." *American Politics Quarterly* 20, no. 1 (January 1992): 26–53.

———. "Bipartisanship, Partisanship, and Ideology in Congressional-Executive Foreign Policy Relations, 1947–1988." *Journal of Politics* 52, no. 4 (November 1990): 1077–98.

McGinniss, Joe. *The Selling of the President, 1968.* New York: Simon & Schuster, 1969.

McGirr, Lisa. *Suburban Warriors: The Origins of the New American Right.* Princeton, NJ: Princeton University Press, 2001.

McMahon, Robert J. "Credibility and World Power: Exploring the Psychological Dimension in Postwar American Diplomacy." *Diplomatic History* 15, no. 4 (Fall 1991): 455–71.

———. *The Limits of Empire: The United States and Southeast Asia since World War II.* New York: Columbia University Press, 1999.

McMaster, H. R. *Dereliction of Duty: Lyndon Johnson, Robert McNamara, the Joint Chiefs of Staff, and the Lies That Led to Vietnam.* New York: HarperCollins, 1997.

McNamara, Robert S. *In Retrospect: The Tragedy and Lessons of Vietnam.* New York: Times Books, 1995.

McNamara, Robert S., James G. Blight, and Robert K. Brigham. *Argument without End: In Search of Answers to the Vietnam Tragedy.* New York: PublicAffairs, 1999.

McPherson, Harry. *A Political Education.* Boston: Little, Brown, 1972.

McQuaid, Kim. *The Anxious Years: America in the Vietnam-Watergate Era.* New York: Basic, 1989.

Meernik, James. "Domestic Politics and the Political Use of Military Force by the United States." *Political Research Quarterly* 54, no. 4 (December 2001): 889–904.

———. "Presidential Support in Congress: Conflict and Consensus on Foreign and Defense Policy." *Journal of Politics* 55, no. 3 (August 1993): 569–87.

Mergel, Sarah Katherine. "A Report Card for Richard Nixon: Conservative Intellectuals and the President." Ph.D. diss., George Washington University, 2007.

Merry, Robert W. *Taking on the World: Joseph and Stewart Alsop—Guardians of the American Century.* New York: Viking, 1996.

Middendorf, J. William, II. *A Glorious Disaster: Barry Goldwater's Presidential Campaign and the Origins of the Conservative Movement.* New York: Basic, 2006.

Miller, Aaron David. "The US-Israeli Relationship: Special but Not Exclusive." *Harvard International Review* 30, no. 2 (Summer 2008): 88.

Milne, David. *America's Rasputin: Walt Rostow and the Vietnam War.* New York: Hill & Wang, 2009.

Milner, Helen V. *Interest, Institutions, and Information: Domestic Politics and International Relations.* Princeton, NJ: Princeton University Press, 1997.

Moïse, Edwin E. *Tonkin Gulf and the Escalation of the Vietnam War.* Chapel Hill: University of North Carolina Press, 1996.

Mollenhoff, Clark R. *George Romney: Mormon in Politics.* New York: Meredith, 1968.

Morgan, Iwan W. *Beyond the Liberal Consensus: A Political History of the United States since 1965.* New York: St. Martin's, 1994.

Morgan, Patrick M., and Keith L. Nelson, eds. *Re-Viewing the Cold War: Domestic Factors and Foreign Policy in the East-West Confrontation*. Westport, CT: Praeger, 2000.

Morris, Roger. *Richard Milhous Nixon: The Rise of an American Politician*. New York: Henry Holt, 1990.

Morton, Thruston. "Only the GOP Can Get Us Out of Vietnam." *Saturday Evening Post*, 6 April 1968, 10–12.

Moser, Charles A. *Promise and Hope: The Ashbrook Presidential Campaign of 1972*. Washington, DC: Free Congress Research and Education Foundation, 1985.

Moyar, Mark. *Triumph Forsaken: The Vietnam War, 1954–1965*. New York: Cambridge University Press, 2006.

Mueller, John E. *War, Presidents, and Public Opinion*. New York: Wiley, 1973.

Nathan, James A., and James K. Oliver. *Foreign Policy Making and the American Political System*. 2nd ed. Boston: Little, Brown, 1987.

Nelson, Keith L. "Nixon, Kissinger, and the Domestic Side of Détente." In *Re-Viewing the Cold War: Domestic Factors and Foreign Policy in the East-West Confrontation*, ed. Patrick M. Morgan and Keith L. Nelson, 127–48. Westport, CT: Praeger, 2000.

Nelson, Justin A. "Drafting Lyndon Johnson: The President's Secret Role in the 1968 Democratic Convention." *Presidential Studies Quarterly* 30, no. 4 (December 2000): 688–713.

Nelson, Michael, ed. *The Presidency and the Political System*. 4th ed. Washington, DC: Congressional Quarterly Press, 1995.

Neustadt, Richard E. *Presidential Power and the Modern Presidents: The Politics of Leadership from Roosevelt to Reagan*. New York: Free Press, 1990.

Neustadt, Richard E., and Ernest R. May. *Thinking in Time: The Uses of History for Decision Makers*. New York: Free Press, 1986.

Newman, John M. *JFK and Vietnam: Deception, Intrigue, and the Struggle for Power*. New York: Warner, 1992.

Nincic, Miroslav. "Elections and U.S. Foreign Policy." In *The Domestic Sources of American Foreign Policy: Insights and Evidence* (4th ed.), ed. Eugene R. Wittkopf and James M. McCormick, 117–28. Lanham, MD: Rowman & Littlefield, 2004.

———. "The National Interest and Its Interpretation." *Review of Politics* 61, no. 1 (Winter 1999): 29–55.

Nixon, Richard. "Asia After Vietnam." *Foreign Affairs* 46, no. 1 (October 1967): 111–25.

———. "Cuba, Castro and John F. Kennedy." *Reader's Digest*, November 1964, 292–301.

———. *In the Arena: A Memoir of Victory, Defeat, and Renewal*. New York: Simon & Schuster, 1990.

———. "Needed in Vietnam: The Will to Win." *Reader's Digest*, August 1964, 37–43.

———. *Real Peace/No More Vietnams*. New York: Touchstone, 1990.

———. *RN: The Memoirs of Richard Nixon*. New York: Touchstone, 1990.

———. "Why Not Negotiate in Vietnam?" *Reader's Digest*, December 1965, 49–54.

Novak, Robert D. *The Agony of the GOP, 1964*. New York: Macmillan, 1965.

Oberdorfer, Don. *Senator Mansfield: The Extraordinary Life of a Great American Statesman and Diplomat*. Washington, DC: Smithsonian Books, 2003.

O'Brien, Charles F. "Aiken and Vietnam: A Dialogue with Vermont Voters." *Vermont History* 61, no. 1 (Winter 1993): 5–17.

Olson, James S., and Randy Roberts. *Where the Domino Fell: America and Vietnam, 1945–1990.* New York: St. Martin's, 1991.

Olson, William C. "The U.S. Congress: An Independent Force in World Politics?" *International Affairs* 67, no. 3 (July 1991): 547–63.

Osgood, Kenneth. "Form Before Substance: Eisenhower's Commitment to Psychological Warfare and Negotiations with the Enemy." *Diplomatic History* 24, no. 3 (Summer 2000): 405–33.

———. *Total Cold War: Eisenhower's Secret Propaganda Battle at Home and Abroad.* Lawrence: University Press of Kansas, 2006.

Osgood, Kenneth, and Andrew K. Frank, eds. *Selling War in a Media Age: The Presidency and Public Opinion in the American Century.* Gainesville: University Press of Florida, 2010.

"Outlook for Republicans Now." *U.S. News and World Report,* 3 October 1966, 59–62. Interview with Richard Nixon.

Pach, Chester J., Jr., and Elmo Richardson. *The Presidency of Dwight D. Eisenhower.* Rev. ed. Lawrence: University Press of Kansas, 1991.

Page, Caroline. *U.S. Official Propaganda during the Vietnam War, 1965–1973: The Limits of Persuasion.* London: Leicester University Press, 1996.

Parmet, Herbert S. *JFK: The Presidency of John F. Kennedy.* New York: Dial, 1983.

———. *Richard Nixon and His America.* New York: Konecky & Konecky, 1990.

Paterson, Thomas G. "Bearing the Burden: A Critical Look at JFK's Foreign Policy." *Virginia Quarterly Review* 54, no. 2 (Spring 1978): 193–212.

———. "Introduction: Kennedy and Global Crisis." In Thomas G. Paterson, ed., *Kennedy's Quest for Victory: American Foreign Policy, 1961–1963,* ed. Thomas G. Paterson, 3–23. New York: Oxford University Press, 1989.

———, ed. *Kennedy's Quest for Victory: American Foreign Policy, 1961–1963.* New York: Oxford University Press, 1989.

———. "Presidential Foreign Policy, Public Opinion, and Congress: The Truman Years." *Diplomatic History* 3, no. 1 (Winter 1979): 1–18.

Patterson, James T. *Grand Expectations: The United States, 1945–1974.* New York: Oxford University Press, 1996.

Peabody, Robert L. "Political Parties: House Republican Leadership." In *American Political Institutions and Public Policy: Five Contemporary Studies,* ed. Allan P. Sindler, 180–229. Boston: Little, Brown, 1969.

Pelz, Stephen E. "John F. Kennedy's 1961 Vietnam War Decisions." *Journal of Strategic Studies* 4, no. 4 (December 1981): 356–85.

———. "'When Do I Have Time to Think?': John F. Kennedy, Roger Hilsman, and the Laotian Crisis of 1962." *Diplomatic History* 3, no. 3 (Summer 1979): 215–29.

*The Pentagon Papers: The Department of Defense History of United States Decision Making on Vietnam.* Senator Mike Gravel Edition. 5 vols. Boston: Beacon, 1971–1972.

Perisco, Joseph E. *The Imperial Rockefeller: A Biography of Nelson A. Rockefeller.* New York: Simon & Schuster, 1982.

Perlstein, Rick. *Nixonland: The Rise of a President and the Fracturing of America.* New York: Scribner, 2008.

Pious, Richard M. *Why Presidents Fail: White House Decision Making from Eisenhower to Bush II.* Lanham, MD: Rowman & Littlefield, 2008.

Plummer, Brenda Gayle. "The Changing Face of Diplomatic History: A Literature Review." *History Teacher* 38, no. 3 (May 2005): 385–400.

Porter, Gareth. *A Peace Denied: The United States, Vietnam, and the Paris Agreement.* Bloomington: Indiana University Press, 1975.

Powell, Lee Riley. *J. William Fulbright and America's Lost Crusade: Fulbright's Opposition to the Vietnam War.* Little Rock, AR: Rose, 1984.

Powers, Thomas. *The War at Home: Vietnam and the American People, 1964–1968.* New York: Grossman, 1973.

Prados, John. *The Hidden History of the Vietnam War.* Chicago: Ivan R. Dee, 1995.

———. *Vietnam: The History of an Unwinnable War, 1945–1975.* Lawrence: University Press of Kansas, 2009.

Prados, John, and Margaret Pratt Porter, eds. *Inside the Pentagon Papers.* Lawrence: University Press of Kansas, 2004.

Preston, Andrew. *The War Council: McGeorge Bundy, the NSC, and Vietnam.* Cambridge, MA: Harvard University Press, 2006.

Prins, Brandon C., and Bryan W. Marshall. "Congressional Support of the President: A Comparison of Foreign, Defense, and Domestic Policy Decision Making during and after the Cold War." *Presidential Studies Quarterly* 31, no. 4 (December 2001): 660–78.

*Public Papers of the President of the United States: Richard Nixon, 1969.* Washington, DC: U.S. Government Printing Office, 1971.

Quandt, William B. "The Electoral Cycle and the Conduct of American Foreign Policy." In *The Domestic Sources of American Foreign Policy: Insights and Evidence,* ed. Charles W. Kegley Jr. and Eugene R. Wittkopf, 87–98. New York: St. Martin's 1988.

Rae, Nicol C. *The Decline and Fall of the Liberal Republicans: From 1952 to the Present.* New York: Oxford University Press, 1989.

Randolph, Stephen P. *Powerful and Brutal Weapons: Nixon, Kissinger, and the Easter Offensive.* Cambridge, MA: Harvard University Press, 2007.

Ray, James Lee. *American Foreign Policy and Political Ambition.* Washington, DC: CQ, 2007.

Record, Jeffrey. *Making War, Thinking History: Munich, Vietnam, and Presidential Uses of Force from Korea to Kosovo.* Annapolis, MD: Naval Institute Press, 2002.

Reeves, Richard. *President Kennedy: Profile of Power.* New York: Simon & Schuster, 1993.

Regnery, Alfred S. *Upstream: The Ascendance of American Conservatism.* New York: Threshold, 2008.

Reich, Cary. *The Life of Nelson Rockefeller.* New York: Doubleday, 1996.

Reinhard, David W. *The Republican Right since 1945.* Lexington: University Press of Kentucky, 1983.

Rhodes, John. *John Rhodes: "I Was There."* With Dean Smith. Salt Lake City, UT: Northwest, 1995.

Riccards, Michael P. "Richard Nixon and the American Political Tradition." *Presidential Studies Quarterly* 23, no. 4 (Fall 1993): 739–45.

Riegle, Donald S. *O Congress.* Garden City, NY: Doubleday, 1972.

Ripon Society. *The Lessons of Victory.* New York: Dial, 1969.

Ritchie, Donald A. *A History of the United States Senate Republican Policy Committee, 1947–1997.* Washington, DC: U.S. Government Printing Office, 1997.

Roper, Jon. "Richard Nixon's Political Hinterland: The Shadows of JFK and Charles de Gaulle." *Presidential Studies Quarterly* 28, no. 2 (Spring 1998): 422–34.

Rosati, Jerel A. *The Politics of American Foreign Policy.* Fort Worth, TX: Harcourt Brace, 1993.

Rostow, Walt W. *The Diffusion of Power: An Essay in Recent History.* New York: Macmillan, 1972.

Rotter, Andrew J. *The Path to Vietnam: Origins of the American Commitment to Southeast Asia.* Ithaca, NY: Cornell University Press, 1988.

Rottinghaus, Brandon. "Opening the President's Mailbag: The Nixon Administration's Use of Public Opinion Mail." *Presidential Studies Quarterly* 38, no. 1 (March 2008): 61–77.

Rust, William J. *The Bitter Heritage: Vietnam and American Democracy, 1941–1966.* Boston: Houghton Mifflin, 1967.

———. *Kennedy in Vietnam: American Vietnam Policy, 1960–1963.* New York: Da Capo, 1985.

Rutland, Robert Allen. *The Republicans: From Lincoln to Bush.* Columbia: University of Missouri Press, 1996.

Safire, William H. *Before the Fall: An Inside View of the Pre-Watergate White House.* Garden City, NY: Doubleday, 1975.

Scanlon, Sandra. "The Conservative Lobby and Nixon's 'Peace with Honor' in Vietnam." *Journal of American Studies* 43, no. 2 (August 2009): 255–77.

Schaffer, Howard B. *Ellsworth Bunker: Global Troubleshooter, Vietnam Hawk.* Chapel Hill: University of North Carolina Press, 2003.

Schaller, Michael, and George Rising. *The Republican Ascendancy: American Politics, 1968–2001.* Wheeling, IL: Harlan Davidson, 2002.

Schandler, Herbert Y. *Lyndon Johnson and Vietnam: The Unmaking of a President.* Princeton, NJ: Princeton University Press, 1977.

Schapsmeier, Edward L., and Frederick H. Schapsmeier. *Dirksen of Illinois: Senatorial Statesman.* Chicago: University of Illinois Press, 1985.

———. *Gerald R. Ford's Date with Destiny: A Political Biography.* New York: Peter Lang, 1989.

Scheele, Henry Z. *Charlie Halleck: A Political Biography.* New York: Exposition, 1966.

———. "Prelude to the Presidency: An Examination of the Gerald R. Ford–Charles A.

Halleck House Minority Leadership Contest." *Presidential Studies Quarterly* 25, no. 4 (Fall 1995): 767–85.

———. "Response to the Kennedy Administration: The Joint Senate-House Republican Leadership Press Conferences." *Presidential Studies Quarterly* 19, no. 4 (Fall 1989): 825–46.

Schell, Jonathan. *Observing the Nixon Years: "Notes and Comment" from the "New Yorker" on the Vietnam War and the Watergate Crisis, 1969–1975.* New York: Pantheon, 1989.

Schlafly, Phyllis. *A Choice, Not an Echo.* Alton, IL: Pere Marquette, 1964.

Schlesinger, Arthur M., Jr. *The Imperial Presidency.* Boston: Houghton Mifflin, 1989.

———. *Robert Kennedy and His Times.* New York: Ballantine, 1978.

———. *A Thousand Days: John F. Kennedy in the White House.* Boston: Houghton Mifflin, 1965.

Schmitz, David F. *The Tet Offensive: Politics, War, and Public Opinion.* Lanham, MD: Rowman & Littlefield, 2005.

———. *Thank God They're on Our Side: The United States and Right-Wing Dictatorships, 1921–1965.* Chapel Hill: University of North Carolina Press, 1999.

———. *The United States and Right-Wing Dictatorships, 1965–1989.* New York: Cambridge University Press, 2006.

Schmitz, David F., and Natalie Fousekis. "Frank Church, the Senate, and the Emergence of Dissent on the Vietnam War." *Pacific Historical Review* 63, no. 4 (November 1994): 561–81.

Schneider, Gregory L. *Cadres for Conservatism: Young Americans for Freedom and the Rise of the Contemporary Right.* New York: New York University Press, 1999.

Schoenbaum, Thomas J. *Waging Peace and War: Dean Rusk in the Truman, Kennedy, and Johnson Years.* New York: Simon & Schuster, 1988.

Schulman, Bruce J. *Lyndon B. Johnson and American Liberalism: A Brief Biography with Documents.* New York: Bedford, 1995.

Schulman, Robert. *John Sherman Cooper: The Global Kentuckian.* Lexington: University Press of Kentucky, 1976.

Schulzinger, Robert D. *Henry Kissinger: Doctor of Diplomacy.* New York: Columbia University Press, 1989.

———. *A Time for Peace: The Legacy of the Vietnam War.* New York: Oxford University Press, 2006.

———. *A Time for War: The United States and Vietnam, 1941–1975.* New York: Oxford University Press, 1997.

Schwab, Orrin. *Defending the Free World: John F. Kennedy, Lyndon Johnson, and the Vietnam War, 1961–1965.* Westport, CT: Praeger, 1998.

Schwartz, Thomas A. *Lyndon Johnson and Europe: In the Shadow of Vietnam.* Cambridge, MA: Harvard University Press, 2003.

———. "'Winning an election is terribly important, Henry': Thinking about Domestic Politics and U.S. Foreign Relations." Presidential address presented at the meeting of the Society of Historians of American Foreign Relations, Columbus, OH, June 2008. Copy in author's possession.

Scott, Hugh. *Come to the Party.* Englewood Cliffs, NJ: Prentice-Hall, 1968.

See, Jennifer W. "A Prophet without Honor: Hans Morgenthau and the War in Vietnam, 1955–1965." *Pacific Historical Review* 70, no. 3 (August 2001): 419–47.

Serewicz, Lawrence W. *America at the Brink of Empire: Rusk, Kissinger, and the Vietnam War.* Baton Rouge: Louisiana State University Press, 2007.

Shannon, William V. "George Romney: Holy and Hopeful." *Harper's,* February 1967, 55–62.

Shapley, Deborah. *Promise and Power: The Life and Times of Robert McNamara.* Boston: Little, Brown, 1993.

Shaw, John M. *The Cambodian Campaign: The 1970 Offensive and America's Vietnam War.* Lawrence: University Press of Kansas, 2005.

Shawcross, William. *Sideshow: Kissinger, Nixon and the Destruction of Cambodia.* London: Andre Deutsch, 1979.

Sheehan, Neil. *A Bright Shining Lie: John Paul Vann and America in Vietnam.* New York: Vintage, 1988.

Sherman, Janann. *No Place for a Woman: A Life of Senator Margaret Chase Smith.* New Brunswick, NJ: Rutgers University Press, 2000.

Sherman, Michael, ed. *The Political Legacy of George D. Aiken: Wise Old Owl of the U.S. Senate.* Montpelier: Vermont Historical Society, 1995.

Sherry, Michael S. *In the Shadow of War: The United States since the 1930s.* New Haven, CT: Yale University Press, 1995.

Shesol, Jeff. *Mutual Contempt: Lyndon Johnson, Robert Kennedy, and the Feud That Defined a Decade.* New York: Norton, 1997.

Sieg, Kent G. "The Lodge Peace Mission of 1969 and Nixon's Vietnam Policy." *Diplomacy and Statecraft* 7, no. 1 (March 1996): 175–96.

———. "The 1968 Presidential Election and Peace in Vietnam." *Presidential Studies Quarterly* 26, no. 4 (Fall 1996): 1062–80.

———. "W. Averell Harriman, Henry Cabot Lodge, and the Quest for Peace in Vietnam." *Peace and Change* 20, no. 2 (April 1995): 237–49.

Siff, Ezra Y. *Why the Senate Slept: The Gulf of Tonkin Resolution and the Beginning of America's Vietnam War.* Westport, CT: Praeger, 1999.

Sindler, Allan P., ed. *American Political Institutions and Public Policy: Five Contemporary Studies.* Boston: Little, Brown, 1969.

Skidmore, David. *Reversing Course: Carter's Foreign Policy, Domestic Politics, and the Failure of Reform.* Nashville: Vanderbilt University Press, 1996.

Skowronek, Stephen. *The Politics Presidents Make: Leadership from John Adams to George Bush.* Cambridge, MA: Belknap, 1993.

Small, Melvin. *Antiwarriors: The Vietnam War and the Battle for America's Hearts and Minds.* Wilmington, DE: Scholarly Resources, 2002.

———. *At the Water's Edge: American Politics and the Vietnam War.* Chicago: Ivan R. Dee, 2005.

———. "Containing Domestic Enemies: Richard M. Nixon and the War at Home." In *Shadow on the White House: Presidents and the Vietnam War, 1945–1975,* ed. David L. Anderson, 130–51. Lawrence, KS: University Press of Kansas, 1993.

———. *Democracy and Diplomacy: The Impact of Domestic Politics on U.S. Foreign Policy, 1789–1994*. Baltimore: Johns Hopkins University Press, 1996.

———. *Johnson, Nixon, and the Doves*. New Brunswick, NJ: Rutgers University Press, 1986.

———. *The Presidency of Richard Nixon*. Lawrence: University Press of Kansas, 2000.

———. "Public Opinion." In *Explaining the History of American Foreign Relations*, ed. Michael J. Hogan and Thomas G. Paterson, 165–76. New York: Cambridge University Press, 1991.

Smiley, Sara Judith. "The Political Career of Thruston B. Morton: The Senate Years, 1956–1968." Ph.D. diss., University of Kentucky, 1975.

Smith, R. B. *An International History of the Vietnam War*. 3 vols. New York: St. Martin's, 1983–1991.

———. "The International Setting of the Cambodia Crisis, 1969–1970." *International History Review* 18, no. 2 (May 1996): 303–35.

Smith, Tony. "New Bottles for New Wine: A Pericentric Framework for the Study of the Cold War." *Diplomatic History* 24, no. 4 (Fall 2000): 567–92.

Snyder, Jack. *Myths of Empire: Domestic Politics and International Ambition*. Ithaca, NY: Cornell University Press, 1991.

Solberg, Carl. *Hubert Humphrey: A Biography*. New York: Norton, 1984.

Sorensen, Theodore C. *Kennedy*. New York: Konecky & Konecky, 1965.

Sorley, Lewis. *A Better War: The Unexamined Victories and Final Tragedy of America's Last Years in Vietnam*. San Diego: Harcourt Brace, 1999.

Spector, Ronald. *Advice and Support: The Early Years, 1941–1960*. Washington, DC: U.S. Government Printing Office, 1983.

———. *After Tet: The Bloodiest Year in Vietnam*. New York: Vintage, 1994.

Statler, Kathryn C. *Replacing France: The Origins of American Intervention in Vietnam*. Lexington: University Press of Kentucky, 2007.

Statler, Kathryn C., and Andrew L. Johns, eds. *The Eisenhower Administration, the Third World, and the Globalization of the Cold War*. Lanham, MD: Rowman & Littlefield, 2006.

Steel, Ronald. *Walter Lippmann and the American Century*. Boston: Little, Brown, 1980.

Steinberg, Blema S. *Shame and Humiliation: Presidential Decision Making on Vietnam*. Pittsburgh, PA: University of Pittsburgh Press, 1996.

Stoler, Mark A. "Aiken, Mansfield, and the Tonkin Gulf Crisis: Notes from the Congressional Leadership Meeting at the White House, August 4, 1964." *Vermont History* 50, no. 2 (Spring 1982): 80–94.

———. "What Did He *Really* Say? The 'Aiken Formula' for Vietnam Revisited." *Vermont History* 46, no. 2 (Spring 1978): 100–108.

———. "The 'Wise Old Owl': George D. Aiken and Foreign Affairs, 1941–1975." In *The Political Legacy of George D. Aiken: Wise Old Owl of the U.S. Senate*, ed. Michael Sherman, 99–116. Montpelier: Vermont Historical Society, 1995.

Stone, Gary. *Elites for Peace: The Senate and the Vietnam War, 1964–1968*. Knoxville: University of Tennessee Press, 2007.

Sullivan, Michael P. "Presidential Rhetoric on Vietnam: Kennedy, Johnson and Nixon." *International Interactions* 9, no. 2 (Spring 1982): 125–46.

Suri, Jeremi. *Henry Kissinger and the American Century.* Cambridge, MA: Belknap, 2007.

Szulc, Tad. *The Illusion of Peace: Foreign Policy in the Nixon Years.* New York: Viking, 1978.

Thelen, Sarah. "'Will you help our nation win the peace?': Americans for Winning the Peace and the Nixon Administration, 1969–1971." Paper presented at the International Graduate Student Conference on the Cold War, Santa Barbara, CA, April 2008. Copy in author's possession.

Thomas, Norman C., Joseph A. Pika, and Richard A. Watson. *The Politics of the Presidency.* 3rd ed. Washington, DC: CQ, 1993.

Thornton, Richard C. *The Nixon-Kissinger Years: The Reshaping of American Foreign Policy.* 2nd ed. St. Paul, MN: Paragon, 2001.

Thucydides. *History of the Peloponnesian War.* Translated by Rex Warner. New York: Penguin, 1972.

Tomes, Robert R. *Apocalypse Then: American Intellectuals and the Vietnam War, 1954–1975.* New York: New York University Press, 1998.

Tower, John G. *Consequences: A Personal and Political Memoir.* Boston: Little, Brown, 1991.

Tuchman, Barbara. *The March of Folly: From Troy to Vietnam.* New York: Ballantine, 1985.

Tudda, Chris. *The Truth Is Our Weapon: The Rhetorical Diplomacy of Dwight D. Eisenhower and John Foster Dulles.* Baton Rouge: Louisiana State University Press, 2006.

Turner, Kathleen J. *Lyndon Johnson's Dual War: Vietnam and the Press.* Chicago: University of Chicago Press, 1985.

Van Atta, Dale. *With Honor: Melvin Laird in War, Peace, and Politics.* Madison: University of Wisconsin Press, 2008.

VanDeMark, Brian. *Into the Quagmire: Lyndon Johnson and the Escalation of the Vietnam War.* New York: Oxford University Press, 1990.

———. "A Way of Thinking: The Kennedy Administration's Initial Assumptions about Vietnam and Their Consequences." In *Vietnam: The Early Decisions,* ed. Lloyd Gardner and Ted Gittinger, 24–36. Austin: University of Texas Press, 1997.

Vandenberg, Arthur H. *The Private Papers of Senator Vandenberg.* Edited by Arthur H. Vandenberg Jr. and Joe Alex Morris. Westport, CT: Greenwood, 1974.

Vandiver, Frank E. *Shadows of Vietnam: Lyndon Johnson's Wars.* College Station: Texas A&M University Press, 1997.

Verba, Sidney, Richard A. Brody, Edwin B. Parker, Norman H. Nie, Nelson W. Polsby, Paul Ekman, and Gordon S. Black. "Public Opinion and the War in Vietnam." *American Political Science Review* 61, no. 2 (June 1967): 317–33.

*The Vietnam Hearings.* With an introduction by J. William Fulbright. New York: Vintage, 1966.

"Vietnam: No Exit." *Saturday Evening Post,* 7 October 1967, 90.

Wainstock, Dennis. *The Turning Point: The 1968 United States Presidential Campaign.* Jefferson, NC: McFarland, 1988.

Wallace, Patricia Ward. *Politics of Conscience: A Biography of Margaret Chase Smith.* Westport, CT: Praeger, 1995.

Wang, Kevin H. "Presidential Responses to Foreign Policy Crises: Rational Choice and Domestic Politics." *Journal of Conflict Resolution* 40, no. 1 (March 1996): 68–97.

Wehrle, Edmund F. "'A Good, Bad Deal': John F. Kennedy, W. Averell Harriman, and the Neutralization of Laos, 1961–1962." *Pacific Historical Review* 67, no. 3 (August 1998): 349–77.

Wells, Tom. *The War Within: America's Battle over Vietnam.* Berkeley and Los Angeles: University of California Press, 1994.

Westad, Odd Arne. *The Global Cold War.* New York: Cambridge University Press, 2005.

Whalen, Richard J. *Catch the Falling Flag: A Republican's Challenge to His Party.* Boston: Houghton Mifflin, 1972.

White, Mark J., ed. *Kennedy: The New Frontier Revisited.* New York: New York University Press, 1998.

White, Theodore H. *The Making of the President, 1960.* New York: Atheneum, 1961.

——. *The Making of the President, 1964.* New York: Atheneum, 1965.

——. *The Making of the President, 1968.* New York: Atheneum, 1969.

——. *The Making of the President, 1972.* New York: Atheneum, 1973.

Wicker, Tom. *JFK and LBJ: The Influence of Personality on Politics.* New York: William Morrow, 1968.

——. *One of Us: Richard Nixon and the American Dream.* New York: Random House, 1995.

Willbanks, James H. *Abandoning Vietnam: How America Left and South Vietnam Lost Its War.* Lawrence: University Press of Kansas, 2004.

Williams, William Appleman. *The Tragedy of American Diplomacy.* 3rd ed. New York: Norton, 1972.

Witcover, Jules. "George Romney: Battered but Unbowed." *Saturday Evening Post,* 2 December 1967, 38–42.

——. *The Resurrection of Richard Nixon.* New York: Putnam's, 1970.

——. *Very Strange Bedfellows: The Short and Unhappy Marriage of Richard Nixon and Spiro Agnew.* New York: PublicAffairs, 2007.

——. *The Year the Dream Died: Revisiting 1968 in America.* New York: Warner, 1997.

Wittkopf, Eugene R., and James M. McCormick. *The Domestic Sources of American Foreign Policy: Insights and Evidence.* 4th ed. Lanham, MD: Rowman & Littlefield, 2004.

Womack, Steven Douglas. "Charles A. Halleck and the New Frontier: Political Opposition through the Madisonian Model." Ph.D. diss., Ball State University, 1980.

Woods, Randall B. *Fulbright: A Biography.* New York: Cambridge University Press, 1995.

————. *J. William Fulbright, Vietnam, and the Search for a Cold War Foreign Policy.* New York: Cambridge University Press, 1998.

————. *LBJ: Architect of American Ambition.* New York: Free Press, 2006.

————, ed. *Vietnam and the American Political Tradition: The Politics of Dissent.* New York: Cambridge University Press, 2003.

Xu, Guangqiu. *Congress and the U.S.-China Relationship, 1949–1979.* Akron, OH: University of Akron Press, 2007.

Young, Marilyn B. *The Vietnam Wars, 1945–1990.* New York: HarperCollins, 1991.

Zaroulis, Nancy, and Gerald Sullivan. *Who Spoke Up? American Protest against the War in Vietnam, 1963–1975.* Garden City, NY: Doubleday, 1984.

Zeiler, Thomas W. "The Diplomatic History Bandwagon: A State of the Field." *Journal of American History* 95, no. 4 (March 2009): 1053–73.

Zelman, Walter A. "Senate Dissent and the Vietnam War, 1964–1968." Ph.D. diss., University of California, Los Angeles, 1971.

Zhai, Qiang. *China and the Vietnam Wars, 1950–1975.* Chapel Hill: University of North Carolina Press, 2000.

# Index

223202LV00001B/1/P
06 April 2011
LaVergne, TN USA